second edition

essentials of international economics

ROBERT C. FEENSTRA
University of California, Davis

ALAN M. TAYLOR
University of California, Davis

WORTH PUBLISHERS

Senior Publisher: Catherine Woods
Executive Editor: Charles Linsmeier
Senior Acquisitions Editor: Sarah Dorger
Development Editors: Jane Tufts and Bruce Kaplan
Media and Supplements Editor: Jaclyn Castaldo
Executive Marketing Manager: Scott Guile
Associate Managing Editor: Tracey Kuehn
Project Editor: Anthony Calcara
Art Director: Babs Reingold
Senior Designer: Kevin Kall
Photo Editor: Cecilia Varas
Photo Researcher: Dena Betz
Production Manager: Barbara Anne Seixas
Composition: TSI Graphics
Printing and Binding: RR Donnelley

Cover Photo Credits: *Globes:* Fusion/Getty Images; *Picking coffee:* Courtesy
TransFair USA © 2007; *Trucks:* David McNew/Getty Images; *Protestors
(Trade):* © Hagerty Patrick/Corbis Sygma; *Zibabwean boy with money:*
Reuters/Howard Burditt/Newscom; *Protestors (Euro vs. Pound):* Stefan
Rousseau/PA Archive/PA Photos

Library of Congress Cataloging in Publication Data: 2010935914

ISBN-13: 978-1-4292-7710-5
ISBN-10: 1-4292-7710-6

Worth Publishers
41 Madison Avenue
New York, NY 10010
www.worthpublishers.com
www.wortheconomics.com

About the Authors

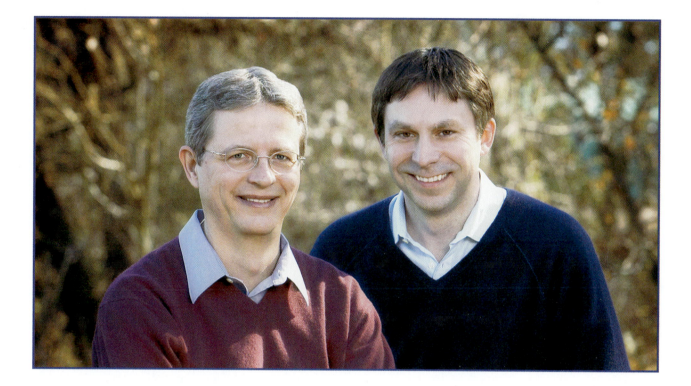

Robert C. Feenstra and **Alan M. Taylor**
are Professors of Economics at the University of
California, Davis.
They each began their studies
abroad: Feenstra received his B.A. in 1977 from the
University of British Columbia, Canada, and Taylor
received his B.A. in 1987 from King's College,
Cambridge, U.K. They trained as professional
economists in the United States, where Feenstra
earned his Ph.D. in economics from MIT in 1981
and Taylor earned his Ph.D. in economics from
Harvard University in 1992. Feenstra has been
teaching international trade at the undergraduate
and graduate levels at UC Davis since 1986, where
he holds the C. Bryan Cameron Distinguished
Chair in International Economics. Taylor has been
teaching international macroeconomics, growth,
and economic history at UC Davis since 1999,
where he directs the Center for the Evolution of
the Global Economy.

Both Feenstra and Taylor are active in research
and policy discussions in international economics.
They are research associates of the National Bureau
of Economic Research, where Feenstra directs the
International Trade and Investment research pro-
gram. They have both published graduate-level
books in international economics: *Offshoring in the
Global Economy* and *Product Variety and the Gains from
Trade* (MIT Press, 2010), by Robert C. Feenstra, and
Global Capital Markets: Integration, Crisis and Growth
(Cambridge University Press, 2004), by Maurice
Obstfeld and Alan M. Taylor. Feenstra received the
Bernhard Harms Prize from the Institute for World
Economics, Kiel, Germany, in 2006, and delivered
the Ohlin Lectures at the Stockholm School of
Economics in 2008. Taylor was awarded a
Guggenheim Fellowship in 2004 and was a visiting
professor at the American University in Paris and
London Business School in 2005–06.

Feenstra lives in Davis, California, with his wife,
Gail, and has two grown children: Heather, who is a
genetics counselor, and Evan, who recently graduat-
ed from Pitzer College. Taylor also lives in Davis,
with his wife, Claire, and has two young children,
Olivia and Sebastian.

To our parents

Brief Contents

v

Contents

CHAPTER 6 Increasing Returns to Scale and Monopolistic Competition 167

PART 3
New Explanations
for International
Trade

CHAPTER 12 Exchange Rates II: The Asset Approach in the Short Run 411

PART 7
Applications and
Policy Issues

Preface

The twenty-first century is an age of unprecedented globalization and dramatic economic developments. Our text incorporates fresh perspectives, current topics, and up-to-date approaches into the study of international economics. With this book, we have expanded the vision of international economics to encompass the latest theory and events in the world today.

In decades past, international economics was taught differently. There was a much greater emphasis on theory and a strong focus on the advanced countries. Policy analysis reflected the concerns of the time, whether strategic trade policy or the Bretton Woods system. Today, the concerns are not the same. In addition to new theoretical developments, there is a much greater emphasis on empirical studies. A wave of applied research in recent years has proved (or refuted) existing theories and taught us important new lessons about the determinants of trade, factor flows, exchange rates, and crises. Trade and capital flows have been liberalized and allowed to grow, and more attention is now devoted to emerging markets and developing countries, regions that now carry substantial weight in the global economy.

Covering new and expanding ground is part of the challenge and excitement of teaching and learning the international economics of the twenty-first century. Our goal is to provide new material that is rigorous enough to meet the challenge yet approachable enough to nurture the excitement. Many of the new topics stand apart from conventional textbook treatments and in the past have been bypassed in lectures or taught through supplementary readings. In our view they deserve a more prominent place in today's curriculum.

In addition to expanding our coverage to include up-to-date theory and policy applications, our other major goal is to present all the material—both new and old—in the most teachable way. To do this, we ensure that all material presented rests on firm and up-to-the-minute empirical evidence. We believe this approach is the right way to study economics, and it is our experience, shared with many instructors, that teaching is more effective and more enlivened when students can see not just an elegant derivation in theory but, right next to it, some persuasive evidence of the economic mechanisms under investigation.

We have taught the chapters of this book ourselves several times, and have benefited from the feedback of professors at colleges and universities in the United States and throughout the world. Like us, they have been enthusiastic about the response from students to our fresh, accessible, and up-to-the-minute approach, and we hope that you too will enjoy the book.

Essentials of International Economics

To answer the needs and feedback of those instructors who teach a one-semester course that combines international trade and macroeconomics, our text now comes in a one-semester, fifteen-chapter version. Again, we have learned from the experience of faculty teaching this course, and include the fifteen chapters most relevant to teaching the one-semester combined course.

Our text is also available in a combined edition *(International Economics)* and in two split editions *(International Trade* and *International Macroeconomics)*, allowing greater flexibility for instructors to assign their preferred text and keep costs down for students.

Features

Each chapter includes several features that bring the material alive for the students:

- **Applications** are integrated into the main text and use material that has been covered to illuminate real-world policies, events, and evidence. Students outside the economics major often take the one-semester combined course. Because of the wealth of applications, we have found that our chapters serve those students very well.
- **Headlines** show how topics in the main text relate directly to media coverage of the global economy.
- **Side Bars** include topics that, while not essential, are nonetheless of interest.
- **Net Work** problems, a separate group of homework problems, provide an opportunity for students to explore chapter concepts on the Internet.

Essentials Topics and Approaches

Reviewers and class testers of the first edition of *International Economics* (the complete volume, which includes 22 chapters) have been enthusiastically supportive of the topics we have included in our presentation. The 15-chapter, one-semester *Essentials* version has an introduction in Chapter 1 that incorporates both international trade and macroeconomic issues. It then moves to Chapters 2–4, the basic trade chapters, followed by labor and capital flows between countries (Chapter 5) and then monopolistic competition (Chapter 6). The international trade section concludes with Chapters 7–9 on tariffs, quotas, trade agreements, and the environment. (An extra chapter on offshoring is available online.) These nine chapters offer students a solid foundation in international trade and trade policy.

The trade chapters are followed by chapters on the core concepts and models of international macroeconomics. Chapters 10–12 cover exchange rates, followed by chapters on national income and the balance of payments (Chapter 13), short-run macroeconomic policy (Chapter 14), and fixed-versus-floating exchange rates (Chapter 15). (An extra chapter on the euro is available online.) These six chapters give students a solid foundation in international macroeconomics.

In writing our chapters we have made every effort to link them analytically. For example, although immigration and foreign direct investment are sometimes treated as afterthoughts in international economics books, we integrate these topics into the discussion of the trade models by covering the movement of labor and capital between countries in Chapter 5. Specifically, we analyze the movement of labor and capital between countries in the short run using the specific-factors model developed in Chapter 3, and explore the long-run implications using the Heckscher-Ohlin model developed in Chapter 4. Chapter 5 therefore builds on the models that the student has learned in earlier chapters, and applies them to issues at the forefront of policy discussion.

In the macroeconomics section of *Essentials*, this analytical linking is seen in the parallel development of fixed and floating exchange rate regimes (a topic introduced in Chapter 1) through the workings of exchange rates in Chapters 10, 11, 12, the discussion of policy in the IS-LM model of Chapter 14, to the discussion of regime choice in Chapter 15. Many textbooks discuss fixed and floating regimes separately, with fixed regimes often treated as an afterthought. But given the widespread use of fixed rates in many countries, the rising macro weight of fixed regimes, and the collapse of fixed rates during crises, we think it is more helpful for the student to grapple with the different workings and cost-benefit tradeoffs of the two regimes by studying them side by side. This approach also allows us to address numerous policy issues such as the implications of the trilemma (Chapter 12) and the optimal choice of exchange rate regime (Chapter 15).

A Roadmap for *Essentials of International Economics*

Part 1: Introduction to International Economics

Chapter 1: The Global Economy

Chapter 1 sets the stage by introducing some basic facts about international trade and macroeconomics. It starts by discussing global flows of goods and services through international trade, of people through migration, and of capital through foreign direct investment. The chapter then introduces the topic of international macroeconomics by explaining the field and surveying the main topics: money and exchange rates, the balance of payments, and the role of policy.

Part 2: Patterns of International Trade

Chapter 2: Trade and Technology: The Ricardian Model

Chapter 2 presents the Ricardian model, where students learn first about comparative advantage and the mutual gains from trade. It also discusses how absolute advantage determines relative wages across countries, and therefore links living standards in different countries to their productivities.

Chapter 3: Gains and Losses from Trade in the Specific-Factors Model

The ordering of topics among Chapters 3, 4, and 5 and many of the applications are new, and these chapters are linked together tightly in their pedagogical approach.

Chapter 3 covers the specific-factors model and shows how the opening of trade has differing effect on the earnings of labor, land, and capital. While some of these factors of production lose and others gains, there are still overall gains from trade for each country. This chapter also discusses Trade Adjustment Assistance in the United States as a policy response to assist workers who are laid off due to import competition.

Chapter 4: Trade and Resources: The Heckscher-Ohlin Model

A streamlined presentation of this model focuses on the Heckscher-Ohlin theorem, the Stolper-Samuelson theorem, and empirical testing of the model. This approach allows an easier resolution of the Leontief Paradox, which is explained by relying on differing productivities of labor across countries.

Chapter 5: Movement of Labor and Capital between Countries

Some of the topics conventionally included in the specific-factors and Heckscher-Ohlin model, such as the effects of changing the endowments of labor (by immigration) or capital (by foreign direct investment), are not covered in those chapters but are instead examined in this chapter. We contrast the effects of immigration and foreign direct investment in the short-run specific-factors models with the long-run Heckscher-Ohlin model. In the long run, changing the endowments of labor or capital will not have any impact on their earnings, which is a surprising result. To illustrate this result, the chapter starts with the Mariel boat lift of migrants from Cuba to Miami in 1980, where it was found that wages in Miami did not change.

Part 3: New Explanations for International Trade

Chapter 6: Increasing Returns to Scale and Monopolistic Competition

Formal models of trade with increasing returns to scale and monopolistic competition have been popular since the early 1980s, but there is no standardized method for presenting this topic in undergraduate textbooks. In Chapter 6, we use the original graphical discussion from Edward Chamberlin, who introduced the DD and dd curves (which we label in Chapter 6 as simply D and d). The D curve represents the share of the market going to each firm and traces out demand if all firms charge the same prices. In contrast, the d curve is the demand facing a firm when other firms keep their prices constant. The distinction between these two demands is crucial when analyzing the impact of trade liberalization: the d curve clearly shows the incentive for each individual firm to lower its price after trade liberalization, but the steeper D curve shows that when all firms lower prices, then losses occur and some firms must exit. This chapter also includes an assessment of NAFTA after 15 years.

Part 4: International Trade Policies

Chapters 7, 8, and 9 present the material on trade policies and international agreements in a more systematic fashion than found elsewhere, using both very recent and historical applications.

Chapter 7: Import Tariffs and Quotas under Perfect Competition

Chapter 7, dealing with tariffs and quotas under perfect competition, is the "bread and butter" of trade policy. We adopt the partial-equilibrium approach, using import demand and export supply curves, along with consumer and producer surplus. Our experience is that students feel very comfortable with this approach from their microeconomics training (so they can usually label the consumer surplus region for example, in each diagram before the labels are shown). The chapter uses the tariffs applied by President George W. Bush on U.S. steel imports and by President Barack Obama on imported tires from China as motivating cases, which we analyze from both a "small country" and a "large country" perspective.

Chapter 8: Import Tariffs and Quotas under Imperfect Competition

Most of the theory in this chapter is familiar, but the organization is new, as are many of the applications, including infant industry protection. Chapter 8 brings in some of the insights from the literature on the strategic role of trade policy, which was developed in the later 1980s and 1990s. Whereas that literature focused on oligopoly interactions between firms, we simplify the analysis by focusing on home or foreign monopoly cases. The topic of dumping is discussed along with trade policy under imperfect competition and General Motors' recent experience in the China market.

Chapter 9: International Agreements: Trade, Labor, and the Environment

This chapter begins by drawing upon tariffs under perfect competition (from Chapter 7), and showing that large countries have a natural incentive to apply tariffs to move the terms of trade to their advantage. The resulting prisoner's dilemma situation is overcome by rules in the WTO. The chapter then moves on to discuss international rules governing labor issues and the environment and includes the failure of the 2009 Copenhagen Climate Summit. Students are especially interested in the environmental applications.

Part 5: Exchange Rates

We depart from the traditional presentation by presenting exchange rates before balance of payments, an approach that we and our students find more logical and appealing. We begin the core macro material with exchange rates because (for macroeconomics) the exchange rate is the key difference between a closed economy and a world of open economies. Our approach, supported by our own experience and that of our reviewers and class testers, first treats all price topics and then moves on to quantity topics.

Chapter 10: Introduction to Exchange Rates and the Foreign Exchange Market

This chapter introduces the basics of exchange rates and the foreign exchange (forex) market and exposes students to real-world data on exchange rate behavior. It describes how the forex market is structured and explains the principles of arbitrage in forex markets. It ends with interest parity conditions, which are covered in more detail in Chapter 12.

Chapter 11: Exchange Rates I: The Monetary Approach in the Long Run

This chapter presents the monetary approach to the determination of exchange rates in the long run. We cover the long run before the short run because long-run expectations are assumed to be known in the short-run model. Topics include goods market arbitrage, the law of one price, and purchasing power parity. We first develop a simple monetary model (the quantity theory) and then look at the standard monetary model, the Fisher effect, and real interest parity. The chapter ends with a discussion of nominal anchors and their relationship to monetary and exchange rate regimes.

Chapter 12: Exchange Rates II: The Asset Approach in the Short Run

Chapter 12 presents the asset approach to the determination of exchange rates in the short run. Uncovered interest parity, first introduced in Chapter 10, is the centerpiece of the asset approach, and the expected future exchange rate is assumed to be given by the long-run model. Short-run interest rates are explained using a money market model. We show how all the building blocks from the monetary and asset approaches fit together for a complete theory of exchange rate determination. Finally, we explain how the complete theory works for fixed as well as floating regimes, and demonstrate the trilemma.

Part 6: The Balance of Payments

Chapter 13: National and International Accounts: Income, Wealth, and the Balance of Payments

A streamlined presentation introduces the key macroeconomic quantities: the national and international accounts and the balance of payments (BOP). The BOP is explained as the need for balancing trade on goods, services, and assets (with allowances for transfers). We discuss how countries have used creative accounting to disguise their economic problems. The chapter ends with an introduction to external wealth and valuation effects, which are of increasing importance in the world economy.

Chapter 14: Output, Exchange Rates, and Macroeconomic Policies in the Short Run

Chapter 14 presents the short-run open economy Keynesian model, which links the balance of payments to output, exchange rates, and macroeconomic policies. We use IS-LM and forex market diagrams, with the interest rate on a common axis. With this presentation, we use tools (IS-LM) that many students have already learned how to use, and avoid inventing new ways to present the same model with new and challenging notation. We look at the issue of how central banks can face difficulties with interest rate policies in the presence of market-risk premiums or at the zero bound. In this chapter we discuss fixed and floating rate regimes side by side, not in different chapters. We think it helpful throughout the book to study these regimes in parallel.

Part 7: Applications and Policy Issues

Chapter 15: Fixed versus Floating: International Monetary Experience

Chapter 15 confronts one of the major policy issues in international macroeconomics, the choice of fixed versus floating exchange rates. The analysis begins with the two classic criteria for two regions to adopt a fixed exchange rate: high levels of integration and symmetry of economic shocks. The chapter then goes on to consider other factors that could make a fixed exchange rate desirable especially in developing countries: a need for a credible nominal anchor and the "fear of floating" that results from significant liability dollarization. These discussions present empirical evidence for all of these influences. A brief section summarizes the debate over the desirability and possibility of coordination in larger exchange rate systems. Finally, a historical survey uses the tools at hand to understand the evolution of international monetary arrangements since the nineteenth century.

Supplements and Media Package

In addition to all its pedagogical innovations, our book brings to the market an innovative supplements and media package. These supplements were given the same careful thought, time, and preparation as the text. We are happy to provide a full suite of teaching materials for instructors along with a complete set of resources to aid students in reviewing the key concepts presented in the text.

www.Aplia.com

The Aplia/Worth course for Feenstra/Taylor is the only fully integrated Aplia solution in International Economics. It enhances students' experiences through Aplia's interactive problem sets, news analyses, and tutorials—all in a format that saves time for professors while encouraging students in their learning.

Full eBook integration—the Feenstra/Taylor Aplia course includes a full eBook as well as offering:

- **Homework sets correlated to the text.** Online homework is easy to assign, and it grades automatically. The course gradebook quickly puts results at your fingertips.

- **Algorithmic problem sets.** All homework problem sets offer **Grade It Now.** Students can attempt any problem set up to three times with variables that randomize on each attempt.

- **Multiple purchase options.** Aplia access can be packaged with any version of the text, or purchased separately online as a less expensive alternative to the book because it includes an eBook. Students who purchase on-line access can also buy a physical textbook directly from Aplia at a significant discount.

Instructor Supplements

Instructor's Manual with Solutions Manual

Instructor's Manuals for each portion of the book, prepared by Philip Luck (University of California, Davis) and Tony Lima (California State University, East Bay) are available. For each chapter in the textbook, the Instructor's Manuals provide:

- *Notes to the instructor:* notes that include a chapter summary with additional comments

- *Lecture notes:* a complete set of notes, including a detailed outline of the chapter for aid in preparing class lectures

- *Teaching tips:* 4 or 5 activities per chapter that instructors can utilize in lectures, for in-class group work, or as take-home assignments

- *In-class problems:* 10 to 15 problems per chapter, including in-depth suggested answers.

- *Solutions to textbook problems:* detailed solutions to all end-of-chapter problems.

Computerized Test Bank

The test bank provides a wide range of creative and versatile questions ranging in levels of difficulty and format to assess students' comprehension, interpretation, analysis, and synthesis skills. Containing over 125 questions per chapter, the test bank offers a variety of multiple-choice, true/false, and short-answer questions. All questions have been checked for continuity with the text content and reviewed extensively for accuracy. The test bank was coordinated by Ron Davies (University College, Dublin) with the help of contributing authors Terry Monson (Finlandia University) and Millicent Taylor (Carson-Newman College). The test bank is available in CD-ROM format for both Windows and Macintosh users. With this Diploma software, instructors can easily create and print tests as well as write and edit questions.

Student and Instructor Supplements

Study Guide with Worked Examples

Students' economic thinking will be challenged and extended by a creative new Study Guide with Worked Examples prepared by Stephen Yeaple of Pennsylvania State

University. This study guide complements the textbook by providing students with additional opportunities to develop their knowledge of international economics through active learning. This innovative resource reinforces the topics and key concepts covered in the text. For each key section of each chapter, the Study Guide with Worked Examples provides:

- *Key themes:* detailed discussions of key concepts.
- *Key terms:* a summary of important vocabulary within the chapter, with space for students to make their own notes
- *Review questions with tips:* detailed, thorough problems for students to test their comprehension, along with tips to help students work through the problems. To identify common mistakes and to demonstrate common features of different types of economic problems, tips are provided immediately following questions that delve into particularly important or difficult topics.
- *Worked-out solutions:* including solutions to all Study Guide review questions.

Companion Website for Students and Instructors

The companion site http://www.worthpublishers.com/feenstrataylor2_essentials is a virtual study guide for students and an excellent resource for instructors. For each chapter in the textbook, the tools on the site include:

Student Tools

- *Detailed learning objectives*
- *Practice quizzes:* A set of questions with feedback and page references to the textbook. Student answers are saved in an online database that can be accessed by instructors.
- *Web exercises*
- *Web links* to relevant research and demonstrations

Instructor Resources

- *Quiz gradebook:* The site gives instructors the ability to track students' interaction with the practice quizzes via an online gradebook. Instructors may choose to have student results emailed directly to them.
- *PowerPoint lecture presentations:* These customizable PowerPoint slides, prepared by Fernando Quijano (Dickinson State University) are designed to assist instructors with lecture preparation and presentation by providing original animations, graphs from the textbook, data tables, key concepts, and bulleted lecture outlines.
- *Image gallery:* A complete set of figures and tables from the textbook in JPEG and PowerPoint formats

CourseSmart eBooks

All four versions (*International Economics, International Trade, International Macroeconomics,* and *Essentials of International Economics*) are available as CourseSmart eBooks. Students who purchase the Feenstra/Taylor CourseSmart eBooks have instant access to their textbooks on any computer or handheld device with an Internet connection. CourseSmart eBooks offer an earth-friendly and wallet-friendly option for students.

CourseSmart eBook features include:

- **Copy and paste text:**

  Easy integration with word processing programs

- **Textbook Search:**

  Find words or topics fast within your online eTextbook

- **Print what you need:**

  From any printer connected to the computer

- **Highlighting and Note-Taking:**

  Highlight relevant sections or take notes on important topics

- **Same "Everything Else":**

  Online eTextbooks share the same page layout and numbering as the print version

- **No Connection Necessary:**

Once you download the eBook and save it to your computer, you don't need the Internet. Just start reading

Web-CT E-pack

The Feenstra/Taylor WebCT e-packs enable you to create a thorough, interactive, and pedagogically sound online course or course Web site. The e-pack, available free, provides you with online materials that facilitate critical thinking and learning, including preprogrammed quizzes, tests, activities, and an array of other materials. This material is preprogrammed and fully functional in the WebCT environment.

BlackBoard

Blackboard

The Feenstra/Taylor BlackBoard Course Cartridge, available free, allows you to combine BlackBoard's popular tools and easy-to-use interface with the Feenstra/Taylor text-specific, rich Web content, including preprogrammed quizzes, tests, activities, and an array of other materials. The result is an interactive, comprehensive online course that allows for effortless implementation, management, and use. The files are organized and pre-built to work within the BlackBoard software. They can be easily downloaded from the BlackBoard content showcases directly onto your department server.

Acknowledgments

A book like this would not be possible without the assistance of many people, which we gratefully acknowledge.

First, the renowned team at Worth has spared no effort to help us; their experience and skill in publishing economics textbooks were invaluable. Numerous individuals have been involved with this project, but we must give special mention to four: the project has been continually and imaginatively guided by acquisitions editor Sarah Dorger, now joined by executive editor Chuck Linsmeier and development editor Bruce Kaplan, and by marketing manager Scott Guile, who successfully brought the book to market. Through it all, the manuscript was improved endlessly by our primary development editor, Jane Tufts. We are greatly in their debt.

We have also relied on the assistance of a number of graduate students in collecting data for applications, preparing problems, and proofreading material. We would like to thank Leticia Arroyo Abad, Chang Hong, David Jacks, Alyson Ma, Ahmed Rahman, Seema Sangita, Radek Szulga, and Yingying Xu for their assistance. We are especially grateful to Benjamin Mandel, who has worked on many of the international trade chapters in the first edition, and to Philip Luck, who worked on all the chapters in this second edition. Thanks also to Christian Broda, Colin Carter, Michele Cavallo, Menzie Chinn, Sebastian Edwards, Ann Harrison, Mervyn King, Philip Lane, Karen Lewis, Christopher Meissner, Gian Maria Milesi-Ferretti, Michael Pakko, Ugo Panizza, Giovanni Peri, Eswar Prasad, Andrés Rodríguez-Clare, Jay Shambaugh, and Martin Wolf for providing data used in the applications.

We have taught the chapters of this book ourselves a number of times, and have benefited from the feedback of colleagues. The book has also been class-tested by a number of individuals.

For the second edition, we benefited from the suggestions of the following reviewers:

Bradley Andrew, *Juniata College*

Damyana Bakardzhieva, *George Washington University*

Mina Baliamoune, *University of North Florida*

Valerie Bencivenga, *University of Texas at Austin*

Emily Blanchard, *University of Virginia*

Nicola Borri, *Boston University*

Drusilla Brown, *Tufts University*

Vera Brusentsev, *University of Delaware*

Colleen Callahan, *American University*

Geoffrey Carliner, *Boston University*

Ron Cronovich, *Carthage College*

Firat Demir, *University of Oklahoma*

Asim Erdilek, *Case Western Reserve University*

John Gilbert, *Utah State University*

William Hauk, *University of South Carolina*

David Hummels, *Purdue University*

Hakan Inal, *Virginia Commonwealth University*

Alan Isaac, *American University*

Robert Jerome, *James Madison University*

Grace Johnson, *Oklahoma State University— Tulsa*

Kathy Kelly, *University of Texas at Arlington*

Bill Kosteas, *Cleveland State University*

Ricardo Lopez, *Indiana University*

Volodymyr Lugovskyy, *Georgia Tech*

Nicolas Magud, *University of Oregon*

Keith Malone, *University of North Alabama*

Maria Muniagurria, *University of Wisconsin— Madison*

Catherine Mann, *Brandeis University*

Steven J. Matusz, *Michigan State University*

Fabio Mendez, *University of Arkansas*

William Mertens, *University of Colorado at Boulder*

Rebecca Neumann, *University of Wisconsin— Milwaukee*

Emanuel Ornelas, *London School of Economics*

Perry Patterson, *Wake Forest University*

Masha Rahnama, *Texas Tech University*

Michael Rinkus, *Walsh College*

Sheikh Shahnawaz, *University of Southern California*

David Sobiechowski, *University of Michigan— Dearborn*

Steve Steib, *University of Tulsa*

Nicholas Stratis, *Florida State University*

Edward Tower, *Duke University*

Elizabeth Wheaton, *Southern Methodist University*

Peter Wylie, *University of British Columbia— Okanagan*

We would like to thank the following instructors for sharing their ideas with us in the development of the first edition. These colleagues have been enthusiastic about the reception of their students to our fresh approach.

Joshua Aizenman, *University of California, Santa Cruz*

Scott Baier, *Clemson University*

Paul Bergin, *University of California, Davis*

Matilde Bombardini, *University of British Columbia—Vancouver*

Drusilla Brown, *Tufts University*

Avik Chakraborty, *University of Tennessee—Knoxville*

Gordon Hanson, *University of California, San Diego*

James Harrigan, *University of Virginia*

Takeo Hoshi, *University of California, San Diego*

David Hummels, *Purdue University*

Samuel Kortum, *University of Chicago*

John McLaren, *University of Virginia*

Marc-Andreas Muendler, *University of California, San Diego*

Robert Murphy, *Boston College*

Constantin Ogloblin, *Georgia Southern University*

Kevin O'Rourke, *Trinity College, Dublin*

Sanjay Paul, *Elizabethtown College*

Priya Ranjan, *University of California, Irvine*

Andrés Rodriguez-Clare, *Pennsylvania State University*

Katheryn Russ, *University of California, Davis*

Stephen Stageberg, *University of Mary Washington*

Bruce Wydick, *University of San Francisco*

Stephen Yeaple, *Pennsylvania State University*

A huge number of colleagues were very helpful in reviewing the first-edition manuscript. We wish to thank the following reviewers:

Joshua Aizenman, *University of California, Santa Cruz*

Mohsen Bahmani-Oskooee, *University of Wisconsin—Milwaukee*

Scott Baier, *Clemson University*

Richard Baillie, *Michigan State University*

Joe Bell, *Missouri State University*

Paul Bergin, *University of California, Davis*

Robert Blecker, *American University*

Roger Butters, *University of Nebraska—Lincoln*

Francisco Carrada-Bravo, *Arizona State University*

Menzie Chinn, *University of Wisconsin—Madison*

Richard Chisik, *Florida International University*

Ann Davis, *Marist College*

Robert Driskill, *Vanderbilt University*

James Fain, *Oklahoma State University*

David H. Feldman, *The College of William & Mary*

Diane Flaherty, *University of Massachusetts, Amherst*

Jean-Ellen Giblin, *Fashion Institute of Technology*

Bill Gibson, *University of Vermont*

Thomas Grennes, *North Carolina State University*

Gordon Hanson, *University of California, San Diego*

Mehdi Haririan, *Bloomsburg University*

James Harrigan, *University of Virginia*

Takeo Hoshi, *University of California, San Diego*

Douglas Irwin, *Dartmouth College*

Michael Klein, *Tufts University*

Kala Krishna, *Pennsylvania State University*

Maria Kula, *Roger Williams University*

Ricardo Lopez, *Indiana University*

Mary Lovely, *Syracuse University*

Barbara Lowrey, *University of Maryland*

Steven J. Matusz, *Michigan State University*

Jose Mendez, *Arizona State University*

Shannon Mitchell, *Virginia Commonwealth University*

Farshid Mojaver Hosseini, *University of California, Davis*

Marc-Andreas Muendler, *University of California, San Diego*

Maria Muniagurria, *University of Wisconsin—Madison*

Robert Murphy, *Boston College*

Ranganath Murthy, *Bucknell University*

Kanda Naknoi, *Purdue University*

Constantin Ogloblin, *Georgia Southern University*

Kevin O'Rourke, *Trinity College, Dublin*

Kerry Pannell, *DePauw University*

Jaishankar Raman, *Valparaiso University*

Raymond Robertson, *Macalester College*

Andrés Rodriguez-Clare, *Pennsylvania State University*

Hadi Salehi-Esfahani, *University of Illinois at Urbana-Champaign*

Andreas Savvides, *Oklahoma State University*

Till Schreiber, *The College of William & Mary*

Gunjan Sharma, *University of Missouri, Columbia*

John Subrick, *James Madison University*

Mark P. Taylor, *University of Warwick*

Linda Tesar, *University of Michigan, Ann Arbor*

Geetha Vaidyanathan, *University of North Carolina at Greensboro*

Kristin Van Gaasbeck, *California State University, Sacramento*

Gary Wells, *Clemson University*

Mark Wohar, *University of Nebraska, Omaha*

Susan Wolcott, *SUNY Binghamton*

Bin Xu, *China Europe International Business School*

Stephen Yeaple, *Pennsylvania State University*

We received useful feedback from focus group participants. We would like to thank the following individuals:

Mohsen Bahmani-Oskooee, *University of Wisconsin—Milwaukee*

Roger Butters, *University of Nebraska—Lincoln*

Francisco Carrada-Bravo, *Arizona State University*

Mitchell Charkiewicz, *Central Connecticut State University*

Menzie Chinn, *University of Wisconsin—Madison*

Carl Davidson, *Michigan State University*

Ann Davis, *Marist College*

Robert Driskill, *Vanderbilt University*

Eric Fisher, *California Polytechnic State University, San Luis Obispo*

Diane Flaherty, *University of Massachusetts, Amherst*

Bill Gibson, *University of Vermont*

Thomas Grennes, *North Carolina State University*

Mehdi Haririan, *Bloomsburg University*

Andreas Hauskrecht, *Indiana University*

Andrew Hughes-Hallett, *George Mason University*

Eckhard Janeba, *University of Mannheim*

Mary Lovely, *Syracuse University*

Marc Melitz, *Harvard University*

Norman Miller, *Miami University of Ohio*

Shannon Mitchell, *Virginia Commonwealth University*

Ranganath Murthy, *Bucknell University*

Rebecca Neumann, *University of Wisconsin—Milwaukee*

Constantin Ogloblin, *Georgia Southern University*

Lucjan Orlowski, *Sacred Heart University*

Jeff Pliskin, *Hamilton College*

Francisca Richter, *Cleveland State University*

Hadi Salehi-Esfahani, *University of Illinois at Urbana-Champaign*

Bin Xu, *China Europe International Business School*

We would like to thank the following instructors who have provided feedback on the initial preliminary version of the first edition of our text:

Scott Baier, *Clemson University*

Paul Bergin, *University of California, Davis*

Luisa Blanco Raynal, *Pepperdine University*

James Cassing, *University of Pittsburgh*

Ted Fu, *Stanford University*

James Harrigan, *University of Virginia*

David Hummels, *Purdue University*

Farshid Mojaver Hosseini, *University of California, Davis*

Maria Muniagurria, *University of Wisconsin—Madison*

Kanda Naknoi, *Purdue University*

Raymond Robertson, *Macalester College*

Andrés Rodriguez-Clare, *Pennsylvania State University*

Jeffrey Rosensweig, *Emory University*

Jennifer Steele, *University of Texas at Austin*

Asha Sundaram, *Syracuse University*

Kristin Van Gaasbeck, *California State University, Sacramento*

Wolfgang Keller, *University of Colorado at Boulder*

We would like to thank the following individuals who have aided us in the preparation and extensive review of the ancillary package.

Francis Ahking, *University of Connecticut*

Ron Davies, *University College, Dublin*

Philip Luck, *University of California, Davis*

Alyson Ma, *University of San Diego*

Terry Monson, *Michigan Technological University*

Robert Murphy, *Boston College*

Sanjay Paul, *Elizabethtown College*

Jaishankar Raman, *Valparaiso University*

Millicent Sites, *Carson-Newman College*

Marie Truesdell, *Marian College*

Kristin Van Gaasbeck, *California State University, Sacramento*

Stephen Yeaple, *Pennsylvania State University*

We would also like to thank our families, especially Claire and Gail, for their sustained support during the time we have devoted to writing this book.

Finally, you will see an accompanying picture of children in Ciudad Darío, Nicaragua, with their teacher, in the classroom of a small schoolhouse that was built for them by Seeds of Learning (www.seedsoflearning.org), a nonprofit organization dedicated to improving educational opportunities in rural Latin America. A portion of the royalties from this book go toward supporting the work of Seeds of Learning.

ROBERT C. FEENSTRA

ALAN M. TAYLOR

Davis, California

June 2010

James Hall

Sixth-grade class with their teacher in La Carreta #2 school in Ciudad Darío, Nicaragua.

The Global Economy

The main losers in today's very unequal world are not those who are too much exposed to globalization. They are those who have been left out.

> Kofi Annan, former secretary general of the United Nations, 2000

So much of barbarism, however, still remains in the transactions of most civilized nations, that almost all independent countries choose to assert their nationality by having, to their inconvenience and that of their neighbors, a peculiar currency of their own.

> John Stuart Mill

In 2007 problems in the U.S. subprime mortgage market acted as a trigger for a worldwide financial crisis that erased roughly $50 trillion dollars of global wealth in a little over 18 months. From April 2008 to March 2009, there was a global decline in output and an alarming 25% drop in world goods exports. At the time this book was written much, but not all, of the lost wealth had been recovered, although output and employment remain below potential, in many countries. Trade has recovered strongly, but not fully, and protectionist policies have so far been largely avoided, despite occasional rhetoric to the contrary. Exchange rates fluctuated dramatically during the crisis and international flows of capital were disrupted, adding to international tensions. During the recession many countries ran up large public debts, and several began to be regarded by financial markets as being at risk of not being able to pay their debts. Despite the trend toward recovery, the events of the world economic crisis demonstrate the importance of the economic forces linking countries of the world. In this book we endeavor to explain how countries are linked by trade and finance.

In the first part of this book, we develop a number of models that help us understand the reasons that countries trade goods and services, that people move from one country to another, and that firms own companies in other countries. All three types of flows between countries—of products (goods and services), people, and capital—are so

1

common today that we take them for granted. When you go into a store to purchase an item, for example, it is possible that it was made in another country, the store itself might be foreign-owned, and the salesperson who assists you may be an immigrant. Why are these international flows so common? What are the consequences of these flows for the countries involved? And what actions do governments take to make their countries more or less open to trade, migration, and foreign direct investment? These are the questions we address in the first part of the book.

In the second part of this book, we study the global macroeconomy and how it is defined by integrated markets for goods, services, and capital. To effectively study macroeconomic outcomes, we must understand how countries are linked to one another through their currencies, their trade, and their capital flows. Why do so many countries have their own currency? How do exchange rates affect output and flows of trade and capital? Why do so many countries choose to open up to economic interaction with other nations? And what costs and benefits do these and other macroeconomic policy decisions impose on a nation's economic well-being? These are the questions we answer in the second half of this book.

1 International Trade

On April 14, 2010, the Eyjafjallajökull volcano in Iceland roared to life after being dormant for more than two centuries. A plume of ash erupted 7 miles into the atmosphere, disrupting air travel in Northern Europe and beyond. An event like this has dramatic consequences for **international trade,** the movement of goods and services across borders. Roughly 100,000 flights to and from Northern Europe were canceled, and billions of dollars in air freight and millions of travelers were delayed, canceled, or re-routed.

The air freight that was disrupted included products as diverse as auto parts being sent from factories in Europe and flowers being shipped from Africa. In Kenya 10 million roses that could not be delivered to Europe had to be thrown away, and as a result, 5,000 Kenyan workers were laid off.[1] Estimates of revenue lost because of this disruption in air freight for two weeks range from $16 to 27 billion of goods imported to the United States from Europe, and $20 to 26 billion of goods exported from the United States to Europe.

In addition to the disruption to international trade in goods, there were also canceled passenger fights, which are an example of international trade in services. The canceled flights between the United States and Europe over two weeks in April 2010 translated into roughly $3.2 billion of lost services trade between the United States and Europe. In this book, we study international trade in goods and services and will learn the economic forces that determine what that trade looks like: what products are traded; who trades them; at what quantities and prices they are traded; and what the benefits and costs of trade are. We also learn about the policies that governments use to shape trade patterns among countries.

---

[1] See Carley Petesch and Karoun Demirjian, "10 Million Roses Ruined, 5K Kenya Workers Laid Off," *The New York Times*, April 19, 2010, p. A1.

Let's begin by looking at a very broad picture of international trade. What country was the world's largest exporter of goods in 2009? If you guessed China, you're right: in that year it overtook Germany as the top exporter, selling some $1.3 trillion in goods to other countries, slightly ahead of the $1.17 trillion exported by Germany. The third largest exporter of goods is the United States, which exported $1.05 trillion of goods in 2009.

These numbers reveal only part of the trade picture, however, because in addition to exporting goods, countries also export services. In 2009 the United States exported $0.5 trillion in services (including business services, education of foreign students, travel by foreigners, etc.). If we combine exports in goods and services, then in 2009 the world's largest exporter was the United States at $1.55 trillion, followed by Germany, China, Japan, the United Kingdom, and France.

The Basics of World Trade

This section begins our study of international economics by defining some important terms and summarizing the overall trends in world trade.

Countries buy and sell goods and services from one another constantly. An **export** is a product sold from one country to another, and an **import** is a product bought by one country from another. We normally think of exports and imports as goods that are shipped between countries, but for services that is not necessarily the case. Construction services, for example, are performed on-site in the importing country rather than being shipped. Travel and tourism are large categories of service exports that also occur on-site: the money spent by a U.S. visitor to the Eiffel Tower is a service export of France, and a Chinese visitor to the Grand Canyon adds to U.S. service exports.

A country's **trade balance** is the difference between its total value of exports and its total value of imports (usually including both goods and services). Countries that export more than they import, such as China in recent years, run a **trade surplus,** whereas countries that import more than they export, such as the United States, run a **trade deficit.** In addition to keeping track of the overall trade balance for a country with the rest of the world, we often see reported in the newspaper the **bilateral trade balance,** meaning the difference between exports and imports between two countries. The U.S. trade deficit with China, for example, was more than $200 billion every year between 2005 and 2009.

In the models we develop to understand trade, we are not concerned with whether a country has a trade deficit or surplus but just assume that each country has balanced trade, with exports equal to imports. There are two reasons why we make this assumption. First, economists believe that an overall trade deficit or surplus arises from macroeconomic conditions, the overall levels of spending and savings in an economy—countries with high spending and low savings will run a trade deficit. Macroeconomic conditions are studied in the second half of this book, which deals with international macroeconomics.

In April 2010 the ash from Iceland's Eyjafjallajökull volcano disrupted air travel in Northern Europe and beyond.

Second, the interpretation of a trade deficit or surplus is problematic when we focus on the bilateral trade balance between two countries, such as the United States and China. To see what the problem is, think about the U.S. import of a particular good from China, such as the iPod (see **Headlines: An iPod Has Global Value. Ask the (Many) Countries That Make It**).

HEADLINES

An iPod Has Global Value. Ask the (Many) Countries That Make It.

Although the iPod sold in the United States is assembled in China, most of its value comes from parts made in other countries.

Who makes the Apple iPod? Here's a hint: It is not Apple. The company outsources the entire manufacture of the device to a number of Asian enterprises, among them Asustek, Inventec Appliances and Foxconn. But this list of companies isn't a satisfactory answer either: They only do final assembly. What about the 451 parts that go into the iPod? Where are they made and by whom?

The retail value of the 30-gigabyte video iPod . . . was $299. The most expensive component in it was the hard drive, which was manufactured by Toshiba and costs about $73. The next most costly components were the display module (about $20), the video/multimedia processor chip ($8) and the controller chip ($5). . . . [T]he final assembly, done in China, costs only about $4 a unit.

One approach to tracing supply chain geography might be to attribute the cost of each component to the country of origin of its maker. So $73 of the cost of the iPod would be attributed to Japan since Toshiba is a Japanese company, and the $13 cost of the two chips would be attributed to the United States, since the suppliers, Broadcom and PortalPlayer, are American companies, and so on.

But this method hides some of the most important details. Toshiba may be a Japanese company, but it makes most of its hard drives in the Philippines and China. So perhaps we should also allocate part of the cost of that hard drive to one of those countries. The same problem arises regarding the Broadcom chips, with most of them manufactured in Taiwan. So how can one distribute the costs of the iPod components across the countries where they are manufactured in a meaningful way?

To answer this question, let us look at the production process as a sequence of steps, each possibly performed by a different company operating in a different country. At each step, inputs like computer chips and a bare circuit board are converted into outputs like an assembled circuit board. The difference between the cost of the inputs and the value of the outputs is the "value added" at that step, which can then be attributed to the country where that value was added. . . .

This value added calculation illustrates the futility of summarizing such a complex manufacturing process by using conventional trade statistics. Even though Chinese workers contribute only about 1 percent of the value of the iPod, the export of a finished iPod to the United States directly contributes about $150 to our bilateral trade deficit with the Chinese.

Ultimately, there is no simple answer to who makes the iPod or where it is made. The iPod, like many other products, is made in several countries by dozens of companies, with each stage of production contributing a different amount to the final value.

The real value of the iPod doesn't lie in its parts or even in putting those parts together. The bulk of the iPod's value is in the conception and design of the iPod. That is why Apple gets $80 for each of these video iPods it sells, which is by far the largest piece of value added in the entire supply chain. Those clever folks at Apple figured out how to combine 451 mostly generic parts into a valuable product. They may not make the iPod, but they created it. In the end, that's what really matters.

Source: Hal R. Varian, "An iPod Has Global Value. Ask the (Many) Countries That Make It," Economic Scene, The New York Times, *June 28, 2007, electronic edition.*

The iPod is valued at about $150 when it leaves the dock in China en route to the United States, and it eventually sells for $299 in the United States, but only $4 of that amount reflects the value of Chinese labor used in the assembly. The rest of the $150 export value was actually imported into China from other countries, including $73 for the hard drive, $20 for the display module, $13 for various chips, and so on. Nevertheless, the entire $150 is counted as an export from China to the United States. This example shows that the bilateral trade deficit or surplus between countries is a slippery concept. It doesn't really make sense to count the entire $150 iPod as a Chinese export to the United States, as is done in official trade statistics, when only $4 is the **value-added** in China; that is, the difference between the value of the iPod when it leaves China and the cost of parts and materials purchased in China and imported from other countries. That shortcoming of official statistics gives us a good reason to not focus on the bilateral trade deficit or surplus between countries, even though that number is often reported in the media.

The iPod example illustrates how the manufacturing of a single final product is often spread across many countries: the iPod and its components are produced in facilities in China, Taiwan, Thailand, Malaysia, Singapore, South Korea, the Czech Republic, Philippines, and the United States. That so many countries are involved in manufacturing a final product and its components is a new phenomenon that illustrates the drop in transportation and communication costs in the modern world economy. In the past, trade occurred in more standardized goods (such as raw materials) that were shipped long distances, but were not shipped back-and-forth between countries during the manufacturing process. This new feature of world trade and production is often called **offshoring.**

Map of World Trade

To show the flow of exports and imports around the world, we use the map in Figure 1-1, which shows trade in billions of dollars for 2006. That year about $11.6 trillion in goods crossed international borders. (Because trade in services is harder to measure between countries, we do not include it in Figure 1-1.) The amount of trade in goods is illustrated by the width of the lines, with the largest trade flows having the heaviest lines and the smallest having dashed lines. For large trade flows, we usually draw two lines indicating the direction of each trade flow. For smaller amounts of trade, we draw a single dashed line, with the amount of the trade flows shown on each arrow. The trade flows within certain regions, such as Europe, are described by a circle, with the total amount of trade shown.

Factors That Explain Trade Patterns Figure 1-1 shows that the amount of trade that occurs among nations ranges from the huge flows we see in Europe to the very small flows between Europe and Africa. What factors determine the amount of trade that occurs between nations and regions?

1. **Low Tariffs** The largest amount of trade shown in Figure 1-1 is the flow of goods within Europe, which was $3.7 trillion in 2006—nearly one-third (31%) of total world trade! The amount of trade among European countries is large because there are so many countries located there and because it is easy to ship from one country to another. Furthermore, trade is high because **import tariffs** (taxes on international trade) are low. Most of the European countries are members of the European Union, a group of countries that trade with each other at zero tariffs.

FIGURE 1-1

Total world trade flows in 2006: $11,600 billion

World Trade in Goods

- - - - - - < $50 billion
————— $50–150 billion
————— $150–500 billion
━━━━━ > $500 billion

World Trade in Goods, 2006 ($ billions) This figure shows the trade in merchandise goods between selected countries and regions of the world for 2006 in billions of dollars. The amount of trade in goods is illustrated by the width of the lines, with the largest trade flows having the heaviest lines and the smallest having dashed lines.

Source: United Nations trade data.

2. **Trade Between Similar Countries** In addition to large trade flows among the European countries, there are also large trade flows between the United States and Europe. The United States exported $243 billion of goods to Europe in 2006 and imported $384 billion of goods from Europe. This fact shows that a large amount of world trade occurs between countries that are similar in their levels of advanced industrialization and great wealth. Why do these countries trade so much with each other?

The many differences among European countries and between Europe and the United States explain, in part, the trade between them. The first model of trade we study, called the Ricardian model, was initially used to explain trade between England and Portugal based on the difference in their climates. Despite their differences, industrialized countries like the United Kingdom and the United States have many similarities in their consumption patterns and in their ability to produce goods and services. Even very similar countries have enough variety in the goods they produce (such as different models of cars or types of cheese) that it is natural for them to trade with each other.

3. **Labor, Capital, and Natural Resources** Why does Asia trade so much? There are many answers to this question. One answer is that wages in many Asian countries are much lower than in the industrialized world. China's low wages allow it to produce goods cheaply and then export them. But why are Chinese wages so low? One explanation is that Chinese workers are less productive. Low wages cannot explain why Japan exports so much, however. Japan's wages are very high because its workers are very productive; it exports a great deal to Europe and the United States because its highly skilled workforce and large amount of capital (factories and machines) make it possible for Japan to produce high-quality goods in abundance. Conversely, its scarcity of raw materials explains why it imports those goods from resource-rich countries such as Australia, Canada, and the United States. Trade patterns based on the amounts of labor, capital, and natural resources found in each country are explained by the Heckscher-Ohlin trade model.

Trade Compared with GDP

So far, we have discussed the value of trade crossing international borders. But there is a second way that trade is often reported, and that is as a ratio of trade to a country's **gross domestic product (GDP),** the value of all final goods produced in a year. For the United States, the average value of imports and exports of goods and services expressed relative to GDP was 15% in 2008. Most other countries have a higher ratio of trade to GDP, as shown in Table 1-1.

At the top of the list are Hong Kong (China) and Malaysia, where the amount of trade exceeds their GDP![2] These two countries are important shipping and processing centers, so they continually import goods, process them, and then export the final product to other countries. As in the iPod example, the value-added involved in the exports ($4 for each iPod) can be much less than the total value of exports ($150). That explains why the total amount that countries trade can be greater than their GDP. At the bottom of the list are the United States and Japan, which have very large economies; Pakistan, which is only starting to engage in international trade; and Brazil and Argentina, which are far away from other importing countries.

TABLE 1-1

Trade/GDP Ratio in 2008 This table shows the ratio of total trade to GDP for each country, where trade is calculated as (Imports + Exports)/2, including both merchandise goods and services. Countries with the highest ratios of trade to GDP tend to be small in economic size and are often important centers for shipping goods, like Hong Kong (China) and Malaysia. Countries with the lowest ratios of trade to GDP tend to be very large in economic size, like Japan and the United States, or are not very open to trade because of trade barriers or their distance from other countries.

Country	Trade/GDP (%)	GDP ($ billion)
Hong Kong, China	207	215
Malaysia	116	222
Hungary	81	155
Thailand	75	272
Switzerland	65	492
Austria	56	414
Denmark	54	341
Sweden	50	479
Germany	44	3,649
Norway	38	452
South Africa	37	276
Canada	33	1,501
China	33	4,327
United Kingdom	30	2,674
Indonesia	29	511
Italy	29	2,303
Mexico	29	1,088
Spain	29	1,604
Greece	28	356
France	28	2,857
Turkey	26	735
Russian Federation	26	1,679
Venezuela	25	314
India	25	1,159
Argentina	23	328
Pakistan	18	165
Japan	16	4,911
United States	15	14,093
Brazil	14	1,575

Source: World Development Indicators, The World Bank.

---

[2] Hong Kong (China) has been a part of the People's Republic of China since July 1, 1997, but its trade statistics are measured separately, so we list Hong Kong in Table 1-1 as a distinct region.

Even though the United States is among the world's largest exporters and importers, it is nearly the smallest trading nation of the countries shown in Table 1-1 when trade is measured as a percent of a country's GDP. What is the reason for this inverse relationship? Very large countries tend to have a lot of trade among states or provinces *within* their borders, trade that is not counted as part of international trade. Other countries that are not quite as large as the United States but are close to their major trading partners, such as Germany, the United Kingdom, Italy, and Spain, and Canada and Mexico, tend to appear in the middle of the list in Table 1-1. Smaller countries with close neighbors, such as Hong Kong, Malaysia, and the smaller European nations, will have more trade spilling across their borders and have the highest ratios of trade to GDP.

Barriers to Trade

Table 1-1 shows the differences across countries in the amount of trade relative to GDP, but this ratio changes over time. There are many reasons for the amount of trade to change. Those reasons include import tariffs, taxes that countries charge on imported goods; transportation costs of shipping from one country to another; events, such as wars and natural disasters, that lead to reduced trade; and so on. The term **trade barriers** refers to all factors that influence the amount of goods and services shipped across international borders.

APPLICATION

The Financial Crisis

In the fall of 2008 there was a financial crisis in the United States that quickly spread to other countries. The full, detailed story of the financial crisis is beyond the scope of this book. Here, we present a highly simplified description of the crisis that allows us to show how and why the crisis affected international trade. The reason this crisis occurred was that the prices for homes rose from 1997 to 2005, and then fell substantially from 2006 up to the present time. As a result, many homeowners **defaulted** on (i.e., stopped paying) their mortgages, and banks began foreclosing on and taking possession of the homes. Mortgage defaults meant that the loans made by the banks became worth much less—they became worth only the value at which the house could be sold, which was often far less than the price for which the house had been purchased. Banks making mortgages therefore lost a great deal of money, and these losses spread throughout the whole financial system in the United States and abroad.

From this brief description of the banking crisis, it is apparent that international trade was not the cause of the crisis. Nevertheless, the crisis had a substantial impact on the amount of international trade, because it sent many countries into recessions that led to a fall in exports and imports. This fall in trade is illustrated in Figure 1-2, where we show the percentage change in value of trade (the average of exports and imports for each country) from the first quarter (January–March) of 2007 to the fourth quarter (October–December) of 2009. For all the countries shown, the pattern is similar: at the end of 2007 or early in 2008, trade began to fall, reaching a quarter-to-quarter fall of about 20% by the end of 2008 or early in 2009. By the last quarter of 2009, trade was expanding by about 10% as compared with the previous quarter, but that was still not

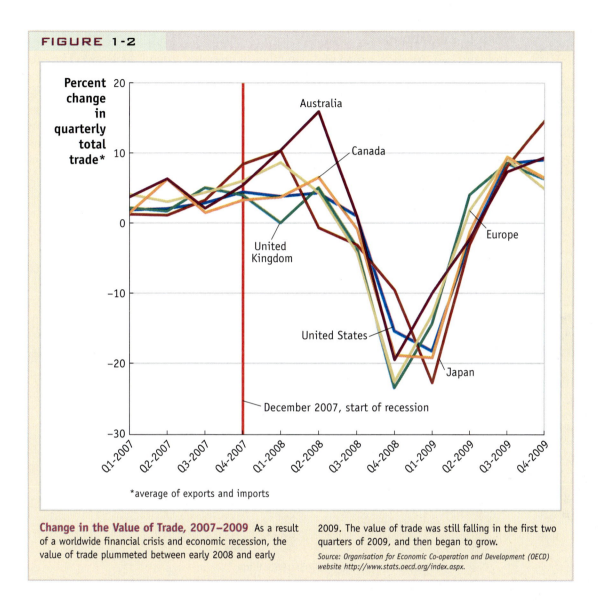

FIGURE 1-2

Percent change in quarterly total trade*

Australia

Canada

United Kingdom

Europe

United States

Japan

December 2007, start of recession

*average of exports and imports

Change in the Value of Trade, 2007–2009 As a result of a worldwide financial crisis and economic recession, the value of trade plummeted between early 2008 and early 2009. The value of trade was still falling in the first two quarters of 2009, and then began to grow.

Source: Organisation for Economic Co-operation and Development (OECD) website http://www.stats.oecd.org/index.aspx.

enough to return trade to its pre-crisis level. It will take some years for the world economy to again reach a level of trade, or ratio of trade to GDP, that is as high as what it has achieved in the past. ■

2 Migration and Foreign Direct Investment

In addition to examining the reasons for and effects of international trade (the flow of goods and services between countries), we also analyze **migration,** the movement of people across borders, and **foreign direct investment (FDI),** the movement of capital across borders. All three of these flows affect the economy of a nation that opens its borders to interact with other nations.

Map of Migration

In Figure 1-3, we show a map of the number of migrants around the world. The values shown are the number of people in 2005 who were living (legally or illegally) in a country other than the one in which they were born. For this map, we combine two different sources of data: (1) the movement of people from one country to another, reported for just the Organisation for Economic Co-operation and Development (OECD) countries and shown by arrows from one country to another,[3] and (2) the number of foreign-born located in each region (but without knowing their country of origin), shown by the bold arrows from World into Asia, Africa, and Latin America.[4]

FIGURE 1-3

Total world migrants in 2005: 195 million

World Migration

- - - - - - < 1 million
———— 1–5 million
———— 5–15 million
━━━━ > 15 million

Foreign-Born Migrants, 2005 (millions) This figure shows the number of foreign-born migrants living in selected countries and regions of the world for 2005 in millions of people. The level of migration is illustrated by the width of the lines, with the largest migrant numbers having the heaviest lines and the smallest having dashed lines.

Source: OECD and UN migration data.

---

[3] The Organization for Economic Cooperation and Development (OECD) consists of 30 member countries, including most European countries as well as Australia, Canada, Japan, Mexico, South Korea, and the United States. See the complete list of countries at http://www.oecd.org.

[4] Data on total immigration for major regions are available from the United Nations at http://www.esa.un.org/migration.

In 2005 there were 62 million foreign-born people living in the OECD countries. But that is less than one-third of the total number of foreign-born people worldwide, which was 195 million. These figures show that unlike trade (much of which occurs between the OECD countries), the majority of immigration occurs *outside* the OECD between countries that are less wealthy. Asia, for example, was home to 53.1 million migrants in 2005, and Africa was home to 17.1 million migrants. Latin America has 6.9 million foreign-born people living there. We expect that many of these immigrants come from the same continent where they are now living but have had to move from one country to another for employment or other reasons such as famine and war.[5]

Given the choice, these migrants would probably rather move to a high-wage, industrial country. But people cannot just move to another country as can the goods and services that move in international trade. All countries have restrictions on who can enter and work there. In many OECD countries, these restrictions are in place because policy makers fear that immigrants from low-wage countries will drive down the wages for a country's own less skilled workers. Whether or not that fear is justified, immigration is a hotly debated political issue in many countries, including Europe and the United States. As a result, the flow of people between countries is *much less* free than the flow of goods.

The limitation on migration out of the low-wage countries is offset to some extent by the ability of these countries to export products instead. International trade can act as a *substitute* for movements of labor or capital across borders, in the sense that trade can raise the living standard of workers in the same way that moving to a higher-wage country can. The increased openness to trade in the world economy since World War II has provided opportunities for workers to benefit through trade by working in export industries, even when restrictions on migration prevent them from directly earning higher incomes abroad.

Map of Foreign Direct Investment

As mentioned earlier in the chapter, foreign direct investment (FDI) occurs when a firm in one country owns (in part or in whole) a company or property in another country. Figure 1-4 shows the principal stocks of FDI in 2006, with the magnitude of the stocks illustrated by the width of the lines. As we did for migration, we again combine two sources of information: (1) stocks of FDI found in the OECD countries that are owned by another country, shown by arrows from the country of ownership to the country of location, and (2) FDI stocks from anywhere in the world found in Africa, Asia, Europe, and Latin America.

In 2006 the total value of FDI stocks located in the OECD countries or owned by those countries was $11.4 trillion. That value is more than 90% of the total world stock of FDI, which was $12.4 trillion in 2006. So unlike our findings for immigration, the vast majority of FDI is located in or owned by firms in the OECD countries. The concentration of FDI among wealthy countries is even more pronounced than the concentration of international trade flows. The FDI stock in Africa ($340 billion) is

---

[5] The United Nations data on migrants include refugees, so other reasons for moving include wars and famines. Of the 50.3 million migrants in Asia in 2000, 8.8 million were refugees; of the 16.5 million migrants in Africa, 3.6 million were refugees; and of the 6.3 million migrants in Latin America, 500,000 were refugees.

FIGURE 1-4

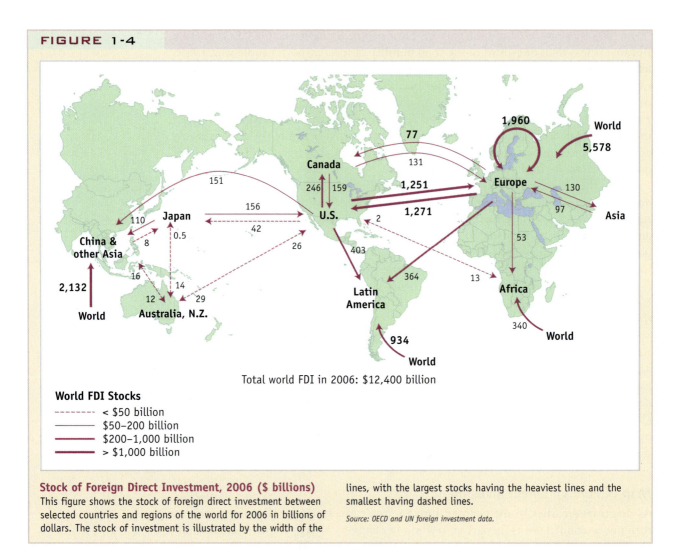

Total world FDI in 2006: $12,400 billion

World FDI Stocks

- - - - - - - < $50 billion
————— $50–200 billion
————— $200–1,000 billion
━━━━━ > $1,000 billion

Stock of Foreign Direct Investment, 2006 ($ billions)
This figure shows the stock of foreign direct investment between selected countries and regions of the world for 2006 in billions of dollars. The stock of investment is illustrated by the width of the lines, with the largest stocks having the heaviest lines and the smallest having dashed lines.

Source: OECD and UN foreign investment data.

approximately one-third of the stock in Latin America ($934 billion), which in turn is less than one-half of the FDI into China and other Asian countries ($2,132 billion). Most of this FDI is from industrial countries, but Chinese firms have begun to acquire land in Africa and Latin America for agriculture and resource extraction, as well as purchase companies in the industrial countries.

There are also substantial amounts of FDI shown in Figure 1-4 among the United States, Canada, and Latin America. The United States had a stock of direct investments of $246 billion in Canada in 2006, and Canada invested $159 billion in the United States. The United States had a stock of direct investments of $403 billion in Latin America, principally in Mexico. Brazil and Mexico are two of the largest recipients of FDI among developing countries, after China. In 2006 Mexico had a FDI stock of $226 billion, and Brazil had a stock of $222 billion, accounting for about one-half of the total $934 billion in FDI to Latin America. These are examples of **vertical FDI,** by which we mean foreign direct investment from developed to developing countries, prompted by the opportunity to produce goods at lower wages than in the industrial countries.

The direct investments between the United States and Japan and between Europe and Japan are **horizontal FDI,** by which we mean foreign direct investment between developed countries. In addition to Japan, the rest of Asia shows a large amount of FDI in Figure 1-4. The United States had direct investments of $151 billion in the rest of Asia, especially China, while Europe had a direct investment of $130 billion in Asia. These stocks are also examples of vertical FDI, foreign direct investment from industrial to developing countries, to take advantage of low wages.

3 International Macroeconomics

Increased globalization has not only affected the trade in goods, services, and capital, but has also greatly affected the global macroeconomy by strengthening the linkages between the economies of the world through financial flows and trade flows. International macroeconomics is the study of large-scale economic issues in interdependent economies. It is macroeconomic because it focuses on key economy-wide variables such as exchange rates, prices, interest rates, income, wealth, and payments between countries.

The most essential features of international macroeconomics can be reduced to three key elements: the world has many monies (not one), countries are financially integrated (not isolated), and in this context economic policy choices are made (but not always very well). In the chapters in the second part of this book, we combine relevant economic theory with compelling empirical evidence to explain the workings of today's global macroeconomy. Here, we briefly explore the road ahead.

Foreign Exchange: Currencies and Crises

In most branches of economics, and even in studying international trade, it is common to assume that all goods are priced in a common currency. Despite this unrealistic assumption, these analyses deliver important insights into the workings of the global economy.

In the real world, however, countries have different currencies, and a complete understanding of how a country's economy works requires that we study the *exchange rate*, the price of foreign currency and learn how and why they fluctuate. In later chapters, we see why exchange rates matter for economic outcomes and why they are an important focus of economic policy making.

How Exchange Rates Behave Economists divide the world into two groups of countries: those with **fixed** (or *pegged*) **exchange rates** and those with **floating** (or *flexible*) **exchange rates.** Fixed exchange rates are officially set to fluctuate within a very narrow range. In contrast, a floating exchange rate moves up and down over a much wider range. In later chapters we investigate how exchange rates are determined, why some exchange rates fluctuate sharply in the short run while others are almost constant, and what explains why exchange rates rise, fall, or stay flat in the long run.

We also examine one type of event that is almost guaranteed to put exchange rates front and center in the news: an **exchange rate crisis.** In such a crisis, a currency experiences a sudden and pronounced loss of value against another currency.

100 Chinese yuan, U.S. dollars, Eurozone euros.

One of the most dramatic currency crises in recent history occurred in Argentina from December 2001 to January 2002. After the crisis, one Argentine peso, which had been worth exactly one U.S. dollar for about ten years, had fallen in value to just $0.25. The Argentine government declared a world-record default (i.e., a suspension of payments) on its $155 billion of debt; the financial system was in a state of near closure for months; inflation climbed; output collapsed and unemployment soared; and more than 50% of Argentine households fell below the poverty line. At the height of the crisis, violence flared and the country had five presidents in the space of two weeks (see **Headlines: Economic Crisis in Argentina**).

Argentina's experience was extreme but not unique. Exchange rate crises are fairly common. Figure 1-5 lists 24 exchange rate crises in the six-year period from 1997 to 2009. The year 1997 was especially eventful, with 7 crises, 5 of them in East Asia. Other notable crises during this period included Russia in 1998, Brazil in 1999, Argentina in

FIGURE 1-5

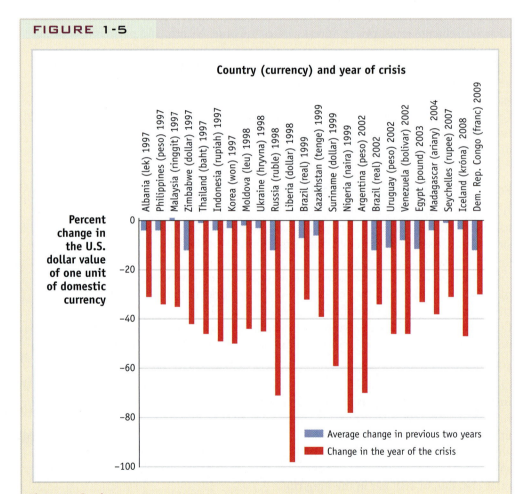

Currency Crashes The chart shows that exchange rate crises are common events.

Note: An exchange rate crisis is defined here as an event in which a currency loses more than 30% of its value in U.S. dollar terms over one year, having changed by less than 20% each of the previous two years.

Source: IMF, International Financial Statistics.

2002. More recently, Iceland experienced an exchange rate crisis during the global financial crisis of 2008.

Crisis episodes display some regular patterns. Output typically falls, banking and debt problems emerge, households and firms suffer. The economic setbacks are often more pronounced in poorer countries. Although we could confine our study of exchange rates to normal times, the frequent and damaging occurrence of crises obliges us to pay some attention to these abnormal episodes, too.

Why Exchange Rates Matter Changes in exchange rates affect an economy in two ways:

■ Changes in exchange rates cause a change in the international relative prices of goods. That is, one country's goods and services become more or less expensive relative to another's when expressed in a common unit of currency. These changes affect a country's imports (goods it buys from other countries) and exports (goods it sells to other countries).

■ Changes in exchange rates can cause a change in the international relative prices of assets. These fluctuations in wealth can then affect firms, governments, and individuals. For example, the Eurozone countries held about $200 billion in U.S. dollar assets at the end of 2002. These assets were worth approximately €200 billion, since €1 was then worth about $1. A year later, at the end of 2003, those same assets were worth the equivalent of only €160 billion. Why? The dollar was then worth only €0.80, and 0.8 times 200 equals 160. Hence, *simply as a result of a change in the exchange rate*, the inhabitants of the Eurozone suffered a €40 billion loss in their total wealth.[6]

In later chapters we study how changes in exchange rates affect the demand for goods from different countries, and hence the levels of national output and how changes in exchange rates affect the values of foreign assets, and hence change national wealth.

Globalization of Finance: Debts and Deficits

Financial development is a defining characteristic of modern economies. Households' use of financial instruments such as credit cards, savings accounts, and mortgages is taken for granted, as is the ability of firms and governments to use the products and services offered in financial markets. A few years ago, very little of this financial activity spilled across international borders; countries were very nearly closed from a financial standpoint. Today many countries are more open: financial globalization has taken hold around the world, starting in the economically advanced countries and spreading to many emerging market countries.

Although you might expect that you need many complex and difficult theories to understand the financial transactions between countries, such analysis requires only the application of familiar household accounting concepts such as income, expenditure, and wealth. We develop these concepts at the national level to understand how flows of goods, services, income, and capital make the global macroeconomy work. We then see how the smooth functioning of international finance can make countries better off by allowing them to lend and borrow. Along the way, we also find that

---

[6] Data for this example are based on U.S. Treasury reports.

HEADLINES

Economic Crisis in Argentina

International macroeconomics can often seem like a dry and abstract subject, but it must be remembered that societies and individuals can be profoundly shaken by the issues we will study. This article was written just after the start of the severe economic crisis that engulfed Argentina in 2002, following the collapse of its fixed exchange rate, a financial crisis, and a government default. Real output shrank by 15% and took years to regain its previous peak, as poverty and unemployment rates remained at high levels. The country sank into an economic depression worse even than those in the 1930s, 1910s, and 1890s.

ROSARIO, Argentina—Word spread fast through the vast urban slums ringing Rosario. There was food on the freeway—and it was still alive.

A cattle truck had overturned near this rusting industrial city, spilling 22 head of prime Angus beef across the wind-swept highway. Some were dead. Most were injured. A few were fine.

A mob moved out from Las Flores, a shantytown of trash heaps and metal shacks boiling over with refugees from the financial collapse of what was once Latin America's wealthiest nation. Within minutes, 600 hungry residents arrived on the scene, wielding machetes and carving knives. Suddenly, according to accounts from some of those present on that March day, a cry went up.

"Kill the cows!" someone yelled. "Take what you can!"

Cattle company workers attempting a salvage operation backed off. And the slaughter began. The scent of blood, death and fresh meat filled the highway. Cows bellowed as they were sloppily diced by groups of men, women and children. Fights broke out for pieces of flesh in bloody tugs of war.

"I looked around at people dragging off cow legs, heads and organs, and I couldn't believe my eyes," said Alberto Banrel, 43, who worked on construction jobs until last January, when the bottom fell out of the economy after Argentina suffered the world's largest debt default ever and a massive currency devaluation.

"And yet there I was, with my own bloody knife and piece of meat," Banrel said. "I felt like we had become a pack of wild animals . . . like piranhas on the Discovery Channel. Our situation has turned us into this."

The desolation of that day, neighbor vs. neighbor over hunks of meat, suggested how profoundly the collapse has altered Argentina. Traditionally proud, Argentines have begun to despair. Talk today is of vanished dignity, of a nation diminished in ways not previously imaginable. . . .

Until last year, Argentines were part of the richest, best-educated and most cultured nation in Latin America. . . . The poor here lived with more dignity than their equals anywhere else in the region. Argentina was, as the Argentines liked to say, very civilized.

Not anymore. . . . With government statistics showing 11,200 people a day falling into poverty—earning less than $3 daily—Buenos Aires, a city once compared to Paris, has become the dominion of scavengers and thieves at night. Newly impoverished homeless people emerge from abandoned buildings and rail cars, rummaging through trash in declining middle- and upper-class neighborhoods. People from the disappearing middle

Beatriz Orresta, 20, holds her malnourished son in Rio Chico. She had been feeding her children soup made with the dried bones of a dead cow that her husband had found.

Silvina Frydlewsky for the *Washington Post*, August 5, 2002.

class, such as Vicente Pitasi, 60 and jobless, have turned to pawn shops to sell their wedding rings.

"I have seen a lot happen in Argentina in my day, but I never lost hope until now," Pitasi said. "There is nothing left here, not even our pride.". . .

Severe hunger and malnutrition have emerged in the rural interior—something almost never seen in a country famous for great slabs of beef and undulating fields of wheat. In search of someone to blame, Argentines have attacked the homes of local politicians and foreign banks. . . .

Economists and politicians differ on the causes of the brutal crisis. Some experts blame globalization and faulty policies imposed by the International Monetary Fund. But just as many blame the Argentine government for runaway spending and systematic corruption. The one thing everyone agrees on, however, is that there is no easy fix. . . .

What had been a snowball of poverty and unemployment has turned into an avalanche since January's default and devaluation. A record number of Argentines, more than half, live below the official poverty line. More than one in five no longer have jobs. . . .

For some rural families, the crisis has gone further. It has generated something rarely seen in Argentina: hunger. In the province of Tucuman, an agricultural zone of 1.3 million people, health workers say cases of malnutrition have risen 20 percent to 30 percent over the previous year.

"I wish they would cry," whispered Beatriz Orresta, 20, looking at her two young sons in a depressed Tucuman sugar cane town in the shadow of the Andes. "I would feel much better if they cried." Jonatan, 2, resting on the dirt floor behind the family's wooden shack, and Santiago, the 7-month-old she cradled in her arms, lay listlessly.

"They don't act it, but they're hungry. I know they are," she said.

Source: Excerpted from Anthony Faiola, "Despair in Once-Proud Argentina: After Economic Collapse, Deep Poverty Makes Dignity a Casualty," Washington Post, *August 6, 2002.*

financial interactions are not always so smooth. Defaults and other disruptions in financial markets can mean that the potential gains from globalization are not so easily realized in practice.

Deficits and Surpluses: The Balance of Payments Do you keep track of your finances? If so, you probably follow two important figures: your income and expenditure. The difference between the two is an important number: if it is positive, you have a surplus; if it is negative, you have a deficit. The number tells you if you are living within or beyond your means. What would you do with a surplus? The extra money could be added to savings or used to pay down debt. How would you handle a deficit? You could run down your savings or borrow and go into deeper debt. Thus, imbalances between income and expenditure require you to engage in financial transactions with the world outside your household.

At the national level, we can make exactly the same kinds of economic measurements of **income, expenditure, deficit,** and **surplus,** many of which are important barometers of economic performance and the subject of heated policy debate.

Because the world *as a whole* is a closed economy (we can't borrow from outer space, as yet), it is impossible for the world to run a deficit. If the United States is a net borrower, running a current account deficit with income less than expenditure, then the rest of the world must be a net lender to the United States, running surpluses with expenditure less than income. Globally, the world's finances must balance in this way, even if individual countries and regions have surpluses or deficits. Figure 1-6 shows the massive scale of some of these recent imbalances, dramatically illustrating the impact of financial globalization.

In later chapters we study how different international economic transactions contribute to current account imbalances, how these imbalances are financed, and the role of current account imbalances in a well-functioning economy.

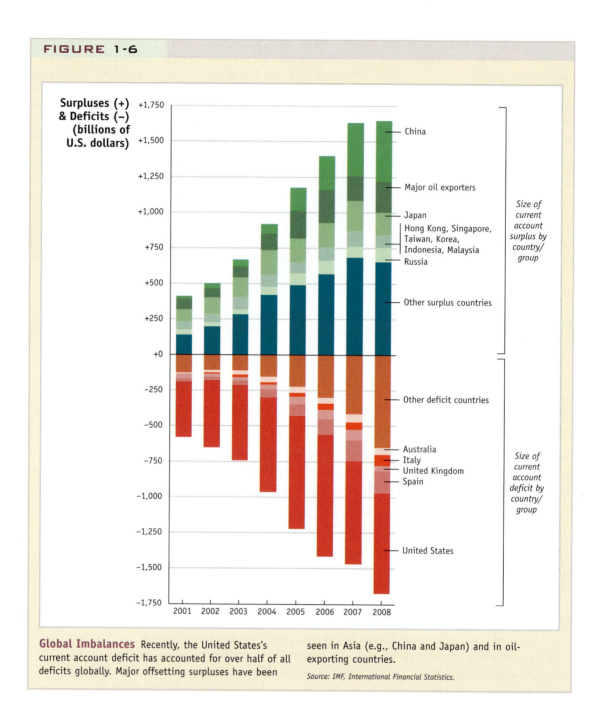

FIGURE 1-6

Global Imbalances Recently, the United States's current account deficit has accounted for over half of all deficits globally. Major offsetting surpluses have been seen in Asia (e.g., China and Japan) and in oil-exporting countries.

Source: IMF, International Financial Statistics.

Debtors and Creditors: External Wealth To understand the role of wealth in international financial transactions, we revisit our household analogy. Your total **wealth** or net worth is equal to your assets (what others owe you) minus your liabilities (what you owe others). When you run a surplus, and save money (buying assets or paying down debt), your total wealth, or net worth, tends to rise. Similarly, when you have a deficit and borrow (taking on debt or running down savings), your wealth tends to fall.

We can use a similar analysis to understand the behavior of nations. From an international perspective, a country's net worth is called its *external wealth* and it equals the difference between its foreign assets (what it is owed by the rest of the world) and its foreign liabilities (what it owes to the rest of the world). Positive external wealth makes a country a creditor nation (other nations owe it money); negative external wealth makes it a debtor nation (it owes other nations money).

What forms can a nation's external wealth take and does the composition of wealth matter? What explains the level of a nation's external wealth and how does it change over time? How important is the current account as a determinant of external wealth? How does it relate to the country's present and future economic welfare?

In later chapters we see how international flows of goods, services, income, and capital allow the global macroeconomy to operate. In our course of study, we build up our understanding gradually, starting with basic accounting and measurement, then moving on the causes and consequences of imbalances in the flows and the accumulations of debts and credits.

Government and Institutions: Policies and Performance

In theory, one could devise a course of study in international economics without reference to government, but the result might not shed much light on reality. As we know from other courses in economics, and as we have already started to see in this chapter, government actions influence economic outcomes in many ways by making decisions about exchange rates, macroeconomic policies, and so on.

To gain a deeper understanding of the global macroeconomy, we can look at government activity on several distinct levels. In the traditional way we will study **policies,** which refers to direct government actions, including familiar textbook topics like monetary and fiscal policy. However, economists also consider the broader context of rules and norms, or **regimes** in which policy choices are made. At the broadest level, research also focuses on **institutions,** a term that refers to the overall legal, political, cultural, and social structures that influence economic and political actions.

Evading control: For years, Zimbabwe imposed capital controls. In theory, U.S. dollars could be traded for Zimbabwe dollars only through official channels at an official rate. On the street, the reality was different.

Three important features of the broad macroeconomic environment play an important role in the remainder of this book: the rules that a government decides to apply to restrict or allow capital mobility; the decision that a government makes between a fixed and a floating exchange rate regime; and the institutional foundations of economic performance, such as the quality of governance that prevails in a country.

Independence and Monetary Policy: The Choice of Exchange Rate Regimes

There are two broad categories of exchange rate behavior: fixed regimes and floating regimes. How common is each type? Figure 1-7 shows that there are many countries operating under each kind of regime. Because fixed and floating are both common regime choices, we have to understand both.

The choice of exchange rate regime is a major policy problem. If you have noticed the attention given by journalists and policy makers in recent years to the exchange rate movements of the dollar, euro, yen, pound, yuan, and other currencies, you know that these are major important issues in debates on the global economy.

FIGURE 1-7

Exchange Rate Regimes The pie chart shows a classification of exchange rate regimes around the world using the most recent data for 2008.

Notes: The fixed category includes countries with no separate legal tender (46 countries), currency boards (7), other fixed pegs (58), pegs within horizontal bands (2), crawling pegs (8), and crawling bands (2). The floating category includes managed floating with no predetermined path for the exchange rate (25) and independently floating (44).

Source: IMF and author's classification. See Figure 10-4 for details.

Exploring the evidence on exchange rate fluctuations, their origins, and their impact is a major goal of this book. On an intuitive level, whether we are confused travelers fumbling to change money at the bank or importers and exporters trying to conduct business in a predictable way, we have a sense that exchange rate fluctuations, especially if drastic, can impose real economic costs. If every country fixed its exchange rates, we could avoid those costs. Or, taking the argument to an extreme, if we had a single world currency, we might think that all currency-related transaction costs could be avoided. With more than 150 different currencies in existence today, however, we are very far from such a monetary utopia!

The existence of multiple currencies in the world dates back centuries, and for a state to possess its own currency has long been viewed as an almost essential aspect of sovereignty. Without control of its own national currency, a government's freedom to pursue its own monetary policy is sacrificed automatically. However, even with your own currency, it still remains to be seen how beneficial monetary independence is.

Despite the profusion of currencies, we also see newly emerging forms of monetary organization. Some groups of countries have sought to simplify their transactions through the adoption of a **common currency** with shared policy responsibility. The most notable example is the Eurozone, a subset of the European Union that in 2009 comprised 16 countries, but with more members expected to join soon. Still other countries have chosen to use currencies over which they have no policy control, as with the recent cases of **dollarization** in El Salvador and Ecuador.

Why do so many countries insist on the "barbarism" of having their own currency (as John Stuart Mill put it)? Why do some countries create a common currency or adopt another nation's currency as their own? Why do some of the countries that have kept their own currencies maintain a fixed exchange rate with another currency? And why do others permit their exchange rate to fluctuate over time, making a floating exchange rate their regime choice?

Institutions and Economic Performance: The Quality of Governance Going beyond specific policy choices, economists also consider the broader institutional context in which such choices are made. The legal, political, social, cultural, ethical, and religious structures of a society set the environment for economic prosperity and stability, or poverty and instability. The functioning of the global macroeconomy is affected in many ways by the actions of governments. Throughout the book, we must pay attention to the possible actions that governments might take and try to understand their possible causes and consequences.

Governance matters: it explains large differences between countries in their economic outcomes. Poor governance generally means that a country is poorer and is subject to more macroeconomic shocks. It may also be subject to more political shocks and a general inability to conduct policy in a reliable and consistent way. These characteristics force us to think carefully about the formulation of optimal policies and policy regimes in rich and poor countries. One size may not fit all, and policies that work well in a stable well-governed country may be less successful in an unstable developing country with poor governance.

Figure 1-8 shows evidence on the importance of the quality of institutions or "governance" using national measures on five dimensions: voice and accountability, political

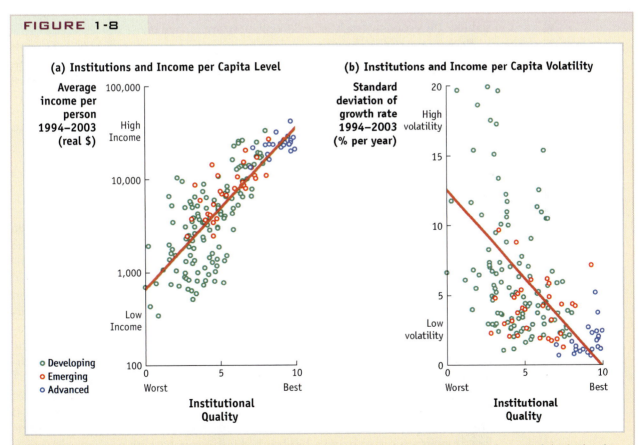

FIGURE 1-8

(a) Institutions and Income per Capita Level

Average income per person 1994–2003 (real $)

(b) Institutions and Income per Capita Volatility

Standard deviation of growth rate 1994–2003 (% per year)

○ Developing
○ Emerging
○ Advanced

Institutional Quality

Institutions and Economic Performance The scatterplots show how an index measuring the quality of a country's institutions is positively correlated with the level of income per capita as shown in panel (a), and is inversely correlated with the volatility of income per capita as shown in panel (b). In each case, the line of best fit is shown.

Source: Real GDP per capita from Penn World Tables. Institutional quality from Daniel Kaufmann, Aart Kraay, and Massimo Mastruzzi, September 2006, "Governance Matters V: Governance Indicators for 1996–2005," World Bank Policy Research.

stability, government effectiveness, regulatory quality, rule of law, and control of corruption. The figure shows that, across countries, an average or composite measure of all these dimensions is strongly correlated with economic outcomes.

First, we see that better institutions are correlated with more **income per capita** in panel (a). A government that is unaccountable, unstable, ineffective, capricious, corrupt, and not based on laws is unlikely to encourage commerce, business, investment, or innovation. The effects of institutions on economic prosperity are very large. In the advanced countries at the top right of the figure, income per person is more than 50 times larger than in the poorest developing countries at the bottom left, probably the largest gap between rich and poor nations we have ever seen in history. Economists refer to this unequal outcome as "The Great Divergence."

We also see that better institutions are correlated with less **income volatility** (i.e., smaller fluctuations in the growth of income per capita, measured by the standard deviation). This result is shown in panel (b) and may also reflect the unpredictability of economic activity in poorly governed economies. There may be periodic shifts in political power, leading to big changes in economic policies. Or there may be internal conflict between groups that sporadically breaks out and leads to conflict over valuable economic resources. Or the state may be too weak to ensure that essential policies to stabilize the economy (such as bank regulation) are carried out.

Recent research has documented these patterns and has sought to show that causality runs from institutions to outcomes and to explore the possible sources of institutional variation. Institutional change is typically very slow, taking decades or even centuries, because vested interests may seek to block efficiency-enhancing reforms. Thus, as the institutional economist Thorstein Veblen famously pointed out, "Institutions are products of the past process, are adapted to past circumstances, and are therefore never in full accord with the requirements of the present."

4 Conclusions

Globalization means many things: the flow of goods and services across borders; the movement of people and firms; the spread of culture and ideas among countries; the cross-border spillovers of macroeconomic policies; and the tight integration of financial markets around the world. Since World War II international trade and financial flows have grown rapidly, even faster than the growth in world GDP, so that the ratio of trade and financial flows to world GDP have risen steadily. International institutions established after World War II have promoted these trends: the General Agreement on Tariffs and Trade (now known as the World Trade Organization), the International Monetary Fund, the United Nations, and the World Bank were all established in the postwar years to promote economic integration and development.

Migration across countries is not as free as international trade, and all countries have restrictions on immigration because of the fear that the inflow of workers will drive down wages. In later chapters we learn that such a fear is not necessarily justified. Immigrants can sometimes be absorbed into a country with no change in wages. Foreign direct investment is largely unrestricted in the industrial countries but often faces some restrictions in developing countries. China, for example, requires approval of all foreign investments and usually requires that foreign firms have a local partner.

Typically, firms invest in developing countries to take advantage of lower wages in those countries. Investments in developing countries and industrial countries enable firms to spread their business and knowledge of production processes across borders. Migration and foreign direct investment are further aspects of the globalization that has become so widespread today.

The world's increasingly integrated markets for goods, services, and capital also shape today's global macroeconomy. To effectively study the international macroeconomy, we must understand the economic linkages between different countries—their currencies, their trade, their capital flows. Only then can we begin to understand some of the most important economic phenomena in the world today, such as the fluctuations in currencies, the determinants of global imbalances, and the problems of economic policy making.

KEY POINTS

1. The trade balance of a country is the difference between the value of its exports and the value of its imports, and is determined by macroeconomic conditions in the country.

2. A large portion of international trade is between industrial countries. Trade within Europe and between Europe and the United States accounts for over one-third of world trade.

3. Many of the trade models we study emphasize the differences between countries, but it is also possible to explain trade between countries that are similar. Similar countries will trade different varieties of goods with each other.

4. Larger countries tend to have smaller shares of trade relative to GDP because so much of their trade occurs internally. Hong Kong (China) and Malaysia have ratios of trade to GDP that exceed 100%, whereas the United States' ratio of trade to GDP in 2008 was 15%.

5. The majority of world migration occurs into developing countries as a result of restrictions on immigration into wealthier, industrial countries.

6. The majority of world foreign direct investment occurs between industrial countries. In 2006 more than one-third of the world stock of FDI was within Europe or between Europe and the United States, and 90% of the world stock of FDI was into or out of the OECD countries.

7. Countries have different currencies, and the price at which these currencies trade is known as the exchange rate. In learning what determines this exchange rate and how the exchange rate is linked to the rest of the economy, we look at some key questions: Why do some countries have fixed exchange rates and others floating? Why do some go from one to the other, often in response to a crisis? Why do some countries have no currency of their own?

8. When countries are financially integrated, it allows them to decouple their level of income from their level of expenditure; the difference between the two is the current account. An important goal is to understand what determines the current account and how the current account is linked to the rest of a nation's economy. Along the way, we learn how a country's current account affects its wealth, how its credits and debts are settled, and how the current account changes.

9. Countries differ in the quality of their policy choices and in the quality of the deeper institutional context in which policies are made. In studying international macroeconomic interactions and events, it is essential to understand how policy regimes and institutions affect policy choices and economic outcomes. How does quality of governance affect economic outcomes? Why might some policies, such as a fixed exchange rate, work better in some contexts than others?

KEY TERMS

international trade, p. 2

export, p. 3

import, p. 3

trade balance, p. 3

trade surplus, p. 3

trade deficit, p. 3

bilateral trade balance, p. 3

value-added, p. 5

offshoring, p. 5

import tariffs, p. 5

gross domestic product (GDP),
   p. 7

trade barriers, p. 8

default, p. 8

migration, p. 9

foreign direct investment (FDI),
   p. 9

vertical FDI, p. 12

horizontal FDI, p. 13

fixed exchange rate, p. 13

floating exchange rate, p. 13

exchange rate crisis, p. 13

income, p. 17

expenditure, p. 17

deficit, p. 17

surplus, p. 17

wealth, p. 18

policies, p. 19

regimes, p. 19

institutions, p. 19

common currency, p. 20

dollarization, p. 20

income per capita, p. 22

income volatility, p. 22

PROBLEMS

1. Figures 1-1 and 1-4 rely on data from 2006, and Figure 1-3 relies on data from 2005, to map worldwide trade, migration, and foreign direct investment. Updated data for migration and foreign direct investment were not available at the time this chapter was written, but it is available for worldwide trade. In this question, you are asked to update the numbers for world trade.

    a. Go to the World Trade Organization website at http://www.wto.org, and look for its trade data under "Resources" and "Statistics."[7] Look for the most recent edition of its *International Trade Statistics* publication, go to "Trade by region," and find the Excel spreadsheet with "Intra- and inter-regional merchandise trade." Print out this table.

    If you cannot find the website or spreadsheet, use the 2008 table for "Intra- and Inter-Regional Merchandise Trade" that appears on the next page.

    b. From this table, what is the total amount of trade within Europe? What percentage of total world trade is this?

    c. What is the total amount of trade (in either direction) between Europe and North America? Add that to the total trade within Europe, and calculate the percentage of this to the world total.

    d. What is the total amount of trade within the Americas (i.e., between North America, Central America, South America, and within each of these regions)? What percentage of total world trade is this?

    e. What is the total value of exports from Europe and the Americas, and what percentage of the world total is this?

    f. What is the total value of exports from Asia, and what percentage of the world total is this?

    g. What is the total value of exports from the Middle East and the Commonwealth of Independent States,[8] and what percentage of the world total is this?

    h. What is the total value of exports from Africa, and what percentage of the world total is this?

---

[7] The trade statistics are available at http://www.wto.org/english/res_e/statis_e/its2009_e/its09_world_trade_dev_e.htm.

[8] The Commonwealth of Independent States consists of Azerbaijan, Armenia, Belarus, Georgia, Kazakhstan, Kyrgyzstan, Moldova, Russia, Tajikistan, Turkmenistan, Ukraine, and Uzbekistan.

Intra- and Inter-Regional Merchandise Trade, 2008 ($ billions)

Region of Origin	North America	South and Central America	Europe	CIS	Africa	Middle East	Asia	World
DESTINATION								
World	**2,708**	**583**	**6,736**	**517**	**458**	**618**	**3903**	**15,717**
North America	1,015	165	369	16	34	60	376	2,036
South and Central America	169	159	121	9	17	12	101	500
Europe	475	96	4,695	240	186	189	487	6,447
Commonwealth of Independent States (CIS)	36	10	405.6	135	11	25	77	703
Africa	122	19	218.1	2	53	14	114	558
Middle East	117	7	125.5	7	37	122	569	1,021
Asia	775	128	801.0	108	121	196	2181	4,353

Source: WTO, International Trade Statistics 2009.

2. Visit the U.S. Bureau of Economic Analysis at http://www.bea.gov to find information for the latest full calendar year (or for the last four quarters). What is the latest estimate of the size of the annual U.S. current account deficit in billions of dollars?

3. Visit http://www.oanda.com and download data on the same exchange rates (yuan per dollar and dollar per euro) for the past 12 months. What are the rates today? What were they a year ago? By what percentage amount did the rates change? At the OANDA website, click on "Currency Tools" and then "FXGraph" and use the tool to plot the last year of data for each exchange rate. Do you think the rates are floating or fixed? Why?

4. The charts below show the growth of real GDP per capita in three pairs of geographically adjacent countries: North and South Korea, Argentina and Chile, Zimbabwe and Botswana (using data from the Penn World Table).

a. Which country in each pair experienced faster growth in GDP per capita? Which one is now richest?

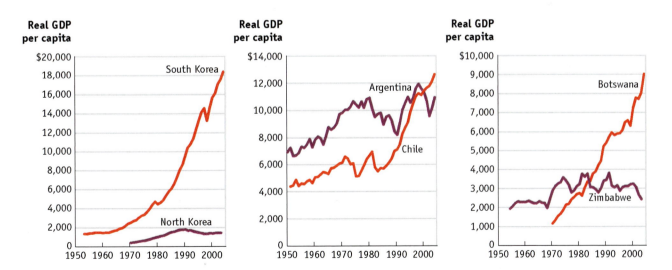

b. The World Bank's World Governance Indicators for each country in 2000 were as follows (higher is better):

	Control of Corruption	Government Effectiveness	Political Stability and Absence of Violence	Rule of Law	Regulatory Quality	Voice and Accountability
South Korea	0.37	0.63	0.49	0.64	0.47	0.76
North Korea	−0.93	−1.10	−0.66	−1.08	−1.70	−2.02
Chile	1.56	1.34	0.85	1.31	1.38	0.56
Argentina	−0.34	0.28	0.48	0.17	0.45	0.44
Botswana	1.02	0.98	0.90	0.67	0.79	0.78
Zimbabwe	−0.87	−1.13	−1.21	−0.74	−1.61	−0.97

Based on these data, do you think institutions
can explain the divergent outcomes in these
countries? Explain. Why do you think it helps
to compare countries that are physically
contiguous?

Trade and Technology: The Ricardian Model

England exported cloth in exchange for wine, because, by so doing her industry was rendered more productive to her; she had more cloth and wine than if she had manufactured both for herself; and Portugal imported cloth and exported wine, because the industry of Portugal could be more beneficially employed for both countries in producing wine. . . .

It would therefore be advantageous for [Portugal] to export wine in exchange for cloth. This exchange might even take place, notwithstanding that the commodity imported by Portugal could be produced there with less labour than in England.

David Ricardo, *On the Principles of Political Economy and Taxation,* 1821

Comparative advantage is the best example of an economic principle that is undeniably true yet not obvious to intelligent people.

Paul Samuelson, "The Way of an Economist," 1969[1]

Pick any manufactured product, and you will most likely find that it is traded among a number of countries. Let's choose snowboards as an example. In 2005 the United States **imported** (i.e., purchased from other countries) $59 million of snowboards from 20 different countries; Table 2-1 identifies the 12 countries with the highest dollar amount of snowboard sales to the United States. In 2009 the value of snowboard imports to the United States had fallen to $38.5 million. This fall occurred because the U.S. recession led to a large drop in imports for many products, including snowboards.

At the top of the list in Table 2-1 is China, **exporting** (i.e., selling to another country) more than $18 million worth of snowboards to the United States in 2005 and $21 million in 2009. The second largest exporter to the United States is Austria, selling

---

[1] Samuelson, Paul A. 1969. "The Way of an Economist." In *International Economic Relations: Proceedings of the Third Congress of the International Economic Association,* edited by Paul A. Samuelson (London: Macmillan), pp. 1–11.

TABLE 2-1

U.S. Imports of Snowboards, 2005 and 2009

Rank	Country	Value of Imports 2005 ($ millions)	Value of Imports 2009 ($ millions)	Quantity of Snowboards 2009 (thousands)	Average Price 2009 ($/board)
1	China	18.15	21.30	365.0	58
2	Austria	17.77	11.04	104.0	106
3	Canada	9.11	3.94	51.8	76
4	Mexico	4.96	0.00	0.0	na
5	Spain	2.17	0.57	6.6	85
6	Poland	1.90	0.04	0.5	71
7	Tunisia	1.29	0.15	4.3	34
8	France	1.12	0.07	0.6	127
9	Germany	1.00	0.02	0.1	227
10	Taiwan	0.49	1.14	37.4	31
11	Bulgaria	0.30	0.00	0.0	na
12	Switzerland	0.18	0.08	0.7	113
13-20	All other countries	0.29	0.18	1.49	123
	Total	58.76	38.51	572	67

Source: U.S. Department of Commerce and the U.S. International Trade Commission.

Where did Shaun White's snowboard come from?

just under $18 million in 2005 and $11 million in 2009. Thus, although China was able to increase its exports even during the U.S. recession, exports from Austria fell. These two countries sell considerably more than the next country on the list, Canada (which sold $3.9 million of snowboards to the United States in 2009). The fourth largest exporter in 2005 was Mexico, selling $5 million of snowboards to the United States, but by 2009 this country does not appear on the list at all: it has been entirely replaced by sales from other countries, most likely China.

Then, a group consisting of mostly European countries—Spain, Poland, France, and Germany, as well as Tunisia, a country on the north coast of Africa that is a former colony of France—sold between $1 million and $2 million each to the United States in 2005. These countries sold less in 2009, and of the other countries shown only Taiwan (in addition to China) managed to increase its sales between these two years.[2] Table 2-1 shows that the value of imports to the United States has fallen in recent years and, in snowboards at least, has become more focused on exports from China and Taiwan. This pattern raises a question: With all the manufacturing capability in the United States, why does it purchase snowboards from these countries at all instead of producing them domestically?

---

[2] Two other countries not shown in Table 2-1, South Korea and the Ukraine, were able to export snowboards to the United States in 2009 even though they did not in 2005.

The first chapters of this book look at various reasons why countries trade goods with one another. These reasons include:

- Differences in the **technology** used in each country (i.e., differences in each country's ability to manufacture products)
- Differences in the total amount of **resources** (including labor, capital, and land) found in each country
- Differences in the costs of **offshoring** (i.e., producing the various parts of a good in different countries and then assembling it in a final location)
- The **proximity** of countries to each other (i.e., how close they are to one another)

In this chapter, we focus on the first of these reasons as an explanation for trade—technology differences across countries. This explanation is often called the **Ricardian model** because it was proposed by the nineteenth-century economist David Ricardo. This model explains how the level of a country's technology affects the wages paid to labor, such that countries with better technologies have higher wages. This, in turn, helps to explain how a country's technology affects its **trade pattern,** the products that it imports and exports.

1 Reasons for Trade

Besides technology differences across countries, which is the focus of the Ricardian model, there are many other reasons why countries trade goods. Before we get into the details of the Ricardian model, let's briefly explore the other reasons for trade.

Proximity

The proximity of countries is a reason for trade primarily because it affects the costs of transportation. Countries that are near one another will usually have lower shipping costs added to the cost of their traded goods. The proximity of countries to one another helps to explain why Canada is among the top exporters of snowboards to the United States and why Canada is the United States' largest trading partner overall. There are many other examples of how the closeness of countries affects trade partners. The largest trading partner of many European countries is another European country, and the largest trading partner of many Asian countries is Japan or China. Sometimes neighboring countries take advantage of their proximity by joining into a **free-trade area,** in which the countries have no restrictions on trade between them.

Resources

Proximity is only a partial explanation for trade patterns. As you can see in Table 2-1, Austria sells at least twice the value of snowboards to the United States as does Canada, despite being farther away, and Mexico went from selling one-half the value as Canada in 2005 to exporting none in 2009, even though it is just as close to the United States as Canada is. Why do Austria and Canada rank higher than Mexico in their sales of snowboards to the United States? Among other reasons, Austria and Canada have cold climates and mountains, making skiing and snowboarding very popular, in contrast to Mexico. In many cases, the local production of (and expertise for) ski and snowboard equipment develops as a result of being in a place where snow sports are common. This local production occurs because of either high demand for equipment or the ready supply of a complementary good (such as a snowy mountain). This is an example of how the geography of a country (mountains and climate, in this case) affects its exports. Ski resorts can also be found in many of the other countries listed in Table 2-1, including France, Switzerland, Spain, and Bulgaria.

Geography includes the **natural resources** (such as land and minerals) found in a country, as well as its **labor resources** (labor of various education and skill levels) and **capital** (machinery and structures). A country's resources are often collectively called its **factors of production,** the land, labor, and capital used to produce goods and services. In the next two chapters, we study how the resources of a country influence its trade patterns and how trade leads to economic gains or losses for different factors of production.

In some cases, a country can export a good without having any advantage in the natural resources needed to produce it. One example is "icewine," which is a type of wine invented in Germany but now also produced in the Niagara Falls region of Canada and the United States (see **Side Bar: Can Comparative Advantage Be Created? The Case of "Icewine"**). For snowboards, having mountains with ski resorts obviously does not apply to Mexico, Tunisia, and Taiwan, which are included among the top twelve sellers of snowboards to the United States in one year or the other. What explains these exports? A hint is provided by noticing that the wholesale price of a snowboard purchased by the United States from these countries is very low: in 2009 Tunisia and Taiwan sold snowboards to the United States for $34 and $31, respectively, and in 2005 Mexico's wholesale price was just $9. These prices are very low compared with the highest-priced countries shown, which are Germany ($227), France ($127), and Switzerland ($113). The very low prices from Mexico, Taiwan, and Tunisia indicate that the snowboards they sell to the United States are not finished products but unfinished boards imported into the United States for further processing. This type of trade in unfinished goods is an example of *offshoring*, a process in which a company spreads its production activities across several countries and trades semifinished products among them.

Absolute Advantage

We've now explained some possible reasons for many countries to export snowboards to the United States, but we haven't yet explained the imports from China, the largest exporter of snowboards to the United States, and from Germany, the ninth largest exporter in 2005 (and having the highest wholesale price in 2009). Germany has the Alps on its southern border, so natural resources are one reason it exports snowboards. Many people, however, may think the primary reason is that Germany has the world's best *technology* for producing snowboards. In fact, Germany is recognized as a world leader in the methods to produce many goods, including chemicals, machine tools, motor vehicles, and steel products. When a country has the best technology for producing a good, it has an **absolute advantage** in the production of that good. Germany has an absolute advantage in many industries, and it produces high-quality goods. But if Germany has an absolute advantage in producing snowboards, why does the United States import so many more snowboards from China, which uses less advanced technologies than Germany in most industries?

SIDE BAR

Can Comparative Advantage Be Created? The Case of "Icewine"

In Ricardo's original example of trade between Portugal and England, he gave Portugal an absolute advantage in both wine and cloth, based on its favorable climate. England would find it very difficult to grow grapes for wine and not so difficult to produce cloth, so it had a comparative advantage in cloth. This raises the question: What if a new technology could be discovered that would allow England to produce world-class grapes and wine? Would it be possible for it to create a new comparative advantage in wine?

Something like this occurred in the Niagara Falls region of Canada, which sells a product called "icewine." First developed in Germany in 1794 (when Ricardo was 21 years old), icewine is produced by allowing grapes to freeze on the vine. Freezing concentrates the sugars and flavors of the grapes, which are picked by hand and then processed into a sweet dessert wine. In 1983 several wineries in the Niagara Falls region of Canada experimented with producing this wine, and it has since taken off to become a local specialty. The cold climate of Niagara Falls offers an advantage in producing icewine, because the temperature should be −10°C to −13°C before picking. The yield from this process is very low—an entire vine might make only one bottle—which is why it

Harvesting frozen grapes to make icewine.

is sold in half-bottles. But demand is high because of the unique flavor of this wine, and the half-bottles often sell for $50 or more. Icewine is now also being produced in the Okanagan Valley region of British Columbia, Canada, which similarly enjoys a climate warm enough in the summer to grow grapes and cold enough in the winter to freeze them. Will England ever be able to develop this wine? If so, the comparative advantage between England and Portugal in Ricardo's original model might be reversed!

Furthermore, although Germany is a world leader in many technologies, so is the United States. So why should the United States import snowboards from Germany or China at all? Why doesn't it just produce all the snowboards it needs with U.S. technology and factors of production?

Comparative Advantage

These questions indicate that absolute advantage is not, in fact, a good explanation for trade patterns. This is one of the key lessons from this chapter. Instead, **comparative advantage** is the primary explanation for trade among countries. To get an idea of what comparative advantage means, let us consider the example of trade between Portugal and England, as described by David Ricardo (see **Side Bar: David Ricardo and Mercantilism**).

To keep things simple, Ricardo considered just two commodities: wine and cloth. Ricardo allowed Portugal to have an absolute advantage in the production of both goods. Portugal's absolute advantage may reflect, for example, its more favorable climate for growing grapes and raising sheep. Even though Portugal can produce wine and cloth more easily than England, England is still able to produce both cloth and wine, but it is *relatively more difficult* to produce wine in England than cloth—as any visitor to England will know, it lacks the regular sunshine needed to produce good grapes! Based on these assumptions, Ricardo argued that England would have a

SIDE BAR

David Ricardo and Mercantilism

David Ricardo (1772–1823) was one of the great classical economists, and the first model we study in this book is named after him. At the time that Ricardo was writing, there was a school of economic thought known as *mercantilism*. Mercantilists believed that exporting (selling goods to other countries) was good because it generated gold and silver for the national treasury and that importing (buying goods from other countries) was bad because it drained gold and silver from the national treasury. To ensure that a country exported a lot and imported only a little, the mercantilists were in favor of high *tariffs* (taxes that must be paid at the border when a good is imported). The mercantilist school of thought was discredited shortly after the time that Ricardo wrote, but some of these old ideas are still advocated today. For example, the United States sometimes insists that other countries should buy more from its companies and sometimes restricts import purchases from other countries; proponents of these ideas are called "mercantilists."

Ricardo was interested in showing that countries could benefit from international trade without having to use tariffs and without requiring exports to be higher than imports. He considered a case that contrasted sharply with what mercantilists believed to be best for a nation: in his writings about trade, Ricardo assumed that the value of exports equaled the value of

imports (a situation called *balanced trade*) and that countries engaged in *free trade,* with no tariffs or other restrictions to limit the flow of goods across borders. Under these assumptions, can international trade benefit every country? Ricardo showed that it could. All countries gain from trade by exporting the goods in which they have comparative advantage.

Ricardo's ideas are so important that it will take some time to explain how and why they work. It is no exaggeration to say that many of the major international institutions in the world today, including the United Nations, the World Bank, and the World Trade Organization, are founded at least in part on the idea that free trade between countries brings gains for all trading partners. This idea comes from the writings of David Ricardo (and Adam Smith, a great classical economist of the eighteenth century).

David Ricardo.

comparative advantage in producing cloth and would export cloth to Portugal, whereas Portugal would have comparative advantage in producing wine and would export wine to England.

From this example, we can see that a country has comparative advantage in producing those goods that it produces best *compared with* how well it produces other goods. That is, Portugal is better at producing wine than cloth, and England is better at producing cloth than wine, even though Portugal is better than England at producing both goods. This is the idea behind the quotation from Ricardo at the start of the chapter—it will be advantageous for Portugal to import cloth from England because England has a comparative advantage in cloth. In our snowboard example, we would expect that China has a disadvantage compared with Germany or the United States in producing many manufactured goods, but it is still better at producing snowboards than some other goods, so it is able to export snowboards to the United States.

It will take us most of the chapter to explain the concept of comparative advantage and why it works as an explanation for trade patterns. As indicated by the other quotation at the beginning of the chapter, from Nobel laureate Paul Samuelson, this concept is far from obvious, and students who master it will have come a long way in their study of international trade.

2 Ricardian Model

In developing the Ricardian model of trade, we will work with an example similar to that used by Ricardo; instead of wine and cloth, however, the two goods will be wheat and cloth. Wheat and other grains (including barley, rice, and so on) are major exports of the United States and Europe, while many types of cloth are imported into these countries. In our example, the home country (we will call it just "Home") will end up with this trade pattern, exporting wheat and importing cloth.

The Home Country

To simplify our example, we will ignore the role of land and capital and suppose that both goods are produced with labor alone. At Home, one worker can produce 4 bushels of wheat or 2 yards of cloth. This production can be expressed in terms of the **marginal product of labor (MPL)** for each good. Recall from your study of microeconomics that the marginal product of labor is the extra output obtained by using one more unit of labor.[3] In Home, one worker produces 4 bushels of wheat, so $MPL_W = 4$. Alternatively, one worker can produce 2 yards of cloth, so $MPL_C = 2$.

Home Production Possibilities Frontier Using the marginal products for producing wheat and cloth, we can graph Home's **production possibilities frontier (PPF)**. Suppose there are $\overline{L} = 25$ workers in the home country (the bar over the letter L indicates our assumption that the amount of labor in Home stays constant). If all these workers were employed in wheat, they could produce $Q_W = MPL_W \cdot \overline{L} = 4 \cdot 25 = 100$ bushels. Alternatively, if they were all employed in cloth, they could produce $Q_C = MPL_C \cdot \overline{L} = 2 \cdot 25 = 50$ yards. The production possibilities frontier is a straight line between these two points at the corners, as shown in Figure 2-1.

The straight-line PPF, a special feature of the Ricardian model, follows from the assumption that the marginal products of labor are *constant*. That is, regardless of how much wheat or cloth is already being produced, one extra hour of labor yields an additional 4 bushels of wheat or 2 yards of cloth. There are *no diminishing returns* in the Ricardian model because it ignores the role of land and capital.

Given this property, the slope of the PPF in Figure 2-1 can be calculated as the ratio of the quantity of cloth produced to the quantity of wheat produced at the corners, as follows:

$$\text{Slope of PPF} = -\frac{50}{100} = -\frac{MPL_C \cdot \overline{L}}{MPL_W \cdot \overline{L}} = -\frac{MPL_C}{MPL_W} = -\frac{1}{2}$$

Ignoring the minus sign, the slope equals the ratio of marginal products of the two goods. The slope is also the **opportunity cost** of wheat, the amount of cloth that must be given up to obtain one more unit of wheat.[4] To see this, suppose that Q_W is increased by 1 bushel. It takes one worker to produce 4 bushels of wheat, so

---

[3] A special assumption of the Ricardian model is that there are no diminishing returns to labor, so the marginal product of labor is constant. That assumption will no longer be made in the next chapter, when we introduce capital and land, along with labor, as factors of production.

[4] Notice that the slope of the PPF is the opportunity cost of the good on the *horizontal* axis—wheat, in this case.

FIGURE 2-1

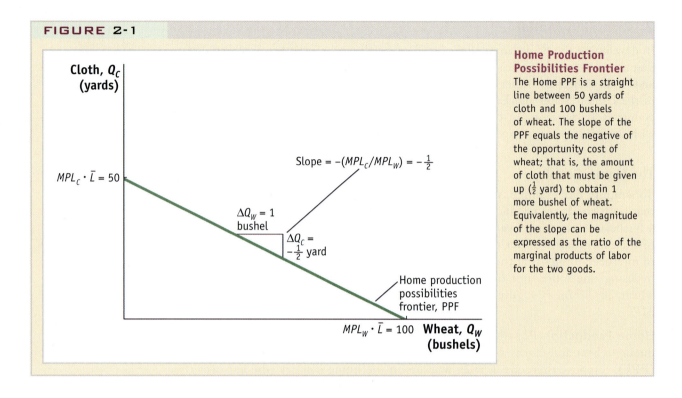

Home Production Possibilities Frontier The Home PPF is a straight line between 50 yards of cloth and 100 bushels of wheat. The slope of the PPF equals the negative of the opportunity cost of wheat; that is, the amount of cloth that must be given up ($\frac{1}{2}$ yard) to obtain 1 more bushel of wheat. Equivalently, the magnitude of the slope can be expressed as the ratio of the marginal products of labor for the two goods.

increasing Q_W by 1 bushel means that one-quarter of a worker's time must be withdrawn from the cloth industry and shifted into wheat production. This shift would reduce cloth output by $\frac{1}{2}$ yard, the amount of cloth that could have been produced by one-quarter of a worker's time. Thus, $\frac{1}{2}$ yard of cloth is the opportunity cost of obtaining 1 more bushel of wheat and is the slope of the PPF.

Home Indifference Curve With this production possibilities frontier, what combination of wheat and cloth will Home actually produce? The answer depends on the country's demand for each of the two goods. There are several ways to represent demand in the Home economy, but we will start by using **indifference curves.** Each indifference curve shows the combinations of two goods, such as wheat and cloth, that a person or economy can consume and be equally satisfied.

In Figure 2-2, the consumer is indifferent between points A and B, for example. Both of these points lie on an indifference curve U_1 associated with a given level of satisfaction, or **utility.** Point C lies on a higher indifference curve U_2, indicating that it gives a higher level of utility, whereas point D lies on a lower indifference curve U_0, indicating that it gives a lower level of utility. It is common to use indifference curves to reflect the utility that an individual consumer receives from various consumption points. In Figure 2-2, we go a step further, however, and apply this idea to an entire country. That is, the indifference curves in Figure 2-2 show the preferences of an entire country. The combinations of wheat and cloth on U_0 give consumers in the country lower utility than the combinations on indifference curve U_1, which in turn gives lower utility than the combinations of wheat and cloth on U_2.

FIGURE 2-2

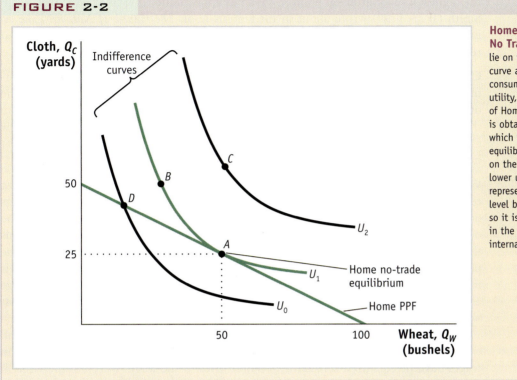

Home Equilibrium with No Trade Points A and B lie on the same indifference curve and give the Home consumers the level of utility, U_1. The highest level of Home utility on the PPF is obtained at point A, which is the no-trade equilibrium. Point D is also on the PPF but would give lower utility. Point C represents a higher utility level but is off of the PPF, so it is not attainable in the absence of international trade.

Home Equilibrium In the absence of international trade, the production possibilities frontier acts like a budget constraint for the country, and with perfectly competitive markets, the economy will produce at the point of highest utility subject to the limits imposed by its PPF. The point of highest utility is at point A in Figure 2-2, where Home consumes 25 yards of cloth and 50 bushels of wheat. This bundle of goods gives Home the highest level of utility possible (indifference curve U_1) given the limits of its PPF. Notice that Home could produce at other points such as point D, but this point would give a lower level of utility than point A (i.e., point D would offer lower utility because U_0 is lower than U_1). Other consumption points, such as C, would give higher levels of utility than point A but cannot be obtained in the absence of international trade because they lie outside of Home's PPF.

We will refer to point A as the "no-trade" or the "pre-trade" equilibrium for Home.[5] What we really mean by this phrase is "no *international* trade." The Home country is able to reach point A by having its own firms produce wheat and cloth and sell these goods to its own consumers. We are assuming that there are many firms in each of the wheat and cloth industries, so the firms act under perfect competition and take the market prices for wheat and cloth as given. The idea that perfectly competitive markets lead to the highest level of well-being for consumers—as illustrated by

---

[5] We also refer to point A as the "autarky equilibrium," because "autarky" means a situation in which the country does not engage in international trade.

the highest level of utility at point *A*—is an example of the "invisible hand" that Adam Smith (1723–1790) wrote about in his famous book *The Wealth of Nations*. Like an invisible hand, competitive markets lead firms to produce the amount of goods that results in the highest level of well-being for consumers.

Opportunity Cost and Prices Whereas the slope of the PPF reflects the opportunity cost of producing one more bushel of wheat, under perfect competition the opportunity cost of wheat should also equal the relative price of wheat, as follows from the economic principle that price reflects the opportunity cost of a good. We can now check that this equality between the opportunity cost and the relative price of wheat holds at point *A*.

Wages We solve for the prices of wheat and cloth using an indirect approach, by first reviewing how wages are determined. In competitive labor markets, firms hire workers up to the point at which the cost of one more hour of labor (the wage) equals the value of one more hour of production. In turn, the value of one more hour of labor equals the amount of goods produced in that hour (the marginal product of labor) times the price of the good (P_W for the price of wheat and P_C for the price of cloth). That is to say, in the wheat industry, labor will be hired up to the point at which the wage equals $P_W \cdot MPL_W$, and in the cloth industry labor will be hired up to the point at which the wage equals $P_C \cdot MPL_C$.

If we assume that labor is perfectly free to move between these two industries and that workers will choose to work in the industry for which the wage is highest, then wages must be equalized across the two industries. If the wages were not the same in the two industries, laborers in the low-wage industry would have an incentive to move to the high-wage industry; this would, in turn, lead to an abundance of workers and a decrease in the wage in the high-wage industry and a scarcity of workers and an increase in the wage in the low-wage industry. This movement of labor would continue until wages are equalized between the two industries.

We can use the equality of the wage across industries to obtain the following equation:

$$P_W \cdot MPL_W = P_C \cdot MPL_C$$

By rearranging terms, we see that

$$P_W / P_C = MPL_C / MPL_W$$

The right-hand side of this equation is the slope of the production possibilities frontier (the opportunity cost of obtaining one more bushel of wheat) and the left-hand side of the equation is the **relative price** of wheat, as we will explain in the next paragraph. This equation says that the relative price of wheat (on the left) and opportunity cost of wheat (on the right) must be equal in the no-trade equilibrium at point *A*.

To understand why we measure the relative price of wheat as the ratio P_W/P_C, suppose that a bushel of wheat costs $3 and a yard of cloth costs $6. Then $3/$6 = $\frac{1}{2}$, which shows that the relative price of wheat is $\frac{1}{2}$, that is, $\frac{1}{2}$ of a yard of cloth (or half of $6) must be given up to obtain 1 bushel of wheat (the price of which is $3). A price ratio like P_W/P_C always denotes the relative price of the good in the numerator (wheat, in this case), measured in terms of how much of the good in the denominator (cloth) must be given up. In Figure 2-2, the slope of the PPF equals the relative price of wheat, the good on the *horizontal axis*.

The Foreign Country

Now let's introduce another country, Foreign, into the model. We will assume that Foreign's technology is inferior to Home's so that it has an absolute *disadvantage* in producing both wheat and cloth as compared with Home. Nevertheless, once we introduce international trade, we will still find that Foreign will trade with Home.

Foreign Production Possibilities Frontier Suppose that one Foreign worker can produce 1 bushel of wheat ($MPL_W^* = 1$), or 1 yard of cloth ($MPL_C^* = 1$), whereas recall that a Home worker can produce 4 bushels of wheat or 2 yards of cloth. Suppose that there are $\overline{L}^* = 100$ workers available in the Foreign country. If all these workers were employed in wheat, they could produce $MPL_W^* \cdot \overline{L}^* = 100$ bushels, and if they were all employed in cloth, they could produce $MPL_C^* \cdot \overline{L}^* = 100$ yards. Foreign's production possibilities frontier (PPF) is thus a straight line between these two points, with a slope of –1, as shown in Figure 2-3.

You might find it helpful to think of the Home country in our example as the United States or Europe and the Foreign country as the "rest of the world." Empirical evidence supports the idea that the United States and Europe have the leading technologies in many goods and an absolute advantage in the production of both wheat and cloth. Nevertheless, they import much of their clothing and textiles from abroad, especially from Asia and Latin America. Why does the United States or Europe import these goods from abroad when they have superior technology at home? To answer this question, we want to focus on the *comparative advantage* of Home and Foreign in producing the two goods.

FIGURE 2-3

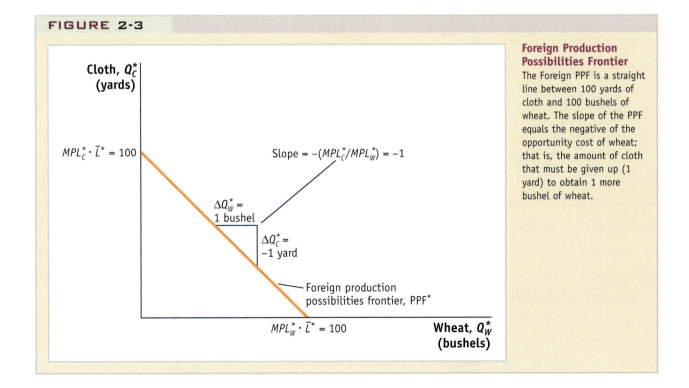

Foreign Production Possibilities Frontier The Foreign PPF is a straight line between 100 yards of cloth and 100 bushels of wheat. The slope of the PPF equals the negative of the opportunity cost of wheat; that is, the amount of cloth that must be given up (1 yard) to obtain 1 more bushel of wheat.

Comparative Advantage   In Foreign, it takes one worker to produce 1 bushel of wheat or 1 yard of cloth. Therefore, the opportunity cost of producing 1 yard of cloth is 1 bushel of wheat. In Home, one worker produces 2 yards of cloth or 4 bushels of wheat. Therefore, Home's opportunity cost of a bushel of wheat is $\frac{1}{2}$ a yard of cloth, and its opportunity cost of a yard of cloth is 2 bushels of wheat. Based on this comparison, Foreign has a *comparative advantage in producing cloth* because its opportunity cost of cloth (which is 1 bushel of wheat) is *lower* than Home's opportunity cost of cloth (which is 2 bushels of wheat). Conversely, Home has a *comparative advantage in producing wheat* because Home's opportunity cost of wheat (which is $\frac{1}{2}$ yard of cloth) is lower than Foreign's (1 yard of cloth). In general, a country has a comparative advantage in a good when it has a lower opportunity cost of producing it than does the other country. Notice that Foreign has a comparative advantage in cloth even though it has an absolute disadvantage in both goods.

As before, we can represent Foreign's preferences for wheat and cloth with indifference curves like those shown in Figure 2-4. With competitive markets, the economy will produce at the point of highest utility for the country, point A^*, which is the no-trade equilibrium in Foreign. The slope of the PPF, which equals the opportunity cost of wheat, also equals the relative price of wheat.[6] Therefore, in Figure 2-4,

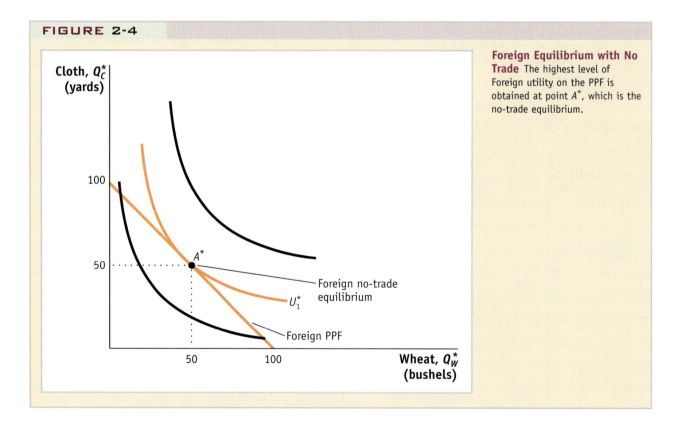

FIGURE 2-4

Foreign Equilibrium with No Trade The highest level of Foreign utility on the PPF is obtained at point A^*, which is the no-trade equilibrium.

---

[6] Remember that the slope of the PPF (ignoring the minus sign) equals the relative price of the good on the *horizontal* axis—wheat in Figure 2-4. Foreign has a steeper PPF than Home as shown in Figure 2-2, so Foreign's relative price of wheat is higher than Home's. The inverse of the relative price of wheat is the relative price of cloth, which is lower in Foreign.

Foreign's no-trade relative price of wheat is $P_W^*/P_C^* = 1$. Notice that this relative price *exceeds* Home's no-trade relative price of wheat, which is $P_W/P_C = \frac{1}{2}$. This difference in these relative prices reflects the comparative advantage that Home has in the production of wheat.[7]

Comparative Advantage in Apparel, Textiles, and Wheat

The U.S. textile and apparel industries face intense import competition, especially from Asia and Latin America. Employment in this industry in the United States fell from about 1.5 million people in 1990 to less than 1 million in 1999. An example of this import competition can be seen from one U.S. fabric manufacturer, Burlington Industries, which announced in January 1999 that it would reduce its production capacity by 25% because of increased imports from Asia. Burlington closed seven plants and laid off 2,900 people, about 17% of its domestic force. After the layoffs, Burlington Industries employed 17,400 people in the United States. With 1999 sales of $1.6 billion, this means that its sales per employee were $1.6 billion/17,400 = $92,000 per worker. This is exactly at the average for all U.S. apparel producers, as shown in Table 2-2. The textile industry, producing the fabric and material inputs for apparel, is even more productive, with annual sales per employee of $140,000 in the United States.

In comparison, the average worker in China produces $13,500 of sales per year in the apparel industry and $9,000 in the textile industry. Thus, a worker in the United

TABLE 2-2

Apparel, Textiles, and Wheat in the United States and China This table shows sales per employee for the apparel and textile industries in the United States and China, as well as bushels per hour in producing wheat. The United States has an absolute advantage in all these products (as shown by the numbers in the right-hand column of the table), but it has a comparative advantage in producing wheat (as shown by the numbers in the bottom rows of the table).

	United States	China	Absolute Advantage
	Sales/Employee	*Sales/Employee*	*U.S./China Ratio*
Apparel	$92,000	$13,500	7
Textiles	$140,000	$9,000	16
	Bushels/Hour	*Bushels/Hour*	*U.S./China Ratio*
Wheat	27.5	0.1	275
	Comparative Advantage		
Wheat/apparel ratio × 1,000	0.3	0.01	
Wheat/textile ratio × 1,000	0.2	0.01	

Note: Data are for years around 1995.

Source: Wheat data from Colin Carter, University of California, Davis; apparel/textiles data from various sources.

---

[7] Taking the reciprocal of the relative price of wheat in each country, we also see that Foreign's no-trade relative price of cloth is $P_C^*/P_W^* = 1$, which is less than Home's no-trade relative price of cloth, $P_C/P_W = 2$. Therefore, Foreign has a comparative advantage in cloth.

States produces $92,000/$13,500 = 7 times more apparel sales than a worker in China and $140,000/$9,000 = 16 times more textile sales. This ratio is shown in Table 2-2 in the column labeled "Absolute Advantage." It illustrates how much more productive U.S. labor is in these industries relative to Chinese labor. The United States clearly has an absolute advantage in both these industries, so why does it import so much of its textiles and apparel from Asia, including China?

The answer can be seen by also comparing the productivities in the wheat industry. The typical wheat farmer in California devotes only 1.35 hours per acre to growing a crop of wheat, and an acre provides 37 bushels of wheat, a marginal product of $37/1.35 = 27.5$ bushels per hour of labor. In comparison, the typical wheat farmer in China obtains only one-tenth of a bushel per hour of labor, so the U.S. farmer is $27.5/0.1 = 275$ times more productive! The United States clearly has an *absolute advantage* in all these industries.

But China has the *comparative advantage* in both apparel and textiles, as illustrated by the rows labeled "Comparative Advantage." To keep the calculations simple, suppose that a farmer spends 1,000 hours per year growing a crop of wheat. Multiplying the marginal product of an hour of labor in wheat by 1,000, to obtain the marginal product of labor per year, and dividing by the marginal product of labor in apparel give us the *opportunity cost of apparel*. In the United States, for example, this ratio is $27,500/92,000 \approx 0.3$ bushels/$, indicating that 0.3 bushels of wheat must be foregone to obtain an extra dollar of sales in apparel. In textiles, the U.S. ratio is $27,500/140,000 \approx 0.2$ bushels/$, so that 0.2 bushels of wheat must be foregone to obtain an extra dollar in textile sales. But these ratios are much smaller in China: only 100/13,500 or $100/9,000 \approx 0.01$ bushels of wheat must be foregone to obtain $1 of extra sales in either textiles or apparel. As a result, China has a lower opportunity cost of both textiles and apparel than the United States, which explains why it exports those goods, while the United States exports wheat, just as predicted by the Ricardian model. ■

3   Determining the Pattern of International Trade

Now that we have examined each country in the absence of trade, we can start to analyze what happens when goods are traded between them. We will see that a country's no-trade relative price determines which product it will export and which it will import when trade is opened. As we have shown earlier, the no-trade relative price in each country equals its opportunity cost of producing that good. Therefore, the pattern of exports and imports will be determined by the opportunity costs of production in each country, or by each country's pattern of comparative advantage. This section examines why this is the case and details each country's choice of how much to produce, consume, and trade of each good.

International Trade Equilibrium

The differences in no-trade prices across the countries create an opportunity for international trade between them. In particular, producers of cloth in Foreign, where the relative price of cloth is $P_C^*/P_W^* = 1$, would want to export cloth to Home, where the relative price, $P_C/P_W = 2$, is higher. Conversely, producers of wheat in Home, where the relative price of wheat is $P_W/P_C = \frac{1}{2}$, would want to export wheat to Foreign, where the relative price of $P_W^*/P_C^* = 1$ is higher. The trade pattern that we expect to arise, then, is that *Home will export wheat*, and *Foreign will export cloth*. Notice that both countries export the good in which they have a comparative advantage, which is what the Ricardian model predicts.

To solidify our understanding of this trade pattern, let's be more careful about explaining where the two countries would produce on their PPFs under international trade and where they will consume. As Home exports wheat, the quantity of wheat sold at Home falls, and this condition bids up the price of wheat in the Home market. As the exported wheat arrives in the Foreign wheat market, more wheat is sold there, and the price of wheat in the Foreign market falls. Likewise, as Foreign exports cloth, the price of cloth in Foreign will be bid up and the price of cloth in Home will fall. The two countries are in an **international trade equilibrium,** or just "trade equilibrium," for short, when the relative price of wheat is the same in the two countries, which means that the relative price of cloth is also the same in both countries.[8]

To fully understand the international trade equilibrium, we are interested in two issues: (1) determining the relative price of wheat (or cloth) in the trade equilibrium and (2) seeing how the shift from the no-trade equilibrium to the trade equilibrium affects production and consumption in both Home and Foreign. Addressing the first issue requires some additional graphs, so let's delay this discussion for a moment and suppose for now that the relative price of wheat in the trade equilibrium is established at a level between the pre-trade prices in the two countries. This assumption is consistent with the bidding up of export prices and bidding down of import prices, as discussed previously. Since the no-trade prices were $P_W/P_C = \frac{1}{2}$ in Home and $P_W^*/P_C^* = 1$ in Foreign, let's suppose that the world relative price of wheat is between these two values, say, at $\frac{2}{3}$. Given the change in relative prices from their pre-trade level to the international trade equilibrium, what happens to production and consumption in each of the two countries?

Change in Production and Consumption The world relative price of wheat that we have assumed is higher than Home's pre-trade price $\left(\frac{2}{3} > \frac{1}{2}\right)$. This relationship between the pre-trade and world relative prices means that Home producers of wheat can earn more than the opportunity cost of wheat (which is $\frac{1}{2}$) by selling their wheat to Foreign. For this reason, Home will shift its labor resources toward the production of wheat and produce more wheat than it did in the pre-trade equilibrium (point A in Figure 2-5). To check that this intuition is correct, let us explore the incentives for labor to work in each of Home's industries.

Recall that Home wages paid in the wheat industry equal $P_W \cdot MPL_W$, and wages paid in the cloth industry equal $P_C \cdot MPL_C$. We know that the relative price of wheat in the trade equilibrium is $P_W/P_C = \frac{2}{3}$, that the marginal product of labor in the Home wheat industry is $MPL_W = 4$, and that the marginal product of labor in the Home cloth industry is $MPL_C = 2$. We can plug these numbers into the formulas for wages to compute the *ratio* of wages in the two industries as

$$\frac{P_W \cdot MPL_W}{P_C \cdot MPL_C} = \left(\frac{2}{3}\right)\left(\frac{4}{2}\right) = \frac{8}{6} > 1, \text{ so that } P_W \cdot MPL_W > P_C \cdot MPL_C$$

---

[8] Notice that if the relative price of wheat P_W/P_C is the same in the two countries, then the relative price of cloth, which is just its inverse (P_C/P_W), is also the same.

FIGURE 2-5

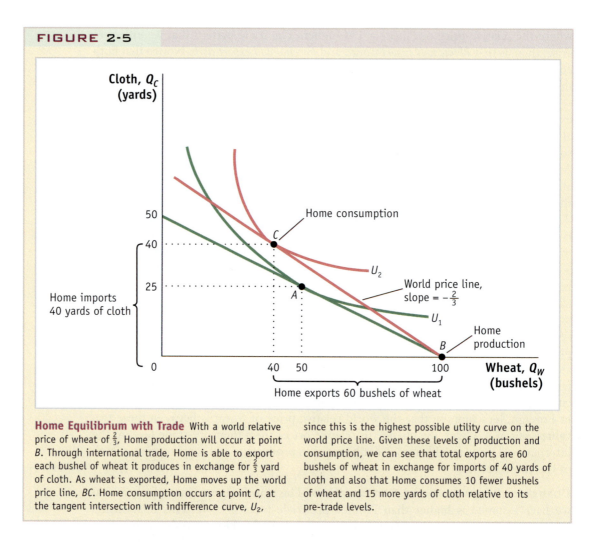

Home Equilibrium with Trade With a world relative price of wheat of $\frac{2}{3}$, Home production will occur at point B. Through international trade, Home is able to export each bushel of wheat it produces in exchange for $\frac{2}{3}$ yard of cloth. As wheat is exported, Home moves up the world price line, BC. Home consumption occurs at point C, at the tangent intersection with indifference curve, U_2, since this is the highest possible utility curve on the world price line. Given these levels of production and consumption, we can see that total exports are 60 bushels of wheat in exchange for imports of 40 yards of cloth and also that Home consumes 10 fewer bushels of wheat and 15 more yards of cloth relative to its pre-trade levels.

This formula tells us that with the world relative price of wheat of $\frac{2}{3}$, wages paid in Home's wheat industry ($P_W \cdot MPL_W$) are greater than those paid in its cloth industry ($P_C \cdot MPL_C$). Accordingly, all of Home's workers will want to work in the wheat industry, and no cloth will be produced. With trade, the Home economy will be fully specialized in wheat production, as occurs at production point B in Figure 2-5.[9]

International Trade Starting at the production point B, Home can export wheat at a relative price of $\frac{2}{3}$. This means that for 1 bushel of wheat exported to Foreign, it receives $\frac{2}{3}$ yard of cloth in exchange. In Figure 2-5, we can trace out its international trades by starting at point B and then exchanging 1 bushel of wheat for $\frac{2}{3}$ yard of cloth, another bushel of wheat for $\frac{2}{3}$ yard of cloth, and so on. From point B, this traces out the line toward point C, with slope $-\frac{2}{3}$. We will call the line starting at point B (the

---

[9] The fully specialized economy (producing only wheat) is a special feature of the Ricardian model because of its straight-line production possibilities frontier.

production point) and with a slope equal to the negative of the world relative price of wheat, the **world price line,** as shown by *BC*. The world price line shows the range of *consumption possibilities* that a country can achieve by specializing in one good (wheat, in Home's case) and engaging in international trade (exporting wheat and importing cloth). We can think of the world price line as a new budget constraint for the country under international trade.

Notice that this budget constraint (the line *BC*) lies *above* Home's original PPF. The ability to engage in international trade creates consumption possibilities for Home that were not available in the absence of trade, when the consumption point had to be on Home's PPF. Now, Home can choose to consume at any point on the world price line, and utility is maximized at the point corresponding to the intersection with the highest indifference curve, labeled *C* with a utility of U_2. Home obtains a higher utility with international trade than in the absence of international trade (U_2 is higher than U_1); the finding that Home's utility increases with trade is our first demonstration of the **gains from trade,** by which we mean the ability of a country to obtain higher utility for its citizens under free trade than with no trade.

Pattern of Trade and Gains from Trade   Comparing production point *B* with consumption point *C*, we see that Home is exporting $100 - 40 = 60$ bushels of wheat, in exchange for 40 yards of cloth imported from Foreign. If we value the wheat at its international price of $\frac{2}{3}$, then the value of the exported wheat is $\frac{2}{3} \cdot 60 = 40$ yards of cloth, and the value of the imported cloth is also 40 yards of cloth. Because Home's exports equal its imports, this outcome shows that Home's trade is balanced.

What happens in Foreign when trade occurs? Foreign's production and consumption points are shown in Figure 2-6. The world relative price of wheat $\left(\frac{2}{3}\right)$ is less than Foreign's pre-trade relative price of wheat (which is 1). This difference in relative prices causes workers to leave wheat production and move into the cloth industry. Foreign specializes in cloth production at point B^*, and from there, trades along the world price line with a slope of (negative) $\frac{2}{3}$, which is the relative price of wheat. That is, Foreign exchanges $\frac{2}{3}$ yard of cloth for 1 bushel of wheat, then $\frac{2}{3}$ yard of cloth for another 1 bushel of wheat, and so on repeatedly, as it moves down the world price line B^*C^*. The consumption point that maximizes Foreign's utility is C^*, at which point 60 units of each good are consumed and utility is U_2^*. Foreign's utility is greater than it was in the absence of international trade (U_2^* is a higher indifference curve than U_1^*), as is true for Home. Therefore, both countries gain from trade.

Foreign produces 100 yards of cloth at point B^*: it consumes 60 yards itself and exports $100 - 60 = 40$ yards of cloth in exchange for 60 bushels of wheat imported from Home. This trade pattern is exactly the opposite of Home's, as must be the case. In our two-country world, everything leaving one country must arrive in the other. We see that Home is exporting wheat, in which it has a comparative advantage (Home's opportunity cost of wheat production is $\frac{1}{2}$ yard of cloth compared with 1 yard in Foreign). Furthermore, Foreign is exporting cloth, in which it has a comparative advantage (Foreign's opportunity cost of cloth production is 1 bushel of wheat compared with 2 bushels in Home). This outcome confirms that *the pattern of trade is determined by comparative advantage,* which is the first lesson of the Ricardian model. We have also established that there are *gains from trade for both countries,* which is the second lesson.

FIGURE 2-6

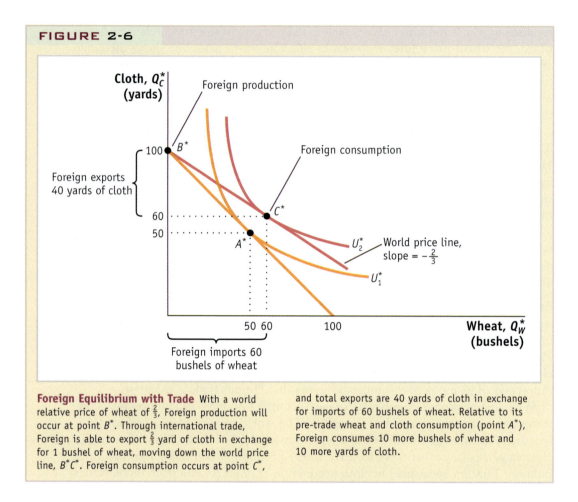

Foreign Equilibrium with Trade With a world relative price of wheat of $\frac{2}{3}$, Foreign production will occur at point B^*. Through international trade, Foreign is able to export $\frac{2}{3}$ yard of cloth in exchange for 1 bushel of wheat, moving down the world price line, B^*C^*. Foreign consumption occurs at point C^*, and total exports are 40 yards of cloth in exchange for imports of 60 bushels of wheat. Relative to its pre-trade wheat and cloth consumption (point A^*), Foreign consumes 10 more bushels of wheat and 10 more yards of cloth.

These two conclusions are often where the Ricardian model stops in its analysis of trade between countries, but the story is incomplete because we have not yet determined the level of wages across countries. We have seen that with trade, the relative price of each good converges to a single equilibrium price in both countries. Does the same occur with wages? As we now show, this is not the case. Wage levels differ across countries with trade, and wages are determined by *absolute* advantage, not *comparative* advantage. This is a third, less emphasized lesson from the Ricardian model, which we explore next.

Solving for Wages across Countries

To understand how wages are determined, we go back to microeconomics. In competitive labor markets, firms will pay workers the value of their marginal product. Home produces and exports wheat, so we can think of Home workers being paid in terms of that good: their real wage is $MPL_W = 4$ bushels of wheat. We refer to this payment as a "real" wage because it is measured in terms of a good that workers consume and not in terms of money. The workers can then sell the wheat they earn on the world market at the relative price of $P_W/P_C = \frac{2}{3}$. Thus, their real wage in terms of units of cloth is $(P_W/P_C) \cdot MPL_W = \frac{2}{3} \cdot 4 = \frac{8}{3}$ yard. Summing up, the Home wage is[10]

$$\text{Home wage} = \begin{cases} MPL_W = 4 \text{ bushels of wheat} \\ \text{or} \\ (P_W/P_C) \cdot MPL_W = \frac{8}{3} \text{ yard of cloth} \end{cases}$$

What happens to Foreign wages? Foreign produces and exports cloth, and the real wage is $MPL_C^* = 1$ yard of cloth. Because cloth workers can sell the cloth they earn for wheat on the world market at the price of $\frac{3}{2}$, their real wage in terms of units of wheat is $(P_C^*/P_W^*) \cdot MPL_C^* = \left(\frac{3}{2}\right) \cdot 1 = \frac{3}{2}$ bushel. Thus, the Foreign wage is[11]

$$\text{Foreign wage} = \begin{cases} (P_C^*/P_W^*) \cdot MPL_C = \frac{3}{2} \text{ bushels of wheat} \\ \text{or} \\ MPL_C = 1 \text{ yard of cloth} \end{cases}$$

Foreign workers earn less than Home workers as measured by their ability to purchase either good. This fact reflects Home's absolute advantage in the production of both goods.

Absolute Advantage   As our example shows, wages are determined by absolute advantage: Home is paying higher wages because it has better technology in both goods. In contrast, the pattern of trade in the Ricardian model is determined by comparative advantage. Indeed, these two results go hand in hand—the only way that a country with poor technology can export at a price others are willing to pay is by having low wages.

This statement might sound like a pessimistic assessment of the ability of less developed countries to pay reasonable wages, but it carries with it a silver lining: as a country develops its technology, its wages will correspondingly rise. In the Ricardian model, a logical consequence of technological progress is that workers will become better off through receiving higher wages. In addition, as countries engage in international trade, the Ricardian model predicts that their real wages will rise.[12] We do not have to look very hard to see examples of this outcome in the world. Per capita income in China in 1978, just as that nation began to open up to international trade, is estimated to have been $779, whereas 29 years later in 2007, per capita income in China had risen by more than 10 times to $8,510. Likewise for India, per capita income more than doubled from $1,430 in 1978 to $3,826 in 2007.[13] Many people believe that the opportunity for these countries to engage in international trade has been crucial in raising their standard of living. As our study

---

[10] Recall that without international trade, Home wages were $MPL_W = 4$ bushels of wheat or $MPL_C = 2$ yards of cloth. Home workers are clearly better off with trade because they can afford to buy the same amount of wheat as before (4 bushels) but more cloth ($\frac{8}{3}$ yards instead of 2 yards). This is another way of demonstrating the gains from trade.

[11] Without international trade, Foreign wages were $MPL_W^* = 1$ bushel of wheat or $MPL_C^* = 1$ yard of cloth. Foreign workers are also better off with trade because they can afford to buy the same amount of cloth (1 yard) but more wheat ($\frac{3}{2}$ bushels instead of 1 bushel).

[12] That result is shown by the comparison of real wages in the trade equilibrium as compared with the no-trade equilibrium in each country, as is done in the previous two footnotes.

[13] These values are expressed in 2005 dollars and are taken from the Penn World Table version 6.3, http://pwt.econ.upenn.edu.

of international trade proceeds, we will try to identify the conditions that have allowed China, India, and many other developing countries to improve their standards of living through trade.

Labor Productivity and Wages

The close connection between wages and labor productivity is evident by looking at data across countries. Labor productivity can be measured by the *value-added per hour* in manufacturing. Value-added is the difference between sales revenue in an industry and the costs of intermediate inputs (e.g., the difference between the value of a car and the cost of all the parts used to build it). Value-added then equals the payments to labor and capital in an industry. In the Ricardian model, we ignore capital, so we can measure labor productivity as value-added divided by the number of hours worked, or value-added per hour.

In Figure 2-7, we show the value-added per hour in manufacturing in 2001 for several different countries. The United States has the highest level of productivity and Taiwan has the lowest for the countries shown. Figure 2-7 also shows the wages per hour paid in each country. These are somewhat less than value-added per hour because value-added is also used to pay capital, but the general ranking of countries—from highest to lowest—in terms of labor productivity is the same as the ranking in terms of wages: countries with higher labor productivity pay higher wages, just as the Ricardian model predicts. The close connection between productivity and wages is also evident if we look at countries over time. These graphs are shown in Figure 2-8. We can see that the general upward movement in labor productivity is matched by upward movement in wages, as the Ricardian model predicts. ■

FIGURE 2-7

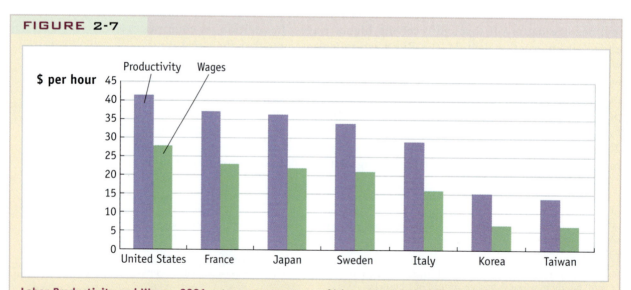

Labor Productivity and Wages, 2001 Labor productivity is measured by value-added per hour of work and can be compared with the wages paid in manufacturing in various countries. The general ranking of countries—from highest to lowest—in terms of labor productivity is the same as the ranking in terms of wages: countries with higher labor productivity pay higher wages, just as the Ricardian model predicts.

Source: U.S. Department of Labor, Bureau of Labor Statistics.

FIGURE 2-8

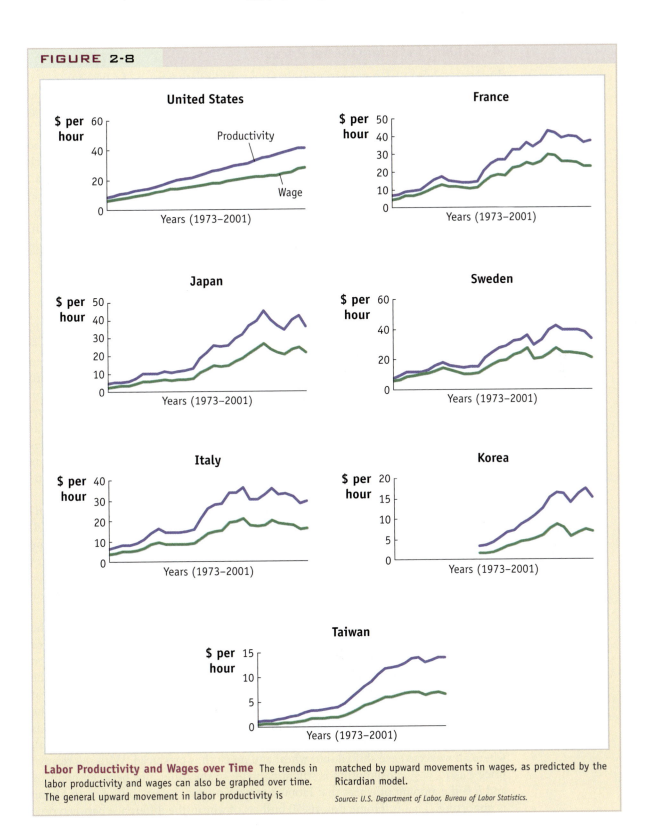

Labor Productivity and Wages over Time The trends in labor productivity and wages can also be graphed over time. The general upward movement in labor productivity is matched by upward movements in wages, as predicted by the Ricardian model.

Source: U.S. Department of Labor, Bureau of Labor Statistics.

4 Solving for International Prices

In Figures 2-5 and 2-6, we assumed that the world relative price of wheat was $\frac{2}{3}$ and that at this level Home's exports of wheat just equaled Foreign's imports of wheat (and vice versa for cloth). Now we will dig a little deeper to show how the world price is determined.

To determine the world relative price of wheat, we will use supply and demand curves. Home exports wheat, so we will derive a Home **export supply curve,** which shows the amount it wants to export at various relative prices. Foreign imports wheat, so we will derive a Foreign **import demand curve,** which shows the amount of wheat that it will import at various relative prices. The international trade equilibrium is the quantity and relative price at which Home exports equal Foreign imports of wheat. This equality occurs where the Home export supply curve intersects the Foreign import demand curve.

Home Export Supply Curve

In panel (a) of Figure 2-9, we repeat Figure 2-5, which shows the trade equilibrium for Home with production at point B and consumption at point C. At the world relative price of $P_W/P_C = \frac{2}{3}$, Home exports 60 bushels of wheat (the difference between wheat production of 100 and consumption of 40). We can use these numbers to construct a new graph, the Home export supply curve of wheat, shown in panel (b). The vertical axis in panel (b) measures the relative price of wheat and the horizontal axis measures the exports of wheat. The points B and C in panel (a), with the relative price of $P_W/P_C = \frac{2}{3}$ and Home exports of 60 bushels of wheat, now appear as point C' in panel (b), with $P_W/P_C = \frac{2}{3}$ on the vertical axis and Home wheat exports of 60 bushels on the horizontal axis. This is our first point on the Home export supply curve.

To derive other points on the export supply curve, consider the no-trade equilibrium in panel (a), which is shown by production and consumption at point A. The no-trade relative price of wheat is $\frac{1}{2}$ (the slope of Home's PPF), and Home exports of wheat are zero because there is no international trade. So the point A in panel (a) can be graphed at point A' in panel (b), with a relative price of $P_W/P_C = \frac{1}{2}$ and zero Home exports of wheat. This gives us a second point on the Home export supply curve.

To get a third point, let us keep the relative price of wheat at $P_W/P_C = \frac{1}{2}$, as in the no-trade equilibrium, but now allow Home to export some wheat in exchange for cloth at this price. Home consumption remains at point A in panel (a), but production can shift from that point. The reason that production can shift to another point on the PPF is that, with the relative price $P_W/P_C = \frac{1}{2}$, the wages of workers are equal in wheat and cloth. This result was shown in our earlier discussion. With wages equal in the two industries, workers are willing to shift between them, so any point on the PPF is a possible production point. Consider, for example, production at point B in panel (a), where all workers have shifted into wheat and no cloth is produced. With the relative price $P_W/P_C = \frac{1}{2}$, consumption is still at point A, so the difference between points A and B is the amount of wheat that Home is exporting and the amount of cloth Home is importing. That is, Home exports 50 bushels of wheat (the difference between production of 100 and consumption of 50) and imports 25 yards of cloth (the difference

FIGURE 2-9

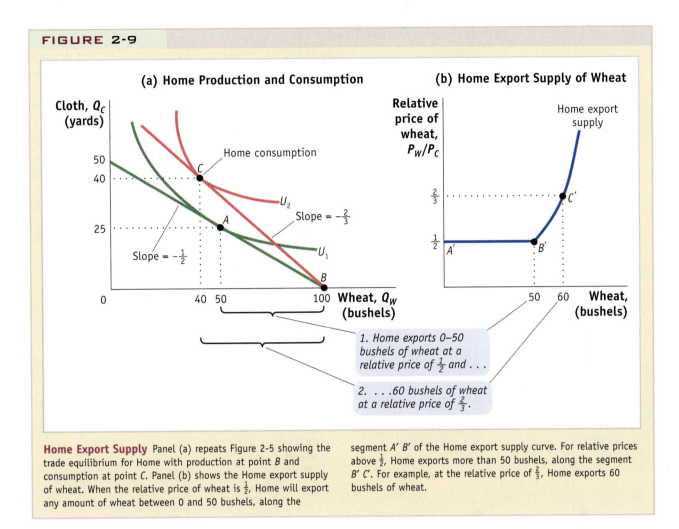

(a) Home Production and Consumption

(b) Home Export Supply of Wheat

1. *Home exports 0–50 bushels of wheat at a relative price of $\frac{1}{2}$ and . . .*

2. *. . . .60 bushels of wheat at a relative price of $\frac{2}{3}$.*

Home Export Supply Panel (a) repeats Figure 2-5 showing the trade equilibrium for Home with production at point B and consumption at point C. Panel (b) shows the Home export supply of wheat. When the relative price of wheat is $\frac{1}{2}$, Home will export any amount of wheat between 0 and 50 bushels, along the segment A' B' of the Home export supply curve. For relative prices above $\frac{1}{2}$, Home exports more than 50 bushels, along the segment B' C'. For example, at the relative price of $\frac{2}{3}$, Home exports 60 bushels of wheat.

between production of 0 and consumption of 25). Therefore, the relative price of $P_W/P_C = \frac{1}{2}$, with wheat exports of 50, is another point on the Home export supply curve, shown by B' in panel (b).

Joining up points A' C', B', and C', we get a Home export supply curve that is flat between A' and B', and then rises between B' and C' and beyond. The flat portion of the export supply curve is a special feature of the Ricardian model that occurs because the PPF is a straight line. That is, with the relative price of $P_W/P_C = \frac{1}{2}$, production can occur anywhere along the PPF as workers shift between industries; meanwhile, consumption is fixed at point A, leading to all the export levels between A' and B' in panel (b). As the relative price of wheat rises above $\frac{1}{2}$, production remains fixed at point B in panel (a), but the consumption point changes, rising above point A. With the relative price $P_W/P_C = \frac{2}{3}$, for example, consumption is at point C. Then Home exports of wheat are calculated as the difference between production at B and consumption at C. Graphing the various relative prices above $\frac{1}{2}$ and the bushels of wheat exported at each price, we get the upward-sloping Home export supply curve between B' and C' in panel (b).

Foreign Import Demand Curve

In Foreign we will again focus on the wheat market and construct an import demand curve for wheat. In panel (a) of Figure 2-10, we repeat Figure 2-6, which shows the Foreign trade equilibrium with production at point B^* and consumption at point C^*. At the world relative price of $P_W/P_C = \frac{2}{3}$, Foreign imports 60 bushels of wheat (the difference between wheat consumption of 60 and production of 0). These numbers are graphed as point $C^{*\prime}$ in panel (b), where we have the relative price of wheat on the vertical axis and the Foreign imports of wheat on the horizontal axis.

Other points on Foreign's import demand curve can be obtained in much the same way as we did for Home. For example, the no-trade equilibrium in Foreign is shown by production and consumption at point A^* in panel (a), with the relative price of wheat equal to 1 (the slope of Foreign's PPF) and zero imports (since there is no international trade). This no-trade equilibrium is graphed as point $A^{*\prime}$ in panel (b). Keeping the relative price of wheat fixed at 1 in Foreign, production can shift away from point A^* in panel (a). This can occur because, as we argued for Home, wages are the same in Foreign's wheat and cloth industries when the relative price is at its no-trade level, so workers are willing to move between industries. Keeping Foreign consumption fixed at point A^* in

(a) Foreign Production and Consumption

(b) Foreign Import Demand for Wheat

1. Foreign imports 0–50 bushels of wheat at a relative price of 1 and . . .

2. . . .60 bushels of wheat at a relative price of $\frac{2}{3}$.

Foreign Import Demand Panel (a) repeats Figure 2-6, showing the Foreign trade equilibrium with production at point B^* and consumption at point C^*. Panel (b) shows Foreign import demand for wheat. When the relative price of wheat is 1, Foreign will import any amount of wheat between 0 and 50 bushels, along the segment $A^{*\prime}B^{*\prime}$ of the Foreign import demand curve. For relative prices below 1, Foreign imports more than 50 bushels, along the segment $B^{*\prime}C^{*\prime}$. For example, at the relative price of $\frac{2}{3}$, Foreign imports 60 bushels of wheat.

panel (a), suppose that all workers shift into the cloth industry, so that production is at point B^*. Then Foreign imports of wheat are 50 bushels (the difference between Foreign consumption of 50 and production of zero), as shown by point $B^{*\prime}$ in panel (b).

Joining up points $A^{*\prime}$, $B^{*\prime}$, and $C^{*\prime}$, we get an import demand curve that is flat between $A^{*\prime}$ and $B^{*\prime}$ and then falls between $B^{*\prime}$ and $C^{*\prime}$ and beyond. The flat portion of the Foreign import demand curve is once again a special feature of the Ricardian model that occurs because the PPF is a straight line. As we investigate other trade models in the following chapters, in which the production possibilities frontiers are curved rather than straight lines, the export supply and import demand curves will no longer have the flat portions. A general feature of these export supply and import demand curves is that they begin at the no-trade relative price for each country and then slope up (for export supply) or down (for import demand).

International Trade Equilibrium

Now that we have derived the Home export supply curve and the Foreign import demand curve, we can put them together in a single diagram, shown in Figure 2-11. The intersection of these two curves at point C' gives the international trade equilibrium, the equilibrium relative price of wheat at which the quantity of Home exports just equals Foreign imports. In Figure 2-11, the equilibrium relative price of wheat is $P_W/P_C = \frac{2}{3}$. This graph looks just like the supply = demand equilibria that you have seen in other economics classes, except that Figure 2-11 now refers to the *world* market for wheat rather than the market in a single country. That is, Home's export supply of wheat is the *excess* of the total Home supply over the quantity demanded by Home consumers, whereas Foreign import demand is the excess of total Foreign demand over the quantity supplied by Foreign suppliers. The intersection of these excess supply and demand curves, or export supply and import demand curves in

FIGURE 2-11

World Market for Wheat
Putting together the Home export supply curve and the Foreign import demand curve for wheat, the world equilibrium is established at point C', where the relative price of wheat is $\frac{2}{3}$. At this price, Home exports of 60 bushels just equal Foreign imports of wheat.

Figure 2-11, determines the relative price of wheat that clears the world market, that is, at which the desired sales of Home equal the desired purchases by Foreign.

The Terms of Trade The price of a country's exports divided by the price of its imports is called the **terms of trade.** Because Home exports wheat, (P_W/P_C) is its terms of trade. Notice that an increase in the price of wheat (Home's export) or a fall in the price of cloth (Home's import) would both *raise* its terms of trade. Generally, an increase in the terms of trade is good for a country because it is earning more for its exports or paying less for its imports, thus making it better off. Foreign exports cloth, so (P_C/P_W) is its terms of trade. In this case, having a higher price for cloth (Foreign's export) or a lower price for wheat (Foreign's import) would make the Foreign country better off.

APPLICATION

The Terms of Trade for Primary Commodities

What has happened over time to the terms of trade? Writing in the 1950s, the Latin American economist Raúl Prebisch and the British economist Hans Singer each put forward the hypothesis that the price of *primary commodities* (i.e., agricultural products and minerals) would decline over time relative to the price of manufactured goods. Because primary commodities are often exported by developing countries, this would mean that the terms of trade in developing countries would decline over time.

There are several reasons why the Prebisch-Singer hypothesis might be true. First, it is well known that as people or countries become richer, they spend a smaller share of their income on food.[14] This means that as world income grows, the demand for food will decline relative to the demand for manufactured goods. Therefore, the price of agricultural products can also be expected to decline relative to manufactured goods. Second, for mineral products, it may be that industrialized countries continually find substitutes for the use of minerals in their production of manufactured products. For example, much less steel is used in cars today because automobile producers have shifted toward the use of plastic and aluminum in the body and frame. We can think of the substitution away from mineral products as a form of technological progress, and as it proceeds, it can lead to a fall in the price of raw minerals.

However, there are also several reasons why the Prebisch-Singer hypothesis may not be true. First, technological progress in manufactured goods can certainly lead to a fall in the price of these goods as they become easier to produce (e.g., think of the reduction in prices of many electronic goods, such as MP3 and DVD players). This is a fall in the terms of trade for industrialized countries rather than developing countries. Second, at least in the case of oil exports, the Organization of Petroleum Exporting Countries (OPEC) has managed to keep oil prices high by restricting supplies on the world market. This has resulted in an increase in the terms of trade for oil-exporting countries, which includes developing and industrialized nations.

Data on the relative price of primary commodities are shown in Figure 2-12.[15] This study considered 24 primary commodities from 1900 to 1998 and measured their

---

[14] This relationship is known as Engel's law after the nineteenth-century German statistician Ernst Engel. It is certainly true for purchases of food eaten at home but might not hold for dining out. As your income rises, you might spend a constant or even increasing share of your budget on restaurant food.

[15] These results are provided by Neil Kellard and Mark E. Wohar, 2006, "Trends and Persistence in Primary Commodity Prices," *Journal of Development Economics*, 79, February 146–167.

FIGURE 2-12

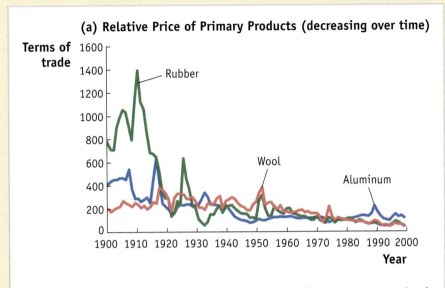

(a) Relative Price of Primary Products (decreasing over time)

Rubber

Wool

Aluminum

Terms of trade

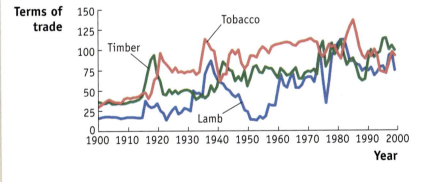

(b) Relative Price of Primary Products (increasing over time)

Tobacco

Timber

Lamb

Terms of trade

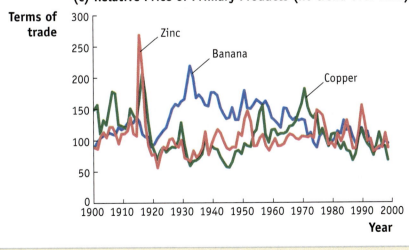

(c) Relative Price of Primary Products (no trend over time)

Zinc

Banana

Copper

Terms of trade

Relative Price of Primary Commodities
Many developing countries export primary commodities (i.e., agricultural products and minerals), whereas industrial countries export manufactured products. Shown here are the prices of various primary commodities relative to an overall manufacturing price, from 1900 to 1998. The relative prices of some primary commodities have fallen over time (panel a), whereas other commodities have had rising relative prices (panel b). Other commodity prices show no consistent trend over time (panel c).

world price relative to the overall price of manufactured goods. Of the 24 commodities, one-half of them showed a decline in their relative price for 50% or more of the time period, including aluminum, cotton, hides, palm oil, rice, sugar, rubber, wheat, and wool. This evidence provides some support for the Prebisch-Singer hypothesis. Several examples of these commodities, with declining relative prices, are shown in panel (a) of Figure 2-12.

However, there are also a number of primary commodities whose prices increased for significant periods of time, or showed no consistent trend over the century. Commodities that had increasing relative prices for 50% or more of the time period include beef, lamb, timber, tin, and tobacco. Several of these commodities are shown in panel (b) of Figure 2-12. Finally, commodities that had no consistent trend in their relative prices between the beginning and end of the century include bananas, coffee, copper, and zinc. Several of these are shown in panel (c) of Figure 2-12. From these results for different commodities, we should conclude that there are some that follow the pattern predicted by Prebisch and Singer, with falling prices relative to manufacturing. This is not a general rule, however, and other primary commodities have had increasing or no consistent change in their prices. ■

5 Conclusions

The Ricardian model was devised to respond to the mercantilist idea that exports are good and imports are bad. Not so, said David Ricardo, and to prove his point, he considered an example in which trade between two countries (England and Portugal) is balanced; that is, the value of imports equals the value of exports for each country. The reason that England and Portugal trade with each other in Ricardo's example is that their technologies for producing wine and cloth are different. Portugal has an absolute advantage in both goods, but England has a comparative advantage in cloth. That is, the opportunity cost of producing cloth in England (measured by how much wine would have to be given up) is lower than in Portugal. Based on this comparative advantage, the no-trade relative price of cloth is also lower in England than in Portugal. When trade is opened, cloth merchants in England export to Portugal, where they can obtain a higher price, and wine vintners in Portugal export to England. Thus, the pattern of trade is determined by comparative advantage, and both countries gain from trade.

For simplicity, the Ricardian model is presented with just a single factor of production—labor. We have used a lesson from microeconomics to solve for wages as the marginal product of labor times the price of each good. It follows from this relationship that the ratio of wages across countries is determined by the marginal product of labor in the goods being produced and by the prices of those goods. Because wages depend on the marginal products of labor in each country, we conclude that wages are determined by absolute advantage—a country with better technology will be able to pay higher wages. In addition, wages depend on the prices prevailing on world markets for the goods exported by each country. We have defined the "terms of trade" as the price of a country's exports divided by the price of its imports. Generally, having higher terms of trade (because of high export prices or low import prices) will lead to higher real wages and therefore will benefit workers.

The fact that only labor is used in the Ricardian model makes it special. Because of this assumption, the PPF in the Ricardian model is a straight line, and the export supply and import demand curves each have a flat segment. These special properties do not occur in other models we consider in the following chapters, where in addition to labor, industries will use capital and land. Once we allow for the more realistic assumption of several factors of production, the gains from trade become more complicated. Even if there are overall gains for a country, some factors of production might gain as other factors of production lose due to opening trade. That is the topic we explore in the next chapter.

KEY POINTS

1. A country has comparative advantage in producing a good when the country's opportunity cost of producing the good is lower than the opportunity cost of producing the good in another country.

2. The pattern of trade between countries is determined by comparative advantage. This means that even countries with poor technologies can export the goods in which they have comparative advantage.

3. All countries experience gains from trade. That is, the utility of an importing or exporting country is at least as high as it would be in the absence of international trade.

4. The level of wages in each country is determined by its absolute advantage; that is, by the amount the country can produce with its labor. This result explains why countries with poor technologies are still able to export: their low wages allow them to overcome their low productivity.

5. The equilibrium price of a good on the world market is determined at the point where the export supply of one country equals the import demand of the other country.

6. A country's terms of trade equal the price of its export good divided by the price of its import good. A rise in a country's terms of trade makes it better off because it is exporting at higher prices or importing at lower prices.

KEY TERMS

import, p. 27
export, p. 27
technology, p. 29
resources, p. 29
offshoring p. 29
proximity, p. 29
Ricardian model, p. 29
trade pattern, p. 29
free-trade area, p. 29
natural resources, p. 30

labor resources, p. 30
capital, p. 30
factors of production, p. 30
absolute advantage, p. 30
comparative advantage, p. 31
marginal product of labor (MPL), p. 33
production possibilities frontier (PPF), p. 33
opportunity cost, p. 33

indifference curves, p. 34
utility, p. 34
relative price, p. 36
international trade equilibrium, p. 41
world price line, p. 43
gains from trade, p. 43
export supply curve, p. 48
import demand curve, p. 48
terms of trade, p. 52

PROBLEMS

1. At the beginning of the chapter, there is a brief quotation from David Ricardo; here is a longer version of what Ricardo wrote:

   > England may be so circumstanced, that to produce the cloth may require the labour of 100 men for one year; and if she attempted to make the wine, it might require the labour of 120 men for the same time. . . . To produce the wine in Portugal, might require only the labour of 80 men for one year, and to produce the cloth in the same country, might require the labour of 90 men for the same time. It would therefore be advantageous for her to export wine in exchange for cloth. This exchange might even take place, notwithstanding that the commodity imported by Portugal could be produced there with less labour than in England.

   Suppose that the amount of labor Ricardo describes can produce 1,000 yards of cloth or 1,000 bottles of wine, in either country. Then answer the following:

   a. What is England's marginal product of labor in cloth and in wine, and what is Portugal's marginal product of labor in cloth and in wine? Which country has absolute advantage in cloth, and in wine, and why?

   b. Use the formula $P_W/P_C = MPL_C/MPL_W$ to compute the no-trade relative price of wine in each country. Which country has comparative advantage in wine, and why?

2. Suppose that each worker in the Home country can produce three cars or two TVs. Assume that Home has four workers.

   a. Graph the production possibilities frontier for the Home country.

   b. What is the no-trade relative price of cars at Home?

3. Suppose that each worker in the Foreign country can produce two cars or three TVs. Assume that Foreign also has four workers.

   a. Graph the production possibilities frontier for the Foreign country.

   b. What is the no-trade relative price of cars in Foreign?

   c. Using the information provided in Problem 2 regarding Home, in which good does Foreign have a comparative advantage, and why?

4. Suppose that in the absence of trade, Home consumes nine cars and two TVs, while Foreign consumes two cars and nine TVs. Add the indifference curve for each country to the figures in Problems 2 and 3. Label the production possibilities frontier (PPF), indifference curve (U_1), and the no-trade equilibrium consumption and production for each country.

5. Now suppose the world relative price of cars is $P_C/P_{TV} = 1$.

   a. In what good will each country specialize? Briefly explain why.

   b. Graph the new world price line for each country in the figures in Problem 4, and add a new indifference curve (U_2) for each country in the trade equilibrium.

   c. Label the exports and imports for each country. How does the amount of Home exports compare with Foreign imports?

   d. Does each country gain from trade? Briefly explain why or why not.

6. Answer the following questions using the information given by the accompanying table:

	Home Country	Foreign Country	Absolute Advantage
Number of bicycles produced per hour	4	2	?
Number of snowboards produced per hour	6	8	?
Comparative advantage	?	?	

   a. Complete the table for this problem in the same manner as Table 2-2.

b. Which country has an absolute advantage in the production of bicycles? Which country has an absolute advantage in the production of snowboards?

c. What is the opportunity cost of bicycles in terms of snowboards at Home? What is the opportunity cost of bicycles in terms of snowboards in Foreign?

d. Which product will Home export, and which product does Foreign export? Briefly explain why.

7. Assume that Home and Foreign produce two goods, TVs and cars, and use the information below to answer the following questions:

In the No-Trade Equilibrium

Home Country		Foreign Country	
$Wage_{TV} = 12$	$Wage_C = ?$	$Wage_{TV}^* = ?$	$Wage_C^* = 6$
$MPL_{TV} = 2$	$MPL_C = ?$	$MPL_{TV}^* = ?$	$MPL_C^* = 1$
$P_{TV} = ?$	$P_C = 4$	$P_{TV}^* = 3$	$P_C^* = ?$

a. What is the marginal product of labor for TVs and cars in the Home country? What is the no-trade relative price of TVs at Home?

b. What is the marginal product of labor for TVs and cars in the Foreign country? What is the no-trade relative price of TVs in Foreign?

c. Suppose the world relative price of TVs in the trade equilibrium is $P_{TV}/P_C = 1$. Which good will each country export? Briefly explain why.

d. In the trade equilibrium, what is the real wage at Home in terms of cars and in terms of TVs? How do these values compare with the real wage in terms of either good in the no-trade equilibrium?

e. In the trade equilibrium, what is the real wage in Foreign in terms of TVs and in terms of cars? How do these values compare with the real wage in terms of either good in the no-trade equilibrium?

f. In the trade equilibrium, do Foreign workers earn more or less than those at Home, measured in terms of their ability to purchase goods? Explain why.

8. Why do some low-wage countries, such as China, pose a threat to manufacturers in industrial countries, such as the United States, whereas other low-wage countries, such as Haiti, do not?

Answer Problems 9 to 11 using the chapter information for Home and Foreign.

9. a. Suppose that the number of workers doubles in Home. What happens to the Home PPF and what happens to the no-trade relative price of wheat?

b. Suppose that there is technological progress in the wheat industry such that Home can produce more wheat with the same amount of labor. What happens to the Home PPF, and what happens to the relative price of wheat? Describe what would happen if a similar change occurred in the cloth industry.

10. a. Using Figure 2-5, show that an increase in the relative price of wheat from its world relative price of $\frac{2}{3}$ will raise Home's utility.

b. Using Figure 2-6, show that an increase in the relative price of wheat from its world relative price of $\frac{2}{3}$ will lower Foreign's utility. What is Foreign's utility when the world relative price reaches 1, and what happens in Foreign when the world relative price of wheat rises above that level?

11. *(This is a harder question.)* Suppose that the Home country is much larger than the Foreign country. For example, suppose we double the number of workers at Home from 25 to 50. Then Home is willing to export up to 100 bushels of wheat at its no-trade price of $P_W/P_C = \frac{1}{2}$ rather than 50 bushels of wheat as shown in Figure 2-11. In the following, we draw a new version of Figure 2-11, with the larger Home country.

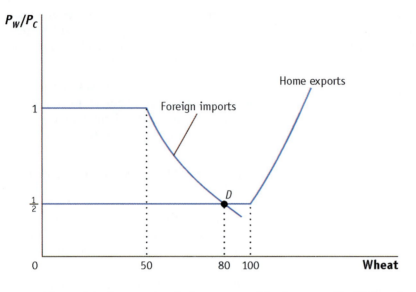

a. From this figure, what is the new world relative price of wheat (at point *D*)?

b. Using this new world equilibrium price, draw a new version of the trade equilibrium in Home and in Foreign, and show the production point and consumption point in each country.

c. Are there gains from trade in both countries? Explain why or why not.

12. Using the results from Problem 11, explain why the Ricardian model predicts that Mexico would gain more than the United States when the two countries signed the North American Free Trade Agreement, establishing free trade between them.

Gains and Losses from Trade in the Specific-Factors Model

The time has come, the awaited day, a historic day in which Bolivia retakes absolute control of our natural resources.

Evo Morales, President of Bolivia, 2006[1]

If we do not take action, those who have the most reason to be dissatisfied with our present rate of growth will be tempted to seek shortsighted and narrow solutions—to resist automation, to reduce the work week to 35 hours or even lower, to shut out imports, or to raise prices in a vain effort to obtain full capacity profits on under-capacity operations. But these are all self-defeating expedients which can only restrict the economy, not expand it.

President John F. Kennedy, New York Economic Club, 1962

Over the span of three years, 2003 to 2005, Bolivia had three presidents. This rapid succession at the highest level of government was largely a result of public dissatisfaction with the distribution of gains that had come from exporting natural gas. Many people, including the indigenous Aymara Indians, believed that most of these gains had gone to multinational oil corporations, with little distributed to the citizens of the country in which the gas deposits and refineries are located.

Violent protests in September 2003 led to the resignation of President Gonzalo Sánchez de Lozada, who was replaced by Carlos Mesa, a writer and television journalist. He promised to respect the views of the indigenous people of Bolivia and in July 2004 held a referendum on whether the country should export natural gas. The referendum included provisions to ensure that more of the profits from natural gas exports would go to the Bolivian government rather than to foreign companies. With these assurances, the referendum passed, and in May 2005 taxes on foreign oil companies were sharply

---

[1] Speech from the San Alberto field operated by Petrobras, "Bolivia Nationalizes Natural Gas Industry," *USA Today*, May 1, 2006.

Evo Morales and his supporters.

increased. But many protestors wanted more and forced President Mesa to resign within the year. Elections were held again in December 2005, and Evo Morales scored a decisive victory, becoming the first Aymara Indian elected to president in Bolivia's 180-year history. In May 2006 he nationalized the gas industry, which meant that all natural gas resources were placed under the control of the state-owned energy company. With this policy change, foreign investors lost their majority ownership claims to gas fields, pipelines, and refineries that they had built and lost a significant portion of the profits from the sales of Bolivian natural gas. This drastic step, which was criticized heavily by foreign governments, followed a trend in some other Latin American countries toward taking control of oil and gas resources.

The Bolivian experience illustrates the difficulty of ensuring that all people within a country share in the gains from trade. Exports of Bolivia's natural gas are expected to generate earnings of some $500 million per year, which are the gains from exporting. But the difficulty of sharing these gains among Bolivia's citizenry makes the export of gas a contentious issue. Although the export of natural gas clearly generated gains for the foreign-owned and state-owned companies that sold the resources, the indigenous peoples have only begun to share in those gains.

The new constitution in 2009 gives indigenous peoples control over natural resources in their territories. In addition to oil and gas, those resources include lithium, a key ingredient to make batteries for electric cars, which is found in abundance in Bolivia. Companies from Japan and Europe are trying to make deals to extract this resource, but the government of Evo Morales is proceeding cautiously. And the indigenous peoples are working to ensure that they also gain from this valuable resource.[2]

A key lesson from this chapter is that in most cases, opening a country to trade generates winners *and* losers. In general, the gains of those who benefit from trade exceed the losses of those who are harmed, and in this sense there are "overall" gains from trade. That was a lesson from the Ricardian model in the last chapter. But our argument in the last chapter that trade generates gains for *all* workers was too simple because, in the Ricardian model, labor was the only factor of production. Once we make the more realistic assumption that capital and land are also factors of production, then trade will generate gains for some factors and losses for others. Our goal in this chapter is to determine who gains and who loses from trade and under what circumstances.

The model we use to analyze the role of international trade in determining the earnings of labor, land, and capital assumes that one industry (agriculture) uses labor and land and the other industry (manufacturing) uses labor and capital. This model is sometimes called the **specific-factors model** because land is *specific* to the agriculture sector and capital is *specific* to the manufacturing sector; labor is used in both sectors, so it is not specific to either one. The idea that land is specific to agriculture and that capital is specific to manufacturing might be true in the short run but does not really hold in the long run. In later chapters, we develop a long-run model, in which capital and other resources can be shifted from use in one industry to use in another. For now we focus on the short-run specific-factors model, which will offer many new insights about the gains from trade beyond those obtained from the Ricardian model.

---

[2] You can read more about this case in Simon Romero, "In Bolivia, Untapped Bounty Meets Nationalism," *New York Times*, February 3, 2009, from which this paragraph is drawn.

1 Specific-Factors Model

We address the following question in the specific-factors model: How does trade affect the earnings of labor, land, and capital? We have already seen from our study of the Ricardian model that when a country is opened to free trade, the relative price of exports rises and the relative price of imports falls. Thus, the question of how trade affects factor earnings is really a question of how changes in *relative prices* affect the earnings of labor, land, and capital. The idea we develop in this section is that the earnings of *specific* or *fixed factors* (such as capital and land) will go up or down the most due to changes in relative prices (i.e., they are the most sensitive to relative price changes) because in the short run they are "stuck" in a sector and cannot be employed elsewhere. In contrast, mobile factors (such as labor) can offset their losses somewhat by seeking employment in other industries.

As in our study of international trade in Chapter 2, we will have two countries, called Home and Foreign. We first discuss the Home country.

The Home Country

Let us call the two industries in the specific-factors model "manufacturing" and "agriculture." Manufacturing uses labor and capital, whereas agriculture uses labor and land. In each industry, increases in the amount of labor used are subject to **diminishing returns;** that is, the marginal product of labor declines as the amount of labor used in the industry increases. Figure 3-1, panel (a), plots output against the amount of labor used in production, and shows diminishing returns for the manufacturing industry. As more labor is used, the output of manufacturing goes up, but it does so at

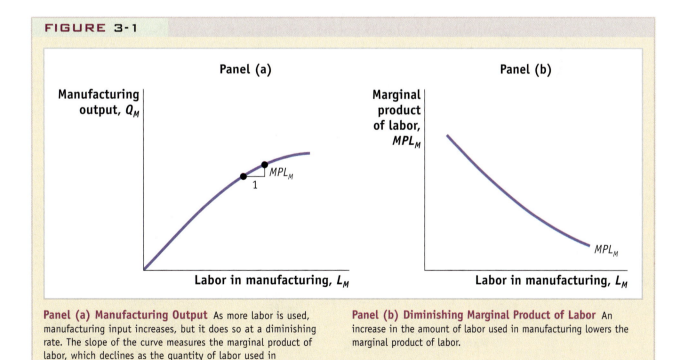

FIGURE 3-1

Panel (a)

Manufacturing output, Q_M

MPL_M

1

Labor in manufacturing, L_M

Panel (b)

Marginal product of labor, MPL_M

MPL_M

Labor in manufacturing, L_M

Panel (a) Manufacturing Output As more labor is used, manufacturing input increases, but it does so at a diminishing rate. The slope of the curve measures the marginal product of labor, which declines as the quantity of labor used in manufacturing increases.

Panel (b) Diminishing Marginal Product of Labor An increase in the amount of labor used in manufacturing lowers the marginal product of labor.

a diminishing rate. The slope of the curve in Figure 3-1 measures the marginal product of labor, which declines as labor increases.

Figure 3-1, panel (b), graphs MPL_M, the marginal product of labor in manufacturing, against the labor used in manufacturing L_M. This curve slopes downward due to diminishing returns. Likewise, in the agriculture sector (not drawn), the marginal product of labor MPL_A also diminishes as the amount of labor used in agriculture L_A increases.

Production Possibilities Frontier Combining the output for the two industries, manufacturing and agriculture, we obtain the production possibilities frontier (PPF) for the economy (Figure 3-2). Because of the diminishing returns to labor in both sectors, the PPF is *bowed out* or concave with respect to the graph's origin. (You may recognize this familiar shape from your introductory economics class.)

By using the marginal products of labor in each sector, we can determine the slope of the PPF. Starting at point A in Figure 3-2, suppose that one unit of labor leaves agriculture and enters manufacturing so that the economy's new output is at point B. The drop in agricultural output is MPL_A, and the increase in manufacturing output is MPL_M. The slope of the PPF between points A and B is the negative of the ratio of marginal products, or $-MPL_A/MPL_M$. This ratio can be interpreted as the opportunity cost of producing one unit of manufacturing, the cost of one unit of manufacturing in terms of the amount of food (the agricultural good) that would need to be given up to produce it.

Opportunity Cost and Prices As in the Ricardian model, the slope of the PPF, which is the opportunity cost of manufacturing, also equals the relative price of manufacturing. To understand why this is so, recall that in competitive markets, firms hire labor up to the point at which the cost of one more hour of labor (the wage) equals the value of one more hour of labor in terms of output. In turn, the value of one more hour of labor equals the amount of goods produced in that hour (the marginal product of labor) times the price of the good. In manufacturing, labor will be hired to the

---

FIGURE 3-2

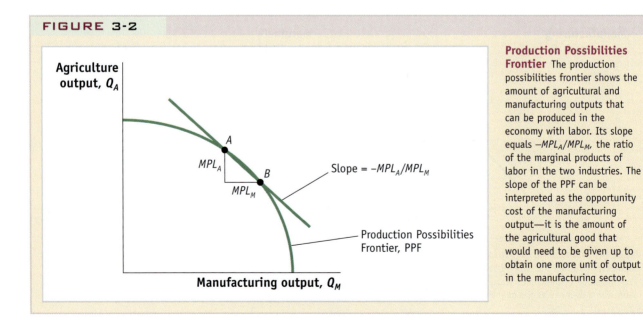

Production Possibilities Frontier The production possibilities frontier shows the amount of agricultural and manufacturing outputs that can be produced in the economy with labor. Its slope equals $-MPL_A/MPL_M$, the ratio of the marginal products of labor in the two industries. The slope of the PPF can be interpreted as the opportunity cost of the manufacturing output—it is the amount of the agricultural good that would need to be given up to obtain one more unit of output in the manufacturing sector.

point at which the wage W equals the price of manufacturing P_M times the marginal product of labor in manufacturing MPL_M:

$$W = P_M \cdot MPL_M$$

Similarly, in agriculture, labor will be hired to the point at which the wage W equals the price of manufacturing P_A times the marginal product of labor in manufacturing MPL_A:

$$W = P_A \cdot MPL_A$$

Because we are assuming that labor is free to move between sectors, the wages in these two equations must be equal. If the wage were not the same in both sectors, labor would move to the sector with the higher wage. This movement would continue until the increase in the amount of labor in the high-wage sector drove down the wage, and the decrease in amount of labor in the low-wage sector drove up the wage, until the wages were equal. By setting the two wage equations equal, we obtain $P_M \cdot MPL_M = P_A \cdot MPL_A$, and by rearranging terms, we get

$$(P_M/P_A) = (MPL_A/MPL_M)$$

This equation shows that the relative price of manufacturing (P_M/P_A) equals the opportunity cost of manufacturing (MPL_A/MPL_M), the slope of the production possibilities frontier. These relative prices also reflect the value that Home consumers put on manufacturing versus food. In the absence of international trade, the equilibrium for the Home economy is at point A in Figure 3-3, where the relative price of manufacturing (P_M/P_A) equals the slope of the PPF as well as the slope of the indifference curve for a representative consumer with utility of U_1. The intuition for the no-trade equilibrium is exactly the same as for the Ricardian model in Chapter 2: equilibrium occurs at the tangency of the PPF and the consumer's indifference curve. This point on the PPF corresponds to the highest possible level of utility for the consumer.

FIGURE 3-3

Increase in the Relative Price of Manufactures In the absence of international trade, the economy produces and consumes at point A. The relative price of manufactures, P_M/P_A, is the slope of the line tangent to the PPF and indifference curve, U_1, at point A. With international trade, the economy is able to produce at point B and consume at point C. The world relative price of manufactures, $(P_M/P_A)^W$, is the slope of the line BC. The rise in utility from U_1 to U_2 is a measure of the gains from trade for the economy.

The Foreign Country

In this chapter, we do not discuss the Foreign country in any detail. Instead, we simply assume that the no-trade relative price of manufacturing in Foreign (P_M^*/P_A^*) differs from the no-trade price (P_M/P_A) at Home. There are several reasons why these prices can differ. In the previous chapter, we showed how differences in productivities across countries cause the no-trade relative prices to differ across countries. That is the key assumption, or starting point, of the Ricardian model. Another reason for relative prices to differ, which we have not yet investigated, is that the amounts of labor, capital, or land found in the two countries are different. (That will be the key assumption of the Heckscher–Ohlin model, which we discuss in the next chapter.)

For now, we will not explain why the no-trade relative prices differ across countries but will take it for granted that this is not unusual. For the sake of focusing on one case, let us assume that the Home no-trade relative price of manufacturing is *lower* than the Foreign relative price, $(P_M/P_A) < (P_M^*/P_A^*)$. This assumption means that Home can produce manufactured goods relatively cheaper than Foreign, or, equivalently, that Home has a comparative advantage in manufacturing.

Overall Gains from Trade

Starting at the no-trade equilibrium point A in Figure 3-3, suppose that the Home country opens up to international trade with Foreign. Once trade is opened, we expect that the world equilibrium relative price; that is, the relative price in *all* countries $(P_M/P_A)^W$, will lie between the no-trade relative prices in the two countries, so

$$(P_M/P_A) < (P_M/P_A)^W < (P_M^*/P_A^*)$$

This equation shows us that when Home opens to trade, the relative price of manufacturing will *rise*, from (P_M/P_A) to $(P_M/P_A)^W$; conversely, for Foreign, the relative price of manufacturing will *fall*, from (P_M^*/P_A^*) to $(P_M/P_A)^W$. With trade, the world relative price $(P_M/P_A)^W$ is represented by a line with that slope that is tangent to Home's PPF, line BC in Figure 3-3. The increase in the Home relative price of manufactured goods is shown by the steeper slope of the world relative price line as compared with the Home no-trade price line (through point A).

What is the effect of this increase in (P_M/P_A) at Home? The higher relative price of the manufactured good at Home attracts more workers into that sector, which now produces at point B rather than A. As before, production takes place at the point along the Home PPF tangent to the relative price line, where equality of wages across industries is attained. The country can then export manufactures and import agricultural products along the international price line BC, and it reaches its highest level of utility, U_2, at point C. The difference in utility between U_2 and U_1 is a measure of the country's overall gains from trade. (These overall gains would be zero if the relative prices with trade were equal to the no-trade relative prices, but they can never be negative—a country can never be made worse off by opening to trade.)

Notice that the good whose relative price goes up (manufacturing, for Home) is exported and the good whose relative price goes down (agriculture, for Home) is imported. By exporting manufactured goods at a higher price and importing food at a lower price, Home is better off than it was in the absence of trade. To measure the gains from trade, economists rely on the price increases for exports and the price decreases for imports to determine how much extra consumption a country can afford. The following application considers the magnitude of the overall gains from trade in historical cases in which the gains have been measured.

How Large Are the Gains from Trade?

How large are the overall gains from trade? There are a few historical examples of countries that have moved from **autarky** (i.e., no trade) to free trade, or vice versa, quickly enough that we can use the years before and after this shift to estimate the gains from trade.

One such episode in the United States occurred between December 1807 and March 1809, when the U.S. Congress imposed a nearly complete halt to international trade at the request of President Thomas Jefferson. A complete stop to all trade is called an **embargo.** The United States imposed its embargo because Britain was at war with Napoleon, and Britain wanted to prevent ships from arriving in France that might be carrying supplies or munitions. As a result, Britain patrolled the eastern coast of the United States and seized U.S. ships that were bound across the Atlantic. To safeguard its own ships and possibly inflict economic losses on Britain, the United States declared a trade embargo for 14 months from 1807 to 1809. The embargo was not complete, however; the United States still traded with some countries, such as Canada and Mexico, that didn't have to be reached by ship.

As you might expect, U.S. trade fell dramatically during this period. Exports (such as cotton, flour, tobacco, and rice) fell from about $49 million in 1807 to $9 million in 1809. The drop in the value of exports reflects both a drop in the quantity exported and a drop in the price of exports. Recall that in Chapter 2 we defined the terms of trade of a country as the price of its export goods divided by the price of its import goods, so a drop in the price of U.S. exports is a fall in its terms of trade, which is a loss for the United States. According to one study, the cost of the trade embargo to the United States was about 5% of gross domestic product (GDP). That is, U.S. GDP was 5% lower than it would have been without the trade embargo. The cost of the embargo was offset somewhat because trade was not completely eliminated and because some U.S. producers were able to shift their efforts to producing goods (such as cloth and glass) that had previously been imported. Thus, we can take 5% of GDP as a lower estimate of what the gains from trade for the United States would have been relative to a situation with no trade.

Is 5% of GDP a large or small number? It is large when we think that a recession that reduced GDP by 5% in one year would be regarded as a very deep downturn.[3] To get another perspective, instead of comparing the costs of the embargo with overall GDP, we can instead compare them with the size of U.S. exports, which were 13% of GDP before the embargo. Taking the ratio of these numbers, we conclude that the cost of the embargo was more than one-third of the value of exports.

Another historical case was Japan's rapid opening to the world economy in 1854, after 200 years of self-imposed autarky. In this case, military action by Commodore Matthew Perry of the United States forced Japan to open up its borders so that the

---

[3] The most severe downturn ever in the United States was the Great Depression of the 1930s. U.S. real GDP fell each year between 1929 and 1933 by an average of 9% per year and then began to recover. It was not until 1939 that the United States regained the same level of real GDP that it had in 1929.

United States could establish commercial ties. When trade was opened, the prices of Japanese exports to the United States (such as silk and tea) rose, and the prices of U.S. imports (such as woolens) fell. These price movements were a terms-of-trade gain for Japan, very much like the movement from the no-trade point A in Figure 3-3 to a trade equilibrium at points B and C. According to one estimate, Japan's gains from trade after its opening were 4 to 5% of GDP.[4] The gains were not one-sided, however; Japan's trading partners—such as the United States—also gained from being able to trade in the newly opened markets. ■

2 Earnings of Labor

Because there are overall gains from trade, at least *someone* in the economy must be better off, but it does not mean that *everyone* is better off. The goal of this chapter is to explore how a change in relative prices, such as that shown in Figure 3-3, feeds back onto the earnings of workers, landowners, and capital owners. We begin our study of the specific-factors model by looking at what happens to the wages earned by labor when there is an increase in the relative price of manufactures.

Determination of Wages

To determine wages, it is convenient to take the marginal product of labor in manufacturing (MPL_M), which was shown in Figure 3-2, and the marginal product of labor in agriculture (MPL_A), and put them in one diagram.

First, we add the amount of labor used in manufacturing L_M and the amount used in agriculture L_A to give us the total amount of labor in the economy $\overline{L}$:

$$L_M + L_A = \overline{L}$$

Figure 3-4 shows the total amount of labor $\overline{L}$ on the horizontal axis. The amount of labor used in manufacturing L_M is measured from left (0_M) to right, while the amount of labor used in agriculture L_A is measured from right (0_A) to left. Each point on the horizontal axis indicates how much labor is used in manufacturing (measured from left to right) and how much labor is used in agriculture (measured from right to left). For example, point L indicates that $0_M L$ units of labor are used in manufacturing and $0_A L$ units of labor are used in agriculture, which adds up to $\overline{L}$ units of labor in total.

The second step in determining wages is to multiply the marginal product of labor in each sector by the price of the good in that sector (P_M or P_A). As we discussed earlier, in competitive markets, firms will hire labor up to the point at which the cost of one more hour of labor (the wage) equals the value of one more hour in production, which is the marginal product of labor times the price of the good. In each industry, then, labor will be hired until

$$W = P_M \cdot MPL_M \text{ in manufacturing}$$

$$W = P_A \cdot MPL_A \text{ in agriculture}$$

In Figure 3-4, we draw the graph of $P_M \cdot MPL_M$ as downward-sloping. This curve is basically the same as the marginal product of labor MPL_M curve in Figure 3-2,

---

[4] Daniel M. Bernhofen and John C. Brown, March 2005, "Estimating the Comparative Advantage Gains from Trade," *American Economic Review*, 95(1), 208–225.

FIGURE 3-4

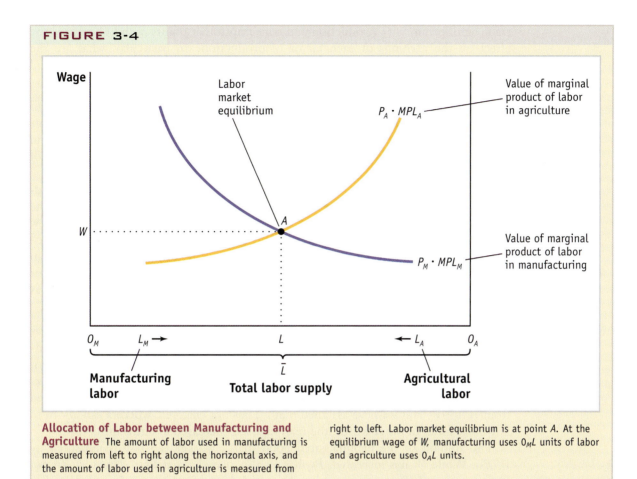

Allocation of Labor between Manufacturing and Agriculture The amount of labor used in manufacturing is measured from left to right along the horizontal axis, and the amount of labor used in agriculture is measured from right to left. Labor market equilibrium is at point A. At the equilibrium wage of W, manufacturing uses $0_M L$ units of labor and agriculture uses $0_A L$ units.

except that it is now multiplied by the price of the manufactured good. When we draw the graph of $P_A \cdot MPL_A$ for agriculture, however, it slopes upward. This is because we are measuring the labor used in agriculture L_A from *right to left* in the diagram: the marginal product of labor in agriculture falls as the amount of labor increases (moving from right to left).

Equilibrium Wage The equilibrium wage is found at point A, the intersection of the curves $P_M \cdot MPL_M$ and $P_A \cdot MPL_A$ in Figure 3-4. At this point, $0_M L$ units of labor are used in manufacturing, and firms in that industry are willing to pay the wage $W = P_M \cdot MPL_M$. In addition, $0_A L$ units of labor are used in agriculture, and farmers are willing to pay the wage $W = P_A \cdot MPL_A$. Because wages are equal in the two sectors, there is no reason for labor to move, and the labor market is in equilibrium.

Change in Relative Price of Manufactures

Now that we have shown how the wage is determined in the specific-factors model, we want to ask how the wage *changes* in response to an increase in the relative price of manufactures. That is, as the relative price of manufactures rises (shown in Figure 3-3), and the economy shifts from its no-trade equilibrium at point A to its trade equilibrium with production and consumption at points B and C, what is the effect on the earnings of each factor of production? In particular, what are the changes in the wage, and in the earnings of capital owners in manufacturing and landowners in agriculture?

Effect on the Wage An increase in the relative price of manufacturing P_M/P_A can occur due to either an increase in P_M or a decrease in P_A. Both these price movements will have the same effect on the **real wage;** that is, on the amount of manufactures and food that a worker can afford to buy. For convenience, let us suppose that the price of manufacturing P_M rises, while the price of agriculture P_A does not change.

When P_M rises, the curve $P_M \cdot MPL_M$ shifts up to $P_M' \cdot MPL_M$, as shown in Figure 3-5. The vertical rise in this curve is exactly $\Delta P_M \cdot MPL_M$, as illustrated in the diagram. (We use the symbol Δ, delta, to stand for the *change* in a variable.) The new intersection of the two curves occurs at point B, where the wage is W' and the allocation of labor between the two sectors is identified by point L'. The equilibrium wage has risen from W to W', the amount of labor used in the manufacturing sector has increased from $0_M L$ to $0_M L'$, and the amount of labor used in agriculture has fallen from $0_A L$ to $0_A L'$.

Effect on Real Wages The fact that the wage has risen does not really tell us whether workers are better off or worse off in terms of the amount of food and manufactured goods they can buy. To answer this question, we have to take into account any change in the prices of these goods. For instance, the amount of food that a worker can afford to buy with his or her hourly wage is W/P_A.[5] Because W has increased from W to W' and we have assumed that P_A has not changed, workers can afford to buy more food. In other words, the real wage has increased in terms of food.

The amount of the manufactured good that a worker can buy is measured by W/P_M. While W has increased, P_M has also increased, so at first glance we do not know whether W/P_M has increased or decreased. However, Figure 3-5 can help us figure this out. Notice that as we've drawn Figure 3-5, the increase in the wage from W to W' is less than the vertical increase $\Delta P_M \cdot MPL_M$ that occurred in the $P_M \cdot MPL_M$ curve. We can write this condition as

$$\Delta W < \Delta P_M \cdot MPL_M$$

To see how W/P_M has changed, divide both sides of this equation by the initial wage W (which equals $P_M \cdot MPL_M$) to obtain

$$\frac{\Delta W}{W} < \frac{\Delta P_M \cdot MPL_M}{P_M \cdot MPL_M} = \frac{\Delta P_M}{P_M}$$

where the final ratio is obtained because we canceled out MPL_M in the numerator and denominator of the middle ratio. The term $\Delta W/W$ in this equation is the *percentage change in wages*. For example, suppose the initial wage is \$8 per hour and it rises to \$10 per hour. Then $\Delta W/W = \$2/\$8 = 0.25$, which is a 25% increase in the wage. Similarly, the term $\Delta P_M/P_M$ is the *percentage change in the price of manufactured goods*. When $\Delta W/W < \Delta P_M/P_M$, then the percentage increase in the wage is *less than* the percentage increase in the price of the manufactured good. This inequality means that the

---

[5] For example, suppose that you earn \$8 per hour, and your favorite snack costs \$2. Then you could afford to buy \$8/\$2 = 4 of these snacks after working for one hour.

FIGURE 3-5

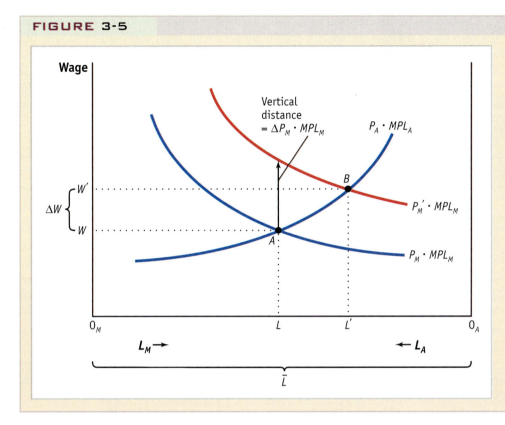

Wage

Vertical distance = $\Delta P_M \cdot MPL_M$

$P_A \cdot MPL_A$

B

$P_M{}' \cdot MPL_M$

W'

ΔW

A

W

$P_M \cdot MPL_M$

O_M L L' O_A

$L_M \rightarrow$ $\leftarrow L_A$

$\bar{L}$

Increase in the Price of Manufactured Goods
With an increase in the price of the manufactured good, the curve $P_M \cdot MPL_M$ shifts up to $P_M{}' \cdot MPL_M$ and the equilibrium shifts from point A to point B. The amount of labor used in manufacturing rises from $O_M L$ to $O_M L'$, and the amount of labor used in agriculture falls from $O_A L$ to $O_A L'$. The wage increases from W to W', but this increase is less than the upward shift $\Delta P_M \cdot MPL_M$.

amount of the manufactured good that can be purchased with the wage has fallen, so the *real wage in terms of the manufactured good W/P_M has decreased*.[6]

Overall Impact on Labor We have now determined that as a result of our assumption of an increase in the relative price of manufactured goods, the *real wage in terms of food has increased and the real wage in terms of the manufactured good has decreased*. In this case, we assumed that the increase in relative price was caused by an increase in the price of manufactures with a constant price of agriculture. Notice, though, that if we had assumed a constant price of manufactures and a decrease in the price of agriculture (taken together, an increase in the relative price of manufactures), then we would have arrived at the same effects on the real wage in terms of both products.

Is labor better off or worse off after the price increase? We cannot tell. A person who spends most of his or her income on manufactured goods is worse off because fewer manufactured goods can be bought, but a person who spends most of his or her income on food is better off because more food is affordable. The bottom line is that in the specific-factors model, the increase in the price of the manufactured good has an ambiguous effect on the real wage and therefore an *ambiguous* effect on the well-being of workers.

---

[6] For example, suppose that the manufactured good is compact discs (CDs), which initially cost $16 and then rise in price to $24. The increase in the price of CDs is $8, and so the percentage increase in the price of CDs is $\Delta P_M / P_M = \$8/\$16 = 0.50 = 50\%$. Suppose also that the wage has increased from $8 to $10 per hour, or 25%. Using the initial prices, by working one hour, you could afford to buy $W/P_M = \$8/\$16 = 0.5$, or one-half of a CD. Using the new prices, by working one hour, you can afford to buy $W/P_M = \$10/\$24 = 0.42$, or about four-tenths of a CD. So, your real wage measured in terms of CDs has gone down.

The conclusion that we cannot tell whether workers are better off or worse off from the opening of trade in the specific-factors model might seem wishy-washy to you, but it is important for several reasons. First, this result is different from what we found in the Ricardian model of Chapter 2, in which the real wage increases with the opening of trade so that workers are always unambiguously better off than in the absence of trade.[7] In the specific-factors model, that is no longer the case; the opening of trade and the shift in relative prices raise the real wage in terms of one good but lower it in terms of the other good. Second, our results for the specific-factors model serve as a warning against making unqualified statements about the effect of trade on workers, such as "Trade is bad for workers" or "Trade is good for workers." Even in the specific-factors model, which is simplified by considering only two industries and not allowing capital or land to move between them, we have found that the effects of opening trade on the real wage are complicated. In reality, the effect of trade on real wages is often more complex still.

Unemployment in the Specific-Factors Model We have ignored one significant, realistic feature in the specific-factors model: unemployment. You may often see online news stories about workers who are laid off because of import competition and who face a period of unemployment. Despite this outcome, most economists do not believe that trade necessarily harms workers overall. It is true that we have ignored unemployment in the specific-factors model: the labor employed in manufacturing L_M plus the labor employed in agriculture L_A always sums to the total labor supply $\bar{L}$, which means that there is no unemployment. One of the reasons we ignore unemployment in this model is that it is usually treated as a macroeconomic phenomenon, caused by business cycles, and it is hard to combine business cycle models with international trade models to isolate the effects of trade on workers. But the other, simpler reason is that even when people are laid off because of import competition, many of them do find new jobs within a reasonable period of time, and sometimes they find jobs with *higher* wages, as shown in the next application. Therefore, even if we take into account spells of unemployment, once we recognize that workers can find new jobs—possibly in export industries that are expanding—then we still cannot conclude that trade is necessarily good or bad for workers.

In the two applications that follow, we look at some evidence from the United States on the amount of time it takes to find new jobs and on the wages earned, and at attempts by governments to compensate workers who lose their jobs because of import competition. This type of compensation is called **Trade Adjustment Assistance (TAA)** in the United States.

APPLICATION

Manufacturing and Services in the United States: Employment and Wages across Sectors

Although the specific-factors model emphasizes manufacturing and agriculture, the amount of labor devoted to agriculture in most industrialized countries is small. A larger sector in industrialized countries is that of **services,** which includes wholesale

---

[7] The only situation in which workers do not gain from trade in the Ricardian model is if the Home country is very large, as discussed in Problem 11 of Chapter 2, such that the international relative price equals the no-trade relative price. In that case, Home workers are no better off from international trade but also no worse off.

and retail trade, finance, law, education, information technology, software engineering, consulting, and medical and government services. In the United States and most industrial countries, the service sector is larger than the manufacturing sector and much larger than the agriculture sector.

In Figure 3-6, we show employment in the manufacturing sector of the United States, both in terms of the number of workers employed in it and as a percentage of total employment in the economy. Using either measure, employment in manufacturing has been falling over time; given zero or negative growth in the agriculture sector, this indicates that the service sector has been growing. In Figure 3-7, we show the real wages earned by production—or blue-collar—workers in manufacturing, in all private services, and in information services (a subset of private services).[8] While wages were slightly higher in manufacturing than in private services from 1974 through 2007, all private service wages have been higher since 2008. This change is due in part to the effect of wages in the *information service* industry, which are substantially higher than those in manufacturing. For example, average hourly earnings in all private services were $18.40 per hour in 2009 and slightly lower—$18.30 per hour—in manufacturing overall. But in information services, average wages were much higher—$25.60 per hour.

FIGURE 3-6

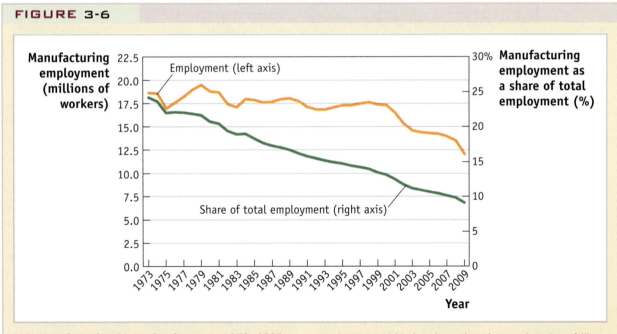

U.S. Manufacturing Sector Employment, 1973–2009
Employment in the U.S. manufacturing sector is shown on the left axis, and the share of manufacturing employment in total U.S. employment is shown on the right axis. Both manufacturing employment and its share in total employment have been falling over time, indicating that the service sector has been growing.

Source: Economic Report of the President, 2010, Table B46.

---

[8] The real wages shown in Figure 3-7 are measured relative to consumer prices in 2008 and represent the average hourly earnings for *production* workers, those workers involved in the assembly of services or products. Production workers are sometimes called "blue-collar" workers and typically earn hourly wages. The other category of workers, *nonproduction* workers, includes managers and all those who work at a desk. They are sometimes called "white-collar" workers and typically earn annual salaries instead of hourly wages.

FIGURE 3-7

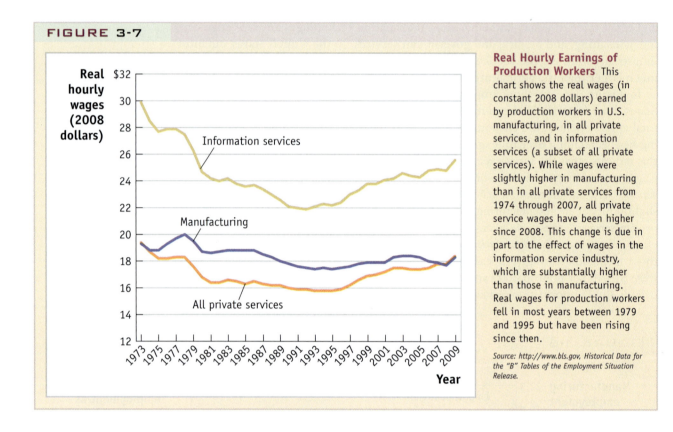

Real Hourly Earnings of Production Workers This chart shows the real wages (in constant 2008 dollars) earned by production workers in U.S. manufacturing, in all private services, and in information services (a subset of all private services). While wages were slightly higher in manufacturing than in all private services from 1974 through 2007, all private service wages have been higher since 2008. This change is due in part to the effect of wages in the information service industry, which are substantially higher than those in manufacturing. Real wages for production workers fell in most years between 1979 and 1995 but have been rising since then.

Source: http://www.bls.gov, Historical Data for the "B" Tables of the Employment Situation Release.

In both manufacturing and services, many workers are *displaced* or laid off each year and need to look for other jobs. In the three years from January 2005 to December 2007, for example, about 0.9 million workers were displaced in manufacturing and 2.3 million in all service industries, as shown in Table 3-1.[9] Of those laid off in manufacturing, 64% were reemployed by January 2008, and about half of these (49%) earned less in their new jobs. For services, however, 68% were reemployed by January 2008, and slightly more than half of these (56%) earned the same *or more* in their new jobs. The recession that began in 2008 clearly increased the number of displaced workers. From January 2008 to December 2009 the total number of displaced workers increased to 5.1 million, of which 2.1 million had been employed in manufacturing.

There are four lessons that we can take away from this comparison of employment and wages in manufacturing and services. First, wages differ across different sectors in the economy, so our theoretical assumption that wages are the same in agriculture and manufacturing is a simplification. Second, many workers are displaced each year and must find jobs elsewhere. Some of these workers may be laid off due to competition from imports, but there are other reasons, too—for instance, products that used to be purchased go out of fashion, firms reorganize as computers and other

---

[9] There were a smaller number of workers displaced in mining and construction (293,000), totaling 3.6 million overall. These were all displaced "long-tenured" people who had worked for at least three years with their former employer. There were another 4.6 million displaced people who had worked for less than three years with their former employer.

TABLE 3-1

Job Losses in Manufacturing and Service Industries, 2005–2009 This table shows the number of displaced (or laid-off) workers in manufacturing and service industries from 2005 to 2009. Between 64 and 68% of the workers displaced from 2005 to 2007 were reemployed by January 2008, with about one-half earning less in their new jobs and one-half earning the same or more, with slightly more workers reemployed in service industries earning more at their new job. However, the recession that began in 2008 clearly increased the number of displaced workers. From January 2008 to December 2009 the total number of displaced workers increased to 5.1 million, of which 2.1 million had been employed in manufacturing.

		PERCENTAGES			
	Total Displaced Workers (thousands) January 2005–		Of the Workers		Total Displaced Workers (thousands) January 2008–
Industry	December 2007	Workers Reemployed by January 2008	Reemployed:		December 2009
			Earn Less in New Job	Earn Same or More in New Job	
Total	3,641	67%	44%	55%	5,087
Manufacturing industries	876	64%	49%	51%	2,117
Service industries	2,312	68%	44%	56%	n.a.

n.a. = not available.

Source: U.S. Bureau of Labor Statistics.

technological advances become available, and firms change locations. Third, the majority of displaced workers find a new job within two or three years but not necessarily at the same wage. Typically, older workers (age 45 to 64) experience earnings losses when shifting between jobs, whereas younger workers (age 25 to 44) are often able to find a new job with the same or higher wages. Finally, when we measure wages in real terms by adjusting for inflation in the price of consumer goods, we see that real wages for all production workers fell in most years between 1979 and 1995 (we examine the reasons for that fall in later chapters) but have been rising slightly since then. ■

APPLICATION

Trade Adjustment Assistance Programs: Financing the Adjustment Costs of Trade

Should the government step in to compensate workers who are looking for jobs or who do not find them in a reasonable period of time? The unemployment insurance program in the United States provides some compensation, regardless of the reason for the layoff. In addition, the *Trade Adjustment Assistance (TAA)* program offers additional unemployment insurance payments and health insurance to workers who are laid off because of import competition and who are enrolled in a retraining program. The quotation from President Kennedy at the beginning of the chapter comes from a speech he made introducing the TAA program in 1962. He believed that this program was needed to compensate those Americans who lost their jobs due to international trade. Since 1993 there has also been a special TAA program under the North

American Free Trade Agreement (NAFTA) for workers who are laid off as a result of import competition from Mexico or Canada.[10] Recently, as part of the jobs stimulus bill signed by President Obama on February 17, 2009, workers in the service sector (as well as farmers) who lose their jobs due to trade can now also apply for TAA benefits. This extension is described in **Headlines: Services Workers Are Now Eligible for Trade Adjustment Assistance.**

Other countries also have programs like TAA to compensate those harmed by trade. A particularly interesting example occurred with the unification of East and West Germany on June 30, 1990. On that date, all barriers to trade between the countries were removed as well as all barriers to the movement of labor and capital between the two regions. The pressure from labor unions to achieve wage parity (equality) between the East and West meant that companies in former East Germany were faced with wages that were far above what they could afford to pay. According to one estimate, only 8% of former East German companies would be profitable at the higher wages paid in the West. In the absence of government intervention, it could be expected that severe bankruptcy and unemployment would result, leading to massive migration of East German workers to the former West Germany.

Economists studying this situation proposed that deep wage subsidies, or "flexible employment bonuses," should be given in former East Germany, thereby allowing factories to employ their workers while paying only a fraction of their wages. Furthermore, they argued that the wage subsidies would essentially pay for themselves because without them the government would have to provide unemployment insurance on a massive scale to the people left without jobs.[11] As it turns out, wage subsidies of this type were not used, and unemployment in the East and migration to the West continue to be challenging policy issues for the united Germany. ■

3 Earnings of Capital and Land

Let us now return to the specific-factors model. We have found that with the opening of trade and an increase in the relative price of manufactures, there are overall gains for the country, but labor does not necessarily gain. What about the gains to the other factors of production, either the capital used in manufacturing or the land used in agriculture? Capital and land are the two specific factors of production that cannot shift between the two industries; let us now look at the effect of the increase in the relative price of manufactures on the earnings of these specific factors.

Determining the Payments to Capital and Land

In each industry, capital and land earn what is left over from sales revenue after paying labor. Labor (L_M and L_A) earns the wage W, so total payments to labor in manufacturing are $W \cdot L_M$ and in agriculture are $W \cdot L_A$. By subtracting the payments to labor from the sales revenue earned in each industry, we end up with the payments

---

[10] We discuss the North American Free Trade Agreement in a later chapter and provide more details there on how many workers applied for benefits under the NAFTA-TAA program.

[11] George Akerlof, Andrew Rose, Janet Yellen, and Helga Hessenius, 1991, "East Germany in from the Cold: The Economic Aftermath of Currency Union," *Brookings Papers on Economic Activity*, Vol.1, 1–87.

HEADLINES

Services Workers Are Now Eligible for Trade Adjustment Assistance

President Kennedy first introduced Trade Adjustment Assistance (TAA) in the United States in 1962, for workers in manufacturing. This article described how it was recently extended to include service workers.

In today's era of global supply chains, high-speed Internet connection, and container shipping, Kennedy's concerns remain relevant: technology and trade mean growth, innovation and better living standards, but also change and instability. (Research early in this decade typically found that international competition accounted for about 2 percent of layoffs.) But while concerns may be permanent, specific programs and policies fade unless they adapt to changing times. And despite its periodic update, until this week TAA remained designed for an older world. Most notably, it barred support for services workers facing Internet-based competition . . . .

In this context, yesterday's stimulus bill signing contained the first fundamen-

tal change to the TAA program in a half-century. An accord three years in the making, overseen by Senators Max Baucus (D-MT) and Charles Grassley (R-IA), reshapes TAA for the 21st century. The new program, set out in 184 pages of legal text, has three basic changes:

- More workers are eligible: Service-industry employees will be fully eligible for TAA services, making the program relevant to the high-tech economy. So will workers whose businesses move abroad, regardless of the destination. The reform also eases eligibility for farmers and fishermen.

- They get more help: The reform raises training support from $220 million to $575 million, hikes support

for health insurance from 65 percent to 80 percent of premiums, gives states $86 million a year to pay for TAA caseworkers, creates a $230 million program to support communities dealing with plant closure, and triples support for businesses managing sudden trade competition.

- They are more likely to know their rights: The bill also creates a special Labor Department TAA office to ensure that eligible workers know their options.

Kennedy's innovation is thus adapted to the 21st-century economy, guaranteeing today's workers the support their grandparents enjoyed. A bit of good news, in a year when it is all too rare.

Source: Excerpted from Progressive Policy Institute trade fact of the week, "Services Workers are Now Eligible for Trade Adjustment Assistance," February 18, 2009.

to capital and to land. If Q_M is the output in manufacturing and Q_A is the output in agriculture, the revenue earned in each industry is $P_M \cdot Q_M$ and $P_A \cdot Q_A$, and the payments to capital and to land are

$$\text{Payments to capital} = P_M \cdot Q_M - W \cdot L_M$$

$$\text{Payments to land} = P_A \cdot Q_A - W \cdot L_A$$

It will be useful to take these payments one step further and break them down into the earnings of each unit of capital and land. To do so, we need to know the quantity of capital and land. We denote the quantity of land used in agriculture as T acres and the quantity of capital (number of machines) used in manufacturing as K. Thus, the earnings of one unit of capital (a machine, for instance), which we call R_K, and the earnings of an acre of land, which we call R_T, are calculated as

$$R_K = \frac{\text{Payments to capital}}{K} = \frac{P_M \cdot Q_M - W \cdot L_M}{K}$$

$$R_T = \frac{\text{Payments to land}}{T} = \frac{P_A \cdot Q_A - W \cdot L_A}{T}$$

Economists call R_K the **rental on capital** and R_T the **rental on land.** The use of the term "rental" does not mean that the factory owners or farmers rent their machines or land from someone else, although they could. Instead, the rental on machines and land reflects what these factors of production earn during a period when they are used in manufacturing and agriculture. Alternatively, the rental is the amount these factors *could* earn if they were rented to someone else over that same time.

There is a second way to calculate the rentals, which will look similar to the formula we have used for wages. In each industry, wages reflect the marginal product of labor times the price of the good, $W = P_M \cdot MPL_M = P_A \cdot MPL_A$. Similarly, capital and land rentals can be calculated as

$$R_K = P_M \cdot MPK_M \text{ and } R_T = P_A \cdot MPT_A$$

where MPK_M is the marginal product of capital in manufacturing, and MPT_A is the marginal product of land in agriculture. These marginal product formulas give the same values for the rentals as first calculating the payments to capital and land, as we just did, and then dividing by the quantity of capital and land. We will use both approaches to obtain rental values, depending on which is easiest.

Change in the Real Rental on Capital Now that we understand how the rentals on capital and land are determined, we can look at what happens to them when the price of the manufactured good P_M rises, holding constant the price in agriculture P_A. From Figure 3-5, we know that the wage rises throughout the economy and that labor shifts from agriculture into manufacturing. As more labor is used in manufacturing, the marginal product of capital will rise because each machine has more labor to work it. In addition, as labor leaves agriculture, the marginal product of land will fall because each acre of land has fewer laborers to work it. The general conclusion is that *an increase in the quantity of labor used in an industry will raise the marginal product of the factor specific to that industry, and a decrease in labor will lower the marginal product of the specific factor.* This outcome does not contradict the law of diminishing returns, which states that an increase in labor will lower the marginal product *of labor* because now we are talking about how a change in labor affects the marginal product of *another factor*.

Using the preceding formulas for the rentals, we can summarize the results so far with

$$P_M \uparrow \Rightarrow \begin{bmatrix} L_M \uparrow, \text{ so that } MPK_M = R_K/P_M\uparrow \\ \\ L_A \downarrow, \text{ so that } MPT_A = R_T/P_A\downarrow \end{bmatrix}$$

That is, the increase in the marginal product of capital in manufacturing means that R_K/P_M also increases. Because R_K is the rental for capital, R_K/P_M is the amount of the manufactured good that can be purchased with this rent. Thus, the fact that R_K/P_M increases means that the real rental on capital in terms of the manufactured good has gone up. For the increase in the real rental on capital to occur even though the price of the manufactured good has gone up, too, the percentage increase in R_K must be greater than the percentage increase in P_M.[12]

The amount of food that can be purchased by capital owners is R_K/P_A. Because R_K has increased, and P_A is fixed, R_K/P_A must also increase; in other words, the real rental

---

[12] For example, if the price of manufactured goods rises by 6% and the rental on capital rises by 10%, then owners of capital can afford to buy 4% more of the manufactured good.

on capital in terms of food has also gone up. Because capital owners can afford to buy more of both goods, they are clearly better off when the price of the manufactured good rises. Unlike labor, whose real wage increased in terms of one good but fell in terms of the other, capital owners clearly gain from the rise in the relative price of manufactured goods.

Change in the Real Rental on Land Let us now consider what happens to the landowners. With labor leaving agriculture, the marginal product of each acre falls, so R_T/P_A also falls. Because R_T is the rental on land, R_T/P_A is the amount of food that can be purchased with this rent. The fact that R_T/P_A falls means that the real rental on land in terms of food has gone down, so landowners cannot afford to buy as much food. Because the price of food is unchanged while the price of the manufactured good has gone up, landowners will not be able to afford to buy as much of the manufactured good either. Thus, landowners are clearly worse off from the rise in the price of the manufactured good because they can afford to buy less of both goods.

Summary The real earnings of capital owners and landowners move in opposite directions, an outcome that illustrates a general conclusion: *an increase in the relative price of an industry's output will increase the real rental earned by the factor specific to that industry but will decrease the real rental of factors specific to other industries.* This conclusion means that the specific factors used in export industries will generally gain as trade is opened and the relative price of exports rises, but the specific factors used in import industries will generally lose as trade is opened and the relative price of imports falls.

Numerical Example

We have come a long way in our study of the specific-factors model and conclude by presenting a numerical example of how an increase in the relative price of manufactures affects the earnings of labor, capital, and land. This example reviews the results we have obtained so far using actual numbers. Suppose that the manufacturing industry has the following payments to labor and capital:

$$\text{Manufacturing:} \quad \text{Sales revenue} = P_M \cdot Q_M = \$100$$

$$\text{Payments to labor} = W \cdot L_M = \$60$$

$$\text{Payments to capital} = R_K \cdot K = \$40$$

Notice that 60% of sales revenue in manufacturing goes to labor, and 40% goes to capital.

In agriculture, suppose that the payments to labor and land are as follows:

$$\text{Agriculture:} \quad \text{Sales revenue} = P_A \cdot Q_A = \$100$$

$$\text{Payments to labor} = W \cdot L_A = \$50$$

$$\text{Payments to land} = R_T \cdot T = \$50$$

In the agriculture industry, we assume that land and labor each earn 50% of the sales revenue.

An increase in the relative price of manufactures P_M/P_A can be caused by an increase in P_M or a decrease in P_A. To be specific, suppose that the price of manufactures P_M rises by 10%, whereas the price of agriculture P_A does not change at all. We have found in our earlier discussion that $\Delta W/W$, the percentage change in the wage, will be between the percentage change in these two industry prices. So let us suppose that $\Delta W/W$, is 5%. We summarize these output and factor price changes as follows:

Manufacturing: Percentage increase in price $= \Delta P_M/P_M = 10\%$

Agriculture: Percentage increase in price $= \Delta P_A/P_A = 0\%$

Both industries: Percentage increase in the wage $= \Delta W/W = 5\%$

Notice that the increase in the wage applies in both industries because wages are always equalized across sectors.

Change in the Rental on Capital   Our goal is to use the preceding data for manufacturing and agriculture to compute the change in the rental on capital and the change in the rental on land. Let's start with the equation for the rental on capital, which was computed by subtracting wage payments from sales revenue and then dividing by the amount of capital:

$$R_K = \frac{\text{Payments to capital}}{K} = \frac{P_M \cdot Q_M - W \cdot L_M}{K}$$

If the price of manufactured goods rises by $\Delta P_M > 0$, holding constant the price in agriculture, then the change in the rental is

$$\Delta R_K = \frac{\Delta P_M \cdot Q_M - \Delta W \cdot L_M}{K}$$

We want to rewrite this equation using percentage changes, like $\Delta P_M/P_M$, $\Delta W/W$, and $\Delta R_K/R_K$. To achieve this, divide both sides by R_K and rewrite the equation as

$$\frac{\Delta R_K}{R_K} = \frac{(\Delta P_M/P_M) \cdot P_M \cdot Q_M - (\Delta W/W) \cdot W \cdot L_M}{R_K \cdot K}$$

You can cancel terms in this equation to check that it is the same as before.

The term $\Delta P_M/P_M$ in this equation is the percentage change in the price of manufacturing, whereas $\Delta W/W$ is the percentage change in the wage. Given this information, along with the preceding data on the payments to labor, capital, and sales revenue, we can compute the percentage change in the rental on capital:

$$\frac{\Delta R_K}{R_K} = \frac{(10\% \cdot 100 - 5\% \cdot 60)}{40} = 17.5\%$$

We see that the percentage increase in the rental on capital, 17.5%, *exceeds* the percentage increase in the relative price of manufacturing, 10% (so $\Delta R_K/R_K > \Delta P_M/P_M > 0$). This outcome holds no matter what numbers are used in the preceding formula, provided that the percentage increase in the wage is less than the percentage increase in the price of the manufactured good (as proved in Figure 3-5).

Change in the Rental on Land   We can use the same approach to examine the change in the rental on land. Continuing to assume that the price of the manufactured good rises, while the price in agriculture stays the same ($\Delta P_A = 0$), the change in the land rental is

$$\Delta R_T = \frac{0 \cdot Q_A - \Delta W \cdot L_A}{T}$$

Because the wage is increasing, $\Delta W > 0$, it follows immediately that the *rental on land is falling*, $\Delta R_T < 0$. The percentage amount by which it falls can be calculated by rewriting the above equation as

$$\frac{\Delta R_T}{R_T} = -\frac{\Delta W}{W}\left(\frac{W \cdot L_A}{R_T \cdot T}\right)$$

Using these earlier data for agriculture in this formula, we get

$$\frac{\Delta R_T}{R_T} = -5\%\left(\frac{50}{50}\right) = -5\%$$

In this case, the land rent falls by the same percentage amount that the wage increases. This equality occurs because we assumed that labor and land receive the same share of sales revenue in agriculture (50% each). If labor receives a higher share of revenue than land, then the rent on land will fall even more; if it receives a lower share, then the rent on land won't fall as much.

General Equation for the Change in Factor Prices By summarizing our results in a single equation, we can see how all the changes in factor and industry prices are related. Under the assumption that the price of the manufactured good increased but the price of the agricultural good did not change, we have shown the following:

$$\underbrace{\Delta R_T / R_T < 0}_{\substack{\text{Real rental} \\ \text{on land falls}}} < \underbrace{\Delta W/W < \Delta P_M / P_M}_{\substack{\text{Change in the real} \\ \text{wage is ambiguous}}} < \underbrace{\Delta R_K / R_K}_{\substack{\text{Real rental} \\ \text{on capital rises}}}, \text{ for an increase in } P_M$$

In other words, wages rise but not as much as the percentage increase in the price of the manufactured good; the rental on capital (which is specific to the manufacturing sector) rises by more than the manufacturing price, so capital owners are better off; and the rental on land (which is the specific factor in the other sector) falls, so landowners are worse off.

What happens if the price of the manufactured good falls? Then the inequalities are reversed, and the equation becomes

$$\underbrace{\Delta R_K / R_K}_{\substack{\text{Real rental} \\ \text{on capital falls}}} < \underbrace{\Delta P_M / P_M < \Delta W/W < 0}_{\substack{\text{Change in the real} \\ \text{wage is ambiguous}}} < \underbrace{\Delta R_T / R_T}_{\substack{\text{Real rental} \\ \text{on land rises}}}, \text{ for a decrease in } P_M$$

In this case, wages fall but by less than the percentage decrease in the manufactured good; the rental on capital (which is specific to the manufacturing sector) falls by more than the manufacturing price, so capital owners are worse off; and the rental on land (which is the specific factor in the other sector) rises, so landowners are better off.

What happens if the *price of the agricultural good rises*? You can probably guess based on the previous example that this change will benefit land and harm capital. The equation summarizing the changes in all three factor earnings becomes

$$\underbrace{\Delta R_K / R_K < 0}_{\substack{\text{Real rental} \\ \text{on capital falls}}} < \underbrace{\Delta W/W < \Delta P_A / P_A}_{\substack{\text{Change in the real} \\ \text{wage is ambiguous}}} < \underbrace{\Delta R_T / R_T}_{\substack{\text{Real rental} \\ \text{on land rises}}}, \text{ for an increase in } P_A$$

Note that it is the specific factor in the agricultural sector that gains and the specific factor in manufacturing that loses. The general result of these summary equations is that *the specific factor in the sector whose relative price has increased gains, the specific factor in the other sector loses, and labor is "caught in the middle," with its real wage increasing in terms of one good but falling in terms of the other*. These equations summarize the response of all three factor prices in the short run, when capital and land are specific to each sector but labor is mobile.

What It All Means

Our results from the specific-factors model show that the earnings of *specific factors* change the most from changes in relative prices due to international trade. Regardless of which good's price changes, the earnings of capital and land show the most extreme changes in their rentals, whereas the changes in the wages paid to labor are in the middle. Intuitively, these extreme changes in factor prices occur because the specific factors are not able to leave their sectors and find employment elsewhere. Labor benefits by its opportunity to move between sectors and earn the same wage in each, but the interests of capital and land are opposed to each other: one gains and the other loses. This suggests that we ought to be able to find real-world examples in which a change in international prices leads to losses for either capitalists or landowners. There are many such examples, and we discuss one in the next application.

APPLICATION

Prices in Agriculture

At the end of the previous chapter, we discussed the Prebisch–Singer hypothesis, which states that the prices of primary commodities tend to fall over time. Although we argued that this hypothesis does not hold for all primary commodities, it does hold for some agricultural goods: the relative prices of cotton, palm oil, rice, sugar, rubber, wheat, and wool declined for more than half the years between 1900 and 1998. Generally, agricultural prices fall as countries become more efficient at growing crops and begin exporting them. From our study of the specific-factors model, it will be landowners (i.e., farmers) who lose in real terms from this decline in the relative price of agricultural products. On the other hand, capital owners gain in real terms, and changes in the real wage are ambiguous. Faced with declining real earnings in the agriculture sector, governments and other groups often take actions to prevent the incomes of farmers from falling.

Coffee Prices An example of an agricultural commodity with particularly volatile prices is coffee. The price of coffee on world markets fluctuates a great deal from year to year because of weather and also because of the entry of new suppliers in Brazil and new supplying countries such as Vietnam. The movements in the real wholesale price of coffee (measured in 2008 dollars) are shown in Figure 3-8. Wholesale prices were at a high of $3.00 per pound in 1986, then fell to a low of 83¢ per pound in 1993, rose to $1.77 in 1995, and then fell to 50¢ per pound in 2001. Since 2001 there has been a sustained increase in both price and quantity, implying a shift in import demand. By 2008 prices had risen to $1.24 per pound. These dramatic fluctuations in prices create equally large movements in the real incomes of farmers, making it difficult for them to sustain a living. The very low prices in 2001 created a crisis in the coffee-growing regions of Central America, requiring humanitarian aid for farmers and their families. The governments of coffee-growing regions in Central America and Asia cannot afford to protect their coffee farmers by propping up prices, as do the industrial countries.

FIGURE 3-8

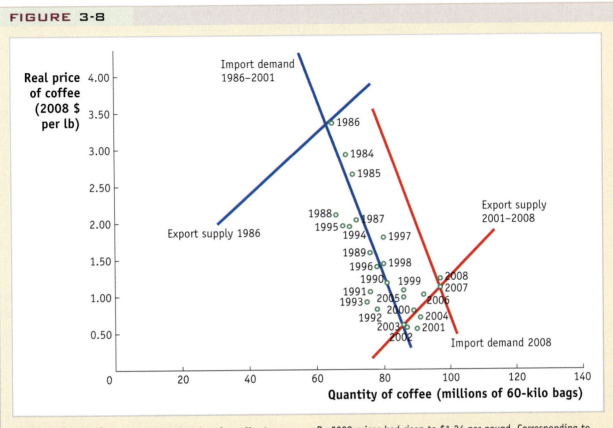

World Coffee Market Real wholesale prices for coffee have fluctuated greatly on world markets. Using 2008 dollars, prices were at a high of about $3.00 per pound in 1986, fell to 83¢ per pound in 1993, rose to $1.77 in 1995, and then fell to 50¢ per pound in 2001. Since 2001 there has been a sustained increase in both price and quantity, implying a shift in import demand.

By 2008 prices had risen to $1.24 per pound. Corresponding to these price fluctuations, the quantity of world coffee exports was at a low in 1986 (65 million bags) and at a high in 2008 (97 million bags), as supplies from Brazil and Vietnam increased.

Source: International Coffee Organization, http://www.ico.org.

According to the specific-factors model, big fluctuations in coffee prices are extremely disruptive to the real earnings of landowners in coffee-exporting developing countries, many of whom are small farmers and their families. Can anything be done to avoid the kind of boom-and-bust cycle that occurs regularly in coffee markets?

Fair-Trade Coffee One idea that is gaining appeal is to sell coffee from developing countries directly to consumers in industrial countries, thereby avoiding the middlemen (such as local buyers, millers, exporters, shippers, and importers) and ensuring a minimum price for the farmers. You may have seen "fair-trade" coffee at your favorite coffeehouse. This coffee first appeared in the United States in 1999, imported by a group called TransFair USA that is committed to passing more of the profits back to the growers. TransFair USA is an example of a nongovernmental organization that

Groups like TransFair USA ensure coffee farmers like Santiago Rivera, pictured here, a more stable source of income over time.

is trying to help farmers by raising prices, and the consumer gets the choice of whether to purchase this higher-priced product. In addition to coffee, TransFair USA has been applying its Fair Trade label to imports of cocoa, tea, rice, sugar, bananas, mangoes, pineapples, and grapes.

World coffee prices recovered in 2005, which meant that groups like TransFair USA faced a dilemma: the fair-trade prices that they had guaranteed to farmers were actually less than the world price of coffee. The accompanying article **Headlines: Rise in Coffee Prices—Great for Farmers, Tough on Co-ops** describes how some farmers were tempted to break their contracts with local co-ops (at fixed, fair-trade prices) to deliver coffee to local middlemen at prevailing world prices. TransFair USA and similar organizations purchase coffee at higher than the market price when the market is low (as in 2001), but in other years (like 2005) the fair-trade price is below the market price. Essentially, TransFair USA is offering farmers a form of *insurance* whereby the fair-trade price of coffee will not fluctuate too much, ensuring them a more stable source of income over time. By protecting farmers against the boom-and-bust cycle of fluctuating prices, they are able to enjoy greater gains from trade by exporting their coffee. So when you consider buying a cup of fair-trade coffee at your favorite coffeehouse, you are supporting coffee farmers who rely on the efforts of groups like TransFair USA to raise their incomes, and applying the logic of the specific-factors model, all at the same time! ■

HEADLINES

Rise in Coffee Prices—Great for Farmers, Tough on Co-ops

TransFair USA guarantees a minimum purchase price for coffee farmers, acting as insurance against a falling market price. But during periods when the market price is rising, it is challenging to ensure that farmers deliver their coffee.

During winter and spring of the 2005 harvest, a dilemma surfaced in rural areas of Central America and Mexico. Fair-trade cooperative managers found it increasingly difficult to get members to deliver coffee to their own organization at fair-trade prices. The co-op managers were holding contracts that were set months before at fixed fair-trade prices of $1.26 per pound, but now the world coffee price was higher. Growers were seeing some of the highest prices paid in five years, and the temptation was great to sell their coffee to the highest local bidder, instead of delivering it as promised to their own co-ops.

In most cases, the co-ops' leaders were able to convince farmers to deliver coffee, but often based on arguments of loyalty, as the fair-trade fixed price was now lower than the premium prices being offered by the local middleman. It was not the model that the founders of fair-trade coffee pricing had envisioned when they created the program.

"It's worth noting that we were pleased to see prices rise in late 2004," says Christopher Himes, TransFair USA's Director of Certification and Finance. "This price rise, in conjunction with the impact fair trade was already having, increased the income and living standards of coffee farmers around the world. The most challenging thing during this time for TransFair USA was the speed with which the local differentials [between the fair-trade price and the world price] rose in Indonesia. They quickly skyrocketed to 80 cents [per pound] or higher, making the market value of farmers' coffee higher than that of some of the . . . fair-trade contracts."

Source: David Griswold, http://www.FreshCup.com, June 2005.

4 Conclusions

In the Ricardian model of Chapter 2, we showed that free trade could never make a country worse off, and in most cases free trade would make it better off. This result remains true when we add land and capital as factors of production, in addition to labor. Provided that the relative price with international trade differs from the no-trade relative price, then a country gains from international trade. This conclusion does not mean, however, that each and every factor of production gains. On the contrary, we have shown in this chapter that the change in relative prices due to the opening of trade creates winners and losers. Some factors of production gain in real terms and other factors of production lose. To demonstrate this result, we have used a short-run model, in which labor is mobile between sectors and land and capital are each specific to their sectors.

Classical economists believed that, in the short run, factors of production that could not move between industries would lose the most from trade. We have found that this is true for the factor that is specific to the import-competing industry. That industry suffers a drop in its relative price because of international trade, which leads to a fall in the real rental on the specific factor in that industry. On the other hand, the specific factor in the export industry—whose relative price rises with the opening of trade—enjoys an increase in its real rental. Labor is mobile between the two industries, which allows it to avoid such extreme changes in its wage—real wages rise in terms of one good but fall in terms of the other good, so we cannot tell whether workers are better off or worse off after a country opens to trade.

Economists have carefully proved that, in theory, the gains of individuals due to opening trade exceed the losses. This result means that, in principle, the government should be able to tax the winners and compensate the losers so that everyone is better off because of trade. In practice, it is very difficult to design programs to achieve that level of compensation. In this chapter, we looked at one compensation program—Trade Adjustment Assistance—that is used in the United States and other countries to compensate people who are laid off because of import competition. There are many other policies (such as import tariffs and quotas) that are intended to protect individuals from the effect of price changes resulting from international trade, and we examine these policies later in the book.

KEY POINTS

1. Opening a country to international trade leads to overall gains, but in a model with several factors of production, some factors of production will lose.

2. The fact that some people are harmed because of trade sometimes creates social tensions that may be strong enough to topple governments. A recent example is Bolivia, where the citizens in the early 2000s could not agree on how to share the gains from exporting natural gas.

3. In the specific-factors model, factors of production that cannot move between industries will gain or lose the most from opening a country to trade. The factor of production that is specific to the import industry will lose in real terms, as the relative price of the import good falls. The factor of production that is specific to the export industry will gain in real terms, as the relative price of the export good rises.

4. In the specific-factors model, labor can move between the industries and earns the same wage in each. When the relative price of either good changes, then the real wage rises when measured in terms of one good but falls when measured in terms of the other good. Without knowing how much of each good workers prefer to consume, we cannot say whether workers are better off or worse off because of trade.

5. Economists do not normally count the costs of unemployment as a loss from trade because people are often able to find new jobs. In the United States, for example, about two-thirds of people laid off from manufacturing or services

companies find new jobs within two or three years, although sometimes at lower wages.

6. Trade Adjustment Assistance policies are intended to compensate those who are harmed due to trade by providing additional income during the period of unemployment. Recently, the Trade Adjustment Assistance program in the United States was expanded to include workers laid off due to trade in service industries.

7. Even when many people are employed in export activities, such as those involved in coffee export from certain developing countries, fluctuations in the world market price can lead to large changes in income for growers and workers.

KEY TERMS

specific-factors model, p. 60
diminishing returns, p. 61
autarky, p. 65
embargo, p. 65

real wage, p. 68
Trade Adjustment Assistance
 (TAA), p. 70
services, p. 70

rental on capital, p. 76
rental on land, p. 76

PROBLEMS

1. Why is the specific-factors model referred to as a short-run model?

2. Figure 3-7 presents wages in the manufacturing and services sectors for the period 1973 to 2009. Is the difference in wages across sectors consistent with either the Ricardian model studied in Chapter 2 or the specific-factors model? Explain why or why not.

3. In the gains from trade diagram in Figure 3-3, suppose that instead of having a rise in the relative price of manufactures, there is instead a fall in that relative price.

   a. Starting at the no-trade point A in Figure 3-3, show what would happen to production and consumption.
   b. Which good is exported and which is imported?
   c. Explain why the overall gains from trade are still positive.

4. Starting from equilibrium in the specific-factors model, suppose the price of manufactured goods falls so that wages fall from W'' to W in Figure 3-5.

   a. Show that the percentage fall in the wage is less than the percentage fall in the price of manufacturing so that the real wage of labor in terms of manufactured goods goes up.
   b. What happens to the real wage of labor in terms of agriculture?
   c. Are workers better off, worse off, or is the outcome ambiguous?

5. Use the information given here to answer the following questions:

   Manufacturing:

   Sales revenue = $P_M \cdot Q_M = 150$
   Payments to labor = $W \cdot L_M = 100$
   Payments to capital = $R_K \cdot K = 50$

Agriculture:

Sales revenue $= P_A \cdot Q_A = 150$
Payments to labor $= W \cdot L_A = 50$
Payments to land $= R_T \cdot T = 100$

Holding the price of manufacturing constant, suppose the increase in the price of agriculture is 10% and the increase in the wage is 5%.

a. Determine the impact of the increase in the price of agriculture on the rental on land and the rental on capital.

b. Explain what has happened to the real rental on land and the real rental on capital.

6. If instead of the situation given in Problem 5, the price of manufacturing were to fall by 10%, would landowners or capital owners be better off? Explain. How would the decrease in the price of manufacturing affect labor? Explain.

7. Read the article by Lori G. Kletzer and Robert E. Litan, "A Prescription to Relieve Worker Anxiety," Policy Brief 01-2 (Washington, D.C.: Peterson Institute for International Economics), available online at http://www.iie.com/publications/pb/PP1-2.htm, which refers to the U.S. recession of 2000 and 2001. Then answer the following:

a. Under the version of Trade Adjustment Assistance (TAA) in the United States that they refer to, how many extra weeks of unemployment insurance are workers eligible for? What two criteria must workers meet to qualify for this extra unemployment insurance?

b. Consider the proposal for "wage insurance" that Kletzer and Litan make in their article. What criteria would workers need to qualify for this insurance? What amount of extra income would they receive from the insurance?

c. If Kletzer and Litan's new plan for "wage insurance" had been adopted by the United States, what would have been the budgetary cost in 1999, when unemployment was 4.2%? How does this compare with the amount that is now spent on unemployment insurance?

8. In the specific-factors model, assume that the price of agricultural goods decreases while the price of manufactured goods is unchanged ($\Delta P_A/P_A < 0$ and $\Delta P_M/P_M = 0$). Arrange the following terms in ascending order:

$\Delta R_T/R_T \quad \Delta R_K/R_K \quad \Delta P_A/P_A \quad \Delta P_M/P_M \quad \Delta W/W$

Hint: Try starting with a diagram like Figure 3-5, but change the price of agricultural goods instead.

9. Suppose two countries, Canada and Mexico, produce two goods: timber and televisions. Assume that land is specific to timber, capital is specific to televisions, and labor is free to move between the two industries. When Canada and Mexico engage in free trade, the relative price of televisions falls in Canada and the relative price of timber falls in Mexico.

a. In a graph similar to Figure 3-5, show how the wage changes in Canada due to a fall in the price of televisions, holding constant the price of timber. Can we predict that change in the real wage?

b. What is the impact of opening trade on the rentals on capital and land in Canada? Can we predict that change in the real rentals on capital and land?

c. What is the impact of opening trade on the rentals on capital and land in Mexico? Can we predict that change in the real rentals on capital and land?

d. In each country, has the specific factor in the export industry gained or lost and has the specific factor in the import industry gained or lost?

10. Home produces two goods, computers and wheat, for which capital is specific to computers, land is specific to wheat, and labor is mobile between the two industries. Home has 100 workers and 100 units of capital but only 10 units of land.

a. Draw a graph similar to Figure 3-1 with the output of wheat on the horizontal axis and the labor in wheat on the vertical axis. What is the relationship between the output of wheat and the marginal product of labor in the wheat industry as more labor is used?

b. Draw the production possibilities frontier for Home with wheat on the horizontal axis and computers on the vertical axis.

c. Explain how the price of wheat relative to computers is determined in the absence of trade.

d. Reproduce Figure 3-4 with the amount of labor used in wheat measuring from left to right along the horizontal axis and the amount of labor used in computers moving in the reverse direction.

e. Assume that due to international trade, the price of wheat rises. Analyze the effect of the increase in the price of wheat on the allocation of labor between the two sectors.

11. Similar to Home in Problem 10, Foreign also produces computers and wheat using capital, which is specific to computers; land, which is specific to wheat; and labor, which is mobile between the two sectors. Foreign has 100 workers and 100 units of land but only 10 units of capital. It has the same production functions as Home.

a. Will the no-trade relative price of wheat be higher in Home or in Foreign? Explain why you expect this outcome.

b. When trade is opened, what happens to the relative price of wheat in Foreign and to the relative price of wheat in Home?

c. Based on your answer to (b), predict the effect of opening trade on the rental on land in each country, which is specific to wheat. What about the rental on capital, which is specific to computers?

12. In the text, we learned that workers displaced by import competition are eligible for compensation through the Trade Adjustment Assistance program. Firms are also eligible for support through Trade Adjustment Assistance for Firms, a federal program that provides financial assistance to manufacturers affected by import competition. Go to http://www.taacenters.org to read about this program, and answer the following:

a. What criteria does a firm have to satisfy to quality for benefits?

b. What amount of money is provided to firms, and for what purpose?

c. Provide an argument for and an argument against the continued funding of this federal program.

N E T W O R K

The Bureau of Labor Statistics regularly releases information on the changes in employment, wages, and displacement of workers at http://www.bls.gov. Find one recent announcement and summarize that information. How does the information in that announcement compare with the trends in the application just discussed on employment and wages in manufacturing and services?

Trade and Resources: The Heckscher-Ohlin Model

God did not bestow all products upon all parts of the earth, but distributed His gifts over different regions, to the end that men might cultivate a social relationship because one would have need of the help of another. And so He called commerce into being, that all men might be able to have common enjoyment of the fruits of the earth, no matter where produced.

Libanius (AD 314–393), *Orations* (III)

Nature, by giving a diversity of geniuses, climates, and soils, to different nations, has secured their mutual intercourse and commerce. . . . The industry of the nations, from whom they import, receives encouragement: Their own is also [i]ncreased, by the sale of the commodities which they give in exchange.

David Hume, *Essays, Moral, Political, and Literary*, 1752, Part II, Essay VI, "On the Jealousy of Trade"

In Chapter 2, we examined U.S. imports of snowboards. We argued there that the resources found in a country would influence its pattern of international trade. Canada's export of snowboards to the United States reflects its mountains and cold climate, as do the exports of snowboards to the United States from Austria, Spain, France, Bulgaria, and Switzerland. Because each country's resources are different and because resources are spread unevenly around the world, countries have a reason to trade the goods made with these resources. This is an old idea, as shown by the quotations at the beginning of this chapter; the first is from the fourth-century Greek scholar Libanius, and the second is from the eighteenth-century philosopher David Hume.

In this chapter, we outline the **Heckscher-Ohlin model,** a model that assumes that trade occurs because countries have different resources. This model contrasts with the Ricardian model, which assumed that trade occurs because countries use their technological comparative advantage to specialize in the production of different goods. The model is named after the Swedish economists Eli Heckscher, who wrote about his views of international trade in a 1919 article, and his student Bertil Ohlin, who further developed these ideas in his 1924 dissertation.

The Heckscher-Ohlin model was developed at the end of a "golden age" of international trade (as described in Chapter 1) that lasted from about 1890 until 1914, when World War I started. Those years saw dramatic improvements in transportation: the steamship and the railroad allowed for a great increase in the amount of international trade. For these reasons, there was a considerable increase in the ratio of trade to GDP between 1890 and 1914. It is not surprising, then, that Heckscher and Ohlin would want to explain the large increase in trade that they had witnessed in their own lifetimes. The ability to transport machines across borders meant that they did not look to differences in technologies across countries as the reason for trade, as Ricardo had done. Instead, they assumed that technologies were the same across countries, and they used the uneven distribution of resources across countries to explain trade patterns.

Even today, there are many examples of international trade driven by the land, labor, and capital resources found in each country. Canada, for example, has a large amount of land and therefore exports agricultural and forestry products, as well as petroleum; the United States, Western Europe, and Japan have many highly skilled workers and much capital and export sophisticated services and manufactured goods; China and other Asian countries have a large number of workers and moderate but growing amounts of capital and export less sophisticated manufactured goods; and so on. We study these and other examples of international trade in this chapter.

Our first goal is to describe the Heckscher-Ohlin model of trade. The specific-factors model that we studied in the previous chapter was a short-run model because capital and land could not move between the industries. In contrast, the Heckscher-Ohlin model is a long-run model because all factors of production can move between the industries. It is difficult to deal with three factors of production (labor, capital, and land) in both industries, so, instead, we assume that there are just two factors (labor and capital).

After predicting the long-run pattern of trade between countries using the Heckscher-Ohlin model, our second goal is to examine the empirical evidence on the Heckscher-Ohlin model. Although you might think it is obvious that a country's exports will be based on the resources the country has in abundance, it turns out that this prediction does not always hold true in practice. To obtain better predictions from the Heckscher-Ohlin model, we extend the model in several directions, first by allowing for more than two factors of production and second by allowing countries to differ in their technologies, as in the Ricardian model. Both extensions make the predictions from the Heckscher-Ohlin model match more closely the trade patterns in the world economy today.

The third goal of the chapter is to investigate how the opening of trade between the two countries affects the payments to labor and to capital in each of them. We use the Heckscher-Ohlin model to predict which factor(s) gain when international trade begins and which factor(s) lose.

1 Heckscher-Ohlin Model

In building the Heckscher-Ohlin (HO) model, we suppose there are two countries, Home and Foreign, each of which produces two goods, computers and shoes, using two factors of production, labor and capital. Using symbols for capital (K) and labor (L), we can add up the resources used in each industry to get the total for the economy. For example, the amount of capital Home uses in shoes K_S, plus the amount of capital used in computers K_C, adds up to the total capital available in the economy $\overline{K}$, so that $K_C + K_S = \overline{K}$. The same applies for Foreign: $K_C^* + K_S^* = \overline{K}^*$. Similarly, the amount of labor Home uses in shoes L_S, and the amount of labor used in computers L_C, add up to the total labor in the economy $\overline{L}$, so that $L_C + L_S = \overline{L}$. The same applies for Foreign: $L_C^* + L_S^* = \overline{L}^*$.

Assumptions of the Heckscher-Ohlin Model

Because the Heckscher-Ohlin (HO) model describes the economy in the long run, the assumptions used differ from those in the short-run specific-factors model of Chapter 3:

Assumption 1: Both factors can move freely between the industries.

This assumption implies that if both industries are actually producing, then capital must earn the same rental R in each of them. The reason for this result is that if capital earned a higher rental in one industry than the other, then all capital would move to the industry with the higher rental and the other industry would shut down. This result differs from the specific-factors model in which capital in manufacturing and land in agriculture earned different rentals in their respective industries. But like the specific-factor model, if both industries are producing, then all labor earns the same wage W in each of them.

Our second assumption concerns how the factors are combined to make shoes and computers:

Assumption 2: Shoe production is labor-intensive; that is, it requires more labor per unit of capital to produce shoes than computers, so that $L_S/K_S > L_C/K_C$

Another way to state this assumption is to say that computer production is capital-intensive; that is, more capital per worker is used to produce computers than to produce shoes, so that $K_C/L_C > K_S/L_S$. The idea that shoes use more labor per unit of capital, and computers use more capital per worker, matches how most of us think about the technologies used in these two industries.

In Figure 4-1, the demands for labor relative to capital in each industry (L_C/K_C and L_S/K_S) are graphed against the wage relative to the rental on capital, W/R (or the wage-rental ratio). These two curves slope down just like regular demand curves: as W/R rises, the quantity of labor demanded relative to the quantity of capital demanded falls. As we work through the HO model, remember that these are *relative* demand curves for labor; the "quantity" on the horizontal axis is the ratio of labor to capital used in production, and the "price" is the ratio of the labor wage to the capital rental. Assumption 2 says that the relative demand curve in shoes, L_S/K_S in Figure 4-1, lies to the right of the relative demand curve in computers L_C/K_C, because shoe production is more labor-intensive.

Whereas the preceding assumptions have focused on the production process within each country, the HO model requires assumptions that apply across countries as well. Our next assumption is that the amounts of labor and capital found in Home and Foreign are different:

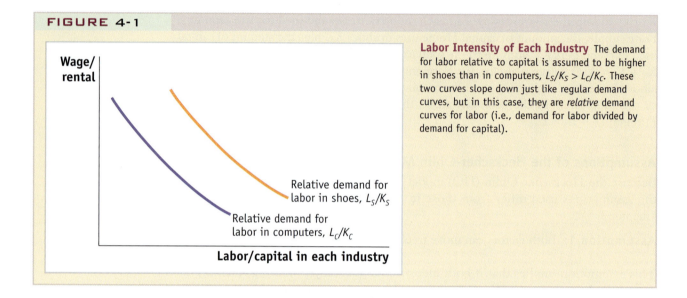

FIGURE 4-1

Labor Intensity of Each Industry The demand for labor relative to capital is assumed to be higher in shoes than in computers, $L_S/K_S > L_C/K_C$. These two curves slope down just like regular demand curves, but in this case, they are *relative* demand curves for labor (i.e., demand for labor divided by demand for capital).

Assumption 3: Foreign is labor-abundant, by which we mean that the labor–capital ratio in Foreign exceeds that in Home, $\overline{L}^*/\overline{K}^* > \overline{L}/\overline{K}$. Equivalently, Home is capital-abundant, so that $\overline{K}/\overline{L} > \overline{K}^*/\overline{L}^*$.

There are many reasons for labor, capital, and other resources to differ across countries: countries differ in their geographic size and populations, previous waves of immigration or emigration may have changed a country's population, countries are at different stages of development and so have differing amounts of capital, and so on. If we were considering land in the HO model, Home and Foreign would have different amounts of usable land due to the shape of their borders and to differences in topography and climate. In building the HO model, we do not consider why the amounts of labor, capital, or land differ across countries but simply accept these differences as important determinants of why countries engage in international trade.

Assumption 3 focuses on a particular case, in which Foreign is labor-abundant and Home is capital-abundant. This assumption is true, for example, if Foreign has a larger workforce than Home ($\overline{L}^* > \overline{L}$) and Foreign and Home have equal amounts of capital, $\overline{K}^* = \overline{K}$. Under these circumstances, $\overline{L}^*/\overline{K}^* > \overline{L}/\overline{K}$, so Foreign is labor-abundant. Conversely, the capital–labor ratio in Home exceeds that in Foreign, $\overline{K}/\overline{L} > \overline{K}^*/\overline{L}^*$, so the Home country is capital-abundant.

Assumption 4: The final outputs, shoes and computers, can be traded freely (i.e., without any restrictions) between nations, but labor and capital do not move between countries.

In this chapter, we do not allow labor or capital to move between countries. We relax this assumption in the next chapter, in which we investigate the movement of labor between countries through immigration as well as the movement of capital between countries through foreign direct investment.

Our final two assumptions involve the technologies of firms and tastes of consumers across countries:

Assumption 5: The technologies used to produce the two goods are identical across the countries.

This assumption is the opposite of that made in the Ricardian model (Chapter 2), which assumes that technological differences across countries are the reason for trade. It is not realistic to assume that technologies are the same across countries because often the technologies used in rich versus poor countries are quite different (as described in the following application). Although assumption 5 is not very realistic, it allows us to focus on a single reason for trade: the different amounts of labor and capital found in each country. Later in this chapter, we use data to test the validity of the HO model and find that the model performs better when assumption 5 is not used.

Our final assumption is as follows:

Assumption 6: Consumer tastes are the same across countries, and preferences for computers and shoes do not vary with a country's level of income.

That is, we suppose that a poorer country will buy fewer shoes and computers, but will buy them in the same ratio as a wealthier country facing the same prices. Again, this assumption is not very realistic: consumers in poor countries do spend more of their income on shoes, clothing, and other basic goods than on computers, whereas in rich countries a higher share of income can be spent on computers and other electronic goods than on footwear and clothing. Assumption 6 is another simplifying assumption that again allows us to focus attention on the differences in resources as the sole reason for trade.

APPLICATION

Are Factor Intensities the Same across Countries?

One of our assumptions for the HO model is that the same good (shoes) is labor-intensive in both countries. Specifically, we assume that in both countries, shoe production has a higher labor–capital ratio than does computer production. Although it might seem obvious that this assumption holds for shoes and computers, it is not so obvious when comparing other products, say, shoes and call centers.

Despite its ninteenth-century exterior, this New Balance factory in Maine houses advanced shoe-manufacturing technology.

In principle, all countries have access to the same technologies for making footwear. In practice, however, the machines used in the United States are different from those used in Asia and elsewhere. While much of the footwear in the world is produced in developing nations, the United States retains a small number of shoe factories. New Balance, which manufactures sneakers, has five plants in the New England states, and 25% of the shoes it sells in North America are produced in the United States. One of their plants is in Norridgewock, Maine, where employees operate computerized equipment that allows one person to do the work of six.[1] This is a far cry from the plants in Asia that produce shoes for Nike, Reebok, and other U.S. producers. Because Asian plants use old

---

[1] This description of the New Balance plant is drawn from Aaron Bernstein, "Low-Skilled Jobs: Do They Have to Move?" *BusinessWeek*, February 26, 2001, 94–95.

technology (such as individual sewing machines), they use more workers to operate less productive machines.

In call centers, on the other hand, technologies (and, therefore, factor intensities) are similar across countries. Each employee works with a telephone and a personal computer, so call centers in the United States and India are similar in terms of the amount of capital per worker that they require. The telephone and personal computer, costing several thousand dollars, are much less expensive than the automated manufacturing machines in the New Balance plant in the United States, which cost tens or hundreds of thousands of dollars. So the manufacture of footwear in the New Balance plant is capital-intensive as compared with a U.S. call center. In India, by contrast, the sewing machine used to produce footwear is cheaper than the computer used in the call center. So footwear production in India is labor-intensive as compared with the call center, which is the opposite of what holds in the United States. This example illustrates a **reversal of factor intensities** between the two countries.

The same reversal of factor intensities is seen when we compare the agricultural sector across countries. In the United States, agriculture is capital-intensive. Each farmer works with tens of thousands of dollars in mechanized, computerized equipment, allowing a farm to be maintained by only a handful of workers. In many developing countries, however, agriculture is labor-intensive. Farms are worked by many laborers with little or no mechanized equipment. The reason that this labor-intensive technology is used in agriculture in developing nations is that capital equipment is expensive relative to the wages earned.

In assumption 2 and Figure 4-1, we assume that the labor–capital ratio (L/K) of one industry exceeds that of the other industry *regardless of the wage-rental ratio (W/R)*. That is, whether labor is cheap (as in a developing country) or expensive (as in the United States), we are assuming that the same industry (shoes, in our example) is labor-intensive in both countries. This assumption may not be true for footwear or for agriculture, as we have just seen. In our treatment of the HO model, we will ignore the possibility of factor intensity reversals. The reason for ignoring these is to get a definite prediction from the model about the pattern of trade between countries so that we can see what happens to the price of goods and the earnings of factors when countries trade with each other. ■

No-Trade Equilibrium

In assumption 3, we outlined the difference in the amount of labor and capital found at Home and in Foreign. Our goal is to use these differences in resources to predict the pattern of trade. To do this, we begin by studying the equilibrium in each country in the absence of trade.

Production Possibilities Frontiers To determine the no-trade equilibria in Home and Foreign, we start by drawing the production possibilities frontiers (PPFs) in each country as shown in Figure 4-2. Under our assumptions that Home is capital-abundant and that computer production is capital-intensive, Home is capable of producing more computers than shoes. The Home PPF drawn in panel (a) is skewed in the direction of computers to reflect Home's greater capability to produce computers. Similarly, because Foreign is labor-abundant and shoe production is labor-intensive, the Foreign PPF shown in panel (b) is skewed in the direction of shoes, reflecting Foreign's greater capability to produce shoes. These particular shapes for the PPFs are reasonable given the assumptions we have made. When we continue our study of the Heckscher-Ohlin (HO) model in

FIGURE 4-2

No-Trade Equilibria in Home and Foreign The Home production possibilities frontier (PPF) is shown in panel (a), and the Foreign PPF is shown in panel (b). Because Home is capital-abundant and computers are capital-intensive, the Home PPF is skewed toward computers. Home preferences are summarized by the indifference curve, U, and the Home no-trade (or autarky) equilibrium is at point A, with a low relative price of computers, as indicated by the flat slope of $(P_C/P_S)^A$. Foreign is labor-abundant and shoes are labor-intensive, so the Foreign PPF is skewed toward shoes. Foreign preferences are summarized by the indifference curve, U^*, and the Foreign no-trade equilibrium is at point A^*, with a higher relative price of computers, as indicated by the steeper slope of $(P_C^*/P_S^*)^{A^*}$.

Chapter 5, we prove that the PPFs must take this shape.[2] For now, we accept these shapes of the PPF and use them as the starting point for our study of the HO model.

Indifference Curves Another assumption of the Heckscher-Ohlin model (assumption 6) is that consumer tastes are the same across countries. As we did in the Ricardian model, we graph consumer tastes using indifference curves. Two of these curves are shown in Figure 4-2 (U and U^* for Home and Foreign, respectively); one is tangent to Home's PPF, and the other is tangent to Foreign's PPF. Notice that these indifference curves are the same shape in both countries, as required by assumption 6. They are tangent to the PPFs at different points because of the distinct shapes of the PPFs just described.

The slope of an indifference curve equals the amount that consumers are willing to pay for computers measured in terms of shoes rather than dollars. The slope of the PPF equals the opportunity cost of producing one more computer in terms of shoes given up. When the slope of an indifference curve equals the slope of a PPF, the relative price that consumers are willing to pay for computers equals the opportunity cost of producing them, so this point is the no-trade equilibrium.[3] The common slope of the indifference curve and PPF at their tangency equals the relative price of computers

---

[2] See Problem 7 in Chapter 5.
[3] Remember that the slope of an indifference curve or PPF reflects the relative price of the good on the *horizontal* axis, which is computers in Figure 4-2.

P_C/P_S. A steeply sloped price line implies a high relative price of computers, whereas a flat price line implies a low relative price for computers.

No-Trade Equilibrium Price   Given the differently shaped PPFs, the indifference curves of each country will be tangent to the PPFs at different production points, corresponding to different relative price lines across the two countries. In Home the no-trade or autarky equilibrium is shown by point A, at which Home produces Q_{C1} of computers and Q_{S1} of shoes at the relative price of $(P_C/P_S)^A$. Because the Home PPF is skewed toward computers, the slope of the Home price line $(P_C/P_S)^A$ is quite flat, indicating a low relative price of computers. In Foreign, the no-trade or autarky equilibrium is shown by point A^* at which Foreign produces Q_{C1}^* of computers and Q_{S1}^* of shoes at the relative price of $(P_C^*/P_S^*)^{A*}$. Because the Foreign PPF is skewed toward shoes, the slope of the Foreign price line $(P_C^*/P_S^*)^{A*}$ is quite steep, indicating a high relative price of computers. Therefore, the result from comparing the no-trade equilibria in Figure 4-2 is that the *no-trade relative price of computers at Home is lower than in Foreign*. (Equivalently, we can say that the no-trade relative price of shoes at Home is higher than in Foreign.)

These comparisons of the no-trade prices reflect the differing amounts of labor found in the two countries: the Foreign country has abundant labor, and shoe production is labor-intensive, so the no-trade relative price of shoes is lower in Foreign than in Home. That Foreigners are willing to give up more shoes for one computer reflects the fact that Foreign resources are suited to making more shoes. The same logic applies to Home, which is relatively abundant in capital. Because computer production is capital-intensive, Home has a lower no-trade relative price of computers than Foreign. Thus, Home residents need to give up fewer shoes to obtain one computer, reflecting the fact that their resources are suited to making more computers.

Free-Trade Equilibrium

We are now in a position to determine the pattern of trade between the countries. To do so, we proceed in several steps. First, we consider what happens when the world relative price of computers is *above* the no-trade relative price of computers at Home, and trace out the Home export supply of computers. Second, we consider what happens when the world relative price is *below* the no-trade relative price of computers in Foreign, and trace out the Foreign import demand for computers. Finally, we put together the Home export supply and Foreign import demand to determine the equilibrium relative price of computers with international trade.

Home Equilibrium with Free Trade   The first step is displayed in Figure 4-3. We have already seen in Figure 4-2 that the no-trade relative price of computers is lower in Home than in Foreign. Under free trade, we expect the equilibrium relative price of computers to lie between the no-trade relative prices in each country (as we already found in the Ricardian model of Chapter 2). Because the no-trade relative price of computers is lower at Home, the free-trade equilibrium price will be above the no-trade price at Home. Therefore, panel (a) of Figure 4-3 shows the Home PPF with a free-trade or world relative price of computers, $(P_C/P_S)^W$, higher than the no-trade Home relative price, $(P_C/P_S)^A$, shown in panel (a) of Figure 4-2.

The no-trade equilibrium at Home, point A, has the quantities (Q_{C1}, Q_{S1}) for computers and shoes, shown in Figure 4-2. At the higher world relative price of computers, Home production moves from point A, (Q_{C1}, Q_{S1}), to point B in Figure 4-3, (Q_{C2}, Q_{S2}),

FIGURE 4-3

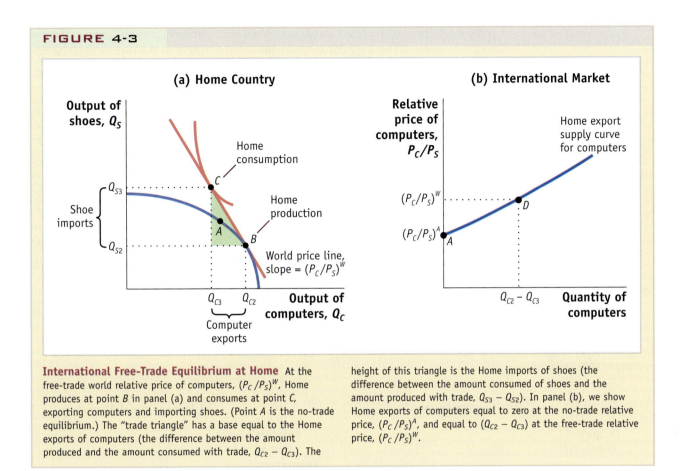

(a) Home Country

Output of shoes, Q_S

Home consumption

Home production

World price line, slope = $(P_C/P_S)^W$

Shoe imports

Q_{S3}

Q_{S2}

C

A

B

Output of computers, Q_C

Q_{C3} Q_{C2}

Computer exports

(b) International Market

Relative price of computers, P_C/P_S

Home export supply curve for computers

$(P_C/P_S)^W$

$(P_C/P_S)^A$

D

A

$Q_{C2} - Q_{C3}$

Quantity of computers

International Free-Trade Equilibrium at Home At the free-trade world relative price of computers, $(P_C/P_S)^W$, Home produces at point B in panel (a) and consumes at point C, exporting computers and importing shoes. (Point A is the no-trade equilibrium.) The "trade triangle" has a base equal to the Home exports of computers (the difference between the amount produced and the amount consumed with trade, $Q_{C2} - Q_{C3}$). The height of this triangle is the Home imports of shoes (the difference between the amount consumed of shoes and the amount produced with trade, $Q_{S3} - Q_{S2}$). In panel (b), we show Home exports of computers equal to zero at the no-trade relative price, $(P_C/P_S)^A$, and equal to $(Q_{C2} - Q_{C3})$ at the free-trade relative price, $(P_C/P_S)^W$.

with more computers and fewer shoes. Thus, with free trade, Home produces fewer shoes and specializes further in computers to take advantage of higher world relative prices of computers. Because Home can now engage in trade at the world relative price, Home's consumption can now lie on any point along the world price line through B with slope $(P_C/P_S)^W$. The highest Home utility is obtained at point C, which is tangent to the world price line $(P_C/P_S)^W$ and has the quantities consumed (Q_{C3}, Q_{S3}).

We can now define the Home "trade triangle," which is the triangle connecting points B and C, shown in panel (a) of Figure 4-3. Point B is where Home is producing and point C is where it is consuming, and the line connecting the two points represents the amount of trade at the world relative price. The base of this triangle is the Home exports of computers (the difference between the amount produced and the amount consumed with trade, or $Q_{C2} - Q_{C3}$). The height of this triangle is the Home imports of shoes (the difference between the amount consumed of shoes and the amount produced with trade, or $Q_{S3} - Q_{S2}$).

In panel (b) of Figure 4-3, we graph the Home exports of computers against their relative price. In the no-trade equilibrium, the Home relative price of computers was $(P_C/P_S)^A$, and exports of computers were zero. This no-trade equilibrium is shown by point A in panel (b). Under free trade, the relative price of computers is $(P_C/P_S)^W$, and exports of computers are the difference between the amount produced and amount consumed with trade, or $(Q_{C2} - Q_{C3})$. This free-trade equilibrium is shown by point D

in panel (b). Joining up points A and D, we obtain the Home export supply curve of computers. It is upward-sloping because at higher relative prices as compared with the no-trade price, Home is willing to specialize further in computers to export more of them.

Foreign Equilibrium with Free Trade   We proceed in a similar fashion for the Foreign country. In panel (a) of Figure 4-4, the Foreign no-trade equilibrium is at point A^*, with the high equilibrium relative price of computers $(P_C^*/P_S^*)^{A^*}$. Because the Foreign no-trade relative price was higher than at Home, and we expect the free-trade relative price to lie between, it follows that the free-trade or world equilibrium price of computers $(P_C/P_S)^W$ is lower than the no-trade Foreign price $(P_C^*/P_S^*)^{A^*}$.

At the world relative price, Foreign production moves from point A^*, (Q_{C1}^*, Q_{S1}^*), to point B^*, (Q_{C2}^*, Q_{S2}^*), with more shoes and fewer computers. Thus, with free trade, Foreign specializes further in shoes and produces fewer computers. Because Foreign can now engage in trade at the world relative price, Foreign's consumption can now lie on any point along the world price line through B^* with slope $(P_C/P_S)^W$. The highest Foreign utility is obtained at point C^*, which is tangent to the world price line $(P_C/P_S)^W$ and has the quantities consumed (Q_{C3}^*, Q_{S3}^*). Once again, we can connect points B^* and C^* to form a "trade triangle." The base of this triangle is Foreign imports of computers

FIGURE 4-4

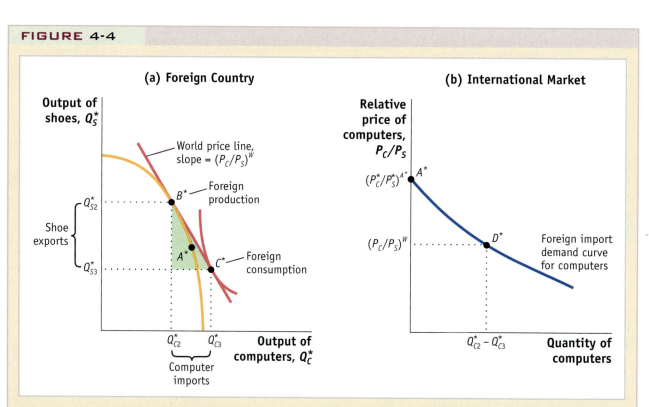

(a) Foreign Country

(b) International Market

International Free-Trade Equilibrium in Foreign At the free-trade world relative price of computers, $(P_C/P_S)^W$, Foreign produces at point B^* in panel (a) and consumes at point C^*, importing computers and exporting shoes. (Point A^* is the no-trade equilibrium.) The "trade triangle" has a base equal to Foreign imports of computers (the difference between the consumption of computers and the amount produced with trade, $Q_{C3}^* - Q_{C2}^*$). The height of this triangle is Foreign exports of shoes (the difference between the production of shoes and the amount consumed with trade, $Q_{S2}^* - Q_{S3}^*$). In panel (b), we show Foreign imports of computers equal to zero at the no-trade relative price, $(P_C^*/P_S^*)^{A^*}$, and equal to $(Q_{C3}^* - Q_{C2}^*)$ at the free-trade relative price, $(P_C/P_S)^W$.

(the difference between consumption of computers and production with trade, or $Q^*_{C3} - Q^*_{C2}$), and the height is Foreign exports of shoes (the difference between production and consumption with trade, or $Q^*_{S2} - Q^*_{S3}$).

In panel (b) of Figure 4-4, we graph Foreign's imports of computers against its relative price. In the no-trade equilibrium, the Foreign relative price of computers was $(P^*_C/P^*_S)^{A*}$, and imports of computers were zero. This no-trade equilibrium is shown by the point A^* in panel (b). Under free trade, the relative price of computers is $(P_C/P_S)^W$, and imports of computers are the difference between the amount produced and amount consumed with trade, or $(Q^*_{C3} - Q^*_{C2})$. This free-trade equilibrium is shown by the point D^* in panel (b). Joining up points A^* and D^*, we obtain the Foreign import demand curve for computers. It is downward-sloping because at lower relative prices as compared with no-trade, Foreign specializes more in shoes and exports these in exchange for computers.

Equilibrium Price with Free Trade As we see in Figure 4-5, the equilibrium relative price of computers with free trade is determined by the intersection of the Home export supply and Foreign import demand curves, at point D (the same as point D in Figure 4-3 or D^* in Figure 4-4). At that relative price, the quantity of computers that the Home country wants to export equals the quantity of computers that Foreign wants to import; that is, $(Q_{C2} - Q_{C3}) = (Q^*_{C3} - Q^*_{C2})$. Because exports equal imports, there is no reason for the relative price to change and so this is a **free-trade equilibrium**. Another way to see the equilibrium graphically is to notice that in panel (a) of Figures 4-3 and 4-4, the trade triangles of the two countries are identical in size—what one country wants to sell is the same as what the other country wants to buy.

Pattern of Trade Using the free-trade equilibrium, we have determined the pattern of trade between the two countries. Home exports computers, the good that uses intensively the factor of production (capital) found in abundance at Home. Foreign exports shoes, the good that uses intensively the factor of production (labor) found in abundance there. This important result is called the **Heckscher-Ohlin theorem.**

FIGURE 4-5

Q^W
$= (Q_{C2} - Q_{C3})$
$= (Q^*_{C3} - Q^*_{C2})$

Determination of the Free-Trade World Equilibrium Price The world relative price of computers in the free-trade equilibrium is determined at the intersection of the Home export supply and Foreign import demand, at point D. At this relative price, the quantity of computers that Home wants to export, $(Q_{C2} - Q_{C3})$, just equals the quantity of computers that Foreign wants to import, $(Q^*_{C3} - Q^*_{C2})$.

Heckscher-Ohlin Theorem: With two goods and two factors, each country will export the good that uses intensively the factor of production it has in abundance and will import the other good.

It is useful to review the assumptions we made at the beginning of the chapter to see how they lead to the Heckscher-Ohlin theorem.

Assumption 1: Labor and capital flow freely between the industries.
Assumption 2: The production of shoes is labor-intensive as compared with computer production, which is capital-intensive.
Assumption 3: The amounts of labor and capital found in the two countries differ, with Foreign abundant in labor and Home abundant in capital.
Assumption 4: There is free international trade in goods.
Assumption 5: The technologies for producing shoes and computers are the same across countries.
Assumption 6: Tastes are the same across countries.

Assumptions 1 to 3 allowed us to draw the PPFs of the two countries as illustrated in Figure 4-2, and in conjunction with assumptions 5 and 6, they allowed us to determine that the no-trade relative price of computers in Home was lower than the no-trade relative price of computers in Foreign; that is, $(P_C/P_S)^A$ was less than $(P_C^*/P_S^*)^{A^*}$. This key result enabled us to determine the starting points for the Home export supply curve for computers (point A) and the Foreign import demand curve for computers (point A^*) in panel (b) of Figures 4-3 and 4-4. Using those starting points, we put together the upward-sloping Home export supply curve and downward-sloping Foreign import demand curve. We see from Figure 4-5 that the relative price of computers in the free-trade equilibrium lies between the no-trade relative prices (which confirms the expectation we had when drawing Figures 4-3 and 4-4).

Therefore, when Home opens to trade, its relative price of computers rises from the no-trade equilibrium relative price $(P_C/P_S)^A$, to the free-trade equilibrium price $(P_C/P_S)^W$, giving Home firms an incentive to export computers. That is, higher prices give Home an incentive to produce more computers than it wants to consume, and export the difference. Similarly, when Foreign opens to trade, its relative price of computers falls from the no-trade equilibrium price $(P_C^*/P_S^*)^{A^*}$, to the trade equilibrium price $(P_C/P_S)^W$, encouraging Foreign consumers to import computers from Home. That is, lower prices give Foreign an incentive to consume more computers than it wants to produce, importing the difference.

You might think that the Heckscher-Ohlin theorem is somewhat obvious. It makes sense that countries will export goods that are produced easily because the factors of production are found in abundance. It turns out, however, that this prediction does not always work in practice, as we discuss in the next section.

2 Testing the Heckscher-Ohlin Model

The first test of the Heckscher-Ohlin theorem was performed by economist Wassily Leontief in 1953, using data for the United States from 1947. We will describe his test below and show that he reached a surprising conclusion, which is called **Leontief's paradox.** After that, we will discuss more recent data for many countries that can be used to test the Heckscher-Ohlin model.

Leontief's Paradox

To test the Heckscher-Ohlin theorem, Leontief measured the amounts of labor and capital used in all industries needed to produce $1 million of U.S. exports and to produce $1 million of imports into the United States. His results are shown in Table 4-1.

Leontief first measured the amount of capital and labor required in the production of $1 million worth of U.S. exports. To arrive at these figures, Leontief measured the labor and capital used *directly* in the production of final good exports in each industry. He also measured the labor and capital used *indirectly* in the industries that produced the intermediate inputs used in making the exports. From the first row of Table 4-1, we see that $2.55 million worth of capital was used to produce $1 million of exports. This amount of capital seems much too high, until we recognize that what is being measured is the total stock, which exceeds that part of the capital stock that was actually used to produce exports that year: the capital used that year would be measured by the depreciation on this stock. For labor, 182 person-years were used to produce the exports. Taking the ratio of these, we find that each person employed (directly or indirectly) in producing exports was working with $14,000 worth of capital.

Turning to the import side of the calculation, Leontief immediately ran into a problem—he could not measure the amount of labor and capital used to produce imports because he didn't have data on foreign technologies. To get around this difficulty, Leontief did what many researchers have done since—he simply used the data on U.S. technology to calculate estimated amounts of labor and capital used in imports from abroad. Does this approach invalidate Leontief's test of the Heckscher-Ohlin model? Not really, because the Heckscher-Ohlin model assumes that technologies are the same across countries, so Leontief is building this assumption into the calculations needed to test the theorem.

Using U.S. technology to measure the labor and capital used directly and indirectly in producing imports, Leontief arrived at the estimates in the last column of Table 4-1: $3.1 million of capital and 170 person-years were used in the production of $1 million worth of U.S. imports, so the capital–labor ratio for imports was $18,200 per worker. Notice that this amount *exceeds* the capital–labor ratio for exports of $14,000 per worker.

Leontief supposed correctly that in 1947 the United States was abundant in capital relative to the rest of the world. Thus, from the Heckscher-Ohlin theorem, Leontief expected that the United States would export capital-intensive goods and import labor-intensive goods. What Leontief actually found, however, was just the opposite: the capital–labor ratio for U.S. imports was *higher* than the capital–labor ratio found for U.S. exports! This finding contradicted the Heckscher-Ohlin theorem and came to be called Leontief's paradox.

Explanations A wide range of explanations has been offered for Leontief's paradox, including the following:

■ U.S. and foreign technologies are not the same, in contrast to what the Heckscher-Ohlin theorem and Leontief assumed.

TABLE 4-1

Leontief's Test Leontief used the numbers in this table to test the Heckscher-Ohlin theorem. Each column shows the amount of capital or labor needed to produce $1 million worth of exports from, or imports into, the United States in 1947. As shown in the last row, the capital–labor ratio for exports was less than the capital–labor ratio for imports, which is a paradoxical finding.

	Exports	Imports
Capital ($ millions)	2.55	3.1
Labor (person-years)	182	170
Capital/labor ($/person)	14,000	18,200

Source: Wassily Leontief, 1953, "Domestic Production and Foreign Trade: The American Capital Position Re-examined," Proceedings of the American Philosophical Society, 97, September, 332–349. Reprinted in Richard Caves and Harry G. Johnson, eds., 1968, Readings in International Economics (Homewood, IL: Irwin).

- By focusing only on labor and capital, Leontief ignored land abundance in the United States.
- Leontief should have distinguished between skilled and unskilled labor (because it would not be surprising to find that U.S. exports are intensive in skilled labor).
- The data for 1947 may be unusual because World War II had ended just two years earlier.
- The United States was not engaged in completely free trade, as the Heckscher-Ohlin theorem assumes.

Several of the additional possible explanations for the Leontief paradox depend on having more than two factors of production. The United States is abundant in land, for example, and that might explain why in 1947 it was exporting labor-intensive products: these might have been agricultural products, which use land intensively and, in 1947, might also have used labor intensively. By ignoring land, Leontief was therefore not performing an accurate test of the Heckscher-Ohlin theorem. Alternatively, it might be that the United States was mainly exporting goods that used skilled labor. This is certainly true today, with the United States being a leading exporter of high-technology products, and was probably also true in 1947. By not distinguishing between skilled versus unskilled labor, Leontief was again giving an inaccurate picture of the factors of production used in U.S. trade.

Research in later years aimed to redo the test that Leontief performed, while taking into account land, skilled versus unskilled labor, checking whether the Heckscher-Ohlin theorem holds in other years, and so on. We now discuss the data that can be used to test the Heckscher-Ohlin theorem in a more recent year—2000.

Factor Endowments in the New Millenium

In Figure 4-6, we show the country shares of six factors of production and world GDP in 2000, broken down by select countries (the United States, China, Japan, India, Germany, the United Kingdom, France, and Canada) and then the rest of the world. To determine whether a country is abundant in a certain factor, we compare the country's share of that factor with its share of world GDP. If its share of a factor exceeds its share of world GDP, then we conclude that the country is **abundant in that factor,** and if its share in a certain factor is less than its share of world GDP, then we conclude that the country is **scarce in that factor.** This definition allows us to calculate factor abundance in a setting with as many factors and countries as we want.

Capital Abundance For example, in the first bar graph of Figure 4-6, we see that in 2000, 24% of the world's physical capital was located in the United States, with 8.7% located in China, 13.3% in Japan, 3.6% in India, 7.5% in Germany, and so on. When we compare these numbers with the final bar in the graph, which shows each country's percentage of world GDP, we see that in 2000 the United States had 21.6% of world GDP, China had 11.2%, Japan 7.5%, India 5.5%, Germany 4.7%, and so on. Because the United States had 24% of the world's capital and 21.6% of world GDP, we can conclude that the United States was abundant in physical capital in 2000. Japan had 13.3% of the world's capital and 7.5% of world GDP, so it was also abundant in capital, as was Germany (with 7.5% of the world's capital and 4.7% of world GDP). The opposite holds for China, India, and the group of countries included in the rest of the world: their shares of world capital were less than their shares of GDP, so they were scarce in capital.

FIGURE 4-6

Country Factor Endowments, 2000 Shown here are country shares of six factors of production in the year 2000, for eight selected countries and the rest of the world. In the first bar graph, we see that 24% of the world's physical capital in 2000 was located in the United States, with 9% located in China, 13% located in Japan, and so on. In the final bar graph, we see that in 2000 the United States had 22% of world GDP, China had 11%, Japan had 8%, and so on. When a country's factor share is larger than its share of GDP, then the country is abundant in that factor, and when a country's factor share is less than its share of GDP, then the country is scarce in that factor.

Notes:
(1) The product of 1990 capital per worker (Penn World Table) and 2000 total labor force (World Bank, World Development Indicators). China figure based on Gregory Chow and Kui-Wai Li, 2002, "China's Economic Growth: 1952–2010," *Economic Development and Cultural Change,* 51, 247–256. There are 63 countries included.
(2) The product of R&D researcher intensity and total population (World Bank, World Development Indicators). There are 55 countries included.

(3) Labor force with tertiary education (World Bank, World Development Indicators); when unavailable, population 25 and over with postsecondary education was used (R. J. Barro and J. W. Lee, 2000, "International Data on Educational Attainment: Updates and Implications," Center for International Development at Harvard University, Working Paper No. 42). There are 123 countries included.
(4) Labor force with primary and/or secondary education (World Bank, World Development Indicators); when unavailable, population 25 and over with primary and/or secondary education was used (R. J. Barro and J. W. Lee, 2000, "International Data on Educational Attainment: Updates and Implications," Center for International Development at Harvard University, Working Paper No. 42). There are 123 countries included.
(5) The product of one minus the adult literacy rate and the adult population in 2004 (World Bank, World Development Indicators). There are 136 countries included.
(6) Hectares of arable land (World Bank, World Development Indicators). There are 196 countries included.
(7) Gross domestic product converted to 2000 international dollars using purchasing power parity rates (World Bank, World Development Indicators). There are 169 countries included.

Labor and Land Abundance We can use a similar comparison to determine whether each country is abundant in R&D scientists, in types of labor distinguished by skill, in arable land, or any other factor of production. For example, the United States was abundant in R&D scientists in 2000 (with 26.1% of the world's total as compared with 21.6%

of the world's GDP) and also skilled labor (workers with more than a high school education) but was scarce in less-skilled labor (workers with a high school education or less) and illiterate labor. India was scarce in R&D scientists (with 2.5% of the world's total as compared with 5.5% of the world's GDP) but abundant in skilled labor, semiskilled labor, and illiterate labor (with shares of the world's total that exceed its GDP share). Canada was abundant in arable land (with 3.3% of the world's total as compared with 1.9% of the world's GDP), as we would expect. But the United States was scarce in arable land (12.6% of the world's total as compared with 21.6% of the world's GDP). That is a surprising result because we often think of the United States as a major exporter of agricultural commodities, so from the Heckscher-Ohlin theorem, we would expect it to be land-abundant.

Another surprising result in Figure 4-6 is that China was abundant in R&D scientists: it had 14.1% of the world's R&D scientists, as compared with 11.2% of the world's GDP in 2000. This finding also seems to contradict the Heckscher-Ohlin theorem, because we do not think of China as exporting highly skill-intensive manufactured goods. These observations regarding R&D scientists (a factor in which both the United States and China were abundant) and land (in which the United States was scarce) can cause us to question whether an R&D scientist or an acre of arable land has the same productivity in all countries. If not, then our measures of factor abundance are misleading: if an R&D scientist in the United States is more productive than his or her counterpart in China, then it does not make sense to just compare each country's share of these with each country's share of GDP; and likewise, if an acre of arable land is more productive in the United States than in other countries, then we should not compare the share of land in each country with each country's share of GDP. Instead, we need to make some adjustment for the differing productivities of R&D scientists and land across countries. In other words, we need to abandon the original Heckscher-Ohlin assumption of identical technologies across countries.

Differing Productivities across Countries

Leontief himself suggested that we should abandon the assumption that technologies are the same across countries and instead allow for differing productivities, as in the Ricardian model. Remember that in the original formulation of the paradox, Leontief had found that the United States was exporting labor-intensive products even though it was capital-abundant at that time. One explanation for this outcome would be that labor is highly productive in the United States and less productive in the rest of the world. If that is the case, then the **effective labor force** in the United States, the labor force times its productivity (which measures how much output the labor force can produce), is much larger than it appears to be when we just count people. If this is true, perhaps the United States is abundant in *skilled* labor after all (like R&D scientists), and it should be no surprise that it is exporting labor-intensive products.

We now explore how differing productivities can be introduced into the Heckscher-Ohlin model. In addition to allowing labor to have a differing productivity across countries, we can also allow capital, land, and other factors of production to have differing productivity across countries.

Measuring Factor Abundance Once Again To allow factors of production to differ in their productivities across countries, we define the **effective factor endowment** as the actual amount of a factor found in a country times its productivity:

Effective factor endowment = Actual factor endowment • Factor productivity

The amount of an effective factor found in the world is obtained by adding up the effective factor endowments across all countries. Then to determine whether a country is abundant in a certain factor, we compare the country's share of that *effective* factor with its share of world GDP. If its share of an effective factor exceeds its share of world GDP, then we conclude that the country is **abundant in that effective factor;** if its share of an effective factor is less than its share of world GDP, then we conclude that the country is **scarce in that effective factor.** We can illustrate this approach to measuring effective factor endowments using two examples: R&D scientists and arable land.

Effective R&D Scientists The productivity of an R&D scientist depends on the laboratory equipment, computers, and other types of material with which he or she has to work. R&D scientists working in different countries will not necessarily have the same productivities because the equipment they have available to them differs. A simple way to measure the equipment they have available is to use a country's *R&D spending per scientist*. If a country has more R&D spending per scientist, then its productivity will be higher, but if there is less R&D spending per scientist, then its productivity will be lower. To measure the effective number of R&D scientists in each country, we take the total number of scientists and multiply that by the R&D spending per scientist:

Effective R&D scientists = Actual R&D scientists • R&D spending per scientist

Using the R&D spending per scientist in this way to obtain effective R&D scientists is one method to correct for differences in the productivity of scientists across countries. It is not the only way to make such a correction because there are other measures that could be used for the productivity of scientists (e.g., we could use scientific publications available in a country, or the number of research universities). The advantage of using R&D spending per scientist is that this information is collected annually for many countries, so using this method to obtain a measure of effective R&D scientists means that we can easily compare the share of each country with the world total.[4] Those shares are shown in Figure 4-7.

In the first bar graph of Figure 4-7, we repeat from Figure 4-6 each country's share of world R&D scientists, not corrected for productivity differences. In the second bar graph, we show each country's share of effective scientists, using the R&D spending per scientist to correct for productivity. The United States had 26.1% of the world's total R&D scientists in 2000 (in the first bar) but 37.1% of the world's effective scientists (in the second bar). So the United States was more abundant in effective R&D scientists in 2000 than it was in the number of scientists. Likewise, Japan and India both had more shares of effective R&D scientists as compared with their number of scientists, with a 13.2% and 2.5% share of scientists for each country compared with 14% and 2.9% in the share of effective scientists, respectively. But China's share of R&D scientists fell by half when correcting for productivity, from a 14.1% share in the number of R&D scientists to a 7% share in effective R&D scientists. Since China's share of world GDP was 11.1% in 2000, it became scarce in effective R&D scientists once we made this productivity correction.

China has increased its spending on R&D in recent years and, according to news reports, exceeded the level of R&D spending in Japan for 2006 and later years. Even

---

[4] Notice that by correcting the number of R&D scientists by the R&D spending per scientist, we end up with the total R&D spending in each country: Effective R&D scientists = Actual R&D scientists • R&D spending per scientist = Total R&D spending. So a country's share of effective R&D scientists equals its share of world R&D spending.

FIGURE 4-7

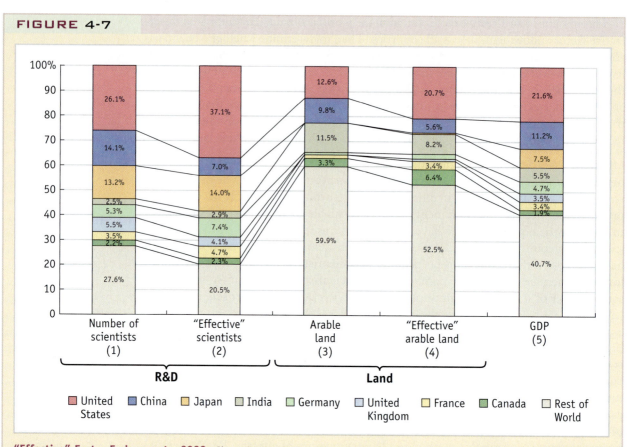

"Effective" Factor Endowments, 2000   Shown here are country shares of R&D scientists and land in 2000, using first the information from Figure 4.6, and then making an adjustment for the productivity of each factor across countries to obtain the "effective" shares. China was abundant in R&D scientists in 2000 (since it had 14% of the world's R&D scientists as compared with 11% of the world's GDP) but scarce in effective R&D scientists (because it had 7% of the world's effective R&D scientists as compared with 11% of the world's GDP). The United States was scarce in arable land when using the number of acres (since it had 13% of the world's land as compared with 22% of the world's GDP) but neither scarce nor abundant in effective land (since it had 21% of the world's effective land, which nearly equaled its share of the world's GDP).

Notes:
(1) The product of R&D researcher intensity and total population (World Bank, World Development Indicators). There are 55 countries included.
(2) R&D expenditure in units of purchasing power parity (World Bank, World Development Indicators). There are 74 countries included.
(3) Hectares of arable land (World Bank, World Development Indicators). There are 196 countries included.
(4) Productivity adjustment based on agriculture TFP estimation (based on data from the Food and Agriculture Organization of the United Nations). There are 152 countries included.
(5) Gross domestic product converted to 2000 international dollars using purchasing power parity rates (World Bank, World Development Indicators). There are 169 countries included.

when compared with the United States, China is taking the lead in some areas of R&D. An example is in research on "green" technologies, such as wind and solar power. As described in **Headlines: China Drawing High-Tech Research from U.S.,** American companies are now being attracted to China by a combination of inexpensive land and skilled labor. According to this article, we would expect China's share of effective R&D scientists to have grown significantly in recent years.

Effective Arable Land   As we did for R&D scientists, we also need to correct arable land for its differing productivity across countries. To make this correction, we use a

HEADLINES

China Drawing High-Tech Research from U.S.

Applied Materials, a well-known firm in Silicon Valley, recently announced plans to establish a large laboratory in Xi'an, China, as described in this article.

XI'AN, China—For years, many of China's best and brightest left for the United States, where high-tech industry was more cutting-edge. But Mark R. Pinto is moving in the opposite direction. Mr. Pinto is the first chief technology officer of a major American tech company to move to China. The company, Applied Materials, is one of Silicon Valley's most prominent firms. It supplied equipment used to perfect the first computer chips. Today, it is the world's biggest supplier of the equipment used to make semiconductors, solar panels and flat-panel displays.

In addition to moving Mr. Pinto and his family to Beijing in January, Applied Materials, whose headquarters are in Santa Clara, Calif., has just built its newest and largest research labs here. Last week, it even held its annu-al shareholders' meeting in Xi'an. It is hardly alone. Companies—and their engineers—are being drawn here more and more as China develops a high-tech economy that increasingly competes directly with the United States. . . .

Not just drawn by China's markets, Western companies are also attracted to China's huge reservoirs of cheap, highly skilled engineers—and the subsidies offered by many Chinese cities and regions, particularly for green energy companies. Now, Mr. Pinto said, researchers from the United States and Europe have to be ready to move to China if they want to do cutting-edge work on solar manufacturing because the new Applied Materials complex here is the only research center that can fit an entire solar panel assembly line. "If you really want to have an impact on this field, this is just such a tremendous laboratory," he said. . . .

Locally, the Xi'an city government sold a 75-year land lease to Applied Materials at a deep discount and is reimbursing the company for roughly a quarter of the lab complex's operating costs for five years, said Gang Zou, the site's general manager. The two labs, the first of their kind anywhere in the world, are each bigger than two American football fields. Applied Materials continues to develop the electronic guts of its complex machines at laboratories in the United States and Europe. But putting all the machines together and figuring out processes to make them work in unison will be done in Xi'an. The two labs, one on top of the other, will become operational once they are fully outfitted late this year. . . .

Source: Keith Bradsher, "China Drawing High-Tech Research from U.S.," The New York Times, March 17, 2010.

measure of agricultural productivity in each country. Then the effective amount of arable land found in a country is

$$\text{Effective arable land} = \text{Actual arable land} \cdot \text{Productivity in agriculture}$$

We will not discuss here the exact method for measuring productivity in agriculture, except to say that it compares the output in each country with the inputs of labor, capital, and land: countries with higher output as compared with inputs are the more productive, and countries with lower output as compared with inputs are the less productive. The United States has very high productivity in agriculture, whereas China has lower productivity.

In the third bar graph of Figure 4-7, we repeat from Figure 4-6 each country's share of arable land, not corrected for productivity differences. In the fourth bar graph, we show each country's share of effective arable land in 2000, corrected for productivity differences. The United States had 12.6% of the world's total arable land (in the third bar), as compared with 21.6% of the world's GDP (in the final bar), so it was scarce in land in 2000 without making any productivity correction. But when measured by effective arable land, the United States had 20.7% of the world's total (in the fourth bar), as compared with 21.6% of the world's GDP (in the final bar). These two numbers are so close that we should conclude *the United States was neither abundant nor scarce in effective arable land*: its share of the world's total approximately equaled its share of the world's GDP.

TABLE 4-2

U.S. Food Trade and Total Agricultural Trade, 2000–2009 This table shows that U.S. food trade has fluctuated between positive and negative net exports since 2000, which is consistent with our finding that the United States is neither abundant nor scarce in land. Total agriculture trade (including nonfood items like cotton) has positive net exports, however.

	2000	2001	2002	2003	2004	2005	2006	2007	2008	2009
U.S. food trade, 2000–2009 (billions of U.S. dollars)										
Exports	41.4	42.5	43.2	48.3	50.0	51.7	57.8	75.4	97.4	82.8
Imports	41.4	42.0	44.7	50.1	55.7	61.6	68.9	74.0	81.3	73.8
Net exports	0.0	0.5	−1.5	−1.8	−5.7	−9.9	−11.1	1.4	16.1	9.0
U.S. agricultural trade, 2000–2009 (billions of U.S. dollars)										
Exports	51.3	53.7	53.1	59.4	61.4	63.2	70.9	90.0	115.3	98.6
Imports	39.2	39.5	42.0	47.5	54.2	59.5	65.5	72.1	80.7	71.9
Net exports	12.1	14.1	11.1	11.9	7.2	3.7	5.5	17.9	34.6	26.7

Source: Total agricultural trade compiled by USDA using data from Census Bureau, U.S. Department of Commerce. U.S. food trade data provided by the USDA, Foreign Agricultural Service.

How does this conclusion compare with U.S. trade in agriculture? We often think of the United States as a major exporter of agricultural goods, but this pattern is changing. In Table 4-2, we show the U.S. exports and imports of food products and total agricultural trade. This table shows that U.S. food trade has fluctuated between positive and negative net exports since 2000, which is consistent with our finding that the United States is neither abundant nor scarce in land. Total agriculture trade (including nonfood items like cotton) continues to have positive net exports, however.

Leontief's Paradox Once Again

Our discussion of factor endowments in 2000 shows that it is possible for countries to be abundant in more that one factor of production: the United States and Japan are both abundant in physical capital and R&D scientists, and the United States is also abundant in skilled labor (see Figure 4-6). We have also found that it is sometimes important to correct that actual amount of a factor of production for its productivity, obtaining the effective factor endowment. Now we can apply these ideas to the United States in 1947 to reexamine the Leontief paradox.

Using a sample of 30 countries for which GDP information is available in 1947, the U.S. share of those countries' GDP was 37%. That estimate of the U.S. share of "world" GDP is shown in the last bar graph of Figure 4-8. To determine whether the United States was abundant in physical capital or labor, we need to estimate its share of the world endowments of these factors.

Capital Abundance It is hard to estimate the U.S. share of the world capital stock in the postwar years. But given the devastation of the capital stock in Europe and Japan due to World War II, we can presume that the U.S. share of world capital was more than 37%. That estimate (or really a "guesstimate") means that the U.S. share of world

FIGURE 4-8

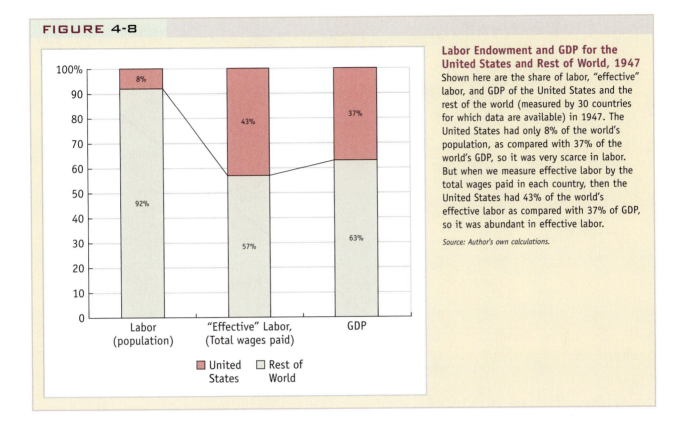

Labor Endowment and GDP for the United States and Rest of World, 1947
Shown here are the share of labor, "effective" labor, and GDP of the United States and the rest of the world (measured by 30 countries for which data are available) in 1947. The United States had only 8% of the world's population, as compared with 37% of the world's GDP, so it was very scarce in labor. But when we measure effective labor by the total wages paid in each country, then the United States had 43% of the world's effective labor as compared with 37% of GDP, so it was abundant in effective labor.

Source: Author's own calculations.

capital exceeds the U.S. share of world GDP, so that the United States was abundant in capital in 1947.

Labor Abundance What about the abundance of labor for the United States? If we do not correct labor for productivity difference across countries, then the population of each country is a rough measure of its labor force. The U.S. share of population for the sample of 35 countries in 1947 was very small, about 8%, which is shown in the first bar graph of Figure 4-8. This estimate of labor abundance is much less than the U.S. share of GDP, 37%. According to that comparison, the United States was scarce in labor (its share of that factor was less than its share of GDP).

Labor Productivity Using the U.S. share of population is not the right way to measure the U.S. labor endowment, however, because it does not correct for differences in the productivity of labor across countries. A good way to make that correction is to use wages paid to workers as a measure of their productivity. To illustrate why this is a good approach, in Figure 4-9 we plot the wages of workers in various countries and the estimated productivity of workers in 1990. The vertical axis in Figure 4-9 measures wages earned across a sample of 33 countries, measured relative to (i.e., as a percentage of) the United States. Only one country—Canada—has wages higher than those in the United States (probably reflecting greater union pressure in that country). All other countries have lower wages, ranging from Austria and Switzerland with wages that are about 95% of the U.S. wage, to Ireland, France, and Finland, with wages at about 50% of the U.S. level, to Bangladesh and Sri Lanka, with wages at about 5% of the U.S. level.

FIGURE 4-9

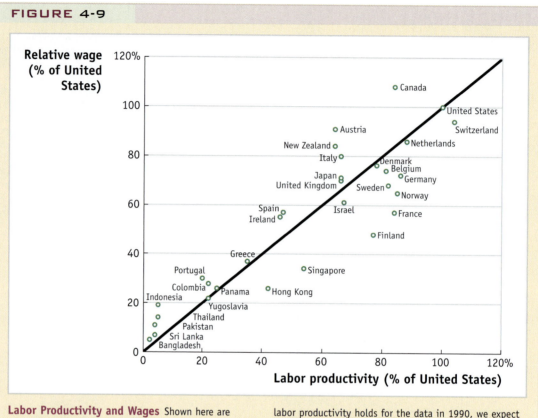

Labor Productivity and Wages Shown here are estimated labor productivities across countries, and their wages, relative to the United States in 1990. Notice that the labor and wages were highly correlated across countries: the points roughly line up along the 45-degree line. While this close connection between wages and labor productivity holds for the data in 1990, we expect that it also held in 1947, so that we can use wages to adjust for labor productivity in explaining the Leontief paradox.

Source: Daniel Trefler, 1993, "International Factor Price Differences: Leontief was Right!" Journal of Political Economy, 101(6), December, 961–987.

The horizontal axis in Figure 4-9 measures labor productivity in various countries relative to that in the United States. For example, labor productivity in Canada is 80% of that in the United States; labor productivity in Austria and New Zealand is about 60% of that in the United States; and labor productivity in Indonesia, Thailand, Pakistan, Sri Lanka, and Bangladesh is about 5% of that in the United States. Notice that the labor productivities (on the horizontal axis) and wages (on the vertical axis) are highly correlated across countries: the points in Figure 4-9 line up approximately along the 45-degree line. This close connection between wages and labor productivity holds for the data in 1990, we expect that it also held in 1947, so that we can use wages to adjust for labor productivity in explaining the Leontief Paradox.

Effective Labor Abundance As suggested by Figure 4-9, wages across countries are strongly correlated with the productivity of labor. Going back to the data for 1947, which Leontief used, we use the wages earned by labor to measure the productivity of labor in each country. Then the *effective* amount of labor found in each country equals the actual amount of labor times the wage. Multiplying the amount of labor in each country by average wages, we obtain total wages paid to labor. That information is available for 30 countries in 1947, and we have already found that the United States accounted for 37% of the GDP of these countries, as shown in the final bar in Figure 4-8. Adding up total wages paid to labor across the 30 countries and comparing it with the United States, we find that the United States accounted for 43% of wages paid to labor in these 30 countries, as shown in the bar labeled "effective" labor. By comparing this estimate with the United States share of world GDP of 37% in 1947, we see that the United States was abundant in effective labor, taking into account the differing productivity of labor across countries. So not only was the United States abundant in capital, it was also abundant in effective—or skilled—labor in 1947, just as we have also found for the year 2000!

Summary In Leontief's test of the Heckscher-Ohlin theorem, he found that the capital–labor ratio for exports from the United States in 1947 was less than the capital–labor ratio for imports. That finding seemed to contradict the Heckscher-Ohlin theorem if we think of the United States as being capital-abundant: in that case, it should be exporting capital-intensive goods (with a high capital–labor ratio). But now we have found that the United States was abundant in *both* capital *and* labor in 1947, once we correct for the productivity of labor by using its wage. Basically, the relatively low population and number of workers in the United States are boosted upward by high U.S. wages, making the effective labor force seem much larger—large enough so that the U.S. share of wordwide wages even exceeds its share of GDP.

Such a finding means the United States was *also* abundant in effective—or skilled—labor in 1947, just as it is today. Armed with this finding, it is not surprising that Leontief found exports from the United States in 1947 used relatively less capital and more labor than did imports: that pattern simply reflects the high productivity of labor in the United States and its abundance of this effective factor. As Leontief himself proposed, once we take into account differences in the productivity of factors across countries, there is no "paradox" after all, at least in the data for 1947. For more recent years, too, taking account of factor productivity differences across countries is important when testing the Heckscher-Ohlin theorem.[5]

3 Effects of Trade on Factor Prices

In the Heckscher-Ohlin model developed in the previous sections, Home exported computers and Foreign exported shoes. Furthermore, we found in our model that the relative price of computers *rose* at Home from the no-trade equilibrium to the trade equilibrium (this higher relative price with trade is why computers are exported). Conversely, the relative price of computers *fell* in Foreign from the no-trade equilibrium to the trade equilibrium (this lower relative price with trade is why computers are imported abroad). The question we ask now is how the changes in the relative prices of goods affect the wage paid to labor in each country and the rental earned by capital. We begin by showing how the wage and rental are determined, focusing on Home.

---

[5] Readers who want to learn more about testing the HO model can consult the appendix to this chapter, which further discusses the Leontief Paradox and summarizes factor endowment and trade data in a recent year.

Effect of Trade on the Wage and Rental of Home

To determine the wage and rental, we go back to Figure 4-1, which showed that the quantity of labor demanded relative to the quantity of capital demanded in each industry at Home depends on the relative wage at Home W/R. We can use these relative demands for labor in each industry to derive an economy-wide relative demand for labor, which can then be compared with the economy-wide relative supply of labor $\overline{L}/\overline{K}$. By comparing the economy-wide relative demand and supply, just as we do in any supply and demand context, we can determine Home's relative wage. Moreover, we can evaluate what happens to the relative wage when the Home relative price of computers rises after Home starts trading.

Economy-Wide Relative Demand for Labor To derive an economy-wide relative demand for labor, we use the conditions that the quantities of labor and capital used in each industry add up to the total available labor and capital: $L_C + L_S = \overline{L}$ and $K_C + K_S = \overline{K}$. We can divide total labor by total capital to get

$$\underbrace{\frac{\overline{L}}{\overline{K}}}_{\substack{\text{Relative} \\ \text{supply}}} = \frac{L_C + L_S}{\overline{K}} = \underbrace{\frac{L_C}{K_C} \cdot \left(\frac{K_C}{\overline{K}}\right) + \frac{L_S}{K_S} \cdot \left(\frac{K_S}{\overline{K}}\right)}_{\substack{\text{Relative} \\ \text{demand}}}$$

The left-hand side of this equation is the economy-wide supply of labor relative to capital, or relative supply. The right-hand side is the economy-wide demand for labor relative to capital, or relative demand. The relative demand is a weighted average of the labor–capital ratio in each industry. This weighted average is obtained by multiplying the labor–capital ratio for each industry, L_C/K_C and L_S/K_S, by the terms $K_C/\overline{K}$ and $K_S/\overline{K}$, the shares of total capital employed in each industry. These two terms must add up to 1, $(K_C/\overline{K}) + (K_S/\overline{K}) = 1$, because capital must be employed in one industry or the other.

The determination of Home's equilibrium relative wage is shown in Figure 4-10 as the intersection of the relative supply and relative demand curves. The supply of labor relative to the supply of capital, the relative supply $(\overline{L}/\overline{K})$, is shown as a vertical line

---

FIGURE 4·10

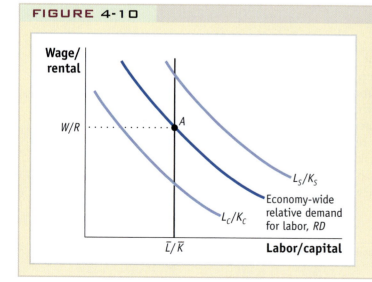

Determination of Home Wage/Rental The economy-wide relative demand for labor, *RD*, is an average of the L_C/K_C and L_S/K_S curves and lies between these curves. The relative supply, $\overline{L}/\overline{K}$, is shown by a vertical line because the total amount of resources in Home is fixed. The equilibrium point *A*, at which relative demand *RD* intersects relative supply $\overline{L}/\overline{K}$, determines the wage relative to the rental, *W/R*.

because the total amounts of labor and capital do not depend on the relative wage; they are fixed by the total amount of factor resources in each country. Because the relative demand (the RD curve in the graph) is an average of the L_C/K_C and L_S/K_S curves from Figure 4-1, it therefore lies *between* these two curves. The point at which relative demand intersects relative supply, point A, tells us that the wage relative to the rental is W/R (from the vertical axis). Point A describes an equilibrium in the labor and capital markets and combines these two markets into a single diagram by showing relative supply equal to relative demand.

Increase in the Relative Price of Computers

When Home opens itself to trade, it faces a higher relative price of computers; that is, P_C/P_S increases at Home. We illustrate this higher relative price using Home's production possibilities frontier in Figure 4-11. At the no-trade or autarky equilibrium, point A, the relative price of computers is $(P_C/P_S)^A$ and the computer industry produces Q_{C1}, while the shoe industry produces Q_{S1}. With a rise in the relative price of computers to $(P_C/P_S)^W$, the computer industry increases its output to Q_{C2}, and the shoe industry decreases its output to Q_{S2}. With this shift in production, labor and capital both move from shoe production to computer production. What is the effect of these resource movements on the relative supply and relative demand for labor?

The effects are shown in Figure 4-12. Relative supply $\overline{L}/\overline{K}$ is the same as before because the total amounts of labor and capital available in Home have not changed. The relative demand for labor changes, however, because capital has shifted to the computer industry. This shift affects the terms used in the weighted average: $(K_C/\overline{K})$ rises and $(K_S/\overline{K})$ falls. The relative demand for labor in the economy is now more weighted toward computers and less weighted toward the shoe industry. In Figure 4-12, the change in the weights shifts the relative demand curve from RD_1 to RD_2. The curve shifts in the direction of the relative demand curve for computers, and the equilibrium moves from point A to B.

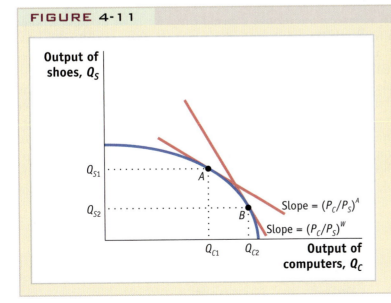

FIGURE 4-11

Output of shoes, Q_S

Q_{S1} ..... A

Q_{S2} ..... B

Slope = $(P_C/P_S)^A$

Slope = $(P_C/P_S)^W$

Q_{C1} Q_{C2} **Output of computers, Q_C**

Increase in the Price of Computers Initially, Home is at a no-trade equilibrium at point A with a relative price of computers of $(P_C/P_S)^A$. An increase in the relative price of computers to the world price, as illustrated by the steeper world price line, $(P_C/P_S)^W$, shifts production from point A to B. At point B, there is a higher output of computers and a lower output of shoes, $Q_{C2} > Q_{C1}$ and $Q_{S2} < Q_{S1}$.

FIGURE 4-12

1. An increase in the relative price of computers shifts the relative demand curve from RD_1 to RD_2.

2. The relative wage decreases from $(W/R)_1$ to $(W/R)_2$.

3. At the new relative wage, the labor/capital ratio in each industry increases.

Effect of a Higher Relative Price of Computers on Wage/Rental An increase in the relative price of computers shifts the economy-wide relative demand for labor, RD_1, toward the relative demand for labor in the computer industry, L_C/K_C. The new relative demand curve, RD_2, intersects the relative supply curve for labor at a lower relative wage, $(W/R)_2$. As a result, the wage relative to the rental falls from $(W/R)_1$ to $(W/R)_2$. The lower relative wage causes both industries to increase their labor–capital ratios, as illustrated by the increase in both L_C/K_C and L_S/K_S at the new relative wage.

The impacts on all the variables are as follows. First, the relative wage W/R falls from $(W/R)_1$ to $(W/R)_2$, reflecting the fall in the relative demand for labor as both factors move into computer production from shoe production. Second, the lower relative wage induces *both* industries to hire more workers per unit of capital (a move down along their relative demand curves). In the shoe industry, for instance, the new, lower relative wage $(W/R)_2$ intersects the relative demand curve for labor L_S/K_S at a point corresponding to a higher L/K level than the initial relative wage $(W/R)_1$. That is, $(L_S/K_S)_2 > (L_S/K_S)_1$, and the same argument holds for the computer industry. As a result, the labor–capital ratio rises in both shoes and computers.

How is it possible for the labor–capital ratio to rise in *both* industries when the amount of labor and capital available in total is fixed? The answer is that more labor per unit of capital is released from shoes than is needed to operate that capital in computers (because computers require fewer workers per machine). As the relative price of computers rises, computer output rises while shoe output falls, and labor is "freed up" to be used more in both industries. In terms of our earlier equation for relative supply and relative demand, the changes in response to the increase in the relative price of computers P_C/P_S are

$$\frac{\overline{L}}{\overline{K}} = \underbrace{\frac{L_C}{K_C} \cdot \left(\frac{K_C}{\overline{K}}\right)}_{} + \underbrace{\frac{L_S}{K_S} \cdot \left(\frac{K_S}{\overline{K}}\right)}_{}$$

$$\underbrace{\qquad}_{\substack{\text{Relative supply} \\ \text{No change}}} \qquad \underbrace{\uparrow \qquad \uparrow \qquad \uparrow \qquad \downarrow}_{\substack{\text{Relative demand} \\ \text{No change in total}}}$$

The relative supply of labor has not changed, so relative demand for labor cannot change overall. Since some of the individual components of relative demand have increased, other components must decrease to keep the overall relative demand the same. After the rise in the price of computers, even more capital will be used in the computer industry ($K_C/\overline{K}$ rises while $K_S/\overline{K}$ falls) because the output of computers rises and the output of shoes falls. This shift in weights on the right-hand side pulls down the overall relative demand for labor (this is necessarily true since $L_C/K_C < L_S/K_S$ by assumption). But because the relative supply on the left-hand side doesn't change, another feature must increase the relative demand for labor: this feature is the increased labor–capital ratios in *both* industries. In this way, relative demand continues to equal relative supply at point B, and at the same time, the labor–capital ratios have risen in both industries.

Determination of the Real Wage and Real Rental

To summarize, we have found that an increase in the relative price of computers—which are capital-intensive—leads to a fall in the relative wage (W/R). In turn, the decrease in the relative wage leads to an increase in the labor–capital ratio used in each industry (L_C/K_C and L_S/K_S). Our goal in this section is to determine who gains and who loses from these changes. For this purpose, it is not enough to know how the *relative* wage changes; instead, we want to determine the change in the *real wage* and *real rental*; that is, the change in the quantity of shoes and computers that each factor of production can purchase. With the results we have already obtained, it will be fairly easy to determine the change in the real wage and real rental.

Change in the Real Rental
Because the labor–capital ratio increases in both industries, the marginal product of capital also increases in both industries. This is because there are more people to work with each piece of capital. This result follows from our earlier argument that when a machine has more labor to work it, it will be more productive, and the marginal product of capital will go up. In both industries, the rental on capital is determined by its marginal product and by the prices of the goods:

$$R = P_C \cdot MPK_C \text{ and } R = P_S \cdot MPK_S$$

Because capital can move freely between industries in the long run, the rental on capital is equalized across them. By using the result that both marginal products of capital increase and by rearranging the previous equations, we see that

$$MPK_C = R/P_C \uparrow \text{ and } MPK_S = R/P_S \uparrow$$

Remember that R/P_C measures that quantity of computers that can be purchased with the rental, whereas R/P_S measures the quantity of shoes that can be bought with the rental. When both of these go up, the real rental on capital (in terms of either good) *increases*. Therefore, capital owners are clearly better off when the relative price of computers increases. Notice that computers is the capital-intensive industry, so the more general result is that *an increase in the relative price of a good will benefit the factor of production used intensively in producing that good.*

Change in the Real Wage
To understand what happens to the real wage when the relative price of computers rises, we again use the result that the labor–capital ratio increases in *both* industries. The law of diminishing returns tells us that the marginal product of labor must fall in both industries (since there are more workers on each

machine). In both industries, the wage is determined by the marginal product of labor and the prices of the goods:

$$W = P_C \cdot MPL_C \text{ and } W = P_S \cdot MPL_S$$

Using the result that the marginal product of labor falls in both industries, we see that

$$MPL_C = W/P_C \downarrow \text{ and } MPL_S = W/P_S \downarrow$$

Therefore, the quantity of computers that can be purchased with the wage (W/P_C) and the quantity of shoes that can be purchased with the wage (W/P_S) both fall. These decreases mean that the real wage (in terms of either good) is *reduced*, and labor is clearly worse off due to the increase in the relative price of computers.

We can summarize our results with the following theorem, first derived by economists Wolfgang Stolper and Paul Samuelson.

Stolper-Samuelson Theorem: In the long run, when all factors are mobile, an increase in the relative price of a good will increase the real earnings of the factor used intensively in the production of that good and decrease the real earnings of the other factor.

For our example, the **Stolper-Samuelson theorem** predicts that when Home opens to trade and faces a higher relative price of computers, the real rental on capital in Home rises and the real wage in Home falls. In Foreign, the changes in real factor prices are just the reverse. When Foreign opens to trade and faces a lower relative price of computers, the real rental falls and the real wage rises. Remember that Foreign is abundant in labor, so our finding that labor is better off there, but worse off at Home, means that workers in the labor-abundant country gain from trade but workers in the capital-abundant country lose. In addition, capital in the capital-abundant country (Home) gains, and capital in the labor-abundant country loses. These results are sometimes summarized by saying that in the Heckscher-Ohlin model, *the abundant factor gains from trade, and the scarce factor loses from trade.*[6]

Changes in the Real Wage and Rental: A Numerical Example

To illustrate the Stolper-Samuelson theorem, we use a numerical example to show how much the real wage and rental can change in response to a change in price. Suppose that the computer and shoe industries have the following data:

Computers: Sales revenue = $P_C \cdot Q_C = 100$

Earnings of labor = $W \cdot L_C = 50$

Earnings of capital = $R \cdot K_C = 50$

Shoes: Sales revenue = $P_S \cdot Q_S = 100$

Earnings of labor = $W \cdot L_S = 60$

Earnings of capital = $R \cdot K_S = 40$

---

[6] This result follows logically from combining the Heckscher-Ohlin theorem with the Stolper-Samuelson theorem.

Notice that shoes are more labor-intensive than computers: the share of total revenue paid to labor in shoes (60/100 = 60%) is more than that share in computers (50/100 = 50%).

When Home and Foreign undertake trade, the relative price of computers rises. For simplicity we assume that this occurs because the price of computers P_C rises, while the price of shoes P_S does not change:

$$\textit{Computers:} \qquad \text{Percentage increase in price} = \Delta P_C/P_C = 10\%$$

$$\textit{Shoes:} \qquad \text{Percentage increase in price} = \Delta P_S/P_S = 0\%$$

Our goal is to see how the increase in the relative price of computers translates into long-run changes in the wage W paid to labor and the rental on capital R. Remember that the rental on capital can be calculated by taking total sales revenue in each industry, subtracting the payments to labor, and dividing by the amount of capital. This calculation gives us the following formulas for the rental in each industry:[7]

$$R = \frac{P_C \cdot Q_C - W \cdot L_C}{K_C}, \text{ for computers}$$

$$R = \frac{P_S \cdot Q_S - W \cdot L_S}{K_S}, \text{ for shoes}$$

The price of computers has risen, so $\Delta P_C > 0$, holding fixed the price of shoes, $\Delta P_S = 0$. We can trace through how this affects the rental by changing P_C and W in the previous two equations:

$$\Delta R = \frac{\Delta P_C \cdot Q_C - \Delta W \cdot L_C}{K_C}, \text{ for computers}$$

$$\Delta R = \frac{0 \cdot Q_C - \Delta W \cdot L_S}{K_S}, \text{ for shoes}$$

It is convenient to work with percentage changes in the variables. For computers, $\Delta P_C/P_C$ is the percentage change in price. Similarly, $\Delta W/W$ is the percentage change in the wage, and $\Delta R/R$ is the percentage change in the rental of capital. We can introduce these terms into the preceding formulas by rewriting them as

$$\frac{\Delta R}{R} = \left(\frac{\Delta P_C}{P_C}\right)\left(\frac{P_C \cdot Q_C}{R \cdot K_C}\right) - \left(\frac{\Delta W}{W}\right)\left(\frac{W \cdot L_C}{R \cdot K_C}\right), \text{ for computers}$$

$$\frac{\Delta R}{R} = -\left(\frac{\Delta W}{W}\right)\left(\frac{W \cdot L_S}{R \cdot K_S}\right), \text{ for shoes}$$

(You should cancel terms in these equations to check that they are the same as before.)
Now we'll plug the above data for shoes and computers into these formulas:

$$\frac{\Delta R}{R} = 10\% \cdot \left(\frac{100}{50}\right) - \left(\frac{\Delta W}{W}\right)\left(\frac{50}{50}\right), \text{ for computers}$$

$$\frac{\Delta R}{R} = -\left(\frac{\Delta W}{W}\right)\left(\frac{60}{40}\right), \text{ for shoes}$$

---

[7] Remember that due to factor mobility, the rental is the same in each industry, but it is helpful here to derive two separate equations for the percentage change in rental by industry.

Our goal is to find out by how much rental and wage change given changes in the relative price of the final goods, so we are trying to solve for two unknowns ($\Delta R/R$ and $\Delta W/W$) from the two equations given here. A good way to do this is to reduce the two equations with two unknowns into a single equation with one unknown. This can be done by subtracting one equation from the other, as follows:

$$\frac{\Delta R}{R} = 10\% \cdot \left(\frac{100}{50}\right) - \left(\frac{\Delta W}{W}\right)\left(\frac{50}{50}\right), \text{ for computers}$$

Minus: $\quad \frac{\Delta R}{R} = 0 - \left(\frac{\Delta W}{W}\right)\left(\frac{60}{40}\right), \text{ for shoes}$

Equals: $\quad 0 = 10\% \cdot \left(\frac{100}{50}\right) + \left(\frac{\Delta W}{W}\right)\left(\frac{20}{40}\right)$

Simplifying the last line, we get $0 = 20\% + \left(\frac{\Delta W}{W}\right)\left(\frac{1}{2}\right)$, so that

$$\left(\frac{\Delta W}{W}\right) = \frac{-20\%}{\left(\frac{1}{2}\right)} = -40\%, \text{ is the change in wages}$$

So when the price of computers increases by 10%, the wage falls by 40%. With the wage falling, labor can no longer afford to buy as many computers (W/P_C has fallen since W is falling and P_C has increased) or as many pairs of shoes (W/P_S has fallen since W is falling and P_S has not changed). In other words, the *real wage* measured in terms of either good has *fallen*, so labor is clearly worse off.

To find the change in the rental paid to capital (R/R), we can take our solution for $W/W = -40\%$, and plug it into the equation for the change in the rental in the shoes[8] sector:

$$\frac{\Delta R}{R} = -\left(\frac{\Delta W}{W}\right)\left(\frac{60}{40}\right) = 40\% \cdot \left(\frac{60}{40}\right) = 60\%, \text{ change in rental}$$

The rental on capital increases by 60% when the price of computers rises by 10%, so the rental increases even more (in percentage terms) than the price. Because the rental increases by more than the price of computers in percentage terms, it follows that (R/P_C) rises: owners of capital can afford to buy more computers, even though their price has gone up. In addition, they can afford to buy more shoes (R/P_S also rises, since R rises and P_S is constant). Thus, the real rental measured in terms of either good has *gone up*, and capital owners are clearly better off.

General Equation for the Long-Run Change in Factor Prices

The long-run results of a change in factor prices can be summarized in the following equation:

$$\underbrace{\Delta W/W < 0}_{\substack{\text{Real wage} \\ \text{falls}}} < \underbrace{\Delta P_C/P_C < \Delta R/R}_{\substack{\text{Real rental} \\ \text{increases}}}, \text{ for an increase in } P_C$$

---

[8] You should check that you get the same answer if instead you plug the change in the wage into the formula for the change in the rental in the computer sector.

That is, the increase in the price of computers (10%) leads to an even larger increase in the rental on capital (60%) and a decrease in the wage (-40%). If, instead, the price of computers falls, then these inequalities are reversed, and we get

$$\underbrace{\Delta R/R < \Delta P_C/P_C}_{\substack{\text{Real rental} \\ \text{falls}}} < 0 < \underbrace{\Delta W/W}_{\substack{\text{Real wage} \\ \text{increases}}}, \text{ for an decrease in } P_C$$

What happens if the relative price of shoes increases? From the Stolper-Samuelson theorem, we know that this change will benefit labor, which is used intensively in shoe production, and will harm capital. The equation summarizing the changes in factor earnings when the price of shoes increases is

$$\underbrace{\Delta R/R < 0}_{\substack{\text{Real rental} \\ \text{falls}}} < \underbrace{\Delta P_S/P_S < \Delta W/W}_{\substack{\text{Real wage} \\ \text{increases}}}, \text{ for an increase in } P_S$$

These equations relating the changes in product prices to changes in factor prices are sometimes called the "magnification effect" because they show how changes in the prices of goods have *magnified effects* on the earnings of factors: even a modest fluctuation in the relative prices of goods on world markets can lead to exaggerated changes in the long-run earnings of both factors. This result tells us that some groups—those employed intensively in export industries—can be expected to support opening an economy to trade because an increase in export prices increases their real earnings. But other groups—those employed intensively in import industries—can be expected to oppose free trade because the decrease in import prices decreases their real earnings. The following application examines the opinions that different factors of production have taken toward free trade.

APPLICATION

Opinions toward Free Trade

Countries sometimes conduct surveys about their citizens' attitudes toward free trade. A survey conducted in the United States by the National Elections Studies (NES) in 1992 included the following question:

> Some people have suggested placing new limits on foreign imports in order to protect American jobs. Others say that such limits would raise consumer prices and hurt American exports. Do you favor or oppose placing limits on imports, or haven't you thought much about this?

Respondents to the survey could either answer that they "favor" placing limits on imports, meaning that they do not support free trade, or that they "oppose" limits on imports, meaning that they support free trade. How do these answers compare with characteristics of the respondents, such as their wages, skills, or the industries in which they work?

According to the specific-factors model, in the short run we do not know whether labor will gain or lose from free trade, but we do know that the specific factor in the export sector gains, and the specific factor in the import sector loses. Think about an extension of this model, in which, in addition to their wage, labor also earns some part of the rental on the specific factor in their industry. This assumption is true for farmers, for example, who work in agriculture and may own their land; it can also be true for workers in manufacturing if their salary includes a bonus that is based on the profits earned by capital. In those situations, we would expect that workers in export industries will support free trade (since the specific factor in that industry gains), but workers in import-competing industries will be against free trade (since the specific factor in that industry loses). In the short run, then, the *industry of employment* of workers will affect their attitudes toward free trade.

In the long-run Heckscher-Ohlin model, however, the industry of employment should not matter. According to the Stolper-Samuelson theorem, an increase in the relative price of exports will benefit the factor of production used intensively in exports and harm the other factor, regardless of the industry in which these factors of production actually work (remember that each factor of production earns the same wage or rental across industries in the long run). In the United States, export industries tend to use skilled labor intensively for research and development and other scientific work. An increase in the relative price of exports will benefit skilled labor in the long run, regardless of whether these workers are employed in export-oriented industries or import-competing industries. Conversely, an increase in the relative price of exports will harm unskilled labor, regardless of where these workers are employed. In the long run, then, the *skill level* of workers should determine their attitudes toward free trade.

In the 1992 NES survey, the industry of employment was somewhat important in explaining the respondents' attitudes toward free trade, but their skill level was much more important.[9] That is, workers in export-oriented industries are somewhat more likely to favor free trade, with those in import-competing industries favoring import restrictions, but this statistical relationship is not strong. A much more important determinant of the attitudes toward free trade is the skill level of workers, as measured by their wages or their years of education. Workers with lower wages or fewer years of education are more likely to favor import restrictions, whereas those with higher wages and more years of education favor free trade. This finding suggests that the respondents to the survey are basing their answer on their *long-run* earnings, as predicted by the Heckscher-Ohlin model and Stolper-Samuelson theorem, rather than on their short-run industry of employment, as predicted by the specific-factors model.

There is an interesting extension to these findings, however. The survey also asked respondents whether they owned a home. It turns out that people who own homes in communities in which the local industries face a lot of import competition are much more likely to oppose free trade. Examples of this are towns in the northeastern states where people have been employed by textiles mills, or in the midwestern states where people have been employed by automobile, steel, and other heavy industries. But people who own homes in communities in which the industries benefit from export opportunities, such as the high-tech areas in Boston or in Silicon Valley, California, are much more likely to support free trade. We can think of a house as a specific factor, since it cannot move locations. So the attitudes in this part of the NES survey conform to the short-run specific-factors model: people are very concerned about the asset value of their homes, just as the owners of specific factors in our model are concerned about the rental earned by the factor of production they own. ■

---

[9] See Kenneth F. Scheve and Matthew J. Slaughter, 2001, "What Determines Individual Trade-Policy Preferences?" *Journal of International Economics*, 54, 267–292.

4 Conclusions

The Heckscher-Ohlin framework is one of the most widely used models in explaining trade patterns. It isolates the effect of different factor endowments across countries and determines the impact of these differences on trade patterns, relative prices, and factor returns. This approach is a major departure from the view that technology differences determine trade patterns as we saw in the Ricardian model and is also a departure from the short-run specific-factors model that we studied in Chapter 3.

In this chapter, we have investigated some empirical tests of the Heckscher-Ohlin theorem; that is, tests to determine whether countries actually export the goods that use their abundant factor intensively. The body of literature testing the theorem originates in Leontief's puzzling finding that U.S. exports just after World War II were relatively labor-intensive. Although the original formulation of his test did not seem to support the HO theorem, later research has reformulated the test to measure the effective endowments of labor, capital, and other factors found in each country. Using this approach, we found that the United States was abundant in effective labor, and we also presume that it was abundant in capital. The United States had a positive factor content of net exports for both labor and capital in 1947, which is consistent with the finding of Leontief, so there was really no "paradox" after all.

By focusing on the factor intensities among goods (i.e., the relative amount of labor and capital used in production), the Heckscher-Ohlin model also provides clear guidance as to who gains and who loses from the opening of trade. In the specific-factors model, an increase in the relative price of a good leads to real gains for the specific factor used in that industry, losses for the other specific factor, and an ambiguous change in the real wage for labor. In contrast, the HO model predicts real gains for the factor used intensively in the export good, whose relative price goes up with the opening of trade, and real losses for the other factor. Having just two factors, both of which are fully mobile between the industries, leads to a very clear prediction about who gains and who loses from trade in the long run.

KEY POINTS

1. In the Heckscher-Ohlin model, we assume that the technologies are the same across countries and that countries trade because the available resources (labor, capital, and land) differ across countries.

2. The Heckscher-Ohlin model is a long-run framework, so labor, capital, and other resources can move freely between the industries.

3. With two goods, two factors, and two countries, the Heckscher-Ohlin model predicts that a country will export the good that uses its abundant factor intensively and import the other good.

4. The first test of the Heckscher-Ohlin model was made by Leontief using U.S. data for 1947. He found that U.S. exports were less capital-intensive and more labor-intensive than U.S. imports. This was a paradoxical finding because the United States was abundant in capital.

5. The assumption of identical technologies used in the Heckscher-Ohlin model does not hold in practice. Current research has extended the empirical tests of the Heckscher-Ohlin model to allow for many factors and countries, along with differing productivities of factors across countries. When we allow for different productivities

of labor in 1947, we find that the United States is abundant in effective—or skilled—labor, which explains the Leontief paradox.

6. According to the Stolper-Samuelson theorem, an increase in the relative price of a good will cause the real earnings of labor and capital to move in opposite directions: the factor used intensively in the industry whose relative price goes up will find its earnings increased, and the real earnings of the other factor will fall.

7. Putting together the Heckscher-Ohlin theorem and the Stolper-Samuelson theorem, we conclude that a country's abundant factor gains from the opening of trade (because the relative price of exports goes up), and its scarce factor loses from the opening of trade.

KEY TERMS

Heckscher-Ohlin model, p. 87
reversal of factor intensities, p. 92
free-trade equilibrium, p. 97
Heckscher-Ohlin theorem, p. 97
Leontief's paradox, p. 98

abundant in that factor, p. 100
scarce in that factor, p. 100
effective labor force, p. 102
effective factor endowment,
 p. 102

abundant in that effective factor,
 p. 103
scarce in that effective factor,
 p. 103
Stolper-Samuelson theorem,
 p. 114

PROBLEMS

1. This problem uses the Heckscher-Ohlin model to predict the direction of trade. Consider the production of handmade rugs and assembly line robots in Canada and India.

   a. Which country would you expect to be relatively labor-abundant, and which is capital-abundant? Why?

   b. Which industry would you expect to be relatively labor-intensive, and which is capital-intensive? Why?

   c. Given your answers to (a) and (b), draw production possibilities frontiers for each country. Assuming that consumer preferences are the same in both countries, add indifference curves and relative price lines (without trade) to your PPF graphs. What do the slopes of the price lines tell you about the direction of trade?

   d. Allowing for trade between countries, redraw the graphs and include a "trade triangle" for each country. Identify and label the vertical and horizontal sides of the triangles as either imports or exports.

2. Leontief's paradox is an example of testing a trade model using actual data observations. If Leontief had observed that the amount of labor needed per $1 million of U.S. exports was 100 person-years instead of 182, would he have reached the same conclusion? Explain.

3. Suppose there are drastic technological improvements in shoe production at Home such that shoe factories can operate almost completely with computer-aided machines. Consider the following data for the Home country:

Computers: Sales revenue = $P_C Q_C = 100$

Payments to labor = $WL_C = 50$

Payments to capital = $RK_C = 50$

Percentage increase in the price = $\Delta P_C/P_C = 0\%$

Shoes: Sales revenue = $P_S Q_S = 100$

Payments to labor = $WL_S = 5$

Payments to capital = $RK_S = 95$

Percentage increase in the price = $\Delta P_S/P_S = 50\%$

a. Which industry is capital-intensive? Is this a reasonable question, given that some industries are capital-intensive in some countries and labor-intensive in others?

b. Given the percentage changes in output prices in the data provided, calculate the percentage change in the rental on capital.

c. How does the magnitude of this change compare with that of labor?

d. Which factor gains in real terms, and which factor loses? Are these results consistent with the Stolper-Samuelson theorem?

4. Using the information in the chapter, suppose Home doubles in size, while Foreign remains the same. Show that an equal proportional increase in capital and labor at Home will change the relative price of computers, wage, rental on capital, and the amount traded but not the pattern of trade.

5. Using a diagram similar to Figure 4-12, show the effect of a decrease in the relative price of computers in Foreign. What happens to the wage relative to the rental? Is there an increase in the labor–capital ratio in each industry? Explain.

6. Suppose when Russia opens to trade, it imports automobiles, a capital-intensive good.

a. According to the Heckscher-Ohlin theorem, is Russia capital-abundant or labor-abundant? Briefly explain.

b. What is the impact of opening trade on the real wage in Russia?

c. What is the impact of opening trade on the real rental on capital?

d. Which group (capital owner or labor) would support policies to limit free trade? Briefly explain.

7. In Figure 4-3, we show how the movement from the no-trade equilibrium point A to a trade equilibrium at a higher relative price of computers leads to an upward-sloping export supply, from points A to D in panel (b).

a. Suppose that the relative price of computers continues to rise in panel (a), and label the production and consumption points at several higher prices.

b. In panel (b), extend the export supply curve to show the quantity of exports at the higher relative prices of computers.

c. What happens to the export supply curve when the price of computers is high enough? Can you explain why this happens? *Hint:* An increase in the relative price of a country's export good means that the country is richer because its terms of trade have improved. Explain how that can lead to fewer exports as their price rises.

8. In 2008 the Ukraine successfully negotiated terms to become a member of the World Trade Organization. Consequently, countries such as those in western Europe are shifting toward free trade with the Ukraine. What does the Stolper-Samuelson theorem predict about the impact of the shift on the real wage of unskilled labor in western Europe? In the Ukraine?

9. The following are data on U.S. exports and imports in 2007 at the two-digit Harmonized Schedule (HS) level. Which products do you think support the Heckscher-Ohlin theorem? Which products are inconsistent?

HS Code	Product	Export ($ billions)	Import ($ billions)
22	Beverages	3.6	14.7
30	Pharmaceutical products	40.7	55.6
52	Cotton	4.9	0.8
61	Apparel	1.9	33.3
64	Footwear	1.0	17.6
72	Iron and steel	15.4	12.4
74	Copper	5.0	6.4
85	Electric machinery	124.9	212.1
87	Vehicles	73.6	131.9
88	Aircraft	83.0	18.4
94	Furniture	7.0	30.1
95	Toys	7.0	27.6

Source: International Trade Administration, U.S. Department of Commerce.

10. Following are data for soybean yield, production, and trade for 2007:

Suppose that the countries listed in the table are engaged in free trade and that soybean production is land-intensive. Answer the following:

a. In which countries does land benefit from free trade in soybeans? Explain.

b. In which countries does land lose from free trade in soybeans? Explain.

c. In which countries does the move to free trade in soybeans have little or no effect on the land rental? Explain.

	Yield (metric ton/hectare)	Production (100,000 metric ton)	Export (100,000 metric ton)	Imports (100,000 metric ton)
Australia	2.44	3.2	0.3	1.0
Brazil	2.81	5,785.7	2,373.4	9.8
Canada	2.30	269.6	186.8	21.3
China	1.45	1,272.5	45.7	3,315.0
France	2.60	8.5	1.7	49.4
Ireland	3.13	40.8	2.0	8.4
Japan	1.64	22.7	0.1	416.1
Mexico	1.41	8.8	0.0	361.1
Russian Federation	0.92	65.0	1.7	12.5
United States	2.81	7,286.0	2,984.0	27.6

Source: Food and Agriculture Organization.

11. According to the Heckscher-Ohlin model, two countries can equalize wage differences by either engaging in international trade in goods or allowing skilled and unskilled labor to freely move between the two countries. Discuss whether this is true or false, and explain why.

12. According to the standard Heckscher-Ohlin model with two factors (capital and labor) and two goods, movement of Turkish migrants to Germany would decrease the amount of capital-intensive products produced in Germany. Discuss whether this is true or false, and explain why.

N E T W O R K

See the New Balance plant in Skowhegan, Maine, at http://www.youtube.com/watch?v=ittvWwCS5QI. What shoes are produced there, and what is the "Super Team 33"?

APPENDIX TO CHAPTER 4

The Sign Test in the Heckscher-Ohlin Model

Modern research on the Heckscher-Ohlin (HO) model allows for many goods, factors, and countries as well as differing technologies across countries. In this appendix, we discuss a method called the "sign test" that can be used to test the HO model. In addition to allowing for many goods, factors, and countries, the sign test can also be extended to allow for differing technologies across countries.

Measuring the Factor Content of Trade

The first question is, How do we measure the factor intensity of exports and imports when there are thousands of products traded between countries? How can we summarize all that information into categories that allow us to test the Heckscher-Ohlin model?

It turns out that Leontief's test gives us a good way to answer this question. Recall that Leontief measured the amount of labor and capital used to produce $1 million worth of U.S. exports and $1 million worth of U.S. imports. His numbers are shown in the second and fourth columns of Table 4A-1. If we multiply his numbers shown in Table 4A-1 by the actual value of U.S. exports, which were $16,700 million in 1947, and U.S. imports, which were $6,200 million, we obtain the values for "total exports" and "total imports" shown in Table 4A-1. These values are called the "factor content of exports" and "factor content of imports," respectively, and they measure the amounts of labor and capital used to produce exports and imports.

TABLE 4A-1

Factor Content of Trade for the United States, 1947 This table extends Leontief's test of the Heckscher-Ohlin model to measure the factor content of net exports. The first column for exports and for imports shows the amount of capital or labor needed per $1 million worth of exports from or imports into the United States, for 1947. The second column for each shows the amount of capital or labor needed for the total exports from or imports into the United States. The final column is the difference between the totals for exports and imports.

	EXPORTS, X		IMPORTS, M		NET EXPORTS (X − M)
	For $1 Million Exports	For Total Exports	For $1 Million Imports	For Total Imports	
Capital ($ millions)	2.55	42,600	3.1	19,200	23,400
Labor (person-years)	182	3.04 million	170	1.05 million	2 million
Capital/labor ($/person)	14,000	14,000	18,200	18,200	16,700

Source: Edward E. Leamer, 1980, "The Leontief Paradox, Reconsidered," Journal of Political Economy, 88(3), 495–503. Reprinted in Edward E. Leamer, ed., 2001, International Economics (New York: Worth), pp. 142–149.

By taking the difference between the factor content of exports and the factor content of imports, we obtain the *factor content of net exports*, shown in the final column of Table 4A-1. In 1947 the net exports of the United States required $23.4 billion worth of capital and 2 million person-years. The fact that both these factor contents are positive indicates that the United States was running a trade surplus (with the value of exports greater than the value of imports) that year. This finding is not surprising. The United States exported large amounts of goods to help the countries of Europe rebuild after the devastation of World War II (which had just ended in 1945).

The Sign Test

We make use of the factor content of trade in developing a test for the Heckscher-Ohlin model, called the sign test. This test states that if a country is abundant in an effective factor, then that factor's content in net exports should be positive, but if a country is scarce in an effective factor, then that factor's content in net exports should be negative. To measure whether a factor is abundant or scarce in a country, we compare the amount of the effective factor found there with that country's share of world GDP, as we did in Figures 4-7 and 4-8. So the form of the sign test is as follows:

Sign of (country's % share of effective factor − % share of world GDP)

= Sign of country's factor content of net exports

For example, the finding in Table 4A-1 that the United States was a net exporter of capital in 1947, as measured by its factor content of net exports, means that according to the sign test, it should also be abundant in capital. That prediction from the sign test is confirmed in our discussion on pages 106–107, where we argued that the U.S. share of the world capital stock in 1947 exceeds its share of world GDP. Likewise, the finding in Table 4A-1 that the United States was a net exporter of labor in 1947 means that according to the sign test, it should also be abundant in effective labor. That prediction is also confirmed in Figure 4-8, where we show that the U.S. share of the world effective labor in 1947 (43%) exceeds its share of world GDP (37%).

The Sign Test in a Recent Year

We now turn to the sign test in a recent year—1990—using 9 factors of production and 33 countries. The factors of production are capital; seven kinds of labor (professional, technical, clerical, sales, service, agricultural, and production workers); and two kinds of arable land (cropland and pasture). We allow capital, seven types of labor, and two types of land to differ in their productivities across countries.

The countries include poor nations, middle-income nations, and countries with per capita incomes nearly equal to those in the United States. Like Leontief, we use the technology of the United States to construct the factor contents of net exports. With 33 countries and 9 factors, there are 33 · 9 = 297 sign tests that can be made. Rather than show the results for every country, we instead group the nations by their GDP per capita, from lowest to highest. The results of the sign test are shown in Table 4A-2.

For the countries with low GDP per capita (less than one-third of the U.S. level), the first row of Table 4A-2 shows that, on average, nearly 6 out of 9 effective factors pass the sign test. When we consider the middle-income countries (with GDP per capita between one-third and two-thirds of the U.S. level), the sign test passes for 5.7 out of

TABLE 4A-2

The Sign Test for 33 Countries with Differing Technologies, 1990 This table shows the sign test for the Heckscher-Ohlin model for 1990, allowing for different technologies across countries. There are 33 countries included in the study and 9 factors of production. All countries have more factors passing the sign test than failing it, especially the low- and medium-income countries. These results show that the sign test holds true when we allow productivities to differ across countries.

Country Group	GDP per Capita (% of U.S. GDP)	Number of Factors Passing Sign Test	Number of Factors Failing Sign Test
Lowest GDP per capita	4–33	5.9	3.1
Middle GDP per capita	33–66	5.7	3.3
Highest GDP per capita	66–100	5.3	3.7
All countries	4–100	5.6	3.4

Note: The countries with low GDP per capita are Bangladesh, Pakistan, Indonesia, Sri Lanka, Thailand, Colombia, Panama, Yugoslavia, Portugal, and Uruguay. The countries with middle GDP per capita are Greece, Ireland, Spain, Israel, Hong Kong, New Zealand, and Austria. The countries with high GDP per capita are Singapore, Italy, the United Kingdom, Japan, Belgium, Trinidad, the Netherlands, Finland, Denmark, former West Germany, France, Sweden, Norway, Switzerland, Canada, and the United States.

Source: Computed from Daniel Trefler, 1995, "The Case of Missing Trade and Other Mysteries," American Economic Review, 85(5), December, 1029–1046. Reprinted in Edward E. Leamer, ed., 2001, International Economics (New York: Worth), pp. 151–175.

9 factors, on average, which is again close to 6 out of 9. In contrast, for the richest countries, the sign test using effective factors of production does not perform as well, passing for 5.3 factors out of 9, while failing for 3.7 factors. Combining all the countries, the sign test is successful in more than one-half of the cases (passing for 5.6 factors out of 9, on average). These results show that the predictions of the Heckscher-Ohlin model hold true, especially for low- and medium-income countries, when they are tested on a global dataset for a recent year.

Movement of Labor and Capital between Countries

After World War I, laws were passed severely limiting immigration. Only a trickle of immigrants has been admitted since then. . . . By keeping labor supply down, immigration policy tends to keep wages high.

Paul Samuelson, *Economics*, 1964

Amidst growing dissent, housing and job shortages as well as a plummeting economy, Cuban Premier Fidel Castro withdrew his guards from the Peruvian embassy in Havana on April 4, 1980. . . . Less than 48 hours after the guards were removed, throngs of Cubans crowded into the lushly landscaped gardens at the embassy, requesting asylum. . . . By mid-April, Carter issued a Presidential Memorandum allowing up to 3,500 refugees sanctuary in the U.S. . . . But the Carter Administration was taken by surprise when on April 21, refugees started arriving on Florida's shores—their numbers would eventually reach 125,000.

"Memories of Mariel, 20 Years Later"[1]

From May to September 1980, boatloads of refugees from Cuba arrived in Miami, Florida. For political reasons, Fidel Castro had allowed them to leave freely from the port of Mariel, Cuba, during that brief period of time. Known as "the Mariel boat lift," this influx of about 125,000 refugees to Miami increased the city's Cuban population by 20% and its overall population by about 7%. The widespread unemployment of many of the refugees during the summer of 1980 led many people to expect that the wages of other workers in Miami would be held down by the Mariel immigrants.

Not surprisingly, the refugees were less skilled than the other workers in Miami, as is confirmed by looking at their wages: the immigrants initially earned about one-third less than other Cubans in Miami. What is surprising, however, is that this influx

---

[1] Judy L. Silverstein, "Memories of Mariel, 20 Years Later," *U.S. Coast Guard Reservist*, 47(3), April/May 2000, electronic edition.

of low-skilled immigrants does not appear to have pulled down the wages of other less skilled workers in Miami.[2] The wages for low-skilled workers in Miami essentially followed national trends over this period, despite the large inflow of workers from Cuba. This finding seems to contradict the prediction of basic supply and demand theory—that a higher supply of workers should bid down their wage and that restricting immigration will raise the wages for local workers. This is the principle stated by Paul Samuelson in the quote at the beginning of this chapter. The fact that wages in Miami did not respond to the inflow of Mariel refugees calls for an explanation, which is one goal of this chapter.

A similar outcome occurred in a more recent case of sudden migration, the emigration of Russian Jews to Israel after 1989, when the Soviet Union relaxed its restrictions on such departures. From late 1989 to 1996, some 670,000 Russian Jews emigrated to Israel, which increased the population in Israel by 11% and its workforce by 14%. This wave of immigration was especially notable because the Russian immigrants were more highly skilled than the existing Israeli population. But despite this large influx of immigrants, the relative wages of high-skilled workers in Israel actually *rose* during the 1990s. Careful studies of this episode can find little or no negative impact of the Russian immigrants on the wages of other high-skilled workers.[3]

These emigrations were of different types of workers—the Cuban workers were low-skilled and the Russian emigrants high-skilled—but they share the finding that large inflows of workers need not depress wages in the areas where they settle. In other cases of large-scale migration—such as occurred from Europe to America during the 1800s and 1900s—wages did indeed fall due to the inflow of immigrants. So the Mariel boat lift and Russian emigration to Israel should be seen as special: they are cases in which the economic principles of supply and demand do not at first glance work as we would expect them to.

In this chapter, we begin our study of the movement of labor across countries by explaining the case in which immigration leads to a fall in wages, as we normally expect. The model we use is the **specific-factors model,** the short-run model introduced in Chapter 3. That model allows labor to move between industries but keeps capital and land specific to each industry. To study migration, we allow labor to move between countries as well as industries, while still keeping capital and land specific to each industry.

Next, we use the long-run Heckscher-Ohlin model, from Chapter 4, in which capital and land can also move between industries. In the long run, an increase in labor *will not* lower the wage, as illustrated by the Mariel boat lift to Miami and the Russian emigration to Israel. This outcome occurs because industries have more time to respond to the inflow of workers by adjusting their outputs. It turns out that by adjusting industry output enough, the economy can absorb the new workers without changing the wage for existing workers. The explanation for this surprising outcome relies on the assumption that industries are able to sell their outputs on international markets.

To give a brief idea of how this long-run explanation will work, think about the highly skilled scientists and engineers emigrating from Russia to Israel. The only

[2] See David Card, January 1990, "The Impact of the Mariel Boatlift on the Miami Labor Market," *Industrial Labor Relations Review*, 43(2), 245–257.

[3] See Neil Gandal, Gordon Hanson, and Matthew Slaughter, 2004, "Technology, Trade and Adjustment to Immigration in Israel," *European Economic Review*, 48(2), 403–428.

way to employ the large number of these workers at the going wages would be to increase the number of scientific and engineering projects in which Israeli companies are engaged. Where does the demand for these new projects come from? It is unlikely this demand would be generated in Israel alone, and more likely that it would come from Israeli *exports* to the rest of the world. We see then that the ability of Israel to export products making use of the highly skilled immigrants is essential to our explanation: with international demand, it is possible for the Russian immigrants to be fully employed in export activities without lowering wages in Israel. Likewise, with the influx of low-skilled Cuban immigrants to Miami, many of whom could work in the textile and apparel industry or in agriculture, it is the ability of Florida to export those products that allows the workers to be employed at the going wages.

After studying what happens in the short run and long run when labor moves across countries, we study the effects of foreign direct investment (FDI), the movement of capital across countries. FDI occurs when a company from one country owns a company in another country. We conclude the chapter by discussing the gains to the host and destination countries, and to the world, from the movement of labor or capital between countries.

1 Movement of Labor between Countries: Migration

We begin with the examples of labor migration described by the Mariel boat lift and the Russian migration to Israel. We can think of each migration as a movement of labor from the Foreign country to the Home country. What is the impact of this movement of labor on wages paid at Home? To answer this question, we make use of our work in Chapter 3, in which we studied how the wages paid to labor and the rentals paid to capital and land are determined by the prices of the goods produced. The prices of goods themselves are determined by supply and demand in world markets. In the analysis that follows, we treat the prices of goods as fixed and ask how the Home wage and the rentals paid to capital and land change as labor moves between countries.

Effects of Immigration in the Short Run: Specific-Factors Model

We begin our study of the effect of factor movements between countries by using the specific-factors model we learned in Chapter 3 to analyze the short run, when labor is mobile among Home industries, but land and capital are fixed. After that, we consider the long run, when all factors are mobile among industries at Home.

Determining the Wage Figure 5-1 shows a diagram that we used in Chapter 3 to determine the equilibrium wage paid to labor. The horizontal axis measures the total amount of labor in the economy $\overline{L}$, which consists of the labor used in manufacturing L_M and the amount used in agriculture L_A:

$$L_M + L_A = \overline{L}$$

In Figure 5-1, the amount of labor used in manufacturing L_M is measured from left (0_M) to right, and the amount of labor used in agriculture L_A is measured from right (0_A) to left.

FIGURE 5-1

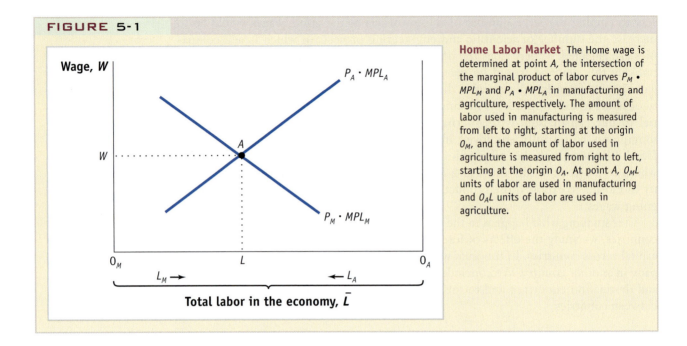

Home Labor Market The Home wage is determined at point A, the intersection of the marginal product of labor curves $P_M \cdot MPL_M$ and $P_A \cdot MPL_A$ in manufacturing and agriculture, respectively. The amount of labor used in manufacturing is measured from left to right, starting at the origin 0_M, and the amount of labor used in agriculture is measured from right to left, starting at the origin 0_A. At point A, $0_M L$ units of labor are used in manufacturing and $0_A L$ units of labor are used in agriculture.

The two curves in Figure 5-1 take the marginal product of labor in each sector and multiply it by the price (P_M or P_A) in that sector. The graph of $P_M \cdot MPL_M$ is downward-sloping because as more labor is used in manufacturing, the marginal product of labor in that industry declines, and wages fall. The graph of $P_A \cdot MPL_A$ for agriculture is upward-sloping because we are measuring the labor used in agriculture L_A from *right to left* in the diagram: as more labor is used in agriculture (moving from right to left), the marginal product of labor in agriculture falls, and wages fall.

The equilibrium wage is at point A, the intersection of the marginal product curves $P_M \cdot MPL_M$ and $P_A \cdot MPL_A$ in Figure 5-1. At this point, $0_M L$ units of labor are used in manufacturing, and firms in that industry are willing to pay the wage $W = P_M \cdot MPL_M$. In addition, $0_A L$ units of labor are used in agriculture, and farmers are willing to pay the wage $W = P_A \cdot MPL_A$. Because wages are equal in the two sectors, there is no reason for labor to move between them, and the Home labor market is in equilibrium.

In the Foreign country, a similar diagram applies. We do not draw this but assume that the equilibrium wage abroad W^* is less than W in Home. This assumption would apply to the Cuban refugees, for example, who moved to Miami and to the Russian emigrants who moved to Israel to earn higher wages as well as enjoy more freedom. As a result of this difference in wages, workers from Foreign would want to immigrate to Home and the Home workforce would increase by an amount ΔL, reflecting the number of immigrants.

Effect of Immigration on the Wage in Home The effects of immigration are shown in Figure 5-2. Because the number of workers at Home has grown by ΔL, we expand the size of the horizontal axis from $\bar{L}$ to $\bar{L}' = \bar{L} + \Delta L$. The right-most point on the horizontal axis, which is the origin 0_A for the agriculture industry, shifts to the right by the amount ΔL. As this origin moves rightward, it carries along with it the

FIGURE 5-2

Wage, W

$P_A \cdot MPL_A$

ΔL

A

W

$(P_A \cdot MPL_A)'$

B

W'

$P_M \cdot MPL_M$

0_M L L' 0_A $0_A'$

$L_M \rightarrow$ $\leftarrow L_A$

$\overline{L}$ ΔL

$\overline{L}'$

Increase in Home labor due to immigration

Increase in Home Labor When the amount of labor at Home increases by the amount ΔL, the origin for agriculture shifts to the right by that amount, from 0_A to $0_A'$. The marginal product of labor curve in agriculture also shifts right by the amount ΔL. Equilibrium in the Home labor market is now at point B: wages have fallen to W' and the amount of labor has increased in manufacturing (to $0_M L'$) and in agriculture (to $0_A' L'$).

marginal product curve $P_A \cdot MPL_A$ for the agriculture industry (because the marginal product of labor curve is graphed relative to its origin). That curve shifts to the right by exactly the amount ΔL, the increase in the Home workforce. There is no shift in the marginal product curve $P_M \cdot MPL_M$ for the manufacturing industry because the origin 0_M for manufacturing has not changed.[4]

The new equilibrium Home wage is at point B, the intersection of the marginal product curves. At the new equilibrium, the wage is lower. Notice that the extra workers ΔL arriving at Home are shared between the agriculture and manufacturing industries: the number of workers employed in manufacturing is now $0_M L'$, which is higher than $0_M L$, and the number of workers employed in agriculture is $0_A' L'$, which is also higher than $0_A L$.[5] Because both industries have more workers but fixed amounts of capital and land, the wage in both industries declines due to the diminishing marginal product of labor.

We see, then, that the specific-factors model predicts that an inflow of labor will lower wages in the country in which the workers are arriving. This prediction has been confirmed in numerous episodes of large-scale immigration, as described in the applications that follow.

---

[4] If, instead, we had added labor to the left-hand side of the graph, the origin and marginal product curve for manufacturing would have shifted and those of agriculture would have remained the same, yielding the same final results as in Figure 5-2—the wage falls and both industries use more labor.

[5] We know that the number of workers employed in agriculture rises because the increase in workers in manufacturing, from $0_M L$ to $0_M L'$, is less than the total increase in labor ΔL.

Immigration to the New World

Between 1870 and 1913, some 30 million Europeans left their homes in the "Old World" to emigrate to the "New World" of North and South America and Australia. The population of Argentina rose by 60% due to immigration, and Australia and Canada gained 30% more people. The population of the United States increased by 17% as a result of immigration (and it absorbed the largest number of people, more than 15 million). The migrants left the Old World for the opportunities present in the New and, most important, for the higher real wages. In Figure 5-3, we show an index of average real wages in European countries and in the New World (an average of the United States, Canada, and Australia).[6] In 1870 real wages were nearly three times higher in the New World than in Europe—120 as compared with 40.

Real wages in both locations grew over time as capital accumulated and raised the marginal product of labor. But due to the large-scale immigration to the New World, wages grew more slowly there. By 1913, just before the onset of World War I, the wage index in the New World was at 160, so real wages had grown by $(160 - 120)/120 = 33\%$ over 43 years. In Europe, however, the wage index reached 75 by 1913, an increase of $(75 - 40)/40 = 88\%$ over 43 years. In 1870 real wages in the New World were three times as high as those in Europe, but by 1913 this wage gap was substantially reduced, and

FIGURE 5-3

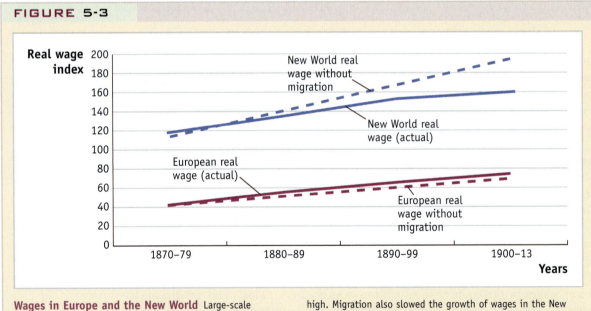

Wages in Europe and the New World Large-scale migration from Europe to the New World in America and Australia closed the wage gap between the two locations. In 1870 wages in the New World were almost three times as high as wages in Europe, whereas in 1910 they were about twice as high. Migration also slowed the growth of wages in the New World relative to what they would have been without migration and allowed for slightly faster growth of wages in Europe.

Source: Alan M. Taylor and Jeffrey G. Williamson, 1997, "Convergence in the Age of Mass Migration," European Review of Economic History, 1, April, 27–63.

---

[6] From Alan M. Taylor and Jeffrey G. Williamson, 1997, "Convergence in the Age of Mass Migration," *European Review of Economic History*, 1, April, 27–63.

wages in the New World were only about twice as high as those in Europe. Large-scale migration therefore contributed to a "convergence" of real wages across the continents.

In Figure 5-3, we also show estimates of what real wages would have been if migration had not occurred. Those estimates are obtained by calculating how the marginal product of labor would have grown with capital accumulation but without the immigration. Comparing the actual real wages with the no-migration estimates, we see that the growth of wages in the New World was slowed due to immigration (workers arriving), while wages in Europe grew slightly faster due to emigration (workers leaving). ■

APPLICATION

Immigration to the United States and Europe Today

The largest amount of migration is no longer from Europe to the "New World." Instead, workers from developing countries immigrate to wealthier countries in the European Union and North America, when they can. In many cases, the immigration includes a mix of low-skilled workers and high-skilled workers. During the 1960s and 1970s, some European countries actively recruited guest workers, called *gastarbeiters* in West Germany, to fill labor shortages in unskilled jobs. Many of these foreign workers have remained in Germany for years, some for generations, so they are no longer "guests" but long-term residents. At the end of 1994, about 2.1 million foreigners were employed in western Germany, with citizens of Turkey, the former Yugoslavia, Greece, and Italy representing the largest groups.

Today, the European Union has expanded to include many of the countries in Eastern Europe, and in principle there is free migration within the European Union.[7] In practice, it can still be difficult for countries to absorb all the workers who want to enter, whether they come from within or outside the Union. That especially has been the case during the recent downturn in the global economy, as described in **Headlines: Europe Sours on Labor Migration.**

In the United States, immigration policy is debated in Congress nearly every year. Indeed, after jobs and health care, immigration ranks among the top issues in surveys of voters. On the same day as the historic vote on health care in the House of Representatives, March 21, 2009, there was a large rally in Washington, D.C., for immigration reform, including a procedure by which illegal immigrants can become legal. It is estimated that there are about 12 million illegal immigrants in the United States, many of them from Mexico. Gaining control over U.S. borders is one goal of immigration policy, but focusing on that goal alone obscures the fact that the majority of immigrants are legal. For example, agricultural workers have been allowed to enter the United States under special visa programs, thereby providing inexpensive labor to harvest crops. More recently, there has been a special program for engineers, scientists, and other skilled workers needed in high-technology industries, who are

---

[7] Prior to 2004, the European Union consisted of 15 countries: Belgium, France, Germany, Italy, Luxembourg, and the Netherlands (founding members in 1952); Denmark, Ireland, and the United Kingdom (added in 1973); Greece (added in 1981); Portugal and Spain (added in 1986); and Austria, Finland, and Sweden (added in 1995). On May 1, 2004, 10 more countries were added: Cyprus, the Czech Republic, Estonia, Hungary, Lithuania, Latvia, Malta, Poland, Slovakia, and Slovenia. Citizens from these countries were then permitted to work anywhere in the European Economic Area (EEA), which consists of the countries of the EU plus Iceland, Liechtenstein, and Norway. However, member countries of the EEA can adopt a seven-year moratorium on allowing labor mobility if they wish.

HEADLINES

Europe Sours on Labor Migration

With unemployment soaring, many EU countries want the migrant workers they once courted to return home as soon as possible.

Chultem Choijusuren was watching television in Ulan Bator when he decided to climb aboard the globalization bandwagon. According to an ad he had seen, companies in the Czech Republic were paying young mechanics "€1,000 a month." Most people in the Mongolian steppes were already familiar with the small Eastern European country. After all, many young people from here had studied in Prague during the two countries' Socialist pasts. . . .

Choijusuren is part of the army of migrants that has moved westward from developing countries in recent years, with one in three choosing Europe as their destination. After the European Union's eastward expansion in 2004, tens of thousands of Asians found jobs in Polish, Czech and Slovak factories, where they were welcomed with open arms to fill the jobs that one million Poles and hundreds of thousands of Czechs, Balts, Slovaks and Hungarians had left behind when they in turn migrated to the wealthier EU countries. Ireland, Great Britain and Sweden, unlike Germany and Austria, had immediately opened their borders to citizens of the new member states, and Spain followed suit two years later.

Construction companies and restaurants in these countries were only too pleased to employ the cheap labor from the East. More and more families hired Polish women to clean their houses or nannies with Slavic accents to put their children to bed. The migrants' wages were modest, and yet in some cases three times as high as they were at home. The newcomers sent as much of their earnings home as possible, injecting capital that helped their hometowns gain unprecedented prosperity.

Once the global economic crisis erupted those days were over. Unemployment has risen twice as fast in Great Britain and Spain as elsewhere in Europe. Now the citizens of Western European countries need the jobs themselves, and their governments are resorting to all kinds of tricks and incentives to get rid of the willing hands they once needed so badly.

Globalization has turned 200 million people into migrant workers in the last few decades. One fifth of them are Europeans, less than one tenth are Africans and 3 percent are from Latin America. Now the trend is reversing itself, a shift that generally affects those who came from Europe's poorest regions and from emerging and developing nations. Officials at the United Nations International Labour Organization (ILO) fear that 30 million people around the globe could lose their livelihoods by the end of the year. . . .

Source: Excerpted from Renate Flottau, Thomas Hüetlin, Jan Puhl, and Helene Zuber, "Europe Sours on Labor Migration," Business Week, March 19, 2009.

Agricultural migrant workers in the United States.

awarded H-1B visas. This program was established under the Clinton administration and continues today.

The combination of legal and illegal immigrants in the United States creates a "U-shaped" pattern between the number of immigrants and their educational level, as shown in Figure 5-4, for 2008. Among those workers in the United States with only 0 to 8 years of education, more than 70% were foreign-born, and for those with 8 to 11 years of education, more than 20% were foreign-born. These two categories of high school dropouts include many illegal immigrants and attract much attention in the U.S. debate over immigration, even though they make up only 10% of U.S. workers. At the other end of the spectrum, 10% of U.S. workers have master's degrees or Ph.D.'s, and in these categories, the foreign-born make up 16% and nearly 30%, respectively, of the U.S. workforce. In the middle educational levels, consisting of high school and

FIGURE 5-4

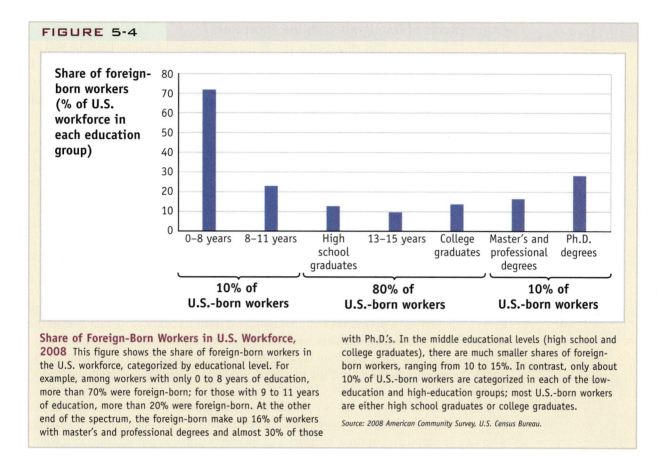

Share of Foreign-Born Workers in U.S. Workforce, 2008 This figure shows the share of foreign-born workers in the U.S. workforce, categorized by educational level. For example, among workers with only 0 to 8 years of education, more than 70% were foreign-born; for those with 9 to 11 years of education, more than 20% were foreign-born. At the other end of the spectrum, the foreign-born make up 16% of workers with master's and professional degrees and almost 30% of those with Ph.D.'s. In the middle educational levels (high school and college graduates), there are much smaller shares of foreign-born workers, ranging from 10 to 15%. In contrast, only about 10% of U.S.-born workers are categorized in each of the low-education and high-education groups; most U.S.-born workers are either high school graduates or college graduates.

Source: 2008 American Community Survey, U.S. Census Bureau.

college graduates and comprising 80% of the U.S. labor force, foreign-born workers have much smaller shares (10–15%). Figure 5-4 shows that immigrants into the United States compete primarily with workers at the lowest and highest ends of the educational levels and much less with the majority of U.S.-born workers with mid-levels of education.

The lesson that we should take from Figure 5-4 is that illegal immigrants into the United States compete primarily with the lowest-educated workers and that legal immigrants compete with workers at the highest educational levels. If we extend the specific-factors model to allow for several types of labor distinguished by educational level but continue to treat capital and land as fixed, then the greatest negative impact of immigration on wages would be for the lowest- and highest-educated U.S. workers. That prediction is supported by estimates of the effect of immigration on U.S. wages: from 1990 to 2004, immigration led to a fall in wages of 9% for high school dropouts and 5% for college graduates. But the impact of immigration on the wages of the majority of U.S. workers (those with mid-levels of education) is much less: wages of high school graduates decreased by 2.4% from 1990 to 2004, and wages of individuals with less than four years of college decreased by less than 1%. The negative impact of immigration on wages is thus fairly modest for most workers and is offset when capital moves between industries, as discussed later in the chapter. ■

Other Effects of Immigration in the Short Run

The previous application shows that the United States and Europe have both welcomed foreign workers into specific industries, such as agriculture and the high-tech industry, even though these workers compete with domestic workers in those industries. This observation suggests that there must be benefits to the industries involved. We can measure the potential benefits by the payments to capital and land, which we refer to as "rentals." We saw in Chapter 3 that there are two ways to compute the rentals: either as the earnings left over in the industry after paying labor or as the marginal product of capital or land times the price of the good produced in each industry. Under either method, the owners of capital and land benefit from the reduction in wages due to immigration.

Rentals on Capital and Land Under the first method for computing the rentals, we take the revenue earned in either manufacturing or agriculture and subtract the payments to labor. If wages fall, then there is more left over as earnings of capital and land, so these rentals are higher. Under the second method for computing rentals, capital and land earn their marginal product in each industry times the price of the industry's good. As more labor is hired in each industry (because wages are lower), the marginal products of capital and land both increase. The increase in the marginal product occurs because each machine or acre of land has more workers available to it, and that machine or acre of land is therefore more productive. So under the second method, too, the marginal products of capital and land rise and so do their rentals.

From this line of reasoning, we should not be surprised that owners of capital and land often support more open borders, which provides them with foreign workers who can be employed in their industries. The restriction on immigration in a country should therefore be seen as a compromise between entrepreneurs and landowners who might welcome the foreign labor; local unions and workers who view migrants as a potential source of competition leading to lower wages; and the immigrant groups themselves, who if they are large enough (such as the Cuban population in Miami) might also have the ability to influence the political outcome on immigration policy.

Effect of Immigration on Industry Output One final effect of labor immigration is its effect on the output of the industries. In Figure 5-2, the increase in the labor force due to immigration led to more workers being employed in each of the industries: employment increased from $0_M L$ to $0_M L'$ in manufacturing and from $0_A L$ to $0'_A L'$ in agriculture. With more workers and the same amount of capital or land, the output of both industries rises. This outcome is shown in Figure 5-5—immigration leads to an outward shift in the production possibilities frontier (PPF). With constant prices of goods (as we assumed earlier, because prices are determined by world supply and demand), the output of the industries rises from point A to point B.

Although it may seem obvious that having more labor in an economy will increase the output of both industries, it turns out that this result depends on the short-run nature of the specific-factors model, when capital and land in each industry are fixed. If instead these resources can move between the industries, as would occur in the long run, then the output of one industry will increase but that of the other industry will decline, as we explain in the next section.

FIGURE 5-5

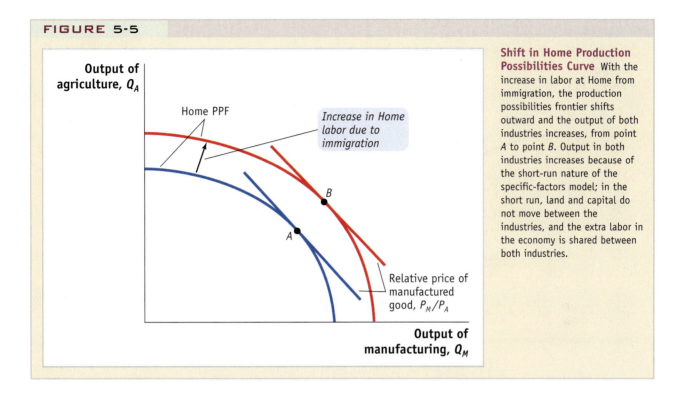

Output of agriculture, Q_A

Home PPF

Increase in Home labor due to immigration

B

A

Relative price of manufactured good, P_M/P_A

Output of manufacturing, Q_M

Shift in Home Production Possibilities Curve With the increase in labor at Home from immigration, the production possibilities frontier shifts outward and the output of both industries increases, from point *A* to point *B*. Output in both industries increases because of the short-run nature of the specific-factors model; in the short run, land and capital do not move between the industries, and the extra labor in the economy is shared between both industries.

Effects of Immigration in the Long Run

We turn now to the long run, in which all factors are free to move between industries. Because it is complicated to analyze a model with three factors of production—capital, land, and labor—all of which are fully mobile between industries, we will ignore land and assume that only labor and capital are used to produce two goods: computers and shoes. The long-run model is just like the Heckscher-Ohlin model studied in the previous chapter except that we will now allow labor to move between countries. (Later in the chapter, we will allow capital to move between the countries.)

The amount of capital used in computers is K_C, and the amount of capital used in shoe production is K_S. These quantities add up to the total capital available in the economy: $K_C + K_S = \overline{K}$. Because capital is fully mobile between the two sectors in the long run, it must earn the same rental R in each. The amount of labor used to manufacture computers is L_C, and the labor used in shoe production is L_S. These amounts add up to the total labor in the economy, $L_C + L_S = \overline{L}$, and all labor earns the same wage of W in both sectors.

In our analysis, we make the realistic assumption that more labor per machine is used in shoe production than in computer production. That assumption means that shoe production is labor-intensive compared with computer production, so the labor–capital ratio in shoes is higher than it is in computers: $L_S/K_S > L_C/K_C$. Computer production, then, is capital-intensive compared with shoes, and the capital–labor ratio is higher in computers: $K_C/L_C > K_S/L_S$.

"You seem familiar, yet somehow strange— are you by any chance Canadian?"

Cartoonbank

FIGURE 5-6

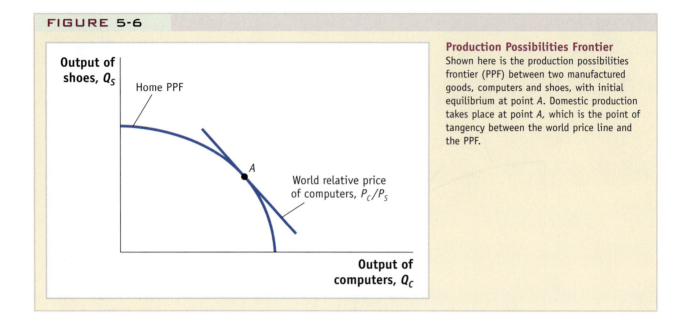

Output of shoes, Q_S

Home PPF

A

World relative price of computers, P_C/P_S

Output of computers, Q_C

Production Possibilities Frontier
Shown here is the production possibilities frontier (PPF) between two manufactured goods, computers and shoes, with initial equilibrium at point A. Domestic production takes place at point A, which is the point of tangency between the world price line and the PPF.

The PPF for an economy producing shoes and computers is shown in Figure 5-6. Given the prices of both goods (determined by supply and demand in world markets), the equilibrium outputs are shown at point A, at the tangency of the PPF and world relative price line. Our goal in this section is to see how the equilibrium is affected by having an inflow of labor into Home as a result of immigration.

Box Diagram To analyze the effect of immigration, it is useful to develop a new diagram to keep track of the amount of labor and capital used in each industry. Shown as a "box diagram" in Figure 5-7, the length of the top and bottom horizontal axes is the total amount of labor $\overline{L}$ at Home, and the length of the right and left vertical axes is the total amount of capital $\overline{K}$ at Home. A point like point A in the diagram indicates that $0_S L$ units of labor and $0_S K$ units of capital are used in shoes, while $0_C L$ units of labor and $0_C K$ units of capital are used in computers. Another way to express this is that the line $0_S A$ shows the amount of labor and capital used in shoes and the line $0_C A$ shows the amount of labor and capital used in computers.

Notice that the line $0_S A$ for shoes is flatter than the line $0_C A$ for computers. We can calculate the slopes of these lines by dividing the vertical distance by the horizontal distance (the rise over the run). The slope of $0_S A$ is $0_S K/0_S L$, the capital–labor ratio used in the shoe industry. Likewise, the slope of $0_C A$ is $0_C K/0_C L$, the capital–labor ratio for computers. The line $0_S A$ is flatter than $0_C A$, so the capital–labor ratio in the shoe industry is less than that in computers; that is, there are fewer units of capital per worker in the shoe industry. This is precisely the assumption that we made earlier. It is a realistic assumption given that the manufacture of computer components such as semiconductors requires highly precise and expensive equipment, which is operated by a small number of workers. Shoe production, on the other hand, requires more workers and a smaller amount of capital.

Determination of the Real Wage and Real Rental In addition to determining the amount of labor and capital used in each industry in the long run, we also need

FIGURE 5-7

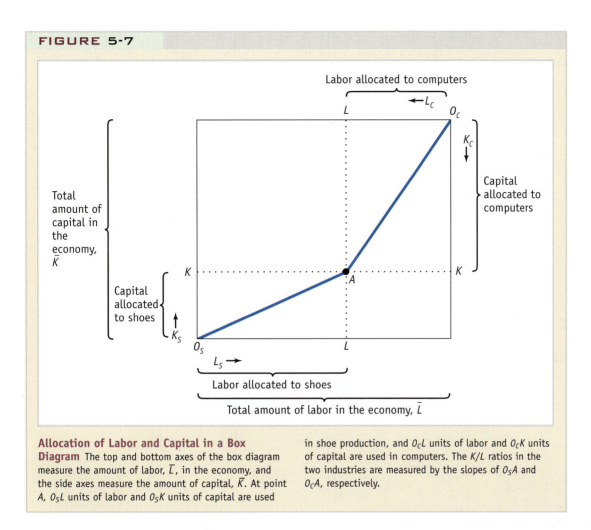

Allocation of Labor and Capital in a Box Diagram The top and bottom axes of the box diagram measure the amount of labor, $\bar{L}$, in the economy, and the side axes measure the amount of capital, $\bar{K}$. At point A, 0_SL units of labor and 0_SK units of capital are used in shoe production, and 0_CL units of labor and 0_CK units of capital are used in computers. The K/L ratios in the two industries are measured by the slopes of 0_SA and 0_CA, respectively.

to determine the wage and rental in the economy. To do so, we use the logic introduced in Chapter 3: the wage and rental are determined by the marginal products of labor and capital, which are in turn determined by the capital–labor ratio in either industry. If there is a higher capital–labor ratio (i.e., if there are more machines per worker), then by the law of diminishing returns, the marginal product of capital and the real rental must be lower. Having more machines per worker means that the marginal product of labor (and hence the real wage) is higher because each worker is more productive. On the other hand, if there is a higher labor–capital ratio (more workers per machine), then the marginal product of labor must be lower because of diminishing returns, and hence the real wage is lower, too. In addition, having more workers per machine means that the marginal product of capital and the real rental are both higher.

The important point to remember is that each amount of labor and capital used in Figure 5-7 along line 0_SA corresponds to a particular capital–labor ratio for shoe manufacture and therefore a particular real wage and real rental. We now consider how the labor and capital used in each industry will change due to immigration at Home. Although the total amount of labor and capital used in each industry changes, we will show that the capital–labor ratios are unaffected by immigration, which means that the immigrants can be absorbed with no change at all in the real wage and real rental.

Increase in the Amount of Home Labor Suppose that because of immigration, the amount of labor at Home increases from $\overline{L}$ to $\overline{L}' = \overline{L} + \Delta L$. This increase expands the labor axes in the box diagram, as shown in Figure 5-8. Rather than allocating $\overline{L}$ labor and $\overline{K}$ capital between the two industries, we must now allocate $\overline{L}'$ labor and $\overline{K}$ capital. The question is how much labor and capital will be used in each industry so that the total amount of both factors is fully employed?

You might think that the only way to employ the extra labor is to allocate more of it to both industries (as occurred in the short-run specific-factors model). This outcome would tend to lower the marginal product of labor in both industries and therefore lower the wage. But it turns out that such an outcome will not occur in the long-run model because when capital is also able to move between the industries, industry outputs will adjust to keep the capital–labor ratios in each industry constant. Instead of allocating the extra labor to both industries, all the extra labor (ΔL) will be allocated to shoes, the *labor*-intensive industry. Moreover, along with that extra labor,

FIGURE 5-8

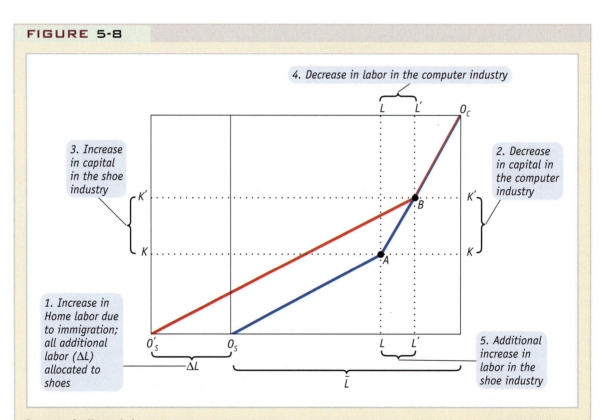

Increase in Home Labor With an increase in Home labor from $\overline{L}$ to $\overline{L} + \Delta L$, the origin for the shoe industry shifts from O_S to O'_S. At point B, $O'_S L'$ units of labor and $O'_S K'$ units of capital are used in shoes, whereas $O_C L'$ units of labor and $O_C K'$ units of capital are used in computers. In the long run, industry outputs adjust so that the capital–labor ratios in each industry at point B (the slopes of $O'_S B$ and $O_C B$) are unchanged from the initial equilibrium at point A (the slopes of $O_S A$ and $O_C A$). To achieve this outcome, all new labor resulting from immigration is allocated to the shoe industry, and capital and *additional* labor are transferred from computers to shoes, keeping the capital–labor ratio in both industries unchanged.

some capital is withdrawn from computers and allocated to shoes. To maintain the capital–labor ratio in the computer industry, some labor will also leave the computer industry, along with the capital, and go to the shoe industry. Because all the new workers in the shoe industry (immigrants plus former computer workers) have the same amount of capital to work with as the shoe workers prior to immigration, the capital–labor ratio in the shoe industry stays the same. *In this way, the capital–labor ratio in each industry is unchanged and the additional labor in the economy is fully employed.*

This outcome is illustrated in Figure 5-8, where the initial equilibrium is at point A. With the inflow of labor due to immigration, the labor axis expands from $\overline{L}$ to $\overline{L} + \Delta L$, and the origin for the shoe industry shifts from 0_S to $0'_S$. Consider point B as a possible new equilibrium. At this point, $0'_S L'$ units of labor and $0'_S K'$ units of capital are used in shoes, while $0_C L'$ units of labor and $0_C K'$ units of capital are used in computers. Notice that the lines $0_S A$ and $0'_S B$ are parallel and have the same slope, and similarly, the lines $0_C A$ and $0_C B$ have the same slope. The extra labor has been employed by *expanding* the amount of labor and capital used in shoes (the line $0'_S B$ is longer than $0_S A$) and *contracting* the amount of labor and capital used in computers (the line $0_C B$ is smaller than $0_C A$). That the lines have the same slope means that the capital–labor ratio used in each industry is exactly the same before and after the inflow of labor.

What has happened to the wage and rentals in the economy? Because the capital–labor ratios are unchanged in both industries, the marginal products of labor and capital are also unchanged. Therefore, the wage and rental do not change at all due to the immigration of labor! This result is very different from what happens in the short-run specific-factors model, which showed that immigration depressed the wage and raised the rental on capital and land. In the long-run model, when capital can move between industries, an inflow of labor has no impact on the wage and rental. Instead, the extra labor is employed in shoes, by combining it with capital and additional labor that has shifted out of computers. In that way, the capital–labor ratios in both industries are unchanged, as are the wage and rental.

Effect of Immigration on Industry Outputs What is the effect of immigration on the output of each industry? We have already seen from Figure 5-8 that more labor and capital are used in the labor-intensive industry (shoes), whereas less labor and capital are used in the capital-intensive industry (computers). Because the factors of production both increase or both decrease, it follows that the output of shoes expands and the output of computers contracts.

This outcome is shown in Figure 5-9, which shows the outward shift of the PPF due to the increase in the labor endowment at Home. Given the prices of computers and shoes, the initial equilibrium was at point A. At this point, the slope of the PPF equals the relative price of computers, as shown by the slope of the line tangent to the PPF. With unchanged prices for the goods, and more labor in the economy, the equilibrium moves to point B, with greater output of shoes but reduced output of computers. Notice that the slope of the PPFs at points A and B is identical because the relative price of computers is unchanged. As suggested by the diagram, the expansion in the amount of labor leads to an uneven outward shift of the PPF—it shifts out more in the direction of shoes (the labor-intensive industry) than in the direction of computers. This asymmetric shift illustrates that the new labor is employed in shoes and that this additional labor pulls capital and additional labor out of computers in the long run, to establish the new equilibrium at point B. *The finding that an increase in labor will expand one industry but contract the other holds only in the long run; in the short run, as we*

FIGURE 5-9

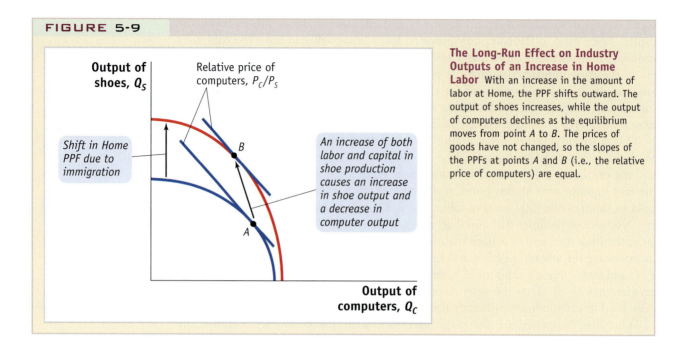

The Long-Run Effect on Industry Outputs of an Increase in Home Labor With an increase in the amount of labor at Home, the PPF shifts outward. The output of shoes increases, while the output of computers declines as the equilibrium moves from point *A* to *B*. The prices of goods have not changed, so the slopes of the PPFs at points *A* and *B* (i.e., the relative price of computers) are equal.

saw in Figure 5-5, both industries will expand. This finding shows how much the long-run model differs from the short-run model. The long-run result is named after the economist T. N. Rybczynski, who first discovered it.

Rybczynski Theorem

In the Heckscher-Ohlin model with two goods and two factors, an increase in the amount of a factor found in an economy will increase the output of the industry using that factor intensively and decrease the output of the other industry.

We have proved the Rybczynski theorem for the case of immigration, where labor in the economy grows. As we argue later in the chapter, the same theorem holds when capital in the economy grows: in this case, the industry using capital intensively expands and the other industry contracts.[8]

Effect of Immigration on Factor Prices The **Rybczynski theorem,** which applies to the long-run Heckscher-Ohlin model with two goods and two factors of production, states that an increase in labor will expand output in one industry but contract output in the other industry. Notice that the change in outputs in the Rybczynski theorem goes hand in hand with the previous finding that the wage and rental will not change due to an increase in labor (or capital). The reason that factor prices do not need to change is that the economy can absorb the extra amount of a factor by increasing the output of the industry using that factor intensively and reducing the output of the other industry. The finding that factor prices do not change is sometimes called the **factor price insensitivity** result.

---

[8] Furthermore, the Rybczynski theorem can be used to compare the output of the same industry across two countries, where the two countries have identical technologies but differing factor endowments as in the Heckscher-Ohlin model. See Problem 7 at the end of the chapter.

Factor Price Insensitivity

In the Heckscher-Ohlin model with two goods and two factors, an increase in the amount of a factor found in an economy can be absorbed by changing the outputs of the industries, without any change in the factor prices.

The applications that follow offer evidence of changes in output that absorb new additions to the labor force, as predicted by the Rybczynski theorem, without requiring large changes in factor prices, as predicted by the factor price insensitivity result.

APPLICATION

The Effects of the Mariel Boat Lift on Industry Output in Miami

Now that we have a better understanding of long-run adjustments due to changes in factor endowments, let us return to the case of the Mariel boat lift to Miami in 1980. We know that the Cuban refugees were less skilled than the average labor force in Miami. According to the Rybczynski theorem, then, we expect some unskilled-labor–intensive industry, such as footwear or apparel, to expand. In addition, we expect that some skill-intensive industry, such as the high-tech industry, will contract. Figure 5-10 shows how this prediction lines up with the evidence from Miami and some comparison cities.[9]

Panel (a) of Figure 5-10 shows real value-added in the apparel industry for Miami and for an average of comparison cities. **Real value-added** measures the payments to labor and capital in an industry corrected for inflation. Thus, real value-added is a way to measure the output of the industry. We divide output by the population of the city to obtain real value-added per capita, which measures the output of the industry adjusted for the city size.

Panel (a) shows that the apparel industry was declining in Miami and the comparison cities before 1980. After the boat lift, the industry continued to decline but at a slower rate in Miami; the trend of output per capita for Miami has a smaller slope (and hence a smaller rate of decline in output) than that of the trend for comparison cities from 1980 onward. Notice that there is an increase in industry output in Miami from 1983 to 1984 (which may be due to new data collected that year), but even when averaging this out as the trend lines do, the industry decline in Miami is slightly slower than in the comparison cities after 1980. This graph provides some evidence of the Rybczynski theorem at work: the reduction in the apparel industry in Miami was slower than it would have been without the inflow of immigrants.

What about the second prediction of the Rybczynski theorem: Did the output of any other industry in Miami fall because of the immigration? Panel (b) of Figure 5-10 shows that the output of a group of skill-intensive industries (including motor vehicles, electronic equipment, and aircraft) fell more rapidly in Miami after 1980. These data may also provide some evidence in favor of the Rybczynski theorem. However, it also happened that with the influx of refugees, there was a flight of homeowners away from Miami, and some of these were probably high-skilled workers. So the decline in the group of skill-intensive industries, shown in panel (b), could instead be due to this population decline.

The change in industry outputs in Miami provides some evidence in favor of the Rybczynski theorem. Do these changes in industry outputs in Miami also provide an

---

[9] Figure 5-10 and the material in this application are drawn from Ethan Lewis, 2004, "How Did the Miami Labor Market Absorb the Mariel Immigrants?" Federal Reserve Bank of Philadelphia Working Paper No. 04-3.

FIGURE 5-10

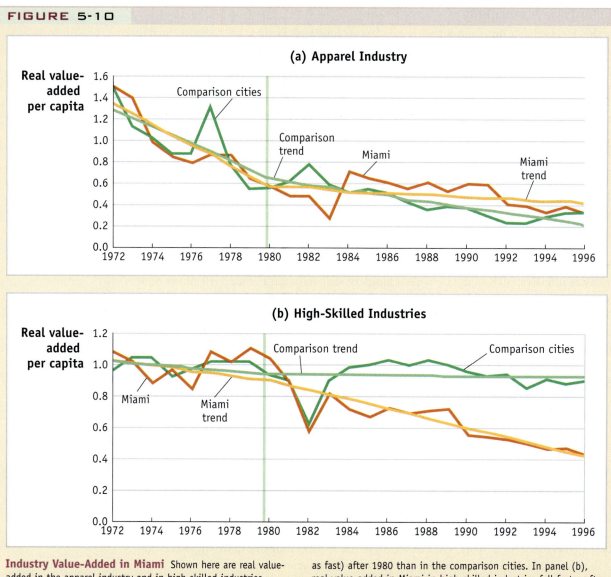

(a) Apparel Industry

Real value-added per capita

Comparison cities

Comparison trend

Miami

Miami trend

(b) High-Skilled Industries

Real value-added per capita

Comparison trend

Comparison cities

Miami

Miami trend

Industry Value-Added in Miami Shown here are real value-added in the apparel industry and in high-skilled industries (measured relative to the city population), for Miami and an average of comparison cities. In panel (a), with the inflow of refugees from Cuba in 1980, real value-added in the apparel industry in Miami rose from 1983 to 1984, and the trend decline of this industry in Miami was slower (i.e., value-added did not fall as fast) after 1980 than in the comparison cities. In panel (b), real value-added in Miami in high-skilled industries fell faster after 1980 than in the comparison cities. Both these findings are consistent with the Rybczynksi theorem.

Source: Ethan Lewis, 2004, "How Did the Miami Labor Market Absorb the Mariel Immigrants?" Federal Reserve Bank of Philadelphia Working Paper No. 04–3.

adequate explanation for why wages of unskilled workers did not decline, or is there some other explanation? An alternative explanation for the finding that wages did not change comes from comparing the use of computers in Miami with national trends. Beginning in the early 1980s, computers became increasingly used in the workplace. The adoption of computers is called a "skill-biased technological change." That is, computers led to an increase in the demand for high-skilled workers and reduced the hiring of low-skilled workers. This trend occurred across the United States and in other countries.

In Miami, however, computers were adopted somewhat more slowly than in cities with similar industry mix and ethnic populations. One explanation for this finding is that firms in many industries, not just apparel, employed the Mariel refugees and other low-skilled workers rather than switching to computer technologies. Evidence to support this finding is that the Mariel refugees were, in fact, employed in many industries. Only about 20% worked in manufacturing (5% in apparel), and the remainder worked in service industries. The idea that the firms may have slowed the adoption of new technologies to employ the Mariel emigrants is hard to prove conclusively, however. We suggest it here as an alternative to the Rybczynski theorem to explain how the refugees could be absorbed across many industries rather than just in the industries using unskilled labor, such as apparel. ■

APPLICATION

Immigration and U.S. Wages, 1990–2004

In 1980, the year of the Mariel boat lift, the percentage of foreign-born people in the U.S. population was 6.2%. The percentage grew to 12.9% in 2005, so there was slightly more than a doubling of foreign-born people in 25 years.[10] How has this wave of recent immigration affected U.S. wages?

Part A of Table 5-1 reports the estimated impact of the immigration from 1990 to 2004 on the wages of various workers, distinguished by their educational level. The first row in part A summarizes the estimates from the specific-factors model, when capital and land are kept fixed within all industries. As we discussed in an earlier application,

TABLE 5-1

Immigration and Wages in the United States This table shows the estimated effect of immigration on the wages of workers, depending on their educational level. Immigration has the greatest impact on workers with very low or high levels of education and only a small impact on those workers with middle levels of education (12–15 years). The impact is even smaller in the long run, when capital adjusts to keep the real return to capital fixed in each industry.

	PERCENTAGE CHANGE IN THE WAGE OF WORKERS WITH EDUCATIONAL LEVEL				
	Less Than 12 Years	12 Years	13–15 Years	16 Years or More	Overall Average
Part A: Effect of Total Immigration, 1990–2004					
Method:					
Capital and land fixed	–9.0	–2.4	–0.8	–5.0	–3.2
Real return to capital fixed	–4.4	1.0	2.2	–0.2	0.3
Part B: Effect of Illegal Immigration, 1990–2004					
Method:					
Real return to capital fixed	–7.9	0.8	0.8	0.8	0.1

Source: Gianmarco I.P. Ottaviano and Giovanni Peri, 2005 "Rethinking Gains from Immigration: Theory and Evidence from the U.S." National Bureau of Economic Research working paper no. 11672.

---

[10] This information on foreign-born people is available from the United Nations, at http://www.esa.un.org/ migration.

the greatest negative impact of immigration is on workers with less than 12 years of education, followed by college graduates (those with greater than 16 years), and then followed by high school graduates and those with some college. Overall, the average impact of immigration on U.S. wages over this period is –3.2%, so there is a fall in wages, consistent with the specific-factors model.

A different story emerges, however, if instead of keeping capital fixed, we hold constant the real rental on capital. Under this approach, we allow capital to grow in each industry to accommodate the inflow of immigrants, so that there is no change in the real rental. This approach is similar to the long-run model we have discussed, except that there are several types of labor, distinguished by their education levels, and the prices of goods and labor are not constant over the period examined. In the second row of part A, we see that total U.S. immigration has a negative impact on workers with the lowest and highest levels of education and a *positive* impact on the other workers (due to the growth in capital). The average U.S. wage now rises by 0.3% due to immigration (combined with capital growth), rather than falling.

In part B of Table 5-1, we focus on the illegal immigration to the United States from 1990 to 2004, rather than total immigration, keeping the real return to capital fixed. In this case, the wages of only the lowest-educated people are negatively affected. All other workers gain from illegal immigration, once we take into account the growth in capital that is expected to occur. ■

2 Movement of Capital between Countries: Foreign Direct Investment

To continue our examination of what happens to wages and rentals when factors can move across borders, we turn now to look at how capital can move from one country to another through **foreign direct investment (FDI),** which occurs when a firm from one country owns a company in another country. How much does the company have to own for foreign direct investment to occur? Definitions vary, but the Department of Commerce in the United States uses 10%: if a foreign company acquires 10% or more of a U.S. firm, then that is counted as an FDI inflow to the United States, and if a U.S. company acquires 10% or more of a foreign firm, then that is counted as an FDI outflow from the United States.

When a company builds a plant in a foreign country, it is sometimes called "greenfield FDI" (because we imagine the site for the plant starting with grass on it). When a firm buys an existing foreign plant, it is called "acquisition FDI" (or sometimes "brownfield FDI"). Having capital move from high-wage to low-wage countries to earn a higher rental is the traditional view of FDI, and the viewpoint we take in this chapter.[11]

Greenfield Investment

Our focus in this section will be on greenfield investment; that is, the building of new plants abroad. We model FDI as a movement of capital between countries, just as we modeled the movement of labor between countries. The key question we ask is: How

---

[11] As discussed in Chapter 1, there are many instances of FDI that do not fit with this traditional view.

does the movement of capital into a country affect the earnings of labor and capital there? This question is similar to the one we asked for immigration, so the earlier graphs that we developed can be modified to address FDI.

FDI in the Short Run: Specific-Factors Model

We begin by modeling FDI in the short run, using the specific-factors model. In that model, the manufacturing industry uses capital and labor and the agriculture industry uses land and labor, so as capital flows into the economy, it will be used in manufacturing. The additional capital will raise the marginal product of labor in manufacturing because workers there have more machines with which to work. Therefore, as capital flows into the economy, it will shift out the curve $P_M \cdot MPL_M$ for the manufacturing industry as shown in panel (a) of Figure 5-11.

Effect of FDI on the Wage As a result of this shift, the equilibrium wage increases, from W to W'. More workers are drawn into the manufacturing industry, and the labor used there increases from $0_M L$ to $0_M L'$. Because these workers are pulled out of agriculture, the labor used there shrinks from $0_A L$ to $0_A L'$ (measuring from right to left).

Effect of FDI on the Industry Outputs It is easy to determine the effect of an inflow of FDI on industry outputs. Because workers are pulled out of agriculture, and there is no change in the amount of land used there, output of the agriculture industry must fall. With an increase in the number of workers used in manufacturing and an increase in capital used there, the output of the manufacturing industry must rise.

FIGURE 5-11

Increase in the Capital Stock in the Short Run In panel (a), an inflow of capital into the manufacturing sector shifts out the marginal product of labor curve in that sector. The equilibrium in the labor market moves from point A to B, and the wage increases from W to W'. Labor used in the manufacturing industry increases from $0_M L$ to $0_M L'$. These workers are pulled out of agriculture, so the labor used there shrinks from $0_A L$ to $0_A L'$.

In panel (b), with the inflow of capital into manufacturing, and the extra labor used in that sector, the output of manufacturing increases. Because labor has been drawn out of agriculture, the output of that sector falls. These changes in outputs are shown by the outward shift of the PPF (due to the increase in capital) and the movement from point A to point B.

These changes in output are shown in panel (b) of Figure 5-11 by the outward shift of the production possibilities frontier. At constant prices for goods (i.e., the relative price lines have the same slope before and after the increase in capital), the equilibrium outputs shift from point A to point B, with more manufacturing output and less agricultural output.

Effect of FDI on the Rentals

Finally, we can determine the impact of the inflow of capital on the rental earned by capital and the rental earned by land. It is easiest to start with the agriculture industry. Because fewer workers are employed there, each acre of land cannot be cultivated as intensively as before, and the marginal product of land must fall. One way to measure the rental on land T is by the value of its marginal product, $R_T = P_A \cdot MPT_A$. With the fall in the marginal product of land (MPT_A), and no change in the price of agricultural goods, the rental on land falls.

Now let us consider manufacturing, which uses more capital and more labor than before. One way to measure the rental on capital is by the value of the marginal product of capital, or $R_K = P_M \cdot MPK_M$. Using this method, however, it is difficult to determine how the rental on capital changes. As capital flows into manufacturing, the marginal product of capital falls because of diminishing returns. That effect reduces the rental on capital. But as labor is drawn into manufacturing, the marginal product of capital tends to rise. So we do not know at first glance how the rental on capital changes overall.

Fortunately, we can resolve this difficulty by using another method to measure the rental on capital. We take the revenue earned in manufacturing and subtract the payments to labor. If wages are higher, and everything else is the same, then there must be a reduced amount of funds left over as earnings of capital, so the rental is lower.

Let us apply this line of reasoning more carefully to see how the inflow of FDI affects the rental on capital. In Figure 5-12, we begin at point A and then assume the capital stock expands due to FDI. Suppose we hold the wage constant, and let the labor used in manufacturing expand up to point C. Because the wage is the same at points A and C, the marginal product of labor in manufacturing must also be the same (since the wage is $W = P_M \cdot MPL_M$). The only way that the marginal product of labor can remain constant is for each worker to have the same amount of capital to work with as he or she had before the capital inflow. In other words, the capital–labor ratio in manufacturing L_M/K_M must be the same at points A and C: the expansion of capital in manufacturing is just matched by a proportional expansion of labor into manufacturing. But if the capital–labor ratio in manufacturing is identical at points A and C, then the marginal product of capital must also be equal at these two points (because each machine has the same number of people working on it). Therefore, the rental on capital, $R_K = P_M \cdot MPK_M$, is also equal at points A and C.

Now let's see what happens as the manufacturing wage increases while holding constant the amount of capital used in that sector. The increase in the wage will move us up the curve $P_M \cdot MPL'_M$ from point C to point B. As the wage rises, less labor is used in manufacturing. With less labor used on each machine in manufacturing, the marginal product of capital and the rental on capital must fall. This result confirms our earlier reasoning: when wages are higher and the amount of capital used in manufacturing is the same, then the earnings of capital (i.e., its rental) must be lower. Because the rental on capital is the same at points A and C but is lower at point B than C, the overall effect of the FDI inflow is to reduce the rental on capital. We learned previously that the FDI inflow also reduces the rental on land, so both rentals fall.

FIGURE 5-12

The Effect of an Increase in Capital Stock on the Rental on Capital By carefully tracing through how the capital–labor ratio in manufacturing is affected by the movement from A to C (where wages and hence the capital–labor ratio do not change), and then the movement from C to B (where wages and the capital–labor ratio both increase), we conclude that the rental on capital is lower at point B than at point A. Therefore, the rental on capital declines when the capital stock increases through FDI.

FDI in the Long Run

The results of FDI in the long run, when capital and labor can move between industries, differ from those we saw in the short-run specific-factors model. To model FDI in the long run, we assume again that there are two industries—computers and shoes—both of which use two factors of production: labor and capital. Computers are capital-intensive as compared with shoes, meaning that K_C/L_C exceeds K_S/L_S.

In panel (a) of Figure 5-13, we show the initial allocation of labor and capital between the two industries at point A. The labor and capital used in the shoe industry are 0_SL and 0_SK, so this combination is measured by the line 0_SA. The labor and capital used in computers are 0_CL and 0_CK, so this combination is measured by the line 0_CA. That amount of labor and capital used in each industry produces the output of shoes and computers shown by point A on the PPF in panel (b).

Effect of FDI on Outputs and Factor Prices An inflow of FDI causes the amount of capital in the economy to increase. That increase expands the right and left sides of the box in panel (a) of Figure 5-13 and shifts the origin up to $0'_C$. The new allocation of factors between the industries is shown at point B. Now the labor and capital used in the shoe industry are measured by 0_SB, which is shorter than the line 0_SA. Therefore, less labor and less capital are used in the production of footwear, and shoe output falls. The labor and capital used in computers are measured by $0'_CB$, which is longer than the line 0_CA. Therefore, more labor and more capital are used in computers, and the output of that industry rises.

The change in outputs of shoes and computers is shown by the shift from point A to point B in panel (b) of Figure 5-13. In accordance with the Rybczynski theorem, the increase in capital through FDI has increased the output of the capital-intensive industry

FIGURE 5-13

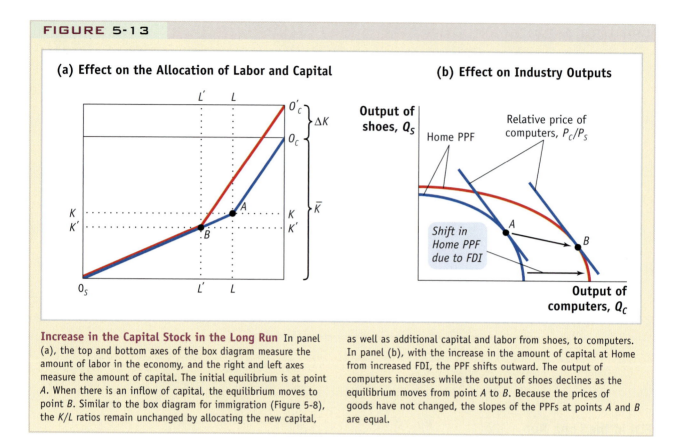

(a) Effect on the Allocation of Labor and Capital

(b) Effect on Industry Outputs

Increase in the Capital Stock in the Long Run In panel (a), the top and bottom axes of the box diagram measure the amount of labor in the economy, and the right and left axes measure the amount of capital. The initial equilibrium is at point A. When there is an inflow of capital, the equilibrium moves to point B. Similar to the box diagram for immigration (Figure 5-8), the K/L ratios remain unchanged by allocating the new capital, as well as additional capital and labor from shoes, to computers. In panel (b), with the increase in the amount of capital at Home from increased FDI, the PPF shifts outward. The output of computers increases while the output of shoes declines as the equilibrium moves from point A to B. Because the prices of goods have not changed, the slopes of the PPFs at points A and B are equal.

(computers) and reduced the output of the labor-intensive industry (shoes). Furthermore, this change in outputs is achieved *with no change* in the capital–labor ratios in either industry: the lines $0'_C B$ and $0_S B$ have the same slopes as $0_C A$ and $0_S A$, respectively.

Because the capital–labor ratios are unchanged in the two industries, the wage and the rental on capital are also unchanged. Each person has the same amount of capital to work with in his or her industry, and each machine has the same number of workers. The marginal products of labor and capital are unchanged in the two industries, as are the factor prices. This outcome is basically the same as that for immigration in the long run: in the long-run model, an inflow of *either* factor of production will leave factor prices unchanged.

When discussing immigration, we found cases in which wages were reduced (the short-run prediction) and other cases in which wages have been constant (the long-run prediction). What about for foreign direct investment? Does it tend to lower rentals or leave them unchanged? There are fewer studies of this question, but we next consider an important application for Singapore.

APPLICATION

The Effect of FDI on Rentals and Wages in Singapore

For many years, Singapore has encouraged foreign firms to establish subsidiaries within its borders, especially in the electronics industry. For example, hard disk drives are assembled in Singapore by Seagate (an American company), Samsung (a Korean company), and Fujitsu (a Japanese company). Singapore has the fourth largest amount of FDI in the world (measured by stock of foreign capital found there), following China, Mexico, and Brazil, even though it is much smaller than those economies.[12] As capital in Singapore has grown, what has happened to the rental and to the wage?

One way to answer this question is to estimate the marginal product of capital in Singapore, using a production function that applies to the entire economy. The overall capital–labor ratio in Singapore has grown by about 5% per year from 1970 to 1990. Because of diminishing returns, it follows that the marginal product of capital (equal to the real rental) has fallen, by an average of 3.4% per year as shown in part A of Table 5-2. At the same time, each worker has more capital to work with, so the marginal product of labor (equal to the real wage) has grown by an average of 1.6% per year, as also shown in part A. These estimates of the falling rental and rising wage are consistent with the short-run specific-factors model.

But there is a second way to calculate a rental on capital besides using the marginal product. Under this second approach, we start with the price P_K of some capital equipment. If that equipment was rented rather than purchased, what would its rental

---

TABLE 5-2

Real Rental and Wages in Singapore This table shows the growth rate in the real rental and real wages in Singapore, depending on the method used to construct these factor prices. In part A, a production function approach is used to construct the factor prices, and the real rental falls over time because of the growth in capital. As a result, implied productivity growth is negative. In part B, the rental and wages are constructed from data on payments to capital and labor in Singapore, and real wages grow over time, while the real rental either grows or falls slightly. As a result, implied productivity growth is positive.

	ANNUAL GROWTH RATE (%)		
	Real Rental	Real Wages	Implied Productivity
Part A: Using Production Function and Marginal Products			
Time Period:			
1970–1980	–5.0	2.6	–1.5
1980–1990	–1.9	0.5	–0.7
1970–1990	–3.4	1.6	–1.1
Part B: Using Calculated Rental and Actual Wages			
Interest Rate Used and Time Period:			
Bank lending rate (1968–1990)	1.6	2.7	2.2
Return on equity (1971–1990)	–0.2	3.2	1.5
Earnings-price ratio (1973–1990)	–0.5	3.6	1.6

Sources: Part A from Alwyn Young, 1995, "The Tyranny of Numbers: Confronting the Statistical Realities of the East Asian Growth Experience," Quarterly Journal of Economics, 110(3), August, 641–680.

Part B from Chang-Tai Hsieh, 2002, "What Explains the Industrial Revolution in East Asia? Evidence from the Factor Markets," American Economic Review, 92(3), 502–526.

---

[12] In 2005 China had $318 billion in foreign capital, with another $533 billion in Hong Kong; Mexico had $210 billion; Brazil $202 billion; and Singapore $189 billion, which was 7% of the total foreign capital in developing countries.

be? Let us suppose that the rental agency needs to make the same rate of return on renting the capital equipment that it would make if it invested its money in some financial asset, such as a savings account in a bank or the stock market. If it invested P_K and the asset had the interest rate of i, then it could expect to earn $P_K \cdot i$ from that asset. On the other hand, if it rents out the equipment, then that machinery also suffers wear and tear, and the rental agency needs to recover that cost, too. If d is the rate of depreciation of the capital equipment (the fraction of it that is used up each year), then to earn the same return on a financial asset as from renting out the equipment, the rental agency must receive $P_K \cdot (i + d)$. This formula is an estimate of R, the rental on capital. Dividing by an overall price index P, the real rental is

$$\frac{R}{P} = \frac{P_K}{P} \cdot (i + d)$$

In part B of Table 5-2, we show the growth rate in the real rental, computed from this formula, which depends on the interest rate used. In the first row, we use the bank lending rate for i, and the computed real rental grows by 1.6% per year. In the next rows, we use two interest rates from the stock market: the return on equity (what you would earn from investing in stocks) and the earnings–price ratio (the profits that each firm earns divided by the value of its outstanding stocks). In both these latter cases, the calculated real rental falls slightly over time, by 0.2% and 0.5% per year, much less than the fall in the real rental in part A. According to the calculated real rentals in part B, there is little evidence of a downward fall in the rentals over time.

In part B, we also show the real wage, computed from actual wages paid in Singapore. Real wages grow substantially over time—between 2.7 and 3.6% per year, depending on the exact interest rate and time period used. This is not what we predicted from our long-run model, in which factor prices would be unchanged by an inflow of capital, because the capital–labor ratios are constant (so the marginal product of labor would not change). That real wages are growing in Singapore, with little change in the real rental, is an indication that there is *productivity growth* in the economy, which leads to an increase in the marginal product of labor *and* in the real wage.

We will not discuss how productivity growth is actually measured[13] but just report the findings from the studies in Table 5-2: in part B, productivity growth is between 1.5 and 2.2% per year, depending on the time period, but in part A, productivity growth is negative! The reason that productivity growth is so much higher in part B is because the average of the growth in the real wage and real rental is rising, which indicates that productivity growth has occurred. In contrast, in part A the average of the growth in the real wage and real rental is zero or negative, indicating that no productivity growth has occurred.

The idea that Singapore might have zero productivity growth contradicts what many people believe about its economy and the economies of other fast-growing Asian countries, which were thought to exhibit "miraculous" growth during this period of time. If productivity growth is zero or negative, then all growth is due only to capital accumulation, and FDI has no spillover benefits to the local economy. Positive productivity growth, as shown in part B, indicates that the free-market policies pursued by Singapore stimulated innovations in the manufacture of goods that have

---

[13] The calculation of productivity growth is discussed in Problem 10.

resulted in higher productivity and lower costs. This is what many economists and policy makers believe happened in Singapore, but this belief is challenged by the productivity calculations in part A. Which scenario is correct—zero or positive productivity growth for Singapore—is a source of ongoing debate in economics. Read the item **Headlines: The Myth of Asia's Miracle** for one interpretation of the growth in Singapore and elsewhere in Asia. ■

3 Gains from Labor and Capital Flows

Foreign investment and immigration are both controversial policy issues. Most countries impose limits on FDI at some time in their development but later become open to foreign investment. Nearly all countries impose limits on the inflow of people. In the United States, controls on immigration were first established by the Quota Law

HEADLINES

The Myth of Asia's Miracle

A CAUTIONARY FABLE: Once upon a time, Western opinion leaders found themselves both impressed and frightened by the extraordinary growth rates achieved by a set of Eastern economies. Although those economies were still substantially poorer and smaller than those of the West, the speed with which they had transformed themselves from peasant societies into industrial powerhouses, their continuing ability to achieve growth rates several times higher than the advanced nations, and their increasing ability to challenge or even surpass American and European technology in certain areas seemed to call into question the dominance not only of Western

power but of Western ideology. The leaders of those nations did not share our faith in free markets or unlimited civil liberties. They asserted with increasing self-confidence that their system was superior: societies that accepted strong, even authoritarian governments and were willing to limit individual liberties in the interest of the common good, take charge of their economics, and sacrifice short-run consumer interests for the sake of long-run growth would eventually outperform the increasingly chaotic societies of the West. And a growing minority of Western intellectuals agreed.

The gap between Western and Eastern economic performance eventually be-

came a political issue. The Democrats recaptured the White House under the leadership of a young, energetic new president who pledged to "get the country moving again"—a pledge that, to him and his closest advisers, meant accelerating America's economic growth to meet the Eastern challenge.

The time, of course, was the early 1960s. The dynamic young president was John F. Kennedy. The technological feats that so alarmed the West were the launch of Sputnik and the early Soviet lead in space. And the rapidly growing Eastern economies were those of the Soviet Union and its satellite nations.

Were you tricked by this fable? Did you think that the "Eastern economies" that the author, Paul Krugman, referred to in the beginning were the Asian economies? Krugman is using this rhetorical trick to suggest that the high growth of the Asian economies is not too different from the growth of the Soviet Union in the 1950s and 1960s, which was due to capital accumulation but without much productivity growth. Other economists disagree and believe that Asian growth is due in significant part to improved productivity, in addition to capital accumulation.

Source: Excerpted from Paul Krugman, 1994, "The Myth of Asia's Miracle," Foreign Affairs, November/December, 63–79.

of 1921, which limited the number of people arriving annually from each country of origin. The Immigration and Nationality Act Amendments of 1965 revised the country-specific limits and allowed immigration on a first-come, first-served basis, up to an annual limit, with special allowances for family members and people in certain occupations. Subsequent revisions to the immigration laws in the United States have established penalties for employers who knowingly hire illegal immigrants, have allowed some illegal immigrants to gain citizenship, or have tightened border controls and deported other illegal immigrants.

Why is immigration so controversial? A glance at articles in the newspaper or on the Internet will show that some groups oppose the spending of public funds on immigrants, such as for schooling, medical care, or welfare. Other groups fear the competition for jobs created by the inflow of foreign workers. We have already seen that immigration creates gains and losses for different groups, often lowering the wage for workers in similar jobs but providing benefits to firms hiring these workers.

This finding raises the important question: Does immigration provide an overall gain to the host country, not including the gains to the immigrants themselves? We presume that the immigrants are better off from higher wages in the country to which they move.[14] But what about the other workers and owners of capital and land in the host country? In the short run, we learned that workers in the host country face competition from the immigrants and receive lower wages, while owners of capital and land benefit from immigration. When we add up these various gains and losses, are there "overall gains" to the destination country, in the same way as we have found overall gains from trade? Fortunately, this outcome turns out to be true.

Immigration benefits the host country in the specific-factors model, not including the income of the immigrants themselves. If we include the immigrant earnings with Foreign income, then we find that emigration benefits the Foreign country, too. The same argument can be made for FDI. An inflow of capital benefits the host country, not including the extra earnings of foreign capital. By counting those extra earnings in Foreign income, then FDI also benefits the source country of the capital. After showing these theoretical results, we discuss how large the overall gains from immigration or FDI flows might be in practice.

Gains from Immigration

To measure the gains from immigration, we will use the specific-factors model. In Figure 5-14, we measure the *world* amount of labor on the horizontal axis, which equals $\bar{L} + \bar{L}^*$. The number of workers in the Home country $\bar{L}$ is measured from left (the origin 0) to right. The number of workers in Foreign $\bar{L}^*$ is measured from right (0^*) to left. Each point on the horizontal axis indicates how many workers are located in the two countries. For example, point L indicates that $0L$ workers are located in Home, and 0^*L workers are located in the Foreign country.

Wages at Home and Abroad We already know from our discussion earlier in the chapter that as immigrants enter the Home country, the wage is reduced. In Figure 5-14, we graph this relationship as a downward-sloping line labeled "Home wage." With Home workers of $0L$ before immigration, the wage is W at point A. If

---

[14] This ignores cases in which the immigrants regret the decision to move because of hardship in making the passage or discrimination once they arrive.

FIGURE 5-14

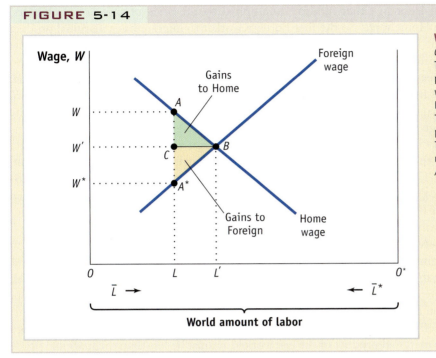

World Labor Market Initially, Home has *OL* workers and Foreign has *0*L* workers. The Home wage is *W,* as determined at point *A,* which is higher than the Foreign wage *W** at *A*.* Workers will move from Foreign to Home to receive higher wages. The equilibrium with full migration is at point *B,* where wages are equalized at *W'.* The gain to Home from migration is measured by triangle *ABC,* and triangle *A*BC* represents the gains to Foreign.

Foreign workers enter and the Home labor force grows to *0L',* then the Home wage is reduced to *W'* at point *B.* The downward-sloping "Home wage" line illustrates the inverse relationship between the number of Home workers and their wage. You can think of this line as a labor demand curve, not for a single industry, but for the economy as a whole.

Similarly, in the Foreign country, there is an inverse relationship between the numbers of workers and their wage. Before any emigration, the labor force in Foreign is 0^*L, and we show the wage at W^* at point A^*. That is lower than the Home wage of *W,* so some workers will want to migrate from Foreign to Home. Remembering that we measure the Foreign workers from right (0^*) to left, when the labor force abroad shrinks from 0^*L to $0^*L'$, the Foreign wages rise from W^* to *W'* at point *B.* We see that as Foreign workers leave, it benefits those left behind by raising their wages.

We will refer to point *B* as the **equilibrium with full migration.** At this point, the wages earned at Home and abroad are equalized at *W'.* It would certainly take a long time for migration to lead to complete wage equality across countries. In our discussion of emigration from the Old World to the New, we saw in Figure 5-3 that real wages in the New World were still twice as high as wages in Europe even after 40 years of large-scale migration. So the equilibrium with full migration is reached only in the very long run. The question we want to answer is whether this migration has benefited the workers (not including the immigrants), labor, and capital in the Home country. In addition, we want to know whether migration has benefited the Foreign country, including the migrants.

Gains for the Home Country To determine whether there are overall gains for Home, we need to measure the contribution of each Foreign worker to the output of one good or the other in that country. This measurement is easy to do. The marginal product of labor in either industry (multiplied by the price of shoes or computers) equals the Home wage. So the first Foreign worker to migrate has a marginal product equal to the Home wage, which is W at point A. As more Foreign workers migrate, the marginal product of labor in both Home industries falls due to diminishing returns. We can measure the immigrants' marginal product by the wage that is paid at Home, which falls from W to W' as we move down the Home wage curve from point A to B.

At the equilibrium with full migration, point B, *all* Foreign immigrants are paid the Home wage of W'. But all Foreign workers except the last one to enter had a marginal product of labor that is above W': the first Foreign worker had a marginal product of W, and the later Foreign immigrants have lower marginal products, ranging from W to W'. Therefore, their contribution to the output of goods in the Home economy *exceeds* the wage that they are paid. The first Foreign immigrant had a marginal product of W but receives the wage W', so the gain to the Home economy from having that worker is $(W - W')$. Likewise, each immigrant to come later has a marginal product between W and W' but is still paid the wage W', so the difference between their marginal products and wages is a gain for the Home economy.

Adding the gains to the Home economy from the Foreign workers, we end up with the triangle ABC, which represents the Home gains as a result of full immigration. The reason for these gains is the law of diminishing returns: as more Foreign immigrants enter the Home workforce, their marginal products fall, and because the wage equals the marginal product of the last worker, it must be less than the marginal products of the earlier immigrants. This economic logic guarantees gains to the Home country from migration.

Gains for the Foreign Country Now consider the Foreign country. To assess the overall gains from emigration, we include the wages received by the migrants who left in calculating Foreign income. These wages are often returned to their families (see **Side Bar: Immigrants and Their Remittances**), but even if they are not, we still incorporate the wages earned by the immigrants in our measure of Foreign income because that is from where the migrants originally came.

In the absence of any emigration, the Foreign wage is W^*, the marginal product of labor in either industry abroad (multiplied by the price of that product in Foreign). As Foreign workers emigrate, the marginal product of labor remaining in Foreign rises, and the Foreign wage rises from W^* to W' (or from points A^* to B in Figure 5-14). Each of these higher marginal products or wages—between W^* and W'—equals the drop in Foreign output (of either good) from having workers leave.

Under full migration, all Foreign migrants earn the wage W' in the Home country. Notice that this wage is *higher* than their Foreign marginal products of labor, which are between W^* and W'. The difference between the wage earned by the migrants and their Foreign marginal products equals the gain to Foreign. Adding up the gains over all Foreign emigrants, we obtain the triangle A^*BC. This gain represents the earnings of the emigrants over and above the drop in output that occurs when they leave Foreign.

World Gains from Migration Combining the gains to the Home and Foreign countries, we obtain the triangular region ABA^*, the world gains from immigration. This magnitude is not too difficult to measure in practice. Turning the triangle on its side, its base equals $(W - W^*)$, the difference in the Home and Foreign wage in the absence of any migration. The height of the triangle is $(L' - L)$, the number of foreign

SIDE BAR

Immigrants and Their Remittances

Immigrants often send a substantial portion of their earnings back home, which we refer to as "remittances." According to estimates from the World Bank, remittances to developing countries were $336 billion in 2008, up from $289 billion in 2007. Economists at the World Bank had believed that the global recession and resulting high global unemployment would limit the ability of migrants to send money to their home countries. However, it appears that in 2008 many migrants reduced their own consumption rather than decreasing their remittances to those they have left behind. A sharp decline in private capital flows in 2008 made remittances an even more important source of external financing throughout the developing world. The strength of remittances in the face of the recession was driven largely by strong growth in flows to South Asia, home to the two largest recipients of remittances: India and China. Remittances declined by 6% in 2009 to $316 billion. Moderate growth in South Asian remittances prevented this slide from being larger.

Especially in times of economic turmoil, remittances are an important supplement to official foreign aid. In Table 5-3, we show the remittances received by some developing countries in 2007, as compared with their net foreign aid. For all countries except Sudan, the income sent home by emigrants is a larger source of income than official aid.

The fact that emigrants return some of their income back home may not be enough to compensate their home countries for the loss of their labor. To calculate any gain to the home countries from the emigration of their workers, we need to include *all the earnings* of the emigrants in their home countries' income. In reality, however, emigrants do not send all their income home, so the countries they leave can lose from their outflow. Consider, for example, the case of highly educated migrants. In 2000 there were 1 million Indian-born people with college educations living in the 30 wealthy countries of the Organization for Economic Co-operation and Development (OECD). That amounts to 4.3% of India's large number of college graduates. In 2008 53% of Indian-born migrants living in the OECD had a post-secondary education. For Asia as a whole, 38% of migrants living in the OECD had a post-secondary education. But for smaller countries, the outflow is much larger. Almost 47% of Ghana's college-educated labor force lives in OECD countries, and for Guyana, the percentage is 89%.[15] Unless these migrants return most of their earnings back home, those countries lose from the outflow of these highly educated workers.

To address this concern, Jagdish Bhagwati (an Indian-born economist now at Columbia University in New York) has proposed that countries impose a "brain drain" tax on the outflow of educated workers. The idea is to tax the earnings of people living outside the countries in which they were born and, through an organization such as the United Nations, return the proceeds from the tax to the countries that lose the most workers. In that way, countries with an outflow of educated workers would be compensated, at least in part, for the outflow. A "brain drain" tax has been widely debated but so far has not actually been used in practice.

TABLE 5-3

Workers' Remittances and Net Foreign Aid, 2007
Shown here are the remittances received by various countries from their citizens working abroad. In many cases, these remittances are larger than the official aid received by the countries. An exception was Sudan, which was experiencing a humanitarian crisis in 2007 so that aid was high.

Country	Remittances Received ($ millions)	Net Aid Received ($ millions)
Albania	1,468	305
Bangladesh	6,562	1,502
Brazil	4,382	297
Colombia	4,523	731
Croatia	1,394	164
Dominican Republic	3,414	128
India	38,666	1,298
Mexico	27,136	121
Morocco	6,730	1,090
Sudan	1,769	2,104
Vietnam	5,500	2,497

Source: World Development Indicators, The World Bank.

---

[15] These percentages are obtained from "Fruit That Falls Far from the Tree," *The Economist*, November 3, 2005, which draws on a World Bank study, and from the 2008 OECD Migration Outlook.

workers that would emigrate in the equilibrium with full migration. So the area of the triangle is $\frac{1}{2}(W - W^*) \cdot (L' - L)$. To solve for the area, we need to know the difference in wages before any migration and the number of people who would emigrate.

One way to think about the world gains from migration is that they equal the *increase in world GDP due to immigration.* To understand why this is so, think about the first person to migrate from Foreign to Home. That person earns the wage W^* in Foreign, which equals his or her marginal product times the price in the industry in which he or she works. When this individual leaves Foreign, GDP in that country falls by W^*. Once he or she moves to Home, he or she earns W, which again reflects the marginal product times the industry price. So W equals the increase in Home GDP when the immigrant begins working. The difference between the Home and Foreign wages therefore equals the net increase in world GDP due to migration. By adding up this amount across all migrants, we obtain the triangular region ABA^*, the increase in world GDP and the world gains due to migration.

In practice, however, there are other costs that immigrants bear that would make the gains from immigration less than the increase in world GDP. Immigrants often face sizable moving costs, including the psychological costs of missing their families and home countries as well as monetary payments to traffickers of illegal immigrants. These costs should be subtracted from the increase in GDP to obtain the net gains. Because all the moving costs are hard to quantify, however, in the next application we measure the net gains from immigration by the increase in Home or world GDP.

APPLICATION

Gains from Migration

How large are the gains from immigration? For the United States, a study by the economist George Borjas puts the net gain from immigration at about 0.1% of GDP (one-tenth of 1% of GDP). That value is obtained by using a stock of immigrants equal to 10% of the workforce in the United States and assuming that the immigrants compete for the same jobs as U.S. workers. If instead we assume the immigrants are lower-skilled on average than the U.S. population, then the low-skilled immigrants can complement the higher-skilled U.S. population, and the gains from immigration in the United States are somewhat higher, up to 0.4% of GDP. These estimates are shown in the first row of Table 5-4. The net gains to the United States in this case equal the increase in U.S. GDP.

Borjas's estimates for the U.S. gains from immigration may seem small, but lying behind these numbers is a larger shift in income from labor to capital and landowners. Labor loses from immigration, while capital and landowners gain, and the net effect of all these changes in real income is the gain in GDP that Borjas estimates. For the net gain of 0.1% of U.S. GDP due to immigration, Borjas estimates that capital would gain 2% and domestic labor would lose 1.9% of GDP. These figures lead him to conclude, "The relatively small size of the immigration surplus [that is, the gain in GDP]—particularly when compared to the very large wealth transfers caused by immigration [that is, the shift in income from labor to capital]—probably explains why the debate over immigration policy has usually focused on the potentially harmful labor market impacts rather than the overall increase in native income."

Other calculations suggest that the overall gains from immigration could be somewhat larger than Borjas's estimates. In the second row of Table 5-4, we report figures

TABLE 5-4

Gains from Immigration The results from several studies of immigration are shown in this table. The second column shows the amount of immigration (as a percentage of the Home labor force), and the third column shows the increase in Home GDP or the increase in GDP of the region.

	AMOUNT OF IMMIGRATION	
	(% of Home labor)	Increase in GDP (%)
Part A: Calculation of Home Gains		
Study used:		
Borjas (1995, 1999), U.S. gains	10	0.1–0.4
Kremer and Watt (2006), Household workers	7	1.2–1.4
Part B: Calculation of Regional Gains		
Study used:		
Walmsley and Winters (2005),		
From developed to developing countries	3	0.6
Klein and Ventura (2006),		
Enlargement of the European Union		
After 10 years	0.8–1.8	0.2–0.7
After 25 years	2.5–5.0	0.6–1.8
After 50 years	4.8–8.8	1.7–4.5
Very long run	na	8
Common Labor Market in NAFTA		
After 10 years	1.0–2.4	0.1–0.4
After 25 years	2.8–5.5	0.4–1.0
After 50 years	4.4–9.1	1.3–3.0
Very long run	na	10.5

na: Not available from the study.

Sources: George Borjas, 1995, "The Economic Benefits from Immigration," Journal of Economic Perspectives, 9(2), 3–22.

George Borjas, 1999, "The Economic Analysis of Immigration." In Orley Ashenfelter and David Card, eds., Handbook of Labor Economics, Vol. 3A (Amsterdam: North Holland), pp. 1697–1760.

Paul Klein and Gustavo Ventura, 2006, "Productivity Differences and the Dynamic Effects of Labour Movements," University of Western Ontario and Pennsylvania State University.

Michael Kremer and Stanley Watt, 2006, "The Globalization of Household Production," Harvard University.

Terrie Louise Walmsley and L. Alan Winters, 2005, "Relaxing the Restrictions on the Temporary Movement of Natural Persons: A Simulation Analysis," Journal of Economic Integration, 20(4), December, 688–726.

from a study by Kremer and Watt that focuses on just one type of immigrant: household workers. Foreign household workers, who are primarily female, make up 10% or more of the labor force in Bahrain, Kuwait, and Saudi Arabia and about 7% of the labor force in Hong Kong and Singapore. The presence of these household workers often allows another member of that household—typically, a highly educated woman—to seek employment in her Home country. Thus, the immigration of low-skilled household workers allows for an increase in the high-skilled supply of individuals at Home, generating higher Home GDP as a result. It is estimated that this type of immigration, if it accounts for 7% of the workforce as in some countries, would increase Home GDP by about 1.2 to 1.4%.

In part B of Table 5-4, we report results from estimates of gains due to migration for several regions of the world. The first study, by Walmsley and Winters, found that an increase in labor supply to developed countries of 3%, as a result of immigration from the developing countries, would create world gains of 0.6% of world GDP. This calculation is similar to the triangle of gains ABA^* shown in Figure 5-14. The next study, by Klein and Ventura, obtains larger estimates of the world gains by modeling the differences in technology across countries. Under this approach, wealthier regions have higher productivity, so an immigrant moving there will be more productive than at home. This productivity increase is offset somewhat by a skill loss for the immigrant (since the immigrant may not find the job for which he or she is best suited, at least initially). Nevertheless, the assumed skill loss is less than the productivity difference between countries, so immigrants are always more productive in the country to which they move.

In their study, Klein and Ventura consider the recent enlargement of the European Union (EU) from 15 countries to 25. Workers from the newly added Eastern European countries are, in principle, permitted to work anywhere in the EU, though in practice this will create some new policy issues for the EU.[16] Klein and Ventura assume that the original 15 EU countries are twice as productive as the newly added countries. During the first 10 years, they find that the population of those 15 EU countries increases by 0.8 to 1.8%, and the combined GDP in the EU increases by 0.2 to 0.7%. The range of these estimates comes from different assumptions on the skill losses of immigrants when they move, and also the psychological costs of their moving, which slow down the extent of migration. As time passes, however, more people flow from Eastern to Western Europe, and GDP continues to rise. In 25 years, they estimate that the combined GDP of the EU will increase by 0.6 to 1.8%, and over 50 years, the increase in GDP will be 1.7 to 4.5%. In the very long run (more than 100 years), much of the population of the eastern EU will have shifted to the west, and GDP will have risen by 8%.

Next, Klein and Ventura consider a common labor market within the North American Free Trade Area (NAFTA), established in 1994, which consists of Canada, Mexico, and the United States. Although NAFTA allows for free international trade between these countries, labor mobility is not free. So the experiment that Klein and Ventura consider is to allow workers from Mexico to migrate freely to the United States and Canada, which are assumed to have workers who are 1.7 times as productive as those from Mexico. During the first 10 years, they predict that the population of the United States and Canada increases by 1.0 to 2.4% due to the immigration from Mexico, and the combined GDP in the NAFTA region increases by 0.1 to 0.4%. After 25 years, they estimate that the combined GDP of the region increases by 0.4 to 1.0%, and over 50 years, the increase in GDP is 1.3 to 3.0%. In the very long run, much of the population of Mexico will have moved to the United States or Canada, and the combined GDP of the NAFTA region will have risen by 10.5%. ■

Gains from Foreign Direct Investment

A diagram very similar to Figure 5-14 can be used to measure the gains from FDI. In Figure 5-15, we show the world amount of capital on the horizontal axis, which equals $\overline{K} + \overline{K}^*$. The rental earned in each country is on the vertical axis. With OK units of

---

[16] See note 7.

FIGURE 5-15

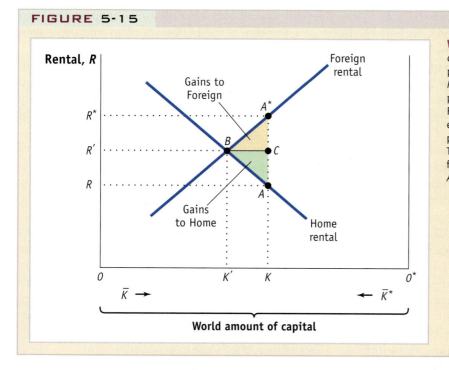

World Capital Market With *OK* units of capital at Home, the Home rental is *R* at point *A*. The remaining capital *O*K* is in *Foreign, and the Foreign rental is R** at point *A**. Capital will move from Home to Foreign to receive a higher rental. The equilibrium with full capital flows is at point *B*, where rentals are equalized at *R′*. Triangle *ABC* measures the gains to Home from the capital outflow, and triangle *A*BC* measures the gains to Foreign.

capital employed at Home (measured from left to right), the Home rental is *R*, determined at point *A*. The remaining capital *O*K* (measured from right to left) is in Foreign, and the Foreign rental is *R**, determined at point *A**.

Because the Foreign rental is higher than that at Home, capital will flow from Home to Foreign. As it enters Foreign, the additional capital will reduce the marginal product of capital and bid down the rental. Likewise, as capital leaves Home, the marginal product of capital will increase, and the Home rental will be bid up. The equilibrium with full capital flows is at point *B*, where rentals are equalized at *R′*. Similar to what we found in the case of immigration, the gains to Home from the capital outflow is the triangle *ABC*, while the gains to Foreign is the triangle *A*BC*, and the world gains are *A*BA*.

4 Conclusions

Immigration, the movement of workers between countries, potentially affects the wages in the host country in which the workers arrive. In the short-run specific-factor model, a larger supply of workers due to immigration will lower wages. Most immigrants into the United States have either the lowest or the highest amounts of education. As a result, after an inflow of labor from other countries, the wages of these two groups of workers fall in the short run. The majority of U.S. workers, those with mid-levels of education, are not affected that much by immigration. Moreover, the arrival of immigrants is beneficial to owners of capital and land in the specific-factors model. As wages are reduced in the short run, the rentals on capital and land will rise. This result helps to explain why landowners lobby for programs to allow agricultural workers to immigrate at least temporarily, and why other industries support increased immigration, such as H1-B visas for workers in the high-technology and other professional industries.

In a long-run framework, when capital can move between industries, the fall in wages will not occur. Instead, the industries that use labor intensively can expand and other industries contract, so that the immigrants become employed without any fall in wages. This change in industry outputs is the main finding of the Rybczynski theorem. The evidence from the Mariel boat lift in 1980 suggests that a readjustment of industry outputs along these lines occurred in Miami after the arrival of immigrants from Cuba: the output of the apparel industry fell by less than predicted from other cities, whereas the output of some skill-intensive industries fell by more than predicted.

The movement of capital between countries is referred to as foreign direct investment (FDI) and has effects analogous to immigration. In the short run, the entry of foreign capital into a country will lower the rental on capital, raise wages, and lower the rental on land. But in the long run, when capital and land can move between industries, these changes in the wage and rentals need not occur. Instead, industry outputs can adjust according to the Rybczynski theorem so that the extra capital is fully employed without any change in the wage or rentals. Evidence from Singapore suggests that foreign capital can be absorbed without a large decline in the rental or the marginal product of capital, though this is an area of ongoing debate in economics.

Both immigration and FDI create world gains as labor and capital move from countries with low marginal products to countries with high marginal products. Gains for the host country are created because the inflow of labor and capital is paid an amount that is less than its full contribution to GDP in the host country. At the same time, there are also gains to the labor and capital in the country they leave, provided that the income earned by the emigrants or capital is included in that country's welfare.

KEY POINTS

1. Holding the amount of capital and land fixed in both industries, as in the specific-factors model, immigration leads to a fall in wages. This was the case, for example, with the mass migration to the New World in the nineteenth century.

2. As wages fall due to immigration, the marginal products of the specific factors (capital and land) rise, and therefore their rentals also increase.

3. Fixing the amount of capital and land in a country is a reasonable assumption in the short run, but in the longer run, firms will move capital between industries, which will change the effect of immigration on wages and rentals.

4. In a long-run model with two goods and two factors, both of which are perfectly mobile between the industries, additional labor from immigration will be absorbed entirely by the labor-intensive industry. Furthermore, the labor-intensive industry will also absorb additional capital and labor from the capital-intensive industry, so its capital–labor ratio does not change in the long run. Because the capital–labor ratio in each industry does not change, the wage and rentals remain the same as well. This results in what is known as factor price insensitivity.

5. According to the Rybczynski theorem, immigration will lead to an increase in output in the labor-intensive industry and a decrease in the

output of the capital-intensive industry. This result is different from that of the short-run specific-factors model, in which immigration leads to increased output in both industries.

6. Besides trade in goods and the movement of labor, another way that countries interact with one another is through investment. When a company owns property, plant, or equipment in another country, it is called foreign direct investment, or FDI.

7. In the short run, FDI lowers the rentals on capital and land and raises wages. In the long run, the extra capital can be absorbed in the capital-intensive industry without any change in the wage or rental.

8. According to the Rybczynski theorem, FDI will lead to an increase in the output of the capital-intensive industry and a decrease in the output of the labor-intensive industry.

9. The movement of capital and labor generates overall gains for both the source and host countries, provided that the income of the emigrants is included in the source country's welfare. Hence, there are global gains from immigration and FDI.

KEY TERMS

specific-factors model, p. 128
Rybczynski theorem, p. 142
factor price insensitivity, p. 142

real value-added, p. 143
foreign direct investment (FDI), p. 146

equilibrium with full migration, p. 155

PROBLEMS

1. In the short-run specific-factors model, examine the impact on a small country following a natural disaster that decreases it population. Assume that land is specific to agriculture and capital is specific to manufacturing, whereas labor is free to move between the two sectors.

   a. In a diagram similar to Figure 5-2, determine the impact of the decrease in the workforce on the output of each industry and the equilibrium wage.

   b. What happens to the rentals on capital and land?

2. How would your answer to Problem 1 change if instead we use the long-run model, with shoes and computers produced using labor and capital?

3. Consider an increase in the supply of labor due to immigration, and use the long-run model. Figure 5-8 shows the box diagram and the left-

ward shift of the origin for the shoe industry. Redraw this diagram but instead shift to the right the origin for computers. That is, expand the labor axis by the amount ΔL but shift it to the right rather than to the left. With the new diagram, show how the amount of labor and capital in shoes and computers is determined, without any change in factor prices. Carefully explain what has happened to the amount of labor and capital used in each industry and to the output of each industry.

4. In the short-run specific-factors model, consider a decrease in the stock of land. For example, suppose a natural disaster decreases the quantity of arable land used for planting crops.

   a. Redraw panel (a) of Figure 5-11 starting from the initial equilibrium at point A.

   b. What is the effect of this change in land on the quantity of labor in each industry and on the equilibrium wage?

c. What is the effect on the rental on land and the rental on capital?

d. Now suppose that the international community wants to help the country struck by the natural disaster and decides to do so by increasing its level of FDI. So the rest of the world increases its investment in physical capital in the stricken country. Illustrate the effect of this policy on the equilibrium wage and rentals.

5. According to part A of Table 5-1, what education level loses most (i.e., has the greatest decrease in wage) from immigration to the United States? Does this result depend on keeping the rental on capital constant? Explain why or why not.

6. Suppose that computers use 2 units of capital for each worker, so that $K_C = 2 \cdot L_C$, whereas shoes use 0.5 units of capital for each worker, so that $K_S = 0.5 \cdot L_S$. There are 100 workers and 100 units of capital in the economy.

a. Solve for the amount of labor and capital used in each industry.

Hint: The box diagram shown in Figure 5-7 means that the amount of labor and capital used in each industry must add up to the total for the economy, so that

$$K_C + K_S = 100 \text{ and } L_C + L_S = 100$$

Use the facts that $K_C = 2 \cdot L_C$ and $K_S = 0.5 \cdot L_S$ to rewrite these equations as

$$2 \cdot L_C + 0.5 \cdot L_S = 100 \text{ and } L_C + L_S = 100$$

Use these two equations to solve for L_C and L_S, and then calculate the amount of capital used in each industry using $K_C = 2 \cdot L_C$ and $K_S = 0.5 \cdot L_S$.

b. Suppose that the number of workers increases to 125 due to immigration, keeping total capital fixed at 100. Again, solve for the amount of labor and capital used in each industry. *Hint:* Redo the calculations from part (a), but using $L_C + L_S = 125$.

c. Suppose instead that the amount of capital increases to 125 due to FDI, keeping the total number of workers fixed at 100. Again solve for the amount of labor and capital used in each industry. *Hint:* Redo the calculations from part (a), using $K_C + K_S = 125$.

d. Explain how your results in parts (b) and (c) are related to the Rybczynski theorem.

The questions 7 and 8 explore the implications of the Rybczynski theorem and the factor price insensitivity result for the Heckscher-Ohlin model from Chapter 4.

7. In this question, we use the Rybczynski theorem to review the derivation of the Heckscher-Ohlin theorem.

a. Start at the no-trade equilibrium point A on the Home PPF in Figure 4-2, panel (a). Suppose that through immigration, the amount of labor in Home grows. Draw the new PPF, and label the point B where production would occur with the same prices for goods. *Hint:* You can refer to Figure 5-9 to see the effect of immigration on the PPF.

b. Suppose that the only difference between Foreign and Home is that Foreign has more labor. Otherwise, the technologies used to produce each good are the same across countries. Then how does the Foreign PPF compare with the new Home PPF (including immigration) that you drew in part (a)? Is point B the no-trade equilibrium in Foreign? Explain why or why not.

c. Illustrate a new point A^* that is the no-trade equilibrium in Foreign. How do the relative no-trade prices of computers compare in Home and Foreign? Therefore, what will be the pattern of trade between the countries, and why?

8. Continuing from Problem 7, we now use the factor price insensitivity result to compare factor prices across countries in the Heckscher-Ohlin model.

a. Illustrate the international trade equilibrium on the Home and Foreign production possibilities frontiers. *Hint:* You can refer to Figure 4-3 to see the international trade equilibrium.

b. Suppose that the only difference between Foreign and Home is that Foreign has more labor. Otherwise, the technologies used to produce each good are the same across countries. Then, according to the factor price insensitivity result, how will the wage and rental compare in the two countries?

c. Call the result in part (b) "factor price equalization." Is this a realistic result? *Hint:* You can refer to Figure 4-9 to see wages across countries.

d. Based on our extension of the Heckscher-Ohlin model at the end of Chapter 4, what is one reason why the factor price equalization result does not hold in reality?

9. Recall the formula from the application "The Effect of FDI on Rentals and Wages in Singapore." Give an intuitive explanation for this formula for the rental rate.
Hint: Describe one side of the equation as a marginal benefit and the other as a marginal cost.

10. In Table 5-2, we show the growth in the real rental and real wages in Singapore, along with the implied productivity growth. One way to calculate the productivity growth is to take the average of the growth in the real rental and real wage. The idea is that firms can afford to pay more to labor and capital if there is productivity growth, so in that case real factor prices should be growing. But if there is no productivity growth, then the average of the growth in the real rental and real wage should be close to zero.

To calculate the average of the growth in the real factor prices, we use the shares of GDP going to capital and labor. Specifically, we multiply the growth in the real rental by the capital share of GDP and add the growth in the

real wage multiplied by the labor share of GDP. Then answer the following:

a. For a capital-rich country like Singapore, the share of capital in GDP is about one-half and the share of labor is also one-half. Using these shares, calculate the average of the growth in the real rental and real wage shown in each row of Table 5-2. How do your answers compare with the productivity growth shown in the last column of Table 5-2?

b. For an industrialized country like the United States, the share of capital in GDP is about one-third and the share of labor in GDP is about two-thirds. Using these shares, calculate the average of the growth in the real rental and real wage shown in each row of Table 5-2. How do your answers now compare with the productivity growth shown in the last column?

11. Figure 5-14 is a supply and demand diagram for the world labor market. Starting at points A and A^*, consider a situation in which some Foreign workers migrate to Home but not enough to reach the equilibrium with full migration (point B). As a result of the migration, the Home wage decreases from W to $W'' > W'$, and the Foreign wage increases from W^* to $W^{**} < W'$.

a. Are there gains that accrue to the Home country? If so, redraw the graph and identify the magnitude of the gains for each country. If not, say why not.

b. Are there gains that accrue to the Foreign country? If so, again show the magnitude of these gains in the diagram and also show the world gains.

12. A housekeeper from the Philippines is contemplating immigrating to Singapore in search of higher wages. Suppose the housekeeper earns approximately $2,000 annually and expects to find a job in Singapore worth approximately $5,000 annually for a period of three years. Furthermore, assume that the cost of living in Singapore is $500 more per year than at home.

a. What can we say about the productivity of housekeepers in Singapore versus the Philippines? Explain.

b. What is the total gain to the housekeeper from migrating?

c. Is there a corresponding gain for the employer in Singapore? Explain.

N E T **W O R K**

Immigration is frequently debated in the United States and other countries. Find the most recent news report dealing with immigration policy in the United States, and briefly summarize the issues discussed.

Increasing Returns to Scale and Monopolistic Competition

Foreign trade, then, . . . [is] highly beneficial to a country, as it increases the amount and variety of the objects on which revenue may be expended.

David Ricardo, *On the Principles of Political Economy and Taxation*, Chapter 7

The idea that a simple government policy [free trade between Canada and the United States] could raise productivity so dramatically is to me truly remarkable.

Professor Daniel Trefler, University of Toronto, 2005

In Chapter 2, we looked at data for U.S. snowboard imports and considered the reasons why the United States imports this product from so many different countries. Now we look at another sporting good that the United States imports *and exports* in large quantities to illustrate how a country can both buy a product and sell it to other countries. In 2009 the United States imported golf clubs from 25 countries and exported them to 83 countries. In Table 6-1, we list the 12 countries that sell the most golf clubs to the United States and the 12 countries to which the United States sells the most golf clubs. The table also lists the amounts bought or sold and their average wholesale prices.

In panel (a), we see that China sells the most clubs to the United States, providing $254 million worth of golf clubs at an average price of $18 each. Next is Thailand, selling $14 million of clubs at an average wholesale price of $102 each. Vietnam comes next, exporting $7 million of clubs at an average price of $14, followed by Japan, selling $6 million of clubs with an average price of $125. The higher average prices of Thai and Japanese clubs compared with Chinese and Vietnamese clubs most likely indicate that the clubs Thailand and Japan sell are of much higher quality. The clubs from most of the other top-selling countries (except Malaysia) have wholesale prices below $55. There are a few other countries (not among the top 12) that export one or two custom-made clubs to the United States, with prices of $2,000 or more![1] In total, the United States imported $284 million of golf clubs in 2009.

---

[1] There was one golf club imported from Ireland in 2009 at a price of $2,096, and one club imported from the Netherlands at a price of $4,000.

TABLE 6-1

U.S. Imports and Exports of Golf Clubs, 2009 This table shows the value, quantity, and average price for golf clubs imported into and exported from the United States. Many of the same countries both sell golf clubs to and buy golf clubs from the United States, illustrating what we call intra-industry trade.

(a) IMPORTS

Rank	Country	Value of Imports (millions)	Quantity of Golf Clubs (thousands)	Average Price ($/club)
1	China	$254.2	14,482	18
2	Thailand	13.5	132	102
3	Vietnam	7.2	504	14
4	Japan	5.8	47	125
5	Taiwan	1.1	69	16
6	Malaysia	1.1	12	89
7	Mexico	0.3	40	8
8	Hong Kong	0.3	16	18
9	Macao	0.2	5	43
10	United Kingdom	0.1	12	10
11	Canada	0.1	3	25
12	Korea	0.1	1	54
13-25	Various countries	0.1	11	8
	All 25 countries	284.2	15,335	19

(b) EXPORTS

Rank	Country	Value of Imports (millions)	Quantity of Golf Clubs (thousands)	Average Price ($/club)
1	Canada	$64.9	837	77
2	Japan	41.7	430	97
3	United Kingdom	35.8	446	80
4	Korea	33.9	419	81
5	Australia	14.1	189	75
6	Singapore	6.8	65	104
7	Hong Kong	6.7	72	92
8	Argentina	2.7	35	77
9	Malaysia	2.5	31	83
10	South Africa	2.3	25	93
11	Netherlands	1.8	18	102
12	Thailand	1.7	22	77
13-83	Various countries	11.3	136	83
	All 83 countries	226.2	2,725	83

Source: U.S. International Trade Commission Interactive Tariff and Trade DataWeb at http://dataweb.usitc.gov/.

On the export side, shown in panel (b), the top destination for U.S. clubs is Canada, followed by Japan and the UnitedKingdom (with its world-famous golf courses in Scotland). Notice that these three countries are also among the top 12 countries selling golf clubs to the United States. The average price for U.S. exports varies between $75 and $104 per club, higher than the price of all the imported clubs except those from Thailand, Japan, and Malaysia, which suggests that the United States is exporting high-quality clubs.

Many of the countries that sell to the United States also buy from the United States: 7 of the top 12 selling countries were also among the top 12 countries buying U.S. golf clubs in 2009. Of the top 25 selling countries, 24 also bought U.S. golf clubs. In fact, the value of U.S. imports ($284 million) and the value of U.S. exports ($226 million) are similar. Why does the United States export and import golf clubs to and from the same countries? The answer to this question is one of the "new" explanations for trade that we study in this chapter and the next. The Ricardian model (Chapter 2) and the Heckscher-Ohlin model (Chapter 4) explained why nations would either import or export a good, but those models do not predict the simultaneous import and export of a product, as we observe for golf clubs and many other goods.

To explain why countries import and export the same product , we need to change some assumptions made in the Ricardian and Heckscher-Ohlin models. In those models, we assumed that markets were perfectly competitive, which means there are many small producers, each producing a homogeneous (identical) product, so none of them can influence the market price for the product. As we know just from walking down the aisles in a grocery or department store, most goods are **differentiated goods;** that is, they are not identical. Based on price differences in Table 6-1, we can see that the traded golf clubs are of different types and quality. So in this chapter, we drop the assumption that the goods are homogeneous, as in perfect competition, and instead will assume that goods are differentiated and allow for **imperfect competition,** in which case firms can influence the price that they charge.

The new explanation for trade explored in this chapter involves a type of imperfect competition called **monopolistic competition,** which has two key features. The first feature, just mentioned, is that the goods produced by different firms are differentiated. By offering different products, firms are able to exert some control over the price they can charge for their particular product. Because the market in which the firms operate is not a perfectly competitive one, they do not have to accept the market price, and by increasing their price, they do not lose all their business to competitors. On the other hand, because these firms are not monopolists (i.e., they are not the only firm that produces this type of product), they cannot charge prices as high as a monopolist would. When firms produce differentiated products, they retain some ability to set the price for their product, but not as much as a monopolist would have.

The second feature of monopolistic competition is **increasing returns to scale,** by which we mean that the average costs for a firm fall as more output is produced. For this reason, firms tend to specialize in the product lines that are most successful—by selling more of those products, the average cost for the production of the successful products falls. Firms can lower their average costs by selling more in their home markets but can possibly attain even lower costs from selling more in foreign markets through exporting. So increasing returns to scale create a reason for trade to occur even when the trading countries are similar in their technologies and factor endowments. Increasing returns to scale set the monopolistic competition trade model apart from the logic of the Ricardian and Heckscher-Ohlin models.

In this chapter, we describe a model of trade under monopolistic competition that incorporates these features of product differentiation and increasing returns to scale. After describing the monopolistic competition model, the next goal of the chapter is to discuss how this model helps us to explain trade patterns that we observe today. In our golf club example, countries specialize in different varieties of the same type of product and trade them; this type of trade is called **intra-industry trade** because it deals with imports and exports in the same industry. The monopolistic competition model explains this trade pattern and also predicts that larger countries will trade more with one another. Just as the force of gravity is strongest between two large objects, the monopolistic competition model implies that large countries (as measured by their GDP) should trade the most.[2] There is a good deal of empirical evidence to support this prediction, which is called the **gravity equation.**

The monopolistic competition model also helps us to understand the effects of **free-trade agreements,** in which free trade occurs among a group of countries. In this chapter, we use the North American Free Trade Agreement (NAFTA) to illustrate the predictions of the monopolistic competition model. The policy implications of free-trade agreements are discussed later in a later chapter.

1 Basics of Imperfect Competition

Monopolistic competition incorporates some aspects of a monopoly (firms have control over the prices they charge) and some aspects of perfect competition (many firms are selling). Before presenting the monopolistic competition model, it is useful to review the case of monopoly, which is a single firm selling a product. The monopoly firm faces the industry demand curve. After that, we briefly discuss the case of **duopoly,** when there are two firms selling a product. Our focus will be on the demand facing each of the two firms. Understanding what happens to demand in a duopoly will help us understand how demand is determined when there are many firms selling differentiated products, as occurs in monopolistic competition.

Monopoly Equilibrium

In Figure 6-1, the industry demand curve is shown by D. For the monopolist to sell more, the price must fall, and so the demand curve slopes downward. This fall in price means that the extra revenue earned by the monopolist from selling another unit is less than the price of that unit—the extra revenue earned equals the price charged for that unit *minus* the fall in price times the quantity sold of all earlier units. The extra revenue earned from selling one more unit is called the **marginal revenue** and is shown by the curve MR in Figure 6-1. The marginal revenue curve lies below the demand curve D because the extra revenue earned from selling another unit is less than the price.

To maximize its profits, the monopolist sells up to the point at which the marginal revenue MR earned from selling one more unit equals the **marginal cost** MC of producing one more unit. In Figure 6-1, the marginal cost curve is shown by

---

[2] If you have read Chapter 1, you will know that large countries do indeed trade the most, as seen in the map of world trade.

FIGURE 6-1

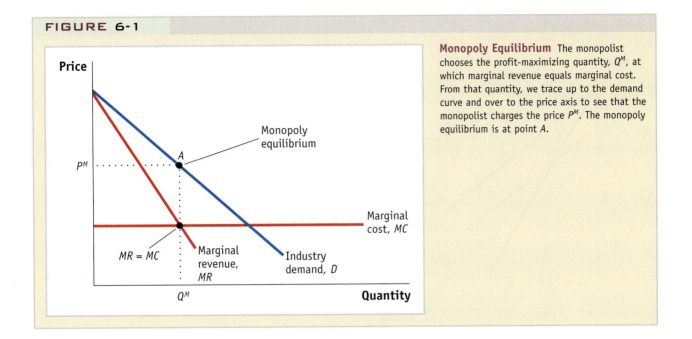

Monopoly Equilibrium The monopolist chooses the profit-maximizing quantity, Q^M, at which marginal revenue equals marginal cost. From that quantity, we trace up to the demand curve and over to the price axis to see that the monopolist charges the price P^M. The monopoly equilibrium is at point A.

MC. Because we have assumed, for simplicity, that marginal costs are constant, the MC curve is flat, although this does not need to be the case. To have marginal revenue equal marginal costs, the monopolist sells the quantity Q^M. To find the profit-maximizing price the monopolist charges, we trace up from quantity Q^M to point A on the demand curve and then over to the price axis. The price charged by the monopolist P^M is the price that allows the monopolist to earn the highest level of profits and is therefore the monopoly equilibrium.

Demand with Duopoly

Let us compare a monopoly with a duopoly, a market structure in which two firms are selling a product. We will not solve for the duopoly equilibrium but will just study how the introduction of a second firm affects the demand facing each of the firms. Knowing how demand is affected by the introduction of a second firm will help us understand how demand is determined when there are many firms, as there are in monopolistic competition.

In Figure 6-2, the industry faces the demand curve D. If there are two firms in the industry and they charge the same price, then the demand curve facing each firm is $D/2$. For example, if both firms charged the price P_1, then the industry demand is at point A, and each firm's demand is at point B on curve $D/2$. The two firms share the market equally, each selling exactly one-half of the total market demand, $Q_2 = Q_1/2$.

If one firm charges a price different from the other firm, however, the demand facing both firms changes. Suppose that one firm charges a lower price P_2, while the other firm keeps its price at P_1. If the firms are selling the same homogeneous product, then the firm charging the lower price would get all the demand (shown by point C), which is Q_3 at the price P_2. Now suppose that the products are not homogeneous but instead are differentiated. In that case, the firm with the lower price P_2 will

FIGURE 6-2

Demand Curves with Duopoly When there are two firms in the market and they both charge the same price, each firm faces the demand curve $D/2$. At the price P_1, the industry produces Q_1 at point A and each firm produces $Q_2 = Q_1/2$ at point B. If both firms produce identical products and one firm lowers its price to P_2, all consumers will buy from that firm only; the firm that lowers its price will face the demand curve, D, and sell Q_3 at point C. Alternatively, if the products are differentiated, the firm that lowers its price will take some, but not all, sales from the other firm; it will face the demand curve, d, and at P_2 it will sell Q_4 at point C'.

capture more of the market than the firm with the higher price P_1, but will not capture the entire market. Because the products are not precisely the same (for instance, in our golf club example the higher-priced club is of better quality than the less expensive club), some consumers will still want to buy the other firm's product even though its price is higher. The firm selling at the lower price P_2 now sells the quantity Q_4, for example, at point C'.

The demand curve d is the demand curve for the firm that lowered its price from P_1 to P_2, even though the other firm held its price at P_1. As we have illustrated, the demand curve d is *flatter* than the demand curve $D/2$. This means that each firm faces a more elastic demand curve than $D/2$: when only one firm lowers its price, it increases its quantity sold by more than when all firms lower their prices. Not only is the quantity demanded in the industry increasing, but in addition, the firm lowering its price is taking away some of the quantity demanded from the other firm. In summary, the demand curve d facing each firm producing in a duopoly is more elastic than the demand curve $D/2$ it faces when the firms charge the same price.

2 Trade under Monopolistic Competition

We begin our study of monopolistic competition by carefully stating the assumptions of the model, which are as follows:

Assumption 1: Each firm produces a good that is similar to but differentiated from the goods that other firms in the industry produce.

Because each firm's product is somewhat different from the goods of the other firms, a firm can raise its prices without losing all its customers to other firms. Thus, each firm faces a downward-sloping demand curve for its product and has some control over the price it charges. This is different from perfect competition, in which all firms produce exactly the same product and therefore must sell at exactly the same market-determined price.

Assumption 2: There are many firms in the industry.

The discussion of duopoly demand in the previous section helps us to think about the demand curve facing a firm under monopolistic competition, when there are many firms in the industry. If the number of firms is N, then D/N is the share of demand that each firm faces when the firms are all charging the same price. When only one firm lowers its price, however, it will face a flatter demand curve d. We will begin describing the model by focusing on the demand curve d and later bring back the demand curve D/N.

The first two assumptions are about the demand facing each firm; the third assumption is about each firm's cost structure:

Assumption 3: Firms produce using a technology with increasing returns to scale.

The assumptions underlying monopolistic competition differ from our usual assumptions on firm costs by allowing for increasing returns to scale, a production technology in which the average costs of production fall as the quantity produced increases. This relationship is shown in Figure 6-3, in which average costs are labeled AC. The assumption that average costs fall as quantity increases means that marginal costs, labeled *MC*, must be *below* average costs. Why? Think about whether a new student coming into your class will raise or lower the class average grade. If the new student's average is below the existing class average, then when he or she enters, the class average will fall. In the same way, when *MC* is less than *AC*, then *AC* must be falling.[3]

FIGURE 6-3

Increasing Returns to Scale This diagram shows the average cost, *AC*, and marginal cost, *MC*, of a firm. Increasing returns to scale cause average costs to fall as the quantity produced increases. Marginal cost is below average cost and is drawn as constant for simplicity.

Cost

Average cost, *AC*

Marginal cost, *MC*

Quantity

---

[3] For simplicity, we assume that marginal costs are constant, but this need not be the case.

Numerical Example As an example of the cost curves in Figure 6-3, suppose that the firm has the following cost data:

$$\text{Fixed costs} = \$100$$

$$\text{Marginal costs} = \$10 \text{ per unit}$$

Given these costs, the average costs for this firm for various quantities are as shown in Table 6-2.

Notice that as the quantity produced rises, average costs fall and eventually become close to the marginal costs of $10 per unit, as shown in Figure 6-3.

Assumption 3 means that average cost is above marginal cost. Assumption 1 means that firms have some control over the price they charge and these firms charge a price that is also above marginal cost (we learn why in a later section).

Whenever the price charged is above average costs, then a firm earns **monopoly profits.** Our final assumption describes what happens to profits in a monopolistically competitive industry in the long run:

Assumption 4: Because firms can enter and exit the industry freely, monopoly profits are zero in the long run.

Recall that under perfect competition, we assume there are many firms in the industry and that in a long-run equilibrium each firm's profits must be zero. In monopolistic competition, there is the same requirement for a long-run equilibrium. We assume that firms can enter and exit the industry freely; this means that firms will enter as long as it is possible to make monopoly profits, and as more firms enter, the profits per firm fall. We will see that this condition leads to a long-run equilibrium in which profits for each firm are zero, just as in perfect competition!

Equilibrium without Trade

Short-Run Equilibrium The short-run equilibrium for a firm under monopolistic competition, shown in Figure 6-4, is similar to a monopoly equilibrium. The demand

---

TABLE 6-2

Cost Information for the Firm This table illustrates increasing returns to scale, in which average costs fall as quantity rises.

Quantity Q	Variable Costs = $Q \cdot MC$ ($MC = \$10$)	Total Costs = Variable Costs + Fixed Costs ($FC = \$100$)	Average Costs = Total Costs/Quantity
10	$100	$200	$20
20	200	300	15
30	300	400	13.3
40	400	500	12.5
50	500	600	12
100	1,000	1,100	11
Large Q	$10 \cdot Q$	$10 \cdot Q + 100$	Close to 10

FIGURE 6-4

Short-Run Monopolistic Competition Equilibrium without Trade The short-run equilibrium under monopolistic competition is the same as a monopoly equilibrium. The firm chooses to produce the quantity Q_0 at which the firm's marginal revenue, mr_0, equals its marginal cost, MC. The price charged is P_0. Because price exceeds average cost, the firm makes monopoly profits.

curve faced by each firm is labeled d_0, the marginal revenue curve is labeled mr_0, and the marginal cost curve of each firm is shown by MC. Each firm maximizes profits by producing Q_0, the quantity at which marginal revenue equals marginal cost. Tracing up from this quantity to the demand curve shows that the price charged by the firms is P_0. Because the price exceeds average costs at the quantity Q_0, the firm earns monopoly profits.

Long-Run Equilibrium In a monopolistically competitive market, new firms continue to enter the industry as long as monopoly profits are earned. In the long run, the entry of new firms draws demand away from existing firms, causing demand curve d_0 to shift to the left until no firm in the industry earns positive monopoly profits (Figure 6-5). Moreover, when new firms enter and there are more product varieties available to consumers, the d_0 curve faced by each firm becomes more elastic, or flatter. We expect the d_0 curve to become more elastic as more firms enter because each product is similar to the other existing products; therefore, as the number of close substitutes increases, consumers become more price-sensitive.

New firms continue to enter the industry until the price charged by each firm is on the average cost curve and monopoly profits are zero. At this point, the industry is in a long-run equilibrium, with no reason for any further entry or exit. The long-run equilibrium without trade is shown in Figure 6-5. Again, the demand curve for the firm is labeled d, with the short-run demand curve denoted d_0 and the long-run demand curve denoted d_1 (with corresponding marginal revenue curve mr_1). Marginal revenue equals marginal cost at quantity Q_1. At this quantity, all firms in the industry charge price P^A. The price P^A equals average cost at point A, where the demand curve d_1 is tangent to the average cost curve. Because the price equals average costs, the firm is earning zero monopoly profits and there is no incentive for firms to enter or exit the industry. Thus, point A is the firm's (and the industry's) long-run equilibrium without trade. Notice that the long-run equilibrium curve d_1 is to the left of and more elastic (flatter) than the short-run curve d_0.

FIGURE 6-5

Long-Run Monopolistic Competition Equilibrium without Trade Drawn by the possibility of making profits in the short-run equilibrium, new firms enter the industry and the firm's demand curve, d_0, shifts to the left and becomes more elastic (i.e., flatter), shown by d_1. The long-run equilibrium under monopolistic competition occurs at the quantity Q_1 where the marginal revenue curve, mr_1 (associated with demand curve d_1), equals marginal cost. At that quantity, the no-trade price, P^A, equals average costs at point A. In the long-run equilibrium, firms earn zero monopoly profits and there is no entry or exit. The quantity produced by each firm is less than in short-run equilibrium (Figure 6-4). Q_1 is less than Q_0 because new firms have entered the industry. With a greater number of firms and hence more varieties available to consumers, the demand for each variety d_1 is less then d_0. The demand curve D/N^A shows the no-trade demand when all firms charge the same price.

Before we allow for international trade, we need to introduce another curve into Figure 6-5. The firm's demand curve d_1 shows the quantity demanded depending on the price charged by that firm, holding the price charged by all other firms fixed. In contrast, there is another demand curve that shows the quantity demanded from each firm when all firms in the industry charge the *same price*. This other demand curve is the total market demand D divided by the number of firms in the absence of trade N^A. In Figure 6-5, we label the second demand curve as D/N^A. We omit drawing total industry demand D itself so we do not clutter the diagram.

The demand curve d_1 is flatter, or more elastic, than the demand curve D/N^A. We discussed why that is the case under duopoly (see Figure 6-2) and can review the reason again now. Starting at point A, consider a drop in the price by just one firm, which increases the quantity demanded along the d_1 curve for that firm. The demand curve d_1 is quite elastic, meaning that the drop in price leads to a large increase in the quantity purchased because customers are attracted away from other firms. If instead all firms drop their price by the same amount, along the curve D/N^A, then each firm will not attract as many customers away from other firms. When all firms drop their prices equally, then the increase in quantity demanded from each firm along industry curve D/N^A is less than the increase along the firm's curve d_1. Thus, demand is less elastic along the demand curve D/N^A, which is why it is steeper than the d_1 curve. As we proceed with our analysis of opening trade under monopolistic competition, it will be helpful to keep track of both of these demand curves.

Equilibrium with Free Trade

Let us now allow for free trade between Home and Foreign in this industry. For simplicity, we assume that Home and Foreign countries are exactly the same, with the same number of consumers, the same factor endowments, the same technology and cost curves, and the same number of firms in the no-trade equilibrium. If there were no increasing returns to scale, there would be no reason at all for international trade to occur. Under the Ricardian model, for example, countries with identical technologies would not trade because their no-trade relative prices would be equal. Likewise, under the Heckscher-Ohlin model, countries with identical factor endowments would not trade because their no-trade relative prices would be the same. Under monopolistic competition, however, two identical countries will still engage in international trade because increasing returns to scale exist.

Short-Run Equilibrium with Trade We will take as given the number of firms in the no-trade equilibrium in each country N^A and use this number of firms to determine the short-run equilibrium with trade. Our starting point is the long-run equilibrium without trade, as shown by point A in Figure 6-5 and reproduced in Figure 6-6. When we allow free trade between Home and Foreign, the number of consumers available to each firm doubles (because there is an equal number of consumers in each country) as does the number of firms (because there is an equal number of firms in each country). Because there are not only twice as many consumers but also twice as many firms, the demand curve D/N^A is the same as it was before, $2D/2N^A = D/N^A$. In other words, point A is still on the demand curve D/N^A, as shown in Figure 6-6.

Free trade doubles the number of firms, which also doubles the product varieties available to consumers. With a greater number of product varieties available to consumers, their demand for each individual variety will be *more elastic*. That is, if one firm drops its price below the no-trade price P^A, then it can expect to attract an even greater number of customers away from other firms. Before trade the firm would attract additional Home customers only, but after trade it will attract additional Home and Foreign consumers. In Figure 6-6, this consumer response is shown by the firm's new demand curve d_2, which is more elastic than its no-trade demand curve d_1. As a result, the demand curve d_2 is no longer tangent to the average cost curve at point A

FIGURE 6-6

Short-Run Monopolistic Competition Equilibrium with Trade When trade is opened, the larger market makes the firm's demand curve more elastic, as shown by d_2 (with corresponding marginal revenue curve, mr_2). The firm chooses to produce the quantity Q_2 at which marginal revenue equals marginal costs; this quantity corresponds to a price of P_2. With sales of Q_2 at price P_2, the firm will make monopoly profits because price is greater than AC. When *all* firms lower their prices to P_2, however, the relevant demand curve is D/N^A, which indicates that they can sell only Q'_2 at price P_2. At this short-run equilibrium (point B'), price is less than average cost and all firms incur losses. As a result, some firms are forced to exit the industry.

but is *above* average costs for prices below P^A. The new demand curve d_2 has a corresponding marginal revenue curve mr_2, as shown in Figure 6-6.

With the new demand curve d_2 and new marginal revenue curve mr_2, the firm again needs to choose its profit-maximizing level of production. As usual, that level will be where marginal revenue equals marginal cost at Q_2. When we trace from Q_2 up to point B on the firm's demand curve d_2, then over to the price axis, we see that the firm will charge P_2. Because P_2 is above average costs at point B, the firm will make positive monopoly profits. We can see clearly the firm's incentive to lower its price: at point A it earns zero monopoly profits and at point B it earns positive profits. Producing Q_2 and selling it at P_2 is the firm's profit-maximizing position.

This happy scenario for the firm is not the end of the story, however. *Every* firm in the industry (in both Home and Foreign) has the same incentive to lower its price in the hope of attracting customers away from all the other firms and earning monopoly profits. When all firms lower their prices at the same time, however, the quantity demanded from each firm increases along the demand curve D/N^A, not along d_2. Remember that the D/N^A curve shows the demand faced by each firm when all firms in the industry charge the same price. With the prices of all firms lowered to P_2, they will each sell the quantity Q'_2 at point B' rather than their expected sales of Q_2 at point B. At point B', the price charged is *less than* average costs, so every firm is incurring a loss. In the short-run equilibrium with trade, firms lower their prices, expecting to make profits at point B, but end up making losses at point B'.

Point B' is not the long-run equilibrium because the losses will bankrupt some firms and cause them to exit from the industry. This exit will increase demand (both d and D/N^A) for the remaining firms and decrease the number of product varieties available to consumers. To understand where the new long-run equilibrium occurs, we turn to a new diagram.

Long-Run Equilibrium with Trade Due to the exit of firms, the number of firms remaining in each country after trade is less than it was before trade. Let us call the number of firms in each country after trade is opened N^T, where $N^T < N^A$. This reduction in the number of firms increases the share of demand facing each one, so that $D/N^T > D/N^A$. In Figure 6-7, the demand D/N^T facing each firm lies to the right of the demand D/N^A in the earlier figures. We show the long-run equilibrium with trade at point C. At point C, the demand curve d_3 facing an individual firm is tangent to the average cost curve AC. In addition, the marginal revenue curve mr_3 intersects the marginal cost curve MC.

How does this long-run equilibrium compare to that without trade? First of all, despite the exit of some firms in each country, we still expect that the world number of products, which is $2N^T$ (the number produced in each country N^T times two countries), exceeds the number of products N^A available in each country before trade, $2N^T > N^A$. It follows that the demand curve d_3 facing each firm must be more elastic than demand d_1 in the absence of trade: the availability of imported products makes consumers more price-sensitive than they were before trade, so the demand curve d_3 is more elastic than demand d_1 in Figure 6-5. At free-trade equilibrium (point C), each firm still in operation charges a lower price than it did with no trade, $P^W < P^A$, and produces a higher quantity, $Q_3 > Q_1$. The drop in prices and increase in quantity for each firm go hand in hand: as the quantity produced by each surviving firm increases, average costs fall due to increasing returns to scale, and so do the prices charged by firms.

FIGURE 6-7

Long-Run Monopolistic Competition Equilibrium with Trade The long-run equilibrium with trade occurs at point C. At this point, profits are maximized for each firm producing Q_3 (which satisfies $mr_3 = MC$) and charging price P^W (which equals AC). Since monopoly profits are zero when price equals average cost, no firms enter or exit the industry. Compared with the long-run equilibrium without trade (Figure 6-5), d_3 (along with mr_3) has shifted out as domestic firms exited the industry and has become more elastic due to the greater total number of varieties with trade, $2N^T > N^A$. Compared with the long-run equilibrium without trade at point A, the trade equilibrium at point C has a lower price and higher sales by all surviving firms.

Gains from Trade The long-run equilibrium at point C has two sources of gains from trade for consumers. First, the price has fallen as compared with point A, so consumers benefit for that reason. A good way to think about this drop in the price is that it reflects increasing returns to scale, with average costs falling as the output of firms rises. The drop in average costs is a rise in productivity for these surviving firms because output can be produced more cheaply. So consumers gain from the drop in price, which is the result of the rise in productivity.

There is a second source of gains from trade to consumers. We assume that consumers obtain higher surplus when there are more product varieties available to buy, and hence the increase in variety is a source of gain for consumers. Within each country, some firms exit the market after trade begins, so fewer product varieties are produced by the remaining domestic firms. However, because consumers can buy products from both Home and Foreign firms, the *total* number of varieties available with trade is greater than the number of varieties available in any one country before trade, $2N^T > N^A$. Thus, in addition to the drop in prices, there is an added consumer gain from the availability of additional product varieties.

Adjustment Costs from Trade Against these long-run gains from trade, there are short-run adjustment costs as some firms in each country shut down and exit the industry. The workers in those firms will experience a spell of unemployment as they look for new jobs. Over the long run, however, we expect these workers to find new positions, so we view these costs as temporary. We do not build these adjustment costs into the model because they are short-term, but we are still interested in how large these costs might be in practice. To compare the short-run adjustment costs with the long-run gains from trade, we next look at the evidence from Canada, Mexico, and the United States under the North American Free Trade Agreement. We will see that the predictions of the monopolistic competition model hold reasonably well in each case.

3 The North American Free Trade Agreement

The idea that free trade will expand the range of products available to consumers is not new—it is even mentioned by David Ricardo in the quote at the beginning of this chapter. But the ability to carefully model the effects of trade under monopolistic competition *is* new and was developed in research during the 1980s by Professors Elhanan Helpman, Paul Krugman, and the late Kelvin Lancaster. That research was not just theoretical but was used to shed light on free-trade agreements, which guarantee free trade among a group of countries. In 1989, for example, Canada and the United States entered into a free-trade agreement, and in 1994 they were joined by Mexico in the North American Free Trade Agreement (NAFTA). The potential for Canadian firms to expand their output (and enjoy lower average costs) by selling in the United States and Mexico was a key factor in Canada's decision to enter into these free-trade agreements. The quote from the Canadian economist Daniel Trefler at the beginning of the chapter shows that there was indeed a rise in productivity in Canada because of the free-trade agreements. We use NAFTA to illustrate the gains and costs predicted by the monopolistic competition model.

Gains and Adjustment Costs for Canada under NAFTA

Studies in Canada dating back to the 1960s predicted substantial gains from free trade with the United States because Canadian firms would expand their scale of operations to serve the larger market and lower their costs. A set of simulations based on the monopolistic competition model performed by the Canadian economist Richard Harris in the mid-1980s influenced Canadian policy makers to proceed with the free-trade agreement with the United States in 1989. Enough time has passed since then to look back and see how Canada has fared under the trade agreements with the United States and Mexico.

Headlines: What Happened When Two Countries Liberalized Trade? Pain, then Gain describes what happened in Canada. Using data from 1988 to 1996, Professor Daniel Trefler of the University of Toronto found short-run adjustment costs of 100,000 lost jobs, or 5% of manufacturing employment. Some industries that faced particularly large tariff cuts saw their employment fall by as much as 12%. These are very large declines in employment. Over time, however, these job losses were more than made up for by the creation of new jobs elsewhere in manufacturing, so there were no long-run job losses as a result of the free-trade agreement.

What about long-run gains? Trefler found a large positive effect on the productivity of firms, with productivity rising as much as 15% over eight years in the industries most affected by tariff cuts, or a compound growth rate of 1.9% per year. For manufacturing overall, productivity rose by 6%, for a compound growth rate of 0.7% per year. The difference between these two numbers, which is 1.9 − 0.7 = 1.2% per year, is an estimate of how free trade with the United States affected the Canadian industries most affected by the tariff cuts over and above the impact on other industries. The productivity growth in Canada allowed for a modest rise in real earnings of 3% over the eight-year period. We conclude that the prediction of the monopolistic competition model that surviving firms increase their productivity is confirmed for Canadian manufacturing. Those productivity gains led to a fall in prices for consumers and a rise in real earnings for workers, which demonstrates the first source of the gains from trade. The second source of gains from trade—increased product variety for Canadian consumers—was not measured in the study by Professor Trefler but has been estimated for the United States, as discussed later in this chapter.

HEADLINES

What Happened When Two Countries Liberalized Trade? Pain, Then Gain

The following article is based on an interview with Professor Daniel Trefler, University of Toronto, who studied the impact of the Canada-U.S. Free Trade Agreement on Canadian manufacturing industries.[4]

Economists argue for free trade. They have two centuries of theory and experience to back them up. And they have recent empirical studies of how the liberalization of trade has increased productivity in less-developed countries like Chile and India. Lowering trade barriers, they maintain, not only cuts costs for consumers but aids economic growth and makes the general public better off.

Even so, free trade is a tough sell. . . . "We talk a lot about the benefits of free trade agreements, but when it comes to academics studying it, we know next to nothing in terms of hard-core facts about what happens when two rich countries liberalize trade," Professor Trefler, of the Rotman School of Management at the University of Toronto, said in an interview. His article, "The Long and Short of the Canada-U.S. Free Trade Agreement," uses detailed data on both Canadian industries and individual companies to address these gaps. . . .

Not surprisingly, the Canadian industries that had relied on tariffs to protect them "were hammered" when those barriers disappeared, Professor Trefler said. "They saw their employment fall by 12 percent," he said, meaning one in eight workers lost their jobs. In manufacturing as a whole, the trade agreement reduced employment by 5 percent.

"Employment losses of 5 percent translate into 100,000 lost jobs and strike me as large," he wrote, "not least because only a relatively small number of industries experienced deep tariff concessions." No wonder free trade agreements touch off so much opposition. As painful as those layoffs were, however, the job losses were a short-term effect. Over the long run, employment in Canada did not drop, and manufacturing employment remains more robust than in other industrialized countries.

"Within 10 years, the lost employment was made up by employment gains in other parts of manufacturing," Professor Trefler found. Although low-productivity plants shut down, high-productivity Canadian manufacturers not only expanded into the United States but further improved their operations. Along the way, they hired enough new workers to make up for losses elsewhere. "The average effect of the U.S. tariff cuts on Canadian employment was thus a wash: the employment losses by less-productive firms offset the employment gains by more productive firms," Professor Trefler wrote in an e-mail message, citing further research. . . .

In addition, he said, "there is absolutely no evidence" that the trade agreement worsened income inequality. The big story is that lowering tariffs set off a productivity boom. Formerly sheltered Canadian companies began to compete with and compare themselves with more efficient American businesses. Some went under, but others significantly improved operations. The productivity gains were huge. In the formerly sheltered industries most affected by the tariff cuts, labor productivity jumped 15 percent, at least half from closing inefficient plants. "This translates into an enormous compound annual growth rate of 1.9 percent," he wrote.

But closing plants is not the whole story, or even half of it. Among export-oriented industries, which expanded after the agreement, data from individual plants show an increase in labor productivity of 14 percent. Manufacturing productivity as a whole jumped 6 percent. "The idea that a simple government policy could raise productivity so dramatically is to me truly remarkable," Professor Trefler said.

---

[4] Daniel Trefler, 2004, "The Long and Short of the Canada-U.S. Free Trade Agreement," *American Economic Review*, 94(4), September, 870–895.

Source: Excerpted from Virginia Postrel, "Economic Scene," New York Times, January 27, 2005, p. C2.

Gains and Adjustment Costs for Mexico under NAFTA

In the mid-1980s Mexican President Miguel de la Madrid embarked on a program of economic liberalization that included land reform and greater openness to foreign investment. Tariffs with the United States were as high as 100% on some goods, and there were many restrictions on the operations of foreign firms. De la Madrid believed that the economic reforms were needed to boost growth and incomes in

Mexico is waiting for its trucks to be allowed to cross the border for long-haul trips into the United States.

Mexico. Joining NAFTA with the United States and Canada in 1994 was a way to ensure the permanence of the reforms already under way. Under NAFTA, Mexican tariffs on U.S. goods declined from an average of 14% in 1990 to 1% in 2001.[5] In addition, U.S. tariffs on Mexican imports fell as well, though from levels that were much lower to begin with in most industries.

How did the fall in tariffs under NAFTA affect the Mexican economy? We will review the evidence on productivity and wages below, but first, you should read **Headlines: NAFTA Turns 15, Bravo!** This editorial was written in 2009, the fifteenth anniversary of the beginning of NAFTA. There were many editorials written that year from differing viewpoints, critiquing various aspects of NAFTA. This article appeared in a U.S.-based pro-business publication focusing on Latin-American businesses. It makes a number of arguments in favor of NAFTA that we have also discussed, including increasing returns to scale and product variety for consumers. But it also points out some defects of NAFTA, including the tardiness of the United States to allow an open border for trucks from Mexico,[6] and the environmental and labor side agreements (discussed in a later chapter).

Productivity in Mexico As we did for Canada, let us investigate the impact of NAFTA on productivity in Mexico. In panel (a) of Figure 6-8, we show the growth in labor productivity for two types of manufacturing firms: the maquiladora plants, which are close to the border and produce almost exclusively for export to the United States, and all other non-maquiladora manufacturing plants in Mexico.[7] The maquiladora plants should be most affected by NAFTA. In panel (b), we also show what happened to real wages and real incomes.

For the maquiladora plants in panel (a), productivity rose 45% from 1994 (when Mexico joined NAFTA) to 2003, a compound growth rate of 4.1% per year over nine years. For the non-maquiladora plants, productivity rose overall by 25% from 1994 to 2003, 2.5% per year. The difference between these two numbers, which is 1.6% per year, is an estimate of the impact of NAFTA on the productivity of the maquiladora plants over and above the increase in productivity that occurred in the rest of Mexico.

Real Wages and Incomes Real wages in the maquiladora and non-maquiladora plants are shown in panel (b) of Figure 6-8. From 1994 to 1997, there was a fall of more than 20% in real wages in both sectors, despite a rise in productivity in the non-maquiladora sector. This fall in real wages is not what we expect from the monopolistic competition model, so why did it occur?

---

[5] Trade was not completely free in 2001 because the tariff reductions under NAFTA were phased in for periods as long as 15 years. Tariff cuts in the agriculture sector in Mexico had the longest phase-in period.
[6] The U.S. spending bill signed by President Obama in 2009 eliminated a pilot program that would have allowed Mexican long-haul trucks to transport cargo throughout the United States. In retaliation, Mexico imposed tariffs on $2.4 billion worth of American goods. See Elisabeth Malkin, "Nafta's Promise, Unfulfilled," *The New York Times*, March 24, 2009, electronic edition.
[7] Labor productivity for the *maquiladoras* is real value-added per worker and for non-*maquiladoras* is real output per worker. Both are taken from Gary C. Hufbauer and Jeffrey J. Schott, 2005, *NAFTA Revisited: Achievements and Challenges* (Washington, D.C.: Peterson Institute for International Economics), Table 1-9, p. 45.

FIGURE 6-8

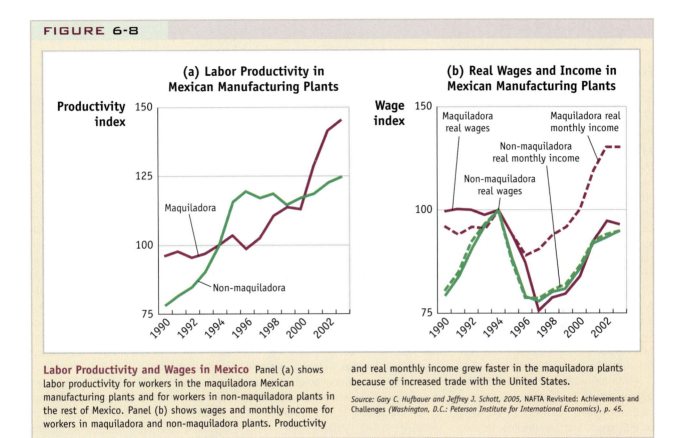

Labor Productivity and Wages in Mexico Panel (a) shows labor productivity for workers in the maquiladora Mexican manufacturing plants and for workers in non-maquiladora plants in the rest of Mexico. Panel (b) shows wages and monthly income for workers in maquiladora and non-maquiladora plants. Productivity and real monthly income grew faster in the maquiladora plants because of increased trade with the United States.

Source: Gary C. Hufbauer and Jeffrey J. Schott, 2005, NAFTA Revisited: Achievements and Challenges (Washington, D.C.: Peterson Institute for International Economics), p. 45.

Shortly after Mexico joined NAFTA, it suffered a financial crisis that led to a large devaluation of the peso. It would be incorrect to attribute the peso crisis to Mexico's joining NAFTA, even though both events occurred the same year. Prior to 1994 Mexico followed a fixed exchange-rate policy, but in late 1994 it switched to a flexible exchange-rate regime instead, and the peso devalued to much less than its former fixed value. Details about exchange-rate regimes and the reasons for switching from a fixed to flexible exchange rate are covered in international macroeconomics. For now, the key idea is that when the peso's value falls, it becomes more expensive for Mexico to import goods from the United States because the peso price of imports goes up. The Mexican consumer price index also goes up, and as a result, real wages for Mexican workers fall.

The maquiladora sector, located beside the U.S. border, was more susceptible to the exchange-rate change and did not experience much of a gain in productivity over that period because of the increased cost of inputs imported from the United States. Workers in both the maquiladora and non-maquiladora sectors had to pay higher prices for imported goods, which is reflected in higher Mexican consumer prices. So the decline in real wages for workers in both sectors is similar. This decline was short-lived, however, and real wages in both sectors began to rise again in 1998. By 2003 real wages in both sectors had risen to nearly equal their value in 1994. This means that workers in Mexico did not gain or lose due to NAFTA on average: the productivity gains were not shared with workers, which is a disappointing finding, but real wages at least recovered from the effects of the peso crisis.

HEADLINES

NAFTA Turns 15, Bravo!

This editorial discussed the impact of NAFTA on the U.S. and Mexican economies. It appeared in a U.S.-based pro-business publication focusing on Latin-American businesses.

As Americans and Mexicans celebrated the start of a new year yesterday, they had reason to celebrate another milestone as well: The North American Free Trade Agreement (NAFTA) turned 15. Despite the slowdown in both the U.S. and Mexican economies, trade between the two nations was expected to set a new record last year. In the first half of 2008, U.S.-Mexico trade grew by 9.6 percent to $183.7 billion. That follows a record $347 billion in trade in 2007. Compare that to the $81.5 billion in total two-way trade in 1993, the last year before NAFTA was implemented.

NAFTA has without a doubt been the primary reason for that success. It dramatically opened up Mexico's economy to U.S. goods and investments, helping boost revenues for many U.S. companies. At the same time, Mexican companies were able to get duty-free access to the world's largest market, resulting in more sales and more jobs there. The trade growth has meant benefits for both consumers and companies on each side of the border.

While China clearly dominates many of the products we buy in U.S. stores these days, Mexico also plays an important role. Mexico ranks third behind Canada and China among the top exporters to the U.S. market. But Mexico beats China when it comes to buying U.S. goods. During the first ten months last year [2008], Mexico imported U.S. products worth $129.4 billion—or more than twice the $61.0 billion China (with a much larger economy) bought from us. . . .

NAFTA has benefited consumers in the U.S. through greater choice of products, in terms of selection, quality, and price, including many that are less expensive than pre-NAFTA. . . . NAFTA has allowed U.S. manufacturing giants from General Motors to General Electric to use economies of scale for their production lines. Prior to NAFTA, GM's assembly plants in Mexico assembled small volumes of many products, which resulted in high costs and somewhat inferior quality, says Mustafa Mohatarem, GM's chief economist. Now its plants in Mexico specialize in few high-volume products, resulting in low cost and high quality, he points out. The result benefits both U.S. and Mexican consumers. . . .

To be sure, NAFTA is not perfect. For one, it didn't even touch on Mexico's sensitive oil sector, which should have been part of a comprehensive free trade agreement. Neither did it offer any teeth when it came to violations. For example, the shameful U.S. disregard for the NAFTA regulations on allowing Mexican trucks to enter the United States. Only in September last year [2008], as part of a pilot program by the Bush Administration, did the first Mexican trucks enter the United States—after a delay of eight years . . . thanks to opposition from U.S. unions and lawmakers. . . . Many economists also are critical of NAFTA's labor and environmental side agreements, which President Bill Clinton negotiated in order to support the treaty.

However, all in all NAFTA has been of major benefit for both the United States and Mexico. Any renegotiation of NAFTA, as president-elect Barack Obama pledged during last year's campaign, would negatively harm both economies just as they now suffer from economic recession. It would also harm our relations with Mexico, our top trading partner in Latin America. Hopefully, pragmatism will win the day in Washington, D.C. this year, as our new president aims to find a way to get the U.S. economy back on track. Leaving NAFTA alone would be a good start.

In the meantime, we congratulate NAFTA on its 15 years. *Feliz Cumpleaños.*

Source: Editors, Latin Business Chronicle, *January 2, 2009, electronic edition.*

The picture is somewhat better if instead of real wages, we look at real monthly income, which includes higher-income employees who earn salaries rather than wages.[8] In panel (b), for the non-maquiladora sector, the data on real wages and real monthly income move together closely. But in the maquiladora sector, real monthly

---

[8] Wage data refer to production workers who are involved in assembly-line and similar activities. Income data refer to all employees, including production and nonproduction workers.

incomes were indeed higher in 2003 than in 1994, indicating some gains for workers in the manufacturing plants most affected by NAFTA. This conclusion is reinforced by other evidence from Mexico, which shows that higher-income workers fared better than unskilled workers in the maquiladora sector and better than workers in the rest of Mexico.[9] From this evidence, the higher-income workers in the maquiladora sector gained most from NAFTA in the long run.

Adjustment Costs in Mexico When Mexico joined NAFTA, it was expected that the short-run adjustment costs would fall especially hard on the agricultural sector in Mexico, such as the corn industry, because it would face strong import competition from the United States. For that reason, the tariff reductions in agriculture were phased in over 15 years. The evidence to date suggests that the farmers growing corn in Mexico did not suffer as much as was feared.[10] There were several reasons for this outcome. First, the poorest farmers do not sell the corn they grow but consume it themselves and buy any extra corn they need. These farmers benefited from cheaper import prices for corn from the United States. Second, the Mexican government was able to use subsidies to offset the reduction in income for other corn farmers. Surprisingly, the total production of corn in Mexico rose following NAFTA instead of falling.

Turning to the manufacturing sector, we should again distinguish the maquiladora and non-maquiladora plants. For the maquiladora plants, employment grew rapidly following NAFTA, from 584,000 workers in 1994 to a peak of 1.29 million workers in 2000. After that, however, the maquiladora sector entered a downturn, due to several factors: the United States entered a recession, reducing demand for Mexican exports; China was competing for U.S. sales by exporting products similar to those sold by Mexico; and the Mexican peso became overvalued, making it difficult to export abroad. For all these reasons, employment in the maquiladora sector fell after 2000, to 1.1 million workers in 2003. It is not clear whether we should count this decline in employment as a short-run adjustment cost due to NAFTA, nor is it clear how long it will take the maquiladora sector to recover. What is apparent is that the maquiladora sector faces increasing international competition (not all due to NAFTA), which can be expected to raise the volatility of its output and employment, and that volatility can be counted as a cost of international trade for workers who are displaced.

Gains and Adjustment Costs for the United States under NAFTA

Studies on the effects of NAFTA on the United States have not estimated its effects on the productivity of American firms, perhaps because Canada and Mexico are only two of many export markets for the United States, and it would be hard to identify the impact of their tariff reductions. Instead, to measure the long-run gains from NAFTA and other trade agreements, researchers have estimated the second source of gains from trade: the expansion of import varieties available to consumers. For the United States, we will compare the long-run gains to consumers from expanded product varieties with the short-run adjustment costs from exiting firms and unemployment.

[9] Gordon H. Hanson, 2007,"Globalization, Labor Income and Poverty in Mexico." In Ann Harrison, ed., *Globalization and Poverty* (Chicago: University of Chicago Press; Washington, D.C.: National Bureau of Economic Research [NBER]), pp. 417–452.

[10] See Margaret McMillan, Alix Peterson Zwane, and Nava Ashraf, 2007, "My Policies or Yours: Does OECD Support for Agriculture Increase Poverty in Developing Countries?" In Ann Harrison, ed., *Globalization and Poverty* (Chicago: University of Chicago Press; Washington, D.C.: NBER), pp. 183–232.

Expansion of Variety to the United States To understand how NAFTA affected the range of products available to American consumers, Table 6-3 shows the variety of goods Mexico exported to the United States in 1990 and 2001. To interpret these numbers, start with the 1990 export variety in agriculture of 42%. That figure means that 42% of all the agricultural products the United States imported in 1990, from any country, also came from Mexico. For instance, avocados, bananas, cucumbers, and tomatoes imported from various Central or South American countries were also imported to the United States from Mexico. Measuring the variety of products Mexico exported to the United States does not take into account the *amount* that Mexico sells of each product; rather, it counts the *number* of different types of products Mexico sells to the United States as compared with the total number of products the United States imports from all countries.

From 1990 to 2001, the range of agricultural products that Mexico exported to the United States expanded from 42 to 51%. That compound growth rate of 1.9% per year is close to the average annual growth rate for export variety in all industries shown in the last column of Table 6-3, which is 2.2% per year. Export variety grew at a faster rate in the wood and paper industry (with a compound growth rate of 2.6% per year), petroleum and plastics (2.5% growth), and electronics (4.6% growth). The industries in which there has traditionally been a lot of trade between the United States and Mexico—such as machinery and transport (including autos) and textiles and garments—have slower growth in export variety because Mexico was exporting a wide range of products in these industries to the United States even before joining NAFTA.

The increase in the variety of products exported from Mexico to the United States under NAFTA is a source of gains from trade for American consumers. The United States has also imported more product varieties over time from many other countries, too, especially developing countries. According to one estimate, the total number of product varieties imported into the United States from 1972 to 2001 has increased by four times. Furthermore, that expansion in import variety has had the same beneficial impact on consumers as a reduction in import prices of 1.2% per year.[11] That

---

TABLE 6-3

Mexico's Export Variety to the United States, 1990–2001 This table shows the extent of variety in Mexican exports to the United States, by industry. From 1990 to 2001, export variety grew in every industry, as U.S. tariffs were reduced due to NAFTA. All figures are percentages.

	Agriculture	Textiles and Garments	Wood and Paper	Petroleum and Plastics	Mining and Metals	Machinery and Transport	Electronics	Average
1990	42%	71%	47%	55%	47%	66%	40%	52%
2001	51	83	63	73	56	76	66	67
Annual growth	1.9	1.4	2.6	2.5	1.7	1.3	4.6	2.2

Source: Robert Feenstra and Hiau Looi Kee, 2007, "Trade Liberalization and Export Variety: A Comparison of Mexico and China," The World Economy, 30(1), 5–21.

---

[11] Christian Broda and David E. Weinstein, 2006, "Globalization and the Gains from Variety," *Quarterly Journal of Economics*, 121(2), May, 541–585.

equivalent price reduction is a measure of the gains from trade due to the expansion of varieties exported to the United States from all countries.

Unfortunately, we do not have a separate estimate of the gains from the growth of export varieties from Mexico alone, which averages 2.2% per year from Table 6-3. Suppose we use the same 1.2% price reduction estimate for Mexico that has been found for all countries. That is, we assume that the growth in export variety from Mexico leads to the same beneficial impact on U.S. consumers as a reduction in Mexican import prices of 1.2% per year, or about one-half as much as the growth in export variety itself. In 1994, the first year of NAFTA, Mexico exported $50 billion in merchandise goods to the United States and by 2001 this sum had grown to $131 billion. Using $90 billion as an average of these two values, a 1.2% reduction in the prices for Mexican imports would save U.S. consumers $90 billion · 1.2% = $1.1 billion per year. We will assume that all these savings are due to NAFTA, though even without NAFTA, there would likely have been some growth in export variety from Mexico.

It is crucial to realize that these consumer savings are *permanent* and that they *increase over time* as export varieties from Mexico continue to grow. Thus, in the first year of NAFTA, we estimate a gain to U.S. consumers of $1.1 billion; in the second year a gain of $2.2 billion, equivalent to a total fall in prices of 2.4%; in the third year a gain of $3.3 billion; and so on. Adding these up over the first nine years of NAFTA, the total benefit to consumers was $49.5 billion, or an average of $5.5 billion per year. In 2003, the tenth year of NAFTA, consumers would gain by $11 billion as compared with 1994. This gain will continue to grow as Mexico further increases the range of varieties exported to the United States.

Adjustment Costs in the United States Adjustment costs in the United States come as firms exit the market because of import competition and the workers employed by those firms are temporarily unemployed. One way to measure that temporary unemployment is to look at the claims under the U.S. **Trade Adjustment Assistance (TAA)** provisions. The TAA program offers assistance to workers in manufacturing who lose their jobs because of import competition. As we discussed in Chapter 3, the North American Free Trade Agreement included a special extension of TAA to workers laid off due to import competition because of NAFTA.

By looking at claims under that program, we can get an idea of the unemployment caused by NAFTA, one of the short-run costs of the agreement. From 1994 to 2002, some 525,000 workers, or about 58,000 per year, lost their jobs and were certified as adversely affected by trade or investment with Canada or Mexico under the NAFTA-TAA program.[12] As a result, these workers were entitled to additional unemployment benefits. This number is probably the most accurate estimate we have of the temporary unemployment caused by NAFTA.

How large is the displacement of 58,000 workers per year due to NAFTA? We can compare this number with overall job displacement in the United States. Over the three years from January 1999 to December 2001, 4 million workers were displaced, about one-third of whom were in manufacturing. So the annual number of workers displaced in manufacturing was 4 million · $(\frac{1}{3})$ · $(\frac{1}{3})$ = 444,000 workers per year. Thus,

---

[12] The information in this paragraph is drawn from Gary Clyde Hufbauer and Jeffrey J. Schott, 2006, *NAFTA Revisited: Achievements and Challenges* (Washington, D.C.: Peterson Institute for International Economics), pp. 38–42.

the NAFTA layoffs of 58,000 workers were about 13% of the total displacement in manufacturing, which is a substantial amount.

Rather than compare the displacement caused by NAFTA with the total displacement in manufacturing, however, we can instead evaluate the wages lost by displaced workers and compare this amount with the consumer gains. In Chapter 3 (see **Application: Manufacturing and Services**), we learned that about two-thirds of workers laid off in manufacturing are reemployed within three years. Some workers are reemployed in less than three years; for some, it takes longer. To simplify the problem, suppose that the *average* length of unemployment for laid-off workers is three years.[13] Average yearly earnings for production workers in manufacturing were $31,000 in 2000, so each displaced worker lost $93,000 in wages (three times the workers' average annual income).[14] Total lost wages caused by displacement would be 58,000 workers displaced per year times $93,000, or $5.4 billion per year during the first nine years of NAFTA.

These private costs of $5.4 billion are nearly equal to the average welfare gains of $5.5 billion per year due to the expansion of import varieties from Mexico from 1994 to 2002, as computed previously. But the gains from increased product variety *continue and grow over time* as new imported products become available to American consumers. Recall from the previous calculation that the gains from the ongoing expansion of product varieties from Mexico were $11 billion in 2003, the tenth year of NAFTA, or twice as high as the $5.4 billion costs of adjustment. As the consumer gains continue to grow, adjustment costs due to job losses fall. Thus, the consumer gains from increased variety, when summed over years, considerably exceed the private losses from displacement. This outcome is guaranteed to occur because the gains from expanded import varieties occur *every year* that the imports are available, whereas labor displacement is a temporary phenomenon.

The calculation we have made shows that the gains to U.S. consumers from greater import variety from Mexico, when summed over time, are more than the private costs of adjustment. In practice, the actual compensation received by workers is much less than their costs of adjustment. In 2002 the NAFTA–TAA program was consolidated with the general TAA program in the United States, so there is no further record of layoffs as a result of NAFTA. Under the Trade Act of 2002, the funding for TAA was increased from $400 million to $1.2 billion per year and some other improvements to the program were made, such as providing a health-care subsidy for laid-off workers. In addition, as part of the jobs stimulus bill signed by President Obama on February 17, 2009, workers in the service sector (as well as farmers) who lose their jobs due to trade can now also apply for TAA benefits, as was discussed in Chapter 3. It would be desirable to continue to expand the TAA program to include more workers who face layoffs due to increased global competition.

Summary of NAFTA In this section, we have been able to measure, at least in part, the long-run gains and short-run costs from NAFTA for Canada, Mexico, and the United States. The monopolistic competition model indicates two sources of gains from trade: the rise in productivity due to expanded output by surviving firms, which leads to lower prices, and the expansion in the overall number of varieties of products

---

[13] We show in Problem 8 at the end of the chapter that this assumption is accurate.
[14] We are not considering the additional losses if the new job has lower wages than earned previously.

available to consumers with trade, despite the exit of some firms in each country. For Mexico and Canada, we measured the long-run gains by the improvement in productivity for exporters as compared with other manufacturing firms. For the United States, we measured the long-run gains using the expansion of varieties from Mexico, and the equivalent drop in price faced by U.S. consumers. It is clear that for Canada and the United States, the long-run gains considerably exceed the short-run costs. The picture is less optimistic for Mexico because the gains have not been reflected in the growth of real wages for production workers (due in part to the peso crisis). The real earnings of higher-income workers in the maquiladora sector have risen, however, so they have been the principal beneficiaries of NAFTA so far.

4 Intra-Industry Trade and the Gravity Equation

In the monopolistic competition model, countries both import and export different varieties of differentiated goods. This result differs from the Ricardian and Heckscher-Ohlin models that we studied in Chapters 2 and 4: in those models, countries either export or import a good but do not export and import the same good simultaneously. Under monopolistic competition, countries will specialize in producing different varieties of a differentiated good and will trade those varieties back and forth. As we saw from the example of golf clubs at the beginning of the chapter, this is a common trade pattern that we call intra-industry trade.

Index of Intra-Industry Trade

To develop the idea of intra-industry trade, let us go back to the golf club example at the beginning of the chapter. In 2009 the United States imported $284.2 million in golf clubs and exported $226.2 million. When the amounts of imports and exports are similar for a good, as they are here, it is an indication that nearly all the trade in that good is intra-industry trade. The **index of intra-industry** trade tells us what proportion of trade in each product involves both imports and exports: a high index (up to 100%) indicates that an equal amount of the good is imported and exported, whereas a low index (0%) indicates that the good is either imported or exported but not both.

The formula for the index of intra-industry trade is

$$(\text{Index of intra-industry trade}) = \frac{\text{Minimum of imports and exports}}{\frac{1}{2}(\text{Imports} + \text{exports})}$$

For golf clubs, shown in Table 6-1, the minimum of imports and exports is $226.2 million, and the average of imports and exports is $\frac{1}{2}(226.2 + 284.2) = \$255.2$ million. So $\frac{226.2}{255.2} = 89\%$ of the U.S. trade in golf clubs is intra-industry trade; that is, it involves both exporting and importing of golf clubs.

In Table 6-4, we show some other examples of intra-industry trade in other products for the United States. Products such as vaccines, small cars, and whiskey have a high index of intra-industry trade. These are all examples of highly differentiated products: for small cars and whiskey, each exporting country sells products that are different from those of other exporting countries, including the United States. So it is not surprising that we both export and import these products. On the other hand, products such as men's shorts, telephones, natural gas, sunglasses, and apples have a low index of intra-industry trade. Some of these goods are homogeneous, such as

TABLE 6-4

Index of Intra-Industry Trade for the United States, 2009 Shown here are value of imports, value of exports, and the index of intra-industry trade for a number of products. When the value of imports is close to the value of exports, such as for golf clubs, then the index of intra-industry trade is highest, and when a product is mainly imported or exported (but not both), then the index of intra-industry trade is lowest.

Product	Value of Imports ($ millions)	Value of Export ($ millions)	Index of Intra-Industry Trade (%)
Golf clubs	284	226	89
Vaccines	2,027	2,763	85
Whiskey	1,166	752	78
Mattresses	133	48	53
Golf carts	29	86	50
Small cars	40,527	11,778	45
Natural gas	12,391	2,790	37
Sunglasses	848	184	36
Frozen orange juice	3	17	33
Apples	139	752	31
Large-passenger aircraft	4,955	31,322	27
Telephones	761	71	17
Men's shorts	542	9	3

Source: U.S. International Trade Commission, Interactive Tariff and Trade DataWeb, at http://dataweb.usitc.gov/.

apples and natural gas. These goods are closer to fitting the assumptions of the Ricardian or Heckscher-Ohlin model of perfect competition with homogeneous goods, which are either imported or exported. Other goods such as fax machines and sunglasses are differentiated but are mostly imported into the United States simply because they can be produced at lower costs abroad. To obtain a high index of intra-industry trade, it is necessary for the good to be differentiated *and* for costs to be similar in the Home and Foreign countries, leading to both imports and exports.

The Gravity Equation

The index of intra-industry trade measures the degree of intra-industry trade for a product but does not tell us anything about the total amount of trade. To explain the value of trade, we need a different equation, called the "gravity equation." This equation was given its name by a Dutch economist and Nobel laureate, Jan Tinbergen. Tinbergen was trained in physics, so he thought about the trade between countries as similar to the force of gravity between objects: Newton's universal law of gravitation states that objects with larger mass, or that are closer to each other, have a greater gravitational pull between them. Tinbergen's gravity equation for trade states that countries with larger GDPs, or that are closer to each other, have more trade between them. Both these equations can be explained simply—even if you have never studied physics, you will be able to grasp their meanings. The point is that just as the force of gravity is strongest between two large objects, the monopolistic competition model predicts that large countries (as measured by their GDP) should trade the most with each other. There is much empirical evidence to support this prediction, as we will show.

Newton's Universal Law of Gravitation Suppose that two objects each have mass M_1 and M_2 and are located distance d apart. According to Newton's universal law of gravitation, the force of gravity F_g between these two objects is

$$F_g = G \cdot \frac{M_1 \cdot M_2}{d^2}$$

where G is a constant that tells us the magnitude of this relationship. The larger each object is, or the closer they are to each other, the greater is the force of gravity between them.

The Gravity Equation in Trade The equation proposed by Tinbergen to explain trade between countries is similar to Newton's law of gravity, except that instead of the mass of two objects, we use the GDP of two countries, and instead of predicting the force of gravity, we are predicting the amount of trade between them. The gravity equation in trade is

$$\text{Trade} = B \cdot \frac{GDP_1 \cdot GDP_2}{dist^n}$$

where Trade is the amount of trade (measured by imports, exports, or their average) between two countries, GDP_1 and GDP_2 are their gross domestic products, and $dist$ is the distance between them. Notice that we use the exponent n on distance, $dist^n$, rather than $dist^2$ as in Newton's law of gravity, because we are not sure of the precise relationship between distance and trade. The term B in front of the gravity equation is a constant that indicates the relationship between the "gravity term" (i.e., $GDP_1 \cdot GDP_2/dist^n$) and Trade. It can also be interpreted as summarizing the effects of all factors (other than size and distance) that influence the amount of trade between two countries; such factors include tariffs (which would lower the amount of trade and reduce B), sharing a common border (which would increase trade and raise B), and so on.

According to the gravity equation, the larger the countries are (as measured by their GDP), or the closer they are to each other, the greater is the amount of trade between them. This connection among economic size, distance, and trade is an implication of the monopolistic competition model that we have studied in this chapter. The monopolistic competition model implies that larger countries trade the most for two reasons: larger countries export more because they produce more product varieties, and they import more because their demand is higher. Therefore, larger countries trade more in both exports and imports.

Deriving the Gravity Equation To explain more carefully why the gravity equation holds in the monopolistic competition model, we can work through some algebra using the GDPs of the various countries. Start with the GDP of Country 1, GDP_1. Each of the goods produced in Country 1 is a differentiated product, so they are different from the varieties produced in other countries. Every other country will demand the goods of Country 1 (because they are different from their home-produced goods), and the amount of their demand will depend on two factors: (1) the relative size of the importing country (larger countries demand more) and (2) the distance between the two countries (being farther away leads to higher transportation costs and less trade).

To measure the relative size of each importing country, we use its share of world GDP. Specifically, we define Country 2's share of world GDP as $Share_2 = GDP_2/GDP_W$. To measure the transportation costs involved in trade, we use distance raised to a power, or $dist^n$. Using these definitions, exports from Country 1 to Country 2 will equal the goods available in Country 1 (GDP_1), times the relative size of Country 2 ($Share_2$), divided by the transportation costs between them ($dist^n$), so that

$$\text{Trade} = B \cdot \frac{GDP_1 \cdot Share_2}{dist^n} = \left(\frac{1}{GDP_W}\right)\frac{GDP_1 \cdot GDP_2}{dist^n}$$

This equation for the trade between Countries 1 and 2 looks similar to the gravity equation, especially if we think of the term ($1/GDP_W$) as the constant term B. We see from this equation that the trade between two countries will be proportional to their relative sizes, measured by the product of their GDPs (the greater the size of the countries, the larger is trade), and inversely proportional to the distance between them (the smaller the distance, the larger is trade). The following application explores how well the gravity equation works in practice.

APPLICATION

The Gravity Equation for Canada and the United States

We can apply the gravity equation to trade between any pair of countries, or even to trade between the provinces or states of one country and another. Panel (a) of Figure 6-9 shows data collected on the value of trade between Canadian provinces and U.S. states in 1993. On the horizontal axis, we show the gravity term:

$$\text{Gravity term} = \frac{GDP_1 \cdot GDP_2}{dist^{1.25}}$$

where GDP_1 is the gross domestic product of a U.S. state (in billions of U.S. dollars), GDP_2 is the gross domestic product of a Canadian province (in billions of U.S. dollars), and $dist$ is the distance between them (in miles). We use the exponent 1.25 on the distance term because it has been shown in other research studies to describe the relationship between distance and trade value quite well. The horizontal axis is plotted as a logarithmic scale, with values from 0.001 to 100. A higher value along the horizontal axis indicates either a large GDP for the trading province and state or a smaller distance between them.

The vertical axis in Figure 6-9 shows the 1993 value of exports (in millions of U.S. dollars) between a Canadian province and U.S. state or between a U.S. state and Canadian province; this is the value of trade for the province–state pair. That axis is also plotted as a logarithmic scale, with values from $0.001 million (or $1,000) to $100,000 million (or $100 billion) in trade. There are 30 states and 10 provinces included in the study, so there are a total of 600 possible trade flows between them (though some of those flows are zero, indicating that no exporting takes place). Each of the points in panel (a) represents the trade flow and gravity term between one state and one province.

We can see from the set of points in panel (a) that states and provinces with a higher gravity term between them (measured on the horizontal axis) also tend to have more trade (measured on the vertical axis). That strong, positive relationship shown by the set of points in panel (a) demonstrates that the gravity equation holds well empirically. Panel (a) also shows the "best fit" straight line through the set of points, which has the following equation:

FIGURE 6-9

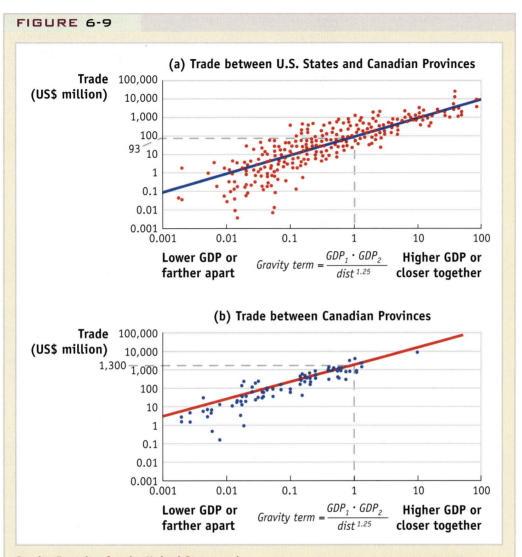

Gravity Equation for the United States and Canada, 1993 Plotted in these figures are the dollar value of exports in 1993 and the gravity term (plotted in log scale). Panel (a) shows these variables for trade between 10 Canadian provinces and 30 U.S. states. When the gravity term is 1, for example, the amount of trade between a province and state is $93 million. Panel (b) shows these variables for trade between 10 Canadian provinces. When the gravity term is 1, the amount of trade between the provinces is $1.3 billion, 14 times larger than between a province and a state. These graphs illustrate two important points: there is a positive relationship between country size (as measured by GDP) and trade volume, and there is much more trade within Canada than between Canada and the United States.

Source: Author's calculations using data from James A. Anderson and Eric van Wincoop, 2003, "Gravity with Gravitas: A Solution to the Border Puzzle," American Economic Review, 170–192.

$$\text{Trade} = 93\ \frac{GDP_1 \cdot GDP_2}{dist^{1.25}}$$

The constant term $B = 93$ gives the best fit to this gravity equation for Canadian provinces and U.S. states. When the gravity term equals 1, as illustrated in panel (a), then the predicted amount of trade between that state and province is $93 million. The closest example to this point is Alberta and New Jersey. In 1993 there were $94 million in exports from Alberta to New Jersey and they had a gravity term of approximately 1.

Trade within Canada Because the gravity equation works well at predicting international trade between provinces and states in different countries, it should also work well at predicting trade *within* a country, or *intra-national* trade. To explore this idea, panel (b) of Figure 6-9 graphs the value of exports (in millions of U.S. dollars) between any two Canadian provinces, along with the gravity term for those provinces. The scale of the axes in panel (b) is the same as in panel (a). From panel (b), we again see that there is a strong, positive relationship between the gravity term between two provinces (measured on the horizontal axis) and their trade (measured on the vertical axis). The "best fit" straight line through the set of points has the following equation:

$$\text{Trade} = 1{,}300 \cdot \frac{GDP_1 \cdot GDP_2}{dist^{1.25}}$$

That is, the constant term $B = 1{,}300$ gives the best fit to this gravity equation for Canadian provinces. When the gravity term equals 1, as illustrated in panel (b), then the predicted amount of trade between two provinces is $1,300 million, or $1.3 billion. The closest example to this combination is between British Columbia and Alberta: in 1993 their gravity term was approximately 1.3 and British Columbia exported $1.4 billion of goods to Alberta.

Comparing the gravity equation for international trade between Canada and the United States with the gravity equation for intra-national trade in Canada, the constant term for Canadian trade is much bigger—1,300 as compared with 93. Taking the ratio of these two constant terms (1,300/93 = 14), we find that on average there is 14 times more trade *within* Canada than occurs across the border! That number is even higher if we consider an earlier year, 1988, just before Canada and the United States signed the Canada-U.S. Free Trade Agreement in 1989. In 1988 intra-national trade within Canada was 22 times higher than international trade between Canada and the United States.[15] Even though that ratio fell from 1988 to 1993 due to the free-trade agreement between Canada and the United States, it is still remarkable that there is so much more trade *within* Canada than across the border, or more generally, so much more intra-national than international trade.

The finding that trade across borders is less than trade within countries reflects all the barriers to trade that occur between countries. Factors that make it easier or more difficult to trade goods between countries are often called **border effects,** and they include the following:

■ Taxes imposed when imported goods enter into a country, **tariffs**

■ Limits on the number of items allowed to cross the border, **quotas**

■ Other administrative rules and regulations affecting trade, including the time required for goods to clear customs

■ Geographic factors such as whether the countries share a border

■ Cultural factors such as whether the countries have a common language that might make trade easier

---

[15] That conclusion comes from John McCallum, 1995, "National Borders Matter," *American Economic Review*, 615–623. The 1993 data used in Figure 6-9 derive from James A. Anderson and Eric van Wincoop, 2003, "Gravity with Gravitas: A Solution to the Border Puzzle," *American Economic Review*, 170–192.

In the gravity equation, all the factors that influence the amount of trade are reflected in the constant B. As we have seen, the value of this constant differs for trade within a country versus trade between countries. In later chapters, we explore in detail the consequences of tariffs, quotas, and other barriers to trade. The lesson from the gravity equation is that such barriers to trade can potentially have a large impact on the amount of international trade as compared with intra-national trade. ■

5 Conclusions

When firms have differentiated products and increasing returns to scale, the potential exists for gains from trade above and beyond those that we studied in earlier chapters under perfect competition. We have demonstrated these additional gains using a model of monopolistic competition. In this model, trade will occur even between countries that are identical because the potential to sell in a larger market will induce firms to lower their prices below those charged in the absence of trade. When all firms lower their prices, however, some firms are no longer profitable and exit the market. The remaining firms expand their output, lowering their average costs through increasing returns to scale. The reduction in average costs lowers the prices charged by firms, creating gains for consumers in the importing country. In addition, because each firm produces a differentiated product, trade between countries allows for the importing of product varieties that are different from those produced domestically, creating a second source of gains for consumers.

When some firms have to exit the market, short-run adjustment costs arise within this model because of worker displacement. Using examples from Canada, Mexico, and the United States, we have argued that the short-run adjustment costs are less than the long-run gains. Regional trade agreements like the North American Free Trade Agreement (NAFTA) are a good application of the monopolistic competition model. Another application is the "gravity equation," which states that countries that are larger or closer to each other will trade more. That prediction is supported by looking at data on trade between countries. Research has also shown that trade within countries is even larger than trade between countries.

KEY POINTS

1. The monopolistic competition model assumes differentiated products, many firms, and increasing returns to scale. Firms enter whenever there are profits to be earned, so profits are zero in the long-run equilibrium.

2. When trade opens between two countries, the demand curve faced by each firm becomes more elastic, as consumers have more choices and become more price-sensitive. Firms then lower their prices in an attempt to capture consumers from their competitors and obtain profits. When all firms do so, however, some firms incur losses and are forced to leave the market.

3. Introducing international trade under monopolistic competition leads to additional gains from trade for two reasons: (i) lower prices as firms expand their output and lower their average costs and (ii) additional imported product varieties available to consumers. There are also short-run adjustment costs, such as unemployment, as some firms exit the market.

4. The assumption of differentiated goods helps us to understand why countries often import and export varieties of the same type of good. That outcome occurs with the model of monopolistic competition.

5. The gravity equation states that countries with higher GDP, or that are close, will trade more. In addition, research has shown that there is more trade within countries than between countries.

KEY TERMS

differentiated goods, p. 169
imperfect competition, p. 169
monopolistic competition, p. 169
increasing returns to scale, p. 169
intra-industry trade, p. 170

gravity equation, p. 170
free-trade agreements, p. 170
duopoly, p. 170
marginal revenue, p. 170
marginal cost, p. 170
monopoly profits, p. 174

Trade Adjustment Assistance (TAA), p. 187
index of intra-industry trade, p. 189
border effects, p. 194
tariffs, p. 194
quotas, p. 194

PROBLEMS

1. Explain how increasing returns to scale in production can be a basis for trade.

2. Why is trade within a country greater than trade between countries?

3. Starting from the long-run equilibrium without trade in the monopolistic competition model, as illustrated in Figure 6-5, consider what happens when the Home country begins trading with two other identical countries. Because the countries are all the same, the number of consumers in the world is three times larger than in a single country, and the number of firms in the world is three times larger than in a single country.

   a. Compared with the no-trade equilibrium, how much does industry demand D increase? How much does the number of firms (or product varieties) increase? Does the demand curve D/N^A still apply after the opening of trade? Explain why or why not.

   b. Does the d_1 curve shift or pivot due to the opening of trade? Explain why or why not.

   c. Compare your answer to (b) with the case in which Home trades with only one other identical country. Specifically, compare the elasticity of the demand curve d_1 in the two cases.

   d. Illustrate the long-run equilibrium with trade, and compare it with the long-run equilibrium when Home trades with only one other identical country.

4. Starting from the long-run trade equilibrium in the monopolistic competition model, as illustrated in Figure 6-7, consider what happens when industry demand D increases. For instance, suppose that this is the market for cars, and lower gasoline prices generate higher demand D.

   a. Redraw Figure 6-7 for the Home market and show the shift in the D/N^T curve and the new short-run equilibrium.

   b. From the new short-run equilibrium, is there exit or entry of firms, and why?

   c. Describe where the new long-run equilibrium occurs, and explain what has happened to the number of firms and the prices they charge.

5. Our derivation of the gravity equation from the monopolistic competition model used the following logic:

   (i) Each country produces many products.
   (ii) Each country demands all of the products that every other country produces.
   (iii) Thus, large countries demand more imports from other countries.

   The gravity equation relationship does not hold in the Heckscher-Ohlin model. Explain how the logic of the gravity equation breaks down in the Heckscher-Ohlin model; that is, which of the statements just listed is no longer true in the Heckscher-Ohlin model?

6. The United States, France, and Italy are among the world's largest producers. To answer the following questions, assume that their markets are monopolistically competitive, and use the gravity equation with $B = 93$ and $n = 1.25$.

	GDP in 2009 ($ billions)	Distance from the United States (miles)
France	2,635	5,544
Italy	2,090	6,229
United States	14,270	—

a. Using the gravity equation, compare the expected level of trade between the United States and France and between the United States and Italy.

b. The distance between Paris and Rome is 694 miles. Would you expect more French trade with Italy or with the United States? Explain what variable (i.e., country size or distance) drives your result.

7. What evidence is there that Canada is better off under the free-trade agreement with the United States?

8. In the section "Gains and Adjustment Costs for the United States under NAFTA," we calculated the lost wages of workers displaced because of NAFTA. Prior experience in the manufacturing sector shows that about two-thirds of these workers obtain new jobs within three years. One way to think about that reemployment process is that one-third of workers find jobs in the first year, and another one-third of remaining unemployed workers find a job each subsequent year. Using this approach, in the table that follows, we show that one-third of workers get a job in the first year (column 2), leaving two-thirds of workers unemployed (column 4). In the second year, another $\left(\frac{1}{3}\right) \cdot \left(\frac{2}{3}\right) = \frac{2}{9}$ of workers get a job (column 2), so that $\frac{1}{3} + \frac{2}{9} = \frac{5}{9}$ of the workers are employed (column 3). That leaves $\frac{4}{9}$ of the workers unemployed (column 4) at the end of the second year.

Year	Fraction Finding Job	Total Fraction Employed	Total Fraction Unemployed
1	$\frac{1}{3}$	$\frac{1}{3}$	$1 - \frac{1}{3} = \frac{2}{3}$
2	$\frac{1}{3} \cdot \frac{2}{3} = \frac{2}{9}$	$\frac{1}{3} + \frac{2}{9} = \frac{5}{9}$	$1 - \frac{5}{9} = \frac{4}{9}$
3	$\frac{1}{3} \cdot \frac{4}{9} = \frac{4}{27}$		
4			
5			
6	$\frac{1}{3} \cdot \left(\frac{2}{3}\right)^{Year-1}$		

a. Fill in two more rows of the table using the same approach as for the first two rows.

b. Notice that the fraction of workers finding a job each year (column 2) has the formula

$$\text{Fraction finding job} = \frac{1}{3} \cdot \left(\frac{2}{3}\right)^{Year-1}$$

Using this formula, fill in six more values for the fraction of workers finding a job (column 2), up to year 10.

c. To calculate the average spell of unemployment, we take the fraction of workers finding jobs (column 2), multiply it by the years of unemployment (column 1), and add up the result over all the rows. By adding up over 10 rows, calculate what the average spell of unemployment is. What do you expect to get when adding up over 20 rows?

d. Compare your answer to (c) with the average three-year spell of unemployment on page 188. Was that number accurate?

9. a. Of two products, rice and paintings, which product do you expect to have a higher index of intra-industry trade? Why?

   b. Access the U.S. TradeStats Express website at http://tse.export.gov/. Click on "National Trade Data" and then "Global Patterns of U.S. Merchandise Trade." Under the "Product" section, change the item to rice (HS 1006) and obtain the export and import values. Do the same for paintings (HS 9701); then calculate the intra-industry trade index for rice and paintings in 2009. Do your calculations confirm your expectation from part (a)? If your answers did not confirm your expectation, explain.

N E T W O R K

In this chapter, we included the editorial **Headlines: NAFTA Turns 15, Bravo!** There were many other editorials written in 2009, for the fifteenth anniversary of NAFTA. Find another editorial on the Web, and summarize the pro and con arguments that it makes for NAFTA.

Import Tariffs and Quotas under Perfect Competition

I take this action to give our domestic steel industry an opportunity to adjust to surges in foreign imports, recognizing the harm from 50 years of foreign government intervention in the global steel market, which has resulted in bankruptcies, serious dislocation, and job loss.

President George W. Bush, in press statement announcing new "safeguard" tariffs on imported steel, March 5, 2002

The president decided to remedy the clear disruption to the U.S. tire industry based on the facts and the law in this case.

President Barack Obama's spokesman, Robert Gibbs, announcing new "safeguard" tariffs on tires imported from China, September 11, 2009

n September 11, 2009, President Barack Obama announced a tariff of 35% on imports of tires made in China, meaning that these products would be taxed as they crossed the U.S. border. This tariff was requested by the United Steelworkers of America, the union that represents American tire workers. After strong lobbying pressure from the union, the tariff was enacted. By approving this tariff, it is believed that President Obama won additional support from the labor movement for the health-care bill that would be considered later that year.

The tariff on Chinese-made tires announced by President Obama was not the first instance of a U.S. president—of either party—approved an import tariff soon after being elected. During the 2000 presidential campaign, George W. Bush promised that he would consider implementing a tariff on imports of steel. That promise was made for political purposes: It helped Bush secure votes in Pennsylvania, West Virginia, and Ohio, states that produce large amounts of steel. After he was elected, the U.S. tariffs on steel were increased in

March 2002, though they were removed less than two years later, as we discuss later in this chapter.

The steel and tire tariffs are examples of **trade policy,** a government action meant to influence the amount of international trade. In earlier chapters, we learned that the opening of trade normally creates both winners and losers. Because the gains from trade are unevenly spread, it follows that firms, industries, and labor unions often feel that the government should do something to help limit their losses (or maximize their gains) from international trade. That "something" is trade policy, which includes the use of **import tariffs** (taxes on imports), **import quotas** (quantity limits on imports), and subsidies for exports. In this chapter, we begin our investigation of trade policies by focusing on the effects of tariffs and quotas in a perfectly competitive industry. In the next chapter, we continue by discussing the use of import tariffs and quotas when the industry is imperfectly competitive.

President Obama and President Bush could not just put tariffs on imports of tires made in China and foreign steel. Rather, they had to follow the rules governing the use of tariffs that the United States and many other countries have agreed to follow. Under these rules, countries can temporarily increase tariffs to safeguard an industry against import competition. This "safeguard" rationale was used to increase the U.S. tariffs on steel and tires. The international body that governs these rules is called the World Trade Organization (WTO); its precursor was the General Agreement on Tariffs and Trade (GATT). This chapter first looks briefly at the history and development of the WTO and GATT.

Once the international context for setting trade policy has been established, the chapter examines in detail the most commonly used trade policy, the tariff. We explain the reasons why countries apply tariffs and the consequences of these tariffs on the producers and consumers in the importing and exporting countries. We show that import tariffs typically lead to welfare losses for "small" importing countries, by which we mean countries that are too small to affect world prices. Following that, we examine the situation for a "large" importing country, meaning a country that is a large enough buyer for its tariff to affect world prices. In that case, we find that the importing country can possibly gain by applying a tariff, but only at the expense of the exporting countries.

A third purpose of the chapter is to examine the use of an import quota, which is a limit on the quantity of a good that can be imported from a foreign country. Past examples of import quotas in the United States include limits on the imports of agricultural goods, automobiles, and steel. More recently, the United States and Europe imposed temporary quotas on the import of textile and apparel products from China. We note that, like a tariff, an import quota often imposes a cost on the importing country. Furthermore, we argue that the cost of quotas can sometimes be even greater than the cost of tariffs. For that reason, the use of quotas has been greatly reduced under the WTO, though they are still used in some cases.

Throughout this chapter, we assume that firms are perfectly competitive. That is, each firm produces a homogeneous good and is small compared with the market, which comprises many firms. Under perfect competition, each firm is a price taker in its market. In the next chapter, we learn that tariffs and quotas have different effects in imperfectly competitive markets.

1 A Brief History of the World Trade Organization

During the period between the First and Second World Wars, unusually high tariffs between countries reduced the volume of world trade. When peace was reestablished following World War II, representatives of the Allied countries met on several occasions to discuss the rebuilding of Europe and issues such as high trade barriers and unstable exchange rates. One of these conferences, held in Bretton Woods, New Hampshire, in July 1944, established the International Monetary Fund (IMF) and the International Bank for Reconstruction and Development, later known as the World Bank. A second conference held at the Palais des Nations, in Geneva, Switzerland, in 1947 established the General Agreement on Tariffs and Trade (GATT), the purpose of which was to reduce barriers to international trade between nations.[1]

Under the GATT, countries met periodically for negotiations, called "rounds," to lower trade restrictions between countries. Each round is named for the country in which the meeting took place. The Uruguay Round of negotiations, which lasted from 1986 to 1994, established the World Trade Organization (WTO) on January 1, 1995. The WTO is a greatly expanded version of the GATT. It keeps most of the GATT's earlier provisions but adds rules that govern an expanded set of global interactions (including trade in services and intellectual property protection) through binding agreements. The most recent round of WTO negotiations, the Doha Round, began in Doha, Qatar, in November 2001.

Although the goal of the WTO is to keep tariffs low, it allows countries to charge a higher tariff on a specific import under some conditions. In **Side Bar: Key Provisions of the GATT,** we show some of the articles of the GATT that still govern trade in the WTO. Some of the main provisions are as follows:

1. A nation must extend the same tariffs to all trading partners that are WTO members. Article I of the GATT, the "most favored nation" clause, states that every country belonging to the WTO must be treated the same: if a country imposes low tariffs on one trading partner, then those low tariffs must be extended to every other trading partner belonging to the WTO.[2]

2. Tariffs may be imposed in response to unfair trade practices such as **dumping.** As we discuss in a later chapter, "dumping" is defined as the sale of export goods in another country at a price less than that charged at home, or alternatively, at a price less than costs of production and shipping. Article VI of the GATT states that an importing country may impose a tariff on goods being dumped into its country by a foreign exporter.

3. Countries should not limit the quantity of goods and services that they import. Article XI states that countries should not maintain quotas against imports. We discuss exceptions to this rule later in this chapter.

4. Countries should declare **export subsidies** provided to particular firms, sectors, or industries. Article XVI deals with export subsidies, benefits such as tax

---

[1] A history of the GATT is provided in Douglas A. Irwin, Petros C. Mavroidis, and Alan O. Sykes, 2008, *The Genesis of the GATT* (New York: Cambridge University Press).
[2] In the United States, the granting of most favored nation trade status to a country is now called "normal trade relations" because most countries now belong to the WTO and enjoy that status.

breaks or other incentives for firms that produce goods specifically for export. The article states that countries should notify each other of the extent of subsidies and discuss the possibility of eliminating them. During the Doha Round of WTO negotiations, the elimination of agricultural subsidies has recently been discussed.

5. Countries can temporarily raise tariffs for certain products. Article XIX, called the **safeguard provision** or the **escape clause,** is our focus in this chapter. Article XIX lists the conditions under which a country can temporarily raise tariffs on particular products. It states that a country can apply a tariff when it imports "any product . . . in such increased quantities and under such conditions as to cause or threaten serious injury to domestic producers." In other words, the importing country can temporarily raise the tariff when domestic producers are suffering due to import competition.

　　The steel tariff of March 2002 is an example of a tariff that was applied by the United States under Article XIX of the GATT. European governments strenuously objected to the steel tariffs, however, and filed a complaint against the United States with the WTO. A panel at the WTO ruled in favor of the European countries. This ruling entitled them to retaliate against the United States by putting tariffs of their own on some $2.2 billion worth of U.S. exports. This pressure from Europe, along with pressure from companies in the United States that had been purchasing the cheaper imported steel, led President Bush to remove the steel tariffs in December 2003. Later in the chapter, we discuss the steel tariff in more detail, and see how Article XIX of the GATT is reflected in U.S. trade laws.

6. **Regional trade agreements** are permitted under Article XXIV of the GATT. The GATT recognizes the ability of blocs of countries to form two types of regional trade agreements: (i) **free-trade areas,** in which a group of countries voluntarily agrees to remove trade barriers between themselves, and (ii) **customs unions,** which are free-trade areas in which the countries also adopt identical tariffs between themselves and the rest of the world. We discuss regional trade agreements in a later chapter.

2　The Gains from Trade

In earlier chapters, we demonstrated the gains from trade using a production possibilities frontier and indifference curves. We now instead demonstrate the gains from trade using Home demand and supply curves, together with the concepts of **consumer surplus** and **producer surplus.** You may already be familiar with these concepts from an earlier economics course, but we provide a brief review here.

Consumer and Producer Surplus

Suppose that Home consumers have the demand curve D in panel (a) of Figure 7-1 and face the price of P_1. Then total demand is D_1 units. For the last unit purchased, the consumer buying it values that unit at close to its purchase price of P_1, so he or

SIDE BAR

Key Provisions of the GATT

ARTICLE I

General Most-Favoured-Nation Treatment

1. With respect to customs duties . . . and with respect to all rules and formalities in connection with importation and exportation . . . any advantage, favour, privilege or immunity granted by any contracting party to any product originating in or destined for any other country shall be accorded immediately and unconditionally to the like product originating in or destined for the territories of all other contracting parties. . . .

ARTICLE VI

Anti-Dumping and Countervailing Duties

1. The contracting parties recognize that dumping, by which products of one country are introduced into the commerce of another country at less than the normal value of the products, is to be condemned if it causes or threatens material injury to an established industry. . . . [A]product is to be considered . . . less than its normal value, if the price of the product exported from one country to another

   a. is less than the comparable price . . . for the like product when destined for consumption in the exporting country, or,

   b. in the absence of such domestic price, is less than either

      i) the highest comparable price for the like product for export to any third country in the ordinary course of trade, or

      ii) the cost of production of the product in the country of origin plus a reasonable addition for selling cost and profit. . . .

ARTICLE XI

General Elimination of Quantitative Restrictions

1. No prohibitions or restrictions other than duties, taxes or other charges, whether made effective through quotas, import or export licenses or other measures, shall be instituted or maintained by any contracting party on the importation of any product of the territory of any other contracting party or on the exportation or sale for export of any product destined for the territory of any other contracting party. . . .

ARTICLE XVI

Subsidies

1. If any contracting party grants or maintains any subsidy, including any form of income or price support, which operates directly or indirectly to increase exports of any product from, or to reduce imports of any product into, its territory, it shall notify the contracting parties in writing of the extent and nature of the subsidization. In any case in which it is determined that serious prejudice to the interests of any other contracting party is caused or threatened by any such subsidization, the contracting party granting the subsidy shall, upon request, discuss with the other contracting party . . . the possibility of limiting the subsidization.

ARTICLE XIX

Emergency Action on Imports of Particular Products

1.

   a. If, as a result of unforeseen developments and of the effect of the obligations incurred by a contracting party under this Agreement, including tariff concessions, any product is being imported into the territory of that contracting party in such increased quantities and under such conditions as to cause or threaten serious injury to domestic producers in that territory of like or directly competitive products, the contracting party shall be free, in respect of such product, and to the extent and for such time as may be necessary to prevent or remedy such injury, to suspend the obligation in whole or in part or to withdraw or modify the concession. . . .

ARTICLE XXIV

Territorial Application—Frontier Traffic—Customs Unions and Free-Trade Areas

4. The contracting parties recognize the desirability of increasing freedom of trade by the development, through voluntary agreements, of closer integration between the economies of the countries party to such agreements. They also recognize that the purpose of a customs union or of a free-trade area should be to facilitate trade between the constituent territories and not to raise barriers to the trade of other contracting parties with such territories.

5. Accordingly, the provisions of this Agreement shall not prevent [the formation of customs unions and free-trade areas, provided that:]

   a. . . . the duties [with outside parties] shall not on the whole be higher or more restrictive than the general incidence of the duties . . . prior to the formation. . . .

Source: http://www.wto.org/english/docs_e/legal_e/gatt47_01_e.htm#articleI.

she obtains little or no surplus over the purchase price. But for all the earlier units purchased (from 0 to D_1 units), the consumers valued the product at *higher than* its purchase price: the consumers' willingness to pay for the product equals the height of the demand curve. For example, the person buying unit D_2 would have been willing to pay the price of P_2, which is the height of the demand curve at that quantity. Therefore, that individual obtains the surplus of $(P_2 - P_1)$ from being able to purchase the good at the price P_1.

For each unit purchased before D_1, the value that the consumer places on the product exceeds the purchase price of P_1. Adding up the surplus obtained on each unit purchased, from 0 to D_1, we can measure consumer surplus (*CS*) as the shaded region below the demand curve and above the price P_1. This region measures the satisfaction that consumers receive from the purchased quantity D_1, over and above the amount $P_1 \cdot D_1$ that they have paid.

Panel (b) of Figure 7-1 illustrates producer surplus. This panel shows the supply curve of an industry; the height of the curve represents the firm's marginal cost at each level of production. At the price of P_1, the industry will supply S_1. For the last unit supplied, the price P_1 equals the marginal cost of production for the firm supplying that unit. But for all earlier units supplied (from 0 to S_1 units), the firms were able to produce those units at a marginal cost *less than* the price P_1. For example, the firm supplying unit S_0 could produce it with a marginal cost of P_0, which is the height of the supply curve at that quantity. Therefore, that firm obtains the producer surplus of $(P_1 - P_0)$ from being able to sell the good at the price P_1.

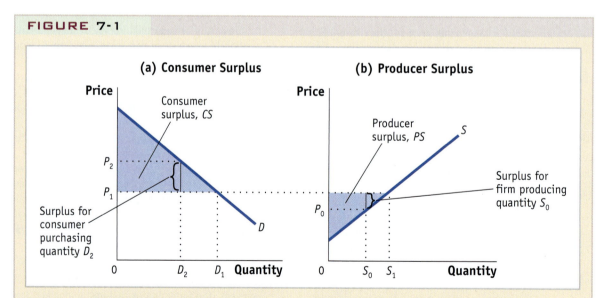

FIGURE 7-1

(a) Consumer Surplus

(b) Producer Surplus

Consumer and Producer Surplus In panel (a), the consumer surplus from purchasing quantity D_1 at price P_1 is the area below the demand curve and above that price. The consumer who purchases D_2 is willing to pay price P_2 but has to pay only P_1. The difference is the consumer surplus and represents the satisfaction of consumers over and above the amount paid. In panel (b), the producer surplus from supplying the quantity S_1 at the price P_1 is the area above the supply curve and below that price. The supplier who supplies unit S_0 has marginal costs of P_0 but sells it for P_1. The difference is the producer surplus and represents the return to fixed factors of production in the industry.

For each unit sold before S_1, the marginal cost to the firm is less than the sale price of P_1. Adding up the producer surplus obtained for each unit sold, from 0 to S_1, we obtain producer surplus (*PS*) as the shaded region in panel (b) above the supply curve and below the price of P_1. It is tempting to think of producer surplus as the profits of firms, since for all units before S_1, the marginal cost of production is less than the sale price of P_1. But a more accurate definition of producer surplus is that it equals the *return to fixed factors of production in the industry*. That is, producer surplus is the difference between the sales revenue $P_1 \cdot S_1$ and the total variable costs of production (i.e., wages paid to labor and the costs of intermediate inputs). If there are fixed factors such as capital or land in the industry, as in the specific-factors model we studied in Chapter 3, then producer surplus equals the returns to these fixed factors of production. We might still loosely refer to this return as the "profit" earned in the industry, but it is important to understand that producer surplus is not *monopoly profits*, because we are assuming perfect competition (i.e., zero monopoly profits) throughout this chapter.[3]

Home Welfare

To examine the effects of trade on a country's welfare, we consider once again a world composed of two countries, Home and Foreign, with each country consisting of producers and consumers. Total Home welfare can be measured by adding up consumer and producer surplus. As you would expect, the greater the total amount of Home welfare, the better off are the consumers and producers overall in the economy. To measure the gains from trade, we will compare Home welfare in no-trade and free-trade situations.

No Trade In panel (a) of Figure 7-2, we combine the Home demand and supply curves in a single diagram. The no-trade equilibrium occurs at the autarky price of P^A, where the quantity demanded equals the quantity supplied, of Q_0. Consumer surplus is the region above the price of P^A and below the demand curve, which is labeled as *CS* in panel (a) and also shown as area *a* in panel (b). Producer surplus is the area below the price of P^A and above the supply curve, which is labeled as *PS* in panel (a) and also shown as area (*b* + *c*) in panel (b). So the sum of consumer surplus and producer surplus is the area between the demand and supply curves, or *CS* + *PS* = area (*a* + *b* + *c*). That area equals Home welfare in the market for this good in the absence of international trade.

Free Trade for a Small Country Now suppose that Home can engage in international trade for this good. As we have discussed in earlier chapters, the world price P^W is determined by the intersection of supply and demand in the world market. Generally, there will be many countries buying and selling on the world market. We will suppose that the Home country is a **small country,** by which we mean that it is small in comparison with all the other countries buying and selling this product. For that reason, Home will be a *price taker* in the world market: it faces the fixed world price of P^W, and its own level of demand and supply for this product has no influence on the world price.

In panel (b) of Figure 7-2, we assume that the world price P^W is *below* the Home no-trade price of P^A. At the lower price, Home demand will increase from Q_0 under

---

[3] Recall from Chapter 6 that under imperfect competition, firms can influence the price of their goods and hence earn positive monopoly profits.

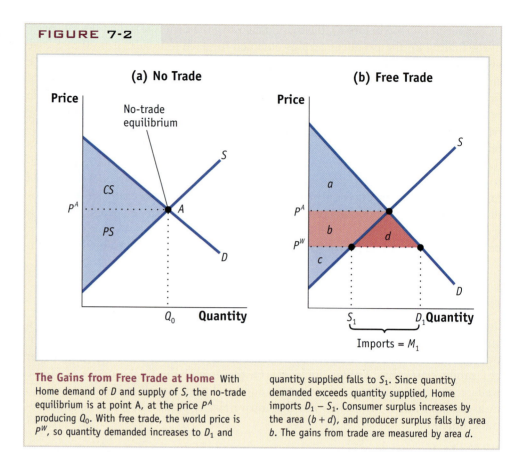

FIGURE 7-2

(a) No Trade

(b) Free Trade

The Gains from Free Trade at Home With Home demand of *D* and supply of *S*, the no-trade equilibrium is at point A, at the price P^A producing Q_0. With free trade, the world price is P^W, so quantity demanded increases to D_1 and

quantity supplied falls to S_1. Since quantity demanded exceeds quantity supplied, Home imports $D_1 - S_1$. Consumer surplus increases by the area $(b + d)$, and producer surplus falls by area *b*. The gains from trade are measured by area *d*.

no trade to D_1, and Home supply will decrease from Q_0 under no trade to S_1. The difference between D_1 and S_1 is *imports* of the good, or $M_1 = D_1 - S_1$. Because the world price P^W is below the no-trade price of P^A, the Home country is an importer of the product at the world price. If, instead, P^W were above P^A, then Home would be an exporter of the product at the world price.

Gains from Trade Now that we have established the free-trade equilibrium at price P^W, it is easy to measure Home welfare as the sum of consumer and producer surplus with trade, and compare it with the no-trade situation. In panel (b) of Figure 7-2, Home consumer surplus at the price P^W equals the area $(a + b + d)$, which is the area below the demand curve and above the price P^W. In the absence of trade, consumer surplus was the area *a*, so the drop in price from P^A to P^W has increased consumer surplus by the amount $(b + d)$. Home consumers clearly gain from the drop in price.

Home firms, on the other hand, suffer a decrease in producer surplus from the drop in price. In panel (b), Home producer surplus at the price P^W equals the area *c*, which is the area above the supply curve and below the price P^W. In the absence of trade, producer surplus was the area $(b + c)$, so the drop in price from P^A to P^W has decreased producer surplus by the amount *b*. Home firms clearly lose from the drop in price.

Comparing the gains of consumers, $(b + d)$, with the losses of producers, area *b*, we see that consumers gain more than the producers lose, which indicates that total

Home welfare (the sum of consumer surplus and producer surplus) has gone up. We can calculate the total change in Home welfare due to the opening of trade by adding the *changes* in consumer surplus and producer surplus:

Rise in consumer surplus:	$+ (b + d)$
Fall in producer surplus:	$- b$
Net effect on Home welfare:	$+d$

The area d is a measure of the *gains from trade* for the importing country due to free trade in this good. It is similar to the gains from trade that we have identified in earlier chapters using the production possibilities frontier and indifference curves, but it is easier to measure: the triangle d has a base equal to free-trade imports $M_1 = D_1 - S_1$, and a height that is the drop in price, $P^A - P^W$, so the gains from trade equal the area of the triangle, $\frac{1}{2} \cdot (P^A - P^W) \cdot M_1$. Of course, with many goods being imported, we would need to add up the areas of the triangles for each good and take into account the net gains on the export side to determine the overall gains from trade for a country. Since gains are positive for each individual good, after summing all imported and exported goods, the gains from trade are still positive.

Home Import Demand Curve

Before introducing a tariff, we use Figure 7-3 to derive the **import demand curve,** which shows the relationship between the world price of a good and the quantity of imports demanded by Home consumers. We first derived this curve in Chapter 2, for

FIGURE 7-3

(a) Home Market   **(b) Import Market**

Home Import Demand With Home demand of D and supply of S, the no-trade equilibrium is at point A, with the price P^A and import quantity Q_0. Import demand at this price is zero, as shown by the point A' in panel (b). At a lower world price of P^W, import demand is $M_1 = D_1 - S_1$, as shown by point B. Joining up all points between A' and B, we obtain the import demand curve, M.

the Ricardian model. We now briefly review the derivation of the import demand curve before analyzing the effect of an import tariff on prices and welfare.

In panel (a) of Figure 7-3, we again show the downward-sloping Home demand curve (D) and the upward-sloping Home supply curve (S). The no-trade equilibrium is at point A, which determines Home's no-trade equilibrium price P^A, and its no-trade equilibrium quantity of Q_0. Because quantity demanded equals quantity supplied, there are zero imports of this product. Zero imports is shown as point A' in panel (b).

Now suppose the world price is at P^W, below the no-trade price of P^A. At the price of P^W, the quantity demanded in Home is D_1, but the quantity supplied by Home suppliers is only S_1. Therefore, the quantity imported is $M_1 = D_1 - S_1$, as shown by the point B in panel (b). Joining points A' and B, we obtain the downward-sloping import demand curve M.

Notice that the import demand curve applies for all prices *below* the no-trade price of P^A in Figure 7-3. Having lower prices leads to greater Home demand and less Home supply and, therefore, positive imports. What happens if the world price is *above* the no-trade price? In that case, the higher price would lead to greater Home supply and less Home demand, so Home would become an exporter of the product.

3 Import Tariffs for a Small Country

We can now use this supply and demand framework to show what happens when a small country imposes a tariff. As we have already explained, an importing country is "small" if its tariff does not have any effect on the world price of the good on which the tariff is applied. As we will see, the Home price of the good will increase due to the tariff. Because the tariff (which is a tax) is applied at the border, the price charged to Home consumers will increase by the amount of the tariff.

Free Trade for a Small Country

In Figure 7-4, we again show the free-trade equilibrium for the Home country. In panel (b), the Foreign export supply curve X^* is horizontal at the world price P^W. The horizontal export supply curve means that Home can import any amount at the price P^W without having an impact on that price. The free-trade equilibrium is determined by the intersection of the Foreign export supply and the Home import demand curves, which is point B in panel (b), at the world price P^W. At that price, Home demand is D_1 and Home supply is S_1, shown in panel (a). Imports at the world price P^W are then just the difference between demand and supply, or $M_1 = D_1 - S_1$.

Effect of the Tariff

With the import tariff of t dollars, the export supply curve facing the Home country shifts up by exactly that amount, reflecting the higher price that must be paid to import the good. The shift in the Foreign export supply curve is analogous to the shift in domestic supply caused by a sales tax, as you may have seen in earlier economics courses; it reflects an effective increase in the costs of the firm. In panel (b) of Figure 7-4,

FIGURE 7-4

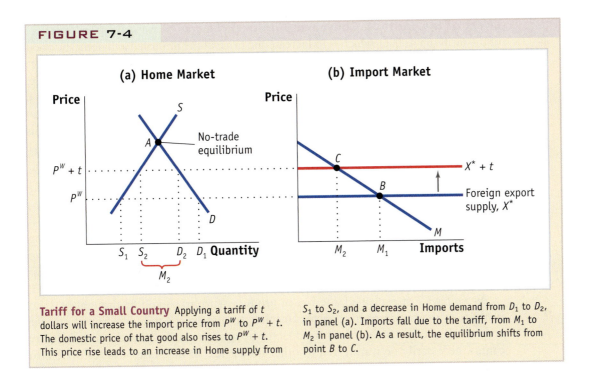

Tariff for a Small Country Applying a tariff of t dollars will increase the import price from P^W to $P^W + t$. The domestic price of that good also rises to $P^W + t$. This price rise leads to an increase in Home supply from S_1 to S_2, and a decrease in Home demand from D_1 to D_2, in panel (a). Imports fall due to the tariff, from M_1 to M_2 in panel (b). As a result, the equilibrium shifts from point B to C.

the export supply curve shifts up to $X^* + t$. The intersection of the post-tariff export supply curve and the import demand curve now occurs at the price of $P^W + t$ and the import quantity of M_2. The import tariff has reduced the amount imported, from M_1 under free trade to M_2 under the tariff, due to its higher price.

We assume that the imported product is identical to the domestic alternative that is available. For example, if the imported product is a women's cruiser bicycle, then the Home demand curve D in panel (a) is the demand for women's cruisers, and the Home supply curve is the supply of women's cruisers. When the import price rises to $P^W + t$, then we expect that the Home price for locally produced bicycles will rise by the same amount. This is because at the higher import price of $P^W + t$, the quantity of cruisers demanded at Home falls from its free-trade quantity of D_1 to D_2. At the same time, the higher price will encourage Home firms to increase the quantity of cruisers they supply from the free-trade quantity of S_1 to S_2. As firms increase the quantity they produce, however, the marginal costs of production rise. The Home supply curve (S) reflects these marginal costs, so the Home price will rise along the supply curve until Home firms are supplying the quantity S_2, at a marginal cost just equal to the import price of $P^W + t$. Since marginal costs equal $P^W + t$, the price charged by Home firms will also equal $P^W + t$, and the domestic price will equal the import price.

Summing up, Home demand at the new price is D_2, Home supply is S_2, and the difference between these are Home imports of $M_2 = D_2 - S_2$. Foreign exporters still receive the "net-of-tariff" price (i.e., the Home price minus the tariff) of P^W, but Home consumers pay the higher price $P^W + t$. We now investigate how the rise in the Home price from P^W to $P^W + t$ affects consumer surplus, producer surplus, and overall Home welfare.

Effect of the Tariff on Consumer Surplus In Figure 7-5, we again show the effect of the tariff of t dollars, which is to increase the price of the imported and domestic good from P^W to $P^W + t$. Under free trade, consumer surplus in panel (a) was the area under the demand curve and above P^W. With the tariff, consumers now pay the higher price, $P^W + t$, and their surplus is the area under the demand curve and above the price $P^W + t$. The fall in consumer surplus due to the tariff is the area between the two prices and to the left of Home demand, which is $(a + b + c + d)$ in panel (a) of Figure 7-5. This area is the amount that consumers lose due to the higher price caused by the tariff.

Effect of the Tariff on Producer Surplus We can also trace the impact of the tariff on producer surplus. Under free trade, producer surplus was the area above the supply curve in panel (a) and below the price of P^W. With the tariff, producer surplus is the area above the supply curve and below the price $P^W + t$: since the tariff increases the Home price, firms are able to sell more goods at a higher price, thus increasing their surplus. We can illustrate this rise in producer surplus as the amount between the two prices and to the left of Home supply, which is labeled as a in panel (a). This area is the amount that Home firms gain due to the higher price caused by the tariff.

As we have just explained, the rise in producer surplus should be thought of as an increase in the return to fixed factors (capital or land) in the industry. Sometimes we even think of labor as a partially fixed factor because the skills learned in one industry cannot necessarily be transferred to other industries. In that case, it is reasonable to think that the increase in Home producer surplus can also benefit Home workers in the import-competing industry, along with capital and land, but this benefit comes at the expense of consumer surplus.

Effect of the Tariff on Government Revenue In addition to affecting consumers and producers, the tariff also affects government revenue. The amount of revenue collected is the tariff t times the quantity of imports $(D_2 - S_2)$. In Figure 7-5, panel (a), this revenue is shown by the area c. The collection of revenue is a gain for the government in the importing country.

Overall Effect of the Tariff on Welfare We are now in a position to summarize the impact of the tariff on the welfare of the Home importing country, which is the sum of producer surplus, consumer surplus, and government revenues. Thus, our approach is to *add up* these impacts to obtain a net effect. In adding up the loss of consumers and the gains of producers, one dollar of consumer surplus is the same as one dollar of producer surplus or government revenue. In other words, we do not care whether the consumers facing higher prices are poor or rich, and do not care whether the specific factors in the industry (capital, land, and possibly labor) earn a lot or a little. Under this approach, transferring one dollar from consumer to producer surplus will have no impact on overall welfare: the decrease in consumer surplus will cancel out the increase in producer surplus.

You may object to this method of evaluating overall welfare, and feel that a dollar taken away from a poor consumer and given to a rich producer represents a net loss of overall welfare, rather than zero effect, as in our approach. We should be careful in evaluating the impact of tariffs on different income groups in the society, especially for poor countries or countries with a high degree of inequality among income groups. But for now we ignore this concern and simply add up consumer surplus, producer surplus, and government revenue. Keep in mind that under this approach we are just evaluating the *efficiency* of tariffs and not their effect on equity (i.e., how fair the tariff is to one group versus another).

FIGURE 7-5

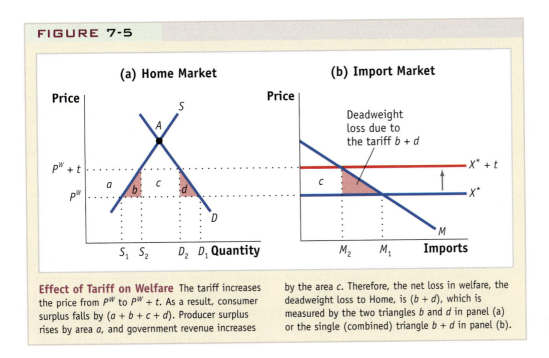

(a) Home Market

(b) Import Market

Effect of Tariff on Welfare The tariff increases the price from P^W to $P^W + t$. As a result, consumer surplus falls by $(a + b + c + d)$. Producer surplus rises by area a, and government revenue increases by the area c. Therefore, the net loss in welfare, the deadweight loss to Home, is $(b + d)$, which is measured by the two triangles b and d in panel (a) or the single (combined) triangle $b + d$ in panel (b).

The overall impact of the tariff in the small country can be summarized as follows:

Fall in consumer surplus:	$-(a + b + c + d)$
Rise in producer surplus:	$+a$
Rise in government revenue:	$+c$
Net effect on Home welfare:	$-(b + d)$

In Figure 7-5(b), the triangle $(b + d)$ is the *net welfare loss* in a small importing country due to the tariff. We sometimes refer to this area as a **deadweight loss,** meaning that it is not offset by a gain elsewhere in the economy. Notice that in panel (a) the area a, which is a gain for producers, just cancels out that portion of the consumer surplus loss; the area a is effectively a transfer from consumers to producers via the higher domestic prices induced by the tariff. Likewise, area c, the gain in government revenue, also cancels out that portion of the consumer surplus loss; this is a transfer from consumers to the government. Thus, the area $(b + d)$ is the remaining loss for consumers that is not offset by a gain elsewhere. This deadweight loss is measured by the two triangles, b and d, in panel (a), or by the combined triangle $(b + d)$ in panel (b). The two triangles b and d of deadweight loss can each be given a precise interpretation, as follows.

Production Loss Notice that the base of triangle b is the net increase in Home supply due to the tariff, from S_1 to S_2. The height of this triangle is the increase in marginal costs due to the increase in supply. The unit S_1 was produced at a marginal cost equal to P^W, which is the free-trade price, but every unit above that amount is produced with higher marginal costs. The fact that marginal costs exceed the world price means that this country is producing the good inefficiently: it would be cheaper to import it rather than produce the extra quantity at home. The area of triangle b equals the increase in marginal costs for the extra units produced and can be interpreted as the **production loss** (or the *efficiency loss*) for the economy due to producing at marginal costs above the world price. Notice that the production loss is only a portion of the overall deadweight loss, which is $(b + d)$ in Figure 7-5.

Consumption Loss The triangle d in panel (a) (the other part of the deadweight loss) can also be given a precise interpretation. Because of the tariff and the price increase from P^W to $P^W + t$, the quantity consumed at Home is reduced from D_1 to D_2. The area of the triangle d can be interpreted as the drop in consumer surplus for those individuals who are no longer able to consume the units between D_1 and D_2 because of the higher price. We refer to this drop in consumer surplus as the **consumption loss** for the economy.

Why and How Are Tariffs Applied?

Our finding that a tariff always leads to deadweight losses for a small importing country explains why most economists oppose the use of tariffs. If a small country suffers a loss when it imposes a tariff, why do so many have tariffs as part of their trade policies? One answer is that a developing country does not have any other source of government revenue. Import tariffs are "easy to collect" because every country has customs agents at major ports checking the goods that cross the border. It is easy to tax imports, even though the deadweight loss from using a tariff is typically higher than the deadweight loss from using "hard-to-collect" taxes, such as income taxes or value-added taxes. These taxes are hard to collect because they require individuals and firms to honestly report earnings, and the government cannot check every report (as they can check imports at the border). Still, to the extent that developing countries recognize that tariffs have a higher deadweight loss, we would expect that over time they would shift away from such easy-to-collect taxes. That is exactly what has occurred, according to one research study.[4] The fraction of total tax revenue collected from "easy to collect" taxes such as tariffs fell during the 1980s and 1990s, especially in developing countries, whereas the fraction of revenue raised from "hard to collect" taxes rose over this same period.

A second reason why tariffs are used even though they have a deadweight loss is politics. The tariff benefits the Home producers, as we have seen, so if the government cares more about producer surplus than consumer surplus, it might decide to use the tariff despite the deadweight loss it incurs. Indeed, the benefits to producers (and their workers) are typically more concentrated on specific firms and states than the costs to consumers, which are spread nationwide. This is our interpretation of the tariff that President George W. Bush granted to the steel industry in 2002: its benefits were concentrated in the steel-producing states of Pennsylvania, West Virginia, and Ohio, and its costs to consumers—in this case, steel-using industries—were spread more widely.[5] For the tariff on tires imported from China, approved by President Barack Obama in 2009, the argument is a bit different. This tariff was requested by

---

[4] Joshua Aizenman and Yothin Jinjarak, January 2006, "Globalization and Developing Countries—A Shrinking Tax Base?" National Bureau of Economic Research (NBER) Working Paper No. 11933.
[5] Although the steel tariff was used to obtain votes from the steel-producing states, it also served another political purpose. In 2002 President George W. Bush faced a vote on whether the president should be granted "fast-track authority" to negotiate trade agreements with other countries. Fast-track authority allows the president to present a new trade agreement to the Congress for an up-or-down vote within 90 days, without having the terms of the trade agreement revised by the Congress. This authority expires every five years. In 2002 the steel tariff prompted some members of Congress to vote in favor of fast-track authority, which passed in Congress by only two votes. More recently, fast-track authority, also called "trade promotion authority," was not renewed by Congress and was allowed to lapse on July 1, 2007.

the United Steelworkers of America, the union who represents workers in the U.S. tire industry, and it is expected to benefit those workers. But U.S. tire producers did not support the tariff because many of them already manufacture tires in other countries—especially China—and this tariff will make it more costly for them to do so.

In both the steel and tire cases, the president was not free to impose just any tariff, but had to follow the rules of the GATT discussed earlier in this chapter. Recall that Article XIX of the GATT, known as the "safeguard" or "escape clause," allows a temporary tariff to be used under certain circumstances. GATT Article XIX is mirrored in U.S. trade law. In **Side Bar: Safeguard Tariffs,** we list the key passages for two sections of the Trade Act of 1974, as amended, both of which deal with safeguard tariffs.

First, Section 201 states that a tariff can be requested by the president, by the House of Representatives, by the Senate, or by any other party such as a firm or union that files a petition with the U.S. International Trade Commission (ITC). That commission determines whether rising imports have been a "a substantial cause of serious injury, or threat thereof, to the U.S. industry. . . ." The commission then makes a recommendation to the president who has the final authority to approve or veto the tariff. Section 201 goes further in defining a "substantial cause" as a "cause that is important and not less than any other cause." Although this kind of legal language sounds quite obscure, it basically means that rising imports have to be *the most important* cause of injury to justify import protection. The steel tariff used by President Bush met this criterion, but as we shall see in later chapters, many other requests for tariffs do not meet this criterion and are not approved.

SIDE BAR

Safeguard Tariffs

The U.S. Trade Act of 1974, as amended, describes conditions under which tariffs can be applied in the United States, and it mirrors the provisions of the GATT and WTO. Two sections of the Trade Act of 1974 deal with the use of "safeguard" tariffs:

Section 201

Upon the filing of a petition. . . , the request of the President or the Trade Representative, the resolution of either the Committee on Ways and Means of the House of Representatives or the Committee on Finance of the Senate, or on its own motion, the [International Trade] Commission shall promptly make an investigation to determine whether an article is being imported into the United States in such increased quantities as to be a *substantial cause of serious injury, or the threat thereof, to the domestic industry* producing an article like or directly competitive with the imported article.

. . . For purposes of this section, the term "substantial cause" means a cause which is *important and not less than any other cause.*

Section 421

Upon the filing of a petition . . . the United States International Trade Commission . . . shall promptly make an investigation to determine whether products of the People's Republic of China are being imported into the United States in such increased quantities or under such conditions as to *cause or threaten to cause market disruption to the domestic producers* of like or directly competitive products.

. . . (1) For purposes of this section, *market disruption* exists whenever imports of an article like or directly competitive with an article produced by a domestic industry are increasing rapidly, either absolutely or relatively, so as to be a *significant cause of material injury, or threat of material injury, to the domestic industry*.

(2) For purposes of paragraph (1), the term "significant cause" refers to a cause which contributes significantly to the material injury of the domestic industry, *but need not be equal to or greater than any other cause*. [Italics added]

Source: http://www4.law.cornell.edu/uscode/19/usc_sec_19_00002252———000-.html and http://www4.law.cornell.edu/uscode/19/usc_sec_19_00002451———000-.html.

A second, more recent amendment to the Trade Act of 1974 is Section 421 that applies only to China. This provision was added by the United States as a condition to China's joining the WTO in 2001.[6] Because the United States was worried about exceptional surges in imports from China, it drafted this legislation so that tariffs could be applied in such a case. Under Section 421, various groups can file a petition with the U.S. International Trade Commission, which makes a recommendation to the president. The commission must determine whether rising imports from China cause "market disruption" in a U.S. industry, which means "a significant cause of material injury, or threat of material injury, to the domestic industry." Furthermore, the term "significant cause" refers to "a cause which contributes significantly to the material injury of the domestic industry, but need not be equal to or greater than any other cause." Again, the legal language can be hard to follow, but it indicates that tariffs can be applied even when rising imports from China *are not the most important* cause of injury to the domestic industry. Section 421 can therefore be applied under weaker conditions than Section 201, and it was used by President Obama to justify the tariff on tires imported from China.

APPLICATION

U.S. Tariffs on Steel and Tires

The U.S. steel and tire tariffs highlight the political motivation for applying tariffs despite the deadweight losses associated with them. We can use our small-country model introduced previously to calculate a rough estimate of how costly these tariffs were in terms of welfare. Although the United States may not be a small country when

Oliphant Universal Press Syndicate

it comes to its influence on import and export prices, it is a good starting point for our analysis, and we will examine the large-country case in the next section. For now, we stay with our small-country model and illustrate the deadweight loss due to a tariff with the U.S. steel tariff in place from March 2002 to December 2003. After that calculation, we compare the steel tariff with the more recent tariff on tires.

To fulfill his campaign promise to protect the steel industry, President George W. Bush requested that the ITC initiate a Section 201 investigation into the steel industry. This was one of the few times that a president had initiated a Section 201 action; usually, firms or unions in an industry apply to the ITC for import protection. After investigating, the ITC determined that the conditions of Section 201 and Article XIX were met and recommended that tariffs be put in place to protect the U.S. steel industry. The tariffs recommended by the ITC varied across products, ranging from 10 to 20% for the first year, as shown in Table 7-1, and then falling over time so as to be eliminated after three years.

---

[6] Section 421 was added to U.S. trade law for 12 years, and is due to expire in 2013.

TABLE 7-1

U.S. ITC Recommended and Actual Tariffs for Steel Shown here are the tariffs recommended by the U.S. International Trade Commission for steel imports, and the actual tariffs that were applied in the first year.

Product Category	U.S. ITC Recommendation (First Year, %)	Actual U.S. Tariff (First Year, %)
Carbon and Alloy Flat Products		
Slab	20	30
Flat products	20	30
Tin mill products	U*	30
Carbon and Alloy Long Products		
Hot-rolled bar	20	30
Cold-finished bar	20	30
Rebar	10	15
Carbon and Alloy Tubular Products		
Tubular products	?**	15
Alloy fittings and flanges	13	13
Stainless and Tool Steel Products		
Stainless steel bar	15	15
Stainless steel rod	?**	15
Stainless steel wire	U*	8

* U: Uncertain—the ITC was divided on whether a tariff should be used or not.

** ?: A specific recommendation was not made by the U.S. ITC.

Source: Robert Read, 2005, "The Political Economy of Trade Protection: The Determinants and Welfare Impact of the 2002 U.S. Emergency Steel Safeguard Measures," The World Economy, 1119–1137.

The ITC decision was based on several factors.[7] First, imports had been rising and prices were falling in the steel industry from 1998 to early 2001, leading to substantial losses for U.S. firms. Those losses, along with falling investment and employment, met the condition of "serious injury." An explanation given by the ITC for the falling import prices was that the U.S. dollar appreciated substantially prior to 2001: as the dollar rises in value, foreign currencies become cheaper and so do imported products such as steel, as occurred during this period. To meet the criterion of Section 201 and Article XIX, rising imports need to be a "substantial cause" of serious injury, which is defined as "a cause which is important and not less than any other cause." Sometimes another cause of injury to U.S. firms can be a domestic recession, but that was not the case in the years preceding 2001, when demand for steel products was rising.[8]

President Bush accepted the recommendation of the ITC but applied even higher tariffs, ranging from 8 to 30%, as shown in Table 7-1, with 30% tariffs applied to the

---

[7] We focus here on the ITC conclusions for flat-rolled carbon steel, from U.S. International Trade Commission, 2001, Steel: Investigation No. TA-201-73, Volume I, Publication 3479, Washington, D.C.

[8] A short recession began in the United States in March 2001 and ended eight months later, in November 2001.

most commonly used steel products (such as flat-rolled steel sheets and steel slab). Initially, the tariffs were meant to be in place for three years and to decline over time. Knowing that U.S. trading partners would be upset by this action, President Bush exempted some countries from the tariffs on steel. The countries exempted included Canada, Mexico, Jordan, and Israel, all of which have free-trade agreements with the United States, and 100 small developing countries that were exporting only a very small amount of steel to the United States.

Deadweight Loss Due to the Steel Tariff To measure the deadweight loss due to the tariffs levied on steel, we need to estimate the area of the triangle $b + d$ in Figure 7-5(b). The base of this triangle is the change in imports due to the tariffs, or $\Delta M = M_1 - M_2$. The height of the triangle is the increase in the domestic price due to the tariff, or $\Delta P = t$. So the deadweight loss equals

$$DWL = \frac{1}{2} \cdot t \cdot \Delta M$$

It is convenient to measure the deadweight loss relative to the value of imports, which is $P^W \cdot M$. We will also use the percentage tariff, which is t/P^W, and the percentage change in the quantity of imports, which is $\%\Delta M = \Delta M/M$. The deadweight loss relative to the value of imports can then be rewritten as

$$\frac{DWL}{P^W \cdot M} = \frac{1}{2} \cdot \frac{t \cdot \Delta M}{P^W \cdot M} = \frac{1}{2} \cdot \left(\frac{t}{P^W}\right) \cdot \%\Delta M$$

For the tariffs on steel, the most commonly used products had a tariff of 30%, so that is the percentage increase in the price: $t/P^W = 0.3$. It turns out that the quantity of steel imports also fell by 30% the first year after the tariff was imposed, so that $\%\Delta M = 0.3$. Therefore, the deadweight loss is

$$\frac{DWL}{P^W \cdot M} = \frac{1}{2} (0.3 \cdot 0.3) = 0.045, \text{ or } 4.5\% \text{ of the import value}$$

The value of steel imports that were affected by the tariff was about $4.7 billion in the year prior to March 2002 and $3.5 billion in the year after March 2002, so average imports over the two years were $\frac{1}{2}$ (4.7 + 3.5) = $4.1 billion (these values do not include the tariffs).[9]

If we apply the deadweight loss of 4.5% to the average import value of $4.1 billion, then the dollar magnitude of deadweight loss is 0.045 · 4.1 billion = $185 million. As we discussed earlier, this deadweight loss reflects the net annual loss to the United States from applying the tariff. If you are a steelworker, then you might think that the price of $185 million is money well spent to protect your job, at least temporarily. On the other hand, if you are a consumer of steel, then you will probably object to the higher prices and deadweight loss. In fact, many of the U.S. firms that purchase steel—such as firms producing automobiles—objected to the tariffs and encouraged President Bush to end them early. But the biggest objections to the tariffs came from exporting countries whose firms were affected by the tariffs, especially the European countries.

---

[9] The drop in imports of 30% corresponds to a fall in import value of $1.2 billion (since 1.2/4.1 ≈ 0.30, or 30%).

Response of the European Countries The tariffs on steel most heavily affected Europe, Japan, and South Korea, along with some developing countries (Brazil, India, Turkey, Moldova, Romania, Thailand, and Venezuela) that were exporting a significant amount of steel to the United States. These countries objected to the restriction on their ability to sell steel to the United States.

The countries in the European Union (EU) therefore took action by bringing the case to the WTO. They were joined by Brazil, China, Japan, South Korea, New Zealand, Norway, and Switzerland. The WTO has a formal **dispute settlement procedure** under which countries that believe that the WTO rules have not been followed can bring their complaint and have it evaluated. The WTO evaluated this case and, in early November 2003, ruled that the United States had failed to sufficiently prove that its steel industry had been harmed by a sudden increase in imports and therefore did not have the right to impose "safeguard" tariffs.

The WTO ruling was made on legal grounds: that the United States had essentially failed to prove its case (i.e., its eligibility for Article XIX protection).[10] But there are also economic grounds for doubting the wisdom of the safeguard tariffs in the first place. Even if we accept that there might be an argument on equity or fairness grounds for temporarily protecting an industry facing import competition, it is hard to argue that such protection should occur because of a change in exchange rates. The U.S. dollar appreciated for much of the 1990s, including the period before 2001 on which the ITC focused, leading to much lower prices for imported steel. But the appreciation of the dollar also lowered the prices for *all other* import products, so many other industries in the United States faced import competition, too. On fairness grounds, there is no special reason to single out the steel industry for protection.

The WTO ruling entitled the European Union and other countries to retaliate against the United States by imposing tariffs of their own against U.S. exports. The European countries quickly began to draw up a list of products—totaling some $2.2 billion in U.S. exports—against which they would apply tariffs. The European countries naturally picked products that would have the greatest negative impact on the United States, such as oranges from Florida, where Jeb Bush, the president's brother, was governor.

The threat of tariffs being imposed on these products led President Bush to reconsider the U.S. tariffs on steel. On December 5, 2003, he announced that they would be suspended after being in place for only 19 months rather than the three years as initially planned. This chain of events illustrates how the use of tariffs by an importer can easily lead to a response by exporters and a **tariff war.** The elimination of the steel tariffs by President Bush avoided such a retaliatory tariff war.

Tariff on Tires The tariff on tires imported from China, announced on September 11, 2009, was applied so recently that the information needed to make a deadweight loss calculation is not available. Instead, we will discuss the similarities and differences with the steel tariff.

---

[10] One of the legal reasons for the WTO ruling was that imports of flat-rolled steel into the United States had fallen from 1998 to 2001, so this product did not meet the requirement that imports had to be increasing to receive Article XIX protection. Even though imports of other steel products were rising, flat-rolled steel was considered one of the most important imported products.

One key difference between these tariffs has already been pointed out: the tire tariff was applied to imports from a single country—China—under Section 421 of U.S. trade law, whereas the steel tariff was applied against many countries under Section 201. The tire tariff is the first time that Section 421, which was added to U.S. trade law when China joined the WTO in 2001, has been used.

A second difference between these cases is that steel producers in the United States supported that tariff, but no U.S. tire producers joined in the request for the tariff on tires. Rather, the petition for a tariff on tires imported from China was brought to the International Trade Commission by the United Steelworkers of American, the union that represents workers in the tire industry. There are ten producers of tires in the United States, and seven of them—including well-known firms like Goodyear, Michelin, Cooper, and Bridgestone—also produce tires in China and other countries. These firms naturally did not want the tariff put in place because it would harm rather than help them. In terms of the model we developed in this chapter, the producer surplus of these U.S. firms would fall rather than increase due to the tariff, which suggests that the deadweight loss from the tariff on tires could be larger than for the steel tariff (where U.S. firms gained producer surplus).

There are also a number of similarities in the two cases. As it did for the steel tariff, the International Trade Commission recommended three years of protection for tires, with tariffs on a declining schedule: 55% in the first year, then 45%, and then 35%, on top of the 4% existing tariff. President Obama instead imposed additional tariffs of 35% in the first year, then 30%, and then 25% in the third year.

Also similar to what occurred in the steel case, the tariff on tires led to retaliation. China responded with actual or potential tariffs on products such as chicken feet (a local delicacy), auto parts, certain nylon products, and even passenger cars. For its part, the United States went on to apply new tariffs on steel pipe imported from China, and also investigated several other products. Although these actions by both countries may not represent a full-fledged trade war, they are at least a skirmish, and they run the risk of not only worsening relations between the countries but also imposing costs on consumers of all these products.

The final, and perhaps most important, similarity with the steel case is that China has made an official complaint to the WTO under its dispute settlement procedure, just as the European countries did in the steel case. On January 11, 2010, the WTO announced that it would review the U.S. tariff on tires to determine whether it was applied in accord with the relevant trade laws. It is too early to know the outcome of this WTO review. As in the steel case, the WTO might find that the United States did not prove the case for the tariff on tires, and therefore allow China to retaliate if the tariff is not removed. Alternatively, because Section 421 allows a tariff to be imposed under weaker conditions than Section 201, the WTO might rule in favor of the United States. In either case, this tariff should not last longer than three years, and it could be removed earlier to avoid retaliation, as occurred in the steel case. ■

4 Import Tariffs for a Large Country

Under the small-country assumption that we have used so far, we know for sure that the deadweight loss is positive; that is, the importing country is always harmed by the tariff. The small-country assumption means that the world price P^W is unchanged by the tariff applied by the importing country. If we consider a large enough importing country or a **large country,** however, then we might expect that its tariff will change the world price. In that case, the welfare for a large importing country can be improved by a tariff, as we now show.

Foreign Export Supply

If the Home country is large, then we can no longer assume that it faces a Foreign export supply curve X^* that is horizontal at the given world price P^W. Instead, we need to derive the Foreign export supply curve using the Foreign market demand and supply curves. In panel (a) of Figure 7-6, we show the Foreign demand curve D^* and supply curve S^*. These intersect at the point A^*, with a no-trade equilibrium price of P^{A*}. Because Foreign demand equals supply at that price, Foreign exports are zero, which we show by point $A^{*\prime}$ in panel (b), where we graph Foreign exports against their price.

Now suppose the world price P^W is above the Foreign no-trade price of P^{A*}. At the price of P^W, the Foreign quantity demanded is lower, at D_1^* in panel (a), but the quantity supplied by Foreign firms is larger, at S_1^*. Because Foreign supply exceeds demand, Foreign will export the amount $X_1^* = S_1^* - D_1^*$ at the price of P^W, as shown by the

---

FIGURE 7-6

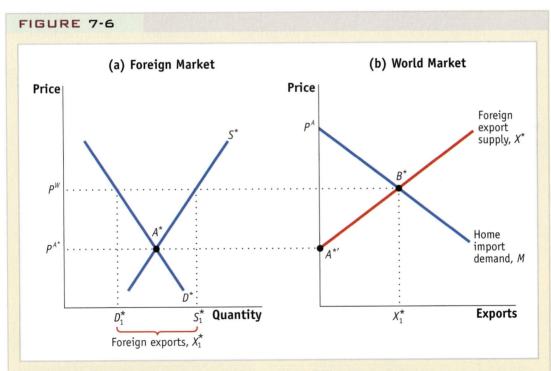

(a) Foreign Market

(b) World Market

Foreign Export Supply In panel (a), with Foreign demand of D^* and Foreign supply of S^*, the no-trade equilibrium in Foreign is at point A^*, with the price of P^{A*}. At this price, the Foreign market is in equilibrium and Foreign exports are zero—point A^* in panel (a) and point $A^{*\prime}$ in panel (b), respectively. When the world price P^W is higher than Foreign's no-trade price, the quantity supplied by Foreign, S_1^*, exceeds the quantity demanded by Foreign, D_1^*, and Foreign exports $X_1^* = S_1^* - D_1^*$. In panel (b), joining up points $A^{*\prime}$ and B^*, we obtain the upward-sloping export supply curve X^*. With the Home import demand of M, the world equilibrium is at point B^*, with the price P^W.

point B^* in panel (b). Drawing a line through points $A^{*\prime}$ and B^*, we obtain the upward-sloping Foreign export supply curve X^*.

We can then combine the Foreign export supply curve X^* and Home import demand curve M, which is also shown in panel (b). They intersect at the price P^W, the world equilibrium price. Notice that the Home import demand curve starts at the no-trade price P^A on the price axis, whereas the Foreign export supply curve starts at the price P^{A*}. As we have drawn them, the Foreign no-trade price is lower, $P^{A*} < P^A$. In Chapters 2 to 5 of this book, a country with comparative advantage in a good would have a lower no-trade relative price and would become an exporter when trade was opened. Likewise, in panel (b), Foreign exports the good since its no-trade price P^{A*} is lower than the world price, and Home imports the good since its no-trade price P^A is higher that the world price. So the world equilibrium illustrated in panel (b) is similar to that in some of the trade models presented in earlier chapters.

Effect of the Tariff

In panel (b) of Figure 7-7, we repeat the Home import demand curve M and Foreign export supply curve X^*, with the world equilibrium at B^*. When Home applies a tariff of t dollars, the cost to Foreign producers of supplying the Home market is t more than it was before. Because of this increase in costs, the Foreign export supply curve shifts up by exactly the amount of the tariff, as shown in panel (b) with the shift from X^* to $X^* + t$. The $X^* + t$ curve intersects import demand M at point C, which establishes the Home price (including the tariff) paid by consumers. On the other hand, the Foreign exporters receive the net-of-tariff price, which is directly below the point C

FIGURE 7-7

(a) Home Market

(b) World Market

Tariff for a Large Country The tariff shifts up the export supply curve from X^* to $X^* + t$. As a result, the Home price increases from P^W to $P^* + t$, and the Foreign price falls from P^W to P^*. The deadweight loss at Home is the area of the triangle $(b + d)$, and Home also has a terms-of-trade gain of area e. Foreign loses the area $(e + f)$, so the net loss in world welfare is the triangle $(b + d + f)$.

by exactly the amount t, at point C^*. Let us call the price received by Foreign exporters P^*, at point C^*, which is the new world price.

The important feature of the new equilibrium is that the price Home pays for its imports, $P^* + t$, rises by *less than* the amount of the tariff t as compared with the initial world price P^W. The reason that the Home price rises by less than the full amount of the tariff is that the price received by Foreign exporters, P^*, has fallen as compared with the initial world price P^W. So Foreign producers are essentially "absorbing" a part of the tariff, by lowering their price from P^W (in the initial free-trade equilibrium) to P^* (after the tariff).

In sum, we can interpret the tariff as driving a wedge between what Home consumers pay and what Foreign producers receive, with the difference (of t) going to the Home government. As is the case with many taxes, the amount of the tariff (t) is shared by both consumers and producers.

Terms of Trade In Chapter 2, we defined the **terms of trade** for a country as the ratio of export prices to import prices. Generally, an improvement in the terms of trade indicates a gain for a country because it is either receiving more for its exports or paying less for its imports. To measure the Home terms of trade, we want to use the net-of-tariff import price P^* (received by Foreign firms) since that is the total amount transferred from Home to Foreign for each import. Because this price has fallen (from its initial world price of P^W), it follows that the Home terms of trade have increased. We might expect, therefore, that the Home country gains from the tariff in terms of Home welfare. To determine whether that is the case, we need to analyze the impact on the welfare of Home consumers, producers, and government revenue, which we do in Figure 7-7.

Home Welfare In panel (a), the Home consumer price increases from P^W to $P^* + t$, which makes consumers worse off. The drop in consumer surplus is represented by the area between these two prices and to the left of the demand curve D, which is shown by $(a + b + c + d)$. At the same time, the price received by Home firms rises from P^W to $P^* + t$, making Home firms better off. The increase in producer surplus equals the area between these two prices, and to the left of the supply curve S, which is the amount a. Finally, we also need to keep track of the changes in government revenue. Revenue collected from the tariff equals the amount of the tariff (t) times the new amount of imports, which is $M_2 = D_2 - S_2$. Therefore, government revenue equals the area $(c + e)$ in panel (a).

By summing the change in consumer surplus, producer surplus, and government revenue, we obtain the overall impact of the tariff in the large country, as follows:

Fall in consumer surplus:	$-(a + b + c + d)$
Rise in producer surplus:	$+a$
Rise in government revenue:	$+(c + e)$
Net effect on Home welfare:	$+e - (b + d)$

The triangle $(b + d)$ is the deadweight loss due to the tariff (just as it is for a small country). But for the large country, there is also a source of gain—the area e—that offsets this deadweight loss. If e exceeds $(b + d)$, then Home is better off due to the tariff; if e is less than $(b + d)$, then Home is worse off.

Notice that the area e is a rectangle whose height is the fall in the price that Foreign exporters receive, the difference between P^W and P^*. The base of this rectangle equals the quantity of imports, M_2. Multiplying the drop in the import price by the quantity of imports to obtain the area e, we obtain a precise measure of the **terms-of-trade gain** for the importer. If this terms-of-trade gain exceeds the deadweight loss of the tariff, which is $(b + d)$, then Home gains from the tariff.

Thus, we see that a large importer might gain by the application of a tariff. We can add this to our list of reasons why countries use tariffs, in addition to their being a source of government revenue or a tool for political purposes. However, for the large country, any net gain from the tariff comes at the expense of the Foreign exporters, as we show next.

Foreign and World Welfare While Home might gain from the tariff, Foreign, the exporting country, definitely loses. In panel (b) of Figure 7-7, the Foreign loss is measured by the area $(e + f)$. We should think of $(e + f)$ as the loss in Foreign producer surplus from selling fewer goods to Home at a lower price. Notice that the area e is the terms-of-trade gain for Home but an equivalent terms of trade *loss* for Foreign; Home's gain comes at the expense of Foreign. In addition, the large-country tariff incurs an extra deadweight loss of f in Foreign, so the combined total outweighs the benefits to Home. For this reason, we sometimes call a tariff imposed by a large country a "beggar thy neighbor" tariff.

Adding together the change in Home welfare and Foreign welfare, the area e cancels out and we are left with a *net loss* in world welfare of $(b + d + f)$, the triangle in panel (b). This area is a deadweight loss for the world. The terms-of-trade gain that Home has extracted from the Foreign country by using a tariff comes at the expense of the Foreign exporters, and in addition, there is an added world deadweight loss. The fact that the large-country tariff leads to a world deadweight loss is another reason that most economists oppose the use of tariffs.

Optimal Tariff for a Large Importing Country We have found that a large importer might gain by the application of tariffs, but have yet to determine what *level* of tariff a country should apply in order to maximize welfare. It turns out there is a shortcut method we can use to evaluate the effect of the tariff on the welfare of a large importing country. The shortcut method uses the concept of the **optimal tariff.**

The optimal tariff is defined as the tariff that leads to the maximum increase in welfare for the importing country. For a large importing country, a small tariff initially increases welfare because the terms-of-trade gain exceeds the deadweight loss. That is, the area of the rectangle e in panel (a) of Figure 7-7 exceeds the area of the triangle $(b + d)$ in panel (b) when the tariff is small enough. The reason for this is that both the height and base of the triangle $(b + d)$ shrink to zero when the tariff is very small, so the area of the triangle is very small indeed; but for the rectangle e, only the height shrinks to zero when the tariff is small, so the area of the rectangle exceeds that of the triangle. By this mathematical reasoning, the Home gains are positive—$e > (b + d)$—when the Home tariff is sufficiently small.

In Figure 7-8, we graph Home welfare against the level of the tariff. Free trade is at point B, where the tariff is zero. A small increase in the tariff, as we have just noted, leads to an *increase* in Home welfare (because the terms-of-trade gain exceeds the deadweight loss). Therefore, starting at point B, the graph of Home welfare must be upward-sloping. But what if the tariff is very large? If the tariff is too large, then welfare will fall *below* the free-trade level of welfare. For example, with a prohibitive tariff so high that no imports are purchased at all, then the importer's welfare will be at the no-trade level, shown by point A. So while the graph of welfare must be increasing for a small tariff from point B, as the tariff increases, welfare eventually falls past the free-trade level at point B' to the no-trade welfare at point A.

FIGURE 7-8

Tariffs and Welfare for a Large Country For a large importing country, a tariff initially increases the importer's welfare because the terms-of-trade gain exceeds the deadweight loss. So the importer's welfare rises from point B. Welfare continues to rise until the tariff is at its optimal level (point C). After that, welfare falls. If the tariff is too large (greater than at B'), then welfare will fall below the free-trade level. For a prohibitive tariff, with no imports at all, the importer's welfare will be at the no-trade level, at point A.

Given that points B and A are both on the graph of the importer's welfare (for free trade and no trade, respectively) and that welfare must be rising after point B, it follows that there must be a highest point of welfare, shown by point C. At this point, the importer's welfare is highest because the difference between the terms-of-trade gain and deadweight loss is maximized. We will call the tariff at that point the "optimal tariff." For increases in the tariff beyond its optimal level (i.e., between points C and A), the importer's welfare falls because the deadweight loss due to the tariff overwhelms the terms-of-trade gain. But whenever the tariff is below its optimal level, between points B and C, then welfare is higher than its free-trade level because the terms-of-trade gain exceeds the deadweight loss.

Optimal Tariff Formula It turns out that there is a simple formula for the optimal tariff. The formula depends on the elasticity of Foreign export supply, which we call E^*_X. Recall that the elasticity of any supply curve is the percentage increase in supply caused by a percentage increase in price. Likewise, the elasticity of the Foreign export supply curve is the percentage change in the quantity exported in response to a percent change in the world price of the export. If the export supply curve is very steep, then there is little response of the quantity supplied, and so the elasticity E^*_X is low. Conversely, if the export supply curve is very flat, there is a large response of the quantity supplied due to a change in the world price, and so E^*_X is high. Recall also that a small importing country faces a perfectly horizontal, or perfectly elastic, Foreign export supply curve, which means that the elasticity of Foreign export supply is infinite.

Using the elasticity of Foreign export supply, the optimal tariff equals

$$\text{optimal tariff} = \frac{1}{E^*_X}$$

That is, the optimal tariff (measured as a percentage) equals the inverse of the elasticity of Foreign export supply. For a small importing country, the elasticity of Foreign export supply is infinite, and so the optimal tariff is zero. That result makes sense, since any tariff higher than zero leads to a deadweight loss for the importer (and no terms-of-trade gain), so the best tariff to choose is zero, or free trade.

For a large importing country however, the Foreign export supply is less than infinite, and we can use this formula to compute the optimal tariff. As the elasticity of Foreign export supply decreases (which means that the Foreign export supply curve is steeper), the optimal tariff is higher. The reason for this result is that with a steep Foreign export supply curve, Foreign exporters will lower their price more in response to the tariff.[11] For instance, if E_X^* decreases from 3 to 2, then the optimal tariff increases from $\frac{1}{3} = 33\%$ to $\frac{1}{2} = 50\%$, reflecting the fact that Foreign producers are willing to lower their prices more, taking on a larger share of the tariff burden. In that case, the Home country obtains a larger terms-of-trade increase and hence the optimal level of the tariff is higher.

APPLICATION

U.S. Tariffs on Steel Once Again

Let us return to the U.S. tariff on steel, and reevaluate the effect on U.S. welfare in the large-country case. The calculation of the deadweight loss that we did earlier in the application assumed that the United States was a small country, facing fixed world prices for steel. In that case, the 30% tariff on steel was fully reflected in U.S. prices, which rose by 30%. But what if the import prices for steel in the United States did not rise by the full amount of the tariff? If the United States is a large enough importer of steel, then the Foreign export price will fall and the U.S. import price will rise by less than the tariff. It is then possible that the United States gained from the tariff.

To determine whether the United States gained from the tariff on steel products, we can compute the deadweight loss (area $b + d$) and the terms-of-trade gain (area e) for each imported steel product using the optimum tariff formula.

Optimal Tariffs for Steel Let us apply this formula to the U.S. steel tariffs to see how the tariffs applied compare with the theoretical optimal tariff. In Table 7-2, we show various steel products along with their respective elasticities of export supply to the United States. By taking the inverse of each export supply elasticity, we obtain the optimal tariff. For example, alloy steel flat-rolled products (the first item) have a low export supply elasticity, 0.27, so they have a very high optimal tariff of $1/0.27 = 3.7 = 370\%$. In contrast, iron and nonalloy steel flat-rolled products (the last item) have a very high export supply elasticity of 750, so the optimal tariff is $1/750 \approx 0\%$. Products between these have optimal tariffs ranging from 1 to 125%.

In the final column of Table 7-2, we show the actual tariffs that were applied to these products. For alloy steel flat-rolled products (the first item), the actual tariff was 30%, which is far below the optimal tariff. That means the terms-of-trade gain for that product was higher than the deadweight loss: the tariff is on the portion of the welfare graph between B and C in Figure 7-8, and U.S. welfare is above its free-trade level. The same holds for iron and steel bars, rods, angles, and shapes, for which the tariffs of 15 to 30% are again less than their optimal level, so the United States obtains a terms-of-trade gain that exceeds the deadweight loss. However, for iron and steel tubes, pipes, and fittings, the U.S. tariffs were 13 to 15%, but the optimal tariff for that product was only 1%. Because of the very high elasticity of export supply, the United States has practically no effect on the world price, so the deadweight loss for that product exceeds the terms-of-trade gain.

---

[11] See Problem 3 at the end of the chapter, where you will show that steeper export supply leads Foreign to absorb more of the tariff.

TABLE 7-2

Optimal Tariffs for Steel Products This table shows optimal tariffs for steel products, calculated with the elasticity formula.

Product Category	Elasticity of Export Supply	Optimal Tariff (%)	Actual Tariff (%)
Alloy steel flat-rolled products	0.27	370	30
Iron and steel rails and railway track	0.80	125	0
Iron and steel bars, rods, angles, shapes	0.80	125	15–30
Ferrous waste and scrap	17	6	0
Iron and steel tubes, pipes, and fittings	90	1	13–15
Iron and nonalloy steel flat-rolled products	750	0	0

Source: Elasticities of export supply provided by Christian Broda and David Weinstein, May 2006, "Globalization and the Gains from Variety," Quarterly Journal of Economics, 121(2), 541–585.

To summarize, for the three product categories in Table 7-2 where the United States applied tariffs, in two products the terms-of-trade gain exceeded the deadweight loss, so U.S. welfare rose due to the tariff, but in a third case the deadweight loss was larger, so U.S. welfare fell due to the tariff. The first two products illustrate the large-country case for tariffs, in which the welfare of the importer can rise due to a tariff, whereas the third product illustrates the small-country case, in which the importer loses from the tariff.

From the information given in Table 7-2, we do not know whether the United States gained or lost overall from the steel tariffs: that calculation would require adding up the gains and losses due to the tariff over all imported steel products, which we have not done. But in the end, we should keep in mind that any rise in U.S. welfare comes at the expense of exporting countries. Even if there was an overall terms-of-trade gain for the United States when adding up across all steel products, that gain would be at the expense of the European countries and other steel exporters. As we have already discussed, the steel exporters objected to the U.S. tariffs at the WTO and were entitled to apply *retaliatory* tariffs of their own against U.S. products. If these tariffs had been applied, they would have eliminated and reversed any U.S. gain. By removing the tariffs in less than two years, the United States avoided a costly tariff war. Indeed, that is one of the main goals of the WTO: by allowing exporting countries to retaliate with tariffs, the WTO prevents importers from using optimal tariffs to their own advantage. In a later chapter, we show more carefully how such a tariff war will end up being costly to all countries involved. ■

5 Import Quotas

On January 1, 2005, China was poised to become the world's largest exporter of textiles and apparel. On that date, a system of worldwide import quotas known as the **Multifibre Arrangement (MFA)** was abolished. Import quotas are a restriction on the amount of a particular good that one country can purchase from another country. Under the Multifibre Arrangement, begun in 1974, import quotas restricted the amount of nearly every textile and apparel product that was imported to Canada, the European countries, and the United States. These countries limited their textile imports to protect their own domestic firms producing those products. With the end of the MFA, China was ready to enjoy greatly increased exports—but this did not occur. The threat of import competition from China led the United States and Europe to negotiate *new* temporary import quotas with China, as we discuss in this section.

Besides the MFA, there are many other examples of import quotas. For example, since 1993 Europe had a quota on the imports of bananas that allowed for a greater number of bananas to enter from its former colonies in Africa than from Latin America. In 2005 that quota was simplified and converted into a tariff, even though that tariff still discriminated among countries based on their colonial past. Then in 2009 Europe agreed to reduce the tariff on Latin American bananas, effectively bringing to an end this "banana war" that had lasted for more than 15 years (see **Headlines: Banana Wars**). Another example is the quota on U.S. imports of sugar, which is still

HEADLINES

Banana Wars

This article discusses a well-known example of a quota that applied to European imports of bananas. The quota and discriminatory tariff on bananas from Latin America finally ended in late 2009.

I can hardly believe the banana wars are over. The dispute started back in 1993 when the European Union set quotas favoring banana imports from Ivory Coast, the Windward Islands and other former colonies at the expense of imports from Latin America. American banana companies and the Latin American countries where they grow their bananas sued the E.U., accusing it of rigging an unfair trade deal, first under the GATT and then under the W.T.O.

The suit dragged on for years, and at several points threatened to spark an all-out trade war between Washington and Europe. In 1999, after a meeting on Kosovo was hijacked by the banana crisis, the secretary of state then, Madeleine Albright, declared in exasperation: "I never in my life thought I would spend so much time on bananas."

It finally ended this month when the E.U. said it would continue to grant tariff-free access to its former colonies but would reduce tariffs on Latin American bananas by 35 percent over seven years. The United States and Latin American producers agreed to drop their case. After all the roiling, what strikes me now is how little people seem to care. That says a lot about how attitudes toward trade have changed.

When this started, trade was trumpeted as the single most important tool for development. Europe insisted that its special treatment of its former colonies was central to its post-imperial responsibilities. The United States and Latin American countries vowed to hold the line for free trade—over bananas at least—to make it a tool of development for all.

Today nobody talks about bananas. Stalled global trade talks (remember Doha?) barely get mentioned. There are a lot of problems out there, including the collapse of world trade in the wake of the global recession and the looming threat of protectionism. Yet there has also been a rethinking about trade's supposed silver bullet role in economic development.

China's growth stands as a beacon for the power of trade. But others that have hitched their economic strategy to trade, like Mexico, have found prosperity elusive. Despite growing banana exports, both the Latin American banana exporters and Europe's impoverished former colonies remain poor.

One thing we have learned over the past 15 years is that trade is necessary but not sufficient for development. Countries also need investment in infrastructure, technology and human capital. They need credit. They need legitimate institutions—like clean courts to battle monopolies—and help building them. Putting up a few barriers against banana imports, or tearing a few of them down, can't do it all.

Source: Eduardo Porter, The New York Times, *December 29, 2009, p. A30.*

HEADLINES

Sweet Opportunity

This article discusses another well-known example of a quota that applies to imports of sugar into the United States. It argues that in 2006 there was an opportunity to remove the quota (since world prices had risen to equal U.S. domestic prices), but that removal did not occur.

It isn't often that circumstances hand the government a chance to remove trade barriers without harming a coddled U.S. industry. But the current surge in world sugar prices is serving up precisely that opportunity to President Bush. The U.S. sugar program is a Rauschenberg painting of farm loans and price supports that guarantees American sugar producers a set price for their crops. If producers cannot sell their sugar at a break-even price after accounting for their loans, they are entitled to sell the excess to the U.S. Department of Agriculture.

To keep U.S. prices high enough to ensure that a mountain of sugar doesn't get dumped on Uncle Sam, the U.S. in turn keeps supplies down by imposing import quotas on its trading partners. But with the world price for raw cane sugar, including delivery, hovering around 18 cents per pound, the farm loan-rate at 18 cents for cane sugar (and 23 cents for beet sugar) and the U.S. economy experiencing sugar shortages, the U.S. market could be opened without incurring huge costs at the USDA. . . .

The U.S. price of sugar has been two to three times higher than the world price for the past 25 years. The longer that imbalance has persisted, the more inefficient U.S. sugar producers have become. And, paradoxically, the more powerful they have become as a special interest blocking U.S. trade expansion. Now that a spike in world prices has put the U.S. on par with foreign producers, there is a window of opportunity to do away with a sugar program that costs American jobs and has become a source of trade friction around the world.

Source: Excerpted from a Wall Street Journal *editorial, February 6, 2006, p. A14.*

in place despite calls for its removal (see **Headlines: Sweet Opportunity**). In this section, we explain how quotas affect the importing and exporting countries and examine the differences between quotas and tariffs. Like a tariff, an import quota often imposes a welfare cost on the importing country. But we will find that quotas can often lead to higher welfare losses for the importer than tariffs.

Import Quota in a Small Country

Applying an import quota for a small country is similar to applying a tariff, so we can use the graphs developed earlier in the chapter to analyze quotas, too.

Free-Trade Equilibrium In panel (a) of Figure 7-9, we show the Home demand curve D and the Home supply curve S. At the free-trade world price of P^W, Home quantity demanded is D_1 and quantity supplied is S_1, so imports are $M_1 = D_1 - S_1$. The import demand curve $M = D - S$ is shown in panel (b). The assumption that the Home country is small means that the fixed world price P^W is not affected by the import quota, so under free trade, the Foreign export supply curve X^* is a horizontal line at the world price P^W. The Home import demand curve M and Foreign export supply curve X^* intersect at point B, resulting in the free-trade level of imports, M_1.

Effect of the Quota Now suppose that an import quota of $M_2 < M_1$ is imposed, meaning that the quantity imported cannot exceed this amount. This quota effectively establishes a vertical export supply curve labeled as $\overline{X}$ in panel (b), which fixes the

FIGURE 7-9

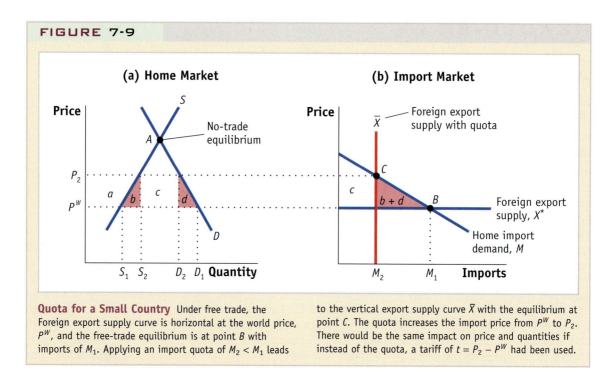

(a) Home Market

(b) Import Market

Quota for a Small Country Under free trade, the Foreign export supply curve is horizontal at the world price, P^W, and the free-trade equilibrium is at point B with imports of M_1. Applying an import quota of $M_2 < M_1$ leads to the vertical export supply curve $\overline{X}$ with the equilibrium at point C. The quota increases the import price from P^W to P_2. There would be the same impact on price and quantities if instead of the quota, a tariff of $t = P_2 - P^W$ had been used.

import quantity at M_2. The vertical export supply curve now intersects import demand at point C, which establishes the Home price of P_2. In panel (a), the price of P_2 leads firms to increase the quantity supplied to S_2 and consumers to decrease their quantity demanded to D_2.

The import quota therefore leads to an increase in the Home price and a reduction in Home imports, just like a tariff. Furthermore, notice that there would be an equivalent effect on the import price and quantity if instead of the quota, the government had imposed an import tariff of $t = P_2 - P^W$. That is, the tariff of $t = P_2 - P^W$ would raise the Home price to P_2 and reduce imports o the level M_2. We conclude that for every level of the import quota, there is an **equivalent import tariff** that would lead to the same Home price and quantity of imports.[12]

Effect on Welfare As we have shown, the quota leads to an increase in the Home price. The rise in the price for consumers leads to a fall in consumer surplus. That fall is measured by the area between the prices P_2 and P^W and to the left of the demand curve, which is the area $(a + b + c + d)$ in panel (a) of Figure 7-9. On the other hand, the increase in the price facing Home producers leads to a gain in producer surplus. That gain is measured by the area between the prices P_2 and P^W and to the left of the supply curve, which is the area a in Figure 7-9(a). These two welfare effects are the same as would occur under a tariff.

---

[12] As we show in the next chapter, this conclusion depends on our assumption of perfect competition and does not hold without that assumption.

The quota and tariff differ, however, in terms of area c, which would be collected as government revenue under a tariff. Under the quota, this area equals the difference between the domestic price P_2 and the world price P^W, times the quantity of imports M_2. Therefore, whoever is actually importing the good will be able to earn the difference between the world price P^W and the higher Home price P_2 by selling the imports in the Home market. We call the difference between these two prices the *rent* associated with the quota, and hence the area c represents the total **quota rents.** There are four possible ways that these quota rents can be allocated:

1. Giving the Quota to Home Firms

First, **quota licenses** (i.e., permits to import the quantity allowed under the quota system) can be given to Home firms, which are then able to import at the world price P^W and sell locally at P_2, earning the difference between these as rents. An example of this is the dairy industry in the United States, in which U.S. producers of cheese receive licenses to import from abroad. With home firms earning the rents c, the net effect of the quota on Home welfare is

Fall in consumer surplus:	$-(a + b + c + d)$
Rise in producer surplus:	$+a$
Quota rents earned at Home	$+c$
Net effect on Home welfare:	$-(b + d)$

We see from this calculation that the net effect on Home welfare is a loss of amount $(b + d)$. That loss is the same as what we found in Section 3 of this chapter for the loss of a tariff in a small country. As in that section, we still refer to $(b + d)$ as a deadweight loss.

2. Rent Seeking

One complication of simply giving valuable quota licenses to Home firms is that these firms may engage in some kind of inefficient activities to obtain them. For example, suppose that Home firms are producing batteries and import the chemical needed as an input. If licenses for the imported chemicals are allocated in proportion to each firm's production of batteries in the previous years, then the Home firms will likely produce more batteries than they can sell (and at lower quality) *just to obtain the import licenses for the following year.* Alternatively, firms might engage in bribery or other lobbying activities to obtain the licenses. These kinds of inefficient activities done to obtain quota licenses are called **rent seeking.** It has been suggested that the waste of resources devoted to rent-seeking activities could be as large as the value of rents themselves so that the area c would be wasted rather than accrue to Home firms. If rent seeking occurs, the welfare loss due to the quota would be

Fall in consumer surplus:	$-(a + b + c + d)$
Rise in producer surplus:	$+a$
Net effect on Home welfare:	$-(b + c + d)$

The waste of resources due to rent seeking leads to a fall in Home welfare of $(b + c + d)$, which is larger than that for a tariff. It is often thought that rent seeking is more severe in some developing countries where rules are not well enforced and officials are willing to take bribes in exchange for the licenses.

3. Auctioning the Quota A third possibility for allocating the rents that come from the quota is for the government of the importing country to auction off the quota licenses. This occurred in Australia and New Zealand during the 1980s. In Australia, the auctions covered imports of textiles, apparel, footwear, and motor vehicles. The quota auctions used for imports of textiles and apparel in Australia were an alternative to the Multifibre Arrangement (MFA). Auctions of import quotas have also been proposed in the United States but have never actually occurred.[13] In a well-organized, competitive auction, the revenue collected should exactly equal the value of the rents, so that area c would be earned by the Home government. Using the auction method to allocate quota rents, the net loss in domestic welfare due to the quota becomes

Fall in consumer surplus:	$-(a + b + c + d)$
Rise in producer surplus:	$+a$
Auction revenue earned at Home	$+c$
Net effect on Home welfare:	$-(b + d)$

The net effect on Home welfare in this case is the deadweight loss of $(b + d)$, which is once again the same loss as incurred from a tariff.

4. "Voluntary" Export Restraint The final possibility for allocating quota rents is for the government of the importing country to give authority for implementing the quota to the government of the *exporting* country. Because the exporting country allocates the quota among its own producers, this is sometimes called a **"voluntary" export restraint (VER),** or a **"voluntary" restraint agreement (VRA).** In the 1980s the United States used this type of arrangement to restrict Japanese automobile imports. In that case, Japan's Ministry of International Trade and Industry (MITI), a government agency that implements Japan's trade policies, told each Japanese auto manufacturer how much it could export to the United States. In this case, the quota rents are earned by foreign producers, so the loss in Home welfare equals

Fall in consumer surplus:	$-(a + b + c + d)$
Rise in producer surplus:	$+a$
Net effect on Home welfare:	$-(b + c + d)$

The VER gives a higher net loss $(b + c + d)$ for the importer than does a tariff because the quota rents are earned by foreign exporters. This result raises the question of why VERs are used at all. One answer is that by giving the quota rents to firms in the exporting country, that country is much less likely to retaliate by adopting import tariffs or quotas of its own. In other words, the transfer of quota rents to the exporter becomes a way to avoid a tariff or quota war.

---

[13] The proposals to auction import quotas in the United States were made during the 1980s; see C. Fred Bergsten, 1987, *Auction Quotas and United States Trade Policy* (Washington, D.C.: Peterson Institute for International Economics). Government auctions have occurred in the United States for bandwidth in radio frequencies and also for off-shore oil drilling.

Costs of Import Quotas in the United States

Table 7-3 presents some estimates of the home deadweight losses, along with the quota rents, for major U.S. quotas in the years around 1985. In all cases except dairy, the rents were earned by foreign exporters. We discuss the case of automobiles in the next chapter, for which the quota rents earned by foreigners range from $2 billion to $8 billion. Textiles and apparel also had very large quota rents and U.S. deadweight losses (about $5 billion each) under the MFA. In addition, the MFA imposed large losses on the Foreign exporting countries, due to rent-seeking activities by exporters to obtain the quota permits. Adding up the costs shown in Table 7-3, the total U.S. deadweight loss from these quotas was in the range of $8 billion to $12 billion annually in the mid-1980s, whereas the quota rents transferred to foreigners were another $7 billion to $17 billion annually.

TABLE 7-3

Annual Cost of U.S. Import Protection ($ billions)
Shown here are estimates of the dead weight losses and quota rents due to U.S. import quotas in the 1980s, for the years around 1985. Many of these quotas are no longer in place today.

	U.S. Deadweight Loss ($) (area $b + d$)	Quota Rents ($) (area c)
Automobiles	0.2–1.2	2.2–7.9
Dairy	1.4	0.25*
Steel	0.1–0.3	0.7–2.0
Sugar	0.1	0.4–1.3
Textiles and apparel	4.9–5.9	4.0–6.1
Import tariffs	1.2–3.4	0
Total	7.9–12.3	7.3–17.3

* In dairy the quota rents are earned by U.S. importers and so are not included in the total.

Source: Robert Feenstra, Summer 1992, "How Costly Is Protectionism?" Journal of Economic Perspectives, 159–178.

Some, but not all, of these costs for the United States are no longer relevant today. The quota in automobiles ceased being applied after 1987 because Japanese producers built plants in the United States and therefore reduced their imports. The quotas in the steel industry were replaced by the "safeguard" tariffs that President Bush temporarily imposed from 2002 to 2003. But the quotas used in sugar remain, and while the MFA expired on January 1, 2005, it has been replaced by a new set of quotas with China. There is the prospect of continuing losses for the United States due to quotas in these industries, as we discuss in the next application to textiles and apparel.

APPLICATION

China and the Multifibre Arrangement

One of the founding principles of GATT was that countries should not use quotas to restrict imports (see Article XI of **Side Bar: Key Provisions of the GATT**). The Multifibre Arrangement (MFA), organized under the auspices of the GATT in 1974, was a major exception to that principle and allowed the industrial countries to restrict imports of textile and apparel products from the developing countries. Importing countries could join the MFA and arrange quotas bilaterally (i.e., after negotiating with exporters) or unilaterally (on their own). In practice, the import quotas established under the MFA were very detailed and specified the amount of each textile and apparel product that each developing country could sell to countries including Canada, Europe, and the United States.

Although the amount of the quotas was occasionally revised upward, it did not keep up with the increasing ability of new supplying countries to sell. Under the Uruguay Round of WTO negotiations held from 1986 to 1994, developing countries were able to negotiate an end to this system of import quotas. The MFA expired on January 1, 2005. The biggest potential supplier of textile and apparel products was China, so the expiration of the MFA meant that China could export as much as it wanted to other countries—or so it thought. The potential for a huge increase in exports from China posed a problem for many other countries. Some developing countries expected that rising exports from China would compete with their own export of apparel items, on which many workers depended for their livelihood. The large producers in importing countries were also concerned with the potential rise in Chinese exports because it could lead to the loss of jobs for their own workers in textiles and apparel.

Growth in Exports from China Immediately after January 1, 2005, exports of textiles and apparel from China grew rapidly. For example, exports of Chinese tights and pantyhose to the European Union increased by 2,000% in January and February, as compared with a year earlier; imports of pullovers and jerseys from China jumped nearly 1,000%; and imports of trousers more than tripled. Overall in 2005, China's textile and apparel imports to the United States rose by more than 40% as compared with the year before, as shown in Figure 7-10, where we include the top 20 exporters to the U.S. market.[14] In panel (a), we show the change in the value of textile and apparel imports from each country. The surge of imports from China came at the expense of some higher-cost exporters, such as South Korea, Hong Kong, and Taiwan, whose exports to the United States declined by 10 to 20%.

In panel (b) of Figure 7-10, we show the percentage change in the prices of textiles and apparel products from each country, depending on whether the products were "constrained goods," subject to the MFA quota before January 1, 2005. China has the largest drop in prices from 2004 to 2005, 38% in the "constrained goods" categories. Many other countries also experienced a substantial fall in their prices due to the end of the MFA quota: 18% for Pakistan; 16% for Cambodia; and 8 to 9% for the Philippines, Bangladesh, India, Indonesia, and Sri Lanka. A drop in price due to the removal of the import quota is exactly what we predict from the theory, as we move from the price P_2 in Figure 7-9 to the free-trade price P^W. Surprisingly, a few countries in Figure 7-10 show increases in their prices, such as Mexico. However, less than 1% of Mexico's sales of textiles and apparel to the United States was constrained by the quota, so that price increase does not appear to be due to the removal of the MFA.

Welfare Cost of MFA Given the drop in prices in 2005 from countries selling to the United States, it is possible to estimate the welfare loss due to the MFA. The United States did not auction the quota licenses for textiles and apparel so the quota rents were earned by foreign exporting firms. That means the welfare loss for the United States due to the MFA is the area $(b + c + d)$ in Figure 7-9. Using the price drops from 2004 to 2005, that area is estimated to be in the range of $6.5 billion to $16.2 billion in 2005.[15] The simple average of these estimates is $11.4 billion as the total cost to the United States. To put that welfare loss in perspective, there were 111 million households in the United States in 2005, and the typical household spent

---

[14] Figure 7-10 and the welfare estimates in the following paragraphs are from James Harrigan and Geoffrey Barrows, 2009, "Testing the Theory of Trade Policy: Evidence from the Abrupt End of the Multifibre Arrangement," *The Review of Economics and Statistics*, vol. 91(2), pp. 282–294.

[15] Notice that this range of estimates for 2005 is comparable with (but wider than) the range of estimates for the welfare costs of textiles and apparel in Table 7-3, which is $8.9 billion to $12 billion for 1985, obtained by adding up the deadweight loss and the quota rents.

FIGURE 7-10

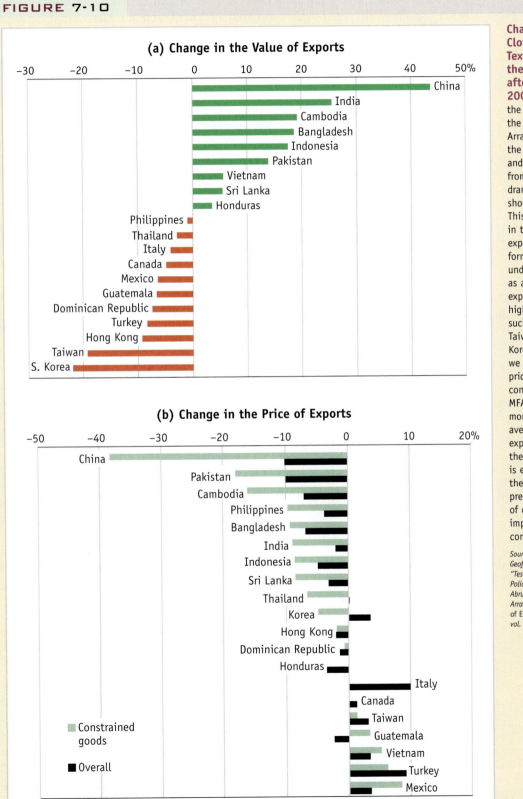

Changes in Clothing and Textile Exports to the United States after the MFA, 2004–2005 After the expiration of the Multifibre Arrangement (MFA), the value of clothing and textile exports from China rose dramatically, as shown in panel (a). This reflects the surge in the quantity of exports that were formerly constrained under the MFA as well as a shift to Chinese exports from other, higher-cost producers such as Hong Kong, Taiwan, and South Korea. In panel (b), we see that the prices of goods constrained by the MFA typically fell by more than the average change in export prices after the MFA's expiry. This is exactly what our theory of quotas predicts: The removal of quotas lowers import prices for consumers.

Source: James Harrigan and Geoffrey Barrows, 2009, "Testing the Theory of Trade Policy: Evidence from the Abrupt End of the Multifibre Arrangement," The Review of Economics and Statistics, vol. 91(2), pp. 282–294.

about $1,400 on apparel. Dividing the loss of $11.4 billion by the 111 million households, we obtain about $100 per household, or 7% of their annual spending on apparel as the welfare cost of the MFA.[16]

Import Quality Besides the overall decline in prices, there was also an interesting pattern to the price drops: the prices of textile and apparel products dropped the most (in percentage terms) for the lower-priced items. So, an inexpensive T-shirt coming from China and priced at $1 had a price drop of more than 38% (more than 38¢), whereas a more expensive item priced at $10 experienced a price drop of less than 38% (less than $3.80). As a result, U.S. demand shifted toward the lower-priced items imported from China: there was "quality downgrading" in the exports from China.

To understand why this quality downgrading occurred, it is easiest to think about the problem in reverse: when a quota like the MFA is applied, what is the effect on quality? The MFA, like most other quotas, was applied to the *quantity* of the import sent to each country: it was applied to yards of cloth, or number of shirts, or dozens of pairs of socks, and so on. Faced with a quota of that type, the exporting firm would have an incentive to *upgrade* the type of cloth, shirts, or socks that it sells, since selling a higher value for the same quantity will still meet the quota limitation. So when the MFA starts, we expect to see "quality upgrading" in the exports for each country. By the same logic, when the MFA was removed, there was "quality downgrading" in the exports from China to the United States and exports from other countries, too.

Reaction of the United States and Europe The surge in exports from China to the United States and Europe was short-lived, however. The European Union threatened to impose new quotas on Chinese exports, and in response, China agreed on June 11, 2005, to "voluntary" export restraints that would limit its growth of textile exports to about 10% per year through the end of 2008. For the United States, the ability to negotiate a new system of quotas with China had been guaranteed by a special agreement with China when it joined the WTO in 2001. Under this agreement, China was limited to a 7.5% annual growth in its textile exports to the United States, from 2005 to 2008. This temporary quota expired at the end of 2008, at which time we might have expected the U.S. textile and apparel industry to renew its call for quota protection once again. But due to the worldwide recession, Chinese exports in this industry were much lower in 2009 than they had been in earlier years. For that reason, China indicated that it would not accept any further limitation on its ability to export textile and apparel products to the United States and to Europe, and both these quotas expired. ■

6 Conclusions

A tariff on imports is the most commonly used trade policy tool. In this chapter, we have studied the effect of tariffs on consumers and producers in both importing and exporting countries. We have looked at several different cases. First, we assumed

---

[16] In comparison, there were 737,000 U.S. workers in the textile and apparel industries in 2004, with an average annual salary of $31,500. If we divide the total loss of $11.4 billion by all these workers, we obtain about $15,500 per job protected in the U.S.industry, or about one-half of the annual salary of each worker.

that the importing country is so small that it does not affect the world price of the imported good. In that case, the price faced by consumers and producers in the importing country will rise by the full amount of the tariff. With a rise in the consumer price, there is a drop in consumer surplus; and with a rise in the producer price, there is a gain in producer surplus. In addition, the government collects revenue from the tariff. When we add together all these effects—the drop in consumer surplus, gain in producer surplus, and government revenue collected—we still get a *net loss* for the importing country. We have referred to that loss as the deadweight loss resulting from the tariff.

The fact that a small importing country always has a net loss from a tariff explains why most economists oppose the use of tariffs. Still, this result leaves open the question of why tariffs are used. One reason that tariffs are used, despite their deadweight loss, is that they are an easy way for governments to raise revenue, especially in developing countries. A second reason is politics: the government might care more about protecting firms than avoiding losses for consumers. A third reason is that the small-country assumption may not hold in practice: countries may be large enough importers of a product so that a tariff will affect its world price. In this large-country case, the decrease in imports demanded due to the tariff causes foreign exporters to lower their prices. Of course, consumer and producer prices in the importing country still go up, since these prices include the tariff, but they rise by less than the full amount of the tariff. We have shown that if we add up the drop in consumer surplus, gain in producer surplus, and government revenue collected, it is possible for a small tariff to generate welfare gains for the importing country.

Still, any gain for the importer in this large-country case comes at the expense of the foreign exporters. For that reason, the use of a tariff in the large-country case is sometimes called a "beggar thy neighbor" policy. We have found that the drop in the exporter's welfare due to the tariff is greater than the gain in the importer's welfare. Therefore, the world loses overall because of the tariff. This is another reason that most economists oppose their use.

In addition to an import tariff, we have also studied import quotas, which restrict the quantity of imports into a country. The WTO has tried to limit the use of import quotas and has been somewhat successful. For example, the Multifibre Arrangement (MFA) was a complex system of quotas intended to restrict the import of textiles and apparel into many industrialized countries. It was supposed to end on January 1, 2005, but both the United States and the European Union then established new quotas against imports of textiles and apparel from China, which expired at the end of 2008. The United States continues to have a quota on imports of sugar, and up until very recently, the European Union had a quota and then a discriminatory tariff on imports of bananas (that "banana war" has now ended). These are some of the best-known import quotas, and there are other examples, too.

Under perfect competition, the effect of applying an import quota is similar to the effect of applying an import tariff: they both lead to an increase in the domestic price in the importing country, with a loss for consumers and a gain for producers. One difference, however, is that under a tariff the government in the importing country collects revenue, whereas under a quota, whoever is able to bring in the import earns the difference between the domestic and world prices, called "quota rents." For example, if firms in the importing country have the licenses to bring in imports, then they earn the quota rents. Alternatively, if resources are wasted by firms trying to capture these rents, then there is an additional deadweight loss. It is more common, however, for the foreign exporters to earn the quota rents, as occurs under a "voluntary" export restraint, administered by the foreign government. A fourth possibility is that the government in the importing country auctions the quota licenses, in which case it earns the equivalent of the quota rents as auction revenue; this case is identical to the tariff in its welfare outcome.

KEY POINTS

1. The government of a country can use laws and regulations, called "trade policies," to affect international trade flows. An import tariff, which is a tax at the border, is the most commonly used trade policy.

2. The rules governing trade policies in most countries are outlined by the General Agreement on Tariffs and Trade (GATT), an international legal convention adopted after World War II to promote increased international trade. Since 1995 the new name for the GATT is the World Trade Organization (WTO).

3. In a small country, the quantity of imports demanded is assumed to be very small compared with the total world market. For this reason, the importer faces a fixed world price. In that case, the price faced by consumers and producers in the importing country will rise by the full amount of the tariff.

4. The use of a tariff by a small importing country always leads to a net loss in welfare. We call that loss the "deadweight loss."

5. In a large country, the decrease in imports demanded due to the tariff causes foreign exporters to lower their prices. Consumer and producer prices in the importing country still go up, since these prices include the tariff, but they rise by less than the full amount of the tariff (since the exporter price falls).

6. The use of a tariff for a large country can lead to a net gain in welfare because the price charged by the exporter has fallen; this is a terms-of-trade gain for the importer.

7. The "optimal tariff" is the tariff amount that maximizes welfare for the importer. For a small country, the optimal tariff is zero since any tariff leads to a net loss. For a large country, however, the optimal tariff is positive.

8. The formula for the optimal tariff states that it depends inversely on the foreign export supply elasticity. If the foreign export supply elasticity is high, then the optimal tariff is low, but if the foreign export supply elasticity is low, then the optimal tariff is high.

9. "Import quotas" restrict the quantity of a particular import, thereby increasing the domestic price, increasing domestic production, and creating a benefit for those who are allowed to import the quantity allotted. These benefits are called "quota rents."

10. Assuming perfectly competitive markets for goods, quotas are similar to tariffs since the restriction in the amount imported leads to a higher domestic price. However, the welfare implications of quotas are different from those of tariffs depending on who earns the quota rents. These rents might be earned by firms in the importing country (if they have the licenses to import the good), or by firms in the exporting country (if the foreign government administers the quota), or by the government in the importing country (if it auctions off the quota licenses). The last case is most similar to a tariff, since the importing government earns the revenue.

KEY TERMS

PROBLEMS

1. The following questions refer to **Side Bar: Key Provisions of the GATT.**

   a. If the United States applies a tariff to a particular product (e.g., steel) imported from one country, what is the implication for its steel tariffs applied to all other countries according to the "most favored nation" principle?

   b. Is Article XXIV an exception to most favored nation treatment? Explain why or why not.

   c. Under the GATT articles, instead of a tariff, can a country impose a quota (quantitative restriction) on the number of goods imported? What has been one exception to this rule in practice?

2. Consider a small country applying a tariff t to imports of a good like that represented in Figure 7-5.

   a. Suppose that the country decides to *reduce* its tariff to t'. Redraw the graphs for the Home and import markets and illustrate this change. What happens to the quantity and price of goods produced at Home? What happens to the quantity of imports?

   b. Are there gains or losses to domestic consumer surplus due to the reduction in tariff?

   Are there gains or losses to domestic producer surplus due to the reduction in tariff? How is government revenue affected by the policy change? Illustrate these on your graphs.

   c. What is the overall gain or loss in welfare due to the policy change?

3. Consider a large country applying a tariff t to imports of a good like that represented in Figure 7-7.

   a. How does the export supply curve in panel (b) compare with that in the small-country case? Explain why these are different.

   b. Explain how the tariff affects the price paid by consumers in the *importing* country and the price received by producers in the *exporting* country. Use graphs to illustrate how the prices are affected if (i) the export supply curve is very elastic (flat) or (ii) the export supply curve is inelastic (steep).

4. Consider a large country applying a tariff t to imports of a good like that represented in Figure 7-7. How does the size of the terms-of-trade gain compare with the size of the deadweight loss when (i) the tariff is very small and (ii) the tariff is very large? Use graphs to illustrate your answer.

5. a. If the foreign export supply is perfectly elastic, what is the optimal tariff Home should apply to increase welfare? Explain.

   b. If the foreign export supply is less than perfectly elastic, what is the formula for the optimal tariff Home should apply to increase welfare?

   c. What happens to Home welfare if it applies a tariff higher than the optimal tariff?

6. Rank the following in ascending order of Home welfare and justify your answers. If two items are equivalent, indicate this accordingly.

   a. Tariff of t in a small country corresponding to the quantity of imports M

   b. Tariff of t in a large country corresponding to the same quantity of imports M

   c. Tariff of t' in a large country corresponding to the quantity of imports $M' > M$

7. Rank the following in ascending order of Home welfare and justify your answers. If two items are equivalent, indicate this accordingly.

   a. Tariff of t in a small country corresponding to the quantity of imports M

   b. Quota with the same imports M in a small country, with quota licenses distributed to Home firms and no rent seeking

   c. Quota of M in a small country with quota licenses auctioned to Home firms

   d. Quota of M in a small country with the quota given to the exporting firms

   e. Quota of M in a small country with quota licenses distributed to rent-seeking Home firms

8. Why did President George W. Bush suspend the U.S. tariffs on steel 17 months ahead of schedule?

9. What provision of U.S. trade law was used by President Barack Obama to apply a tariff on tires imported from China? Does this provision make it easier or harder to apply a tariff than Section 201?

10. No U.S. tire producers joined in the request for the tariff on tires in 2009. Rather, the petition for a tariff on tires imported from China was brought by the United Steelworkers of American, the union who represents workers in the tire industry. Why did major tire manufactures operating in the United States, such as Goodyear, Michelin, Cooper, and Bridgestone, not support the tariff?

11. Suppose Home is a small country. Use the graphs below to answer the questions.

(a) Home Market

(b) Import Market

   a. Calculate Home consumer surplus and producer surplus in the absence of trade.

   b. Now suppose that Home engages in trade and faces the world price, $P^* = \$6$. Determine the consumer and producer surplus under free trade. Does Home benefit from trade? Explain.

c. Concerned about the welfare of the local producers, the Home government imposes a tariff in the amount of $2 (i.e., $t = \$2$). Determine the net effect of the tariff on the Home economy.

12. Refer to the graphs in Problem 11. Suppose that instead of a tariff, Home applies an import quota limiting the amount Foreign can sell to 2 units.

   a. Determine the net effect of the import quota on the Home economy if the quota licenses are allocated to local producers.
   b. Calculate the net effect of the import quota on Home welfare if the quota rents are earned by Foreign exporters.
   c. How do your answers to parts (a) and (b) compare with part (c) of Problem 11?

13. Consider a small country applying a tariff t as in Figure 7-5. Instead of a tariff on *all* units imported, however, we will suppose that the tariff applies only to imports *in excess* of some quota amount M (which is less than the total imports). This is called a "tariff-rate quota" (TRQ) and is commonly used on agricultural goods.

   a. Redraw Figure 7-5, introducing the quota amount M. Remember that the tariff applies only to imports *in excess* of this amount. With this in mind, what is the rectangle of tariff revenue collected? What is the rectangle of quota rents? Explain briefly what quota rents mean in this scenario.
   b. How does the use of a TRQ rather than a tariff at the same rate affect Home welfare? How does the TRQ, as compared with a tariff at the same rate, affect Foreign welfare? Does it depend on who gets the quota rents?
   c. Based on your answer to (b), why do you think TRQs are used quite often?

14. Consider the following hypothetical information pertaining to a country's imports, consumption, and production of T-shirts following the removal of the MFA quota:

	With MFA	Without MFA (Free Trade)
World price ($/shirt)	2.00	2.00
Domestic price ($/shirt)	2.50	2.00
Domestic consumption (million shirts/year)	100	125
Domestic production (million shirts/year)	75	50
Imports (million shirts/year)	25	75

   a. Graph the effects of the quota removal on domestic consumption and production.
   b. Determine the gain in consumer surplus from the removal of the quota.
   c. Determine the loss in producer surplus from the removal of the quota.
   d. Calculate the quota rents that were earned under the quota.
   e. Determine how much the country has gained from removal of the quota.

15. Suppose that a producer in China is constrained by the MFA to sell a certain number of shirts, regardless of the type of shirt. For a T-shirt selling for $2.00 under free trade, the MFA quota leads to an increase in price to $2.50. For a dress shirt selling for $10.00, the MFA will also lead to an increase in price.

	With MFA	Without MFA (Free Trade)
Domestic price of T-shirt ($/shirt)	2.50	2.00
Domestic price of dress shirt ($/shirt)	?	10.00

   a. Suppose that the MFA leads to an increase in the price of dress shirts from $10 to $11. Will the producer be willing to export both T-shirts and dress shirts? (Remember that only a fixed number of shirts can be exported, but of any type.) Explain why or why not.
   b. For the producer to be willing to sell *both* T-shirts and dress shirts, what must be the price of dress shirts under the MFA?

c. Based on your answer to part (b), calculate the price of dress shirts *relative* to T-shirts before and after the MFA. What has happened to the relative price due to the MFA?

d. Based on your answer to part (c), what will happen to the relative demand in the United States for dress shirts versus T-shirts from this producer due to the MFA?

e. Thinking now of the total export bundle of this producer, does the MFA lead to quality upgrading or downgrading? How about the removal of the MFA?

N E T **W O R K**

Go to http://www.wto.org/, and find out how many countries belong to the WTO. Which countries joined most recently?

Go to http://www.usitc.gov/trade_remedy/about_global_safeguard_inv.htm, and read about Section 201 and Section 421 of U.S. Trade Act of 1974. What are the differences between these sections? What are some recent cases?

Import Tariffs and Quotas under Imperfect Competition

If there were an Economist's Creed, it would surely contain the affirmations "I understand the Principle of Comparative Advantage" and "I advocate Free Trade." . . . Yet the case for free trade is currently more at doubt than at any time since since the 1817 publication of Ricardo's Principles of Political Economy.

Paul Krugman, "Is Free Trade Passé?' *Journal of Economic Perspectives*, 1(2), Fall 1987, p. 131

The case for free trade, as brought up-to-date from 1817 to 1987, is therefore alive and well. This is not to say that we have not learned its strengths and weaknesses, its nuances and subtleties, with greater understanding in light of the new developments.

Jagdish Bhagwati, "Is Free Trade Passé After All?" *Weltwirtschaftliches Archiv/ Review of World Economics*, 125(1), March 1989, p. 43

If the case of heavyweight motorcycles is to be considered the only successful escape-clause [tariff], it is because it caused little harm and it helped Harley-Davidson get a bank loan so it could diversify.

John Suomela, chief economist, U.S. International Trade Commission, 1993[1]

In a recent survey of economists, 87% agreed with the statement "tariffs and import quotas usually reduce general economic welfare."[2] It is no exaggeration to say that this belief has been a guiding principle of the international institutions established to govern the world economy since World War II, especially the World Trade Organization. That belief is the message from the previous chapter, which showed that the application of tariffs and quotas will reduce welfare for a small country. We also found that

---

[1] Cited in Douglas A. Irwin, 2002, *Free Trade under Fire* (Princeton, NJ: Princeton University Press), pp. 136–137.
[2] Robert Whaples and Jac C. Heckelman, 2005, "Public Choice Economics: Where Is There Consensus?" *American Economist*, 49(1), pp. 66-78.

although a large country might gain from the application of a tariff, that gain would come at the expense of its trading partners, so the *world* as a whole would still lose. So there is really no good economic argument for the use of tariffs or quotas.

Still, you might wonder if that is really the whole story. We gave several recent examples of tariffs and quotas in the previous chapter, and there are many more examples if we look to countries at earlier stages in their development. For example, during the 1800s the United States had average tariff rates that fluctuated between 10 and 50%. These tariff rates were at times even higher than the Smoot–Hawley tariff that was applied during the Great Depression and peaked at 25%. Likewise, countries that industrialized after World War II, like Japan, South Korea, and Taiwan, started with high tariffs and quotas that were eliminated only slowly and incompletely. More recently, China had very high tariffs before it joined the World Trade Organization in 2001, and it still enjoys tariffs in some industries that are well above those in the United States or Europe.

These observations can lead us to wonder if there are some arguments in favor of tariffs that are missing from our treatment in the previous chapter, which dealt with perfect competition. Do the effects of trade policies differ when markets are imperfectly competitive? We explore the answer to this question in this chapter and the next.

This question received a good deal of attention from trade economists in the 1980s, in a body of research that became known as **strategic trade policy.** The idea of strategic trade policy was that government trade policies could give a strategic advantage to Home firms in imperfectly competitive markets that would enable them to compete more effectively with Foreign firms. Initially, the economists writing in this area thought that their research would challenge the idea that free trade is best for a country, an idea expressed in Paul Krugman's quote at the beginning of the chapter. As more research was done, however, supporters of strategic trade policy theory realized that the new arguments were limited in their scope: in some cases, the use of tariffs or quotas would backfire and harm the Home country, and in other cases, their use would give results similar to the large country case we analyzed in the previous chapter. We will give examples of both outcomes. Taken together, these example of strategic trade policy lead to the conclusion expressed in the opening quotation from Jagdish Bhagwati, that the case for free trade is "alive and well," but that we have "learned its strengths and weaknesses, its nuances and subtleties."

To explore strategic trade policy, we need to abandon the assumption that markets are perfectly competitive, an assumption that was central to the treatment of the tariff and quota in the previous chapter. Instead, we need to allow for imperfect competition which we defined in Chapter 6 as the market conditions that exist when firms have influence over the price that they charge, and can charge a price above marginal costs for their goods. Recall that imperfect competition can arise when there is a small number of producers, as in a monopoly or oligopoly, or if products are differentiated from one another, as we assumed in our model of monopolistic competition in Chapter 6. In this chapter, we use the extreme case of a single producer—a Home or Foreign monopoly—to see how tariffs and quotas affect prices, trade, and welfare. In practice, imperfectly competitive industries often have more than one firm, but focusing on the monopoly case will give us the clearest sense of how the effects of these policy tools differ from those under perfect competition.

In this chapter, we begin by analyzing the effects of tariffs and quotas under the assumption of a Home monopoly. In the perfectly competitive framework of the previous chapter, quotas and tariffs have an equivalent impact on Home prices. In imperfectly competitive markets, however, these two trade policy instruments have *different* effects on Home prices, so the choice of which, if any, trade policy to implement must take these different effects into account.

The second case we analyze is a Foreign monopoly that exports to the Home market. We analyze the effect of an import tariff applied by the Home country and find that the tariff has effects similar to those in the large-country case under perfect competition (described in the previous chapter) in which the Home country can potentially gain from the tariff. A specific example of a Foreign monopolist is the Foreign **discriminating monopoly,** which charges a lower price to Home than to firms in its own local market and is therefore **dumping** its product into the Home market. A tariff applied against the Foreign discriminating monopoly is called an **antidumping duty.** Because of the special way in which antidumping duties are applied, they are unlikely to result in gains for the Home country and instead result in losses.

The final case we analyze is an **infant industry** at Home, by which we mean an industry that is too young to have achieved its lowest costs. Often these industries comprise a small number of firms. In our analysis, we assume there is only one firm, so it is again a case of Home monopoly. The special feature of this Home firm is that it cannot compete effectively under free trade, because the world price is below its minimum cost of production today, so the firm makes a loss. But by increasing its output today, the firm will learn how to produce its output more efficiently, and therefore have lower costs in the future, so that it can compete profitably at the world price. One way to achieve this end is for the government to step in and offer assistance, such as with a tariff, that will help the firm to survive long enough to achieve lower, world-competitive costs. This policy is called an "infant industry tariff."

Although we include the infant industry tariff argument in this chapter on strategic trade policy, it is actually a much older argument, dating back to the writings of John Stuart Mill (1806–1873). We will give several examples of infant industries, including the automobile industry in China, which imposed very high tariffs and quotas on foreign cars before it joined the WTO in 2001. We also use this argument to analyze the tariff used in the 1980s to protect Harley-Davidson motorcycles in the United States. The key policy question for an infant industry is whether a government should impose a temporary tariff today, to protect infant industry from competition, thereby keeping it in business long enough for it to learn how to achieve lower costs (and thus competitive prices) in the future.

1 Tariffs and Quotas with Home Monopoly

To illustrate the effect of tariffs and quotas under imperfect competition, we will start with the example of a Home monopolist—a single firm selling a homogeneous good. In this case, free trade introduces many more firms selling the same good into the Home market, which eliminates the monopolist's ability to charge a price higher than its marginal cost (the free-trade equilibrium results in a perfectly competitive Home market). As we will show, tariffs and quotas affect this trade equilibrium differently because of their impact on the Home monopoly's **market power,** the extent to which a firm can choose its price. With a tariff, the Home monopolist still competes against a large number of importers and so its market power is limited.

With an import quota, on the other hand, once the quota limit is reached, the monopolist is the only producer able to sell in the Home market; hence, the Home monopolist can exercise its market power once again. This section describes the Home equilibrium with and without trade and explains this difference between tariffs and quotas.

No-Trade Equilibrium

We begin by showing in Figure 8-1 the no-trade equilibrium with a Home monopoly. The Home demand curve is shown by D, and because it is downward-sloping, as the monopolist sells more, the price will fall. This fall in price means that the extra revenue earned by the monopolist from selling one more unit is less than the price: the extra revenue earned equals the price charged for that unit *minus* the fall in price times the quantity sold of all earlier units. The extra revenue earned from selling one more unit, the **marginal revenue,** is shown by curve MR in Figure 8-1.

To maximize its profits, the monopolist produces at the point where the marginal revenue MR earned from selling one more unit equals the marginal cost MC of producing one more unit. As shown in Figure 8-1, the monopolist produces quantity Q^M. Tracing up from Q^M to point A on the demand curve and then over to the price axis, the price charged by the monopolist is P^M. This price enables the monopolist to earn the highest profits and is the monopoly equilibrium in the absence of international trade.

Comparison with Perfect Competition We can contrast the monopoly equilibrium with the perfect competition equilibrium in the absence of trade. Instead of a single firm, suppose there are many firms in the industry. We assume that all these firms combined have the same cost conditions as the monopolist, so the industry marginal cost is identical to the monopolist's marginal cost curve of MC. Because a perfectly competitive industry will produce where price equals marginal cost, the MC curve is also the industry supply curve. The no-trade equilibrium under perfect competition

---

FIGURE 8-1

No-Trade Equilibrium In the absence of international trade, the monopoly equilibrium at Home occurs at the quantity Q^M, where marginal revenue equals marginal cost. From that quantity, we trace up to the demand curve at point A, and the price charged is P^M. Under perfect competition, the industry supply curve is MC, so the no-trade equilibrium would occur where demand equals supply (point B), at the quantity Q^C and the price P^C.

occurs where supply equals demand (the quantity Q^C and the price P^C). The competitive price P^C is less than the monopoly price P^M, and the competitive quantity Q^C is higher than the monopoly quantity Q^M. This comparison shows that in the absence of trade, the monopolist restricts its quantity sold to increase the market price. Under free trade, however, the monopolist cannot limit quantity and raise price, as we investigate next.

Free-Trade Equilibrium

Suppose now that Home engages in international trade. We will treat Home as a "small country," which means that it faces the fixed world price of P^W. In Figure 8-2, we draw a horizontal line at that price and label it as X^*, the Foreign export supply curve. At that price, Foreign will supply any quantity of imports (because Home is a small country, the Foreign export supply is perfectly elastic). Likewise, the Home monopolist can sell as much as it desires at the price of P^W (because it is able to export at the world price) but cannot charge any more than that price at Home. If it charged a higher price, Home consumers would import the product instead. Therefore, the Foreign supply curve of X^* is *also* the new demand curve facing the Home monopolist: the original no-trade Home demand of D no longer applies.

Because this new demand curve facing the Home monopolist is horizontal, the Home firm's new marginal revenue curve is the same as the demand curve, so $X^* = MR^*$. To understand why this is so, remember that marginal revenue equals the price earned from selling one more unit *minus* the fall in price times the quantity sold of all earlier units. For a horizontal demand curve, there is no fall in price from selling more because additional units sell for P^W, the same price for which the earlier units sell. Thus, marginal revenue is the price earned from selling another unit, P^W. Therefore, the demand curve X^* facing the Home monopolist is identical to the marginal revenue curve; the no-trade marginal revenue of MR no longer applies.

FIGURE 8-2

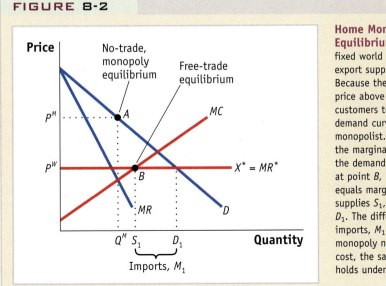

Home Monopoly's Free-Trade Equilibrium Under free trade at the fixed world price P^W, Home faces Foreign export supply of X^* at that price. Because the Home firm cannot raise its price above P^W without losing all its customers to imports, X^* is now also the demand curve faced by the Home monopolist. Because the price is fixed, the marginal revenue MR^* is the same as the demand curve. Profits are maximized at point B, where marginal revenue equals marginal costs. The Home firm supplies S_1, and Home consumers demand D_1. The difference between these is imports, $M_1 = D_1 - S_1$. Because the Home monopoly now sets its price at marginal cost, the same free-trade equilibrium holds under perfect competition.

To maximize profits under the new free-trade market conditions, the monopolist will set marginal revenue equal to marginal cost (point B in Figure 8-2) and will supply S_1 at the price P^W. At the price P^W, Home consumers demand D_1, which is more than the Home supply of S_1. The difference between demand and supply is Home imports under free trade, or $M_1 = D_1 - S_1$.

Comparison with Perfect Competition Let us once again compare this monopoly equilibrium to the perfect competition equilibrium, now with free trade. As before, we assume that the cost conditions facing the competitive firms are the same as those facing the monopolist, so the industry supply curve under perfect competition is equal to the monopolist's marginal cost curve of MC. With free trade and perfect competition, the industry will supply the quantity S_1, where the price P^W equals marginal cost, and consumers will demand the quantity D_1 at the price P^W. Under free trade for a small country, then, a Home monopolist produces the same quantity and charges the same price as a perfectly competitive industry. The reason for this result is that free trade for a small country eliminates the monopolist's control over price; that is, its market power. It faces a horizontal demand curve, equal to marginal revenue, at the world price of P^W. Because the monopolist has no control over the market price, it behaves just as a competitive industry (with the same marginal costs) would behave.

This finding that free trade eliminates the Home monopolist's control over price is an extra source of gains from trade for the Home consumers because of the reduction in the monopolist's market power. We have already seen this extra gain in Chapter 6, in which we first discussed monopolistic competition. There we showed that with free trade, a monopolistically competitive firm faces more-elastic demand curves for its differentiated product, leading it to expand output and lower its prices. The same result holds in Figure 8-2, except that now we have assumed that the good produced by the Home monopolist and the imported good are homogeneous products, so they sell at exactly the same price. Because the Home good and the import are homogeneous, the demand curve X^* facing the Home monopolist in Figure 8-2 is perfectly elastic, leading the monopolist to behave in the same way under free trade as in a competitive industry.

Effect of a Home Tariff

Now suppose the Home country imposes a tariff of t dollars on imports, which increases the Home price from P^W to $P^W + t$. In Figure 8-3, the effect of the tariff is to raise the Foreign export supply curve from X^* to $X^* + t$. The Home firm can sell as much as it desires at the price of $P^W + t$ but cannot charge any more than that price. If it did, the Home consumers would import the product. Thus, the Foreign supply curve of $X^* + t$ is also the new demand curve facing the Home monopolist.

Because this new demand curve is horizontal, the new marginal revenue curve is once again the same as the demand curve, so $MR^* = X^* + t$. The reasoning for this result is similar to the reasoning under free trade: with a horizontal demand curve, there is no fall in price from selling more, so the Home firm can sell as much as it desires at the price of $P^W + t$. So the demand curve $X^* + t$ facing the Home monopolist is identical to its marginal revenue curve.

To maximize profits, the monopolist will once again set marginal revenue equal to marginal costs, which occurs at point C in Figure 8-3, with the price $P^W + t$ and

FIGURE 8-3

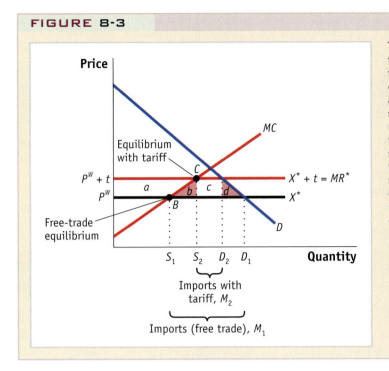

Tariff with Home Monopoly Initially, under free trade at the fixed world price P^W, the monopolist faces the horizontal demand curve (and marginal revenue curve) X^*, and profits are maximized at point B. When a tariff t is imposed, the export supply curve shifts up since Foreign firms must charge $P^W + t$ in the Home market to earn P^W. This allows the Home monopolist to increase its domestic price to $P^W + t$, but no higher, since otherwise it would lose all its customers to imports. The result is fewer imports, M_2, because Home supply S increases and Home demand D decreases. The deadweight loss of the tariff is measured by the area $(b + d)$. This result is the same as would have been obtained under perfect competition because the Home monopolist is still charging a price equal to its marginal cost.

supply of S_2. At the price $P^W + t$, Home consumers demand D_2, which is more than Home supply of S_2. The difference between demand and supply is Home imports, $M_2 = D_2 - S_2$. The effect of the tariff on the Home monopolist relative to the free-trade equilibrium is to raise its production from S_1 to S_2 and its price from P^W to $P^W + t$. The supply increase in combination with a decrease in Home demand reduces imports from M_1 to M_2.

Comparison with Perfect Competition Let us compare this monopoly equilibrium with the tariff to what would happen under perfect competition. The tariff-inclusive price facing a perfectly competitive industry is $P^W + t$, the same price faced by the monopolist. Assuming that the industry supply curve under perfect competition is the same as the monopolist's marginal cost MC, the competitive equilibrium is where price equals marginal cost, which is once again at the quantity S_2 and the price $P^W + t$. So with a tariff, a Home monopolist produces the same quantity and charges the same price as would a perfectly competitive industry. This result is similar to the result we found under free trade. This similarity occurs because the tariff still limits the monopolist's ability to raise its price: it can raise the price to $P^W + t$ but no higher because otherwise consumers will import the product. Because the monopolist has limited control over its price, it behaves in the same way a competitive industry would when facing the tariff.

Home Loss Due to the Tariff Because the tariff and free-trade equilibria are the same for a Home monopoly and a perfectly competitive industry, the deadweight loss from the tariff is also the same. As was discussed in the previous chapter, the deadweight loss under perfect competition is found by taking the total fall in consumer surplus due to the rise in price from P^W to $P^W + t$, adding the gain in producer surplus from the rise in price, and then adding the increase in government revenue due to the tariff. Summing all these components shows a net welfare loss of $(b + d)$:

Fall in consumer surplus:	$-(a + b + c + d)$
Rise in producer surplus:	$+ a$
Rise in government revenue:	$+ c$
Net effect on Home welfare:	$-(b + d)$

Under Home monopoly, the deadweight loss from the tariff is the same. Home consumers still have the loss of $(a + b + c + d)$ because of the rise in price, while the Home monopolist gains the amount a in profits because of the rise in price. With the government collecting area c in tariff revenue, the deadweight loss is still area $(b + d)$.

Effect of a Home Quota

Let us now contrast the tariff with an import quota imposed by the Home government. As we now show, the quota results in a higher price for Home consumers, and therefore a larger Home loss, than would a tariff imposed on the same equilibrium quantity of imports. The reason for the higher costs is that the quota creates a "sheltered" market for the Home firm, allowing it to exercise its monopoly power, which leads to higher prices than under a tariff. Economists and policy makers are well aware of this additional drawback to quotas, which is why the WTO has encouraged countries to replace many quotas with tariffs.

To show the difference between the quota and tariff with a Home monopoly, we use Figure 8-4, in which the free-trade equilibrium is at point B and the tariff equilibrium is at point C (the same points that appear in Figure 8-3). Now suppose that instead of the tariff, a quota is applied. We choose the quota so that it equals the imports under the tariff, which are M_2. Since imports are fixed at that level, the effective demand curve facing the Home monopolist is the demand curve D *minus* the amount M_2. We label this effective demand curve $D - M_2$. Unlike the situation under the tariff, the monopolist now retains the ability to influence its price: it can choose the optimal price and quantity along $D - M_2$. We graph the marginal revenue curve MR for the effective demand curve $D - M_2$. The profit-maximizing position for the monopolist is where marginal revenue equals marginal cost, at point E, with price P_3 and supply S_3.

Let us now compare the tariff equilibrium, at point C, with the quota equilibrium, at point E. It will definitely be the case that the price charged under the quota is higher, $P_3 > P^W + t$. The higher price under the quota reflects the ability of the monopolist to raise its price once the quota amount has been imported. The higher price occurs even though the quota equilibrium *has the same level of imports as the tariff*, M_2. Therefore, the effects of a tariff and a quota are no longer equivalent as they were under perfect competition: the quota enables a monopolist to exercise its market power and raise its price.

What about the quantity produced by the monopolist? Because the price is higher under the quota, the monopolist will definitely produce a lower quantity under the quota, $S_3 < S_2$. What is more surprising, however, is that it is even possible that the quota could lead to a fall in output as compared with free trade: in Figure 8-4, we have shown $S_3 < S_1$. This is not a necessary result, however, and instead we could have drawn the MR curve so that $S_3 > S_1$. It is surprising that the

FIGURE 8-4

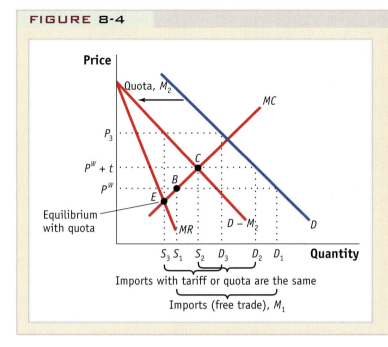

Effect of Quota with Home Monopoly Under free trade, the Home monopolist produces at point B and charges the world price of P^W. With a tariff of t, the monopolist produces at point C and charges the price of $P^W + t$. Imports under the tariff are $M_2 = D_2 - S_2$. Under a quota of M_2, the demand curve shifts to the left by that amount, resulting in the demand $D - M_2$ faced by the Home monopolist. That is, after M_2 units are imported, the monopolist is the only firm able to sell at Home, and so it can choose a price anywhere along the demand curve $D - M_2$. The marginal revenue curve corresponding to $D - M_2$ is MR, and so with a quota, the Home monopolist produces at point E, where MR equals MC. The price charged at point E is $P_3 > P^W + t$, so the quota leads to a higher Home price than the tariff.

case $S_3 < S_1$ is even possible because it suggests that workers in the industry would *fail to be protected* by the quota; that is, employment could fall because of the reduction in output under the quota. We see, then, that the quota can have undesirable effects as compared with a tariff when the Home industry is a monopoly.

Home Loss Due to the Quota Our finding that Home prices are higher with a quota than with a tariff means that Home consumers suffer a greater fall in surplus because of the quota. On the other hand, the Home monopolist earns higher profits from the quota because its price is higher. We will not make a detailed calculation of the deadweight loss from the quota with Home monopoly because it is complicated. We can say, however, that the deadweight loss will always be *higher* for a quota than for a tariff because the Home monopolist will always charge a higher price. That higher price benefits the monopolist but harms Home consumers and creates an extra deadweight loss because of the exercise of monopoly power.

Furthermore, the fact that the Home monopolist is charging a higher price also increases the quota rents, which we defined in the previous chapter as the ability to import goods at the world price and sell them at the higher Home price (in our example, this is the difference between P_3 and P^W times the amount of imports M_2). In the case of Home monopoly, the quota rents are greater than government revenue would be under a tariff. Recall that quota rents are often given to Foreign countries in the case of "voluntary" export restraints (VERs), when the government of the exporting country implements the quota, or else quota rents can even be wasted completely when rent-seeking activities occur. In either of these cases, the increase in quota rents adds to Home's losses if the rents are given away or wasted.

In the next application, we examine a quota used in the United States during the 1980s to restrict imports of Japanese cars. Because the car industry has a small number of producers, it is imperfectly competitive. So our predictions from the case of monopoly discussed previously can serve as a guide for what we expect in the case of Home oligopoly.

APPLICATION

U.S. Imports of Japanese Automobiles

A well-known case of a "voluntary" export restraint (VER) for the United States occurred during the 1980s, when the U.S. limited the imports of cars from Japan. To understand why this VER was put into place, recall that during the early 1980s, the United States suffered a deep recession. That recession led to less spending on durable goods (such as automobiles), and as a result, unemployment in the auto industry rose sharply.

In 1980 the United Automobile Workers and Ford Motor Company applied to the International Trade Commission (ITC) for protection under Article XIX of GATT and Section 201 of U.S. trade laws. As described in the previous chapter, Section 201 protection can be given when increased imports are a "substantial cause of serious injury to the domestic industry," where "substantial cause" must be "not less than any other cause." In fact, the ITC determined that the U.S. recession was a more important cause of injury to the auto industry than increased imports. Accordingly, it did not recommend that the auto industry receive protection.

With this negative determination, several members of Congress from states with auto plants continued to pursue import limits by other means. In April 1981 Senators John Danforth from Missouri and Lloyd Bentsen from Texas introduced a bill in the U.S. Senate to restrict imports. Clearly aware of this pending legislation, the Japanese government announced on May 1 that it would "voluntarily" limit Japan's export of automobiles to the U.S. market. For the period April 1981 to March 1982, this limit was set at 1.83 million autos. After March 1984 the limit was raised to 2.02 million and then to 2.51 million vehicles annually. By 1988 imports fell *below* the VER limit because Japanese companies began assembling cars in the United States.

We are interested in whether American producers were able to exercise their monopoly power and raise their prices under the quota restriction. We are also interested in how much import prices increased. To measure the increase in import prices, we need to take into account a side effect of the 1980 quota: it led to an increase in the features of Japanese cars being sold in the United States such as size, weight, horsepower, and so on, or what we call an increase in quality.[3] The overall increase in auto import prices during the 1980s needs to be broken up into the increases due to (1) the quality upgrading of Japanese cars; (2) the "pure" increase in price because of the quota, which equals the quota rents; and (3) any price increase that would have occurred anyway, even if the auto industry had not been subject to protection.

Price and Quality of Imports The impact of the VER on the price of Japanese cars is shown in Figure 8-5. Under the VER on Japanese car imports, the average price rose from $5,150 to $8,050 between 1980 and 1985. Of that $2,900 increase, $1,100 was the result of quota rents earned by Japanese producers in 1984 and

---

[3] The previous chapter discusses the quality effect of a U.S. import quota on Chinese textile and apparel exports to the United States.

FIGURE 8-5

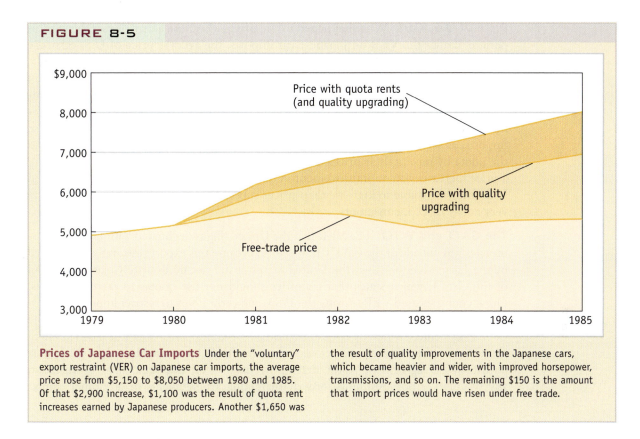

Prices of Japanese Car Imports Under the "voluntary" export restraint (VER) on Japanese car imports, the average price rose from $5,150 to $8,050 between 1980 and 1985. Of that $2,900 increase, $1,100 was the result of quota rent increases earned by Japanese producers. Another $1,650 was the result of quality improvements in the Japanese cars, which became heavier and wider, with improved horsepower, transmissions, and so on. The remaining $150 is the amount that import prices would have risen under free trade.

1985. Another $1,650 was from quality improvements in the Japanese cars, which became heavier and wider, with improved horsepower, transmissions, and so on. The remaining $150 is the amount that import prices would have risen under free trade.

Quota Rents If we multiply the quota rents of $1,100 per car by the imports of about 2 million cars, we obtain total estimated rents of $2.2 billion, which is the lower estimate of the annual cost of quota rents for automobiles. The upper estimate of $7.9 billion comes from also including the increase in price for European cars sold in the United States. Although European cars were not restricted by a quota, they did experience a significant increase in price during the quota period; that increase was due to the reduced competition from Japanese producers.

The Japanese firms benefited from the quota rents that they received. In fact, their stock prices *rose* during the VER period, though only after it became clear that the Japanese Ministry of International Trade and Industry (MITI) would administer the quotas to each producer (so that the Japanese firms would capture the rents). Moreover, because each producer was given a certain number of cars it could export to the United States, but no limit on the value of the cars, producers had a strong incentive to export more expensive models. That explains the quality upgrading that occurred during the quota, which was when Japanese producers started exporting more luxurious cars to the United States.

Price of U.S. Cars What happened to the prices of American small cars during this period? Under the VER on Japanese car imports, the average price of U.S. cars rose very rapidly when the quota was first imposed: from $4,200 in 1979 to $6,000 in 1981, a 43% increase over two years. That price increase was due to the exercise of market power by the U.S. producers, who were sheltered by the quota on their Japanese competitors. Only a small part of that price increase was explained by quality improvements since the quality of U.S. cars did not rise by as much as the quality of Japanese imports, as seen in Figure 8-6. So the American producers were able to benefit from the quota by raising their prices, and the Japanese firms also benefited by combining a price increase with an improvement in quality. The fact that both the Japanese and U.S. firms were able to increase their prices substantially indicates that the policy was very costly to U.S. consumers.

The GATT and WTO The VER that the United States negotiated with Japan in automobiles was outside of the GATT framework: because this export restraint was enforced by the Japanese rather than the United States, it did not necessarily violate Article XI of the GATT, which states that countries should not use quotas to restrict imports. Other countries used VERs during the 1980s and early 1990s to restrict imports in products such as automobiles and steel. All these cases were exploiting a loophole in the GATT agreement whereby a quota enforced by the *exporter* was not a violation of the GATT. This loophole was closed when the WTO was established in 1995. Part of the WTO agreement states that "a Member shall not seek, take or maintain any voluntary export restraints, orderly marketing arrangements or any other similar

FIGURE 8-6

Prices of American Small Cars Under the VER on Japanese car imports, the average price of U.S. cars rose very rapidly when the quota was first imposed: from $4,200 in 1979 to $6,000 in 1981, or a 43% increase over two years. Only a very small part of that increase was explained by quality improvements, and in the later years of the quota, U.S. quality did not rise by as much as it did in the Japanese imports.

measures on the export or the import side. These include actions taken by a single Member as well as actions under agreements, arrangements and understandings entered into by two or more Members."[4] As a result of this rule, VERs can no longer be used unless they are a part of some other agreement in the WTO.[5] ■

2 Tariffs with Foreign Monopoly

So far in this chapter, we have studied the effects of a tariff or quota under Home monopoly. For simplicity, we have focused on the case in which the Home country is small, meaning that the world price is fixed. Let us now examine a different case, in which we treat the Foreign exporting firm as a monopoly. We will show that applying a tariff under a Foreign monopoly leads to an outcome similar to that of the large-country case in the previous chapter; that is, the tariff will lower the price charged by the Foreign exporter. In contrast to the small-country case, a tariff may now benefit the Home country.

Foreign Monopoly

To focus our attention on the Foreign monopolist selling to the Home market, we will assume that there is no competing Home firm, so the Home demand D in Figure 8-7 is supplied entirely by exports from the Foreign monopolist. This assumption is not very realistic because normally a tariff is being considered when there is also a Home firm. But ignoring the Home firm will simplify our analysis while still helping us to understand the effect of an imperfectly competitive Foreign exporter.

Free-Trade Equilibrium In addition to the Home demand of D in Figure 8-7, we also show Home marginal revenue of MR. Under free trade, the Foreign monopolist maximizes profits in its export market where Home marginal revenue MR equals Foreign marginal cost MC^*, at point A in Figure 8-7. It exports the amount X_1 to the Home market and charges the price of P_1.

Effect of a Tariff on Home Price If the Home country applies an import tariff of t dollars, then the marginal cost for the exporter to sell in the Home market increases to $MC^* + t$. With the increase in marginal costs, the new intersection with marginal revenue occurs at point B in Figure 8-7, and the import price rises to P_2.

Under the case we have drawn in Figure 8-7, where the MR curve is steeper than the demand curve, the increase in price from P_1 to P_2 is *less than* the amount of the tariff t. In other words, the vertical rise along the MR curve caused by the tariff (the vertical distance from point A to B, which is the tariff amount) corresponds to a smaller vertical rise moving along the demand curve (the difference between P_1 and P_2). In this case, the net-of-tariff price received by the Foreign exporter, which is $P_3 = P_2 - t$, has *fallen* from its previous level of P_1 because the price rises by less than the tariff. Since the Home country is paying a lower net-of-tariff price P_3 for its import, it has experienced a terms-of-trade gain as a result of the tariff.

---

[4] From Article 11, "Prohibition and Elimination of Certain Measures," of the WTO Agreement on Safeguards.
[5] An example is the quota in textiles that the United States negotiated with China in 2005, which was allowed under the provisions of China's entry into the WTO, as discussed in the previous chapter.

FIGURE 8-7

Tariff with a Foreign Monopoly Under free trade, the Foreign monopolist charges prices P_1 and exports X_1, where marginal revenue MR equals marginal cost MC^*. When an antidumping duty of t is applied, the firm's marginal cost rises to $MC^* + t$, so the exports fall to X_2 and the Home price rises to P_2. The decrease in consumer surplus is shown by the area $c + d$, of which c is collected as a portion of tax revenues. The net-of-tariff price that the Foreign exporter receives falls to $P_3 = P_2 - t$. Because the net-of-tariff price has fallen, the Home country has a terms-of-trade gain, area e. Thus, the total welfare change depends on the size of the terms-of-trade gain e relative to the deadweight loss d.

The effect of the tariff applied against a Foreign monopolist is similar to the effect of a tariff imposed by a large country (analyzed in the previous chapter). There we found that a tariff would lower the price charged by Foreign firms because the quantity of exports decreased, so Foreign marginal costs also fell. Now that we have assumed a Foreign monopoly, we get the same result but for a different reason. The marginal costs of the monopolist are constant at MC^* in Figure 8-7, or $MC^* + t$ including the tariff. The rise in marginal costs from the tariff leads to an increase in the tariff-inclusive Home price as the quantity of Home imports falls, but the monopolist chooses to increase the Home price by *less than* the full amount of the tariff. In that way, the quantity exported to Home does not fall by as much as it would if the Foreign firm increased its price by the full amount of the tariff. So, the Foreign firm is making a strategic decision to absorb part of the tariff itself (by lowering its price from P_1 to P_3) and pass through only a portion of the tariff to the Home price (which rises from P_1 to P_2).

Summary To preserve its sales to Home, the Foreign monopolist chooses to increase the Home price by less than the amount of the tariff. This result depends on having MR steeper than D, as shown in Figure 8-7. It is not necessarily the case that MR is steeper than D for all demand curves, but this is usually how we draw them. In the case of a straight-line demand curve such as the one drawn in Figure 8-7, for example, the marginal revenue curve is exactly twice as steep as the demand curve.[6] In this case, the Home import price rises by exactly half of the tariff amount, and the Foreign export price falls by exactly half of the tariff amount.

Effect of the Tariff on Home Welfare With the rise in the Home price from P_1 to P_2, consumers are worse off. The decline in consumer surplus equals the area between the two prices and to the left of the demand curve, which is $(c + d)$ in Figure 8-7. The increase in the Home price would in principle benefit Home firms, but we have assumed for simplicity that there is no Home producer, so we do not need to keep track of the change in Home producer surplus. We do need to take account of tariff revenue collected by the Home government, however. Tariff revenue equals the amount of the tariff t times Foreign exports X_2, which is area $(c + e)$. Therefore, the effect of the tariff on Home welfare is

Fall in Home consumer surplus:	$-(c + d)$
Rise in Home government revenue:	$+(c + e)$
Net change in Home welfare:	$\mathbf{+ (e - d)}$

We can interpret the area e as the terms-of-trade gain for the Home country, whereas the area d is the deadweight loss from the tariff. If the terms-of-trade gain exceeds the deadweight loss, $e > d$, then Home gains overall by applying a tariff, similar to the result we found for a large country in the previous chapter. As we discussed there, we can expect the terms-of-trade gain to exceed the deadweight loss when the tariff is small, so that Home welfare initially rises for small tariffs. Welfare then reaches some maximum level and then falls as the tariff is increased beyond its optimal level. The same results apply when a tariff is placed against a Foreign monopolist, provided that the marginal revenue curve is steeper than demand, as we have assumed.

To illustrate how a tariff can affect the prices charged by a Foreign monopolist in practice, we once again use the automobile industry as an example. Because there are a small number of firms in that industry, it is realistic to expect them to respond to a tariff in the way that a Foreign monopolist would.

APPLICATION

Import Tariffs on Japanese Trucks

We have found that in the case of a Foreign monopolist, Home will experience a terms-of-trade gain from a small tariff. The reason for this gain is that the Foreign firm will lower its net-of-tariff price to avoid too large an increase in the price paid by consumers in the importing country. To what extent do Foreign exporters actually behave that way?

To answer this question, we can look at the effects of the 25% tariff on imported Japanese compact trucks imposed by the United States in the early 1980s and still in place today. The history of how this tariff came to be applied is an interesting story. Recall from the application earlier in the chapter that in 1980 the United Automobile

---

[6] You are asked to show this result in Problem 6.

Workers and Ford Motor Company applied for a tariff under Article XIX of the GATT and Section 201 of U.S. trade law. They were turned down for the tariff, however, because the International Trade Commission determined that the U.S. recession was a more important cause of injury in the auto industry than growing imports. For cars, the voluntary export restriction (VER) with Japan was pursued. But for compact trucks imported from Japan, it turned out that another form of protection was available.

At that time, most compact trucks from Japan were imported as cab/chassis with some final assembly needed. These were classified as "parts of trucks," which carried a tariff rate of only 4%. But another category of truck—"complete or unfinished trucks"—faced a tariff rate of 25%. That unusually high tariff was a result of the "chicken war" between the United States and West Germany in 1962. At that time, Germany joined the European Economic Community (EEC) and was required to adjust its external tariffs to match those of the other EEC countries. This adjustment resulted in an increase in its tariff on imported U.S. poultry. In retaliation, the United States increased its tariffs on trucks and other products, so the 25% tariff on trucks became a permanent item in the U.S. tariff code.

That tariff created an irresistible opportunity to reclassify the Japanese imports and obtain a substantial increase in the tariff, which is exactly what the U.S. Customs Service did with prodding from the U.S. Congress. Effective August 21, 1980, imported cab/chassis "parts" were reclassified as "complete or unfinished" trucks. This reclassification raised the tariff rate on all Japanese trucks from 4 to 25%, which remains in effect today.

How did Japanese exporters respond to the tariff? According to one estimate, the tariff on trucks was only *partially* reflected in U.S. prices: of the 21% increase, only 12% (or about 60% of the increase) was passed through to U.S. consumer prices; the other 9% (or about 40% of the increase) was absorbed by Japanese producers.[7] Therefore, this tariff led to a terms-of-trade gain for the United States, as predicted by our theory: for a straight-line demand curve (as in Figure 8-7), marginal revenue is twice as steep, and the tariff will lead to an equal increase in the Home import price and decrease in the Foreign export price.[8] The evidence for Japanese trucks is not too different from what we predict in that straight-line case.

Notice that the terms-of-trade gain from the tariff applied on a Foreign monopolist is similar to the terms-of-trade gain from a tariff applied by a "large" country, as we discussed in the previous chapter. In both cases, the Foreign firm or industry absorbs part of the tariff by lowering its price, which means that the Home price rises by less than the full amount of the tariff. If the terms-of-trade gain, measured by the area *e* in Figure 8-7 exceed the deadweight loss *d*, then the Home country gains from the tariff. This is our first example of strategic trade policy that leads to a potential gain for Home.

In principle, this potential gain arises from the tariff that the United States has applied on imports of compact trucks, and that is still in place today. But some economists feel that this tariff has the undesirable side effect of encouraging the U.S. automobile industry to focus on the sales of trucks, since compact trucks have higher

---

[7] Robert Feenstra, 1989, "Symmetric Pass-Through of Tariffs and Exchange Rates under Imperfect Competition: An Empirical Test," *Journal of International Economics*, 27(1/2), 25–45.

[8] You are asked to derive this relationship numerically in Problem 7 at the end of the chapter.

prices due to the tariff.[9] That strategy by U.S. producers can work when gasoline price are low, so consumers are willing to buy trucks. At times of high prices, however, consumers instead want fuel-efficient cars, which have not been the focus of the American industry. So high fuel prices can lead to a surge in imports and fewer domestic sales, exactly what happened after the oil price increase of 1979 and again in 2008, just before the financial crisis. Some industry experts believe that these factors contributed to the losses faced by the American industry during the crisis, as explained in **HEAD-LINES: The Chickens Have Come Home to Roost.** ■

HEADLINES

The Chickens Have Come Home to Roost

This article discusses the history of the 25% tariff that still applies to U.S. imports of lightweight trucks. The author argues that this tariff caused some of the difficulties in the U.S. automobile industry today.

Although we call them the big three automobile companies, they have basically specialized in building trucks. This left them utterly unable to respond when high gas prices shifted the market towards hybrids and more fuel efficient cars.

One reason is that Americans like to drive SUVs, minivans and small trucks when gasoline costs $1.50 to $2.00 a gallon. But another is that the profit margins have been much higher on trucks and vans because the US protects its domestic market with a twenty-five percent tariff. By contrast, the import tariff on regular automobiles is just 2.5 percent and US duties from tariffs on all imported goods are just one percent of the overall value of merchandise imports. Since many of the inputs used to assemble trucks are not subject to tariffs anywhere near 25 percent—US tariffs on all goods average only 3.5 percent—the effective protection and subsidy equivalent of this policy has been huge.

It is no wonder much of the initial foray by Japanese transplants to the US involved setting up trucks assembly plants, no wonder that Automakers only put three doors on SUVs so they can qualify as vans and no wonder that Detroit is so opposed to the US-Korea Free Trade Agreement that would eventually allow trucks built in Korea Duty-Free access to the US market.

What accounts for this distinctive treatment of trucks? An accident of history that shows how hard it is for the government to withdraw favors even when they have no sound policy justification.

It all comes down to the long forgotten chicken wars of the 1960s. In 1962, when implementing the European Common Market, the Community denied access to US chicken producers. In response after being unable to resolve the issue diplomatically, the US responded with retaliatory tariffs that included a twenty five percent tariffs on trucks that was aimed at the German Volkswagen Combi-Bus that was enjoying brisk sales in the US.

Since the trade (GATT) rules required that retaliation be applied on a non-discriminatory basis, the tariffs were levied on all truck-type vehicles imported from all countries and have never been removed. Over time, the Germans stopped building these vehicles and today the tariffs are mainly paid on trucks coming from Asia. The tariffs have bred bad habits, steering Detroit away from building high-quality automobiles towards trucks and truck-like cars that have suddenly fallen into disfavor.

If Congress wants an explanation for why the big three have been so uncompetitive it should look first at the disguised largess it has been providing them with for years. It has taken a long time—nearly 47 years—but it seems that eventually the chickens have finally come home to roost.

Source: Robert Lawrence, guest blogger on Dani Rodrik's weblog, posted May 4, 2009. http://www.rodrik.typepad.com/dani_rodriks_weblog/2009/05/the-chickens-have-come-home-to-roost.html.

---

[9] Larger trucks and SUVs imported into the United States do not have this tariff, but there is another reason why U.S. firms sell many of these products: fuel-economy regulations, which apply to cars but not to trucks or SUVs. These regulations require that the fleet of cars and light trucks sold by each U.S. firms meet a certain average fuel economy, which is expensive for the firms to achieve. Since larger trucks and SUVs do not have to meet the same standard, they are cheaper to produce.

3 Dumping

With imperfect competition, firms can charge *different* prices across countries and will do so whenever that pricing strategy is profitable. Recall that we define imperfect competition as the firm's ability to influence the price of its product. With international trade, we extend this idea: not only can firms charge a price that is higher than their marginal cost, they can also choose to charge different prices in their domestic market than in their export market. This pricing strategy is called **price discrimination** because the firm is able to choose how much different groups of customers pay. To discriminate in international trade, there must be some reason that consumers in the high-price market cannot import directly from the low-cost market; for example, that reason could be transportation costs or tariffs between the markets.

Dumping occurs when a foreign firm sells a product abroad at a price that is either less than the price it charges in its local market, or less than its average cost to produce the product. Dumping is common in international trade, even though the rules of the World Trade Organization (WTO) discourage this activity. Under the rules of the WTO, an importing country is entitled to apply a tariff any time a foreign firm dumps its product on a local market. Such a tariff is called an antidumping duty. We study antidumping duties in detail in the next section. In this section, we want to ask the more general question: Why do firms dump at all? It might appear at first glance that selling abroad at prices less than local prices or less than the average costs of production must be unprofitable. Is that really the case? It turns out the answer is no. It can be profitable to sell at low prices abroad, even at prices lower than average cost.

Discriminating Monopoly To illustrate how dumping can be profitable, we use the example of a Foreign monopolist selling both to its local market and exporting to Home. As described previously, we assume that the monopolist is able to charge different prices in the two markets; this market structure is sometimes called a **discriminating monopoly.** The diagram for a Foreign discriminating monopoly is shown in Figure 8-8. The local demand curve for the monopolist is D^*, with marginal revenue MR^*. We draw these curves as downward-sloping for the monopolist because to induce additional consumers to buy its product, the monopolist lowers its price (downward-sloping D^*), which decreases the revenue received from each additional unit sold (downward-sloping MR^*).

In the export market, however, the Foreign firm will face competition from other firms selling to the Home market. Because of this competition, the firm's demand curve in the export market will be more elastic; that is, it will lose more customers by raising prices than it would in its local market. If it faces enough competition in its export market, the Foreign monopolist's export demand curve will be horizontal at the price P, meaning that it cannot charge more than the competitive market price. If the price for exports is fixed at P, selling more units does not depress the price or the extra revenue earned for each unit exported. Therefore, the marginal revenue for exports equals the price, which is labeled as P in Figure 8-8.

Equilibrium Condition We can now determine the profit-maximizing level of production for the Foreign monopolist, as well as its prices in each market. For the discriminating monopoly, profits are maximized when the following condition holds:

$$MR = MR^* = MC^*$$

FIGURE 8-8

Foreign Discriminating Monopoly The Foreign monopoly faces different demand curves and charges different prices in its local and export markets. Locally, its demand curve is D^* with marginal revenue MR^*. Abroad, its demand curve is horizontal at the export price, P, which is also its marginal revenue of MR. To maximize profits, the Foreign monopolist chooses to produce the quantity Q_1 at point B, where local marginal cost equals marginal revenue in the export market, $MC^* = MR$. The quantity sold in the local market, Q_2 (at point C), is determined where local marginal revenue equals export marginal revenue, $MR^* = MR$. The Foreign monopolist sells Q_2 to its local market at P^*, and $Q_1 - Q_2$ to its export market at P. Because $P < P^*$ (or alternatively $P < AC_1$), the firm is dumping.

This equation looks similar to the condition for profit maximization for a single-market monopolist, which is marginal revenue = marginal cost, except that now the marginal revenues should also be equal in the two markets.

We illustrate this equilibrium condition in Figure 8-8. If the Foreign firm produces quantity Q_1, at point B, then the marginal cost of the last unit equals the export marginal revenue MR. But not all of the supply Q_1 is exported; some is sold locally. The amount sold locally is determined by the equality of the firm's local marginal revenue MR^* with its export marginal revenue MR (at point C), *and* the equality of its local marginal cost MC^* with MR (at point B). All three variables equal P, though the firm charges the price P^* (by tracing up the Foreign demand curve) to its local consumers. Choosing these prices, the profit-maximization equation just given is satisfied, and the discriminating monopolist is maximizing profits across both markets.

The Profitability of Dumping The Foreign firm charges P^* to sell quantity Q_2 in its local market (from Q_2, we go up to the local demand curve D^* and across to the price). The local price exceeds the price P charged in the export market. Because the

Foreign firm is selling the same product at a lower price to the export market, it is dumping its product into the export market.

What about the comparison of its export price with average costs? At total production of Q_1 at point B, the firm's average costs are read off the average cost curve above that point, so average costs equal AC_1, lower than the local price P^* but higher than the export price P. Because average costs AC_1 are above the export price P, the firm is also dumping according to this cost comparison. But we will argue that the Foreign firm still earns positive profits from exporting its good at the low price of P. To see why that is the case, we turn to a numerical example.

Numerical Example of Dumping

Suppose the Foreign firm has the following cost and demand data:

$$
\begin{aligned}
\text{Fixed costs} &= \$100 \\
\text{Marginal costs} &= \$10 \text{ per unit} \\
\text{Local price} &= \$25 \\
\text{Local quantity} &= 10 \\
\text{Export price} &= \$15 \\
\text{Export quantity} &= 10
\end{aligned}
$$

The profits earned from selling in its local market are

$$\underbrace{(\$25 \cdot 10)}_{\text{Revenue}} - \underbrace{\$10 \cdot 10}_{\substack{\text{Variable} \\ \text{cost}}} - \underbrace{\$100}_{\substack{\text{Fixed} \\ \text{cost}}} = \underbrace{\$50}_{\text{Profits}}$$

Notice that the average costs for the firms are

$$\text{Average costs} = \frac{\$200}{10} = \$20$$

Now suppose that this firm sells an additional 10 units abroad, at the price of $15, which is less than its average cost of production. It is *still* worthwhile to sell these extra units because profits become

$$\underbrace{(\$25 \cdot 10 + \$15 \cdot 10)}_{\text{Revenue}} - \underbrace{\$10 \cdot 20}_{\substack{\text{Variable} \\ \text{cost}}} - \underbrace{\$100}_{\substack{\text{Fixed} \\ \text{cost}}} = \underbrace{\$100}_{\text{Profits}}$$

Profits have increased because the extra units are sold at $15 but produced at a *marginal cost* of $10, which is less than the price received in the export market. Therefore, each unit exported will increase profits by the difference between the price and marginal costs. Thus, even though the export price is less than average costs, profits still rise from dumping in the export market.

4 Policy Response to Dumping

In the previous section, we learned that dumping is not unusual: a Foreign monopolist that discriminates between its local and export markets by charging different prices in each can end up charging a lower price in its export market. Furthermore, the price it charges in its export market might be less than its average cost of production and still be profitable. Our interest now is in understanding the policy response in the Home importing country.

Antidumping Duties

Under the rules of the WTO, an importing country is entitled to apply an antidumping tariff any time that a foreign firm is dumping its product. An imported product is being dumped if its price is below the price that the exporter charges in its own local market; if the exporter's local price is not available, then dumping is determined by comparing the import price to (1) a price charged for the product in a third market or (2) the exporter's average costs of production.[10] If one of these criteria is satisfied, then the exporting firm is dumping and the importing country can respond with a tariff called an antidumping duty.[11] The amount of the antidumping duty is calculated as the difference between the exporter's local price and the "dumped" price in the importing country.

An example of an antidumping duty is the tariff that the European Union applies to imports of shoes from China and Vietnam. Since 2006 the European Union has applied tariffs of 10% to 16.5% on shoes imported from China and 10% on shoes imported from Vietnam. These antidumping duties were justified because of the low prices that the imported shoes are sold for in Europe. On January 3, 2010, the European Union voted to extend the duties for another 15 months, through March 2011. That decision was protested by the European Footwear Alliance, which represents major footwear firms who import shoes into Europe, and also by China, which filed an official complaint with the WTO, as described in **Headlines: China Escalates Trade Fight Over European Shoe Tariff.** The WTO will have to determine whether the European Union was entitled to extend this duty; that is, whether shoes from China and Vietnam were still being sold at prices below those in their local market, or below their costs of production.

Strategic Trade Policy? The purpose of an antidumping duty is to raise the price of the dumped good in the importing country, thereby protecting the domestic producers of that good. Because we are dealing with dumping by a Foreign monopolist, we might expect that the antidumping duty, which is a tariff, will lead to a terms-of-trade gain for the Home country. That is, we might expect that the Foreign monopolist will absorb part of the tariff through lowering its own price, as was illustrated in Figure 8-7. It follows that the rise in the consumer price in the importing country is less than the full amount of the tariff, as was illustrated in the previous application dealing with Japanese compact trucks.

Does the application of antidumping duties lead to a terms-of-trade gain for the Home country, making this another example of strategic trade policy that can potentially benefit the Home country? In the upcoming analysis, we'll find that the answer to this question is "no," and that the antidumping provisions of U.S. trade law are

---

[10] See Article VI of the GATT in Side Bar: Key Provisions of the GATT in the previous chapter.
[11] There is another type of tariff, similar to the antidumping duty, that is also used to offset low prices in the importing country, and that is the *countervailing duty*. A countervailing duty is used when the Foreign government subsidizes its own exporting firms so that they can charge lower prices for the exports. We will examine export subsidies in the next chapter.

HEADLINES

China Escalates Trade Fight Over European Shoe Tariff

This article discusses an ongoing case before the World Trade Organization dealing with European tariffs on shoes made in China, and the Chinese response.

China complained to the World Trade Organization on Thursday [February 4, 2010] about antidumping duties imposed by the European Union on Chinese-made shoes, raising tensions between the trading giants. . . . In a statement issued by its mission in Geneva, where the W.T.O. is based, the Chinese government said Europe's actions "violated various obligations under the W.T.O., and consequently caused damage to the legitimate rights and interests of Chinese exporters." It added that China "had repeatedly consulted" with the European Union but said that its concerns "had not been properly addressed or settled." In an eight-page legal complaint, the Chinese government requested consultations on both the original 2006 decision to impose the shoe duties and last year's move to extend them.

. . . While some European Union countries with footwear manufacturers, like Italy, have welcomed the antidumping duties, others support the position of large retailers that argue the duties hurt consumers by pushing up prices. As a compromise, the European Union decided late last year on a 15-month extension of charges that add 9.7 percent to 16.5 percent to the import price of Chinese shoes and 10 percent to Vietnamese shoes.

The European Footwear Alliance, which represents several big global footwear brands, including Adidas, Ecco and Timberland, opposes the duties. It said in a statement that it "shares China's view" that the European Union decision was based on flawed analysis. "Ironically the measure hurts European business and consumers the most," it said. In a letter sent last year to Catherine Ashton, then the European Union trade commissioner, the alliance said its members had paid around 800 million euros ($1.2 billion) in antidumping duties in the previous three and a half years, "and we fail to understand who has benefited."

Until recently, China had made little use of the W.T.O. procedures in trade disputes with Europe. But in 2009, when the European Union applied antidumping tariffs on imports of iron and steel fasteners from China, Beijing dragged the European Union into the W.T.O. dispute settlement process for the first time. Under W.T.O. rules, the European Union and China have 60 days to resolve the shoe dispute through bilateral consultations. If no deal is reached, China can ask the 153 members of the organization to establish a panel of three experts to examine the issue. Europe could block that once, but establishment is automatic if China makes a second request. A final decision can take 18 months or longer.

Source: Excerpted from Stephen Castle and David Jolly, "China Escalates Trade Fight Over European Shoe Tariff," The New York Times, February 5, 2010, electronic edition.

overused and create a much greater cost for consumers and larger deadweight losses than does the less frequent application of tariffs under the safeguard provision, Article XIX of the GATT.[12]

Comparison with Safeguard Tariff It is important to recognize that the tariff on compact trucks, discussed in the previous application, was not an antidumping duty. Rather, it was a **safeguard tariff** applied under Section 201 of the U.S. tariff code, or Article XIX of the GATT. Because the tariff on trucks was increased in the early 1980s and has not been changed since, it fits our assumption that Foreign firms treat the tariff as fixed. That assumption does not hold for antidumping duties, however, because Foreign exporting firms can *influence* the amount of an antidumping duty by their own

---

[12] See Article XIX of the GATT in Side Bar: Key Provisions of the GATT in the previous chapter.

choice of prices. In fact, the evidence shows that Foreign firms often change their prices and *increase* the price charged in the importing country even before an antidumping tariff is applied. To see why this occurs, let us review how the antidumping duty is calculated.

Calculation of Antidumping Duty The amount of an antidumping duty is calculated based on the Foreign firm's local price. If its local price is $10 (after converting from Foreign's currency to U.S. dollars), and its export price to the Home market is $6, then the antidumping tariff is calculated as the difference between these prices, $4 in our example. This method of calculating the tariff creates an incentive for the Foreign firm to *raise* its export price even before the tariff is applied so that the duty will be lower. If the Foreign firm charges an export price of $8 instead of $4 but maintains its local price of $10, then the antidumping tariff would be only $2. Alternatively, the Foreign firm could charge $10 in its export market (the same as its local price) and avoid the antidumping tariff altogether!

Thus, the calculation of an antidumping duty creates a strong incentive for Foreign firms to raise their export prices to reduce or avoid the duty. This increase in the import price results in a terms-of-trade *loss* for the Home country. Such an increase in the import price is illustrated in Figure 8-9 as the rise from price P_1 to P_2. This price increase leads to a gain for Home firms of area a but a loss for Home consumers of area $(a + b + c + d)$. There is no revenue collected when the duty is not imposed, so the net loss for the Home country is area $(b + c + d)$. This loss is higher than the deadweight loss from a tariff (which is area $b + d$) and illustrates the extra costs associated with the threat of an antidumping duty.

FIGURE 8-9

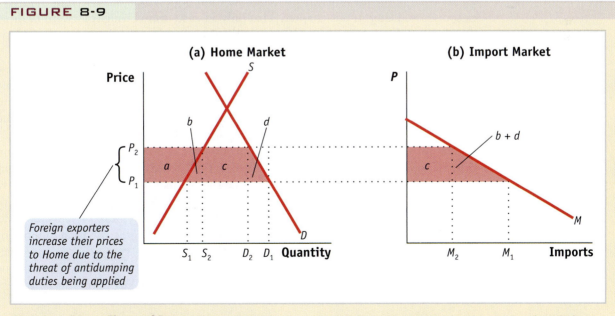

Home Loss Due to Threat of Duty A charge of dumping can sometimes lead Foreign firms to increase their prices, even without an antidumping duty being applied. In that case, there is a loss for Home consumers $(a + b + c + d)$ and a gain for Home producers (a). The net loss for the Home country is area $(b + c + d)$.

Furthermore, the fact that Foreign firms will raise their prices to reduce the potential duty gives Home firms an incentive to charge Foreign firms with dumping, even if none is occurring: just the *threat* of an antidumping duty is enough to cause Foreign firms to raise their prices and reduce competition in the market for that good. As the following application shows, these incentives lead to excessive filings of antidumping cases.

APPLICATION

Antidumping Duties Versus Safeguard Tariffs

In the previous chapter, we discussed the "safeguard" provision in Article XIX of the GATT **(Side Bar: Key Provisions of the GATT)** and Section 201 of U.S. trade law. This provision, which permits temporary tariffs to be applied, is used infrequently. As shown in Table 8-1, from 1980 to 1989, only 19 safeguard (also called "escape clause") cases were filed in the United States. In the following decade there were only nine, and from 2000 to 2009 only three such cases were filed. In each case, the U.S. International Trade Commission must determine whether rising imports are the "most important cause of serious injury, or threat thereof, to the domestic industry." Of the 31 cases filed from 1980 to 2009, the ITC made a *negative* recommendation (i.e., it did not approve the tariff requests) in 16, or about one-half the cases. One of those negative recommendations was for the tariff on Japanese compact trucks discussed in the previous application: the ITC made a negative recommendation for both cars and trucks in 1980, but trucks still obtained a tariff by reclassifying the type of trucks being imported.

The ITC made an affirmative ruling for protection in 12 cases, which then went for a final ruling to the president, who recommended import protection in only nine cases.[13] An example of a positive recommendation was the tariff on the import of steel, as discussed in the previous chapter, and the tariff imposed on heavyweight motorcycles, discussed later in this chapter. That only 31 cases were brought forward in three decades, and that tariffs were approved by the president in only nine cases, shows how infrequently this trade provision is used.

In the next panel of Table 8-1, we show the number of China-specific safeguard cases. This new trade provision, discussed in the previous chapter, took effect in 2001. Since that time, seven cases have been filed, of which two were denied by the ITC and five were approved. Of these five approved tariffs, the president also ruled in favor only once—the tariff imposed on imports of tires from China, approved by President Obama in 2009.

The infrequent use of the safeguard provision can be contrasted with the many cases of antidumping duties. The cases filed in the United States under this provision are also listed in Table 8-1, which shows that the number of antidumping cases vastly exceeds safeguard cases. From 1980 to 1989 and from 1990 to 1999, there were more than 400 antidumping cases filed in the United States. In the next 10 years, 2000 to 2009, there were another 300 or so antidumping cases, bringing the total number of antidumping cases from 1980 to 2009 to more than 1,200!

To have antidumping duties applied, a case must first go to the U.S. Department of Commerce (DOC), which rules on whether imports are selling domestically at "less

---

[13] In addition to the 12 affirmative ITC safeguard cases, there were two ties and one terminated case.

TABLE 8-1

Import Protection Cases in the United States, 1980–2009 This table shows the use of safeguard tariffs as compared with antidumping duties in the United States. Safeguard tariffs are used much less often.

Safeguard or Escape Clause

Total 1980–1989	Total 1990–1999	Total 2000–2009	TOTAL 1980–2009		
			Negative ITC	Affirmative ITC*	Affirmative President
19	9	3	16	12	9

China-Specific Safeguard

Total 1980–1989	Total 1990–1999	Total 2000–2009	TOTAL 1980–2009		
			Negative ITC	Affirmative ITC*	Affirmative President
NA	NA	7	2	5	1

Antidumping

Total 1980–1989	Total 1990–1999	Total 2000–2009	TOTAL 1980–2009		
			Duty Levied	Case Rejected	Withdrawn
468	428	313	545	447	148

* In addition to the 12 affirmative ITC safeguard cases, there were two ties and one terminated case.

NA – not applicable since the China-specific safeguard began in 2001.

Sources: Wendy Hansen and Thomas J. Prusa, 1995, "The Road Most Taken: The Rise of Title VII Protection," The World Economy, 295–313. Update for 1989 to 1994, I. M. Destler, 2005, American Trade Politics, Washington, D.C.: Peterson Institute for International Economics, pp. 149, 165. Update for 1995 to 2009, Chad P. Bown, October 2009, "Global Antidumping Database" [Version 5.1], http://www.brandeis.edu/~cbown/global_ad/ .

than fair value"; that is, below the price in their own market or below the average cost of making them. These rulings were positive in 93% of cases during this period. The case is then brought before the ITC, which must rule on whether imports have caused "material injury" to the domestic industry (defined as "harm that is not inconsequential, immaterial, or unimportant"). This criterion is much easier to meet than the "substantial cause of serious injury" provision for a safeguard tariff, and as a result, the ITC more frequently rules in favor of antidumping duties. Furthermore, the application of duties does not require the additional approval of the president. Of the 1,200 antidumping cases filed from 1980 to 2009, about 450 were rejected and another 550 had duties levied.

The remaining 150 antidumping cases fall into a surprising third category: those that are *withdrawn* prior to a ruling by the ITC. It turns out that the U.S. antidumping law actually permits U.S. firms to withdraw their case and, acting through an intermediary at the Department of Commerce (DOC), agree with the foreign firm on the level of prices and market shares! As we would expect, these withdrawn and settled cases result in a significant increase in market prices for the importing country.

Why do firms make claims of dumping so often? If a dumping case is successful, a duty will be applied against the Foreign competitor, and the import price will increase. If the case is withdrawn and settled, then the Foreign competitor will also raise its price. Even if the case is not successful, imports often decline during the period that the DOC or ITC is making an investigation, and the smaller quantity of imports also causes their price to rise. So regardless of the outcome of a dumping case, the increase in the price of Foreign imports benefits Home firms by allowing them to charge more for their own goods. As a result, Home producers have a strong incentive to file for protection from dumping, whether it is occurring or not. ■

5 Infant Industry Protection

We now turn to the final application of tariffs that we will study in this chapter, and that is a tariff applied to an industry that is too young to withstand foreign competition, and so will suffer losses when faced with world prices under free trade. Given time to grow and mature, the industry will be able to compete in the future. The only way that a firm in this industry could cover its losses today would be to borrow against its future profits. But if banks are not willing to lend to this firm—perhaps because it is small and inexperienced—then it will go bankrupt today unless the government steps in and offers some form of assistance, such as with a tariff or quota. This argument is called the "infant industry case" for protection. Although we include the infant industry tariff argument in this chapter on strategic trade policy, the idea of protecting a young industry dates back to the writings of John Stuart Mill (1806–1873).

To analyze this argument and make use of our results from the previous sections, we assume there is only one Home firm, so it is again a case of Home monopoly. The special feature of this Home firm is that increasing its output today will lead to lower costs in the future because it will learn how to produce its output more efficiently and at a lower cost. The question, then, is whether the Home government should intervene with a temporary protective tariff or quota today, so that the firm can survive long enough to achieve lower costs and higher profits in the future.

There are two cases in which infant industry protection is potentially justified. First, protection may be justified if a tariff today leads to an increase in Home output that, in turn, helps the firm learn better production techniques and reduce costs in the future. This is different from increasing returns to scale as discussed in Chapter 6. With increasing returns to scale, lower costs arise from producing farther down along a decreasing average cost curve; while a tariff might boost Home production and lower costs, removing the tariff would reduce production to its initial level and still leave the firm uncompetitive at world prices. For infant industry protection to be justified, the firm's learning must *shift down* the entire average cost curve to the point where it is competitive at world prices in the future, even without the tariff.

If the firm's costs are going to fall in the future, then why doesn't it simply borrow today to cover its losses and pay back the loan from future profits? Why does it need import protection to offset its current losses? The answer was already hinted at above: banks may be unwilling to lend to this firm because they don't know with certainty that the firm will achieve lower costs and be profitable enough in the future to repay the loan. In such a situation, a tariff or quota offsets an imperfection in the market for borrowing and lending (the capital market). What is most essential for the infant industry argument to be valid is not imperfect competition (a single Home firm), but rather, this imperfection in the Home capital market.

A second case in which import protection is potentially justified is when a tariff in one period leads to an increase in output and reductions in future costs *for other firms in the industry,* or even for firms in other industries. This type of **externality** occurs when firms learn from each other's successes. For instance, consider the high-tech semiconductor industry. Each firm innovates its products at a different pace, and when one firm has a technological breakthrough, other firms benefit by being able to copy the newly developed knowledge. In the semiconductor industry, it is not unusual for firms to mimic the successful innovations of other firms, and benefit from a **knowledge spillover.** In the presence of spillovers, the infant industry tariff promotes a positive externality: an increase in output for one firm lowers the costs for everyone. Because firms learn from each other, each firm on its own does not have much incentive to invest in learning by increasing its production today. In this case, a tariff is needed to offset this externality by increasing production, allowing for these spillovers to occur among firms so that there are cost reductions.

As both of these cases show, the infant industry argument supporting tariffs or quotas depends on the existence of some form of **market failure.** In our first example, the market does not provide loans to the firm to allow it to avoid bankruptcy; in the second, the firm may find it difficult to protect its intellectual knowledge through patents, which would enable it to be compensated for the spillover of knowledge to others. These market failures create a potential role for government policy. In practice, however, it can be very difficult for a government to correct market failure. If the capital market will not provide loans to a firm because it doesn't think the firm will be profitable in the future, then why would the government have better information about that firm's future prospects? Likewise, in the case of a spillover of knowledge to other firms, we cannot expect the government to know the extent of spillovers. Thus, we should be skeptical about the ability of government to distinguish the industries that deserve infant industry protection from those that do not.

Furthermore, even if either of the two conditions we have identified to potentially justify infant industry protection hold, these market failures do not guarantee that the protection will be worthwhile—we still need to compare the future benefits of protection (which are positive) with its costs today (the deadweight losses). With these warnings in mind, let's look at how infant industry protection can work when we have enough information to calculate the costs and benefits.

Free-Trade Equilibrium

In panel (a) of Figure 8-10, we show the situation a Home firm faces today, and in panel (b) we show its situation in the future. We assume that the Home country is small and therefore faces a fixed world price. As discussed earlier in the chapter, even a Home monopolist will behave in the same manner as a perfectly competitive industry under free trade, assuming that they have the same marginal costs. We also assume that any increase in the firm's output today leads to a reduction in costs in the future (i.e., a downward shift in the firm's average cost curve).

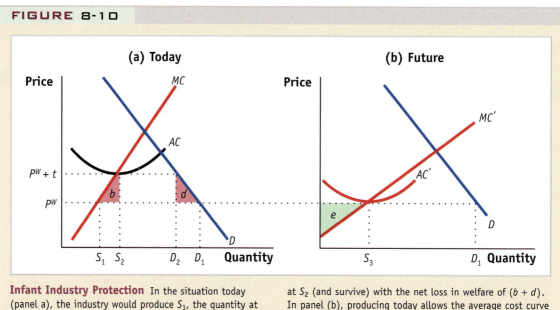

FIGURE 8-10

Infant Industry Protection In the situation today (panel a), the industry would produce S_1, the quantity at which $MC = P^W$. Because P^W is less than average costs at S_1, the industry would incur losses at the world price of P^W and would be forced to shut down. A tariff increases the price from P^W to $P^W + t$, allowing the industry to produce at S_2 (and survive) with the net loss in welfare of $(b + d)$. In panel (b), producing today allows the average cost curve to fall through learning to AC'. In the future, the firm can produce the quantity S_3 at the price P^W without tariff protection and earn producer surplus of e.

Equilibrium Today

With free trade today, the Home firm faces the world price of P^W (which, you will recall from earlier in this chapter, is also its marginal revenue curve) and will produce to the point at which its marginal cost of production equals P^W. The Home firm therefore supplies the quantity S_1. To verify that S_1 is actually the Home supply, however, we need to check that profits are not negative at this quantity. To do so, we compare the firm's average costs with the price. The average cost curve is shown as AC in panel (a), and at the supply of S_1, average costs are much higher than the price P^W. That means the Home firm is suffering losses and would shut down today instead of producing S_1.

Tariff Equilibrium

To prevent the firm from shutting down, the Home government could apply an import tariff or quota to raise the Home price. Provided that the Home firm increases its output in response to this higher price, we assume that this increased size allows the firm to learn better production techniques so that its future costs are reduced. Given the choice of an import tariff or quota to achieve this goal, the Home government should definitely choose the tariff. The reason is that when a Home monopolist is faced with a quota rather than a tariff, it will produce *less* output under the quota so that it can further raise its price. The decrease in output leads to additional deadweight loss today, as discussed earlier in the chapter. Furthermore, because we have assumed that the firm's learning depends on how much it produces and output is lower under the quota, there would be less learning and a smaller reduction in future costs under a quota than a tariff. For both reasons, a tariff is a better policy than a quota when the goal is to nurture an infant industry.

Equilibrium Today If the government applies an import tariff of t dollars today, the Home price increases from P^W to $P^W + t$. We assume that the government sets the tariff high enough so that the new Home price, $P^W + t$, just covers the infant industry's average costs of production. At this new price, the firm produces the quantity S_2 in panel (a). As illustrated, the price $P^W + t$ exactly equals average costs, AC, at the quantity S_2, so the firm is making zero profits. Making zero profits means that the Home firm will continue to operate.

Equilibrium in the Future With the firm producing S_2 today rather than S_1, it can learn about better production methods and lower its costs in the future. The effect of learning on production costs is shown by the downward shift of the average cost curve from AC in panel (a) to AC' in panel (b).[14] The lower average costs in the future mean that the firm can produce quantity S_3 without tariff protection at the world price P^W in panel (b) and still cover its average costs. So the temporary tariff today allows the firm to operate in the future without the tariff, which is what infant industry protection is trying to achieve.

Effect of the Tariff on Welfare The application of the tariff today leads to a deadweight loss, and in panel (a), the deadweight loss is measured by the triangles $(b + d)$. But we also need to count the gain from having the firm operating in the future. In panel (b) of Figure 8-10, the producer surplus earned in the future by the firm is shown by the region e. We should think of the region e as the present value (i.e., the discounted sum over time) of the firm's future producer surplus; it is this amount that would be forgone if the firm shut down today.

To evaluate whether the tariff has been successful, we need to compare the future gain of e with the deadweight loss today of $(b + d)$. If e exceeds $(b + d)$, then the infant industry protection has been worthwhile, but if e is less than $(b + d)$, then the costs of protection today do not justify the future benefits. The challenge for government policy is to try to distinguish worthwhile cases (those for which future benefits exceed present costs) from those cases that are not. In the application that follows, we will see whether the governments of China, Brazil, and the United States have been able to distinguish between these cases.

APPLICATION

Examples of Infant Industry Protection

There are many examples of infant industry protection in practice, and we will consider three: (1) a U.S. tariff imposed to protect Harley-Davidson motorcycles in the United States during the 1980s; (2) a complete ban on imports imposed from 1977 to the early 1990s to protect the computer industry in Brazil; and (3) tariffs and quotas imposed to protect the automobile industry in China, which were reduced when China joined the WTO in 2001. The last two of these examples are for developing countries, in which we normally think of infant industry tariffs being applied. However, this is not necessarily always the case, as shown in the first example for the United States.

---

[14] The marginal cost curve might also shift down, from MC in panel (a) to MC' in panel (b), although that shift is not essential to our argument.

U.S. Tariff on Heavyweight Motorcycles

Harley-Davidson does not really fit the usual description of an "infant" industry: the first plant opened in 1903 in Milwaukee, Wisconsin, and it was owned and operated by William Harley and the three Davidson brothers. Until the late 1970s it did not face intense import competition from Japanese producers; but by the early 1980s, Harley-Davidson was on the verge of bankruptcy. Even though it had been around since 1903, Harley-Davidson had many of the characteristics we associate with an infant industry: the inability to compete at the international price today and (as we will see) the potential for lower costs in the future. By including this case in our discussion of infant industries, we are able to make a precise calculation of the effect of the tariffs on consumers and producers to determine whether the infant industry protection was successful.

In 1983 Harley-Davidson, the legendary U.S.-based motorcycle manufacturer, was in trouble. It was suffering losses due to a long period of lagging productivity combined with intense competition from Japanese producers. Two of these producers, Honda and Kawasaki, not only had plants in the United States but also exported Japan-made goods to the United States. Two other Japanese producers, Suzuki and Yamaha, produced and exported their products from Japan. In the early 1980s these four Japanese firms were engaged in a global price war that spilled over into the U.S. market, and inventories of imported heavyweight cycles rose dramatically in the United States. Facing this intense import competition, Harley-Davidson applied to the International Trade Commission (ITC) for Section 201 protection.

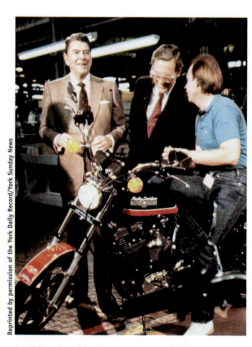

As required by law, the ITC engaged in a study to determine the source of injury to the industry, which in this case was identified as heavyweight (more than 700 cc) motorcycles. Among other factors, it studied the buildup of inventories by Japanese producers in the United States. The ITC determined that there was more than nine months' worth of inventory of Japanese motorcycles already in the United States, which could depress the prices of heavyweight cycles and threaten bankruptcy for Harley-Davidson. As a result, the ITC recommended to President Ronald Reagan that import protection be placed on imports of heavyweight motorcycles. This case is interesting because it is one of the few times that the *threat* of injury by imports has been used as a justification for tariffs under Section 201 of U.S. trade law.

President Reagan approved the recommendation from the ITC, and tariffs were imposed on imports of heavyweight motorcycles. These tariffs were initially very high, but they declined over five years. The initial tariff, imposed on April 16, 1983, was 45%; it then fell annually to 35, 20, 15, and 10% and

President Ronald Reagan visits the Harley-Davidson plant.

was scheduled to end in April 1988. In fact, Harley-Davidson petitioned the ITC to end the tariff one year early, after the 15% rate expired in 1987, by which time it had cut costs and introduced new and very popular products so that profitability had been restored. Amid great fanfare, President Reagan visited the Harley-Davidson plant in Milwaukee, Wisconsin, and declared that the tariff had been a successful case of protection.

Calculation of Deadweight Loss Was the tariff on heavyweight motorcycles really successful? To answer this, we need to compare the deadweight loss of the tariff with the future gain in producer surplus. In our discussion of the steel tariff in the previous chapter, we derived a formula for the deadweight loss from using a tariff, measured relative to the import value:

$$\frac{DWL}{P \cdot M} = \frac{1}{2} \cdot \left(\frac{t}{P^W}\right) \cdot \%\Delta M$$

The information on imports of heavyweight cycles is shown in Table 8-2. Before the tariff was imposed, import sales in 1982 were $452 million and the import quantity was 164,000 motorcycles. After the tariff was imposed in April 1983, imports dropped to 139,000 in calendar year 1983, and 40,000 to 80,000 each year thereafter. The average import quantity between 1982 and 1983 was therefore (164,000 + 139,000)/2 = 151,000, so the percentage drop in import quantity between these years is calculated using a midpoint formula as (164 − 139)/151 = 0.17, or 17%. This percentage drop is reported in Table 8-2, along with the tariff of 45% in 1983.

The deadweight loss relative to import value in 1983 is measured as

$$\frac{DWL}{P \cdot M} = \tfrac{1}{2} \, (0.45 \cdot 0.17) = 0.038, \text{ or } 3.8\%$$

We can calculate the average import sales from 1982 to 1983 as (452 + 410)/2 = $431 million. Multiplying the percentage loss by average imports, we obtain the deadweight loss in 1983 of 0.038 × 431 = $16.3 million. That deadweight loss is reported in the last column of Table 8-2, along with the loss for each following year. Adding up these deadweight losses, we obtain a total loss of $112.5 million over the four years that the tariff was used.[15]

TABLE 8-2

U.S. Imports of Heavyweight Motorcycles This table shows the effects of the tariff on imports of heavyweight motorcycles in the United States.

Year	Import Sales ($ millions)	Import Quantity	% Fall in Imports (from 1982)	Tariff (%)	Net Loss/ Average Sales (%)	Deadweight Loss (% millions)
1982	452	164,000				
1983	410	139,000	17	45	3.8	16.3
1984	179	80,000	69	35	12.1	38.4
1985	191	72,000	78	20	7.8	25.2
1986	152	43,000	116	15	8.7	26.4
January–March 1987	59	14,000	98	15	7.3	6.3
Total, 1983–1987						112.5

Source: Heavy Weight Motorcycles. Report to the President on Investigation No. TA-203-17, under Section 203 of the Trade Act of 1974. U.S. International Trade Commission, June 1987, and author's calculations.

---

[15] This calculation is not quite accurate because we have used the calendar years 1983 to 1986 rather than the 12 months from April of each year to March of the next year, during which the tariff was effective.

Future Gain in Producer Surplus To judge whether the tariff was effective, we need to compare the deadweight loss of $112.5 million with the *future* gain in producer surplus (area *e* in Figure 8-10). How can we assess these future gains? We can use a technique that economists favor: we can evaluate the future gains in producer surplus by examining the stock market value of the firm around the time that the tariff was removed.

During the time that the tariff was in place, the management of Harley-Davidson reduced costs through several methods: implementing a "just-in-time" inventory system, which means producing inventory on demand rather than having excess amounts in warehouses; reducing the workforce (and its wages); and implementing "quality circles," groups of assembly workers who volunteer to meet together to discuss workplace improvements, along with a "statistical operator control system" that allowed employees to evaluate the quality of their output. Many of these production techniques were copied from Japanese firms. The company also introduced a new engine. These changes allowed Harley-Davidson to transform losses during the period from 1981 to 1982 into profits for 1983 and in following years.

In July 1986 Harley-Davidson became a public corporation and issued stock on the American Stock Exchange: 2 million shares at $11 per share, for a total offering of $22 million. It also issued debt of $70 million, which was to be repaid from future profits. In June 1987 it issued stock again: 1.23 million shares at $16.50 per share, for a total offering of $20.3 million. The sum of these stock and debt issues is $112.3 million, which we can interpret as the present discounted value of the producer surplus of the firm. This estimate of area *e* is nearly equal to the consumer surplus loss, $112.5 million, in Table 8-2. Within a month after the second stock offering, however, the stock price rose from $16.50 to $19 per share. Using that price to evaluate the outstanding stock of 3.23 million, we obtain a stock value of $61 million, plus $70 million in repaid debt, to obtain $131 million as the future producer surplus.

By this calculation, the future gain in producer surplus from tariff protection to Harley-Davidson ($131 million) exceeds the deadweight loss of the tariff ($112.5 million). Furthermore, since 1987 Harley-Davidson has become an even more successful company. Its sales and profits have grown every year, and many model changes have been introduced, so it is now the Japanese companies that copy Harley-Davidson. By March 2005 Harley-Davidson had actually surpassed General Motors in its stock market value: $17.7 billion versus $16.2 billion. Both these companies suffered losses during the financial crisis of 2008 and 2009, but Harley-Davidson continued to operate as usual (with a stock market value of $4.3 billion in mid-2009), whereas General Motors declared bankruptcy and required a government bailout (its stock market value fell to less than $0.5 billion). Although both companies can be expected to recover after the crisis, it is clear that General Motors—which once had the world's highest stock market value—has been surpassed by Harley-Davidson.

Was Protection Successful? Does this calculation mean that the infant industry protection was successful? A complete answer to that question involves knowing what would have happened if the tariff had *not* been put in place. When we say that infant industry protection is successful if the area *e* of future producer surplus gain ($131 million) exceeds the deadweight loss ($112.5 million), we are assuming that the firm would not have survived at all without the tariff protection. That assumption may be true for Harley-Davidson. It is well documented that Harley-Davidson was on the brink of bankruptcy from 1982 to 1983. Citibank had decided that it would not extend more loans to cover Harley's losses, and Harley found alternative financing on December 31, 1985, just one week before filing for bankruptcy.[16] If the tariff saved the company, then this was clearly a case of successful infant industry protection.

On the other hand, even if Harley-Davidson had not received the tariff and had filed for bankruptcy, it might still have emerged to prosper again. Bankruptcy does not mean that a firm stops producing; it just means that the firm's assets are used to repay all possible debts. Even if Harley-Davidson had gone bankrupt without the tariff, some or all of the future gains in producer surplus might have been realized. So we cannot be certain whether the turnaround of Harley-Davidson required the use of the tariff.[17]

Despite all these uncertainties, it still appears that the tariff on heavyweight motorcycles bought Harley-Davidson some breathing room. This is the view expressed by the chief economist at the ITC at that time, in the quotation at the beginning of the chapter: "If the case of heavyweight motorcycles is to be considered the only successful escape-clause [tariff], it is because it caused little harm and it helped Harley-Davidson get a bank loan so it could diversify."[18] We agree with this assessment that the harm caused by the tariff was small compared with the potential benefits of avoiding bankruptcy, which allowed Harley-Davidson to become the very successful company that it is today.

Computers in Brazil

There are many cases in which infant industry protection has not been successful. One well-known case involves the computer industry in Brazil. In 1977 the Brazilian government began a program to protect domestic firms involved in the production of personal computers (PCs). It was thought that achieving national autonomy in the computer industry was essential for strategic military reasons. Not only were imports of PCs banned, but domestic firms also had to buy from local suppliers whenever possible, and foreign producers of PCs were not allowed to operate in Brazil.

The Brazilian ban on imports lasted from 1977 to the early 1990s. This was a period of rapid innovations in PC production worldwide, with large drops in the cost of computing power. In Figure 8-11, we show the effective price of computing power in the United States and Brazil between 1982 and 1992, which fell very rapidly in both countries. The price we are graphing is "effective" because it is not just the retail price of a new PC but a price index that reflects the improvements over time in the PC's speed of calculations, storage capacity, and so on.

---

[16] See Peter C. Reid, 1990, *Made Well in America: Lessons from Harley-Davidson on Being the Best* (New York: McGraw-Hill).
[17] The chairman of Harley-Davidson stated in 1987 that the tariff had not actually helped the company that much because the Japanese producers were able to downsize some of their motorcycles to 699 cc engine size, and thereby avoid the tariff (*Wall Street Journal*, March 20, 1987, p. 39).
[18] John Suomela, chief economist at the U.S. International Trade Commission, as cited in Douglas A. Irwin, 2002, *Free Trade under Fire* (Princeton, NJ: Princeton University Press), pp. 136–137.

FIGURE 8-11

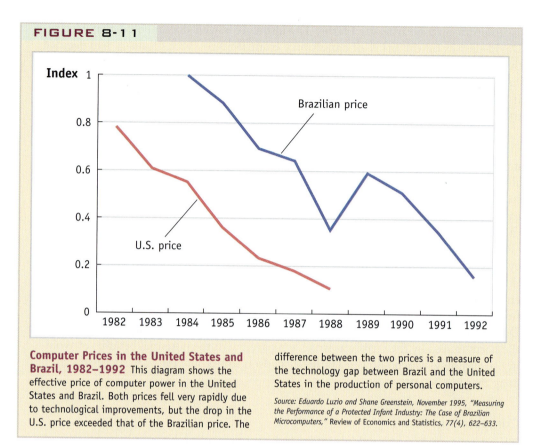

Computer Prices in the United States and Brazil, 1982–1992 This diagram shows the effective price of computer power in the United States and Brazil. Both prices fell very rapidly due to technological improvements, but the drop in the U.S. price exceeded that of the Brazilian price. The difference between the two prices is a measure of the technology gap between Brazil and the United States in the production of personal computers.

Source: Eduardo Luzio and Shane Greenstein, November 1995, "Measuring the Performance of a Protected Infant Industry: The Case of Brazilian Microcomputers," Review of Economics and Statistics, 77(4), 622–633.

Prices in Brazil Brazilian firms were adept at reverse engineering the IBM PCs being sold from the United States. But the reverse engineering took time, and the fact that Brazilian firms were required to use local suppliers for many parts within the computers added to the costs of production. We can see from Figure 8-11 that Brazil *never achieved the same low prices* as the United States. By 1992, for example, the effective prices in Brazil were between the prices that had been achieved in the United States four or five years earlier. The persistent gap between the prices in Brazil and the United States means that Brazil was never able to produce computers at competitive prices without tariff protection. This fact alone means that the infant industry protection was not successful.

Consumer and Producer Surplus In Table 8-3, we show the welfare calculation for Brazil, as well as other details of the PC industry. Local sales peaked at about $750 million in 1986, and the following year, the Brazilian prices rose to within 20% of those in the United States. But that is as close as the Brazilian industry ever got to world prices. In 1984 prices in Brazil were nearly double those in the United States, which led to a producer surplus gain of $29 million but a consumer surplus loss in Brazil of $80 million. The net loss was therefore $80 million – $29 million = $51 million, which was 0.02% of Brazilian gross domestic product (GDP) that year. By 1986 the net loss had grown to $164 million, or 0.06% of GDP. This net loss was the deadweight loss from the tariff during the years it was in place. The industry was never able to produce in the absence of tariffs, so there are no future gains (like area *e* in Figure 8-10) that we can count against those losses.

TABLE 8-3

Brazilian Computer Industry This table shows the effects of the government ban on imports of personal computers into Brazil.

Year	Sales ($ millions)	Brazil/U.S. Price (%)	Producer Surplus Gain ($ millions)	Consumer Surplus Loss ($ millions)	Net Loss ($ millions)	Net Loss (% of GDP)
1984	126	189	29	80	51	0.02
1985	384	159	70	179	109	0.04
1986	746	143	113	277	164	0.06
1987	644	119	50	112	62	0.02
1988	279	127	29	68	39	0.01

Source: Eduardo Luzio and Shane Greenstein, November 1995, "Measuring the Performance of a Protected Infant Industry: The Case of Brazilian Microcomputers," Review of Economics and Statistics, 77(4), 622–633.

Other Losses The higher prices in Brazil imposed costs on Brazilian industries that relied on computers in manufacturing, as well as on individual users, and they became increasingly dissatisfied with the government's policy. During his campaign in 1990, President Fernando Collor de Mello promised to abolish the infant industry protection for personal computers, which he did immediately after he was elected.

A number of reasons have been given for the failure of this policy to develop an efficient industry in Brazil: imported materials such as silicon chips were expensive to obtain, as were domestically produced parts that local firms were required to use; in addition, local regulations limited the entry of new firms into the industry. Whatever the reasons, this case illustrates how difficult it is to successfully nurture an infant industry and how difficult it is for the government to know whether temporary protection will allow an industry to survive in the future.

Protecting the Automobile Industry in China

The final example of infant industry protection that we discuss involves the automobile industry in China. In 2009 China overtook the United States as the largest automobile market in the world (measured by domestic sales plus imports). Strong competition among foreign firms located in China, local producers, and import sales have resulted in new models and falling prices so that the Chinese middle class can now afford to buy automobiles. In 2009 there were over 13 million vehicles sold in China, as compared with 10.4 million cars and light trucks sold in the United States.

Growth in automotive production and sales has been particularly strong since 2001, when China joined the World Trade Organization (WTO). With its accession to the WTO, China agreed to reduce its tariffs on foreign autos, which were as high as 260% in the early 1980s, then fell to 80 to 100% by 1996, and 25% by July 2006. The tariff on automobile parts was further cut from 25 to 10% in 2009. China has loosened its import quotas, as well. Those tariffs and quotas, in addition to restrictions at the province and city level on what type of cars could be sold, had limited China's imports and put a damper on the auto industry in that country. Prices were high and foreign producers were reluctant to sell their newest models to China. That situation has changed dramatically. Now, foreign firms scramble to compete in

Workers at the Shanghai General Motors Plant assemble a Buick.

China with their latest designs and are even making plans to export cars from China. Is the Chinese automobile industry a successful case of infant industry protection? Are the benefits gained by the current production and export of cars greater than the costs of the tariffs and quotas imposed in the past? To answer this, we begin by briefly describing the history of the Chinese auto industry.

Production in China Beginning in the early 1980s, China permitted a number of joint ventures between foreign firms and local Chinese partners. The first of these in 1983 was Beijing Jeep, which was a joint venture between American Motors Corporation (AMC—later acquired by Chrysler Corporation) and a local firm in Beijing. The following year, Germany's Volkswagen signed a 25-year contract to make passenger cars in Shanghai, and France's Peugeot agreed to another passenger car project to make vehicles in Guangzhou.

Although joint venture agreements provided a window for foreign manufacturers to tap the China market, there were limits on their participation. Foreign manufacturers could not own a majority stake in a manufacturing plant—Volkswagen's venture took the maximum of 50% foreign ownership. The Chinese also kept control of distribution networks for the jointly produced automobiles. These various regulations, combined with high tariff duties, helped at least some of the new joint ventures achieve success. Volkswagen's Shanghai plant was by the far the winner under these rules, and it produced more than 200,000 vehicles per year by the late 1990s, more than twice as many as any other plant. Volkswagen's success was also aided by some Shanghai municipal efforts. Various restrictions on engine size, as well as incentives offered to city taxi companies that bought Volkswagens, helped ensure that only Volkswagen's models could be sold in the Shanghai market; essentially, the Shanghai Volkswagen plant had a local monopoly.

That local monopoly has been eroded by entry into the Shanghai market, however. A recent example occurred in early 2009, when General Motors opened two new plants in Shanghai, at a cost of $1.5 billion and $2.5 billion each. General Motors is a leading producer in China, and locally produced 1.8 million of the 13 million vehicles sold in China in 2009. In fact, its profits from the Chinese market were the only bright spot on its global balance sheet that year, and served to offset some of its losses in the American market, as described in **HEADLINES: Shanghai Tie-Up Drives Profits for GM.**

Cost to Consumers The tariffs and quotas used in China kept imports fairly low throughout the 1990s, ranging from a high of 222,000 cars imported in 1993 to a low of 27,500 imports in 1998 and 160,000 cars in 2005. Since tariffs were in the range of 80 to 100% by 1996, import prices were approximately doubled because of the tariffs. But the quotas imposed on auto imports probably had at least as great an impact on prices of imports *and* domestically produced cars. Our analysis earlier in the chapter showed that quotas have a particularly large impact on domestic prices when the Home firm is a monopoly. That situation applied to the sales of Volkswagen's joint venture, in Shanghai, which enjoyed a local monopoly on the sales of its vehicles.

The effect of this local monopoly was to substantially increase prices in the Shanghai market. In Figure 8-12, we show the estimated markups of price over marginal costs for autos sold in China from 1995 to 2001, by various producers. The markups for Shanghai Volkswagen are the highest, reaching a high of 54% in 1998 and then falling to 28% in 2001, for an average of 42% for the period from 1995 to 2001. In comparison, the average markup charged by Tianjin Auto was 19%, and the average markup charged by Shanghai GM was 14%. All the other producers shown in Figure 8-12 have even lower markups.

From this evidence, it is clear that Shanghai Volkswagen was able to substantially raise its prices because of the monopoly power granted by the local government. Furthermore, the Jetta and Audi models produced by Shanghai Volkswagen during the 1990s were outdated models. That plant had the highest production through 2001, despite its high prices and outdated models, so a large number of consumers in the Shanghai area and beyond bore the costs of that local protection. This example illustrates how a Home monopoly can gain from protection at the expense of consumers. The example also illustrates how protection can stifle the incentive for firms to introduce the newest models and production techniques.

Gains to Producers For the tariffs and quotas used in China to be justified as infant industry protection, they should lead to a large enough drop in future costs so that the protection is no longer needed. China has not reached that point entirely, since it still

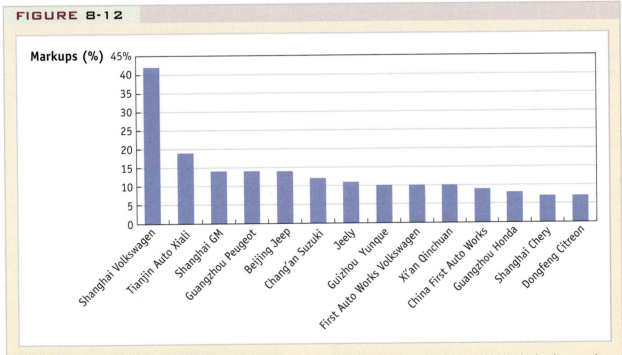

FIGURE 8-12

Markups (%)

Automobile Markups by Firms in China, 1995–2001
This diagram shows the percentage markups (price over marginal cost) applied to automobiles sold in China from 1995 to 2001, by various producers. The highest markup was charged by Shanghai Volkswagen, which had a local monopoly in Shanghai.

Source: Haiyan Deng, 2006, "Market Structure and Pricing Strategy of China's Automobile Industry."

HEADLINES

Shanghai Tie-Up Drives Profits for GM

This article discusses how partnerships in China have helped GM's profits.

If General Motors believes in God, it must be thanking Him right now for China.

Mainland Chinese sales were by far the brightest spot in GM's universe last year: sales in China rose 66 per cent while US sales fell by 30 per cent. One in four GM cars is now made in China. Even those cars made in Detroit were partly designed in Shanghai. GM managed to offload distressed assets to Chinese companies: the loss-making, environment-harming Hummer was sold to a previously unknown heavy equipment manufacturer, Sichuan Tengzhong [this sale was, however, blocked by the Chinese government in February 2010], and Beijing Automotive (BAIC) took some Saab technology off GM's hands. Perhaps most importantly of all, though, China agreed last year to bankroll GM's expansion in Asia.

In exchange for a deal to sell Chinese minicommercial vehicles in India, GM agreed to give up the 50-50 ownership of its leading mainland joint venture, Shanghai General Motors, ceding 51 per cent majority control to its Chinese partner, Shanghai Automotive Industry Corp (SAIC). The Sino-American partnership said this would be only the first of many such deals. Will observers one day look back at that deal and say that was the day GM signed over its future to the Chinese? And does that deal demonstrate how China can save GM—or hint that it might gobble it up?

"The quick answer is that Chinese consumers have already saved GM," says Klaus Paur of TNS auto consultancy in Shanghai, referring to stratospheric Chinese auto sales last year. Longer term, China cannot save the US carmaker singlehandedly. "If GM cannot save itself in the US and Europe, it's not going to be saved," says one GM insider who asked not to be named.

GM does not disclose its China profits but they are estimated at . . . perhaps $500 [million] last year when the Chinese car market had such a good year. "Half a billion in profits is not going to save a company that is losing $1[billion]-plus a quarter in the US," says the GM insider. But without China, GM probably cannot be saved at all. "Take China out of the GM portfolio, then that light at the end of the GM tunnel abruptly goes dim," says Mike Dunne of Dunne & Co, an Asia-based auto consultancy.

That is a remarkable reversal from a decade ago, when the Chinese auto industry was just getting on its feet and desperately needed GM investment. In 1997, when SGM was founded, China produced only 1.3m light vehicles. Next year's Chinese sales will be more than 10 times that figure. Kevin Wale, head of GM in China, defends the decision to cede majority control to his Chinese partner: "Relationships [in a joint venture] are much stronger than numbers. If you have a bad relationship, it doesn't matter if you have 70 per cent, you have a bad relationship. We have a fantastic relationship with SAIC." Whatever role China plays in GM's future, having a symbiotic relationship with the mainland looks like the smart bet for the time being.

Source: Patti Waldmeir, "Shanghai Tie-Up Drives Profits for GM," Financial Times, January 21, 2010.

imposes a tariff of 25% on autos, and a 10% tariff on auto parts. These tariff rates are much lower than in the past but still substantially protect the local market. So it is premature to point to the Chinese auto industry as a successful case of infant industry protection. Still, there are some important lessons that can be learned from its experience. First, there is no doubt that past protection contributed to the inflow of foreign firms to the Chinese market. All the foreign auto companies that entered China prior to its WTO accession in 2001 did so under high levels of protection, so that acquiring a local partner was the only way to sell locally: tariffs were too high to allow significant imports to China. As a result, local costs fell as Chinese partners gained from the technology transferred to them by their foreign partners. The **Headlines: Thanks to Detroit, China Is Poised to Lead** article explains that American firms are now transferring their best technologies to China. We can conclude that tariff protection combined with the ownership restrictions for joint ventures has led to a great deal of learning and reduced costs by the Chinese partners.

HEADLINES

Thanks to Detroit, China Is Poised to Lead

This article discusses the growth in the automobile industry in China, which has benefited from the investment of multinational firms from the United States and Europe.

CHONGQING, China—Volkswagen and other carmakers used to prosper by sending outdated factory equipment to China to produce older models no longer salable in the West. But competition has become so fierce here that Honda is about to introduce its latest version of the Civic only several months after it went on sale in Europe, Japan and the United States. Toyota, meanwhile, is assembling its Prius gasoline-electric sedan only in Japan and China.

When Ford Motor opened its first production line here in western China just three years ago, it used a layout copied from a Ford factory in the Philippines to produce 20,000 sedans a year based on a small car design taken from Ford operations in India. But this winter, Ford opened a second production line next door that is practically identical to one of its most advanced factories, the Saarlouis operation in southwestern Germany. The new line produces the Focus, the same small car it builds in

Germany (but different from the Focus sold in the United States). And with continuing improvements to the first line, it will bring total capacity here to 200,000 cars a year by June.

The Chinese managers here are not even satisfied with that. "I want to learn from Germany and then improve on it," said Li Jianping, the factory's vice director of manufacturing. Ford's success in rapidly expanding the scale and sophistication of its Chongqing operations illustrates how quickly the overall auto industry is expanding and modernizing in China. One requirement for a country to become an automobile exporter is to develop a highly competitive domestic market that demands excellent quality and efficiency, and China has managed to create just such a market. American and European carmakers, including Ford, General Motors, DaimlerChrysler and Volkswagen, as well as Toyota, Honda and Nissan of Japan are introducing their best technology to their plants in

China, and not only to compete against one another. They also face rapidly growing competition in the Chinese market from purely local companies like Geely, Chery and Lifan.

. . . Chinese automakers are also buying modern technology and design themselves. Chery has hired some of the best-known Italian auto design firms to spruce up its cars. When the MG Rover Group of Britain entered bankruptcy proceedings last year, the Nanjing Automobile Group outbid Shanghai Automotive to take control of Rover and its fairly modern engine-producing subsidiary, Powertrain Ltd., and move it to China. The Lifan Group, a car and motorcycle maker with headquarters several miles from the Ford plant here, is bidding to buy one of the world's most advanced engine factories, a joint venture of DaimlerChrysler and BMW in southern Brazil.

Source: Excerpted from Keith Bradsher and Jeremy W. Peters, "Thanks to Detroit, China Is Poised to Lead," New York Times, March 12, 2006.

Second, when we look carefully at which firms in China are now beginning to export, it is not necessarily those firms that benefited the most from protection. The **Headlines** article concludes by mentioning that the Lifan Group is bidding to buy one of the world's most advanced engine factories from Brazil and move it to China. Lifan is a Chinese motorcycle manufacturer and is leapfrogging into the automobile industry by purchasing ready-made plants. It is planning to export midsize sedans costing less than $10,000 to developing countries in Asia, the Mideast, and the Caribbean and then has its sights set on the United States. Two other Chinese firms, Geely and Chery, also intend to start exporting cars, but as of 2010 have not yet been successful.

Third, at least as important as the tariffs themselves is the rapid growth of income in China, which has led to a boom in domestic sales and to additional firms entering the market, such as Lifan. It is that rapid growth in income that has led

China to overtake the United States to become the largest automobile market in the world in 2009. Tariffs have contributed to the inflow of foreign investment, but it is now the consumers in China who are forcing firms to offer the newest models built with the most efficient techniques. For now, we must leave open the question of whether the high tariffs and quotas in China are responsible for the current success of its auto industry, or whether they just resulted in high prices and lagging model designs that slowed the development of the industry. It will be some years before researchers can look back at the development of this industry and identify the specific causes of its success. ■

6 Conclusions

In the previous chapter, we discussed the use of import tariffs and quotas under perfect competition and highlighted the difference between the small-country and large-country cases. With perfect competition, a small importing country loses from a tariff (because it cannot affect world prices), but the large importing country can potentially gain from a tariff (because the tariff depresses the world price). Import quotas have effects similar to those of import tariffs under perfect competition, so we often refer to quotas and tariffs as "equivalent."

We can contrast the results obtained under perfect competition with the results we learned in this chapter, in which we assume imperfect competition—either Home or Foreign monopoly. Under Home monopoly, the effects of a tariff and quota are very different. With a tariff, the Home monopolist can increase its price by the amount of the tariff (as would a competitive industry) but cannot exercise its monopoly power. With an import quota, however, the Home firm is able to charge a higher price than it could with a tariff because it enjoys a "sheltered" market. So the import quota leads to higher costs for Home consumers than the tariff, and these two policies are no longer "equivalent," as they are under perfect competition.

Under Foreign monopoly, the results are similar to those of the large-country case analyzed in the previous chapter: the tariff leads to a fall in the price received by the Foreign monopolist, so the price paid by Home consumers rises by *less than* the full amount of the tariff. The tariff is shared between an increase in the Home price and a decrease in the Foreign price, and the Home importer obtains a terms-of-trade gain. For small tariffs, the terms-of-trade gain exceeds the deadweight loss, and the Home country gains from the tariff. So this is a case where the use of a tariff as strategic trade policy can benefit the Home country, but at the expense of the Foreign firm.

A specific example of a tariff applied against a Foreign monopoly occurs when the Foreign firm is a discriminating monopoly and it dumps its output into Home at a lower price than it charges in its own local market. When dumping occurs, the importing country is permitted by WTO rules to respond with a tariff, which is called an antidumping duty. In principle, we might expect Home to gain from the duty because the Foreign firm will lower its price (as occurs for a tariff applied against a Foreign monopolist). But we have argued that the potential for Home gains from the antidumping duty are unlikely to arise because of special features in the way these duties are applied. Instead, the expected outcome from antidumping duties is that Foreign exporters raise prices even when a duty is *not* applied, leading to Home losses. Because of these losses, the use of antidumping duties as strategic trade policy is not effective.

Another topic discussed in this chapter is the infant industry case for protection. We studied three industries as examples of infant industry protection: Harley-Davidson motorcycles in the United States, computers in Brazil, and automobiles in China. The tariff given to protect Harley-Davidson motorcycles in the United States during the 1980s appears to have been successful because Harley-Davidson survived and has become very profitable. For computers in Brazil, the ban on imports during the 1980s was not successful because the industry was never able to learn enough from the world leaders to reach the same level of efficiency and competitive prices. Finally, automobile production in China has grown rapidly and overtaken the United States, but it is still protected by a 25% tariff, so it is too early to judge whether this is a successful case of infant industry protection. In addition, the rapid growth in the domestic income of Chinese consumers has been at least as important as past tariffs to the recent growth in production and sales.

KEY POINTS

1. Free trade will lead a Home monopoly in a small country to act in the same way as a perfectly competitive industry and charge a price equal to marginal cost. Therefore, competition from imports eliminates the monopoly power of the Home firm.

2. Quotas are not equivalent to tariffs when the Home firm is a monopolist. Because a quota limits the number of imports, the Home monopolist can charge higher prices than under a tariff, which results in greater costs to consumers.

3. When a tariff is applied against a Foreign monopolist, the results are similar to those of the large-country case analyzed in the previous chapter: the Foreign monopolist increases the price in the importing country by less than the full amount of the tariff and allows its own net-of-tariff price to fall. Hence, the tariff is shared between an increase in the Home price and a decrease in the Foreign price, a terms-of-trade gain for Home.

4. Dumping is the practice of a Foreign firm exporting goods at a price that is below its own domestic price or below its average cost of production. If the price charged for the exported good is above the firm's marginal cost, then dumping is profitable. We expect to observe dumping when the Foreign firm is acting like a discriminating monopolist.

5. Countries respond to dumping by imposing antidumping duties on imports. Antidumping duties are calculated as the difference between a Foreign firm's local price (or average costs) and its export price. To reduce or avoid the antidumping duties, Foreign firms can raise their export prices. That increase in price is a terms-of-trade loss for the importer and occurs because the Foreign firm can influence the duty.

6. In the United States and other countries, the use of antidumping tariffs far exceeds the use of safeguard tariffs. It is easy for domestic firms to bring a charge of dumping, and in many cases upholding the charge results in an increase in foreign prices and a decrease in competition for the domestic firm. The excessive use of antidumping cases also invites other countries to respond with their own charges of dumping.

7. An infant industry is a firm that requires protection to compete at world prices today. When a government applies a temporary tariff, it expects that costs for the firm or the industry overall will fall due to learning, thereby allowing it to compete at world prices in the future.

KEY TERMS

strategic trade policy, p. 242
discriminating monopoly, p. 243
dumping, p. 243
antidumping duty, p. 243
infant industry, p. 243

market power, p. 243
marginal revenue, p. 244
price discrimination, p. 258
discriminating monopoly, p. 258
safeguard tariff, p. 262

externality, p. 267
knowledge spillover, p. 267
market failure, p. 267

PROBLEMS

1. Figure 8-1 shows the Home no-trade equilibrium under perfect competition (with the price P^C) and under monopoly (with the price P^M). In this problem, we compare the welfare of Home consumers in these two situations.

   a. Under perfect competition, with the price P^C, label the triangle of consumer surplus and the triangle of producer surplus. Outline the area of total Home surplus (the sum of consumer surplus and producer surplus).

   b. Under monopoly, with the price P^M, label the consumer surplus triangle.

   c. Producer surplus is the same as the profits earned by the monopolist. To measure this, label the point in Figure 8-1 where the MR curve intersects MC as point B'. For selling the units between zero and Q^M, marginal costs rise along the MC curve, up to B'. The monopolist earns the difference between the price P^M and MC for each unit sold. Label the difference between the price and the MC curve as producer surplus, or profits.

   d. Outline the area of total Home surplus with a Home monopoly.

   e. Compare your answer to parts (a) and (d), and outline what the difference between these two areas is. What is this difference called and why?

2. Figure 8-2 shows the free-trade equilibrium under perfect competition and under monopoly (both with the price P^W). In this problem,

we compare the welfare of Home consumers in the no-trade situation and under free trade.

   a. Under perfect competition, with the price P^W, label the triangle of consumer surplus and the triangle of producer surplus. Outline the area of total Home surplus (the sum of consumer surplus and producer surplus).

   b. Based on your answer to part (a) in this problem and part (a) of the last problem, outline the area of gains from free trade under perfect competition.

   c. Under monopoly, still with the price P^W, again label the triangle of consumer surplus and the triangle of producer surplus.

   d. Based on your answer to part (c) in this problem and part (d) in the last problem, outline the area of gains from free trade under Home monopoly.

   e. Compare your answer to parts (b) and (d). That is, which area of gains from trade is higher and why?

3. Rank the following in ascending order of Home welfare and justify your answers. If two items are equivalent, indicate this accordingly.

   a. Tariff t in a small country with perfect competition

   b. Tariff t in a small country with a Home monopoly

   c. Quota with the same imports M in a small country, with a Home monopoly

   d. Tariff t in a country facing a Foreign monopoly

4. Refer to the prices of Japanese auto imports under the VER (Figure 8-5) and answer the following:

   a. What component of the price of imported automobiles from Japan rose the most over the period 1980 to 1985?

   b. Sketch how Figures 8-5 and 8-6 might have looked if the United States had applied a tariff to Japanese auto imports instead of the VER (with the same level of imports). In words, discuss how the import prices and U.S. prices might have compared under a tariff and the VER.

   c. Which policy—a tariff or the VER—would have been least costly to U.S. consumers?

5. In this problem, we analyze the effects of an import quota applied by a country facing a Foreign monopolist. In Figure 8-7, suppose that the Home country applies an import quota of X_2, meaning that the Foreign firm cannot sell any more than that amount.

   a. To achieve export sales of X_2, what is the highest price that the Foreign firm can charge?

   b. At the price you have identified in part (a), what is the Home consumer surplus?

   c. Compare the consumer surplus you identify in part (b) with the consumer surplus under free trade. Therefore, outline in Figure 8-7 the Home losses due to the quota. *Hint:* Remember that there is no Home firm, so you do not need to take into account Home producer surplus or tariff revenue. Assume that quota rents go to Foreign firms.

   d. Based on your answer to (c), which has the greater loss to the Home country—a tariff or a quota, leading to the same level of sales X_2 by the Foreign firm?

6. Suppose that the demand curve for a good is represented by the straight line

   $$P = 10 - Q$$

Fill in the missing information in the following chart:

Quantity	Price	Total Revenue	Marginal Revenue
0			NA
1			
2			
3			
4			
5			
6			
7			
8			
9			
10			

   a. Draw a graph containing both the demand curve and marginal revenue curve.

   b. Is the marginal revenue curve a straight line as well? What is the slope of the marginal revenue curve? How does that slope compare with that of the demand curve?

   c. Does the marginal revenue curve contain negative values over the specified range of quantities? Explain why or why not.

7. Consider the case of a Foreign monopoly with no Home production, shown in Figure 8-7. Starting from free trade at point A, consider a $10 tariff applied by the Home government.

   a. If the demand curve is linear, as in Problem 6, what is the shape of the marginal revenue curve?

   b. How much does the tariff-inclusive Home price increase because of the tariff, and how much does the net-of-tariff price received by the Foreign firm fall?

   c. Discuss the welfare effects of implementing the tariff. Use a graph to illustrate under what conditions, if any, there is an increase in Home welfare.

8. Suppose the Home firm is considering whether to enter the Foreign market. Assume that the Home firm has the following costs and demand:

Fixed costs	=	$140
Marginal costs	=	$10 per unit
Local price	=	$25
Local quantity	=	20
Export price	=	$15
Export quantity	=	10

a. Calculate the firm's total costs from selling only in the local market.

b. What is the firm's average cost from selling only in the local market?

c. Calculate the firm's profit from selling only in the local market.

d. Should the Home firm enter the Foreign market? Briefly explain why.

e. Calculate the firm's profit from selling to both markets.

f. Is the Home firm dumping? Briefly explain.

9. Suppose that in response to a *threatened* antidumping duty of *t*, the Foreign monopoly raises its price by the amount *t*.

a. Illustrate the losses for the Home country.

b. How do these losses compare with the losses from a safeguard tariff of the amount *t*, applied by the Home country against the Foreign monopolist?

c. In view of your answers to (a) and (b), why are antidumping cases filed so often?

10. Why is it necessary to use a market failure to justify the use of infant industry protection?

11. What is a positive externality? Explain the argument of knowledge spillovers as a potential reason for infant industry protection.

12. If infant industry protection is justified, is it better for the Home country to use a tariff or a quota, and why?

13. Figures A, B, and C are taken from a paper by Chad Bown: "The Pattern of Antidumping and Other Types of Contingent Protection" (World Bank, PREM Notes No. 144, October 21, 2009).

a. Figure A shows the number of newly initiated trade remedy investigations, including safeguard (SF), China safeguard (CSF), antidumping (AD), and countervailing duty (CVD) (a countervailing duty is used when foreign firms receive a subsidy from their government, and then the CVD prevents them from charging lower prices in the importing country). Each bar shows the number of new cases in each quarter of the year (Q1, Q2, etc.) for 2007 through 2009. The number of cases is graphed separately for developing countries and developed countries. What does this graph tell us about what has happened to the number of such cases since 2007? What might have caused this pattern?

b. Figure B shows the number of safeguard (SF) tariff initiations by WTO members. Since 1995 what three years saw the largest numbers of safeguards? What might explain these increases? (Hint: Consider the U.S. business cycle over these years.)

c. According to Figure B, year 2002 had the most safeguards actions by WTO members. How many action were started that year, and what U.S. safeguard case that year was discussed in this chapter?

FIGURE A

FIGURE B

FIGURE C

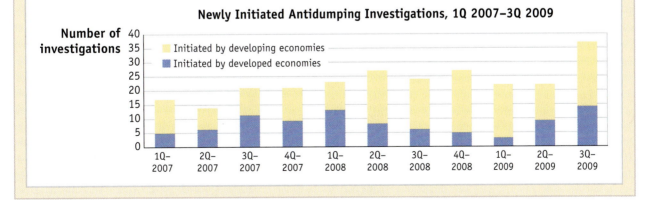

Source: Chad P. Bown, "The Pattern of Antidumping and Other Types of Contingent Protection," World Bank, PREM Notes No. 144, October 21, 2009.

http://www.web.worldbank.org/WBSITE/EXTERNAL/EXTABOUTUS/ORGANIZATION/EXTPREMNET/0,,contentMDK:22357994~pagePK:64159605~
piPK:64157667~theSitePK:489961,00.html.

d. Figure C shows the number of newly initiated antidumping (AD) investigations, for quarters of the year from 2007 through 2009. Compare the number of cases in this graph with Figure A, which included safe-guard (SF), China safeguard (CSF), antidumping (AD), and countervailing duty (CVD). What can you conclude about the total number of SF, CSF, and CVD cases as compared with the number of AD cases?

International Agreements: Trade, Labor, and the Environment

Seattle was a riot, they tried to pin on us.
But we didn't show up, with gas and billy clubs
An un-armed mass of thousands, just trying to be heard.
But there are no world leaders that want to hear our words.

Lyrics from "Seattle Was a Riot" by the punk-rock band Anti-Flag, 1999

We now have a Copenhagen Accord which I think contains a number of very significant elements. . . . But not an accord that is legally binding. Not an accord that, at this moment, pins down industrialised countries to individual targets. Not an accord that at this stage specifies what major developing countries will do.

Yvo de Boer, Executive Secretary of the United Nations Framework Convention on Climate Change, December 19, 2009

In 1999 policy makers from around the world met in Seattle, Washington, to discuss the next round of trade negotiations under the World Trade Organization (WTO). But the meeting never achieved that goal because it was disrupted by large groups of protesters who filled the streets. The protest at times turned violent (as described in the lyrics above from "Seattle Was a Riot"). The scale of these protests took many people by surprise; after all, discussions about trade reform had been occurring since the General Agreement on Trade and Tariffs (GATT) was formed in 1947, but never before had there been such an organized protest against it. What explains this grassroots movement against the WTO?

In past rounds of negotiations, the GATT and now the WTO have been successful in lowering tariffs in most sectors of its members' economies. The barriers to trade remaining for the WTO to address now go beyond tariffs and involve issues of national interest that are indirectly related to trade. One of those issues is the environment. Most countries have national laws governing environmental

In protests at the 1999 meeting of the World Trade Organization in Seattle, Washington, environmentalists dressed as turtles and other endangered species that had been affected by recent WTO rulings.

issues, such as the use of pesticides or genetically modified organisms, the protection of endangered species, the extent to which firms can release pollutants into the atmosphere, the harvesting of renewable and nonrenewable resources, and so on. Inevitably, some of these rules will also affect international trade, and that is where the WTO comes in. Under the Uruguay Round of negotiations (1986–1994), the WTO toughened its own rules governing the extent to which national laws can affect international trade. Countries that believed they were excluded from a foreign market because of unreasonable environmental standards there could bring a dispute before the WTO, where a panel of judges in Geneva would rule on the case. In principle, the panel's ruling would be binding on the countries involved.

The new WTO rules governing environmental regulations infuriated grassroots groups in the United States and abroad. Just before the Seattle meeting, these environmental groups formed a coalition with union leaders, religious groups, third-world activists, and others who believed that the WTO might threaten the interests of those whom they represent. In addition, a wide range of political groups—from conservatives to anarchists—believed it was undesirable for a WTO panel in Geneva to make rulings that would affect U.S. regulations. Members of all these groups gathered in Seattle to voice their dissatisfaction with the WTO. The environmentalists dressed as dolphins, turtles, and other endangered species that had been affected by recent WTO rulings. The scenes of these costumed creatures marching arm in arm with steelworkers gave an entirely new image to protests against the WTO.

Protesters at the U.N. climate change conference, Copenhagen, December 2009.

Protests over the environment were also evident at a meeting 10 years later, in December 2009, held in Copenhagen, Denmark. Called the Copenhagen Climate Summit, this international meeting was supposed to establish binding reductions for countries' emissions of greenhouse gases. Hundreds of protesters were arrested and thousands more attended rallies, some dressed as polar bears and panda bears to highlight the threat of gobal warming to the habitat of those animals. Although expectations for the summit were high, the meeting unfortunately broke up without any binding commitments from countries to reduce their greenhouse gas emissions, as indicated in the quotation at the beginning of the chapter from Yvo de Boer, Executive Secretary of the United Nations Framework Convention on Climate Change.[1]

The goal of this chapter is to examine why international agreements like those negotiated under the WTO for trade, and those negotiated for environmental reasons like the Copenhagen Climate Summit, are needed. We begin by reviewing the reasons why international agreements dealing with tariffs

---

[1] Two months after the Copenhagen Climate Summit, Mr. Yvo de Boer resigned his position.

are needed. As we discussed in an earlier chapter, countries that are large can influence the price they pay for imports by applying an import tariff: the tariff increases the import price for consumers in the large country but lowers the price received by foreign exporting firms. The reduction in the price received by exporters is a **terms-of-trade gain** for the importing country. We show in this chapter that when two or more countries apply tariffs against each other in an attempt to capture this terms-of-trade gain, they both end up losing. The terms-of-trade gain for one country is canceled by the use of a tariff in another country, so both countries wind up losing as a result of the tariffs.

To avoid such losses, international agreements to reduce tariffs and move toward free trade are needed. These international agreements take several forms. The WTO is a **multilateral agreement,** involving many countries, with agreement to lower tariffs between all the members. There are also smaller **regional trade agreements,** involving several countries, often located near each other. The North American Free Trade Agreement (NAFTA) and the European Union are both examples of regional trade agreements, which lead to free trade among the countries who are parties to the agreement. A very recent example is an agreement between China and the Association of Southest Asian Nations (ASEAN) for the China-ASEAN free-trade area. That agreement eliminated tariffs on 90% of products traded between China and six members of ASEAN—Brunei, Indonesia, Malaysia, Philippines, Singapore, and Thailand—on January 1, 2010, with the remaining four countries of the association (Cambodia, Laos, Myanmar, and Vietnam) added by 2015. This Asian free-trade area covers nearly 1.9 billion people, or more than one-quarter of the world's population. In economic terms, it is the third largest free-trade area in the world, after the European Union and NAFTA.

Besides eliminating tariffs on trade, the NAFTA agreement had two other "side agreements": one involved the rights of workers in each country, and the other involved the environment. In this chapter, we discuss the extent to which NAFTA and other labor agreements protect the rights of workers, then we discuss international agreements on the environment. Rulings at the WTO have an indirect impact on the environment, which is what concerned many protesters in Seattle. But other international agreements, such as that attempted at the Copenhagen Climate Summit and its precursor, the Kyoto Protocol, have a more direct impact. Both of these agreements were intended to reduce carbon dioxide emissions worldwide and therefore slow global warming. We argue that for "global" pollutants such as carbon dioxide, countries do not fully recognize the environmental costs of their economic activity. International agreements are needed to ensure that countries recognize these environmental costs, and such agreements are in the best interests of the world community, even though they are hard to achieve.

1 International Trade Agreements

When countries seek to reduce trade barriers between themselves, they enter into a **trade agreement**—a pact to reduce or eliminate trade restrictions. Multilateral trade agreements occur among a large set of countries, such as the members of the WTO, that have negotiated many "rounds" of trade agreements. Under the **most favored nation principle** of the WTO, the lower tariffs agreed to in multilateral negotiations must be extended *equally* to all WTO members (see Article I in **Side Bar: Key Provisions of the GATT,** in a previous chapter). Countries joining the

WTO enjoy the low tariffs extended to all member countries but must also agree to lower their own tariffs.

The WTO is an example of a multilateral trade agreement, which we analyze first in this section. To demonstrate the logic of multilateral agreements, we assume for simplicity that there are only two countries in the world that enter into an agreement; however, the theoretical results that we obtain also apply when there are many countries. The important feature of multilateral agreements is that no countries are *left out* of the agreement.

Following our discussion of multilateral agreements, we analyze regional trade agreements that occur between smaller groups of countries and find that the implications of regional trade agreements differ from those of multilateral trade agreements. When entering into a regional trade agreement, countries agree to eliminate tariffs between themselves but do not reduce tariffs against the countries left out of the agreement. For example, the United States has many regional trade agreements, including those with Israel, Jordan, Chile, with the countries of Central America and the Dominican Republic (through an agreement called CAFTA-DR), and new agreements being planned with South Korea, Panama, and Colombia, which have not been ratified.[2] In South America, the countries of Argentina, Brazil, Paraguay, Uruguay, and Venezuela belong to a free-trade area called Mercosur. In fact, there are more than 200 free-trade agreements worldwide, which some economists feel threaten the WTO as the major forum for multilateral trade liberalization.

The Logic of Multilateral Trade Agreements

Before we begin our analysis of the effects of multilateral trade agreements, let's review the effects of tariffs imposed by large countries under perfect competition.

Tariffs for a Large Country In Figure 9-1, we show the effects of a large-country (Home) tariff, repeated from an earlier chapter. We previously found that a tariff leads to a deadweight loss for Home, which is the sum of consumption and production losses, of area $(b + d)$ in Figure 9-1. In addition, the tariff leads to a terms-of-trade gain for Home, which is area e, equal to the reduction in Foreign price due to the tariff, $(P^W - P^*)$, multiplied by the amount of Home imports under the tariff, $(D_2 - S_2)$. If Home applies an optimal tariff, then its terms-of-trade gain exceeds its deadweight loss, so that $e > (b + d)$. Panel (b) shows that for the rest of the world (which in our two-country case is just Foreign), the tariff leads to a deadweight loss f from producing an inefficiently low level of exports relative to free trade, and a terms-of-trade loss e due to the reduction in its export prices. That is, the Home terms-of-trade gain comes at the expense of an equal terms-of-trade loss e for Foreign, plus a Foreign deadweight loss f.

Payoff Matrix This quick review of the welfare effects of a large-country tariff under perfect competition can be used to derive some new results. Although our earlier analysis indicated that it is optimal for large countries to impose small positive tariffs, that rationale ignored the strategic interaction among *multiple* large countries. If every country imposes even a small positive tariff, is it still optimal behavior for each country individually? We can use game theory to model the strategic choice of whether or

---

[2] The free-trade agreements with these three countries were negotiated by President George W. Bush before leaving office in January 2009, but not ratified by Congress. President Obama mentioned these agreements in his State of the Union address on January 27, 2010, saying that: "we will strengthen our trade relations in Asia and with key partners like South Korea and Panama and Colombia."

FIGURE 9-1

(a) Home Market

(b) World Market

Tariff for a Large Country The tariff shifts up the export supply curve from X^* to $X^* + t$. As a result, the Home price increases from P^W to $P^* + t$, and the Foreign price falls from P^W to P^*. The deadweight loss at Home is the area of the triangle $(b + d)$, and Home also has a terms-of-trade gain of area e. Foreign loses the area $(e + f)$, so the net loss in world welfare is the triangle $(b + d + f)$.

not to apply a tariff, and use a payoff matrix to determine the Nash equilibrium outcome for each country's tariff level. A Nash equilibrium occurs when each player is taking the action that is the best response (i.e., yielding the highest payoff) to the action of the other player.

In Figure 9-2, we show a payoff matrix between the Home and Foreign countries (both large), each of which has to decide whether to impose a tariff against the other country. Each quadrant of the matrix includes Home's payoff in the lower-left corner and Foreign's payoff in the upper-right corner. We will start with a situation of free trade and then measure the change in welfare for Home or Foreign by applying a tariff. For convenience, we will also assume that the two countries are exactly the same size, so their payoffs are symmetric.

Free Trade When both countries do not impose tariffs, we are in a free-trade situation, shown in the upper-left quadrant. For convenience, let us write the payoffs for the two countries under free trade as zero, which means that we will measure the payoffs in any other situation as *relative to* free trade.

Tariffs First, suppose that Home imposes a tariff but Foreign does not. Then the Home payoff as compared with free trade is $e - (b + d)$ (which is positive for an optimal tariff), and the Foreign payoff is $-(e + f)$, the terms-of-trade and deadweight losses described previously. These payoffs are shown in the lower-left quadrant of the matrix. Now suppose that Foreign imposes a tariff but Home does not. Because we have assumed that the Home and Foreign countries are the same size, they have the same potential payoffs from using a tariff. Under these circumstances, the Foreign

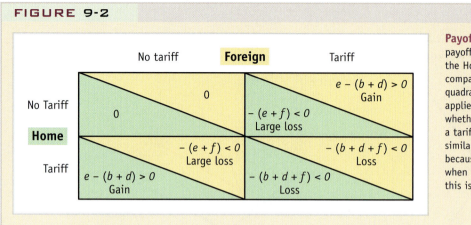

FIGURE 9-2

Payoffs in a Tariff Game This payoff matrix shows the welfare of the Home and Foreign countries as compared with free trade (upper-left quadrant in which neither country applies a tariff). Welfare depends on whether one or both countries apply a tariff. The structure of payoffs is similar to the "prisoner's dilemma" because both countries suffer a loss when they both apply tariffs, and yet this is the unique Nash equilibrium.

payoff from its own tariff is $e - (b + d) > 0$, and the Home payoff is the loss $-(e + f)$. These two payoffs are shown in the upper-right quadrant of the matrix.

Finally, suppose that *both* countries impose optimal tariffs and that the tariffs are the same size. Then the terms-of-trade gain that each country gets from its own tariff is canceled out by the terms-of-trade loss it suffers because of the other country's tariff. In that case, neither country gets any terms-of-trade gain but both countries still suffer a deadweight loss. That deadweight loss is $(b + d)$ from each country's own tariffs plus area f, the deadweight loss from the other country's tariff. The total deadweight loss for each country is $-(b + d + f)$, as shown in the lower-right quadrant of the matrix.

Prisoner's Dilemma The pattern of payoffs in Figure 9-2 has a special structure called the **prisoner's dilemma.** The "prisoner's dilemma" refers to a game in which two accomplices are caught for a crime that they committed, and each has to decide whether to confess. They are kept in separate cells, so they cannot communicate with each other. If one confesses and the other does not, then the person confessing will get a much lighter jail sentence and is better off than taking the chance of being found guilty in a trial. But if they both confess, then they both go to jail for the full sentence. This is like the pattern in Figure 9-2, in which each country acting on its own has an incentive to apply a tariff, but if they both apply tariffs, they will both be worse off.

Nash Equilibrium The only Nash equilibrium in Figure 9-2 is for both countries to apply a tariff (lower-right quadrant). Starting at that point, if either country eliminates its tariff, then it loses $(e + f)$ as compared with free trade, rather than $(b + d + f)$. Because we know that $e > (b + d)$ for an optimal tariff, it follows that each country acting on its own is worse off by moving to free trade (i.e., removing its tariff). That is, the loss $(e + f)$ is greater than the loss $(b + d + f)$. As a result, the Nash equilibrium is for both countries to apply a tariff.

But, like having both prisoners confess, the outcome for both countries when each country applies a tariff is quite bad. They both suffer the deadweight losses that arise from their own tariff and their partner's tariff, without any terms-of-trade gain. The Nash equilibrium in this case leads to an outcome that is undesirable for both countries even though it is the best outcome for each country given that the other country is imposing a tariff.

Trade Agreement This bad outcome can be avoided if the countries enter into some kind of trade agreement. In an earlier chapter, for example, we saw how the WTO dispute-settlement mechanism came into play when the steel tariffs applied by President Bush became problematic for the United States' trading partners. The EU filed a case at the WTO objecting to these tariffs, and it was ruled that the tariffs did not meet the criterion for a safeguard tariff. As a result, the WTO ruled that European countries could *retaliate* by imposing tariffs of their own against U.S. exports. The threat of these tariffs led President Bush to eliminate the steel tariffs ahead of schedule, and the outcome moved from both countries potentially applying tariffs to both countries having zero tariffs. Likewise, China has requested that the WTO launch an investigation to determine whether the tariff on tires applied by President Obama meets the criterion of the relevant trade laws. If not, then China would be entitled to retaliate, and this threat could possibly lead to the removal of the tariff on tires before its three-year expiration date.

Thus, the WTO mechanism eliminated the prisoner's dilemma by providing an incentive to remove tariffs; the outcome was in the preferred upper-left quadrant of the payoff matrix in Figure 9-2, rather than the original Nash equilibrium in the lower-right quadrant. The same logic comes into play when countries agree to join the WTO. They are required to reduce their own tariffs, but in return, they are also assured of receiving lower tariffs from other WTO members. That assurance enables countries to mutually reduce their tariffs and move closer to free trade.

Regional Trade Agreements

Under regional trade agreements, several countries eliminate tariffs among themselves but maintain tariffs against countries outside the region. Such regional trade agreements are permitted under Article XXIV of the GATT (see **Side Bar: Key Provisions of the GATT,** in an earlier chapter). That article states that countries can enter into such agreements provided they do not jointly increase their tariffs against outside countries.

Although they are authorized by the GATT, regional trade agreements contradict the most favored nation principle, which states that every country belonging to the GATT/WTO should be treated equally. The countries included in a regional trade agreement are treated better (since they face zero tariffs) than the countries excluded. For this reason, regional trade agreements are sometimes called **preferential trade agreements,** to emphasize that the member countries are favored over other countries. Despite this violation of the most favored nation principle, regional trade agreements are permitted because it is thought that the removal of trade barriers among expanding groups of countries is one way to achieve freer trade worldwide.

Regional trade agreements can be classified into two basic types: free-trade areas and customs unions.

Free-Trade Area A **free-trade area** is a group of countries agreeing to eliminate tariffs (and other barriers to trade) among themselves but keeping whatever tariffs they formerly had with the rest of the world. In 1989 Canada entered into a free-trade agreement with the United States under which tariffs between the two countries were eliminated over the next decade. Known as the Canada-U.S. Free Trade Agreement, it was signed five years before the agreement with Mexico, in 1994, that created free trade among all three countries under the North American Free Trade Agreement (NAFTA). Each of these countries has its own tariffs with all other countries of the world.

Customs Union A **customs union** is similar to a free-trade area, except that in addition to eliminating tariffs among countries in the union, the countries within a customs union also agree to a *common* schedule of tariffs with each country outside the union. Examples of customs unions include the countries in the European Union (EU) and the signatory countries of Mercosur in South America. All countries in the EU have identical tariffs with respect to each outside country; the same holds for the countries in Mercosur.[3]

Rules of Origin The fact that the countries in a free-trade area do not have common tariffs for outside countries, as do countries within a customs union, leads to an obvious problem with free-trade areas: if China, for example, wants to sell a good to Canada, what would prevent it from first exporting the good to the United States or Mexico, whichever has the lowest tariff, and then shipping it to Canada? The answer is that free-trade areas have complex **rules of origin** that specify what type of goods can be shipped duty-free within the free-trade area.

A good entering Mexico from China, for example, is not granted duty-free access to the United States or Canada, unless that good is first incorporated into another product in Mexico, giving the new product enough "North American content" to qualify for duty-free access. So China or any other outside country cannot just choose the lowest-tariff country through which to enter North America. Rather, products can be shipped duty-free between countries only if most of their production occurred within North America. To determine whether this criterion has been satisfied, the rules of origin must specify—for each and every product—how much of its production (as determined by value-added or the use of some key inputs) took place in North America. As you can imagine, it takes many pages to specify these rules for each and every product, and it is said that the rules of origin for NAFTA take up more space in the agreement than all other considerations combined!

Notice that these rules are not needed in a customs union because in that case the tariffs on outside members are the same for all countries in the union: there is no incentive to import a good into the lowest-tariff country. So why don't countries just create a customs union, making the rules of origin irrelevant? The answer is that modifying the tariffs applied against an outside country is a politically sensitive issue. The United States, for example, might want a higher tariff on textiles than Canada or Mexico, and Mexico might want a higher tariff on corn. NAFTA allows each of these three countries to have its own tariffs for each commodity on outside countries. So despite the complexity of rules of origin, they allow countries to enter into a free-trade agreement without modifying their tariffs on outside countries.

Now that we understand the difference between free-trade areas and customs unions, let us set that difference aside and focus on the main economic effects of regional trade agreements, by which we mean free-trade areas or customs unions.

---

[3] When new countries enter the EU or Mercosur, they must adjust their outside tariffs to the customs union level. Sometimes that will mean *increasing* a tariff on an outside member, as occurred when West Germany joined the European Economic Community in 1962. Germany increased the tariff that it charged on imported U.S. poultry, to be in accordance with the tariffs charged by the European Economic Community on U.S. imports, and in retaliation, the United States increased its tariffs on trucks and other products imported from Germany. This episode became known as the "chicken war." The tariff of 25% on trucks applied by the United States became a permanent item in the U.S. tariff code and today applies to compact trucks imported by the United States from Japan (see Application: Import Tariffs on Japanese Trucks in an earlier chapter).

Trade Creation and Trade Diversion

When a regional trade agreement is formed and trade increases between member countries, the increase in trade can be of two types. The first type of trade increase, **trade creation,** occurs when a member country imports a product from another member country that formerly it produced for itself. In this case, there is a gain in consumer surplus for the importing country (by importing greater amounts of goods at lower prices) and a gain in producer surplus for the exporting country (from increased sales). These gains from trade are analogous to those that occur from the opening of trade in the Ricardian or Heckscher–Ohlin models. No other country inside or outside the trade agreement is affected because the product was not traded before. Therefore, trade creation brings welfare gains for both countries involved.

The second reason for trade to increase within a regional agreement is due to **trade diversion,** which occurs when a member country imports a product from another member country that it formerly imported *from a country outside of the new trade region.* The article **Headlines: China-ASEAN Treaty Threatens Indian Exporters** gives an example of trade diversion that could result from the free-trade agreement between the China and the ASEAN countries, implemented on January 1, 2010.

HEADLINES

China-ASEAN Treaty Threatens Indian Exporters

This article discusses the China-ASEAN free-trade area, implemented on January 1, 2010. By eliminating tariffs between China and the ASEAN countries, this free-trade area will make it more difficult for India to export to those countries, which is an example of trade diversion.

BEIJING—Indian exporters are faced with a new challenge as the free trade agreement between China and members of the Association of Southeast Asian Nations became operational on Friday. It will mean nearly zero duty trade between several Asian nations making it difficult for Indian businesses to sell a range of products.

India has been planning to enlarge its trade basket to include several commodities that are now supplied to China by ASEAN countries. These products include fruits, vegetables and grains. Indian products, which will face 10–12 per cent import duty [tariff], may find it extremely difficult to survive the competition from ASEAN nations. China is cutting tariffs on imports from ASEAN nations from an average of 9.8 per cent to about 0.1 per cent. The original members of ASEAN—Brunei, Indonesia, Malaysia, the Philippines, Singapore and Thailand—have also agreed to dramatically cut import duty on Chinese products from an average of 12.8 per cent to just 0.6 per cent. The newly created free trade area involves 11 countries will a total population of 1.9 billion and having a combined gross domestic product of $6 trillion.

The successful implementation of the FTA is bound to force New Delhi to expatiate similar trade agreements with countries in the ASEAN region besides China. India is in the process of discussing trade agreements with several countries including China. New Delhi has also inked agreements with Beijing on the supply of fruits, vegetables and Basmati rice. But they remain to be implemented. At present, 58 per cent of Indian exports to China consists of iron ore with very little component of value added goods. India has been trying to widen the trade basket to include manufactured goods, fruits and vegetables. This effort might be severely hit because goods from ASEAN nations will now cost much less to the Chinese consumer. . . .

Source: Excerpted from Saibal Dasgupta, "China-ASEAN Treaty Threatens Indian Exporters," The Times of India, January 3, 2010.

Numerical Example of Trade Creation and Diversion

To illustrate the potential for trade diversion, we use an example from NAFTA, in which the United States might import auto parts from Mexico that it formerly imported from Asia.[4] Let us keep track of the gains and losses for the countries involved. Asia will lose export sales to North America, so it suffers a loss in producer surplus in its exporting industry. Mexico gains producer surplus by selling the auto parts. The problem with this outcome is that Mexico is not the most efficient (lowest cost) producer of auto parts: we know that Asia is more efficient because that is where the United States initially purchased its auto parts. Because the United States is importing from a less efficient producer, there is some potential loss for the United States due to trade diversion. We can determine whether this is indeed the case by numerically analyzing the cases of trade creation and trade diversion.

Suppose that the costs to the United States of importing an auto part from Mexico or from Asia are as shown in Table 9-1. The rightmost columns show the total costs of the part under free trade (zero tariff), with a 10% tariff and 20% tariff, respectively. Under free trade, the auto part can be produced in Mexico for $20 or in Asia for $19. Thus, Asia is the most efficient producer. If the United States purchased the part from an American supplier, it would cost $22, as shown in the last row of the table. With a tariff of 10%, the costs of importing from Mexico or Asia are increased to $22 and $20.90, respectively. Similarly, a 20% tariff would increase the cost of importing to $24 and $22.80, respectively. Under NAFTA, however, the cost of importing from Mexico is $20 regardless of the tariff.

With the data shown in Table 9-1, we can examine the effect of NAFTA on each country's welfare. First, suppose that the tariff applied by the United States is 20%, as shown in the last column. Before NAFTA, it would have cost $24 to import the auto part from Mexico, $22.80 to import it from Asia, and $22 to produce it locally in the United States. Before NAFTA, then, producing the part in the United States for $22 is the cheapest option. With the tariff of 20%, therefore, there are no imports of this auto part into the United States.

Trade Creation When Mexico joins NAFTA, it pays no tariff to the United States, whereas Asia continues to have a 20% tariff applied against it. After NAFTA, the United States will import the part from Mexico for $20 because the price is less than the U.S. cost of $22. Therefore, all the auto parts will be imported from Mexico. This is an example of trade creation. The United States clearly gains from the

TABLE 9-1

Cost of Importing an Automobile Part This table shows the cost to the United States of purchasing an automobile part from various source countries, with and without tariffs. If there is a 20% tariff on all countries, then it would be cheapest for the United States to buy the auto part from itself (for $22). But when the tariff is eliminated on Mexico after NAFTA, then the United States would instead buy from that country (for $20), which illustrates the idea of trade creation. If instead we start with a 10% tariff on all countries, then it would be cheapest for the United States to buy from Asia (for $20.90). When the tariff on Mexico is eliminated under NAFTA, then the United States would instead buy there (for $20), illustrating the idea of trade diversion.

	U.S. Tariff		
	0%	10%	20%
From Mexico, before NAFTA	$20	$22	$24
From Asia, before NAFTA	$19	$20.90	$22.80
From Mexico, after NAFTA	$20	$20	$20
From Asia, after NAFTA	$19	$20.90	$22.80
From the United States	$22	$22	$22

---

[4] The largest exporters of auto parts to the United States currently are Canada, Mexico, and Japan. So the Asian country in this example can be thought of as Japan. In the future, however, China is expected to become a major exporter of auto parts, especially for the labor-intensive parts now produced in Mexico.

lower cost of the auto part; Mexico gains from being able to export to the United States; and Asia neither gains nor loses, because it never sold the auto part to the United States to begin with.

Trade Diversion Now suppose instead that the U.S. tariff on auto parts is 10% (the middle column of Table 9-1). Before NAFTA, the United States can import the auto part from Mexico for $22 or from Asia for $20.90. It still costs $22 to produce the part at home. In this case, the least-cost option is for the United States to import the auto part from Asia. When Mexico joins NAFTA, however, this outcome changes. It will cost $20 to import the auto part from Mexico duty-free, $20.90 to import it from Asia subject to the 10% tariff, and $22 to produce it at home. The least-cost option is to import the auto part from Mexico. Because of the establishment of NAFTA, the United States *switches* the source of its imports from Asia to Mexico, an example of trade diversion.

Producer surplus in Asia falls because it loses its export sales to the United States, whereas producer surplus in Mexico rises. What about the United States? Before NAFTA, it imported from Asia at a price of $20.90, of which 10% (or $1.90 per unit) consisted of the tariff. The net-of-tariff price that Asia received for the auto parts was $19. After NAFTA the United States instead imports from Mexico, at the price of $20, but it does not collect any tariff revenue at all. So the United States gains 90¢ on each unit from paying a lower price, but it also loses $1.90 in tariff revenue from not purchasing from Asia. From this example, it seems that importing the auto part from Mexico is not a very good idea for the United States because it no longer collects tariff revenue. To determine the overall impact on U.S. welfare, we can analyze the same example in a graph.

Trade Diversion in a Graph

In Figure 9-3, we show the free-trade price of the auto part from Asia as P_{asia}, and the free-trade export supply curve from Asia is the horizontal line labeled S_{asia}. By treating this price as fixed, we are supposing that the United States is a small country relative to the potential supply from Asia. Inclusive of the tariff, the cost of imported parts from Asia becomes $P_{asia} + t$, and the supply curve is $S_{asia} + t$. The free-trade supply from Mexico is shown as the upward-sloping curve labeled S_{mex}; inclusive of the tariff, the supply curve is $S_{mex} + t$.

Before NAFTA, both Mexico and Asia face the same tariff of t. So the equilibrium imports occur at point A, where the quantity imported is Q_1 and the tariff-inclusive price to the United States is $P_{asia} + t$. Of the total imports Q_1, the amount Q_2 comes from Mexico at point B, since under perfect competition these imports have the same tariff-inclusive price as those from Asia. Thus, tariff revenue is collected on imports from both Mexico and Asia, so the total tariff revenue is the area $(a + b + c + d)$ in Figure 9-3.

After Mexico joins NAFTA, it is able to sell to the United States duty-free. In that case, the relevant supply curve is S_{mex}, and imports from Mexico expand to Q_3 at point C. Notice that the price charged by Mexico at point C still equals the tariff-inclusive price from Asia, which is $P_{asia} + t$, even though Mexican imports do not have any tariff. Mexico charges that price because its marginal costs have risen along its supply curve, so even though the tariff has been removed, the price of its imports to the United States has not changed.

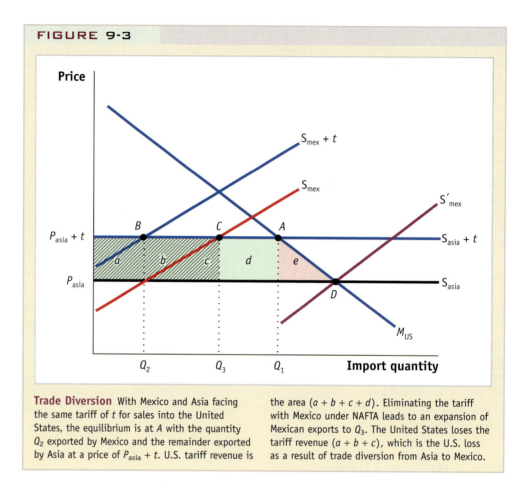

Trade Diversion With Mexico and Asia facing the same tariff of t for sales into the United States, the equilibrium is at A with the quantity Q_2 exported by Mexico and the remainder exported by Asia at a price of $P_{asia} + t$. U.S. tariff revenue is the area $(a + b + c + d)$. Eliminating the tariff with Mexico under NAFTA leads to an expansion of Mexican exports to Q_3. The United States loses the tariff revenue $(a + b + c)$, which is the U.S. loss as a result of trade diversion from Asia to Mexico.

Because the imports from Mexico enter the United States duty-free, the United States loses tariff revenue of $t \cdot Q_3$, which is the area $(a + b + c)$ in Figure 9-3. The price of imports to the United States has not changed, so the United States is worse off due to NAFTA by the loss in its tariff revenue. Mexico is better off because of the increase in its producer surplus from charging the price $P_{asia} + t$, without paying any tariff on its expanded amount of exports. Mexico's producer surplus rises by $(a + b)$, the area to the left of the supply curve S_{mex}. If we add together the changes in U.S. and Mexican welfare, the combined change in their welfare is

Loss in U.S. tariff revenue:	$-(a + b + c)$
Gain in Mexico's producer surplus:	$+(a + b)$
Combined effect due to NAFTA:	$-c$

So we see that the combined welfare of the United States and Mexico actually *falls* as a result of NAFTA. This is a very counterintuitive result because we normally expect that countries will be better off when they move toward free trade. Instead, in this example, we see that one of the countries within the regional agreement is worse off (the United States), and so much so that its fall in welfare exceeds the gains for Mexico, so that their combined welfare falls!

Interpretation of the Loss This is one of the few instances in this textbook in which a country's movement toward free trade makes that country worse off. What is the reason for this result? Asia is the most efficient producer of auto parts in this example for units $Q_3 - Q_2$: its marginal costs equal P_{asia} (not including the tariff). By diverting production to Mexico, the marginal costs of Mexico's extra exports to the United States rise from P_{asia} (which is the marginal cost at quantity Q_2, not including the tariff) to $P_{\text{asia}} + t$ (which is Mexico's marginal cost at quantity Q_3). Therefore, the United States necessarily loses from trade diversion, and by more than Mexico's gain.

The combined loss to the United States and Mexico of area c can be interpreted as the average difference between Mexico's marginal cost (rising from P_{asia} to $P_{\text{asia}} + t$) and Asia's marginal cost (P_{asia}), multiplied by the extra imports from Mexico. This interpretation of the net loss area c is similar to the "production loss" or "efficiency loss" due to a tariff for a small country. However, in this case, the net loss comes from *removing* a tariff among the member countries of a regional agreement rather than from adding a tariff.

What you should keep in mind in this example of the adverse effects of trade diversion is that the tariff between the United States and Mexico was removed, but the tariff against imports of auto parts from Asia was maintained. So it is really only a halfway step toward free trade. We have shown that this halfway step can be bad for the countries involved rather than good. This effect of trade diversion explains why some economists oppose regional trade agreements but support multilateral agreements under the WTO.

Not All Trade Diversion Creates a Loss We should stress that the loss due to a regional trade agreement in this example is not a *necessary* result, but a *possible* result, depending on our assumptions of Mexico's marginal costs. There could also be a gain to the importing country. In Figure 9-3, for example, suppose that after joining NAFTA, Mexico has considerable investment in the auto parts industry, and its supply curve shifts to S'_{mex} rather than S_{mex}. Then equilibrium imports to the United States will occur at point D, at the price P_{asia}, and Mexico will *fully* replace Asia as a supplier of auto parts. As compared with the initial situation with the tariff, the United States will lose all tariff revenue of area $(a + b + c + d)$. But the import price drops to P_{asia}, so it has a gain in consumer surplus of area $(a + b + c + d + e)$. Therefore, the net change in U.S. welfare is

Gain in consumer surplus:	$+ (a + b + c + d + e)$
Loss in tariff revenue:	$- (a + b + c + d)$
Net effect on U.S. welfare:	$+ e$

The United States experiences a net gain in consumer surplus in this case, and Mexico's producer surplus rises because it is exporting more.

This case combines elements of trade diversion (Mexico has replaced Asia) and trade creation (Mexico is exporting more to the United States than total U.S. imports before NAFTA). Thus, we conclude that NAFTA and other regional trade agreements have the potential to create gains among their members, but only if the amount of trade creation exceeds the amount of trade diversion. In the following application we look at what happened to Canada and the United States when free trade opened between them, to see whether the extent of trade creation for Canada exceeded the amount of trade diversion.

APPLICATION

Trade Creation and Diversion for Canada

In 1989 Canada formed a free-trade agreement with the United States and, five years later, entered into the North American Free Trade Agreement with the United States and Mexico. Research by Professor Daniel Trefler at the University of Toronto has analyzed the effect of these free-trade agreements on Canadian manufacturing industries. As summarized in Chapter 6, initially there was unemployment in Canada, but that was a short-term result. A decade after the free-trade agreement with the United States, employment in Canadian manufacturing had recovered and that sector also enjoyed a boom in productivity.

In his research, Trefler also estimated the amount of trade creation versus trade diversion for Canada in its trade with the United States. He found that the reduction in Canadian tariffs on U.S. goods increased imports of those goods by 54%. This increase was trade creation. However, since Canada was now buying more tariff-free goods from the United States, those tariff reductions reduced Canadian imports from the rest of the world by 40% (trade diversion). To compare these amounts, keep in mind that imports from the United States make up 80% of all Canadian imports, whereas imports from the rest of the world make up the remaining 20%. So the 54% increase in imports from the United States should be multiplied (or weighted) by its 80% share in overall Canadian imports to get the amount of trade creation. Likewise, the 40% reduction in imports from the rest of the world should be multiplied by its 20% share in Canadian imports to get trade diversion. Taking the difference between the trade created and diverted, we obtain

$$\underset{\substack{\text{Share of}\\ \text{U.S. imports}}}{\underline{80}\%} \times \underset{\substack{\text{Increase in}\\ \text{U.S. imports}}}{\underline{54}\%} - \underset{\substack{\text{Share of}\\ \text{other imports}}}{\underline{20}\%} \times \underset{\substack{\text{Decrease in}\\ \text{other imports}}}{\underline{40}\%} \approx 35\% > 0$$

Because this calculation gives a positive number, Trefler concludes that trade creation exceeded trade diversion when Canada and the United States entered into the free-trade agreement. Therefore, Canada definitely gained from the free-trade agreement with the United States. ■

2 International Agreements on Labor Issues

Regional agreements often include issues other than tariffs and trade. For example, the NAFTA agreement included two side agreements that were negotiated by President Clinton to help ensure its passage through the U.S. Congress. One side agreement dealt with the environment (discussed later in this chapter), and the other dealt with labor issues.

We use the term **labor standards** to refer to all issues that directly affect workers, including occupational health and safety, child labor, minimum wages, and so on. Labor standards were included in NAFTA to satisfy several groups. First, consumers and policy makers are often concerned with the working conditions in factories abroad and want to avoid "sweat shop" conditions that exploit workers. Second, unions in the industrial countries are also concerned with these conditions, partly because of solidarity with foreign workers and partly because of the concern that poor labor standards abroad will create more competition for U.S. workers (imports will be cheaper because manufacturers don't have to spend as much on safer working conditions and other labor standards).

Economists are sometimes skeptical about such concerns for foreign workers, however, and view attempts to enforce minimum labor standards as a form of "disguised protection" in the industrial countries. For example, the Indian economist T. N. Srinivasan of Yale University states, "The demand for linkage between trading rights and observance of standards with respect to the environment and labor would seem to arise largely from protectionist motives."[5] Likewise, the World Bank writes, "The real danger of using trade sanctions as an instrument for promoting basic rights is that the trade-standards linkage could become highjacked by protectionist interests attempting to preserve activities rendered uncompetitive by cheaper imports."[6] The former prime minister of Malaysia, Mahathir bin Mohammed, goes even further: "Western countries openly propose to eliminate the competitive edge of East Asia. . . . [T]he professed concern about workers welfare is motivated by selfish interest . . . to put as many obstacles as possible in the way of anyone attempting to catch up and compete with the West."[7] Whether you agree with these sentiments or not, economics teaches that we need to be careful that enforcing labor standards abroad does not worsen the situation for foreign workers by leading to unemployment. We will discuss some examples in which such an outcome has occurred.

Labor Side Agreement under NAFTA

The labor side agreement negotiated under NAFTA does not change the existing labor laws in these countries but is meant to improve the *enforcement* of such laws. If one country believes that another is failing to enforce its own laws in these areas, then a complaint can be brought before a commission of the North American Agreement on Labor Cooperation (NAALC), which includes representatives from each country and which attempts to resolve the dispute through consultation and cooperation. Although many cases deal with conditions in the *maquiladora* plants in Mexico, operating just south of the Mexico-U.S. border, complaints have also been brought against the United States, as with a case in 1998 involving farm workers picking apples in the State of Washington, for example.[8] In that case, the petitioners in Mexico charged that the United States failed to protect the rights of workers, especially migrant labor. The resolution of this case, reached in 2000, called for "planned outreach sessions at which these issues were to be discussed with migrant workers as well as a public forum for workers, unions, employers, and government officials."[9]

---

[5] T. N. Srinivasan, 1994, "International Labor Standards Once Again." In U.S. Department of Labor, Bureau of International Affairs, *International Labor Standards and Global Economic Integration: Proceedings of a Symposium* (Washington, D.C.), p. 36. All quotations in this paragraph are cited in Richard B. Freeman, 1996, "International Labor Standards and World Trade: Friends or Foes?" In Jeffrey J. Schott, ed., *The World Trading System: Challenges Ahead* (Washington, D.C.: Peterson Institute for International Economics), Chap. 5.
[6] World Bank, *World Development Report*, 1995, p. 79.
[7] *International Herald Tribune*, May 17, 1994, p. 6.
[8] The annual reports of the North American Commission for Labor Cooperation are available at http://www.naalc.org; choose "Publications" and then "Annual Reports."
[9] See the summary of this and other NAALC cases in Joel Solomon, 2001, "Trading Away Rights: The Unfulfilled Promise of NAFTA's Labor Side Agreement," http://www.hrw.org.

Critics of the NAALC agreement have argued that the procedures for resolving disputes are slow and include major exceptions that render them ineffective. For example, a study at the University of California, Los Angeles, concluded, "The NAALC has failed to protect workers' rights to safe jobs and is in danger of fading into oblivion."[10] Others argue that the agreement has created an institutional forum in which unions and labor activists from the three countries can build solidarity and that even the review of cases alone can lead firms to modify their practices.

Other Labor Agreements

Besides the labor side agreement in NAFTA, there are many other examples of international agreements that monitor the conditions of workers in foreign countries. Unions and other organizations are concerned with issues such as job safety, the right of workers to unionize, workers' entitlement to breaks and not being forced to work overtime, and so on. In some cases, the pressure from unions and grassroots organizations can lead to positive changes in the situation faced by workers in other countries. Consumers also have an important role to play through their purchasing power: if consumers are more likely to buy a product that has been produced using methods that respect the rights of workers, then companies will implement such methods more quickly.

Consumer Responsibility How much do consumers value the idea that the clothing they purchase is made under conditions that do not exploit foreign workers? A survey conducted by the National Bureau of Economic Research asked people to respond to this question, with the results shown in Table 9-2.[11]

Individuals in the first group, Sample *A*, were asked whether they cared about "the condition of workers who make the clothing they buy," and 84% responded that they care a lot or somewhat. Then they were asked, "How much more would you be willing to pay for items made under good working conditions," for items worth $10 and $100. The premium they were willing to pay was $2.80 for a $10 item and $15 for a $100 item.

Individuals in the second group, Sample *B*, were asked about the premium they would pay for a T-shirt made under "good" conditions, but also about the discount needed to buy a T-shirt made under "bad" conditions. In this group, 84% said that they would choose an identically priced alternative to a T-shirt "with a nice logo" if local students told them that the one with the nice logo was made under poor working conditions. Furthermore, 65% said they would not buy the T-shirt made under poor working conditions at all. Among the 35% who were willing to consider buying it, the average discount to buy it was $4.30, whereas the premium they were willing to pay if assured the T-shirt was made under good conditions was $1.83.

The results of this survey highlight several interesting observations about people's attitudes toward labor standards. One such observation is that consumers have a downward-sloping demand curve for labor standards; that is, many people are willing

[10] "NAFTA's Labor Side Agreement: Fading into Oblivion? An Assessment of Workplace Health and Safety Cases," March 2004, UCLA Center for Labor Research and Education.

[11] See Kimberly Ann Elliott and Richard B. Freeman, 2003, "White Hats or Don Quixotes: Human Rights Vigilantes in the Global Economy." In Richard B. Freeman, Joni Hersch, and Lawrence Mishel, eds., *Emerging Labor Market Institutions for the 21st Century* [Chicago: University of Chicago Press for the National Bureau of Economic Research (NBER)]; and Kimberly Ann Elliott and Richard B. Freeman, 2003, *Can Labor Standards Improve under Globalization?* (Washington, D.C.: Peterson Institute for International Economics), Chap. 2.

TABLE 9-2

Survey Responses This table summarizes the responses from a survey conducted by the National Bureau of Economic Research that asked individuals their attitudes toward an item made under good working conditions and under poor working conditions.

Sample A

Consumers who say they care about the condition of workers who make the clothing they buy:

A lot	46%
Somewhat	38%
Only a little	8%
Not at all (or no response)	8%
Consumers willing to pay more for an item if assured it was made under good working conditions:	81%
Additional amount willing to pay for $10 item	$2.80
Additional amount willing to pay for $100 item	$15

Sample B

Would choose an alternative to a T-shirt "with a nice logo" that local students say is made under poor working conditions if alternative is the same price	84%
Would not buy T-shirt made under poor working conditions at all	65%
Would buy T-shirt made under poor working conditions at average discount of	$4.30
Would pay more for T-shirt if came with assurance it was made under good conditions	78%
Average additional amount would pay (including as zeros those who did not offer to pay more or were inconsistent)	$1.83

Source: Kimberly Ann Elliott and Richard B. Freeman, 2003, Can Labor Standards Improve under Globalization? *(Washington, D.C.: Peterson Institute for International Economics), Chap. 2, Table 2.1, Sample A.*

to pay at least a small amount to ensure good labor standards (or simply switch to an alternative with the same price), though relatively few are willing to pay a lot. For example, for a higher-priced good, consumers were willing to pay a smaller percentage of its value to ensure good labor conditions. A second observation is that individuals had to receive a higher discount to purchase a shirt made under poor conditions than they were willing to pay for a shirt made under good conditions. This finding indicates that consumers are more worried about potential losses (paying more) than potential gains (the discount), which is a commonly observed characteristic of consumer behavior. Results similar to those reported in Table 9-2 have also been found in larger-scale surveys of consumers in the United States and the United Kingdom. We conclude that a sizable number of consumers are willing to adjust their shopping patterns in response to the conditions faced by foreign workers.

Corporate Responsibility Because of the pressure from consumers and unions, corporations have started to monitor and improve the conditions in their overseas plants and the plants of their overseas subcontractors. One example of this monitoring is reported in **Headlines: Wal-Mart Orders Chinese Suppliers to Lift Standards.** Wal-Mart insisted that its factories in China meet strict guidelines on both labor and environmental standards, or lose its business.

Country Responsibility Beyond the actions of consumers, unions, and corporations, should national governments monitor and enforce labor regulations in foreign countries? Several U.S. trade laws give the president the power to withhold trade privileges from countries that do not give their workers basic rights, including the right to organize. One study showed that these provisions have been used by the president

HEADLINES

Wal-Mart Orders Chinese Suppliers to Lift Standards

In response to criticism from activists in the United States, Wal-Mart has established strict labor and environmental standards that its overseas suppliers must follow. This article reports on these standards for factories in China.

Wal-Mart, the world's biggest retailer, yesterday told its Chinese suppliers to meet strict environmental and social standards or risk losing its business. "Meeting social and environmental standards is not optional," Lee Scott, Wal-Mart's chief executive, told a gathering of more than 1,000 suppliers in Beijing. "A company that cheats on overtime and on the age of its labour, that dumps its scraps and its chemicals in our rivers, that does not pay its taxes or honour its contracts will ultimately cheat on the quality of its products."

Wal-Mart has been pursuing a drive to improve its reputation on environmental and social issues over the past three years in response to growing criticism in the US over issues that include labour conditions in its supplier factories. . . . The requirements include a clear demonstration of compliance with Chinese environmental laws, an improvement of 20 per cent in energy efficiency at the company's 200 largest China suppliers and disclosure of the names and addresses of every factory involved in the production process. The company will require a 25 per cent rise in the efficiency of energy-intensive products such as flat-screen TVs by 2011.

Source: Excerpted from Tom Mitchell and Jonathan Birchall, "Wal-Mart Orders Chinese Suppliers to Lift Standards," The Financial Times, *October 23, 2008, p. 19.*

32 times from 1985 to 1994, but only one-half of the cases are judged to have been effective in improving workers' rights.[12]

There are two problems with trying to withhold trade privileges. First, denying preferences to a foreign country across all industries is a very broad foreign policy action, when the problems may occur only in particular companies. Second, these laws involve a comparison of U.S. labor standards with those found abroad and the judgment that foreign practices are inadequate. Many people believe that countries should choose their own domestic policies, even when they conflict with established norms abroad, and that countries should not impose their preferences on each other.[13]

An alternative approach to government sanctions is for nongovernmental organizations (NGOs) to take actions that limit undesirable sweatshop activities. According to one research study focusing on Indonesia, actions by NGOs are actually more effective than government action.[14] This study showed that when the U.S. government threatened to withdraw tariff privileges for Indonesia, the minimum wage was doubled in real terms. That increase in the wage reduced the employment of unskilled workers by as much as 10%, so these workers were harmed. The anti-sweatshop activism by NGOs targeted at textile, apparel, and footwear plants raised real wages as well, by ensuring that plants paid the minimum wage. But this activism did not

---

[12] Kimberly Ann Elliott and Richard B. Freeman, 2003, *Can Labor Standards Improve under Globalization?* (Washington, D.C.: Peterson Institute for International Economics), p. 79.
[13] An important example here is child labor, which is avoided in industrial countries but may be necessary for families' survival in developing countries.
[14] Ann Harrison and Jason Scorse, May 2004, "Moving Up or Moving Out? Anti-Sweatshop Activists and Labor Market Outcomes," NBER Working Paper No. 10492.

reduce employment to the same extent. Plants targeted by activists were more likely to close, but those losses were offset by employment gains at surviving plants, which benefited from the growth in exports in these industries. So there was no significant decline in employment from the pressure exerted by NGOs.

The message of this study is that pressure from the U.S. government to raise wages was too blunt a tool to be effective, whereas the actions of NGOs, which were better targeted at particular plants, resulted in higher wages with little or no net loss in employment. In addition, the pressure from activists can sometimes make U.S. companies more willing to reveal their foreign plants, as Nike has done, thereby making them open to monitoring.

Living Wage The final question we can ask about labor issues is whether it is fair to expect foreign firms to pay a **living wage** to their workers; that is, a wage above the norm in the developing country. This issue is perhaps the most controversial part of labor standards because it involves a difficult judgment: How high should foreign wages be to make them acceptable to activists in industrial countries? Economists have a ready answer: the wages should be as high as the market will allow, and not any higher. Raising wages above their equilibrium level will very likely lead to unemployment. In extreme cases, workers laid off from manufacturing jobs in developing countries might be forced into prostitution or other illegal activities that are far worse than the low-wage factory positions they held.

These types of concerns lead many economists and policy makers to reject calls for a "living wage." But this rejection *does not* mean that we should abandon other types of labor standards. Workers in all countries are entitled to conditions that are safe and clean, honesty in payment, the right to unionize, and so on. Consumers, corporations, and unions all play an important role in advocating for such conditions in foreign countries, and that advocacy needs to continue. The enforcement of labor standards can ensure that workers benefit from trade without being exploited in the workplace.

3 International Agreements on the Environment

Many of the protesters at the 1999 Seattle meeting of the WTO, shown in the photo at the start of this chapter, were concerned about how WTO rulings affect the environment. The WTO does not directly address environmental issues; other international agreements, called **multilateral environmental agreements,** deal specifically with the environment. There are some 200 multilateral environmental agreements, including the Convention on International Trade in Endangered Species (CITES) and the Montreal Protocol on Substances that Deplete the Ozone Layer (which has eliminated the use of chlorofluorocarbons, CFCs, which deplete the ozone layer). But the WTO still indirectly affects the environment as the protesters in Seattle were well aware. We begin by clarifying the role of the GATT and WTO in environmental issues.

Environmental Issues in the GATT and WTO

In an earlier chapter (see **Side Bar: Key Provisions of the GATT**), we summarized some of the founding articles of the GATT. Not mentioned there was Article XX, known as the "green provision." Article XX allows countries to adopt their own laws in relation to environmental issues, provided that these laws are applied uniformly to domestic and foreign producers so that the laws do not discriminate against imports.

In its full text, Article XX of the GATT states that "subject to the requirement that such measures are not applied in a manner which would constitute a . . . disguised restriction on international trade, nothing in this Agreement shall be construed to prevent the adoption or enforcement by any contracting party of measures: . . . (b) necessary to protect human, animal or plant life or health; . . . (g) relating to the conservation of exhaustible natural resources if such measures are made effective in conjunction with restrictions on domestic production or consumption."

If the provisions of the GATT and WTO permit countries to apply their own environmental regulations, why were people dressed as turtles and dolphins protesting WTO rulings at the 1999 Seattle meetings? To understand the concerns of these protesters, we need to dig into the details of some specific GATT/WTO cases, summarized in Table 9-3.[15]

Tuna-Dolphin Case In 1991, before the WTO was formed, Mexico brought a GATT case against the United States. The reason for the case was that the United States had banned imports of tuna from Mexico because Mexican fishermen did not catch tuna using nets that safeguarded against the accidental capture of dolphins. The U.S. Marine Mammal Protection Act requires that U.S. tuna fishermen use nets that are safe for dolphins, and by Article XX(g) of the GATT, the United States reasoned that the same requirement could be extended to Mexican fishermen. But the U.S. ban on imports of tuna from Mexico ran afoul of the GATT.

GATT concluded that the United States could not ban the import of tuna because the United States applied the import restriction to the *production process method* and not the product itself. The idea that the production process could not be a basis for a trade restriction was a principle of GATT that was upheld in this case. In addition, the GATT panel ruled that "GATT rules did not allow one country to take trade action for the purpose of attempting to enforce its own domestic laws in another country—even to protect animal health or exhaustible natural resources." Both of these conclusions were a blow to environmentalists interested in protecting the dolphins, and this is the reason that some of the Seattle protesters were dressed as dolphins.

Even though the GATT panel ruled in favor of Mexico and against the United States in this case, the strong consumer response led to the dolphins being protected. Interested parties in the United States and Mexico worked out a system of labeling that now appears on cans of tuna in the United States, declaring the product to be "dolphin-safe." Since 1990 the major companies have sold only this "dolphin friendly" product from Mexico, and the labeling procedure was found to be consistent with GATT. So despite the initial ruling against the United States, the outcome of this case has had the desired effect of protecting dolphins in Mexican waters (in addition to the protection they already received in U.S. waters).

---

[15] These cases are drawn from Jeffrey A. Frankel, November 2003, "The Environment and Globalization," NBER Working Paper No. 10090. Environmental cases are summarized on the WTO webpage at http://www.wto.org/English/tratop_e/envir_e/edis00_e.htm, and details are also provided at the Trade and Environmental Database at the American University, http://www.american.edu/TED/ted.htm.

TABLE 9-3

Environmental Cases at the GATT and WTO This table shows the outcome of environmental cases ruled upon by the GATT and WTO.

Case	Issue	Outcome
Tuna-Dolphin In 1991 Mexico appealed to the GATT against a U.S. ban on Mexican tuna imports.	The United States put a ban on imports of tuna from Mexico that were not caught with nets which were safe for dolphins (as required in the United States under the Marine Mammal Protection Act).	In 1992 the GATT ruled in favor of Mexico that the U.S. import ban violated GATT rules. But the strong consumer response led to labeling of imported tuna as "dolphin friendly."
Shrimp-Turtle In 1996 India, Malaysia, Pakistan, and Thailand appealed to the WTO against a U.S. ban on shrimp imports.	The United States put a ban on imports of shrimp from India, Malaysia, Pakistan, and Thailand that were not caught with nets safe for sea turtles (as required in the United States under the Endangered Species Act).	In 1998 the WTO ruled in favor of India, Malaysia, Pakistan, and Thailand that the U.S. import ban violated WTO rules. But the United States could still require these countries to use turtle-safe nets, provided that adequate notice and consultation were pursued.
Gasoline In 1994 Venezuela and Brazil appealed to the GATT against a U.S. ban on gasoline imports.	The United States put a ban on imports of gasoline from Venezuela and Brazil because the gas exceeded the maximum amount allowed of a smog-causing chemical (under the U.S. Clean Air Act).	In 1996 the WTO ruled in favor of Venezuela and Brazil that the U.S. import restriction violated equal treatment of domestic and foreign producers. The United States adjusted the rules to be consistent with the WTO and still pursued its own clean air goals.
Biotech Food In 2003 the United States appealed to the WTO that Europe was keeping out genetically modified food and crops.	Since 1998 no imports of genetically modified food or crops had been approved in the European Union.	In 2006 the WTO ruled that the European actions violated the principle that import restrictions must be based on "scientific risk assessments." Labeling and consumer concerns in Europe will still limit such imports.

Source: Updated from Jeffrey A. Frankel, 2005, "The Environment and Globalization." In Michael Weinstein, ed., Globalization: What's New, (New York: Columbia University Press), pp. 129–169. Reprinted in R. Stavins, ed., 2005, Economics of the Environment (New York: W. W. Norton), pp. 361–398.

Shrimp-Turtle Case In 1996, just after the WTO was formed, a second closely related case arose involving shrimp and sea turtles. In this case, India, Malaysia, Pakistan, and Thailand appealed to the WTO against a U.S. ban on shrimp imports. The United States had banned imports of shrimp from these countries because they were not caught with nets that were safe for sea turtles, as required in the United States under the Endangered Species Act of 1987. Again, by Article XX(g) of the GATT, the United States reasoned that the same requirement could be extended against fishermen from these Asian countries.

Although this case has a number of similarities to the earlier tuna-dolphin case, the outcome at the WTO was different. The WTO still ruled against the United States, but in this case it *did not rule* against the principle that one country could restrict imports based on the production process method used in another country. On the contrary, the WTO ruled that the United States was consistently applying its laws to American and Asian producers in requiring that turtle-safe nets be used. The problem with the U.S. import ban was that it was applied without due notice and consultation with the exporting countries involved, which did not allow the countries sufficient time to employ turtle-safe devices. In other words, the WTO ruling against the United States was on narrow, technical grounds and not on the principle of protecting endangered species in foreign waters.

In many ways, this WTO ruling was more favorable to environmentalists than the earlier tuna-dolphin ruling at the GATT. The WTO panel explicitly recognized that "the conservation of exhaustible natural resources" referred to in Article XX(g) applies to living resources, especially if they are threatened with extinction. After the United States allowed more flexibility in its regulations and made good-faith efforts to develop an agreement with the Asian producers, the laws requiring the use of turtle-safe nets for exporters were found to be consistent with the WTO in a 2001 ruling.

Gasoline from Venezuela and Brazil A third GATT/WTO case that involves environmental issues was brought against the United States by Venezuela and Brazil in 1994. The United States had restricted imports of gasoline from these countries because the gas did not meet the requirements of the U.S. Clean Air Act (which mandates a maximum amount of certain smog-causing chemicals). In this case, the WTO ruled in 1996 that the United States violated the principle that national and foreign producers should be treated equally. The issue was that refineries in the United States were given a three-year grace period to meet the Clean Air Act goals, whereas that grace period was not extended to refineries abroad. So the U.S. import restriction discriminated against the refineries in Venezuela and Brazil.

This gasoline case is often seen as a loss for environmentalists, but economists would argue that U.S. regulations were in fact acting like "disguised protection" against the import of Venezuelan gasoline. From the perspective of promoting free trade and treating foreign producers fairly, the WTO was correct in ruling against the United States. The United States was not blocked by the WTO in pursuing clean air goals, but it had to modify its requirements so that they were applied equally to U.S. and foreign producers.

Biotech Food in Europe A final, ongoing case concerns whether food that has been genetically modified can be imported into Europe. In 2003 the United States (joined by Argentina and Canada) appealed to the WTO that the European Union was keeping out genetically modified food and crops. Since 1998 no such imports had been approved in the European Union, though it denied that there was any "moratorium" on these imports. Rather, Europe claimed that it needed more time to study the health effects of genetically modified organisms and was not approving such imports for precautionary reasons.

The WTO ruled in 2006 that the European actions violated the principle that import restrictions must be based on "scientific risk assessments." That is, countries cannot keep out imports based on precautionary reasons but must have some scientific evidence to back up the import restriction. Despite this ruling, Europe can use consumer labeling to allow the buyers to decide whether to purchase foods that have been genetically modified. As in our earlier discussion of the labeling of U.S. tuna imports from Mexico, it is expected that the labeling of genetically modified organisms in Europe will allow consumers to exert their power in limiting purchases of these foods if they so choose.

Summary of GATT/WTO Cases The cases in Table 9-3 show that WTO rulings have not adversely affected the environment: in the tuna-dolphin case, the reaction of consumers in the United States was enough to ensure that dolphin-safe nets were used in Mexico; in the shrimp-turtle case, the WTO did not object to the principle of requiring foreign countries to use turtle-friendly nets, as do U.S. companies; in the gasoline case, the imports from Venezuela and Brazil had to meet the requirements of the Clean Air Act, after the same grace period given to U.S. firms; and in the case of biotech foods, labeling in Europe is expected to limit such imports if consumers so choose.

These outcomes have led some observers to conclude that even though environmentalists have lost some specific cases at the WTO, they have gained the upper hand in ensuring that environmental concerns are respected: environmentalists may have lost some battles, but they have won the war! This conclusion does not mean that environmental concerns can now be dropped. On the contrary, the lobbying activity of environmental groups, including the costumed protesters at the Seattle meetings, has been important in shifting public opinion and WTO rulings in directions that support the environment, and such lobbying activities should continue to be pursued.

Does Trade Help or Harm the Environment?

Having clarified the role of the WTO in resolving specific cases brought between particular countries, let us turn to the more general question of whether trade helps or harms the environment. Some of the protesters at the 1999 WTO meetings in Seattle believe that trade is bad for the environment and have examples to support that belief. But there are other examples to support the claim that trade is good for the environment. So the answer to the question of whether trade helps or harms the environment is that *either* outcome is possible, depending on the case being considered. Let us turn to some examples to see the possible outcomes.

U.S. Sugar Quota The United States maintains an import quota on sugar. The import quota leads to higher prices for American buyers, both consumers and firms, who pay domestic prices that can be as high as twice the world price. One source of demand for imported sugarcane comes from firms that are producing ethanol, an alternative (or additive) to gasoline that can be produced from sugar or corn. Because of the high import price for sugarcane, however, these firms instead purchase corn from American farmers, who are themselves subsidized by the U.S. government. As a result of the quota for sugar imports and the subsidies for corn production, much more corn than sugar is used to produce ethanol.

The problem with this arrangement is that producing ethanol from corn is much less energy-efficient than producing it from sugarcane. As described in the article **Headlines: The Power of Big Corn,** corn depletes the soil and requires fertilizers to grow, which themselves use energy in their production. Because the net energy savings by making ethanol from corn and using it as a gasoline substitute are poor, it would be better to use sugarcane to produce ethanol, *if* it could be purchased at world prices. This example shows how the U.S. quota on sugar has an indirect and negative

HEADLINES

The Power of Big Corn

Because of the U.S. import quota on imports of sugarcane, corn is used instead to produce ethanol. This editorial argues that the corn-based ethanol does not save energy, and it would be better to use sugarcane.

The nation's growing appetite for ethanol as an alternative motor fuel is so great that one environmental group warns of a corn shortage, which could raise prices for the many corn-based food and drink products the nation consumes. This competition for corn, though, could be easily avoided if Congress would do away with the tariffs and import restrictions that keep the United States from making greater use of sugar-based ethanol, which requires much less energy than the corn-based version. . . .

The country is relying on corn for ethanol even though it is far from ideal for the purpose. The ratio of energy gained versus the energy needed to plant, fertilize, and harvest the crop is poor, and corn crops are notoriously hard on soil. With technological advances, scientists hope to be able to replace corn with agricultural waste or a non-food plant like switchgrass.

In the meantime, sugar cane could be used to produce ethanol with much less investment in energy. But domestic sugar growers get such a high price for their product due to government price-fixing, tariffs, and import restrictions that it would be uneconomic for them to turn to ethanol production. Those same tariffs and import limits make it impossible to import any of the world's abundant supply of sugar and turn it into ethanol. And just to make sure that no one imports cheap Brazilian sugar-based ethanol, Congress has protected the Corn Belt with a 51 cent per gallon tariff on foreign ethanol.

The result is that ethanol in the United States uses more energy and costs more than it has to, and American drivers use less of it than they would with a freer market. The Earth Policy Institute report points to a further cost to corn farmers' grip on Congress: excessive use of the crop for ethanol could drive up food prices. The country would benefit if Congress would get out of the way and let sugar-based ethanol compete on a level playing field.

Source: Excerpted from "The Power of Big Corn," *Boston Globe, January 15, 2007, editorial.*

impact on the environment. Eliminating the quota, and allowing free trade in sugar, would benefit the environment because it would allow more sugarcane to be used to produce ethanol, rather than corn.

U.S. Automobile VER The sugar quota example is not the only case in which a U.S. trade restriction has worked to harm the environment. In an earlier chapter, we discussed the "voluntary" export restraint (VER) on exports of Japanese cars to the United States, which began in 1981. The VER limited the number of cars that Japanese firms could export each year, but not their value, so there was an incentive for the Japanese firms to export larger and/or more luxurious models. As the quality of the Japanese cars rose, so did the engine size and weight of the vehicles; as a result, the average gas mileage of the imported cars fell.

The impact of the VER on gas mileage is shown in Figure 9-4, where we use data on the Japanese imported cars from 1979 to 1982, before and after the VER began. The horizontal axis shows the change in the quantity sold (in percent) between these years, and the vertical axis shows the gas mileage of each model. The data show that the luxury models with the lowest gas mileage—such as the Maxima, Cressida, and Mazda 626—experienced the greatest increase in sales between these years. Sales went up despite the limit on total imports because the prices of these more luxurious models did not rise as much as the prices of the economy models. U.S. consumers shifted

FIGURE 9-4

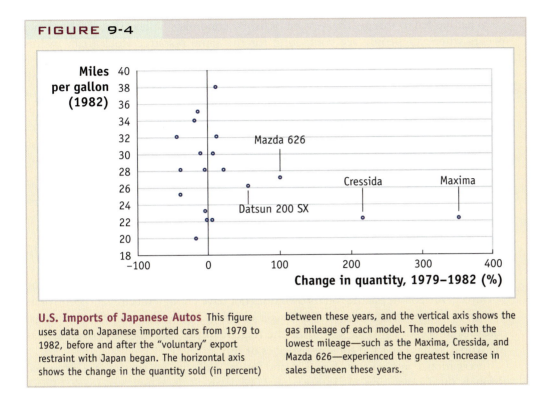

U.S. Imports of Japanese Autos This figure uses data on Japanese imported cars from 1979 to 1982, before and after the "voluntary" export restraint with Japan began. The horizontal axis shows the change in the quantity sold (in percent) between these years, and the vertical axis shows the gas mileage of each model. The models with the lowest mileage—such as the Maxima, Cressida, and Mazda 626—experienced the greatest increase in sales between these years.

their purchases toward the luxury models, and because those models had worse gas mileage, the VER increased the use of energy and led to greater carbon dioxide emissions from the vehicles, therefore harming the environment. Conversely, a free-trade policy would have allowed consumers to continue to import more fuel-efficient cars from Japan during the 1980s and would have been better for the environment.

The Tragedy of the Commons

The two previous examples, dealing with trade in sugar and automobiles, illustrate how free trade can be good for the environment. We now turn to two other cases in which free trade has harmed the environment by threatening endangered species.

Trade in Fish Because of overharvesting, many species of fish are no longer commercially viable and, in some extreme cases, are close to extinction. Examples include the Atlantic cod, tuna in the Mediterranean, and sturgeon in European and Asian waters. According to one scientific study, 29% of fish and seafood species have collapsed; that is, their catch has declined by 90% or more between 1950 and 2003. The same authors writing in 2009 find that the "exploitation rates" of some species were reduced, but that "63% of assessed fish stocks worldwide still require rebuilding, and even lower exploitation rates are needed to reverse the collapse of vulnerable species."[16]

---

[16] Juliet Eilperin, "World's Fish Supply Running Out, Researchers Warn," *Washington Post*, November 3, 2006, p. A01, citing an article from *Science*; and Boris Worm, et al., "Rebuilding Global Fisheries," *Science* 2009, 325, pp. 578–585.

What has led to this overharvesting of fish? Economists believe that this outcome occurs whenever people are competing for the same resource stock (fish, in this case) and refer to this phenomena as the **tragedy of the commons.** When a resource such as fish is treated as **common property** that anyone can harvest, it will be subject to overfishing and its stocks will diminish rapidly over time as each producer seeks to maximize its own share of the resource. International trade can exacerbate the tragedy of the commons by directing global demand toward the resources of a particular country or region so that there is even more overharvesting of fish under free trade.[17]

The Solution to the Tragedy of the Commons The fundamental cause of the tragedy is not that the resource is traded internationally but that the resource is treated as common property by the people who are harvesting it. If instead there was a system of rules that assigned property rights to the resource and limited the harvest of each person, then the overharvesting could be avoided. When a resource is truly global in nature, however, then it is not enough to assign property rights within a country; instead, an international agreement is needed to prevent overharvesting of the resource. One country acting on its own does not have enough incentive to control its harvest if other countries do not also enact controls. In the absence of international controls, international trade will make the tragedy of the commons and overharvesting worse, as has occurred for some species of fish.

International agreements for fish and other endangered species are arranged through the Convention on International Trade in Endangered Species (CITES). The article **Headlines: Europe Leans Toward Bluefin Trade Ban** describes recent action taken by European officials under CITES to limit international trade in bluefin tuna (which is prized for sushi) from European waters. If the bluefin tuna is listed as endangered under CITES, then international trade in this species would have to stop not only for Europe but also for American fishermen. The fishing industry is opposed to this ban, as is Japan as the principal consuming nation.

Trade in Buffalo The example of trade in fish is not the only case in which international trade has interacted with the tragedy of the commons to result in the near extinction of a species. A historical case from America occurred with the slaughter of the Great Plains buffalo in a 10-year period from 1870 to 1880. Various reasons are often given for the slaughter: the railroad allowed hunters to reach the Great Plains easier; the buffalo were killed by the U.S. military in its fight against Native Americans; and climate change on the Great Plains, which had a wet period up to the 1850s followed by 30 years of drought, combined with overhunting by Native Americans. But recent research has uncovered a new reason that dominates all others for the slaughter of the buffalo: an invention in London circa 1871 that allowed the buffalo hides to be tanned for industrial use (such as for belts), creating a huge demand from Europe for the hides.[18] As a result, the price of hides increased in

---

[17] See James A. Brander and M. Scott Taylor, April 1998, "Open Access Renewable Resources: Trade and Trade Policy in a Two-Country World," *Journal of International Economics*, 44(2), 181–210, for a theoretical model in which international trade interacts with the tragedy of the commons to result in losses from trade for the exporter.

[18] See M. Scott Taylor, March 2007, "Buffalo Hunt: International Trade and the Virtual Extinction of the North American Bison," NBER Working Paper No. 12969.

America, and the vast majority of untanned hides were exported to Europe for use in industry.

An estimate of the import of untanned hides from the United States to the United Kingdom and France is shown in Figure 9-5. These estimates come from comparing import demand in the United Kingdom and France with demand in Canada, where the invention allowing buffalo hides to be tanned for industrial use was not known. We are therefore looking at the *extra* demand in the United Kingdom and France after the invention was put to use. We can see from Figure 9-5 that the amount of imports into these countries (in excess of imports into Canada) was small or negative before 1871, but then grew rapidly and peaked in 1875. That year the United Kingdom and France combined imported more than 1 million hides and, over the entire period from 1871 to 1878, imported some 3.5 million hides, which can plausibly account for the slaughter of the entire Great Plains herd.[19] A further slight increase in imports in the 1880s likely reflects hides from the Northern herd of buffalo in the United States.

FIGURE 9-5

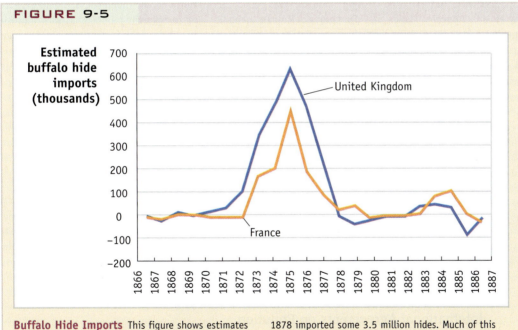

Buffalo Hide Imports This figure shows estimates of the imports to the United Kingdom and France of buffalo hides from the United States. The amount of imports into these countries (in excess of imports to Canada) was small or negative before 1871, but then grew rapidly and peaked in 1875. That year the United Kingdom and France combined imported more than 1 million hides and over the entire period from 1871 to 1878 imported some 3.5 million hides. Much of this trade volume can be attributed to an invention in London in 1871 that allowed buffalo hides to be tanned for industrial use.

Source: M. Scott Taylor, March 2007, "Buffalo Hunt: International Trade and the Virtual Extinction of the North American Bison," NBER Working Paper No. 12969.

---

[19] The import data for the United Kingdom and France are in pounds, so these estimates of imports assume that each four hides weigh 112 pounds.

HEADLINES

Europe Leans Toward Bluefin Trade Ban

This article reports on actions taken by European officials to classify the bluefin tuna as an endangered species, which would ban international trade in this species.

PARIS—European officials are increasing pressure for an international ban on the commercial fishing of bluefin tuna, a threatened species whose fatty belly is prized for sushi. But they are facing a delicate balancing act as they try to weigh economic interests of a Mediterranean fishing industry, a sushi-loving Japan, and a species that some experts say is on the verge of extinction. . . .

In July [2009], Monaco proposed that bluefin tuna be listed as an "Appendix 1" endangered species under the Convention on International Trade in Endangered Species of Wild Fauna and Flora. Such a listing would provide the same level of protection accorded pandas and some whales, effectively banning international trade in the fish. A panel of the United Nations Food and Agriculture Organization concluded in December that the species met the criteria for an Appendix 1 listing. Monaco's proposal will be lodged officially when the 175 nations that are parties to the treaty meet [in March 2010] in Doha, Qatar. . . .

The fishing industry was quick to voice its disapproval. Mourad Kahoul, president of an association representing industrial fishing fleets in France, Italy and Spain, said that his group "is doing everything it can to change the government's mind on this," and that there were differing scientific views on the outlook for the fish. . . . The United States fishing industry is "strongly opposed" to listing the fish under the endangered species convention, said Rich Ruais, executive director of the American Bluefin Tuna Association, who said the trade ban "would create a huge black market" . . . .

Japan has not yet made its own position official, though it is widely expected to fight the proposal, as was the case in 1992 when Sweden sought to have the bluefin listed. The United States initially said it supported Monaco, but it has not made clear its position.

Source: Excerpted from David Jolly, "Europe Leans Toward Bluefin Trade Ban," New York Times, February 4, 2010.

Figure 9-5 shows convincingly that international trade, combined with the innovation in tanning technology in London and the absence of any property rights over the buffalo, was responsible for the slaughter of the buffalo. That is a sad result of market forces and one that we want to avoid today through agreements such as CITES. Multilateral environmental agreements are needed to prevent international trade from exacerbating the tragedy of the commons. We now turn to a final case in which this problem can occur, and that is with global pollution.

International Agreements on Pollution

Pollution is a by-product of many manufacturing activities. The tragedy of the commons applies to pollution, too, because companies and countries can treat the air and water as a common-property resource, allowing pollutants to enter it without regard for where these pollutants end up. Pollution is an international issue because it can often cross borders in the water or atmosphere. We will use the term "global pollutants" for substances that cross country borders. Examples include chlorofluorocarbons (CFCs), which result in a depletion of the ozone layer in the atmosphere, and carbon dioxide (CO_2), which contributes to global warming. In contrast, we use the term "local pollutants" for substances that, for the most part, stay within a country. An example is smog, which is caused by the carbon monoxide (CO) in factory emissions and automobile exhaust.

Global Pollutants For global pollutants, a prisoner's dilemma similar to that illustrated in Figure 9-2 for tariffs again applies. Because the pollution crosses international borders, each country does not face the full cost of its own pollution. It follows that there is little incentive to regulate global pollutants. In the absence of regulation, however, countries will end up with the bad outcome of having too much global pollution, so international agreements are needed to control the amount.

Payoff Matrix To make this argument more carefully, in Figure 9-6 we show the payoff matrix for two countries, each of which decides whether to regulate the emissions of a pollutant. The regulations could take the form of limits on how much of the pollutant an industry can emit, which means that the industry must install special equipment to reduce its emissions, at its own expense. Each quadrant of the matrix includes Home's payoff in the lower-left corner and Foreign's payoff in the upper-right corner. We start with a situation of regulation and then measure the change in welfare for Home or Foreign when there are no pollution regulations (or when pollution regulations are not enforced).

Starting in the upper-left cell, when both countries regulate emissions of the pollutant, consumers are better off as compared with no regulations, while producers are worse off because of the expense of the regulations. If one country—say, Home—decides to not regulate, then its producers would gain because they no longer have to install the extra equipment to reduce emissions, but consumers in Home and Foreign would lose if regulations are not used because of the extra pollution. The outcome is similar if Foreign decides to not regulate: its producers gain, and consumers in both countries lose. Finally, if neither country regulates, then there is a large loss for consumers from the extra pollution and a small gain for producers due to the cost savings from not installing the equipment (this gain is small because neither producer is subject to the regulations, so competition can eliminate most of their gains).

Nash Equilibrium Let us use the structure of payoffs in Figure 9-6 to determine the Nash equilibrium. Start in the upper-left quadrant, where both countries regulate their pollution emissions. If either country deviates from this position and does not

---

FIGURE 9-6

	Regulate	**Foreign**	Don't regulate

Regulate:
- Gain for Foreign consumers, loss for producers / Gain for Home consumers, loss for producers
- Gain for Foreign producers, loss for consumers / Loss for Home producers and consumers

Don't regulate:
- Loss for Foreign producers and consumers / Gain for Home producers, loss for consumers
- Small gain for Foreign producers, large loss for consumers / Small gain for Home producers, large loss for consumers

Payoffs in an Environmental Game This payoff matrix shows the gains and losses for Home and Foreign countries, depending on whether they adopt environmental regulations. If governments weigh producer surplus more than consumer surplus, then the structure of payoffs is similar to the prisoner's dilemma because the Nash equilibrium is to have both countries not adopt regulations. That outcome can occur with "global" pollutants.

regulate, it will experience a gain for producers and a loss for consumers. If pollution is local, then the country might realize that the costs to consumers outweigh the gains to producers. That is why the Environmental Protection Agency (EPA) in the United States regulates the pollution from factories and from cars: the gains to consumers from reducing pollution outweigh the costs to producers.

In the case of global pollution, however, this calculation changes. If a country's pollution crosses international borders, as with CO_2 emissions, then the perceived gains to a country's *own* consumers from regulating the pollution may be less than the costs to producers. In that case, neither country will want to stay in the regulated quadrant in the upper left of Figure 9-6 and will have an incentive to *not* regulate its global pollution. Given that one country does not regulate its global pollution, the other country will have an even greater incentive to not regulate: if Home does not regulate in Figure 9-6 so that we are in the bottom row, then Foreign's best decision will likely be to not regulate either because the additional loss to its consumers will be offset by a gain to producers.[20]

Thus, the payoffs shown in Figure 9-6 can lead us to a situation in which neither country regulates pollution, in the lower-right quadrant, despite the large losses to consumers. That outcome is similar to the prisoner's dilemma that we discussed for the tariff game (Figure 9-2): both countries can end up with a bad outcome (with high tariffs or high pollution), even though they are individually making their best decisions. Just like the tariff game, multilateral agreements are needed to ensure that countries end up instead in the upper-left quadrant, with both countries regulating the global pollution.

Multilateral Agreements One example of an international agreement is the Montreal Protocol on Substances that Deplete the Ozone Layer, which has successfully eliminated the use of chlorofluorocarbons (CFCs). In that case, the scientific evidence showing that CFCs were creating a "hole" in the ozone layer above Australia and New Zealand was conclusive. In addition, the CFCs that were used in refrigerators, air conditioners, and other appliances could be replaced with alternative chemicals at relatively low cost. So it was not that difficult to get all countries to agree to a ban on the use of CFCs, which began in 1989 and has already reduced the damage to the ozone layer. A more difficult case is that of global warming, which is regulated by an agreement known as the Kyoto Protocol, and more recently by the Copenhagen Accord, as discussed in our final application.

The Kyoto Protocol and the Copenhagen Accord

In December 1997 representatives from many nations met in Kyoto, Japan, to discuss nonbinding targets for reducing emissions of greenhouse gases. The principal greenhouse gas is carbon dioxide (CO_2), which is released by cars, factories, home heating, the generation of electricity through coal plants, and basically nearly every activity that involves combustion. Carbon dioxide creates a "greenhouse" effect, whereby heat is trapped inside the atmosphere, slightly increasing the earth's temperature. Even small increases in temperature can have dramatic consequences through the melting

---

[20] In the problems at the end of the chapter, you are asked to work through examples using specific numbers for the gains and losses in Figure 9-6, to determine the Nash equilibrium.

of ice caps, which raises the level of oceans; changes weather patterns; affects agriculture, tourism, and other economic activities; endangers species; and may have even worse consequences.

The **Kyoto Protocol** built on the United Nations' 1992 treaty on climate change, which was ratified by 189 countries, including the United States. Five years later, in 1997, the Kyoto Protocol established specific targets for reduction in greenhouse gas emissions: the industrial countries should cut their emissions of greenhouse gases by a collective 5.2% less than their 1990 levels (which is estimated to be a reduction of 29% from what 2010 levels are predicted to occur without the agreement). Targets for individual countries range from an 8% reduction for the European Union, 7% for the United States, 6% for Japan, 0% for Russia, and permitted increases for Australia and Iceland. In addition, a market for emissions targets was established so that Russia, for example, could sell its credits to other countries if it produces less than its 1990 level of greenhouse gases.

More than 160 have countries ratified this agreement, including about 40 industrial countries. Russia ratified the treaty on November 18, 2004, bringing the amount of greenhouse gases accounted for by the members to more than 55% of the world total. The treaty then took effect three months later, on February 16, 2005. However, the United States did not ratify this treaty and is the only large industrial country to not join the effort. Why did the United States refuse to join, and what actions can be taken instead to reduce global emissions?

There are four reasons often given to explain why the United States did not join the Kyoto Protocol:[21] (1) although the evidence toward global warming is strong, we still do not understand all the consequences of policy actions; (2) while the United States is the largest emitter of greenhouse gases, meeting the Kyoto targets would negatively affect its economy; (3) Kyoto failed to include the developing countries, especially China and India; (4) there are other ways to pursue reductions in greenhouse gas emissions.

The first point has become less plausible over time, as the evidence for and consequences of global warming become more apparent. The second point is true: the United States is the largest emitter of greenhouse gases (because of its very large economy), and meeting the Kyoto goals would certainly impose significant costs on the economy. The costs to the United States would probably be higher than the costs to Germany, for example, because East Germany had plants that were highly polluting in 1990 that have now been shut down. The percentage reduction in German pollution is calculated from a baseline that includes the highly polluting plants, whereas the percentage reduction in the United States is calculated from a baseline using plants that were already polluting less in 1990, due to U.S. regulations.

Nevertheless, the fact that costs are high should not prevent countries from trying to reduce greenhouse gas emissions. A 2006 report by the Stern Commission in the United Kingdom argues that the costs of *not* reducing greenhouse gas emissions are unacceptably high: as high as "the great wars and the economic depression of the first half of the twentieth century" and damage from climate change that is potentially irreversible.[22]

---

[21] These reasons are all mentioned in a speech given by President George W. Bush to the United Nations in 2001. See "In the President's Words: 'A Leadership Role on the Issue of Climate Change,'" *New York Times*, June 12, 2001, electronic edition.

[22] "The Economics of Climate Change," available at http://www.hm-treasury.gov.uk, as cited in Martin Wolf, "A Compelling Case for Action to Avoid a Climatic Catastrophe," *Financial Times*, November 1, 2006, p. 13.

The third point—that the Kyoto Protocol leaves out developing countries such as China and India—is perhaps the major reason why the United States did not ratify the treaty. Just as in the prisoner's dilemma game illustrated in Figure 9-6, if one player does not regulate its emissions, then there is less incentive for the other player to also regulate. For this reason, the Copenhagen Climate Summit, held in Copenhagen in December 2009, brought together all the major countries with an interest in climate change—119 nations in total—to try and hammer out a new agreement. Unfortunately, the meeting ended with only modest goals, called the **Copenhagen Accord**: a recognition that further increases in global average temperature should be kept below 2 degrees centigrade; an agreement that industrialized countries will submit goals for greenhouse gas emissions reductions, while developing countries will communicate their efforts in this regard; and the establishment of a fund to finance the needs of developing countries in fighting the effect of climate change. But as indicated in **Headlines: Dismal Outcome at Copenhagen Fiasco,** these goals come without any firm means to enforce them.

HEADLINES

Dismal Outcome at Copenhagen Fiasco

In the introduction to the chapter, we discussed the Copenhagen Climate Summit, held in December 2009, which was intended to establish new guidelines for reductions in greenhouse gas emissions. The summit did not achieve that goal, unfortunately, and this article discusses possible next steps.

The [Copenhagen Accord] agreement cobbled together by the US, China, India, Brazil and South Africa is merely an expression of aims. It recognises the scientific case for keeping the rise in global temperatures to 2°C. It calls on developed countries to provide $100 [billion] a year in support of poor nations' efforts by 2020, but without saying who pays what to whom. It appears to commit none of the signatories to anything.

. . . Climate change requires global co-operation, to be sure, because the global stock of greenhouse gases is the driver. Collective action is essential. The free-rider problem is obvious and has to be addressed. But the maximalist approach to this, a global treaty with binding caps on emissions, is going to be extraordinar-ily difficult to achieve. Even if the will were there, enforcing the caps would be a problem, as the Kyoto Protocol amply attests. If the maximalist model can be revived in time for next December's [2010] scheduled conference in Mexico, well and good: the key thing, though, is that progress should not be held hostage to it. The need is for greater pragmatism and flexibility.

The US and China can take the lead. In Copenhagen, friction between the two was evident, with the US calling for independent verification of emissions reductions, and China resisting infringe-ments of its sovereignty. In fact the two countries are not so far apart: the US Congress is as jealous of national sover-eignty, and as wary of international ob-ligations, as China. Both countries should lead by example, with unilateral low-cost carbon-abatement policies al-ready announced or under consideration: cap and trade in the US, measures to re-duce carbon intensity in China. The in-ternational framework need not insist on lock-step agreement. Above all, it should not obstruct policies that push the right way. . . .

Generous aid to developing countries for greenhouse gas abatement is war-ranted, but should be negotiated sepa-rately. Again, the need is to unpack the problem into manageable pieces. Copenhagen has shown the limits to the current approach. Reviving international co-operation is of paramount impor-tance. This can best be done by asking less of it.

Source: Excerpted from "Dismal Outcome at Copenhagen Fiasco," Financial Times, December 21, 2009, p. 8.

The **Headlines** article recognizes that action on global climate change requires global cooperation. But the multilateral deal that was attempted at Copenhagen is not the only way to go. Countries can and should pursue domestic policies that limit greenhouse gas emmissions. Europe already has a well-functioning market for carbon emissions, which allows companies and countries to buy and sell credits for such emissions. The United States is considering the same type of market under a "cap and trade" system, which puts a cap (upper limit) on the carbon emissions of each firm, but allows them to trade credits with other firms. Although China does not yet envisage such a system, it is making another type of contribution by focusing on alternative energy, becoming the world's largest producer and exporter of solar panel cells and wind turbines. Furthermore, in March 2010, China and India agreed to join the Copenhagen Accord, as has the United States and more than 100 other countries. These actions show that the modest goals of the Copenhagen Accord have made it easier for countries to join that agreement than the earlier, binding limits of the Kyoto Protocol. Even though this accord does not include a means of enforcement, it could form the basis for future international cooperation on climate change. ■

4 Conclusions

Throughout this book, we have referred to international agreements on trade, including multilateral agreements such as the GATT and WTO and regional agreements such as NAFTA. In this chapter, we have explored the rationale for these agreements more carefully, and we also discussed the areas other than trade—such as labor standards and the environment—that these agreements encompass.

The first issue we addressed is why international agreements are needed at all. The answer is that there are strong temptations for countries to use tariffs for their own benefit, or to avoid adopting environmental regulations, as occurs when countries do not face the costs of their own global pollutants. In these situations, countries have an incentive to use tariffs or not regulate, but when all countries act in this manner, they end up losing: the outcome can be high tariffs or high pollution. This outcome can occur because the countries are in a "prisoner's dilemma" type of game in which the Nash equilibrium leads both parties to act in ways that seem right taken on their own but result in a poor outcome (i.e., both use tariffs or pollute). International agreements are needed to avoid these bad equilibria and restore a free-trade or low-pollution outcome.

A second issue we have addressed is that *halfway* steps toward the complete use of markets (as with complete free trade) can also have bad results. We found that such an outcome was a possibility with regional trade agreements, also called "preferential trade agreements," if the amount of trade diversion caused by the agreement is more than the amount of trade creation. Because preferential trade agreements provide zero tariffs only to the countries included in the agreement but maintain tariffs against all outside countries, they are a halfway step toward free trade. Countries that are not members of the agreement are worse off from being excluded. We have also shown that such agreements *might* make the member countries worse off, too, because the lowest-cost producers can be excluded from the agreement.

Another case in which a halfway step toward open markets can make countries worse off is with the overharvesting of resources. We have argued that in the absence of property rights for an exhaustible resource such as fish, opening countries to free trade can lead to even more harvesting of the resource, to the point of near extinction or extinction. That outcome is bad for the exporting country, at least. So free trade *in the absence of well-defined property rights* can lead to losses. Economists think of this case as opening one market (i.e., free trade between countries) without having a properly functioning market for the resource (i.e., no property rights). Viewed in that way, the overharvesting of an exhaustible resource is similar to trade diversion in a regional trade agreement, since the trade agreement also opens one market (i.e., free trade between member countries) without having complete free trade (i.e., tariffs are applied against the nonmember countries). Both overharvesting and trade diversion are bad outcomes that arise in settings in which markets are not functioning properly.

Finally, we have argued that actions by consumers, unions, and firms to improve labor standards and the environment are important. Such actions, including the protests at the 1999 WTO meetings, *have* made a difference in the rulings of the WTO in environmental cases: although environmentalists have lost some battles at the WTO, some observers believe they have won the war. We can also expect that such actions make a difference to the labor standards enjoyed by workers and the environmental safeguards used by firms.

KEY POINTS

1. There are two primary types of free-trade agreements: multilateral and regional. Multilateral agreements are negotiated among large groups of countries (such as all countries in the WTO) to reduce trade barriers among them, whereas regional agreements operate among a smaller group of countries, often in the same region.

2. Under perfect competition, we can analyze the benefits of multilateral agreements by considering the Nash equilibrium of a two-country game in which the countries are deciding whether to apply a tariff. The unique Nash equilibrium for two large countries is to apply tariffs against each other, which is an example of a "prisoner's dilemma." By using an agreement to remove tariffs, both countries become better off by eliminating the deadweight losses of the tariffs.

3. Regional trade agreements are also known as "preferential trade agreements," because they give preferential treatment (i.e., free trade) to the countries included within the agreement, but maintain tariffs against outside countries. There are two types of regional trade agreements: free-trade areas (such as NAFTA) and customs unions (such as the European Union).

4. The welfare gains and losses that arise from regional trade agreements are more complex than those that arise from multilateral trade agreements because only the countries included within the agreement have zero tariffs, while tariffs are maintained against the countries outside the agreement. Under a free-trade area, the countries within the regional trade agreement each have their own tariffs against outside countries; whereas under a customs union, the countries within the regional trade agreement have the same tariffs against outside countries.

5. Trade creation occurs when a country within a regional agreement imports a product from another member country that formerly it produced for itself. In this case, there is a welfare gain for both the buying and the selling country.

6. Trade diversion occurs when a member country imports a product from another member country that it formerly imported from a country outside of the new trade region. Trade diversion leads to losses for the former exporting country and possibly for the importing country and the new trading region as a whole.

7. Labor standards refer to all issues that directly affect workers, including occupational health and safety, child labor, minimum wages, the right to unionize, and so on. The enforcement of labor standards is sometimes included within trade agreements and is an issue on which consumer groups and unions often demand action.

8. The WTO does not deal directly with the environment, but environmental issues come up as the WTO is asked to rule on specific cases. A review of these cases shows that the WTO has become more friendly to environmental considerations in its rulings.

9. International agreements on the environment are needed for the same reasons that agreements on tariffs are needed—to avoid a prisoner's dilemma type of outcome, which is bad for all countries. The Kyoto Protocol of 2005 had only limited success because the United States did not agree to participate, and developing countries such as China and India were excluded. The Copenhagen Accord of 2009 also did not achieve international commitments with firm enforcement, but at least the United States, China, India, and more than 100 other countries have agreed to participate.

KEY TERMS

terms-of-trade gain, p. 289
multilateral agreement, p. 289
regional trade agreement, p. 289
trade agreement, p. 289
most favored nation principle, p. 289
prisoner's dilemma, p. 292
preferential trade agreements, p. 293

free-trade area, p. 293
customs union, p. 294
rules of origin, p. 294
trade creation, p. 295
trade diversion, p. 295
labor standards, p. 300
living wage, p. 305
multilateral environmental agreements, p. 305

tragedy of the commons, p. 312
common property, p. 312
Kyoto Protocol, p. 317
Copenhagen Accord, p. 318

PROBLEMS

1. a. How is a customs union different from a free-trade area? Provide examples of each.
   b. Why do some economists prefer multilateral trade agreements over regional trade agreements?

2. Figure 9-2 shows the tariff game among large countries.
   a. Redraw the payoff matrix for a game between a large and small country.
   b. What is/are the Nash equilibrium/equilibria, assuming that the large country applies an optimal tariff?
   c. What does your answer to (b) tell you about the role of the WTO in a situation like this?

3. Consider the following variation of Table 9-1 for the U.S. semiconductor market:

	U.S. TARIFF		
	0%	10%	20%
From Canada, before NAFTA	$46	$W	$55.2
From Asia, before NAFTA	$42	$X	$Y
From Canada, after NAFTA	$46	$Z	$Z
From Asia, after NAFTA	$42	$X	$Y
From the United States	$47	$47	$47

a. Fill in the values for W, X, Y, and Z.

b. Suppose that before NAFTA, the United States had a 20% tariff on imported semiconductors. Which country supplied the U.S. market? Is it the lowest-cost producer?

c. After NAFTA, who supplies the U.S. market? Has either trade creation or diversion occurred because of NAFTA? Explain.

d. Now suppose that before NAFTA, the United States had a 10% tariff on imported semiconductors. Then repeat parts (b) and (c).

e. In addition to the assumptions made in (d), consider the effect of an increase in high-technology investment in Canada due to NAFTA, allowing Canadian firms to develop better technology. As a result, *three years after the initiation of NAFTA*, Canadian firms can begin to sell their products to the United States for $46. What happens to the U.S. trade pattern three years after NAFTA? Has either trade creation or diversion occurred because of NAFTA? Explain.

4. Assume that Thailand and India are potential trading partners of China. Thailand is a member of ASEAN but India is not. Suppose the import price of textiles from India (P_{India}) is 50 per unit under free trade and is subject to a 20% tariff. As of January 1st 2010, China and Thailand entered into the China-ASEAN free-trade area, eliminating tariffs on Thai imports. Use the following figure to answer these questions:

a. Before the China-ASEAN free-trade area, how much does China import from each trading partner? What is the import price? Calculate the tariff revenue.

b. After the China-ASEAN free-trade area, how much does China import from each trade partner? What is the import price? What is the total tariff revenue of China?

c. Based on your answer to part (b), what is the impact of the China-ASEAN free-trade area on the welfare of China?

d. What is the effect of the China-ASEAN free-trade area on the welfare of Thailand and India?

e. As mentioned in the **Headlines: China-ASEAN Treaty Threatens Indian Exporters,** the China-ASEAN agreement may lead to a similar one between China and India. How would this affect China's imports from each country? What would be the effect on welfare in China, Thailand, and India if such an agreement was signed?

5. Redraw the graph of trade diversion (Figure 9-3) with the S'_{mex} curve intersecting the M_{US} curve *between* points A and D.

a. When the United States and Mexico join NAFTA, who supplies auto parts to the United States? Does the United States import a larger quantity of auto parts after NAFTA; that is, does trade creation occur?

b. What is the change in government revenue compared to before NAFTA?

c. Is the United States better off for joining NAFTA?

6. Refer to the survey in Table 9-2 regarding consumers' attitudes toward working conditions.

a. Fill in the survey questions for yourself and at least five friends.

b. Average your results, and compare them with those in Table 9-2. Are there any consistent differences in the answers from your friends and those in Table 9-2?

c. Do the answers from your friends show the following two characteristics?

   i. Many people are willing to pay at least a small amount to ensure good labor standards (or simply switch to an alternative with the same price), though relatively few are willing to pay a lot.

   ii. Individuals had to receive a higher discount to purchase a T-shirt made under poor conditions than they were willing to pay for a T-shirt made under good conditions.

   Explain whether these characteristics apply to your friends or not.

7. Using Table 9-3, explain why environmentalists have "lost the battle but won the war" in their dealings with the WTO. Refer to specific WTO cases in your answer.

8. Refer to following variations of the payoff matrix for the environmental game shown in Figure 9-6. In this problem, a number is assigned to represent the welfare level of each outcome for Home and Foreign.

   a. First, consider the case of global pollution in which the government puts more weight on producer profits than consumer well-being when calculating welfare (this is so since a portion of consumer costs are borne by the other country). How can you tell that the government favors producers over consumers from the following payoff matrix? What is the Nash equilibrium for this environmental game? Is it a prisoner's dilemma? Briefly explain.

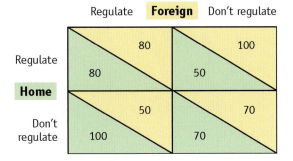

   b. Next, consider the case of local pollution in which the government puts more weight on

consumer well-being than producer profits when calculating welfare. How can you tell that the government favors consumers over producers from the following payoff matrix? What is the Nash equilibrium for this environmental game? Is it a prisoner's dilemma? Briefly explain.

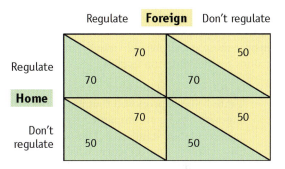

9. Consider the case of protecting the bluefin tuna discussed in **Headlines: Europe Leans Toward Bluefin Trade Ban.** Refer to question 8, and relate this real-world example to the payoff matrices in parts (a) and (b), assuming that Home and Foreign are the United States and Europe. "Regulate" means that the bluefin tuna is classified as endangered, so there is no international trade in this species, whereas "don't regulate" means that it is not classified as endangered.

   a. Which of the two payoff matrices corresponds with both the United States and Europe being more concerned with the fishing industry than with the well-being of the bluefin tuna? What is the Nash equilibrium of that game?

   b. Which of the two payoff matrices corresponds with both the United States and Europe being more concerned with the bluefin species itself than with the fishing industry? What is the Nash equilibrium of that game?

   c. Suppose that Europe is more concerned with the continuation of the bluefin species, and the United States is more concerned with the fishing industry. Draw a payoff matrix for this case and solve for the Nash equilibrium of the game.

Longer study questions: The following questions ask you to consider a real-life situation involving international trade agreements, dealing with trade, labor, or the environment. For each question, you are asked to develop an "agree" or "disagree" position on each situation. These situations are drawn from recent press reports, which are available in the instructor's manual. You can research the issues on the Web and also rely on any relevant information from this textbook. Your instructor might ask you to answer these questions individually, in pairs, or in groups for presentation in class.

10. In 2007, several members of Congress in the United States proposed that any further trade negotiations be accompanied by a "grand bargain" on labor standards. The problem with this action is that the current labor practices of the United States sometimes run afoul of the guidelines of the International Labour Organization (ILO), which would open up the United States to criticism and potentially sanctions from that agency. The article "Why a 'Grand Deal' on Labour Could End Trade Talks" describes these concerns and argues that such a "grand deal" would be a mistake for the United States. A full text of this article is available at http://www.iie.com/publications/opeds/oped.cfm?ResearchID=716.

Answer the following: Do you agree or disagree with the proposal for the United States to pursue a "grand deal" on labor standards, bringing its own laws into line with those of the International Labour Organization?

11. In March 2007 it was announced that several restaurants in the greater San Francisco area would no longer provide bottled water to their patrons to save on the environmental costs of transporting that water: do a web search for the phrase "bottled water backlash" to find articles about the San Francisco restaurants and other companies taking this action. Instead, these companies would install filtering equipment that would allow them to serve local water. Although these actions are intended to be more environmentally friendly, they will affect firms and countries that sell bottled water. One of these countries is Fiji, which obtains a major portion of its export earnings from bottled water.

Answer the following: Do you agree or disagree with the actions taken by the restaurants in San Francisco?

NETWORK

Google "corporate responsibility" to find an example, other than Nike, of a corporation or group of companies that is adopting procedures to protect workers' rights or the environment. Briefly describe the procedures being adopted.

Introduction to Exchange Rates and the Foreign Exchange Market

The chapter on the Fall of the Rupee you may omit. It is somewhat too sensational.
Miss Prism, in Oscar Wilde's *The Importance of Being Earnest*, 1895

The people who benefit from roiling the world currency market are speculators and as far as I am concerned they provide not much useful value.
Paul O'Neill, U.S. Secretary of the Treasury, 2002

Every few years, George, an American, takes a vacation in Paris. To make purchases in Paris, he buys foreign currency, or *foreign exchange*. He can purchase euros, the currency used in France, by trading his U.S. dollars for them in the *market for foreign exchange* at the prevailing market *exchange rate*. In 2003, 1 euro could be purchased for $1.10, so the €100 he spent on a night at the hotel cost him $110 in U.S. currency. In 2007, 1 euro cost $1.32, so each night at the same hotel (where the room price hadn't changed) made a $132 dent in his vacation budget. In 2010, 1 euro cost $1.24, not as much as in 2007, but still expensive enough in dollar terms to make George think about vacationing in northern California, where he reckoned he might find equally good hotels, restaurants, fine food, and wine at prices that were more affordable.

Tourists like George are not the only people affected by exchange rates. Exchange rates affect large flows of international trade by influencing the prices in different currencies of the imported goods and services we buy and the exported goods and services we sell. Foreign exchange also facilitates massive flows of international investment, which include the direct investments made by multinationals in overseas firms as well as the stock and bond trades made by individual investors and fund managers seeking to diversify their portfolios.

Individual foreign exchange transactions are far removed from deep macroeconomic and political consequences. In the aggregate, however, activity in the foreign exchange market can be responsible for "sensational" events (and we are not being ironic, unlike Oscar Wilde in the chapter opening quote) and can arouse strong passions (Paul O'Neill is only one of many to criticize the activities of foreign exchange traders). In the foreign exchange market, trillions of dollars are traded each day and the economic implications of shifts in the market can be dramatic. In times of crisis, the fates of nations and their leaders seem to hang, in part, on the state of the currency market. Why is that so?

In this chapter, we begin to study the nature and impact of activity in the foreign exchange market. We first survey exchange rate basics: the key definitions of exchange rates and related concepts. We then examine the evidence to see how exchange rates behave in the real world and establish some basic facts about exchange rate behavior that require explanation. We next look at the workings of the foreign exchange market, including the role of private participants as well as interventions by governments. Finally, we look in detail at how foreign exchange markets work, and we emphasize two key market mechanisms: *arbitrage* and *expectations*.

1 Exchange Rate Essentials

An **exchange rate** (E) is the price of some foreign currency expressed in terms of a home (or domestic) currency. Because an exchange rate is the relative price of two currencies, it may be quoted in either of two ways:

1. The number of home currency units that can be exchanged for one unit of foreign currency. For example, if the United States is considered home, the dollar/euro exchange rate might be $1.15 per euro (or 1.15 $/€). To buy one euro, you would have to pay $1.15.

2. The number of foreign currency units that can be exchanged for one unit of home currency. For example, the 1.15$/€ exchange rate can also be expressed as €0.87 per U.S. dollar (or 0.87 €/$). To buy one dollar, you would have to pay €0.87.

Knowing the format in which exchange rates are quoted is essential to avoid confusion, so we now establish a systematic rule, even if it is arbitrary.

Defining the Exchange Rate

It is common practice to quote the prices of items traded, whether goods or assets, as units of home currency per unit purchased. In the United States, coffee might be sold at 10 dollars per pound ($/lb); in France, at 20 euros per kilogram (€/kg).[1]

The usual way to quote the price of foreign currency is no different: units of home currency per unit of foreign currency. Confusion may arise because the price then depends on the perspective of the observer. Consider the dollar-euro exchange rate. For the U.S. citizen, who is accustomed to prices expressed as $/unit, the price of a foreign currency (say, the euro) is in terms of $/€. For someone in the Eurozone, however, the convention is to quote prices as €/unit, so €/$ would be the natural choice.

To avoid confusion, we must specify which country is the home country and which is foreign. Throughout the remaining chapters of this book, when we refer to a particular

---

[1] Coffee prices could also be quoted as 0.1 lb/$ or 0.05 kg/€, but this format is not the norm.

country's exchange rate, we will quote it in terms of units of home currency per units of foreign currency. For example, Denmark's exchange rate with the Eurozone is quoted as Danish krone per euro (or kr/€).

From now on, $E_{1/2}$ will denote the exchange rate in units of country 1 currency per unit of country 2 currency; it is the rate at which country 1's currency can be exchanged for one unit of country 2's currency. For example, $E_{\$/€}$ is the U.S. exchange rate (against the euro) in U.S. dollars per euro. In our previous example, $E_{\$/€}$ was 1.15 $/€.

We see different expressions of the same exchange rate all the time—even on the same page in the same publication! So it is important to keep things straight. Table 10-1 presents a typical display of exchange rate information as one might see it in the financial press.[2] Column (1) shows the reported price of U.S. dollars in various currencies (e.g., €/$); columns (2) and (3) show, respectively, the most recent price of British pounds sterling (e.g., $/£) and euros (e.g., $/€) on June 30, 2010.[3] Thus, the first three entries show the Canadian dollar's exchange rate against the U.S. dollar, the pound, and the euro. For comparison, columns (4) to (6) show the same rates one year earlier.

TABLE 10-1

Exchange Rate Quotations This table shows major exchange rates as they might appear in the financial media. Columns (1) to (3) show rates on June 30, 2010. For comparison, columns (4) to (6) show rates on June 30, 2009. For example, column (1) shows that on June 30, 2010, one U.S. dollar was worth 1.063 Canadian dollars, 6.081 Danish krone, 0.816 euros, and so on. The euro-dollar rates appear in bold type.

Country (currency)	Currency Symbol	EXCHANGE RATES ON JUNE 30, 2010			EXCHANGE RATES ON JUNE 30, 2009 *ONE YEAR PREVIOUSLY*		
		(1)	(2)	(3)	(4)	(5)	(6)
		Per $	Per £	Per €	Per $	Per £	Per €
Canada (dollar)	C$	1.063	1.590	1.302	1.161	1.913	1.629
Denmark (krone)	DKr	6.081	9.098	7.449	5.309	8.743	7.447
Euro (euro)	€	**0.816**	1.221	—	**0.713**	1.174	—
Japan (yen)	¥	88.49	132.39	108.39	96.49	158.90	135.34
Norway (krone)	NKr	6.503	9.729	7.966	6.437	10.600	9.028
Sweden (krona)	SKr	7.782	11.643	9.532	7.748	12.760	10.868
Switzerland (franc)	SFr	1.078	1.613	1.321	1.088	1.791	1.526
United Kingdom (pound)	£	0.668	—	0.819	0.607	—	0.852
United States (dollar)	$	—	1.496	**1.225**	—	1.647	**1.403**

Source: ft.com

---

[2] These are typically *midrange* or *central* rates—an end-of-day average of buying and selling rates from the market. As we discuss later in the chapter, such rates do not allow for the differences or *spreads*, between the prices at which currencies are bought and sold. In any market in which intermediaries are present, commissions and fees push buying prices above selling prices.

[3] The currency's price in terms of itself equals 1 and is omitted.

The four bold entries in this table correspond to the dollar-euro exchange rate. On June 30, 2010, for example, the euro was quoted at $1.225 per euro. According to our definition, this is the price from the U.S. perspective and it is sometimes called the *American terms*. Conversely, the dollar is quoted at €0.816 per dollar, the *European terms*.

We write these exchange rates using mathematical symbols as follows, with care given to the explicit expression of the relevant units:

$$E_{\$/\euro} = 1.225 = \text{U.S. exchange rate (American terms)}$$

$$E_{\euro/\$} = 0.816 = \text{Eurozone exchange rate (European terms)}$$

Just as there is complete equivalence when we express the relative price of coffee and dollars at 10 $/lb or 0.1 lb/$, the price of the euro in terms of dollars always equals the reciprocal (or inverse) of the price of dollars in terms of euros. Hence,

$$E_{\$/\euro} = \frac{1}{E_{\euro/\$}}$$

In our example,

$$1.225 = \frac{1}{0.816}$$

Similar calculations and notations apply to any pair of currencies.

Appreciations and Depreciations

Like many financial tables, Table 10-1 includes information on how prices have changed over time. Over the previous 12 months, the Eurozone exchange rate *increased* from $E_{\euro/\$} = 0.713$ a year ago to $E_{\euro/\$} = 0.816$ on June 30, 2010. The value of the euro relative to the dollar went down—more euros were needed to buy one dollar. This change is often described by saying that the euro got "weaker" or "weakened" against the dollar.

Symmetrically, the value of the dollar in euro terms also changed. We see this by computing the reciprocal American terms. Over the same year, the U.S exchange rate *decreased* from $E_{\$/\euro} = 1/0.713 = 1.403$ a year ago to $E_{\$/\euro} = 1/0.816 = 1.225$ on June 30, 2010. The value of the dollar relative to the euro went up—fewer dollars were needed to buy one euro. This change is often described by saying that the dollar got "stronger" or "strengthened" against the euro.

If one currency buys more of another currency, we say it has experienced an **appreciation**—its value has *risen*, *appreciated*, or *strengthened*. If a currency buys less of another currency, we say it has experienced a **depreciation**—its value has *fallen*, *depreciated*, or *weakened*.

In our example, we can understand appreciation and depreciation from both the U.S. and European perspective; this lesson generalizes to all other currency pairs.

In U.S. terms, the following holds true:

■ When the U.S. exchange rate $E_{\$/\euro}$ *rises*, more dollars are needed to buy one euro. The price of one euro goes up in dollar terms, and the U.S. dollar experiences a depreciation.

■ When the U.S. exchange rate $E_{\$/\euro}$ *falls*, fewer dollars are needed to buy one euro. The price of one euro goes down in dollar terms, and the U.S. dollar experiences an appreciation.

Similarly, in European terms, the following holds true:

■ When the Eurozone exchange rate $E_{€/\$}$ *rises*, the price of one dollar goes up in euro terms and the euro experiences a depreciation.

■ When the Eurozone exchange rate $E_{€/\$}$ *falls*, the price of one dollar goes down in euro terms and the euro experiences an appreciation.

If the dollar is appreciating against the euro, the euro must simultaneously be depreciating against the dollar. Because they are the reciprocal of each other, changes in $E_{\$/€}$ and $E_{€/\$}$ must always move in opposite directions.

It may seem confusing or counterintuitive that a fall in the U.S. exchange rate means the dollar is appreciating. Yet it is reasonable because we express the price of foreign currency in dollars, just as we express the prices of other goods. When the price of coffee falls from $10 to $9 per pound, it seems sensible to say that coffee is depreciating or falling in value—but relative to what? The dollars—the currency in which the price is denominated. Conversely, dollars are *appreciating* against coffee because it takes fewer dollars to buy the same amount of coffee! If we keep this analogy in mind, it makes sense that when the dollar price of a euro falls, the dollar has appreciated against the euro.

Exchange rate humor.

In addition to knowing whether a currency has appreciated or depreciated, we are often interested in the knowing the size of an appreciation or depreciation. To do this, we can calculate the proportional or fractional change in the foreign-currency value of the home currency. This proportional change is usually expressed in percentage terms.

In the previous example, we would describe these changes as follows:

■ In 2009, at time t, the dollar value of the euro was $E_{\$/€,t} = \$1.403$.

■ In 2010, at time $t + 1$, the dollar value of the euro was $E_{\$/€,t+1} = \$1.225$.

■ The change in the dollar value of the euro was $\Delta E_{\$/€,t} = 1.225 - 1.403 = \${-}0.178$.

■ The percentage change was $\Delta E_{\$/€,t}/E_{\$/€,t} = -0.178/1.403 = -12.7\%$.

■ Thus, the euro *depreciated* against the dollar by 12.7%.

Similarly, over the same year:

■ In 2009, at time t, the euro value of the dollar was $E_{€/\$,t} = €0.713$.

■ In 2010, at time $t + 1$, the euro value of the dollar was $E_{€/\$,t+1} = €0.816$.

■ The change in the euro value of the dollar was $\Delta E_{€/\$,t} = 0.816 - 0.713 = €{+}0.103$.

■ The percentage change was $\Delta E_{€/\$,t}/E_{€/\$,t} = +0.103/0.713 = +14.4\%$.

■ Thus, the dollar *appreciated* against the euro by 14.4%.

Note that the size of one country's appreciation (here 14.4%) does not exactly equal the size of the other country's depreciation (here 12.7%). For small changes, however, the opposing movements are *approximately* equal. For example, if the

U.S. terms move slightly from $1.00 to $1.01 per euro, the European terms move from €1.00 to €0.99099; a 1% euro appreciation is approximately a 1% dollar depreciation.[4]

Multilateral Exchange Rates

Our discussion of exchange rates has focused on the simplest type of exchange rate between two countries or currencies, what economists refer to as a *bilateral* exchange rate. In reality, we live in a world of many countries and many currencies, and it is of great practical importance to ask whether a particular currency has strengthened or weakened not just against one other currency, but against other currencies in general.

The answer is not always obvious. For example, the U.S. dollar may be depreciating against some currencies, while remaining fixed or appreciating against others. To aggregate these different trends in bilateral exchange rates into one measure, economists calculate *multilateral* exchange rate changes for baskets of currencies using *trade weights* to construct an average of all the bilateral changes for each currency in the basket. The resulting measure is called the change in the **effective exchange rate.**

For example, suppose 40% of Home trade is with country 1 and 60% is with country 2; Home's currency appreciates 10% against 1 but depreciates 30% against 2. To calculate the change in Home's effective exchange rate, we multiply each exchange rate change by the corresponding trade share and then add up: $(-10\% \cdot 40\%) + (30\% \cdot 60\%) = (-0.1 \cdot 0.4) + (0.3 \cdot 0.6) = -0.04 + 0.18 = 0.14 = +14\%$. In this example, Home's effective exchange rate has depreciated by 14%.

In general, suppose there are N currencies in the basket, and Home's trade with the N partners is $\text{Trade} = \text{Trade}_1 + \text{Trade}_2 + \ldots + \text{Trade}_N$. Applying trade weights to each bilateral exchange rate change, the home country's effective exchange rate ($E_{\text{effective}}$) will change according to the following weighted average:

$$\frac{\Delta E_{\text{effective}}}{E_{\text{effective}}} = \underbrace{\frac{\Delta E_1}{E_1}\frac{\text{Trade}_1}{\text{Trade}} + \frac{\Delta E_2}{E_2}\frac{\text{Trade}_2}{\text{Trade}} + \ldots + \frac{\Delta E_N}{E_N}\frac{\text{Trade}_N}{\text{Trade}}}_{\text{Trade-weighted average of bilateral nominal exchange rate changes}}$$

Many discussions among policy makers and in the financial press focus on the effective exchange rate. An especially contentious topic in the last decade has been the path of the United States' effective exchange rate, shown in Figure 10-1. It is clear that, since

---

[4] In general, suppose that the home exchange rate is a, so one unit of home currency buys $1/a$ units of foreign currency. Now the home exchange rate depreciates to $b > a$, and one unit of home currency buys $1/b$ units of foreign currency, with $1/b < 1/a$. The size of the depreciation D of the home currency is

$$D = \left(\frac{1}{a} - \frac{1}{b}\right)\bigg/\left(\frac{1}{a}\right) = \left(1 - \frac{a}{b}\right) = \left(\frac{b-a}{b}\right)$$

Symmetrically, the foreign currency was initially worth a units of home currency but is now worth b. Thus, the size of the appreciation A of the foreign currency is

$$A = \frac{(b-a)}{a} = \frac{b}{a}D$$

Thus, the percentage appreciation A will be approximately equal to the percentage depreciation D when b/a is close to 1, or when b is approximately equal to a, that is, when the change in the exchange rate is small.

FIGURE 10-1

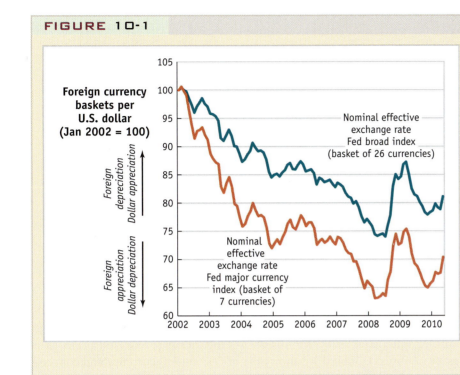

Effective Exchange Rates: Change in the Value of the U.S. Dollar, 2002–2010 The chart shows the value of the dollar measured by the U.S. Federal Reserve using two different baskets of foreign currencies, starting with the index set to 100 foreign baskets in January 2002. Against a basket of 7 major currencies, the dollar had depreciated by more than 25% by late 2004, and 35% by early 2008. But against a broad basket of 26 currencies, the dollar had lost only 15% of its value by 2004, and 25% by 2008. This is because the dollar was floating against the major currencies, but the broad basket included important U.S. trading partners (such as China and other Asian economies) that maintained fixed or tightly managed exchange rates against the dollar. These trends reversed somewhat after the global financial crisis of 2008.

Source: U.S. Federal Reserve.

2002, the U.S. dollar steadily has fallen in value against a basket of other currencies. It lost quite a lot of value against many well-known major currencies, such as the euro, the pound sterling, the Canadian dollar, and the Swiss franc. But on average, the weakening of the dollar was not as pronounced when measured against *all* U.S. trading partners. The simple reason for this was the fact that Japan and China, along with several other developing countries in Asia, sought to peg or control their exchange rates to limit their appreciation against the dollar. Thus in the figure, the downward trend for the broad basket of currencies is not as steep as that for the basket of seven major currencies.

Example: Using Exchange Rates to Compare Prices in a Common Currency

To make comparisons of prices across nations, we must convert prices to a common currency. The following examples show how we use exchange rates to accomplish this task.

James Bond is back from another mission and, what with all the explosions and shootouts, his wardrobe is looking ragged. He needs a new tuxedo. Bond will be in numerous cities On Her Majesty's Secret Service in the next few days, so he can shop around the globe. Although style is important, price is a key factor in Bond's choice, given the paltry MI6 clothing allowance. Should he visit a new tailor in Manhattan? Go back to his favorite cutter in Hong Kong? Or simply nip around the corner to Savile Row in London?

The London tailor sells a tux for £2,000; the Hong Kong shop is asking HK$30,000; and in New York, the going rate is $4,000. In the near future, when the decision must be made, these prices are fixed in their respective home currencies. Which tux will 007 choose?

TABLE 10-2

Using the Exchange Rate to Compare Prices in a Common Currency Now pay attention, 007! This table shows how the hypothetical cost of James Bond's next tuxedo in different locations depends on the exchange rates that prevail.

Scenario		1	2	3	4
Cost of the tuxedo in local currency	London	£2,000	£2,000	£2,000	£2,000
	Hong Kong	HK$30,000	HK$30,000	HK$30,000	HK$30,000
	New York	$4,000	$4,000	$4,000	$4,000
Exchange rates	HK$/£	15	16	14	14
	$/£	2.0	1.9	2.1	1.9
Cost of the tuxedo in pounds	London	£2,000	£2,000	£2,000	£2,000
	Hong Kong	£2,000	£1,875	£2,143	£2,143
	New York	£2,000	£2,105	£1,905	£2,105

To choose among goods priced in different currencies, Bond must first convert all the prices into a common currency; for this he uses the exchange rate (and a calculator disguised as a toothbrush). Table 10-2 shows the prices, in local currency and converted into pounds, under different hypothetical exchange rates.

Scenario 1 In the first column, the Hong Kong suit costs HK$30,000 and the exchange rate is HK$15 per £. Dividing HK$30,000 by 15, we find that this suit costs £2,000 in British currency. The U.S. suit has a price of $4,000, and at an exchange rate of $2 per pound we obtain a British currency price of £2,000. Here the exchange rates are such that all prices are the same when measured in a common currency (pounds). Bond has a difficult choice.

Scenario 2 Moving to the next column, the Hong Kong dollar has depreciated against the pound compared with scenario 1: it takes more HK$ (16 instead of 15) to buy £1. In contrast, the U.S. dollar has appreciated against the pound: it takes fewer dollars (1.9 instead of 2.0) to buy £1. At the new exchange rates, the cost of the New York tux has gone up to £2,105 (4,000/1.9), and the Hong Kong tux has fallen to £1,875 (30,000/16). Hong Kong now has the lowest price.

Scenario 3 Compared with scenario 1, the Hong Kong dollar has appreciated: it takes fewer $HK to buy £1 (14 instead of 15), and the price of the Hong Kong tux has risen to £2,143 (30,000/14). The U.S. dollar, on the other hand, has depreciated: it takes more dollars (2.1 instead of 2) to buy £1. With the dollar's depreciation, New York now has the best price of £1,905 (4,000/2.1).

Scenario 4 In this case, compared with scenario 1, the pound has depreciated against both of the other currencies, and they have each appreciated against the pound. It takes fewer Hong Kong dollars (14 instead of 15) and fewer U.S. dollars (1.9 instead of 2.0) to buy £1. Now London has the bargain price of £2,000 and the other cities have higher prices.

This example illustrates a key point. We assumed that while exchange rates may change, the prices of goods in each country are fixed in the short run (in domestic-currency terms). An economist would say the prices are *sticky* in the short run, and, as we see later, this is not an unreasonable assumption. Given that assumption, changes in exchange rates will cause changes in the common-currency prices of goods from different countries.

Generalizing The same logic applies to any exchange rate. All else equal, when the prices of goods are constant in each country, the following conclusions will apply:

- *Changes in the exchange rate cause changes in prices of foreign goods expressed in the home currency.*
- *Changes in the exchange rate cause changes in the relative prices of goods produced in the home and foreign countries.*
- *When the home country's exchange rate depreciates, home exports become less expensive as imports to foreigners, and foreign exports become more expensive as imports to home residents.*
- *When the home country's exchange rate appreciates, home exports become more expensive as imports to foreigners, and foreign exports become less expensive as imports to home residents.*

2 Exchange Rates in Practice

Having seen Table 10-1, it might be tempting to use the same figures as a guide to today's exchange rates between countries, but this would be a big mistake. Exchange rates fluctuate. They depreciate and appreciate. A lot. On a single day, in a matter of hours or even minutes, they can change substantially. Over a year, they move up and down, and may drift considerably in one direction or another. Any complete theory of exchange rate determination must account for observed behavior, so we should familiarize ourselves with the various patterns we seek to explain.

Exchange Rate Regimes: Fixed Versus Floating

Economists group different patterns of exchange rate behavior into categories known as **exchange rate regimes.** These regimes reflect choices made by governments, and the causes and consequences of exchange rate regimes are a major focus of our study.
There are two major regime types:

- **Fixed** (or **pegged**) exchange rate regimes are those in which a country's exchange rate fluctuates in a narrow range (or not at all) against some *base currency* over a sustained period, usually a year or longer. A country's exchange rate can remain rigidly fixed for long periods only if the government intervenes in the foreign exchange market in one or both countries.
- **Floating** (or **flexible**) exchange rate regimes are those in which a country's exchange rate fluctuates in a wider range, and the government makes no attempt to fix it against any base currency. Appreciations and depreciations may occur from year to year, each month, by the day, or every minute.

For example, earlier in the book we saw data for two of the most talked about exchange rates in the world today: the U.S. dollar-euro and the Chinese yuan-U.S. dollar rates. The dollar-euro rate fluctuated considerably and was said to be floating; the yuan-dollar rate held steady or changed very slowly and was said to be fixed.

However, the "fixed versus floating" classification is not without its problems. First, in practice, to judge whether a regime is fixed or floating, we have to decide where we draw the line between "narrow" and "wide" fluctuations. One rule of thumb is to use the size of annual variations (say, within ±2% or ±1%) as the sign of a fixed regime. Second, "fixed versus floating" is only a very broad description of exchange rate regimes. In reality, the distinctions are not so cut and dried. Fixed and floating provide important benchmarks throughout this book and deliver great insights, but we sometimes need more precise ways of describing *intermediate regimes*, as the following application illustrates.

APPLICATION

Recent Exchange Rate Experiences

If we spend a moment looking at recent exchange rate experiences in a variety of countries, we see not only some helpful illustrations of the differences between floating and fixed rate regimes but also some of the different varieties of fixed and floating behavior. We also encounter the phenomenon of regime change, in which one type of regime gives way to another, either smoothly or catastrophically.

Evidence from Developed Countries Figure 10-2 shows the daily exchange rates from 1996 to 2010 for various currency pairs. The top row shows the U.S. dollar exchange rate against two major currencies (the Japanese yen, the British pound) and against the currency of a neighboring country (the Canadian dollar, also called the *loonie* because it has a loon on it). The bottom row shows the exchange rate of the euro against the yen, the pound, and the Danish krone. In all six charts, the vertical scale varies by a factor of 2 from maximum to minimum, so all of these charts are comparable in terms of their representation of these exchange rates' volatility.

We can clearly see that the U.S. dollar is in a floating relationship with all three foreign currencies shown in the top row—the yen, pound, and loonie. How volatile are the exchange rates? The range of variation in each case is about the same, with the maximum being about one and a half times the minimum: the yen ranges from about $0.0065 to $0.0110, the pound from $1.3 to almost $2, the loonie from $0.6 to about $1. The movements between these peaks and troughs may take many months or years to occur, but the exchange rate also shows a great deal of short-run volatility, with lots of up-and-down movement from day to day. A floating regime of this sort is called a **free float**.

Similarly, the bottom row of Figure 10-2 shows that the euro floats against the yen and the pound. In the sixth and final chart, the Danish krone provides a contrast—an example of a fixed exchange rate in a developed country. Denmark is part of the European Union, but like Britain, it has kept its own national currency, at least for now, and does not use the euro as its currency. Unlike Britain, however, Denmark has fixed its exchange rate against the euro, keeping it very close to 7.44 krone per euro (0.134 euro per krone). There is only a tiny variation around this rate, no more than plus or minus 2%. This type of fixed regime is known as a **band**.

Evidence from Developing Countries Figure 10-3 shows the daily exchange rates against the U.S. dollar from 1996 to 2010 for some developing countries. Exchange rates in developing countries can be much more volatile than those in developed countries. The charts in the top row illustrate exchange rate behavior in three Asian

FIGURE 10-2

Exchange Rate Behavior: Selected Developed Countries, 1996–2010 This figure shows exchange rates of three currencies against the U.S. dollar and three against the euro. The euro rates begin in 1999 when the currency was introduced. The yen, pound, and Canadian dollar all float against the U.S. dollar. The pound and yen float against the euro. The Danish krone is fixed against the euro. The vertical scale ranges by a factor of 2 on all charts.

Source: oanda.com.

countries (India, Thailand, and South Korea); the maximum on the vertical axis is three times the minimum.

India had what looked like a fixed rate of about 35 rupees per dollar until a depreciation in 1997; there was then a period of pronounced movement more like a float. However, the government still acted to prevent abrupt currency movements even after 1997. This middle ground, somewhere between a fixed rate and a free float, is called a **managed float** (also known as a *dirty float*, or a policy of *limited flexibility*).

Thailand and South Korea show more extreme versions of the same pattern, except that in these cases the depreciation in 1997 was large and sudden, with the baht and the won exchange rates more than doubling in a matter of weeks. Such dramatic depreciations are called **exchange rate crises** and they are more common in developing countries than in developed countries. Indeed, South Korea had another mini-crisis in 2008.

FIGURE 10-3

Exchange Rate Behavior: Selected Developing Countries, 1996–2010 Exchange rates in developing countries show a wide variety of experiences and greater volatility. Pegging is common but is punctuated by periodic crises (you can see the effects of these crises in graphs for Thailand, South Korea, and Argentina). Rates that are unpegged may show some flexibility (India). Some rates crawl gradually (Colombia). Dollarization can occur (Ecuador). The vertical scale ranges by a factor of 3 on the upper charts and by a factor of 10 on the lower charts.

Source: oanda.com.

The bottom row of Figure 10-3 shows some Latin American countries and more varieties of exchange rate experience. The maximum on the vertical scale is now ten times the minimum, a change made necessary by the even more volatile exchange rates in this region.

Argentina initially had a fixed rate (of one peso per dollar), followed in 2001 by an exchange rate crisis. After a period of limited flexibility, Argentina returned to an almost fixed rate with a band that appeared to be centered at about three pesos per dollar, before drifting higher after 2008.

Colombia presents an example of a different kind of fixed exchange rate. Here the authorities did not target the level of the Colombian peso but allowed it to steadily depreciate at an almost constant rate for several years from 1996 to 2002. This type of fixed arrangement is called a **crawl** (if the exchange rate follows a simple trend, it is a *crawling peg;* if some variation about the trend is allowed, it is termed a *crawling band*).

In the final figure, Ecuador displays a different crisis pattern. Here a period of floating was followed by a fixed rate rather than the other way around. Episodes of very rapid depreciation like this represent a distinct form of exchange rate behavior; some economists have suggested, not jokingly, that these regimes be identified separately as *freely falling* exchange rate regimes.[5] The Ecuadorean currency stabilized at a fixed rate of 25,000 sucres per dollar, but then the sucre ceased to be. Ecuador took the remarkable step of dollarizing: abolishing its own national currency and adopting the U.S. dollar as its legal tender.

Currency Unions and Dollarization Almost every economy issues its own currency and jealously guards this sovereign right. There are only two exceptions: groups of economies that agree to form a currency or monetary union and adopt a common currency and individual economies that dollarize by adopting the currency of another country as their own.

Under a **currency union** (or **monetary** union), there is some form of transnational structure such as a single central bank or monetary authority that is accountable to the member nations. The most prominent example of a currency union is the Eurozone. Other currency unions include the CFA and CFP Franc zones (among some former French colonies in Africa and the Pacific) and the Eastern Caribbean Currency Union of nine member states.

Under **dollarization** one country unilaterally adopts the currency of another country. The reasons for this choice can vary. The adopting country may be very small, so the costs of running its own central bank and issuing its own currency may be prohibitive. Such is the case, for example, for the 50 or so Pitcairn Islanders (who use New Zealand as their standard currency). Other countries may have a poor record of managing their own monetary affairs and may end up "importing" a better policy from abroad. The currency changeover could be a de jure policy choice; or it may happen de facto if people are so fed up that they stop using the national currency and switch en masse to an alternative. Many of these economies use the U.S. dollar, but other popular choices include the euro, and the Australian and New Zealand dollars.

Exchange Rate Regimes of the World To move beyond specific examples, Figure 10-4 shows an IMF classification of exchange rate regimes around the world, which allows us to see the prevalence of different regime types across the whole spectrum from fixed to floating.[6]

The classification covers 192 economies for the year 2008, and regimes are ordered from the most rigidly fixed to the most freely floating. The first 46 countries are those

---

[5] Carmen M. Reinhart and Kenneth S. Rogoff, February 2004, "The Modern History of Exchange Rate Arrangements: A Reinterpretation," *Quarterly Journal of Economics*, 119(1), 1–48.

[6] The IMF now uses an unofficial classification based on observed exchange rate behavior. Most economists prefer this type of classification to the often misleading official classifications that were based on countries' official policy announcements. For example, as we saw in Figure 10-3, Thailand pegged to the dollar before the 1997 crisis, even though official statements denied this and the Thai authorities claimed the baht was floating. On unofficial or de facto classifications, see Carmen M. Reinhart and Kenneth S. Rogoff, February 2004, "The Modern History of Exchange Rate Arrangements: A Reinterpretation," *Quarterly Journal of Economics*, 119(1), 1–48. Jay C. Shambaugh, February 2004, "The Effect of Fixed Exchange Rates on Monetary Policy," *Quarterly Journal of Economics*, 119(1), 301–352. Eduardo Levy Yeyati and Federico Sturzenegger, August 2005, "Classifying Exchange Rate Regimes: Deeds vs. Words," *European Economic Review*, 49(6), 1603–1635.

FIGURE 10-4

Increasingly fixed ↑	**No separate legal tender (46 countries)**	*Another currency as legal tender*: East Timor, Ecuador, El Salvador, Kiribati, Marshall Islands, Micronesia, Montenegro, Palau, Panama, San Marino *Eastern Caribbean Currency Union*: Antigua and Barbuda, Dominica, Grenada, St. Kitts and Nevis, St. Lucia, St. Vincent and the Grenadines *West African CFA Franc Zone*: Benin, Burkina Faso, Côte d'Ivoire, Guinea-Bissau, Mali, Niger, Senegal, Togo *Central African CFA Franc Zone*: Cameroon, Central African Rep., Chad, Rep. of Congo, Equatorial Guinea, Gabon *Eurozone*: Austria, Belgium, Cyprus, Finland, France, Germany, Greece, Ireland, Italy, Luxembourg, Malta, Netherlands, Portugal, Slovakia, Slovenia, Spain
	Currency boards (7)	Bosnia and Herzegovina, Brunei, Bulgaria, Djibouti, Estonia, Hong Kong, Lithuania
	Other fixed pegs (58)	Angola, Argentina, Aruba, Bahamas, Bahrain, Bangladesh, Barbados, Belarus, Belize, Bhutan, Capre Verde, Comoros, Croatia, Denmark, Eritrea, Fiji, Guyana, Honduras, Jordan, Kazakhstan, Kuwait, Latvia, Lebanon, Lesotho, Libya, Macedonia, Malawi, Maldives, Mongolia, Morocco, Namibia, Nepal, Netherlands Antillies, Oman, Qatar, Russia, Rwanda, Samoa, Saudi Arabia, Seychelles, Sierra Leone, Solomon Islands, Sri Lanka, Suriname, Swaziland, Tajikistan, Trinidad and Tobago, Tunisia, Turkmenistan, United Arab Emirates, Venezuela, Vietnam, Yemen, Zimbabwe
	Pegged within horizontal bands (2)	Syria, Tonga
	Crawling pegs (8)	Bolivia, Botswana, China, Ethiopia, Iran, Iraq, Nicaragua, Uzbekistan
	Crawling bands (2)	Azerbaijan, Costa Rica
Increasingly floating ↓	**Managed floating with no predetermined path for the exchange rate (44)**	Afghanistan, Algeria, Armenia, Bangladesh, Burundi, Cambodia, Colombia, Dominican Rep., Egypt, Gambia, Georgia, Ghana, Guatemala, Guinea, Haiti, India, Indonesia, Jamaica, Kenya, Kyrgyzstan, Laos, Liberia, Madagascar, Malaysia, Mauritania, Mauritius, Moldova, Mozambique, Myanmar, Nigeria, Pakistan, Papua New Guinea, Paraguay, Peru, Romania, São Tomé and Príncipe, Serbia, Singapore, Sudan, Tanzania, Thailand, Uganda, Ukraine, Uruguay, Vanuatu
	Independently floating (25)	Albania, Australia, Brazil, Canada, Chile, Czech Rep. Dem. Rep. of Congo, Hungary, Iceland, Israel, Japan, Mexico, New Zealand, Norway, Philippines, Poland, Somalia, South Africa, South Korea, Sweden, Switzerland, Turkey, United Kingdom, United States, Zambia

A Spectrum of Exchange Rate Regimes The chart shows a recent classification of exchange rate regimes around the world.

Source: With the exception of Slovakia (which joined the Eurozone on January 1, 2009, and is classified as such) all classifications are for April 2008 and based on the IMF's "De Facto Classification of Exchange Rate Regimes and Monetary Policy Frameworks." Note that Estonia is expected to join the Eurozone on January 1, 2011.

that have no currency of their own—they are either dollarized or in a currency union. Next are 7 countries using an ultrahard peg called a **currency board,** a type of fixed regime that has special legal and procedural rules designed to make the peg "harder"— that is, more durable. Then come 58 conventional pegs, with variations of less than ±1%, some fixed to a single currency and a few pegging against a basket of currencies. These are followed by the less rigidly fixed arrangements such as the 2 bands, 8 crawling pegs, and 2 crawling bands. We then encounter two kinds of flexible regimes: the 44 regimes of managed floating rates, in which the authorities seem to restrict exchange rate movements to a noticeable degree, and lastly the 25 independently floating regimes.

Looking Ahead This brief look at the evidence supplies important motivation for the analysis in the remainder of this book. First, the world is divided into fixed and floating rate regimes, so we need to understand how *both* types of regime work. Studying fixed and floating regimes side by side will occupy much of our attention for the next few chapters. Second, when we look at who is fixed and who is floating, we start to notice patterns. Most of the floaters are advanced countries and most of the fixers are developing countries (the major exception is the euro area). The important question of why some countries fix while others float is covered in more detail in later chapters. ■

3 The Market for Foreign Exchange

Day by day, and minute by minute, exchange rates the world over are set in the **foreign exchange market** (or **forex** or **FX** market), which, like any market, is a collection of private individuals, corporations, and some public institutions that buy and sell. When two currencies are traded for each other in a market, the exchange rate is the price at which the trade was done, a price that is determined by market forces.

The forex market is not an organized exchange: trade is conducted "over the counter" between parties at numerous interlinked locations around the world. The forex market is massive and has grown dramatically in recent years. According to the Bank for International Settlements, in April 2007 the global forex market traded $3,210 billion per day in currency, 70% more than in 2004 and 290% more than in 1992. The three major foreign exchange centers—the United Kingdom ($1,359 billion per day, almost all in London), the United States ($664 billion, mostly in New York), and Japan ($238 billion, principally in Tokyo)—played home to more than half of the trade.[7] Other important centers for forex trade include Hong Kong, Paris, Singapore, Sydney, and Zurich. Thanks to time-zone differences, when smaller trading centers are included, there is not a moment in the day when foreign exchange is not being traded somewhere in the world. This section briefly examines the basic workings of this market.

The Spot Contract

The simplest forex transaction is a contract for the immediate exchange of one currency for another between two parties. This is known as a **spot contract** because it happens "on the spot." Accordingly, the exchange rate for this transaction is often called the **spot exchange rate.** In this book, the use of the term "exchange rate" always refers to the spot rate. Spot trades are now essentially riskless: technology permits settlement for most trades in real time, so that the risk of one party failing to deliver on its side of the transaction (*default risk* or *settlement risk*) is essentially zero.[8]

Most of our personal transactions in the forex market are small spot transactions via retail channels, but this represents just a tiny fraction of the activity in the foreign

---

[7] Data from BIS, *Triennial Central Bank Survey: Foreign Exchange and Derivatives Market Activity in 2007* (Basle, Switzerland: Bank for International Settlements, December 2007).
[8] Spot trades formerly took two days for settlement. If a bank failed in that period, spot trades could suffer occasional settlement failure. However, since 1997 a *continuously linked settlement* (CLS) system has been used by the major trading banks and now covers a substantial majority of cross-currency transactions all over the world.

exchange market each day. The vast majority of trading involves commercial banks in major financial centers around the world. But even there the spot contract is the most common type of trade and appears in almost 90% of all forex transactions, either on its own as a single contract or in trades where it is combined with other forex contracts.

Transaction Costs

When individuals buy a little foreign currency through a retail channel (such as a bank), they pay a higher price than the midrange quote typically seen in the press; and when they sell, they are paid a lower price. The difference or **spread** between the "buy at" and "sell for" prices may be large, perhaps 2% to 5%. These fees and commissions go to the many middlemen that stand between the person on the street and the forex market. But when a big firm or a bank needs to exchange millions of dollars, the spreads and commissions are very small. Spreads are usually less than 0.1%, and for actively traded major currencies, they are approximately 0.01% to 0.03%.

Spreads are an important example of **market frictions** or **transaction costs.** These frictions create a wedge between the price paid by the buyer and the price received by the seller. Although spreads are potentially important for any microeconomic analysis of the forex market, macroeconomic analysis usually proceeds on the assumption that, in today's world of low-cost trading, the transaction-cost spreads in markets are so low for the key investors that they can be ignored for all purposes.

Derivatives

The spot contract is undoubtedly the most important contract in the forex market, but there are many other related forex contracts. These contracts include *forwards, swaps, futures,* and *options*. Collectively, all these related forex contracts are termed **derivatives** because the contracts and their pricing are derived from the spot rate.

With the exception of forwards, the forex derivatives market is small relative to the entire global forex market. According to April 2007 data from the Bank for International Settlements, the trade in spot contracts amounted to $1,005 billion per day, while the trade in forward contracts (including swaps) was $2,076 billion per day. All other derivative trades amounted to just $291 billion per day, or less than 10% of all forex trades.

For the rest of this chapter, we focus on the two most important contracts—the spot and the forward. Figure 10-5 shows recent trends in the spot and forward rates in the dollar-euro market. The forward rate tends to track the spot rate fairly closely, and we will explore this relationship further in a moment.

The full study of derivative markets requires an in-depth analysis of risk that is beyond the scope of a course

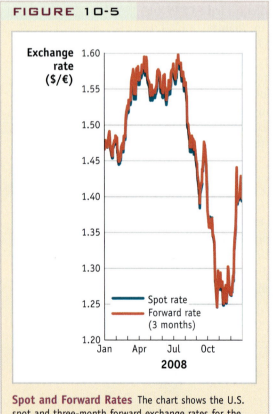

FIGURE 10-5

Spot and Forward Rates The chart shows the U.S. spot and three-month forward exchange rates for the euro in dollars per euro in the year 2008. The spot and forward rates closely track each other.

Source: Federal Reserve Bank of New York.

in international macroeconomics. Such topics are reserved for advanced courses in finance that explore derivative contracts in great detail. The following application supplies a basic guide to derivatives.

APPLICATION

Foreign Exchange Derivatives

There are many derivative contracts in the foreign exchange market, of which the following are the most common.

Forwards A **forward** contract differs from a spot contract in that the two parties make the contract today, but the *settlement date* for the delivery of the currencies is in the future, or forward. The time to delivery, or *maturity*, varies—30 days, 90 days, six months, a year, or even longer—depending on the contract. However, because the price is fixed as of today, the contract carries no risk.

Swaps A **swap** contract combines a spot sale of foreign currency with a forward repurchase of the same currency. This is a common contract for counterparties dealing in the same currency pair over and over again. Combining two transactions reduces transactions costs because the broker's fees and commissions are lower than on a spot and forward purchased separately.

Futures A **futures** contract is a promise that the two parties holding the contract will deliver currencies to each other at some future date at a prespecified exchange rate, just like a forward contract. Unlike the forward contract, however, futures contracts are standardized, mature at certain regular dates, and can be traded on an organized futures exchange. Hence, the futures contract does not require that the parties involved at the delivery date be the same two parties that originally made the deal.

Options An **option** provides one party, the buyer, with the right to buy (*call*) or sell (*put*) a currency in exchange for another at a prespecified exchange rate at a future date. The other party, the seller, must perform the trade if asked to do so by the buyer, but a buyer is under no obligation to trade and, in particular, will not exercise the option if the spot price on the expiration date turns out to be more favorable.

All of these products exist to allow investors to trade foreign currency for delivery at different times or with different contingencies. Thus, derivatives allow investors to engage in *hedging* (risk avoidance) and *speculation* (risk taking).

- Example 1: Hedging. As chief financial officer of a U.S. firm, you expect to receive payment of €1 million in 90 days for exports to France. The current spot rate is $1.20 per euro. Your firm will incur losses on the deal if the euro weakens to less than $1.10 per euro. You advise that the firm buy €1 million in call options on dollars at a rate of $1.15 per euro, ensuring that the firm's euro receipts will sell for at least this rate. This locks in a minimal profit even if the spot rate falls below $1.15. This is hedging.

- Example 2: Speculation. The market currently prices one-year euro futures at $1.30, but you think the dollar will weaken to $1.43 in the next 12 months. If you wish to make a bet, you would buy these futures, and if you are proved right, you will realize a 10% profit. Any level above $1.30 will generate a profit. If the dollar is at or below $1.30 a year from now, however, your investment in futures will be a total loss. This is speculation. ■

Private Actors

The key actors in the forex market are the traders. Most forex traders work for **commercial banks.** These banks trade for themselves and also serve clients who want to import or export goods, services, or assets. Such transactions usually involve a change of currency, and commercial banks are the principal financial intermediaries that provide this service.

For example, suppose Apple Computer Inc. has sold €1 million worth of computers to a German distributor and wishes to receive payment for them in U.S. dollars. The German distributor informs its commercial bank, Deutsche Bank, which then debits €1 million from the distributor's bank account. Deutsche Bank then sells the €1 million bank deposit in the forex market in exchange for a $1.3 million deposit and credits that $1.3 million to Apple's bank in California, which, in turn, deposits $1.3 million into Apple's account. (In this example, we assume a euro is worth $1.3.)

This is an example of **interbank trading.** This business is highly concentrated: about three-quarters of all forex market transactions globally are handled by just ten banks, led by names such as Deutsche Bank, UBS, Citigroup, HSBC, and Barclays. They trade currencies not just for their clients but also on their own account in search of profit. The vast majority of forex transactions are profit-driven interbank trades, and it is the exchange rates for these trades that underlie quoted market exchange rates. Consequently, we focus on profit-driven trading as the key force in the forex market that affects the determination of the spot exchange rate.

Other actors are increasingly participating directly in the forex market. Some **corporations** may trade in the market if they are engaged in extensive transactions either to buy inputs or sell products in foreign markets. It may be costly for them to do this, but by doing so, they can bypass the fees and commissions charged by commercial banks. Similarly, some **nonbank financial institutions** such as mutual fund companies may invest so much overseas that they can justify setting up their own foreign exchange trading operations.

Government Actions

We have so far described the forex market in terms of the private actors. Our discussion of the forex market is incomplete, however, without mention of actions taken by government authorities. Such activities are by no means present in every market at all times, but they are sufficiently frequent that we need to fully understand them. In essence, there are two primary types of actions taken by governments in the forex market.

At one extreme, it is possible for a government to try to completely control the market by preventing its free operation, by restricting trading or movement of forex, or by allowing the trading of forex only through government channels. Policies of this kind are a form of **capital control,** a restriction on cross-border financial transactions. In the wake of the 1997 Asian exchange rate crisis, the Malaysian government temporarily imposed capital controls, an event that prompted Prime Minister Mahathir Mohamad to declare that "currency trading is unnecessary, unproductive and totally immoral. It should be stopped, it should be made illegal."[9]

---

[9] From a speech at the World Bank meeting in Hong Kong, September 20, 1997, in which Mr. Mohamad also referred to the legendary currency trader George Soros as a "moron." See Edward A. Gargan, "Premier of Malaysia Spars with Currency Dealer; Mahathir Says Soros and His Ilk Are 'Impoverishing Others' for Profit," *New York Times*, September 22, 1997, p. A1.

Capital controls are never 100% successful, however. Illegal trades will inevitably occur and are almost impossible to stop. The government may set up an **official market** for foreign exchange and issue a law requiring people to buy and sell in that market at officially set rates. But illicit dealings can persist "on the street" in **black markets** or *parallel markets* where individuals may trade at exchange rates determined by market forces and not set by the government. For example, in Italy in the 1930s, the Mussolini regime set harsh punishments for trading in foreign currency that gradually rose to include the death penalty, but trading still continued on the black market.

A less drastic action taken by the authorities is to let the private market for foreign exchange function but to fix or control forex prices in the market through **intervention,** a job typically given to a nation's central bank.

How do central banks intervene in the forex market? Indeed, how can a government control a price in any market? This is an age-old problem. Consider the issue of food supply in medieval and premodern Europe, one of the earliest examples of government intervention in markets. Rulers faced the problem that droughts or harvest failures lead to famines—and political unrest. Governments reacted by establishing state-run granaries, where wheat would be stored up in years of plenty and then released to the market in years of scarcity. The price could even be fixed if the government stood ready to buy or sell grain at a preset price—*and always had enough grain in reserve to do so.* Some authorities successfully followed this strategy for many years. Others failed when they ran out of grain reserves. Once a reserve is gone, market forces take over. If there is a heavy demand that is no longer being met by the state, a rapid price increase will inevitably follow.

Government intervention in the foreign exchange market works similarly. To maintain a fixed exchange rate, the central bank must stand ready to buy or sell its own currency, in exchange for the base foreign currency, at a fixed price. In practice, this means keeping some foreign currency reserves as a buffer, but having this buffer raises many problems. For one thing, it is costly—resources are tied up in foreign currency when they could be invested in more profitable activities. Second, these reserves are not an unlimited buffer, and if they run out, the game is up. In later chapters, we will explore why countries peg, how a peg is maintained, and under what circumstances pegs fail, leading to an exchange rate crisis.

To conclude, the extent of government intervention can vary. However, even with complete and watertight capital controls, including the suppression of the black market, private actors are always present in the market. Our first task is to understand how private economic motives and actions affect the forex market.

4 Arbitrage and Spot Exchange Rates

The most basic of activities pursued by private actors in any market is **arbitrage,** a trading strategy that exploits any profit opportunities arising from price differences. Understanding arbitrage is one of the keys to thinking like an economist in any situation and is essential in studying exchange rates.

In the simplest terms, arbitrage means to buy low and sell high. If such profit opportunities exist in a market, then it is considered to be out of equilibrium. If no such profit opportunities exist, there will be no arbitrage; the market is in **equilibrium** and satisfies a **no-arbitrage condition.**

Arbitrage with Two Currencies

Suppose you trade dollars and pounds for a bank with branches in New York and London. You can electronically transfer the funds cost free between the two branch locations. Forex trading commissions are the same in each city and so small as to be negligible. Suppose the exchange rate in New York is $E_{£/\$}^{\text{N.Y.}} = £0.50$ per dollar, in London $E_{£/\$}^{\text{London}} = £0.55$ per dollar. Can you make a profit for the bank?

Yes. You can buy \$1 for £0.50 in New York and sell it for £0.55 in London for an instant, riskless profit. Indeed, everyone would buy in New York and sell in London.

In general, one of the three outcomes can occur in the forex market. The spot rate can be higher in London: $E_{£/\$}^{\text{N.Y.}} < E_{£/\$}^{\text{London}}$; the spot rate can be higher in New York: $E_{£/\$}^{\text{N.Y.}} > E_{£/\$}^{\text{London}}$; or the spot rate can be the same in both locations: $E_{£/\$}^{\text{N.Y.}} = E_{£/\$}^{\text{London}}$. Arbitrage will occur in the first two cases. Only in the last case, in which spot rates are equal, does no arbitrage occur. Hence, the no-arbitrage condition for spot rates is

$$E_{£/\$}^{\text{N.Y.}} = E_{£/\$}^{\text{London}}$$

The no-arbitrage condition is shown diagrammatically in Figure 10-6. Following both sets of arrows, we see that on each path we start with a dollar and end up with pounds, but we are indifferent between these paths only when the end result is identical. That would be an equilibrium, where no arbitrage is possible.

If the market were out of equilibrium, arbitrage would drive up the price in the low-price market and drive down the price in the high-price market. In our example,

FIGURE 10-6

Arbitrage and Spot Rates Arbitrage ensures that the trade of currencies in New York along the path AB occurs at the same exchange rate as via London along path ACDB. At B the pounds received must be the same. Regardless of the route taken to get to B, $E_{£/\$}^{\text{N.Y.}} = E_{£/\$}^{\text{London}}$.

everyone buying dollars in New York and selling them in London would bid up the spot rate in New York from £0.50 and would bid down the spot rate in London from £0.55. This process would continue until the prices converged, arbitrage ceased, and equilibrium was attained. In forex markets, these adjustments happen nearly instantaneously, whether in the high-tech electronic markets of world financial centers or in the markets on street corners in the developing world.

Arbitrage with Three Currencies

The same logic that we just applied to transactions between two currencies can also be applied to transactions involving three currencies. Again, as the trader in New York, you are considering trading dollars and pounds, but you also consider indirect or "triangular" trade via a third currency, say, the euro. Triangular arbitrage works as follows: you sell dollars in exchange for euros, then immediately sell the same euros in exchange for pounds. This roundabout way to acquire pounds is feasible, but is it sensible? Perhaps.

Forex traders at their desks in London and money changers on the street in Kabul.

For example, suppose euros can be obtained at $E_{€/\$} = €0.8$ per dollar, and pounds can be obtained at $E_{£/€} = £0.7$ per euro. Starting with $1, you can obtain 0.8 euros, and with those 0.8 euros, you can obtain 0.7×0.8 pounds. Thus, setting aside the negligibly small commissions, the resulting pound-dollar exchange rate on the combined trade is $E_{£/€} \times E_{€/\$} = 0.7 \times 0.8 = 0.56$ pounds per dollar. If, say, the exchange rate on the direct trade from dollars to pounds is a less favorable $E_{£/\$} = 0.5$, we can trade $1 for £0.56 via the euro, and then trade the £0.56 for $1.12 by way of a direct trade (because $1.12 = 0.56/0.5$), a riskless profit of 12 cents.

In general, three outcomes are again possible. The direct trade from dollars to pounds has a better rate: $E_{£/\$} > E_{£/€}E_{€/\$}$; the indirect trade has a better rate: $E_{£/\$} < E_{£/€}E_{€/\$}$; or the two trades have the same rate and yield the same result: $E_{£/\$} = E_{£/€}E_{€/\$}$. Only in the last case are there no profit opportunities. This no-arbitrage condition can be written in two ways:

$$\underbrace{E_{£/\$}}_{\substack{\text{Direct}\\ \text{exchange rate}}} = E_{£/€}E_{€/\$} = \underbrace{\frac{E_{£/€}}{E_{\$/€}}}_{\text{Cross rate}}$$

The right-hand expression, a ratio of two exchange rates, is called a **cross rate**. Examine the units carefully and notice how the two € cancel out. This no-arbitrage condition applies to all currency combinations. It is shown diagrammatically in Figure 10-7, and you can see why it is called *triangular arbitrage*.

The cross rate formula is very convenient. It means that we do not need to keep track of the exchange rate of every currency at all times. For example, if we know the exchange rates against, say, the dollar, for every currency, then for *any* pair of currencies A and B we can use the dollar rates of each currency and the cross rate formula to work out the rate at which the two currencies will trade: $E_{A/B} = E_{A/\$}/E_{B/\$}$. In practice, this is how most exchange rates are calculated.

FIGURE 10-7

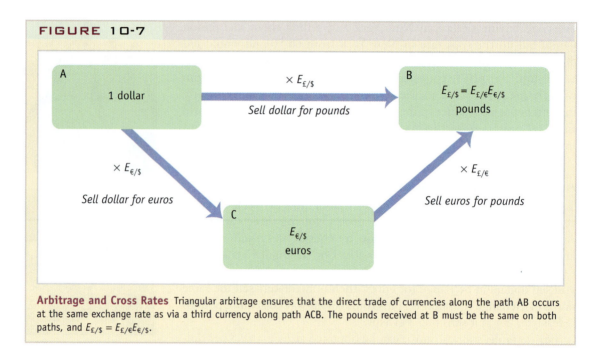

Arbitrage and Cross Rates Triangular arbitrage ensures that the direct trade of currencies along the path AB occurs at the same exchange rate as via a third currency along path ACB. The pounds received at B must be the same on both paths, and $E_{£/\$} = E_{£/€}E_{€/\$}$.

Cross Rates and Vehicle Currencies

The study of cross rates is not just an academic exercise because the vast majority of currency pairs are exchanged for one another through a third currency. There are 160 distinct currencies in the world at the time of this writing. If you write down every possible currency pair, then count them up, you would be expecting to see 12,720 forex markets in operation. You would be disappointed, however, and find only a fraction of this number. Why?

The vast majority of the world's currencies trade directly with only one or two of the major currencies, such as the dollar, euro, yen, or pound, and perhaps a few other currencies from neighboring countries. This is not too surprising. After all, to take some obscure examples, how often does somebody want to trade a Kenyan shilling for a Paraguayan guaraní? Or Mauritanian ouguiya for a Tongan pa'anga? These are small, far-apart countries between which there is very little international trade or investment. It is hard to find counterparties for forex trade in these currencies—so hard that the costs of trading become prohibitive. And there is no need to bear these costs because, to continue our example, Kenya, Paraguay, Mauritania, and Tonga do conduct a lot of business in major currencies such as the U.S. dollar, so individuals always have the option to engage in a triangular trade at the cross rate to convert shillings to dollars to guaraníes (or ouguiyas to dollars to pa'angas), all for a reasonable commission.

When a third currency, such as the U.S. dollar, is used in these transactions, it is called a **vehicle currency** because it is not the home currency of either of the parties involved in the trade and is just used for intermediation. Market data illustrate the importance of vehicle currencies. According to year 2007 data from the Bank for International Settlements, the most common vehicle currency is the U.S. dollar, which appears on one side of more than 86% of all global trades. The euro is next, playing a role in 37% of all trades (many of them with the U.S. dollar). The yen appears in 17% of all trades and the British pound in 15% (many with the U.S. dollar and the euro).

5 Arbitrage and Interest Rates

So far, our discussion of arbitrage has shown how actors in the forex market—for example, the banks—exploit profit opportunities if currencies trade at different prices. But this is not the only type of arbitrage activity affecting the forex market.

An important question for investors is in which currency they should hold their liquid cash balances. Their cash can be placed in bank deposit accounts denominated in various currencies where it will earn a modest interest rate. For example, a trader working for a major bank in New York could leave the bank's cash in a euro deposit for one year earning a 2% euro interest rate or she could put the money in a U.S. dollar deposit for one year earning a 4% dollar interest rate. How can she decide which asset, the euro or the dollar deposit, is the best investment?

This is the final problem that we address in this chapter, and this analysis provides the tools we need to understand the forex market in the rest of this book. The analysis again centers on arbitrage. Would selling euro deposits and buying dollar deposits make a profit for the banker? Decisions like these drive the demand for dollars versus euros and the exchange rate between the two currencies.

The Problem of Risk A key issue for the trader is the exchange rate risk. The trader is in New York, and her bank cares about returns in U.S. dollars. The dollar deposit pays a known return, in dollars. But the euro deposit pays a return in euros, and one year from now we cannot know for sure what the dollar-euro exchange rate will be. Thus, how we analyze arbitrage in the sections that follow depends on how exchange rate risk is handled by the investor.

As we know from our discussion of derivatives, an investor may elect to cover or hedge their exposure to exchange rate risk by using a forward contract, and their decision then simplifies to a case of *riskless arbitrage*. On the other hand, an investor may choose not to use a forward, and instead wait to use a spot contract when their investment matures, whereupon their decision is a case of *risky arbitrage*. These two ways of doing arbitrage lead to two important implications, called *parity conditions*, which describe equilibria in the forward and spot markets. We now examine each one in turn.

Riskless Arbitrage: Covered Interest Parity

Suppose that contracts to exchange euros for dollars in one year's time carry an exchange rate of $F_{\$/€}$ dollars per euro. This is known as the **forward exchange rate** and it allows investors to be absolutely sure of the price at which they can trade forex in the future.

Assume you are trading for the bank in New York, and you have to decide whether to invest $1 for one year in either a dollar or euro bank deposit that pays interest. The interest rate offered in New York on dollar deposits is $i_\$$ and in Europe the interest rate offered on euro deposits is $i_€$. Which investment offers the higher return?

If you invest in a dollar deposit, your \$1 placed in a U.S. bank account will be worth $(1 + i_\$)$ dollars in one year's time. The dollar value of principal and interest for the U.S. dollar bank deposit is called the *dollar return*. Note that we explicitly specify in what currency the return is measured, so that we may compare returns.

If you invest in a euro deposit, you first need to convert the dollar to euros. Using the spot exchange rate, \$1 buys $1/E_{\$/\euro}$ euros today. These $1/E_{\$/\euro}$ euros would be placed in a euro account earning $i_\euro$, so in a year's time they would be worth $(1 + i_\euro)/E_{\$/\euro}$ euros. You would then convert the euros back into dollars, but you cannot know for sure what the future spot rate will be. To avoid that risk, you engage in a forward contract today to make the future transaction at a forward rate $F_{\$/\euro}$. The $(1 + i_\euro)/E_{\$/\euro}$ euros you will have in one year's time can then be exchanged for $(1 + i_\euro)F_{\$/\euro}/E_{\$/\euro}$ dollars, the dollar value of principal and interest, or the dollar return on the euro bank deposit.[10]

Three outcomes are possible when you compare the dollar returns from the two deposits. The U.S. deposit has a higher dollar return, the euro deposit has a higher dollar return, or both deposits have the same dollar return. In the first case, you would advise your bank to sell its euro deposits and buy dollar deposits; in the second case, you would advise the bank to sell its dollar deposits and buy euro deposits. Only in the third case is there no expected profit from arbitrage, so the corresponding no-arbitrage condition can be written as follows:

$$\text{Covered interest parity (CIP): } \underbrace{(1 + i_\$)}_{\substack{\text{Dollar return on} \\ \text{dollar deposits}}} = \underbrace{(1 + i_\euro)\frac{F_{\$/\euro}}{E_{\$/\euro}}}_{\substack{\text{Dollar return on} \\ \text{euro deposits}}} \qquad (10\text{-}1)$$

This expression is called **covered interest parity (CIP)** because all exchange rate risk on the euro side has been "covered" by use of the forward contract. We say that such a trade employs *forward cover*. The condition is illustrated in Figure 10-8.

What Determines the Forward Rate? Covered interest parity is a no-arbitrage condition that describes an equilibrium in which investors are indifferent between the returns on interest-bearing bank deposits in two currencies and exchange risk has been eliminated by the use of a forward contract. Because one of the returns depends on the forward rate, covered interest parity can be seen as providing us with a theory of what determines the forward exchange rate. We can rearrange the above equation and solve for the forward rate:

$$F_{\$/\euro} = E_{\$/\euro}\frac{1 + i_\$}{1 + i_\euro}$$

Thus, if covered interest parity holds, we can calculate the forward rate if we know all three right-hand side variables: the spot rate $E_{\$/\euro}$, the dollar interest rate $i_\$$, and the euro interest rate $i_\euro$. For example, suppose the euro interest rate is 3%, the dollar interest rate is 5%, and the spot rate is \$1.30 per euro. Then the preceding equation says the forward rate would be $1.30 \times (1.05)/(1.03) = \$1.3252$ per euro.

---

[10] Note that this arbitrage strategy requires a spot and a forward contract. The two can be combined in a swap contract, and this helps explain the prevalence of swaps in the forex market.

FIGURE 10-8

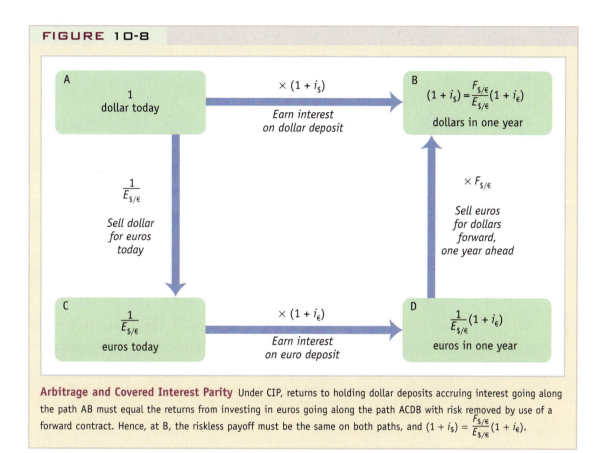

Arbitrage and Covered Interest Parity Under CIP, returns to holding dollar deposits accruing interest going along the path AB must equal the returns from investing in euros going along the path ACDB with risk removed by use of a forward contract. Hence, at B, the riskless payoff must be the same on both paths, and $(1 + i_\$) = \frac{F_{\$/€}}{E_{\$/€}}(1 + i_€)$.

In practice, this is exactly how the forex market works and how the price of a forward contract is set. Traders at their computers all around the world can see the interest rates on bank deposits in each currency, and the spot exchange rate. We can now also see why the forward contract is called a "derivative" contract: to establish the price of the forward contract (the forward rate F), we first need to know the price of the spot contract (the spot rate E). That is, the pricing of the forward contract is derived from the pricing of the underlying spot contract, using additional information on interest rates.

This result raises a new question: How are the interest rates and the spot rate determined? We return to that question in a moment, after looking at some evidence to verify that covered interest parity does indeed hold.

APPLICATION

Evidence on Covered Interest Parity

Does covered interest parity hold? We expect returns to be equalized only if arbitrage is possible. But if governments impose capital controls, there is no way for traders to exploit profit opportunities and no reason for the returns on different currencies to equalize.

For example, Figure 10-9 shows that covered interest parity held for the United Kingdom and Germany after the two countries abolished their capital controls in

FIGURE 10-9

Financial Liberalization and Covered Interest Parity: Arbitrage between the United Kingdom and Germany The chart shows the difference in monthly pound returns on deposits in British pounds and German marks using forward cover from 1970 to 1995. In the 1970s, the difference was positive and often large: traders would have profited from arbitrage by moving money from pound deposits to mark deposits, but capital controls prevented them from freely doing so. After financial liberalization, these profits essentially vanished, and no arbitrage opportunities remained. The CIP condition held, aside from small deviations resulting from transactions costs and measurement errors.

Source: Maurice Obstfeld and Alan M. Taylor, 2004, Global Capital Markets: Integration, Crisis, and Growth, Japan-U.S. Center Sanwa Monographs on International Financial Markets (Cambridge, UK: Cambridge University Press).

the period from 1979 to 1981. (The German deposits shown here were denominated in marks prior to 1999; after 1999, the euro replaced the mark as the German currency.)

The chart shows the profit that could have been made (measured in percent per annum in British currency, before transaction costs) if the investor had been able to move funds from the United Kingdom to Germany with forward cover (or, when the line is in negative territory, the profit from moving funds from Germany to the United Kingdom). From Equation (10-1), we know that the profit from this riskless arbitrage would be

$$\text{Profit} = \underbrace{(1 + i_{GER})\frac{F_{UK/GER}}{E_{UK/GER}}}_{\substack{\text{Pound return on} \\ \text{German deposits}}} - \underbrace{(1 + i_{UK})}_{\substack{\text{Pound return on} \\ \text{U.K. deposits}}}$$

This profit would be zero only if covered interest parity held. In the 1960s and 1970s, the *hypothetical* profits implied by this expression were large—or would have been had arbitrage been allowed. Instead, capital controls in both countries prevented arbitrage. Covered interest parity therefore failed to hold. Following the financial liberalization from 1979 to 1981, arbitrage became possible. From that time until the present, profits have been essentially zero. Computed profits are not exactly zero because of regulations, fees, other transaction costs, and measurement error. Once we allow for these factors, there are no profit opportunities left. Covered interest parity holds when capital markets are open, and, using similar calculations, this can be confirmed for all freely traded currencies today. ■

Risky Arbitrage: Uncovered Interest Parity

As we noted above, the second way to engage in arbitrage is to use spot contracts, and accept that the future exchange rate is then subject to risk. We now examine this case, and by doing so, we will arrive at an understanding of how the exchange rate is determined in the spot market.

To keep things simple, let us suppose, for now, that investors focus *exclusively* on the expected dollar return of the two bank deposits and not on any other characteristics of the investment. (See **Side Bar: Assets and Their Attributes.**) Imagine you are

SIDE BAR
....

Assets and Their Attributes

The bank deposits traded in the forex market pay interest and are part of the wider portfolio of assets held by banks and other private actors. As we have argued, the forex market is heavily influenced by the demand for these deposits as assets.

An investor's entire portfolio of assets may include stocks, bonds, real estate, art, bank deposits in various currencies, and so on. What influences the demand for all these different kinds of assets? Viewed from a financial viewpoint (i.e., setting aside the beauty of a painting or sea-side mansion), all assets have three key attributes that influence demand: return, risk, and liquidity.

An asset's **rate of return** is the total net increase in wealth (measured in a given currency) resulting from holding the asset for a specified period of time, typically one year. For example, you start the year by buying one share of DotBomb Inc., a hot Internet stock, for $100. At year's end, the share is worth $150 and has paid you a dividend of $5. Your total return is $55: a $50 capital gain from the change in the stock price plus a $5 dividend. Your total annual rate of return is 55/100, or 55%. The next year, the stock falls from $150 to $75 and pays no dividend. You lose half of your money in the second year: your rate of return for that year equals –75/150, or –50%. All else equal, investors prefer investments with high returns.

The **risk** of an asset refers to the volatility of its rate of return. The **liquidity** of an asset refers to the ease and speed with which it can be liquidated, or sold. A stock may seem to have high risk because its rate of return bounces up and down quite a lot, but its risk must be considered in relation to the riskiness of other investments. Its degree of risk could be contrasted with the rate of interest your bank offers on a money market deposit, a return that is usually very stable over time. You will lose your bank deposit only if your bank fails, which is unlikely. Your bank deposit is also very liquid. You can go to a cash machine or write a check to instantly access that form of wealth. In contrast, a work of art, say, is much less liquid. To sell the art for the greatest amount, you usually need the services of an auctioneer. Art is also risky. Works by different artists go in and out of fashion. All else equal, investors prefer assets with low risk and high liquidity.

This discussion of an asset's attributes allows us to make two observations. First, because all else is never equal, investors are willing to trade off among these attributes. You may be willing to hold a relatively risky and illiquid asset if you expect it will pay a relatively high return. Second, what you expect matters. Most investments, like stocks or art, do not have a fixed, predictable, guaranteed rate of return. As a result, all investors have to forecast. We refer to the forecast of the rate of return as the **expected rate of return.**

....

once again trading for a bank in New York, and you must decide whether to invest $1 for one year in a dollar or euro bank deposit that pays interest. This time, however, you use spot contracts only and make no use of the forward contract to hedge against the riskiness of the future exchange rate.

The $1 invested in a dollar deposit will be worth $(1 + i_\$)$ in one year's time; this is the dollar return, as before.

If you invest in a euro deposit, a dollar buys $1/E_{\$/€}$ euros today. With interest, these will be worth $(1 + i_€)/E_{\$/€}$ euros in one year. At that time, you will convert the euros back into dollars using a spot contract at the exchange rate that will prevail in one year's time. In this case, traders like you face exchange rate risk and must make a *forecast* of the future spot rate. We refer to the forecast as $E^e_{\$/€}$, which we call the **expected exchange rate.** Based on the forecast, you expect that the $(1 + i_€)/E_{\$/€}$ euros you will have in one year's time will be worth $(1 + i_€)E^e_{\$/€}/E_{\$/€}$ when converted into dollars; this is the *expected dollar return* on euro deposits; that is, the expected dollar value of principal and interest for euro deposits.

Again, three outcomes are possible: the U.S. deposit has a higher expected dollar return, the euro deposit has a higher expected dollar return, or both deposits have the same expected dollar return.

We have assumed that traders like you are indifferent to risk and care only about expected returns. Thus, in the first two cases, you have expected profit opportunities and risky arbitrage is possible: you would sell the deposit with the low expected return and buy the deposit with the higher expected return. Only in the third case is there no expected profit from arbitrage. This no-arbitrage condition can be written as follows:

$$\text{Uncovered interest parity (UIP):} \quad \underbrace{(1 + i_\$)}_{\substack{\text{Dollar return on} \\ \text{dollar deposits}}} = \underbrace{(1 + i_€)\frac{E^e_{\$/€}}{E_{\$/€}}}_{\substack{\text{Expected dollar return} \\ \text{on euro deposits}}} \qquad (10\text{-}2)$$

This expression is called **uncovered interest parity (UIP)** because exchange rate risk has been left "uncovered" by the decision not to hedge against exchange rate risk by using a forward contract and instead simply wait to use a spot contract in a year's time. The condition is illustrated in Figure 10-10.

What Determines the Spot Rate? Uncovered interest parity is a no-arbitrage condition that describes an equilibrium in which investors are indifferent between the returns on unhedged interest-bearing bank deposits in two currencies (where forward contracts are not employed). Because one of the returns depends on the spot rate, uncovered interest parity can be seen as providing us with a theory of what determines the spot exchange rate. We can rearrange the above equation and solve for the spot rate:

$$E_{\$/€} = E^e_{\$/€}\frac{1 + i_€}{1 + i_\$}$$

Thus, if uncovered interest parity holds, we can calculate today's spot rate if we know all three right-hand-side variables: the expected future exchange rate $E^e_{\$/€}$; the

FIGURE 10-10

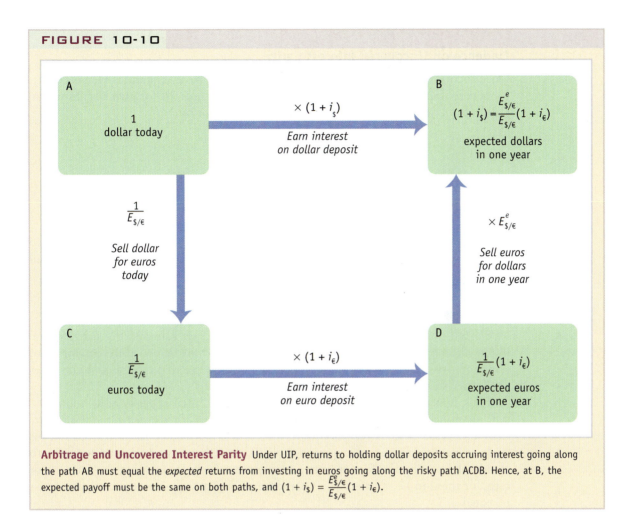

Arbitrage and Uncovered Interest Parity Under UIP, returns to holding dollar deposits accruing interest going along the path AB must equal the *expected* returns from investing in euros going along the risky path ACDB. Hence, at B, the expected payoff must be the same on both paths, and $(1 + i_\$) = \frac{E^e_{\$/€}}{E_{\$/€}}(1 + i_€)$.

dollar interest rate $i_\$$; and the euro interest rate $i_€$. For example, suppose the euro interest rate is 2%, the dollar interest rate is 4%, and the expected future spot rate is $1.40 per euro. Then the preceding equation says today's spot rate would be $1.40 \times (1.02)/(1.04) = \$1.3731$ per euro.

However, this result raises more questions: How can the expected future exchange rate $E^e_{\$/€}$ be forecast? And, as we asked in the case of covered interest parity, how are the two interest rates determined?

In the next two chapters, we will address these unanswered questions, as we continue to develop the building blocks needed for a complete theory of exchange rate determination. We start by looking at the determinants of the expected future exchange rate $E^e_{\$/€}$, and developing a model of exchange rates in the long run, and then by looking at the determinants of the interest rates $i_\$$ and $i_€$. We will soon appreciate that future expectations make the solution of forward-looking economic problems tricky: we have to solve backward from the future to the present, and this motivates the order of the material in this textbook—we must understand exchange rates in the long run before we can understand them in the short run.

APPLICATION

Evidence on Uncovered Interest Parity

Does uncovered interest parity hold? The two interest parity equations seen previously are very similar. Equation (10-1), the CIP equation, uses the forward rate; Equation
(10-2), the UIP equation, uses the expected future spot rate:

$$\text{CIP: } (1 + i_\$) = (1 + i_{\text{€}})\frac{F_{\$/\text{€}}}{E_{\$/\text{€}}}$$

$$\text{UIP: } (1 + i_\$) = (1 + i_{\text{€}})\frac{E^e_{\$/\text{€}}}{E_{\$/\text{€}}}$$

To allow us to see what this implies about the relationship between the expected
future spot rate and the forward rate, we divide the second equation by the first, to obtain

$$1 = E^e_{\$/\text{€}}/F_{\$/\text{€}}, \text{ or}$$

$$F_{\$/\text{€}} = E^e_{\$/\text{€}}$$

We can now clearly see how the expected future spot rate and the forward rate
differ: although they may be the instruments employed in two different forms of
arbitrage—risky and riskless—in equilibrium, we now see that they should not differ
at all; they should be exactly the same!

Thus, if *both* covered interest parity *and* uncovered interest parity hold, an important relationship emerges: *the forward rate $F_{\$/\text{€}}$ must equal the expected future spot rate
$E^e_{\$/\text{€}}$*. The result is intuitive. In equilibrium, and *if investors do not care about risk* (as
we have assumed in our presentation of UIP), then they have no reason to prefer to
avoid risk by using the forward rate, or to embrace risk by awaiting the future spot
rate; for them to be indifferent, as market equilibrium requires, the two rates must
be equal.

With this result we can find an approach to testing UIP that is fairly easy to
describe and implement. Because the evidence in favor of CIP is strong, as we have
seen, we may assume that it holds. In that case, the previous equation then provides
a test for whether UIP holds. But if the forward rate equals the expected spot rate,
then we can also express this equivalence relative to today's spot rate, to show that
the **expected rate of depreciation** (between today and the future period) equals
the **forward premium** (the proportional difference between the forward and spot
rates):

$$\underbrace{\frac{F_{\$/\text{€}}}{E_{\$/\text{€}}} - 1}_{\substack{\text{Forward} \\ \text{premium}}} = \underbrace{\frac{E^e_{\$/\text{€}}}{E_{\$/\text{€}}} - 1}_{\substack{\text{Expected rate} \\ \text{of depreciation}}}$$

For example, if the spot rate is $1.00 per euro, and the forward rate is $1.05, the
forward premium is 5%. But if $F_{\$/\text{€}} = E^e_{\$/\text{€}}$, the expected future spot rate is also $1.05,
and there is a 5% expected rate of depreciation.

The left-hand side of the preceding equation, the forward premium, is easily
observed, since both the current spot and forward rates are data we can collect in the
market. The difficulty is on the right-hand side: expectations are typically unobserved.

FIGURE 10-11

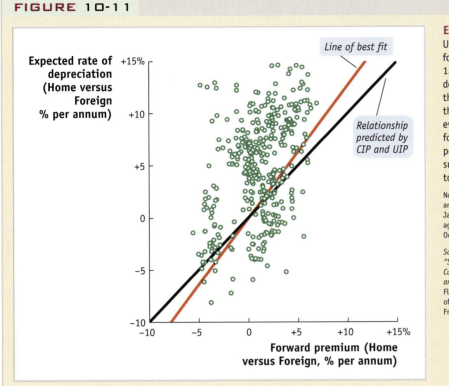

Expected rate of depreciation (Home versus Foreign % per annum)

Line of best fit

Relationship predicted by CIP and UIP

Forward premium (Home versus Foreign, % per annum)

Evidence on Interest Parity When UIP and CIP hold, the 12-month forward premium should equal the 12-month expected rate of depreciation. A scatterplot showing these two variables should be close to the diagonal 45-degree line. Using evidence from surveys of individual forex traders' expectations over the period 1988 to 1993, UIP finds some support, as the line of best fit is close to the diagonal.

Notes: Line of best fit is through the origin. Data are monthly for the German mark, Swiss franc, Japanese yen, British pound, and Canadian dollar against the U.S. dollar from February 1988 to October 1993.

Source: Menzie Chinn and Jeffrey A. Frankel, 2002, "Survey Data on Exchange Rate Expectations: More Currencies, More Horizons, More Tests." In W. Allen and D. Dickinson, eds., Monetary Policy, Capital Flows and Financial Market Developments in the Era of Financial Globalisation: Essays in Honour of Max Fry (London: Routledge), pp. 145–167.

Still, the test can be attempted using surveys in which traders are asked to report their expectations. Using data from one such test, Figure 10-11 shows a strong correlation between expected rates of depreciation and the forward premium, with a slope close to 1. Still, the points do not lie exactly on the 45-degree line, so sometimes expected depreciation does not equal the interest differential. Does this profit opportunity mean that arbitrage is not working? Not necessarily. The deviations may be caused by sampling errors or noise (differences in opinion of individual traders). In addition, there may be limits to risky arbitrage in reality because of various factors such as transactions costs (market frictions) and aversion to risk, which we have so far neglected, but which we discuss in more detail in later chapters. That the slope "on average" is close to 1 provides some support for UIP. ■

Uncovered Interest Parity: A Useful Approximation

Because it provides a theory of how the spot exchange rate is determined, the uncovered interest parity equation (10-2) is one of the most important conditions in international macroeconomics. Yet for most purposes, a simpler and more convenient concept can be used.

The intuition behind the approximation is as follows. Holding dollar deposits rewards the investor with dollar interest. Holding euro deposits rewards investors in two ways: they receive euro interest, but they also receive a gain (or loss) on euros equal to the rate of euro appreciation that approximately equals the rate of dollar depreciation. Thus, for UIP to hold, and for an investor to be indifferent between dollar deposits and euro deposits, any interest shortfall (excess) on the euro side must be off-set by an expected gain (loss) in the form of euro appreciation or dollar depreciation.

We can write the approximation formally as follows:

$$\text{UIP approximation:} \quad \underbrace{i_\$}_{\substack{\text{Interest rate} \\ \text{on dollar} \\ \text{deposits =} \\ \text{Dollar rate of} \\ \text{return on} \\ \text{dollar deposits}}} = \underbrace{\underbrace{i_\euro}_{\substack{\text{Interest rate on} \\ \text{euro deposits}}} + \underbrace{\frac{\Delta E^e_{\$/\euro}}{E_{\$/\euro}}}_{\substack{\text{Expected rate of} \\ \text{depreciation of the} \\ \text{dollar}}}}_{\substack{\text{Expected dollar rate of return on} \\ \text{euro deposits}}} \quad (10\text{-}3)$$

There are three terms in this equation. The left-hand side is the interest rate on dollar deposits. The first term on the right is the interest rate on euro deposits. The second term on the right can be expanded as $\Delta E^e_{\$/\euro}/E_{\$/\euro} = (E^e_{\$/\euro} - E_{\$/\euro})/E_{\$/\euro}$ and is the expected fractional change in the euro's value, or the expected rate of appreciation of the euro. As we have seen, this expression equals the appreciation of the euro exactly, but for small changes it approximately equals the expected rate of depreciation of the dollar.[11]

The UIP approximation equation, Equation (10-3), says that the home interest rate equals the foreign interest rate plus the expected rate of depreciation of the home currency.

A numerical example illustrates the UIP approximation formula. Suppose the dollar interest rate is 4% per year and the euro interest rate 3% per year. If UIP is to hold, then the expected rate of dollar depreciation over a year must be 1%. In that case, a dollar investment put into euros for a year will grow by 3% due to euro interest and in dollar terms will grow by an extra 1% due to euro appreciation, so the total dollar return on the euro deposit is approximately equal to the 4% that is offered by dollar deposits.[12]

To sum up, the uncovered interest parity condition, whether in its exact form (10-2) or its approximate form (10-3), states that there must be parity between expected returns, *expressed in a common currency*, in the two markets.

Summary

All economic models produce an output (some unknown or *endogenous* variable to be explained) and require a set of inputs (some known or *exogenous* variables that are treated as given). The two interest parity conditions provide us with models that

---

[11] To derive Equation (10-3), we can write $E^e_{\$/\euro}/E_{\$/\euro} = (1 + \Delta E^e_{\$/\euro}/E_{\$/\euro})$, and so Equation (10-2) becomes

$$1 + i_\$ = (1 + i_\euro)\left(1 + \frac{\Delta E^e_{\$/\euro}}{E_{\$/\euro}}\right) = 1 + i_\euro + \frac{\Delta E^e_{\$/\euro}}{E_{\$/\euro}} + \left[i_\euro \frac{\Delta E^e_{\$/\euro}}{E_{\$/\euro}}\right]$$

When the euro interest rate and the expected rate of depreciation are small, the last term in brackets is very small and may be neglected in an approximation. We can then cancel out the 1 that appears in the first and third terms of the above equation to obtain Equation (10-3).

[12] Note that the $1 investment in euros will be worth $(1.03) \times (1.01) = \$1.0403$ after one year, which is very close to $1.04, the value of the dollar deposit after one year. The difference is just the approximation error. See the previous footnote.

FIGURE 10-12

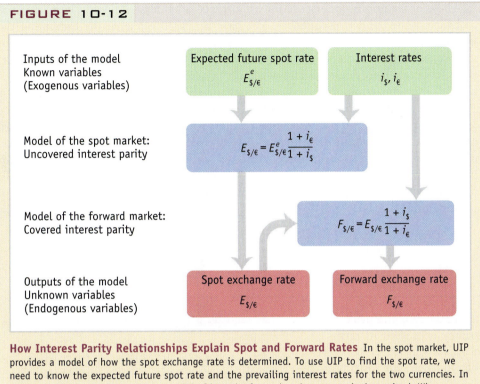

How Interest Parity Relationships Explain Spot and Forward Rates In the spot market, UIP provides a model of how the spot exchange rate is determined. To use UIP to find the spot rate, we need to know the expected future spot rate and the prevailing interest rates for the two currencies. In the forward market, CIP provides a model of how the forward exchange rate is determined. When we use CIP, we derive the forward rate from the current spot rate (from UIP) and the interest rates for the two currencies.

explain how the prices of the two most important forex contracts are determined in market equilibrium with no arbitrage possibilities. Uncovered interest parity applies to the spot market and determines the spot rate, based on interest rates and exchange rate expectations. Covered interest parity applies to the forward market and determines the forward rate based on interest rates and the spot rate. Figure 10-12 sums up what we have learned.

6 Conclusions

The foreign exchange market has a long and often tumultuous record and, in today's globalized world, exchange rates matter more than ever. They affect the prices of international transactions, can be a focus of government policy, and often play a major role in economic and political crises.

This chapter has set the stage for our study of exchange rates. We learned what exchange rates are and how they are used. We have also seen how they have behaved in reality under different exchange rate regimes. History shows a vast range of past experiences, and this experimentation continues.

These observations underscore the importance of understanding different regimes and their causes and consequences. We have prepared ourselves by examining the workings of the foreign exchange market in some detail. Government intervention (or its absence) in this market determines the nature of the exchange rate regime in operation, from fixed to floating. The workings of actors in the forex market then ultimately determine equilibrium values of exchange rates.

How is forex market equilibrium determined? We can now see that two key forces operate in the foreign exchange market: arbitrage and expectations. Through expectations, news about the future can affect expected returns. Through arbitrage, differences in expected returns are equalized, as summed up by the two important interest parity conditions, covered interest parity and uncovered interest parity. In the next two chapters, we build on these ideas to develop a complete theory of exchange rates.

KEY POINTS

1. The exchange rate in a country is the price of a unit of foreign currency expressed in terms of the home currency. This price is determined in the spot market for foreign exchange.

2. When the home exchange rate rises, less foreign currency is bought/sold per unit of home currency; the home currency has depreciated. If home currency buys $x\%$ less foreign currency, the home currency is said to have depreciated by $x\%$.

3. When the home exchange rate falls, more foreign currency is bought/sold per unit of home currency; the home currency has appreciated. If home currency buys $x\%$ more foreign currency, the home currency is said to have appreciated by $x\%$.

4. The exchange rate is used to convert the prices of goods and assets into a common currency to allow meaningful price comparisons.

5. Exchange rates may be stable over time or they may fluctuate. History supplies examples of the former (fixed exchange rate regimes) and the latter (floating exchange rate regimes)

as well as a number of intermediate regime types.

6. An exchange rate crisis occurs when the exchange rate experiences a sudden and large depreciation. These events are often associated with broader economic and political turmoil, especially in developing countries.

7. Some countries may forgo a national currency to form a currency union with other nations (e.g., the Eurozone), or they may unilaterally adopt the currency of another country ("dollarization").

8. Looking across all countries today, numerous fixed and floating rate regimes are observed, so we must understand both types of regime.

9. The forex market is dominated by spot transactions, but many derivative contracts exist, such as forwards, swaps, futures, and options.

10. The main actors in the market are private investors and (frequently) the government authorities, represented usually by the central bank.

11. Arbitrage on currencies means that spot exchange rates are approximately equal in different forex markets. Cross rates (for indirect trades) and spot rates (for direct trades) are also approximately equal.

12. Riskless interest arbitrage leads to the covered interest parity (CIP) condition. CIP says that the dollar return on dollar deposits must equal the dollar return on euro deposits, where forward contracts are used to cover exchange rate risk.

13. Covered interest parity says that the forward rate is determined by home and foreign interest rates and the spot exchange rate.

14. Risky interest arbitrage leads to the uncovered interest parity (UIP) condition. UIP says that when spot contracts are used and exchange rate risk is not covered, the dollar return on dollar deposits must equal the expected dollar returns on euro deposits.

15. Uncovered interest parity explains how the spot rate is determined by the home and foreign interest rates and the expected future spot exchange rate.

KEY TERMS

exchange rate, p. 326
appreciation, p. 328
depreciation, p. 328
effective exchange rate, p. 330
exchange rate regimes, p. 333
fixed (or pegged) exchange rate regime, p. 333
floating (or flexible) exchange rate regime, p. 333
free float, p. 334
band, p. 334
managed float, p. 335
exchange rate crises, p. 335
crawl, p. 336
currency (or monetary) union, p. 337
dollarization, p. 337
currency board, p. 338
foreign exchange (forex or FX) market, p. 339

spot contract, p. 339
spot exchange rate, p. 339
spread, p. 340
market friction, p. 340
transaction costs, p. 340
derivatives, p. 340
forward, p. 341
swap, p. 341
futures, p. 341
option, p. 341
commercial banks, p. 342
interbank trading, p. 342
corporations, p. 342
nonbank financial institutions, p. 342
capital control, p. 342
official market, p. 343
black market, p. 343
intervention, p. 343
arbitrage, p. 343

equilibrium, p. 343
no-arbitrage condition, p. 343
cross rate, p. 345
vehicle currency, p. 346
forward exchange rate, p. 347
covered interest parity (CIP), p. 348
rate of return, p. 351
risk, p. 351
liquidity, p. 351
expected rate of return, p. 351
expected exchange rate, p. 352
uncovered interest parity (UIP), p. 352
expected rate of depreciation, p. 354
forward premium, p. 354

PROBLEMS

1. Refer to the exchange rates given in the following table:

Country	Today June 25, 2010		One Year Ago June 25, 2009	
	Per $	Per £	Per €	Per $
Australia	1.152	1.721	1.417	1.225
Canada	1.037	1.559	1.283	1.084
Denmark	6.036	9.045	7.443	5.238
Euro	0.811	1.215	1.000	0.703
Hong Kong	7.779	11.643	9.583	7.750
India	46.36	69.476	57.179	48.16
Japan	89.35	134.048	110.308	94.86
Mexico	12.697	18.993	15.631	13.22
Sweden	7.74	11.632	9.577	7.460
United Kingdom	0.667	1.000	0.822	0.609
United States	1.000	1.496	1.232	1.000

Source: U.S. Federal Reserve Board of Governors, H.10 release: Foreign Exchange Rates.

Based on the table provided, answer the following questions:

a. Compute the U.S. dollar-yen exchange rate $E_{\$/¥}$ and the U.S. dollar-Canadian dollar exchange rate $E_{\$/C\$}$ on June 25, 2010, and June 25, 2009.

b. What happened to the value of the U.S. dollar relative to the Japanese yen and Canadian dollar between June 25, 2009, and June 25, 2010? Compute the percentage change in the value of the U.S. dollar relative to each currency using the U.S. dollar-foreign currency exchange rates you computed in (a).

c. Using the information in the table for June 25, 2010, compute the Danish krone-Canadian dollar exchange rate $E_{krone/C\$}$.

d. Visit the website of the Board of Governors of the Federal Reserve System at http://www.federalreserve.gov/. Click on "Economic Research and Data" and then "Statistics: Releases and Historical Data." Download the H.10 release Foreign Exchange Rates (weekly data available). What has happened to the value of the U.S. dollar relative to the Canadian dollar, Japanese yen, and Danish krone since June 25, 2010?

e. Using the information from (d), what has happened to the value of the U.S. dollar relative to the British pound and the euro? *Note:* The H.10 release quotes these exchange rates as U.S. dollars per unit of foreign currency in line with long-standing market conventions.

2. Consider the United States and the countries it trades with the most (measured in trade volume): Canada, Mexico, China, and Japan. For simplicity, assume these are the only four countries with which the United States trades. Trade shares and exchange rates for these four countries are as follows:

Country (currency)	Share of Trade	$ per FX in 2009	$ per FX in 2010
Canada (dollar)	36%	0.9225	0.9643
Mexico (peso)	28%	0.0756	0.0788
China (yuan)	20%	0.1464	0.1473
Japan (yen)	16%	0.0105	0.0112

a. Compute the percentage change from 2009 to 2010 in the four U.S. bilateral exchange rates (defined as U.S. dollars per units of foreign exchange, or FX) in the table provided.

b. Use the trade shares as weights to compute the percentage change in the nominal effective exchange rate for the United States between 2009 and 2010 (in U.S. dollars per foreign currency basket).

c. Based on your answer to (b), what happened to the value of the U.S. dollar against this basket between 2009 and 2010? How does this compare with the change in the value of the U.S. dollar relative to the Mexican peso? Explain your answer.

3. Go to the website for Federal Reserve Economic Data (FRED): http://research.stlouisfed.org/fred2/. Locate the monthly exchange rate data for the following:

a. Canada (dollar), 1980–2009

b. China (yuan), 1999–2005 and 2005–2009

c. Mexico (peso), 1993–1995 and 1995—2009
d. Thailand (baht), 1986–1997 and 1997—2009
e. Venezuela (bolivar), 2003–2009

Look at the graphs and make a judgment as to whether each currency was fixed (peg or band), crawling (peg or band), or floating relative to the U.S. dollar during each time frame given.

4. Describe the different ways in which the government may intervene in the foreign exchange market. Why does the government have the ability to intervene in this way, while private actors do not?

5. Suppose quotes for the dollar-euro exchange rate $E_{\$/€}$ are as follows: in New York $1.50 per euro, and in Tokyo $1.55 per euro. Describe how investors use arbitrage to take advantage of the difference in exchange rates. Explain how this process will affect the dollar price of the euro in New York and Tokyo.

6. Consider a Dutch investor with 1,000 euros to place in a bank deposit in either the Netherlands or Great Britain. The (one-year) interest rate on bank deposits is 2% in Britain and 4.04% in the Netherlands. The (one-year) forward euro-pound exchange rate is 1.575 euros per pound and the spot rate is 1.5 euros per pound. Answer the following questions, using the *exact* equations for UIP and CIP as necessary.

   a. What is the euro-denominated return on Dutch deposits for this investor?
   b. What is the (riskless) euro-denominated return on British deposits for this investor using forward cover?
   c. Is there an arbitrage opportunity here? Explain why or why not. Is this an equilibrium in the forward exchange rate market?
   d. If the spot rate is 1.5 euros per pound, and interest rates are as stated previously, what is the equilibrium forward rate, according to covered interest parity (CIP)?
   e. Suppose the forward rate takes the value given by your answer to (d). Compute the forward premium on the British pound for the Dutch investor (where exchange rates are in euros per pound). Is it positive or

negative? Why do investors require this premium/discount in equilibrium?
   f. If uncovered interest parity (UIP) holds, what is the expected depreciation of the euro (against the pound) over one year?
   g. Based on your answer to (f), what is the expected euro-pound exchange rate one year ahead?

7. You are a financial adviser to a U.S. corporation that expects to receive a payment of 40 million Japanese yen in 180 days for goods exported to Japan. The current spot rate is 100 yen per U.S. dollar ($E_{\$/¥} = 0.01000$). You are concerned that the U.S. dollar is going to appreciate against the yen over the next six months.

   a. Assuming the exchange rate remains unchanged, how much does your firm expect to receive in U.S. dollars?
   b. How much would your firm receive (in U.S. dollars) if the dollar appreciated to 110 yen per U.S. dollar ($E_{\$/¥} = 0.00909$)?
   c. Describe how you could use an options contract to hedge against the risk of losses associated with the potential appreciation in the U.S. dollar.

8. Consider how transactions costs affect foreign currency exchange. Rank each of the following foreign exchanges according to their probable spread (between the "buy at" and "sell for" bilateral exchange rates) and justify your ranking.

   a. An American returning from a trip to Turkey wants to exchange his Turkish lira for U.S. dollars at the airport.
   b. Citigroup and HSBC, both large commercial banks located in the United States and United Kingdom, respectively, need to clear several large checks drawn on accounts held by each bank.
   c. Honda Motor Company needs to exchange yen for U.S. dollars to pay American workers at its Ohio manufacturing plant.
   d. A Canadian tourist in Germany pays for her hotel room using a credit card.

N E T **W O R K**

Visit the ft.com website (or another financial website such as oanda.com or xe.com), and download the same exchange rates shown in Table 10-1 for today's date. For all currencies (other than the dollar), compute the one-year percentage appreciation or depreciation against the dollar. For the dollar, compute the one-year percentage appreciation or depreciation against each currency. (*Hint:* Google "ft.com cross rates.")

Visit the OANDA website (oanda.com) to explore recent exchange rate trends for any pair of countries in the world. Download some series to a spreadsheet for manipulation, or use the FXGraph online graphing tools to plot trends. Try to plot examples of some fixed and floating rates. See whether you can locate data for an exchange rate crisis during recent years. Can you tell from the data which countries are fixed and which are floating?

Next visit the IMF's website (imf.org) and locate the latest classification of the de facto exchange rate regimes in all countries around the world, the same source used in Figure 10-4. Do your regime classifications agree with the IMF's?

Exchange Rates I: The Monetary Approach in the Long Run

Our willingness to pay a certain price for foreign money must ultimately and essentially be due to the fact that this money possesses a purchasing power as against commodities and services in that foreign country.

Gustav Cassel, of the Swedish school of economics, 1922

The fundamental things apply / As time goes by.

Herman Hupfeld, songwriter, 1931 (featured in the film *Casablanca*, 1942)

The cost of living is usually rising, but it rises in some places more than others. From 1970 to 1990, for example, a standardized Canadian basket of consumer goods rose in price considerably. In 1970 a Canadian would have spent C$100 (100 Canadian dollars) to purchase this basket; by 1990 the same basket cost C$392. Thus, Canadian prices rose by 292%. Over the same period, in the United States, a basket of goods that initially cost $100 in 1970 had risen in cost to $336 by 1990. Thus, U.S. prices rose by only 236%. Both countries witnessed serious inflation, but Canadian prices rose more.

Did these price changes cause U.S. goods to appear relatively cheaper? Would they have caused Canadians to start spending more on U.S. goods, or Americans to spend less on Canadian goods?

The answer to all three questions is no. In 1970 C$1 was worth almost exactly $1 (1 U.S. dollar). So in 1970 both baskets cost the same *when their cost was expressed in a common currency*, about C$100 = $100. By 1990, however, the Canadian dollar (also called the loonie) had depreciated relative to its 1970 value and C$1.16 was needed to buy $1.00. Thus, the $336 U.S. basket in 1990 actually cost $336 × 1.16 = C$390 when expressed in Canadian currency—almost the same price as the C$392 Canadian basket! (Conversely, expressed in U.S. currency, the Canadian basket cost about 392/1.16 = $338, almost the same as the $336 U.S. basket.)

In this example, although Canadian prices rose about 16% more than U.S. prices, U.S. residents also found that each of their U.S. dollars could buy about 16% more loonies. From the U.S. point of view, the cost of the baskets in each country *expressed in U.S. dollars* rose by about the same amount. The same was true from the Canadian perspective with all prices expressed in loonies. Economists (such as Gustav Cassel, quoted previously) would say that the relative *purchasing power* of each currency (in terms of U.S. versus Canadian goods) had remained the same.

Is it a coincidence that the changes in prices and exchange rates turned out that way? A fundamental economic hypothesis, which we explore in this chapter, asserts that this outcome is *not* a coincidence at all—and that *in the long run*, prices and exchange rates will always adjust so that the purchasing power of each currency remains comparable over baskets of goods in different countries (as here, where $100 and C$100 could purchase comparable amounts of goods in 1970, and also in 1990). This hypothesis provides another key building block in the theory of how exchange rates are determined. How?

In the last chapter, uncovered interest parity provided us with a theory of how the spot exchange rate is determined, given knowledge of three variables: the expected future exchange rate, the home interest rate, and the foreign interest rate. In this chapter we look at the long run to see how the expected future exchange rate is determined; then, in the next chapter, we turn to the short run and discuss how interest rates are determined in each country. When all the pieces are put together, we will have a complete theory of how exchange rates are determined in the short run and the long run.

If investors are to make forecasts of future exchange rates, they need a plausible theory of how exchange rates are determined in the long run. The theory we develop in this chapter has two parts. The first part involves the theory of purchasing power, which links the exchange rate to price levels in each country in the long run. This theory provides a partial explanation of the determinants of long-run exchange rates, but it raises another question: How are price levels determined? In the second part of the chapter, we explore how price levels are related to monetary conditions in each country. Combining the monetary theory of price level determination with the purchasing power theory of exchange rate determination, we emerge with a *long-run* theory known as the **monetary approach to exchange rates.** The goal of this chapter is to set out the long-run relationships between money, prices, and exchange rates.

1 Exchange Rates and Prices in the Long Run: Purchasing Power Parity and Goods Market Equilibrium

Just as arbitrage occurs in the international market for financial assets, it also occurs in the international markets for goods. The result of goods market arbitrage is that the prices of goods in different countries expressed in a common currency must tend to be equalized. Applied to a single good, this idea is referred to as the *law of one price*; applied to an entire basket of goods, it is called the theory of *purchasing power parity*.

Why should these "laws" hold? If the price of a good were not the same in two locations, buyers would rush to buy at the cheap location (forcing prices up there) and would shy away from the expensive location (forcing prices down there). Some factors, such as the costs of transporting goods between locations, may hinder the process of arbitrage, and more refined models take such frictions into account. For now, however, our goal is to develop a simple yet useful theory based on an idealized world of *frictionless trade* where transaction costs can be neglected. We start at the microeconomic level with single goods and the law of one price. We then move to the macroeconomic level to consider baskets of goods and purchasing power parity.

The Law of One Price

The **law of one price (LOOP)** states that in the absence of trade frictions (such as transport costs and tariffs), and under conditions of free competition and price flexibility (where no individual sellers or buyers have power to manipulate prices and prices can freely adjust), identical goods sold in different locations must sell for the same price when prices are expressed in a common currency.

To see how the law of one price operates, consider the trade in diamonds that takes place between the United States and the Netherlands. Suppose that a diamond of a given quality is priced at €5,000 in the Amsterdam market, and the exchange rate is $1.20 per euro. If the law of one price holds, the same-quality diamond should sell in New York for (€5,000 per diamond) × (1.20 $/€) = $6,000 per diamond.

Why will the prices be the same? Under competitive conditions and frictionless trade, arbitrage will ensure this outcome. If diamonds were more expensive in New York, arbitragers would buy at a low price in Holland and sell at a high price in Manhattan. If Dutch prices were higher, arbitragers would profit from the reverse trade. *By definition*, in a market equilibrium there are no arbitrage opportunities. If diamonds can be freely moved between New York and Amsterdam, both markets must offer the same price. Economists refer to this situation in the two locations as an *integrated market*.

We can mathematically state the law of one price as follows, for the case of any good g sold in two locations, say, Europe (EUR, meaning the Eurozone) and the United States (US). The *relative price* of good g (denoted $q^g_{US/EUR}$) is the ratio of the good's price in Europe relative to the good's price in the United States where both prices are expressed in a common currency.

Using subscripts to indicate locations and currencies, the relative price can be written

$$\underbrace{q^g_{US/EUR}}_{\substack{\text{Relative price of good } g \\ \text{in Europe versus U.S.}}} = \underbrace{(E_{\$/\epsilon}P^g_{EUR})}_{\substack{\text{European price} \\ \text{of good } g \text{ in \$}}} / \underbrace{P^g_{US}}_{\substack{\text{U.S. price of} \\ \text{good } g \text{ in \$}}}$$

where P^g_{US} is the good's price in the United States, P^g_{EUR} is the good's price in Europe, and $E_{\$/\epsilon}$ is the dollar-euro exchange rate used to convert euro prices into dollar prices.

Notice that $q^g_{US/EUR}$ expresses the rate at which goods can be exchanged: it tells us how many units of the U.S. good are needed to purchase one unit of the same good in Europe (hence, the subscript uses the notation US/EUR). This contrasts with the nominal exchange rate $E_{\$/\epsilon}$ which expresses the rate at which currencies can be exchanged ($/€).

The law of one price may or may not hold. Recall from Chapter 10 that there are three possibilities in an arbitrage situation of this kind: the ratio exceeds 1 and the good is costlier in Europe; the ratio is less than 1 and the good is cheaper in Europe; or $E_{\$/\epsilon}P^g_{EUR} = P^g_{US}$, the ratio is $q^g_{US/EUR} = 1$, and the good is the same price in both locations. Only in the final case is there no arbitrage, the condition that defines market equilibrium. In equilibrium, European and U.S. prices, expressed in the same currency, are equal; the relative price q equals 1, and the law of one price holds.

How does the law of one price further our understanding of exchange rates? We can rearrange the equation for price equality, $E_{\$/\epsilon}P^g_{EUR} = P^g_{US}$, to show that if the law of one price holds, then the exchange rate must equal the ratio of the goods' prices expressed in the two currencies:

$$\underbrace{E_{\$/\epsilon}}_{\substack{\text{Exchange} \\ \text{rate}}} = \underbrace{P^g_{US}/P^g_{EUR}}_{\substack{\text{Ratio of} \\ \text{goods' prices}}}$$

One final word of caution: given our concerns in the previous chapter about the right way to define the exchange rate, we must take care when using expressions that are ratios to ensure that the units on each side of the equation correspond. In the last equation, we know we have it right because the left-hand side is expressed in dollars per euro and the right-hand side is also a ratio of dollars to euros ($ per unit of goods divided by € per unit of goods).

Purchasing Power Parity

The principle of **purchasing power parity (PPP)** is the macroeconomic counterpart to the microeconomic law of one price (LOOP). The law of one price relates exchange rates to the relative prices of an individual good, while purchasing power parity relates exchange rates to the relative prices of a basket of goods. In studying international macroeconomics, purchasing power parity is the more relevant concept.

We can define a *price level* (denoted P) in each location as a weighted average of the prices of all goods g in a basket, using the same goods and weights in both locations. Let P_{US} be the basket's price in the United States and P_{EUR} the basket's price in Europe. *If the law of one price holds for each good in the basket, it will also hold for the price of the basket as a whole.*[1]

To express PPP algebraically, we can compute the relative price of the two baskets of goods in each location, denoted $q_{US/EUR}$:

$$\underbrace{q_{US/EUR}}_{\substack{\text{Relative price of} \\ \text{basket in Europe} \\ \text{versus U.S.}}} = \underbrace{(E_{\$/\epsilon}P_{EUR})}_{\substack{\text{European} \\ \text{price of basket} \\ \text{expressed in \$}}} / \underbrace{P_{US}}_{\substack{\text{U.S. price} \\ \text{of basket} \\ \text{expressed in \$}}}$$

Just as there were three possible outcomes for the law of one price, there are three possibilities for PPP: the basket is cheaper in United States; the basket is cheaper in Europe; or $E_{\$/\epsilon}P_{EUR} = P_{US}$; or the basket is the same price in both locations $q_{US/EUR} = 1$. In the first two cases, the basket is cheaper in one location and profitable arbitrage on the baskets is possible. Only in the third case is there no arbitrage. PPP holds *when price levels in two countries are equal when expressed in a common currency.* This statement about equality of price levels is also called **absolute PPP.**

---

[1] For example, if the law of one price holds and $P^g_{US} = (E_{\$/\epsilon}) \times (P^g_{EUR})$ for all goods g, this implies that for N goods, the *arithmetic* weighted average satisfies $\sum_{g=1}^N \omega^g P^g_{US} = (E_{\$/\epsilon}) \times \sum_{g=1}^N \omega^g P^g_{EUR}$ for any set of weights ω^g that sum to 1, so PPP holds. The same is also true for *geometric* averages. Technically speaking, this follows for *any* price index definition that satisfies the usually required property that the index be homogeneous of degree 1 in the individual goods' prices.

For example, suppose the European basket costs €100, and the exchange rate is $1.20 per euro. For PPP to hold, the U.S. basket would have to cost $1.20 \times 100 = \$120$.

The Real Exchange Rate

The relative price of the two countries' baskets (denoted q) is the macroeconomic counterpart to the microeconomic relative price of individual goods (q^g). The relative price of the baskets is one of the most important variables in international macroeconomics, and it has a special name: it is known as the **real exchange rate.** The real exchange rate $q_{US/EUR} = E_{\$/€}P_{EUR}/P_{US}$ tells us how many U.S. baskets are needed to purchase one European basket.

As with the nominal exchange rate, we need to be careful about what is in the numerator of the real exchange rate and what is in the denominator. According to our definition (based on the case we just examined), we will refer to $q_{US/EUR} = E_{\$/€}P_{EUR}/P_{US}$ as the home country, or U.S. real exchange rate: it is the price of the European basket in terms of the U.S. basket (or, if we had a Home–Foreign example, the price of a Foreign basket in terms of a Home basket).

To avoid confusion, it is essential to understand the difference between nominal exchange rates (which we have studied so far) and real exchange rates. The exchange rate for currencies is a *nominal* concept; it says how many dollars can be exchanged for one euro. The real exchange rate is a *real* concept; it says how many U.S. baskets of goods can be exchanged for one European basket.

The real exchange rate has some terminology similar to that used with the nominal exchange rate:

- If the real exchange rate rises (more Home goods are needed in exchange for Foreign goods), we say Home has experienced a **real depreciation.**

- If the real exchange rate falls (fewer Home goods are needed in exchange for Foreign goods), we say Home has experienced a **real appreciation.**

Absolute PPP and the Real Exchange Rate

We can restate absolute PPP in terms of real exchange rates: *purchasing power parity states that the real exchange rate is equal to 1*. Under absolute PPP, all baskets have the same price when expressed in a common currency, so their relative price is 1.

It is common practice to use the absolute PPP-implied level of 1 as a benchmark or reference level for the real exchange rate. This leads naturally to some new terminology:

- If the real exchange rate $q_{US/EUR}$ is below 1 by $x\%$, then Foreign goods are relatively cheap, $x\%$ cheaper than Home goods. In this case, the Home currency (the dollar) is said to be *strong*, the euro is *weak*, and we say the euro is **undervalued** by $x\%$.

- If the real exchange rate $q_{US/EUR}$ is above 1 by $x\%$, then Foreign goods are relatively expensive, $x\%$ more expensive than Home goods. In this case, the Home currency (the dollar) is said to be *weak*, the euro is *strong*, and we say the euro is **overvalued** by $x\%$.

For example, if a European basket costs $E_{\$/€}P_{EUR} = \$550$ in dollar terms, and a U.S. basket costs only $P_{US} = \$500$, then $q_{US/EUR} = E_{\$/€}P_{EUR}/P_{US} = \$550/\$500 = 1.10$, the euro is strong, and the euro is 10% overvalued against the dollar.

Absolute PPP, Prices, and the Nominal Exchange Rate

Finally, just as we did with the law of one price, we can rearrange the no-arbitrage equation for the equality of price levels, $E_{\$/€}P_{EUR} = P_{US}$, to allow us to solve for the exchange rate that would be implied by absolute PPP:

$$\text{Absolute PPP:} \quad \underbrace{E_{\$/€}}_{\substack{\text{Exchange} \\ \text{rate}}} = \underbrace{P_{US}/P_{EUR}}_{\substack{\text{Ratio of} \\ \text{price levels}}} \tag{11-1}$$

This is one of the most important equations in our course of study because it shows how PPP (or absolute PPP) makes a clear prediction about exchange rates:

Purchasing power parity implies that the exchange rate at which two currencies trade equals the relative price levels of the two countries.

For example, if a basket of goods costs \$460 in the United States and the same basket costs €400 in Europe, the theory of PPP predicts an exchange rate of \$460/€400 = \$1.15 per euro.

Thus, if we know the price levels in different locations, we can use PPP to determine an implied exchange rate, subject to all of our earlier assumptions about frictionless trade, flexible prices, free competition, and identical goods. The PPP relationship between the price levels in two countries and the exchange rate is therefore a key building block in our theory of how exchange rates are determined, as shown in Figure 11-1. Moreover, the theory is not tied to any point in time: if we can forecast future price levels, then we can also use PPP to forecast the expected future exchange rate implied by those forecasted future price levels, which is the main goal of this chapter.

Relative PPP, Inflation, and Exchange Rate Depreciation

PPP in its absolute PPP form involves price levels, but in macroeconomics we are often more interested in the rate at which price levels change than we are in the price levels themselves. The rate of change of the price level is known as the *rate of inflation*, or simply **inflation.** For example, if the price level today is 100, and one year from now it is 103.5, then the rate of inflation is 3.5% (per year). Because inflation is such an important variable in macroeconomics, we examine the implications of PPP for the study of inflation.

To consider changes over time, we introduce a subscript t to denote the time period, and calculate the rate of change of both sides of Equation (11-1) from period t to

FIGURE 11-1

Home

Input of the model: known variables (exogenous variables)

Price level, P_{US}

Foreign

Price level, P_{EUR}

Output of the model: unknown variables (endogenous variables)

Exchange rate, $E_{\$/€}$

Building Block: Price Levels and Exchange Rates in the Long Run According to the PPP Theory In this model, the price levels are treated as known exogenous variables (in the green boxes). The model uses these variables to predict the unknown endogenous variable (in the red box), which is the exchange rate.

period $t + 1$. On the left-hand side, the rate of change of the exchange rate in Home is the rate of exchange rate depreciation in Home given by [2]

$$\underbrace{\frac{\Delta E_{\$/\euro,t}}{E_{\$/\euro,t}}}_{\text{Rate of depreciation of the nominal exchange rate}} = \frac{E_{\$/\euro,t+1} - E_{\$/\euro,t}}{E_{\$/\euro,t}}$$

On the right of Equation (11-1), the rate of change of the ratio of two price levels equals the rate of change of the numerator minus the rate of change of the denominator: [3]

$$\frac{\Delta(P_{US}/P_{EUR})}{(P_{US}/P_{EUR})} = \frac{\Delta P_{US,t}}{P_{US,t}} - \frac{\Delta P_{EUR,t}}{P_{EUR,t}}$$

$$= \underbrace{\left(\frac{P_{US,t+1} - P_{US,t}}{P_{US,t}}\right)}_{\substack{\text{Rate of inflation in} \\ \text{U.S. } \pi_{US,t}}} - \underbrace{\left(\frac{P_{EUR,t+1} - P_{EUR,t}}{P_{EUR,t}}\right)}_{\substack{\text{Rate of inflation in} \\ \text{Europe } \pi_{EUR,t}}} = \pi_{US} - \pi_{EUR}$$

where the terms in brackets are the inflation rates in each location, denoted π_{US} and π_{EUR}, respectively.

If Equation (11-1) holds for levels of exchange rates and prices, then it must also hold for rates of change in these variables. By combining the last two expressions, we obtain

$$\text{Relative PPP:} \qquad \underbrace{\frac{\Delta E_{\$/\euro,t}}{E_{\$/\euro,t}}}_{\substack{\text{Rate of depreciation of the} \\ \text{nominal exchange rate}}} = \underbrace{\pi_{US,t} - \pi_{EUR,t}}_{\text{Inflation differential}} \qquad (11\text{-}2)$$

This way of expressing PPP is called **relative PPP**, and it *implies that the rate of depreciation of the nominal exchange rate equals the difference between the inflation rates of two countries (the inflation differential)*.

We saw relative PPP in action in the example at the start of this chapter. Over 20 years, Canadian prices rose 16% more than U.S. prices, and the Canadian dollar depreciated 16% against the U.S. dollar. Converting these to annual rates, Canadian prices rose by 0.75% per year more than U.S. prices (the inflation differential), and the loonie depreciated by 0.75% per year against the dollar. Relative PPP held in this case. [4]

Two points should be kept in mind about relative PPP. First, unlike absolute PPP, relative PPP predicts a relationship between *changes* in prices and *changes* in exchange rates, rather than a relationship between their levels. Second, remember that relative PPP is *derived from* absolute PPP. Hence, the latter always implies the former: *if absolute PPP holds, this implies that relative PPP must hold also.* But the converse need not be true: *relative PPP does not necessarily imply absolute PPP* (if relative PPP holds, absolute PPP can hold or fail). For example, imagine that all goods consistently cost 20% more in country A than in country B, so absolute PPP fails; however, it still can be the case that the inflation differential between A and B (say, 5%) is always equal to the rate of depreciation (say, 5%), so relative PPP will still hold.

---

[2] The rate of depreciation at Home and the rate of appreciation in Foreign are approximately equal, as we saw in the previous chapter.
[3] This expression is exact for small changes and otherwise holds true as an approximation.
[4] Note that the rates of change are approximate, with $1.0075^{20} = 1.16$.

Summary

The purchasing power parity theory, whether in the absolute PPP or relative PPP form, suggests that price levels in different countries and exchange rates are tightly linked, either in their absolute levels or in the rates at which they change. To assess how useful this theory is, let's look at some empirical evidence to see how well the theory matches reality. We can then reexamine the workings of PPP and reassess its underlying assumptions.

APPLICATION

Evidence for PPP in the Long Run and Short Run

Is there evidence for PPP? The data offer some support for relative PPP most clearly over the long run, when even moderate inflation mounts and leads to large cumulative changes in price levels and, hence, substantial cumulative inflation differentials.

The scatterplot in Figure 11-2 shows average rates of depreciation and inflation differentials for a sample of countries compared with the United States over three decades from 1975 to 2005. If relative PPP were true, then the depreciation of each country's currency would exactly equal the inflation differential, and the data would line up on the 45-degree line. We see that this is not literally true in the data, but the correlation

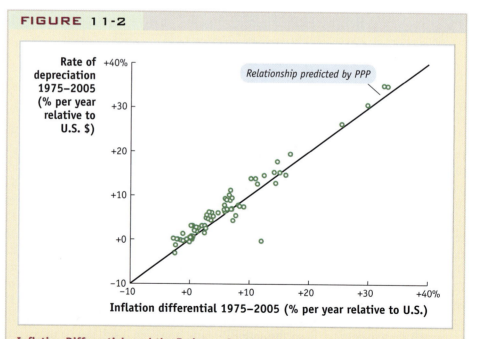

FIGURE 11-2

Inflation Differentials and the Exchange Rate, 1975–2005 This scatterplot shows the relationship between the rate of exchange rate depreciation against the U.S. dollar (the vertical axis) and the inflation differential against the United States (horizontal axis) over the long run, based on data for a sample of 82 countries. The correlation between the two variables is strong and bears a close resemblance to the theoretical prediction of PPP that all data points would appear on the 45-degree line.

Source: IMF, International Financial Statistics.

is close. Relative PPP is an approximate, useful guide to the relationship between prices and exchange rates in the long run, over horizons of many years or decades.

But the purchasing power theory turns out to be a fairly useless theory in the short run, over horizons of just a few years. This is easily seen by examining the time series of relative price ratio and exchange rates for any pair of countries, and looking at the behavior of these variables from year to year and not just over a long period. If absolute PPP held at all times, then the exchange rate would always be equal to the relative price ratio. Figure 11-3 shows 35 years of data for the United States and United Kingdom from 1975 to 2009. This figure confirms the relevance of absolute and relative PPP in the long run because the price-level ratio and the exchange rate have similar levels and drift together along a common trend. In the short run, however, the two series show substantial and persistent differences. In any given year the differences can be 10%, 20%, or more. These year-to-year differences in levels and changes show that absolute and relative PPP fail in the short run. For example, from 1980 to 1985, the pound depreciated by 45% (from $2.32 to $1.28), but the cumulative inflation differential over these five years was only 9%. ■

How Slow Is Convergence to PPP?

If PPP were taken as a strict proposition for the short run, it would require price adjustment via arbitrage to happen fully and instantaneously, rapidly closing the gap between common-currency prices in different countries for all goods in the basket. This doesn't happen. The evidence suggests that PPP works better in the long run. But how long is the long run?

Research shows that price differences—the deviations from PPP—can be quite persistent. Estimates suggest that these deviations may die out at a rate of about 15% per year. This kind of measure is often called a *speed of convergence*: in this case, it implies that after one year, 85% (0.85) of an initial price difference persists; compounding, after two years, 72% of the gap persists ($0.72 = 0.85^2$); and after four years, 52%

FIGURE 11-3

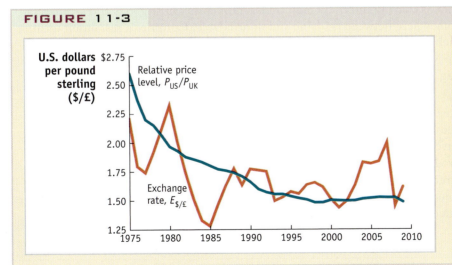

Exchange Rates and Relative Price Levels Data for the United States and United Kingdom for 1975 to 2009 show that the exchange rate and relative price levels do not always move together in the short run. Relative price levels tend to change slowly and have a small range of movement; exchange rates move more abruptly and experience large fluctuations. Therefore, relative PPP does *not* hold in the short run. However, it is a better guide to the long run, and we can see that the two series do tend to drift together over the decades.

Source: Penn World Tables, version 6.3, updated using IMF data for 2008–2009.

$(0.52 = 0.85^4)$. Thus, approximately half of any PPP deviation still remains after four years: economists would refer to this as a four-year *half-life*.

Such estimates provide a rule of thumb that is useful as a guide to forecasting real exchange rates. For example, suppose the home basket costs $100 and the foreign basket $90, in home currency. Home's real exchange rate is 0.900, and the home currency is overvalued, with foreign goods less expensive than home goods. The deviation of the real exchange rate from the PPP-implied level of 1 is −10% (or −0.1). Our rule of thumb tells us that next year 15% of this deviation will have disappeared (i.e., 0.015), so the new deviation will be only −0.085, meaning that Home's real exchange rate would be forecast to be 0.915 after one year and thus end up a little bit closer to 1, after a small depreciation. Similarly, after four years, all else being equal, 52% of the deviation (or 0.052) would have been erased, and the real exchange rate would by then be 0.952, only −5% from PPP. (See **Side Bar: Forecasting When the Real Exchange Rate Is Undervalued or Overvalued.**)

What Explains Deviations from PPP?

If it takes four years for even half of any given price difference to dissipate, as research has indicated, it is no surprise that PPP does not hold in the short run. But how can arbitrage take so long to eliminate price differences? Economists have found a variety of reasons why PPP fails in the short run:

■ *Transaction costs.* Trade is not frictionless as we have assumed thus far because the costs of international transportation are significant for most goods and because some goods also bear additional costs, such as tariffs and duties, when they cross borders. By some recent estimates, transportation costs may add about 20% on average to the price of goods moving internationally, while tariffs (and other policy barriers) may add another 10%.[5] Other costs arise due to the time it takes to ship goods, and the costs and time delays associated with developing distribution networks and satisfying legal and regulatory requirements in foreign markets.

■ *Nontraded goods.* Some goods are inherently nontradable; one can think of them as having infinitely high transaction costs. Most goods and services fall somewhere between tradable and nontradable. Consider a restaurant meal; it includes traded goods such as some raw foods and nontraded goods such as the work of the chef. As a result, PPP may not hold. (See **Headlines: The Big Mac Index.**)

■ *Imperfect competition and legal obstacles.* Many goods are not simple undifferentiated commodities, as LOOP and PPP assume, but are differentiated products with brand names, copyrights, and legal protection. For example, consumers have the choice of cheaper generic acetaminophen or a pricier brand-name product such as Tylenol, but these are not seen as perfect substitutes. Such differentiated goods create conditions of *imperfect competition* because firms have some power to set the price of their good. With this kind of *market power*, firms can charge different prices not just across brands but also across countries

---

[5] There is also evidence of other significant border-related barriers to trade. See James Anderson and Eric van Wincoop, September 2004, "Trade Costs," *Journal of Economic Literature*, 42, 691–751.

SIDE BAR

Forecasting When the Real Exchange Rate Is Undervalued or Overvalued

When relative PPP holds, forecasting exchange rate changes is simple: just compute the inflation differential. But how do we forecast when PPP doesn't hold, as is often the case? Even if the real exchange rate is not equal to 1, knowing the real exchange rate and the convergence speed may still allow us to construct a forecast of real and nominal exchange rates.

To see how, let's take an example. Start with the definition of the real exchange rate, $q_{US/EUR} = E_{\$/€}P_{EUR}/P_{US}$. Rearranging, we find $E_{\$/€} = q_{US/EUR} \times (P_{US}/P_{EUR})$. By taking the rate of change of that expression, we find that the rate of change of the nominal exchange rate equals the rate of change of the real exchange rate plus home inflation minus foreign inflation:

$$\underbrace{\frac{\Delta E_{\$/€,t}}{E_{\$/€,t}}}_{\substack{\text{Rate of depreciation} \\ \text{of the nominal} \\ \text{exchange rate}}} = \underbrace{\frac{\Delta q_{US/EUR,t}}{q_{US/EUR,t}}}_{\substack{\text{Rate of depreciation} \\ \text{of the real exchange} \\ \text{rate}}} + \underbrace{\pi_{US,t} - \pi_{EUR,t}}_{\text{Inflation differential}}$$

When the real exchange rate q is constant, the first term on the right is zero and we are back to the simple world of relative PPP and Equation (11-2). For forecasting purposes, the predicted nominal depreciation is then just the second term on the right, the inflation differential. For example, if the forecast is for U.S. inflation to be 3% next year and for European inflation to be 1%, then the inflation differential is +2% and we would forecast a U.S. dollar depreciation, or rise in $E_{\$/€}$, of +2% next year.

What if q isn't constant and PPP fails? If there is currently a deviation from absolute PPP, but we still think that there will be convergence to absolute PPP in the long run, the first term on the right of the formula is not zero and we can estimate it given the right information.

To continue the example, suppose you are told that a U.S. basket of goods currently costs $100, but the European basket of the same goods costs $130. You would compute a U.S. real exchange rate $q_{US/EUR}$ of 1.30 today. But what will it be next year? If you expect absolute PPP to hold in the long run, then you expect that the U.S. real exchange rate will move toward 1. How fast? At this point, you need to know the convergence speed. Using the 15% rule of thumb, you estimate that 15% of the 0.3 gap between 1 and 1.3 (i.e., 0.045) will dissipate over the coming year. Hence, you forecast that the U.S. real exchange will fall from 1.3 to 1.255, implying a change of −3.46% in the coming year. In this case, adding the two terms on the right of the expression given previously, you forecast that the approximate change in E next year will be the change in $q_{US/EUR}$ of −3.46% plus the inflation differential of +2%, for a total of −1.46%; that is, a dollar appreciation of 1.46% against the euro.

The intuition for the result is as follows: the U.S. dollar is undervalued against the euro. If convergence to PPP is to happen, then some of that undervaluation will dissipate over the course of the year through a real appreciation of the dollar (predicted to be 3.46%). That real appreciation can be broken down into two components:

1. U.S. goods will experience higher inflation than European goods (we have predicted that the inflation differential will be +2%).

2. The remainder of the real appreciation will be accomplished via a 1.46% nominal dollar appreciation (predicted based on a convergence speed of 15% per year).

(pharmaceutical companies, e.g., charge different prices for drugs in different countries). This practice is possible because arbitrage can be shut down by legal threats or regulations. If you try to import large quantities of a firm's pharmaceutical and resell them, then, as an unauthorized distributor, you will probably hear very quickly from the firm's lawyers and/or from the government regulators. The same would apply to many other goods such as automobiles and consumer electronics.

■ *Price stickiness.* One of the most common assumptions of macroeconomics is that prices are "sticky" in the short run—that is, they do not or cannot adjust quickly and flexibly to changes in market conditions. PPP assumes that arbitrage can force prices to adjust, but adjustment will be slowed down by price stickiness. Empirical evidence shows that many goods' prices do not adjust quickly in the short run. For example, in Figure 11-3, we saw that the nominal exchange rate moves up and down in a very dramatic fashion but that price levels are much more sluggish in their movements and do not fully match exchange rate changes.

Despite these problems, the evidence suggests that as a long-run theory of exchange rates, PPP is still a useful approach.[6] And PPP may become even more relevant in the future as arbitrage becomes more efficient and more goods and services are traded. Years ago we might have taken it for granted that certain goods and services (such as pharmaceuticals, customer support, health-care services) were strictly nontraded and thus not subject to arbitrage, at the international level. Today, many consumers shop for pharmaceuticals overseas to save money. If you dial a U.S. software support call center, you may find yourself being assisted by an operator in India. In some countries, citizens motivated by cost considerations may travel overseas for dental treatment, eye care, hip replacements, and other health services (so-called medical tourism or health tourism). These globalization trends may well continue.

HEADLINES

The Big Mac Index

For more than 20 years, The Economist newspaper has engaged in a whimsical attempt to judge PPP theory based on a well-known, globally uniform consumer good: the McDonald's Big Mac. The over- or undervaluation of a currency against the U.S. dollar is gauged by comparing the relative prices of a burger in a common currency, and expressing the difference as a percentage deviation from one:

$$\text{Big Mac Index} = q^{\text{Big Mac}} - 1 = \left(\frac{E_{\$/\text{local currency}} P_{\text{local}}^{\text{Big Mac}}}{P_{\text{US}}^{\text{Big Mac}}} \right) - 1.$$

Home of the undervalued burger?

Table 11-1 shows the July 2009 survey results, and some examples will illustrate how the calculations work. Row 1 shows the average U.S. dollar price of the Big Mac of $3.57. An example of undervaluation appears in Row 2, where we see that the Buenos Aires correspondent found the same burger cost 11.5 pesos, which, at an actual exchange rate of 3.81 pesos per dollar, worked out to be $3.02 in U.S. currency, or 15%

less than the U.S. price. So the peso was 15% undervalued against the U.S. dollar according to this measure, and Argentina's exchange rate would have had to appreciate to 3.22 pesos per dollar to attain the level implied by a burger-based PPP theory. An example of overevaluation appears in Row 4, in the case of neighboring Brazil. There a Big Mac cost 8.03 reais, or $4.02 in U.S. currency at the prevailing exchange rate

of 2.00 reais per dollar, making the Brazilian burgers 13% more expensive than their U.S. counterparts. To get to its PPP-implied level, and put the burgers at parity, Brazil's currency would have needed to depreciate to 2.25 reais per dollar. Looking through the table, burger disparity is typical, with only Britain, Costa Rica, Czech Republic, Hungary, Japan, and Turkey coming within ±5% of PPP.

---

[6] Alan M. Taylor and Mark P. Taylor, Fall 2004, "The Purchasing Power Parity Debate," *Journal of Economic Perspectives*, 8, 135–158.

TABLE 11-1

The Big Mac Index The table shows the price of a Big Mac in July 2009 in local currency (column 1) and converted to U.S. dollars (column 2) using the actual exchange rate (column 4). The dollar price can then be compared with the average price of a Big Mac in the United States ($3.57 in column 1, row 1). The difference (column 5) is a measure of the overvaluation (+) or undervaluation (−) of the local currency against the U.S. dollar. The exchange rate against the dollar implied by PPP (column 3) is the hypothetical price of dollars in local currency that would have equalized burger prices, which may be compared with the actual observed exchange rate (column 4).

| | Big Mac Prices | | Exchange rate (local currency per U.S. dollar) | | Over (+)/ under (−) valuation against dollar, % |
	In local currency (1)	In U.S. dollars (2)	Implied by PPP (3)	Actual, July 13th (4)	(5)
United States	$ 3.57	3.57			
Argentina	Peso 11.5	3.02	3.22	3.81	−15
Australia	A$ 4.34	3.37	1.22	1.29	−6
Brazil	Real 8.03	4.02	2.25	2.00	+13
Britain	£ 2.29	3.69	0.64	0.62	+3
Canada	C$ 3.89	3.35	1.09	1.16	−6
Chile	Peso 1750	3.19	490	549	−11
China	Yuan 12.5	1.83	3.50	6.83	−49
Colombia	Peso 7000	3.34	1,961	2,096	−6
Costa Rica	Colones 2000	3.43	560	583	−4
Czech Rep.	Koruna 67.92	3.64	19.0	18.7	+2
Denmark	DK 29.5	5.53	8.26	5.34	+55
Estonia	Kroon 32	2.85	8.96	11.2	−20
Egypt	Pound 13	2.33	3.64	5.58	−35
Euro area	€ 3.31	4.62	0.93	0.72	+29
Hong Kong	HK$ 13.3	1.72	3.73	7.75	−52
Hungary	Forint 720	3.62	202	199	+1
Iceland	Kronur 640	4.99	179	128	+40
Indonesia	Rupiah 20900	2.05	5,854	10,200	−43
Israel	Shekel 15	3.77	4.20	3.97	+6
Japan	Yen 320	3.46	89.6	92.6	−3
Latvia	Lats 1.55	3.09	0.43	0.50	−13
Lithuania	Litas 7.1	2.87	1.99	2.48	−20
Malaysia	Ringgit 6.77	1.88	1.90	3.60	−47
Mexico	Peso 33	2.39	9.24	13.8	−33
New Zealand	NZ$ 4.9	3.08	1.37	1.59	−14
Norway	Kroner 40	6.15	11.2	6.51	+72
Pakistan	Rupee 190	2.30	53.2	82.6	−36
Peru	New Sol 8.056	2.66	2.26	3.03	−25
Philippines	Peso 99.39	2.05	27.8	48.4	−42
Poland	Zloty 7.6	2.41	2.13	3.16	−33
Russia	Rouble 67	2.04	18.8	32.8	−43
Saudi Arabia	Riyal 11	2.93	3.08	3.75	−18
Singapore	S$ 4.22	2.88	1.18	1.46	−19
South Africa	Rand 17.95	2.17	5.03	8.28	−39
South Korea	Won 3400	2.59	952	1,315	−28
Sri Lanka	Rupee 210	1.83	58.8	115	−49
Sweden	SKr 39	4.93	10.9	7.90	+38
Switzerland	SFr 6.50	5.98	1.82	1.09	+68
Taiwan	Taiwan$ 75	2.26	21.0	33.2	−37
Thailand	Baht 64.49	1.89	18.1	34.2	−47
Turkey	Lire 5.65	3.65	1.58	1.55	+2
UAE	Dirhams 10	2.72	2.80	3.67	−24
Ukraine	Hryvnia 14	1.83	3.92	7.66	−49
Uruguay	Peso 61	2.63	17.1	23.2	−26

Source: "Cheesed Off," The Economist, July 16, 2009, and author's calculations.

2 Money, Prices, and Exchange Rates in the Long Run: Money Market Equilibrium in a Simple Model

It is time to take stock of the theory developed so far in this chapter. Up to now, we have concentrated on PPP, which says that in the long run the exchange rate is determined by the ratio of the price levels in two countries. But this prompts a question: What determines those price levels?

Monetary theory supplies an answer: according to this theory, in the long run, price levels are determined in each country by the relative demand and supply of money. You may recall this theory from previous macroeconomics courses in the context of a closed economy. This section recaps the essential elements of monetary theory and shows how they fit into our theory of exchange rates in the long run.

What Is Money?

We recall the distinguishing features of this peculiar asset that is so central to our everyday economic life. Economists think of **money** as performing three key functions in an economy:

1. Money is a *store of value* because, as with any asset, money held from today until tomorrow can still be used to buy goods and services in the future. Money's rate of return is low compared with many other assets. Because we earn no interest on it, there is an opportunity cost to holding money. If this cost is low, we will hold money more willingly than we hold other assets (stocks, bonds, etc.).

2. Money also gives us a *unit of account* in which all prices in the economy are quoted. When we enter a store in France, we expect to see the prices of goods to read something like "100 euros"—not "10,000 Japanese yen" or "500 bananas," even though, in principle, the yen or the banana could also function as a unit of account in France (bananas would, however, be a poor store of value).

3. Money is a *medium of exchange* that allows us to buy and sell goods and services without the need to engage in inefficient barter (direct swaps of goods). The ease with which we can convert money into goods and services is a measure of how *liquid* money is compared with the many illiquid assets in our portfolios (such as real estate). Money is the most liquid asset of all.

The Measurement of Money

What counts as money? Clearly, the currency in circulation is money. But do checking accounts count as money? What about savings accounts, mutual funds, and other securities? Figure 11-4 depicts the most widely used measures of the money supply and illustrates their relative magnitudes with recent data from the United States. The most basic concept of money is currency in circulation (i.e., in the hands of the nonbank public). After that, M0 is typically the narrowest definition of money (also called "base money"), and it includes both currency in circulation and the reserves of commercial banks (liquid cash held in their vaults or on deposit at the Fed). Normally, in recent years, banks' reserves have been very small indeed (they have been permitted, and preferred, to rely on other securities to provide liquidity *and* some interest income) and so M0 has been virtually identical to currency in circulation. This changed dramatically after the financial crisis of 2008 gave rise to liquidity problems, and banks began to

FIGURE 11-4

The Measurement of Money
This figure shows the major kinds of monetary aggregates (currency, M0, M1, and M2) for the United States from 2004 to 2010. Normally, bank reserves are very close to zero, so M0 and currency are virtually identical, but reserves spiked up during the financial crisis in 2008, as private banks sold securities to the Fed and stored up the cash proceeds in their Fed reserve accounts as a precautionary hoard of liquidity.

Source: Federal Reserve Economic Data (FRED).

maintain huge reserves at the Fed as a precaution. (When and how this unprecedented hoard of cash will be unwound remains to be seen, and this is a matter of some concern to economists and policy makers.)

A different narrow measure of money, M1, includes currency in circulation plus highly liquid instruments such as demand deposits in checking accounts and traveler's checks, but it *excludes* bank's reserves, and thus may be a better gauge of money available for transactions purposes. A much broader measure of money, M2, includes slightly less liquid assets such as savings and small time deposits.[7]

For our purposes, money is defined as the *stock of liquid assets that are routinely used to finance transactions*, in the sense implied by the "medium of exchange" function of money. So when we speak of money (denoted M), we will generally mean M1, currency in circulation plus demand deposits. Many important assets are excluded from M1, including longer-term assets held by individuals and the voluminous interbank deposits used in the foreign exchange market discussed in the previous chapter. These assets do not count as money in the sense used here because they are relatively illiquid and not used routinely for transactions.

The Supply of Money

How is the supply of money determined? In practice, a country's **central bank** controls the **money supply.** Strictly speaking, by issuing notes and coins, the central bank controls directly only the level of M0, or base money, the amount of currency in the

---

[7] There is little consensus on the right broad measure of money. Until 2006 the U.S. Federal Reserve collected data on M3, which included large time deposits, repurchase agreements, and money market funds. This was discontinued because the data were costly to collect and thought to be of limited use to policy makers. In the United Kingdom, a slightly different broad measure, M4, is still used. Some economists now prefer a money aggregate called MZM, or "money of zero maturity," as the right broad measure, but its use is not widespread.

economy. However, it can *indirectly* control the level of M1 by using monetary policy to influence the behavior of the private banks that are responsible for checking deposits. The intricate mechanisms by which monetary policy affects M1 are beyond the scope of this book. In our analysis, we make the simplifying assumption that the central bank's policy tools are sufficient to allow it to control indirectly, but accurately, the level of M1.[8]

The Demand for Money: A Simple Model

A simple theory of household money demand is motivated by the assumption that the need to conduct transactions is in proportion to an individual's income. For example, if an individual's income doubles from $20,000 to $40,000, we expect his or her demand for money (expressed in dollars) to double also.

Moving from the individual or household level up to the aggregate or macroeconomic level, we can infer that the aggregate **money demand** will behave similarly. *All else equal, a rise in national dollar income (nominal income) will cause a proportional increase in transactions and, hence, in aggregate money demand.*

This insight suggests a simple model in which the demand for money is proportional to dollar income. This model is known as the **quantity theory of money:**

$$\underbrace{M^d}_{\substack{\text{Demand} \\ \text{for money (\$)}}} = \underbrace{\overline{L}}_{\text{A constant}} \times \underbrace{PY}_{\substack{\text{Nominal} \\ \text{income (\$)}}}$$

Here, PY measures the total nominal dollar value of income in the economy, equal to the price level P times real income Y. The term $\overline{L}$ is a constant that measures how much demand for liquidity is generated for each dollar of nominal income. To emphasize this point, we assume for now that every $1 of nominal income requires $\$\overline{L}$ of money for transactions purposes and that this relationship is constant. (Later, we relax this assumption.)

The intuition behind the equation is clear. If the price level rises by 10% and real income is fixed, we are paying a 10% higher price for all goods, so the dollar cost of transactions rises by 10%. Similarly, if real income rises by 10% but prices stay fixed, the dollar amount of transactions will rise by 10%. Hence, the *demand for nominal money balances*, M^d, is proportional to the *nominal* income PY.

Another way to look at the quantity theory is to convert all quantities into real quantities by dividing the previous equation by P, the price level (the price of a basket of goods). Quantities are then converted from nominal dollars to real units (specifically, into units of baskets of goods). These conversions allow us to derive the *demand for real money balances*:

$$\underbrace{\frac{M^d}{P}}_{\substack{\text{Demand for} \\ \text{real money}}} = \underbrace{\overline{L}}_{\text{A constant}} \times \underbrace{Y}_{\text{Real income}}$$

Real money balances are simply a measure of the purchasing power of the stock of money in terms of goods and services. The expression just given says that the

---

[8] A full treatment of this topic can be found in a textbook on money and banking. See Laurence M. Ball, *Money, Banking, and Financial Markets* 2nd edition (New York: Worth, 2010 forthcoming).

demand for real money balances is strictly proportional to real income. The more real income we have, the more real transactions we have to perform, so the more real money we need.

Equilibrium in the Money Market

The condition for equilibrium in the money market is simple to state: the demand for money M^d must equal the supply of money M, which we assume to be under the control of the central bank. Imposing this condition on the last two equations, we find that nominal money supply equals nominal money demand:

$$M = \overline{L}PY$$

and, equivalently, that real money supply equals real money demand:

$$\frac{M}{P} = \overline{L}Y$$

A Simple Monetary Model of Prices

We are now in a position to put together a simple model of the exchange rate, using two building blocks. The first building block, the quantity theory, is a model that links prices to monetary conditions. The second building block, PPP is a model that links exchange rates to prices.

We consider two countries, as before, and for simplicity we will consider the United States as the home country and Europe as the foreign country. (The model generalizes to any pair of countries.)

Let's consider the last equation given and apply it to the United States, adding U.S. subscripts for clarity. We can rearrange this formula to obtain an expression for the U.S. price level:

$$P_{US} = \frac{M_{US}}{\overline{L}_{US}Y_{US}}$$

Note that the price level is determined by how much nominal money is issued relative to the demand for real money balances: the numerator on the right-hand side is the total supply of *nominal* money; the denominator is the total demand for *real* money balances.

We can do the same rearrangement for Europe to obtain the analogous expression for the European price level:

$$P_{EUR} = \frac{M_{EUR}}{\overline{L}_{EUR}Y_{EUR}}$$

The last two equations are examples of the **fundamental equation of the monetary model of the price level.** Two such equations, one for each country, give us another important building block for our theory of prices and exchange rates as shown in Figure 11-5.

In the long run, we assume prices are flexible and will adjust to put the money market in equilibrium. For example, if the amount of money in circulation (the nominal money supply) rises, say, by a factor of 100, and real income stays the same, then there will be "more money chasing the same quantity of goods." This leads to inflation, and

FIGURE 11-5

Building Block: The Monetary Theory of the Price Level According to the Long-Run Monetary Model In these models, the money supply and real income are treated as known exogenous variables (in the green boxes). The models use these variables to predict the unknown endogenous variables (in the red boxes), which are the price levels in each country.

in the long run, the price level will rise by a factor of 100. In other words, we will be in the same economy as before except that all prices will have two zeros tacked on to them.

A Simple Monetary Model of the Exchange Rate

A long-run model of the exchange rate is close at hand. If we take the last two equations, which use the monetary model to find the price level in each country, and plug them into Equation (11-1), we can use absolute PPP to solve for the exchange rate:

$$\underset{\substack{\text{Exchange} \\ \text{rate}}}{E_{\$/€}} = \underset{\substack{\text{Ratio of} \\ \text{price levels}}}{\frac{P_{US}}{P_{EUR}}} = \frac{\left(\dfrac{M_{US}}{\overline{L}_{US}Y_{US}}\right)}{\left(\dfrac{M_{EUR}}{\overline{L}_{EUR}Y_{EUR}}\right)} = \underset{\substack{\text{Relative nominal money} \\ \text{supplies divided by relative} \\ \text{real money demands}}}{\frac{(M_{US}/M_{EUR})}{(\overline{L}_{US}Y_{US}/\overline{L}_{EUR}Y_{EUR})}} \qquad (11\text{-}3)$$

This is the **fundamental equation of the monetary approach to exchange rates.** By substituting the price levels from the monetary model into PPP, we have put together the two building blocks from Figures 11-1 and 11-5. The implications of this equation are intuitive.

■ Suppose the U.S. money supply increases, all else equal. The right-hand side increases (the U.S. nominal money supply increases relative to Europe), causing the exchange rate to increase (the U.S. dollar depreciates against the euro). For example, if the U.S. money supply doubles, then all else equal, the U.S. price level doubles. That is, a bigger U.S. supply of money leads to a weaker dollar. That makes sense—there are more dollars around, so you expect each dollar to be worth less.

■ Now suppose the U.S. real income level increases, all else equal. Then the right-hand side decreases (the U.S. real money demand increases relative to Europe), causing the exchange rate to decrease (the U.S. dollar appreciates against the euro). For example, if the U.S. real income doubles, then all else equal, the U.S. price level falls by a factor of one-half. That is, a stronger U.S. economy leads to a stronger dollar. That makes sense—there is more demand for the same quantity of dollars, so you expect each dollar to be worth more.

Money Growth, Inflation, and Depreciation

The model just presented uses absolute PPP to link the level of the exchange rate to the level of prices and uses the quantity theory to link prices to monetary conditions in each country. But as we have said before, macroeconomists are often more interested in rates of change of variables (e.g., inflation) rather than levels.

Can our theory be extended for this purpose? Yes, but this task takes a little work. We convert Equation (11-3) into growth rates by taking the rate of change of each term.

The first term of Equation (11-3) is the exchange rate $E_{\$/€}$. Its rate of change is the rate of depreciation $\Delta E_{\$/€}/E_{\$/€}$. When this term is positive, say, 1%, the dollar is depreciating at 1% per year; if negative, say, −2%, the dollar is appreciating at 2% per year.

The second term of Equation (11-3) is the ratio of the price levels P_{US}/P_{EUR}, and as we saw when we derived relative PPP at Equation (11-2), its rate of change is the rate of change of the numerator (U.S. inflation) minus the rate of change of the denominator (European inflation), which equals the inflation differential $\pi_{US,t} - \pi_{EUR,t}$.

What is the rate of change of the third term in Equation (11-3)? The numerator represents the U.S. price level, $P_{US} = M_{US}/\overline{L}_{US}Y_{US}$. Again, the growth rate of a fraction equals the growth rate of the numerator minus the growth rate of the denominator. In this case, the numerator is the money supply M_{US}, and its growth rate is μ_{US}:

$$\mu_{US,t} = \underbrace{\frac{M_{US,t+1} - M_{US,t}}{M_{US,t}}}_{\text{Rate of money supply growth in U.S.}}$$

The denominator is $\overline{L}_{US}Y_{US}$, which is a constant $\overline{L}_{US}$ times real income Y_{US}. Thus, $\overline{L}_{US}Y_{US}$ grows at a rate equal to the growth rate of real income g_{US}:

$$g_{US,t} = \underbrace{\frac{Y_{US,t+1} - Y_{US,t}}{Y_{US,t}}}_{\text{Rate of real income growth in U.S.}}$$

Putting all the pieces together, the growth rate of $P_{US} = M_{US}/\overline{L}_{US}Y_{US}$ equals the money supply growth rate μ_{US} minus the real income growth rate g_{US}. We have already seen that the growth rate of P_{US} on the left-hand side is the inflation rate π_{US}. Thus, we know that

$$\pi_{US,t} = \mu_{US,t} - g_{US,t} \tag{11-4}$$

The denominator of the third term of Equation (11-3) represents the European price level, $P_{EUR} = M_{EUR}/\overline{L}_{EUR}Y_{EUR}$, and its rate of change is calculated similarly:

$$\pi_{EUR,t} = \mu_{EUR,t} - g_{EUR,t} \tag{11-5}$$

The intuition for these last two expressions echoes what we said previously. When money growth is higher than real income growth, we have "more money chasing fewer goods" and this leads to inflation.

Combining Equation (11-4) and Equation (11-5), we can now solve for the inflation differential in terms of monetary fundamentals and finish our task of computing the rate of depreciation of the exchange rate:

$$\underbrace{\frac{\Delta E_{\$/€,t}}{E_{\$/€,t}}}_{\substack{\text{Rate of depreciation of the} \\ \text{nominal exchange rate}}} = \underbrace{\pi_{US,t} - \pi_{EUR,t}}_{\text{Inflation differential}} = (\mu_{US,t} - g_{US,t}) - (\mu_{EUR,t} - g_{EUR,t}) \quad \text{(11-6)}$$

$$= \underbrace{(\mu_{US,t} - \mu_{EUR,t})}_{\substack{\text{Differential in} \\ \text{nominal money supply} \\ \text{growth rates}}} - \underbrace{(g_{US,t} - g_{EUR,t})}_{\substack{\text{Differential in real} \\ \text{output growth rates}}}$$

The last term here is the rate of change of the fourth term in Equation (11-3).

Equation (11-6) is the fundamental equation of the monetary approach to exchange rates expressed in rates of change, and much of the same intuition we applied in explaining Equation (11-3) carries over here.

■ If the United States runs a looser monetary policy in the long run measured by a faster money growth rate, the dollar will depreciate more rapidly, all else equal. For example, suppose Europe has a 5% annual rate of change of money and a 2% rate of change of real income; then its inflation would be the difference, 5% minus 2% equals 3%. Now suppose the United States has a 6% rate of change of money and a 2% rate of change of real income; then its inflation would be the difference, 6% minus 2% equals 4%. And the rate of depreciation of the dollar would be U.S. inflation minus European inflation, 4% minus 3%, or 1% per year.

■ If the U.S. economy grows faster in the long run, the dollar will appreciate more rapidly, all else equal. In the last numerical example, suppose the U.S. growth rate of real income in the long run increases from 2% to 5%, all else equal. U.S. inflation equals the money growth rate of 6% minus the new real income growth rate of 5%, so inflation is just 1% per year. Now the rate of dollar depreciation is U.S. inflation minus European inflation, that is, 1% minus 3%, or −2% per year (meaning the U.S. dollar would now appreciate at 2% per year).

With a change of notation to make the United States the foreign country, the same lessons could be derived for Europe and the euro.

3 The Monetary Approach: Implications and Evidence

The monetary approach is the workhorse model in the study of long-run exchange rate movements. In this section, we look at some applications and empirical evidence.

Exchange Rate Forecasts Using the Simple Model

An important application of the monetary approach to exchange rate determination is to provide a forecast of the future exchange rate. Remember from the previous chapter that forex market arbitragers need such a forecast to be able to make arbitrage calculations using uncovered interest parity. Using Equation (11-3), we can see that a forecast of future exchange rates (the left-hand side) can be constructed as long as we know how to forecast future money supplies and real income (the right-hand side).

In practice, this is why expectations about money and real income in the future attract so much attention in the financial media, and especially in the forex market. The discussion returns with obsessive regularity to two questions. The first question, "What are central banks going to do?" leads to all manner of attempts to decode the statements of central bank officials. The second question, "How is the economy expected to grow in real terms?" leads to a keen interest in any economic indicators, such as productivity or investment, that might hint at changes in the rate of income growth.

Any such forecasts come with at least two major caveats. First, there is great uncertainty in trying to answer these questions, and forecasts of economic variables years in the future are inevitably subject to large errors. Nonetheless, this is one of the key tasks of financial markets. Second, whenever one uses the monetary model for forecasting, one is answering a hypothetical question: What path would exchange rates follow from now on *if prices were flexible and PPP held*? As forecasters know, in the short run there might be deviations from this prediction about exchange rate changes, but in the longer run, we expect the prediction will supply a more reasonable guide.

Forecasting Exchange Rates: An Example To see how forecasting might work, let's look at a simple scenario and focus on what would happen under flexible prices. Assume that U.S. and European real income growth rates are identical and equal to zero (0%) so that real income levels are constant. Assume also that the European money supply is constant. If the money supply and real income in Europe are constant, then the European price level is constant, and European inflation is zero, as we can see from Equation (11-5). These assumptions allow us to perform a controlled thought-experiment, and focus on changes on the U.S. side of the model, all else equal. Let's look at two cases.

Case 1: A one-time unanticipated increase in the money supply. In the first, and simpler, case, suppose at some time T that the U.S. money supply rises by a fixed proportion, say, 10%, all else equal. Assuming that prices are flexible, what does our model predict will happen to the level of the exchange rate after time T? To spell out the argument in detail, we look at the implications of our model for some key variables.

a. There is a 10% increase in the money supply M.

b. Real money balances M/P remain constant, because real income is constant.

c. These last two statements imply that price level P and money supply M must move in the same proportion, so there is a 10% increase in the price level P.

d. PPP implies that the exchange rate E and price level P must move in the same proportion, so there is a 10% increase in the exchange rate E; that is, the dollar depreciates by 10%.

A quicker solution uses the fundamental equation of the monetary approach at Equation (11-3): the price level and exchange rate are proportional to the money supply, all else equal.

Case 2: An unanticipated increase in the rate of money growth. The model also applies to more complex scenarios. Consider a second case in which the U.S. money supply is not constant, but grows at a steady fixed rate μ. Then suppose we learn at time T that the United States will raise the rate of money supply growth from some previously fixed rate μ to a slightly higher rate $\mu + \Delta\mu$. How would people expect the exchange rate to behave, assuming price flexibility? Let's work through this case step by step:

a. Money supply M is growing at a constant rate.

b. Real money balances M/P remain constant, as before.

c. These last two statements imply that price level P and money supply M must move in the same proportion, so P is always a constant multiple of M.

d. PPP implies that the exchange rate E and price level P must move in the same proportion, so E is always a constant multiple of P (and hence of M).

Corresponding to these four steps, the four panels of Figure 11-6 illustrate the path of the key variables in this example. This figure shows that if we can forecast the

FIGURE 11-6

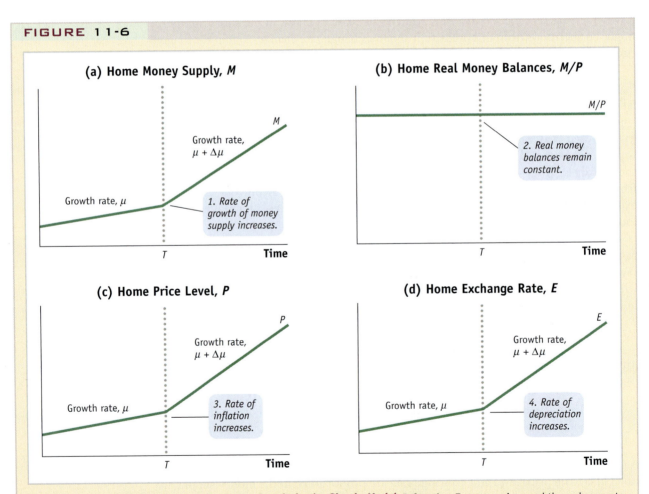

An Increase in the Growth Rate of the Money Supply in the Simple Model Before time T, money, prices, and the exchange rate all grow at rate μ. Foreign prices are constant. In panel (a), we suppose at time T there is an increase $\Delta\mu$ in the rate of growth of home money supply M. In panel (b), the quantity theory assumes that the level of real money balances remains unchanged. After time T, if real money balances (M/P) are constant, then money M and prices P still grow at the same rate, which is now $\mu + \Delta\mu$, so the rate of inflation rises by $\Delta\mu$, as shown in panel (c). PPP and an assumed stable foreign price level imply that the exchange rate will follow a path similar to that of the domestic price level, so E also grows at the new rate $\mu + \Delta\mu$, and the rate of depreciation rises by $\Delta\mu$, as shown in panel (d).

money supply at any future period as in (a), and if we know real money balances re-main constant as in (b), then we can forecast prices as in (c) and exchange rates as in (d). These forecasts are good in any future period, under the assumptions of the mon-etary approach. Again, Equation (11-3) supplies the answer more quickly; under the assumptions we have made, money, prices, and exchange rates all move in proportion to one another.

APPLICATION

Evidence for the Monetary Approach

The monetary approach to prices and exchange rates suggests that, all else equal, in-creases in the rate of money supply growth should be the same size as increases in the rate of inflation and the rate of exchange rate depreciation. Looking for evidence of this relationship in real-world data is one way to put this theory to the test.

The scatterplots in Figure 11-7 and Figure 11-8 show data from the 1975 to 2005 period for a large sample of countries. The results offer fairly strong support for the monetary theory. All else equal, Equation (11-6) predicts that an $x\%$ difference in money growth rates (relative to the United States) should be associated with an $x\%$ difference in inflation rates (relative to the United States) and an $x\%$ depreciation of the home exchange rate (against the U.S. dollar). If this association were literally true in the data, then each country in the scatterplot would be on the 45-degree line. This is not exactly true, but the actual relationship is very close and offers some support for the monetary approach.

One reason the data do not sit on the 45-degree line is that all else is *not* equal in this sample of countries. In Equation (11-6), countries differ not only in their relative

FIGURE 11-7

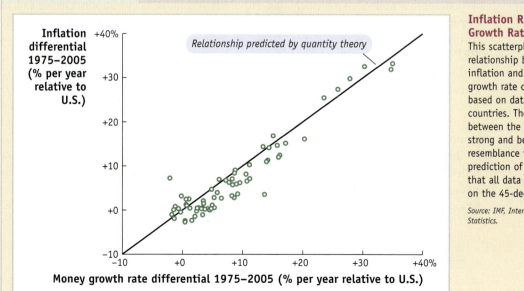

Money growth rate differential 1975–2005 (% per year relative to U.S.)

Inflation Rates and Money Growth Rates, 1975–2005
This scatterplot shows the relationship between the rate of inflation and the money supply growth rate over the long run, based on data for a sample of 76 countries. The correlation between the two variables is strong and bears a close resemblance to the theoretical prediction of the monetary model that all data points would appear on the 45-degree line.

Source: IMF, International Financial Statistics.

FIGURE 11-8

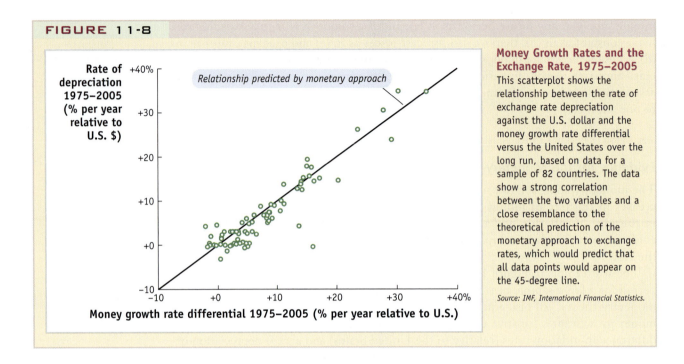

Rate of depreciation 1975–2005 (% per year relative to U.S. $)

Relationship predicted by monetary approach

Money growth rate differential 1975–2005 (% per year relative to U.S.)

Money Growth Rates and the Exchange Rate, 1975–2005 This scatterplot shows the relationship between the rate of exchange rate depreciation against the U.S. dollar and the money growth rate differential versus the United States over the long run, based on data for a sample of 82 countries. The data show a strong correlation between the two variables and a close resemblance to the theoretical prediction of the monetary approach to exchange rates, which would predict that all data points would appear on the 45-degree line.

Source: IMF, International Financial Statistics.

money supply growth rates but also in their real income growth rates. Another explanation is that we have been assuming the money demand parameter L is constant, and this may not be true in reality. This is an issue we must now confront.[9] ■

APPLICATION

Hyperinflations of the Twentieth Century

The monetary approach assumes long-run PPP, which has some support as we saw in Figure 11-2. But we have been careful to note, again, that PPP generally works poorly in the short run. However, there is one notable exception to this general failure of PPP in the short run: hyperinflations.

Economists traditionally define a **hyperinflation** as occurring when the inflation rises to a sustained rate of more than 50% *per month* (which means that prices are doubling every 51 days). In common usage, some lower-inflation episodes are also called hyperinflations; for example, an inflation rate of 1,000% *per year* is a common rule of thumb (when inflation is "only" 22% per month).

There have been many hyperinflations worldwide since the early twentieth century. They usually occur when governments face a budget crisis, are unable to borrow to finance a deficit, and instead choose to print money to cover their financing needs. The situation is not sustainable and usually leads to economic, social, or political crisis,

---

[9] Economists can use sophisticated statistical techniques to address these issues and still find results favorable to the monetary approach in the long run. See David E. Rapach and Mark E. Wohar, 2002, "Testing the Monetary Model of Exchange Rate Determination: New Evidence from a Century of Data," *Journal of International Economics*, 58(2), 359–385.

which is eventually resolved with a return to price stability. (For more discussion of hyperinflations and their consequences, see **Headlines: The First Hyperinflation of the Twenty-First Century** and **Side Bar: Currency Reform.**)

PPP in Hyperinflations   Each of these crises provides a unique laboratory for testing the predictions of the PPP theory. The scatterplot in Figure 11-9 looks at the data using changes in levels (from start to finish, expressed as multiples). The change in the exchange rate (with the United States) is on the vertical axis and the change in the price level (compared with the United States) is on the horizontal axis. Because of the huge changes involved, both axes use log scales in powers of 10. For example, 10^{12} on the vertical axis means the exchange rate rose (the currency depreciated) by a factor of a trillion against the U.S. dollar during the hyperinflation.

If PPP holds, changes in prices and exchange rates should be equal and all observations would be on the 45-degree line. The changes follow this pattern very closely, providing support for PPP. What the hyperinflations have in common is that a very large depreciation was about equal to a very large inflation differential. In an economy with fairly stable prices and exchange rates, large changes in exchange rates and prices only develop over the very long run of years and decades; in a hyperinflation, large inflations and large depreciations are compressed into the short run of years or months, so this is one case where PPP holds quite well even in the short run.

FIGURE 11-9

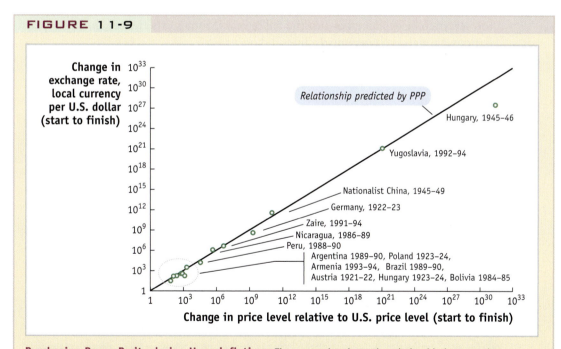

Purchasing Power Parity during Hyperinflations   The scatterplot shows the relationship between the cumulative start-to-finish exchange rate depreciation against the U.S. dollar and the cumulative start-to-finish rise in the local price level for hyperinflations in the twentieth century. Note the use of logarithmic scales. The data show a strong correlation between the two variables and a very close resemblance to the theoretical prediction of PPP that all data points would appear on the 45-degree line.

Sources: IMF, International Financial Statistics; Global Financial Data; Phillip Cagan, "The Monetary Dynamics of Hyperinflation," in Milton Friedman, ed., 1956, Studies in the Quantity Theory of Money (Chicago: University of Chicago Press), pp. 25–117; Pavle Petrovic and Zorica Mladenovic, 2000, "Money Demand and Exchange Rate Determination under Hyperinflation: Conceptual Issues and Evidence from Yugoslavia," Journal of Money, Credit and Banking, 32, 785–806.

Above top to bottom are an Argentine 500,000 austral bill of 1990; a 1923 one billion German mark note (1 German billion = 1 U.S. trillion); and a Hungarian 100 Million B-pengö of 1946, with the "B" denoting the Hungarian billion, or a million million: this 100,000,000,000,000,000,000 pengö note is the highest denomination of currency ever issued by any country.

Some price changes were outrageously large. Austria's hyperinflation of 1921 to 1922 was the first one on record, and prices rose by a factor of about 100 (10^2). In Germany from 1922 to 1923, prices rose by a factor of about 20 billion (2×10^{10}); in the worst month, prices were doubling on average every two days. In Hungary from 1945 to 1946, pengö prices rose by a factor of about 10^{31}, the current record, and in July 1946, prices were doubling on average every 15 hours. Serbia's inflation from 1992 to 1994 came close to breaking the record for cumulative price changes. In comparison, Argentina's 700-fold inflation and Brazil's 200-fold inflation from 1989 to 1990 look deceptively modest.

Money Demand in Hyperinflations There is one other important lesson to be learned from hyperinflations. In our simple monetary model, the money demand parameter L was assumed to be *constant* and equal to $\overline{L}$. This implied that real money balances were proportional to real income, with $M/P = \overline{L}Y$ as shown in Equation (11-5). Is this assumption of stable real money balances justified?

The evidence shown in Figure 11-10 suggests this assumption is not justified, based on a subset of the hyperinflations. For each point, on the horizontal axis of this figure, we see the peak monthly inflation rate (the moment when prices were rising most rapidly); on the vertical axis, we see the level of real money balances in that month relative to their initial level (in the month just before the hyperinflation began). If real money balances were stable, there ought to be no variation in the vertical dimension aside from fluctuations in real income. But there is, and with a clear pattern: the higher the level of inflation, the lower the level of real money balances. These declines are far too severe to be explained by just the fall in real incomes experienced during hyperinflations, though such income declines did occur.

FIGURE 11-10

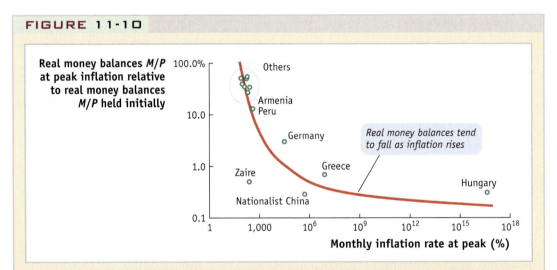

The Collapse of Real Money Balances during Hyperinflations This figure shows that real money balances tend to collapse in hyperinflations as people economize by reducing their holdings of rapidly depreciating notes. The horizontal axis shows the peak monthly inflation rate (%), and the vertical axis shows the ratio of real money balances in that peak month relative to real money balances at the start of the hyperinflationary period. The data are shown using log scales for clarity.

Sources: Global Financial Data; Phillip Cagan, "The Monetary Dynamics of Hyperinflation," in Milton Friedman, ed., 1956, Studies in the Quantity Theory of Money (Chicago: University of Chicago Press), pp. 25–117.

HEADLINES

The First Hyperinflation of the Twenty-First Century

By 2007 Zimbabwe was almost at an economic standstill, except for the printing presses churning out the banknotes. A creeping inflation—58% in 1999, 132% in 2001, 385% in 2003, and 586% in 2005—was about to become hyperinflation, and the long-suffering people faced an accelerating descent into even deeper chaos. Three years later, shortly after this news report, the local currency disappeared from use, replaced by U.S. dollars and South African rand.

. . . Zimbabwe is in the grip of one of the great hyperinflations in world history. The people of this once proud capital have been plunged into a Darwinian struggle to get by. Many have been reduced to peddlers and paupers, hawkers and black-market hustlers, eating just a meal or two a day, their hollowed cheeks a testament to their hunger.

Like countless Zimbabweans, Mrs. Moyo has calculated the price of goods by the number of days she had to spend in line at the bank to withdraw cash to buy them: a day for a bar of soap; another for a bag of salt; and four for a sack of cornmeal.

The withdrawal limit rose on Monday, but with inflation surpassing what independent economists say is an almost unimaginable 40 million percent, she said the value of the new amount would quickly be a pittance, too.

"It's survival of the fittest," said Mrs. Moyo, 29, a hair braider who sells the greens she grows in her yard for a dime a bunch. "If you're not fit, you will starve."

Economists here and abroad say Zimbabwe's economic collapse is gaining velocity, radiating instability into the heart of southern Africa. As the bankrupt government prints ever more money, inflation has gone wild, rising from 1,000 percent in 2006 to 12,000 percent in 2007. . . . In fact, Zimbabwe's hyperinflation is probably among the five worst of all time, said Jeffrey D. Sachs, a Columbia University economics professor, along with Germany in the 1920s, Greece and Hungary in the 1940s and Yugoslavia in 1993. . . .

Basic public services, already devastated by an exodus of professionals in recent years, are breaking down on an ever larger scale as tens of thousands of teachers, nurses, garbage collectors and janitors have simply stopped reporting to their jobs because their salaries, more worthless literally by the hour, no longer cover the cost of taking the bus to work. . . .

The bodies of paupers in advanced states of decay were stacking up in the mortuary at Beitbridge District Hospital because not even government authorities were seeing to their burial. . . . Harare Central Hospital slashed admissions by almost half because so much of its cleaning staff could no longer afford to get to work.

Most of the capital, though lovely beneath its springtime canopy of lavender jacaranda blooms, was without water because the authorities had stopped paying the bills to transport the treatment chemicals. Garbage is piling up uncollected. Sixteen people have died in an outbreak of cholera in nearby Chitungwiza, spread by contaminated water and sewage. . . .

Vigilantes in Kwekwe killed a man suspected of stealing two chickens, eggs and a bucket of corn. . . . And traditional chiefs complained about corrupt politicians and army officers who sold grain needed for the hungry to the politically connected instead.

Ink on their hands: Under President Robert Mugabe and Central Bank Governor Gideon Gono (seen clutching a Z$50 million note), Zimbabwe became the latest country to join a rather exclusive club.

Source: Excerpted from Celia W. Dugger, "Life in Zimbabwe: Wait for Useless Money," The New York Times, *October 2, 2008.*

SIDE BAR

Currency Reform

Hyperinflations help us understand how some currencies become extinct if they cease to function well and lose value rapidly. Dollarization in Ecuador is a recent example. Other currencies survive such travails, only to be reborn. But the low denomination bills—the ones, fives, tens—usually become essentially worthless and normal transactions can require you to be a millionaire. The eradication of a few pesky zeros might then be a good idea. A government may then *redenominate* a new unit of currency equal to 10^N (10 raised to the power N) old units.

Sometimes N can get quite large. In the 1980s, Argentina suffered hyperinflation. On June 1, 1983, the *peso argentino* replaced the (old) peso at a rate of 10,000 to 1. Then on June 14, 1985, the *austral* replaced the peso argentino at 1,000 to 1. Finally, on January 1, 1992, the *convertible peso* replaced the austral at a rate of 10,000 to 1 (i.e., 10,000,000,000 old pesos). After all this, if you had owned 1 new peso in 1983

(and had changed it into the later monies), it would have lost 99.99997% of its U.S. dollar value by 2003.

In 1946 the Hungarian *pengö* became so worthless that the authorities no longer printed the denomination on each note in numbers, but only in words—perhaps to avert distrust (unsuccessful), to hide embarrassment (also unsuccessful), or simply because there wasn't room to print all those zeros. By July 15, 1946, there were 76,041,000,000,000,000,000,000,000 pengö in circulation. A stable new currency, the *forint*, was finally introduced on July 26, 1946, with each forint worth 400,000 quadrillion pengö (4×10^{20} = 400,000,000,000,000,000,000 pengö). The dilution of the Zimbabwean dollar from 2005 to 2009 was even more extreme, as the authorities lopped off 25 zeros in a series of reforms before the currency finally vanished from use.

This finding may not strike you as very surprising. If prices are doubling every few days (or every few hours), the money in people's pockets is rapidly turning into worthless pieces of paper. They will try to minimize their money holdings—and will do so even more as inflation rises higher and higher, just as the figure shows. It becomes just too costly to hold very much money, despite one's need to use it for transactions.

If you thought along these lines, you have an accurate sense of how people behave during hyperinflations. You also anticipated the extensions to the simple model that we make in the next section so it is more realistic. Even during "normal" inflations—situations that are less pathological than a hyperinflation—it is implausible to assume that real money balances are perfectly stable. In our extension of the simple model, we will assume that people make the trade-off highlighted previously: comparing the benefits of holding money for transactions purposes with the costs of holding money as compared with other assets. ■

4 Money, Interest Rates, and Prices in the Long Run: A General Model

So far we have a long-run theory that links exchange rates to the price levels in each country: PPP. We also have a simple long-run monetary model that links price levels in each country to money supply and demand: the *quantity theory*.

These building blocks provide some basic intuition for the links between price levels, money, and exchange rates. The trouble is that the quantity theory's assumption that the demand for money is stable is implausible. In this section, we explore a more general model that addresses this shortcoming by allowing money demand to vary with the nominal interest rate. But this theory, in turn, brings another variable into play: How is the nominal interest rate determined in the long run? Answering this question will lead us to consider the links between inflation and the nominal interest rate in an open economy. With these new models in hand, we then return to the question of how best to understand what determines exchange rates in the long run.

The Demand for Money: The General Model

The general model of money demand is motivated by two insights, the first of which carries over from the quantity theory, the simple model we studied earlier in this chapter.

■ *There is a benefit from holding money.* As is true in the simple quantity theory, the benefit of money is that individuals can conduct transactions with it, and we continue to assume that transactions demand is in proportion to income, all else equal.

■ *There is a cost to holding money.* The nominal interest rate on money is zero, $i_{money} = 0$. By holding money and not earning interest, people incur the opportunity cost of holding money. For example, an individual could hold an interest-earning asset paying $i_\$$. The difference in nominal returns between this asset and money would be $i_\$ - i_{money} = i_\$ > 0$. This is one way of expressing the opportunity cost.

Moving from the individual or household level up to the macroeconomic level, we can infer that aggregate money demand in the economy as a whole will behave similarly:

All else equal, a rise in national dollar income (nominal income) will cause a proportional increase in transactions and, hence, in aggregate money demand.

All else equal, a rise in the nominal interest rate will cause the aggregate demand for money to fall.

Thus, we arrive at a general model in which money demand is proportional to nominal income, and is a decreasing function of the nominal interest rate:

$$\underbrace{M^d}_{\substack{\text{Demand for}\\\text{money (\$)}}} = \underbrace{L(i)}_{\substack{\text{A decreasing}\\\text{function}}} \times \underbrace{P \times Y}_{\substack{\text{Nominal}\\\text{income (\$)}}}$$

Recall that, formerly, in the quantity theory, the parameter L (the liquidity ratio, the amount of money needed for transactions per dollar of nominal GDP) was a constant. In this general model, we assume that L is a decreasing function of the nominal interest rate i. Dividing by P, we can derive the demand for real money balances:

$$\underbrace{\frac{M^d}{P}}_{\substack{\text{Demand for}\\\text{real money}}} = \underbrace{L(i)}_{\substack{\text{A decreasing}\\\text{function}}} \times \underbrace{Y}_{\substack{\text{Real}\\\text{income}}}$$

Figure 11-11(a) shows a typical **real money demand function** of this form, with the quantity of real money balances demanded on the horizontal axis and the nominal interest rate on the vertical axis. The downward slope of the demand curve reflects the inverse relationship between the demand for real money balances and the nominal interest rate *at a given level of real income (Y)*.

Figure 11-11(b) shows what happens when real income increases from Y_1 to Y_2. When real income increases (by $x\%$), the demand for real money balances increases (by $x\%$) at each level of the nominal interest rate and the curve shifts.

FIGURE 11-11

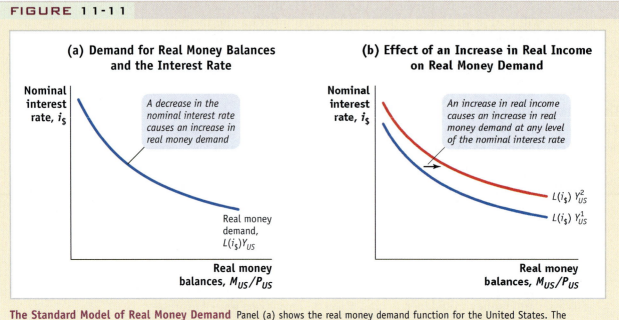

(a) Demand for Real Money Balances and the Interest Rate

Nominal interest rate, $i_\$$

A decrease in the nominal interest rate causes an increase in real money demand

Real money demand, $L(i_\$)Y_{US}$

Real money balances, M_{US}/P_{US}

(b) Effect of an Increase in Real Income on Real Money Demand

Nominal interest rate, $i_\$$

An increase in real income causes an increase in real money demand at any level of the nominal interest rate

$L(i_\$)\ Y^2_{US}$

$L(i_\$)\ Y^1_{US}$

Real money balances, M_{US}/P_{US}

The Standard Model of Real Money Demand Panel (a) shows the real money demand function for the United States. The downward slope implies that the quantity of real money demand rises as the nominal interest rate $i_\$$ falls. Panel (b) shows that an increase in real income from Y^1_{US} to Y^2_{US} causes real money demand to rise at all levels of the nominal interest rate $i_\$$.

Long-Run Equilibrium in the Money Market

The money market is in equilibrium when the real money supply (determined by the central bank) equals the demand for real money balances (determined by the nominal interest rate and real income):

$$\underbrace{\frac{M}{P}}_{\substack{\text{Real money} \\ \text{supply}}} = \underbrace{L(i)Y}_{\substack{\text{Real money} \\ \text{demand}}} \tag{11-7}$$

We will continue to assume that prices are flexible in the long run and that they adjust to ensure that equilibrium is maintained.

We now have a model that describes equilibrium in the money market which will help us on the way to understanding the determination of the exchange rate. Before we arrive at the long-run exchange rate, however, we need one last piece to the puzzle. Under the quantity theory, the nominal interest rate was ignored. Now, in our general model, it is a key variable in the determination of money demand. So we need a theory to tell us what the level of the nominal interest rate i will be in the long run. Once we have solved this problem, we will be able to apply this new, more complex, but more realistic model of the money market to the analysis of exchange rate determination in the long run.

Inflation and Interest Rates in the Long Run

The tools we need to determine the nominal interest rate in an open economy are already at hand. So far in this chapter, we have developed the idea of purchasing power parity (PPP), which links prices and exchange rates. In the last chapter, we developed another parity idea, uncovered interest parity (UIP), which links exchange rates and interest rates. With only these two relationships in hand, PPP and UIP, we can derive a powerful and striking result concerning interest rates that has profound implications for our study of open economy macroeconomics.

Relative PPP, as indicated in Equation (11-2), states that the rate of depreciation equals the inflation differential at time *t*. When market actors use this equation to forecast future exchange rates, we use a superscript *e* to denote such expectations. Equation (11-2) is recast to show expected depreciation and inflation at time *t*:

$$\underbrace{\frac{\Delta E^e_{\$/€}}{E_{\$/€}}}_{\substack{\text{Expected rate of} \\ \text{dollar depreciation}}} = \underbrace{\pi^e_{US} - \pi^e_{EUR}}_{\text{Expected inflation differential}}$$

Next we recall that uncovered interest parity (UIP) in the approximate form (Equation 10-3) can be rearranged to show that the expected rate of depreciation equals the interest differential at time *t*:

$$\underbrace{\frac{\Delta E^e_{\$/€}}{E_{\$/€}}}_{\substack{\text{Expected rate of} \\ \text{dollar depreciation}}} = \underbrace{i_\$}_{\substack{\text{Net dollar} \\ \text{interest rate}}} - \underbrace{i_€}_{\substack{\text{Net euro} \\ \text{interest rate}}}$$

This way of writing the UIP equation says that traders will be indifferent to a higher U.S. interest rate relative to the euro interest rates (making U.S. deposits look more attractive) only if the higher U.S. rate is offset by an expected dollar depreciation (making U.S. deposits look less attractive). For example, if the U.S. interest rate is 4% and the euro interest rate is 2%, the interest differential is 2% and the forex market can be in equilibrium only if traders expect a 2% depreciation of the U.S. dollar against the euro, which would exactly offset the higher U.S. interest rate.

The Fisher Effect

Because the left sides of the previous two equations are equal, the right sides must also be equal. Thus, the nominal interest differential equals the expected inflation differential:

$$\underbrace{i_\$ - i_€}_{\substack{\text{Nominal interest} \\ \text{rate differential}}} = \underbrace{\pi^e_{US} - \pi^e_{EUR}}_{\substack{\text{Nominal inflation rate} \\ \text{differential (expected)}}} \tag{11-8}$$

What does this important result say? To take an example, suppose expected inflation is 4% in the United States and 2% in Europe. The inflation differential on the right is then +2% (4%−2% = +2%). If interest rates in Europe are 3%, then to make the interest differential the same as the inflation differential, +2%, the interest rate in the United States must equal 5% (5%−3% = +2%).

Now suppose expected inflation in the United States changes, rising by one percentage point to 5%. If nothing changes in Europe, then the U.S. interest rate must also rise by one percentage point to 6% for the equation to hold. In general, this equation predicts that changes in the expected rate of inflation will be fully incorporated (one for one) into changes in nominal interest rates.

All else equal, a rise in the expected inflation rate in a country will lead to an equal rise in its nominal interest rate.

This result is known as the **Fisher effect,** named for the American economist Irving Fisher (1867–1947). Note that because this result depends on an assumption of PPP, it is therefore likely to hold only in the long run.

The Fisher effect makes clear the link between inflation and nominal interest rates under flexible prices, a finding that is widely applicable. For a start, it makes sense of the evidence we just saw on money holdings during hyperinflations (see Figure 11-10). As inflation rises, the Fisher effect tells us that the nominal interest rate i must rise by the same amount; the general model of money demand then tells us that $L(i)$ must fall because it is a decreasing function of i. Thus, for a given level of real income, real money balances must fall as inflation rises.

In other words, the Fisher effect predicts that the change in the opportunity cost of money is equal not just to the change in the nominal interest rate but also to the change in the inflation rate. In times of very high inflation, people should, therefore, want to reduce their money holdings—and they do.

Real Interest Parity

As just described, the Fisher effect tells us something about nominal interest rates, but we can quickly derive the implications for real interest rates, too. Rearranging the last equation, we find

$$i_\$ - \pi^e_{US} = i_\text{€} - \pi^e_{EUR}$$

The expressions on either side of this equation might look familiar from previous courses in macroeconomics. When the inflation rate (π) is subtracted from a *nominal* interest rate (i), the result is a **real interest rate** (r), the inflation-adjusted reurn on an interest-bearing asset. Given this definition, we can simplify the last equation further. On the left is the expected real interest rate in the United States ($r^e_{US} = i_\$ - \pi^e_{US}$). On the right is the expected real interest rate in Europe ($r^e_{EUR} = i_\text{€} - \pi^e_{EUR}$).

Thus, using only two assumptions, PPP and UIP, we have shown that

$$r^e_{US} = r^e_{EUR} \tag{11-9}$$

This remarkable result states the following: *If PPP and UIP hold, then expected real interest rates are equalized across countries.*

This powerful condition is called **real interest parity** and because it depends on an assumption of PPP, it is therefore likely to hold only in the long run.[10]

We have arrived at a strong conclusion about the potential for globalization to cause convergence in economic outcomes, because real interest parity implies the following: *Arbitrage in goods and financial markets alone is sufficient, in the long run, to cause the equalization of real interest rates across countries.*

We have considered two countries, but this argument applies to all countries integrated into the global capital market. In the long run, they will all share a common expected real interest rate, the long-run expected **world real interest rate** denoted r^*, so

$$r^e_{US} = r^e_{EUR} = r^*$$

---

[10] You may have encountered other theories in which real interest rates are equalized across countries by other means. Countries may share common technologies (due to technology diffusion) or might have similar saving behavior (due to similar preferences). Such assumptions could lead to identical real interest rates even in two *closed* economies. But here we have derived the real interest parity condition *only* from UIP and PPP, meaning that, in *open* economies, these are *sufficient* conditions for real interest rates to be equalized. No other assumptions are needed!

From now on, unless indicated otherwise, we treat r^* as a given, exogenous variable, something outside the control of a policy maker in any particular country.[11]

Under these conditions, the Fisher effect is even clearer, because, by definition,

$$i_\$ = r^e_{US} + \pi^e_{US} = r^* + \pi^e_{US}, \qquad i_€ = r^e_{EUR} + \pi^e_{EUR} = r^* + \pi^e_{EUR}$$

Thus, in each country, the long-run expected nominal interest rate is the long-run world real interest rate plus that country's expected long-run inflation rate. For example, if the world real interest rate is $r^* = 2\%$, and the country's long-run expected inflation rate goes up by two percentage points from 3% to 5%, then its long-run nominal interest rate also goes up by two percentage points from the old level of $2 + 3 = 5\%$ to a new level of $2 + 5 = 7\%$.

APPLICATION

Evidence on the Fisher Effect

Are the Fisher effect and real interest parity supported by empirical evidence? One might expect a problem here. We derived them from purchasing power parity. The evidence we have seen on PPP offers support only in the long run. Thus, we do not expect the Fisher effect and real interest parity to hold exactly in the short run, but we might expect them to hold (at least approximately) in the long run.

Figure 11-12 shows that the Fisher effect is close to reality in the long run: on average, countries with higher inflation rates tend to have higher nominal interest rates, and the data line up fairly well with the predictions of the theory. Figure 11-13 shows that,

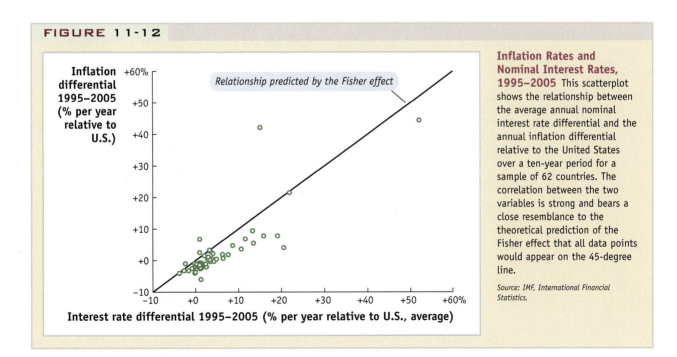

FIGURE 11-12

Inflation Rates and Nominal Interest Rates, 1995–2005 This scatterplot shows the relationship between the average annual nominal interest rate differential and the annual inflation differential relative to the United States over a ten-year period for a sample of 62 countries. The correlation between the two variables is strong and bears a close resemblance to the theoretical prediction of the Fisher effect that all data points would appear on the 45-degree line.

Source: IMF, International Financial Statistics.

---

[11] In advanced economic theories, the determinants of the world real interest rate are explored, with reference to consumption preferences of households and the extent to which they discount the future.

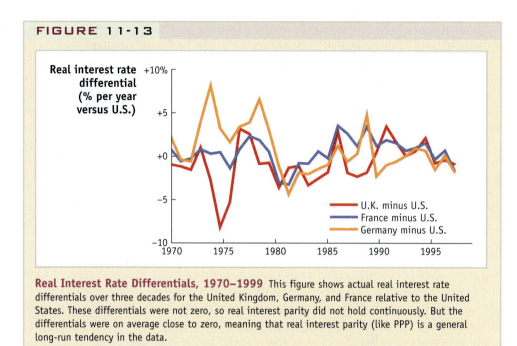

FIGURE 11-13

Real Interest Rate Differentials, 1970–1999 This figure shows actual real interest rate differentials over three decades for the United Kingdom, Germany, and France relative to the United States. These differentials were not zero, so real interest parity did not hold continuously. But the differentials were on average close to zero, meaning that real interest parity (like PPP) is a general long-run tendency in the data.

Source: Maurice Obstfeld and Alan M. Taylor, 2004, Global Capital Markets: Integration, Crisis, and Growth, Japan-U.S. Center Sanwa Monographs on International Financial Markets (Cambridge, UK: Cambridge University Press).

for three developed countries, real interest parity holds fairly well in the long run: real interest differentials are not always zero, but they tend to fluctuate around zero in the long run. This could be seen as evidence in favor of long-run real interest parity. ■

The Fundamental Equation under the General Model

Now that we understand how the nominal interest rate is determined in the long run, our general model is complete. This model differs from the simple model (the quantity theory) *only* by allowing L to vary as a function of the nominal interest rate *i*.

We can therefore update our fundamental equations to allow for this change in how we treat *L*. For example, the fundamental equation of the monetary approach to exchange rates, Equation (11-3), can now be suitably modified:

$$\underbrace{E_{\$/\mathfrak{e}}}_{\substack{\text{Exchange} \\ \text{rate}}} = \underbrace{\frac{P_{US}}{P_{EUR}}}_{\substack{\text{Ratio of} \\ \text{price levels}}} = \frac{\left(\dfrac{M_{US}}{L_{US}(i_{\$})Y_{US}}\right)}{\left(\dfrac{M_{EUR}}{L_{EUR}(i_{\mathfrak{e}})Y_{EUR}}\right)} = \underbrace{\frac{(M_{US}/M_{EUR})}{(L_{US}(i_{\$})Y_{US}/L_{EUR}(i_{\mathfrak{e}})Y_{EUR})}}_{\substack{\text{Relative nominal money supplies} \\ \text{divided by relative real money demands}}} \qquad (11\text{-}10)$$

What have we gained from this refinement? We know that the simple model will remain valid for cases in which nominal interest rates remain unchanged in the long run. It is only when nominal interest rates change that the general model has different implications, and we now have the right tools for that situation. To put those tools to work, we revisit the example of an exchange rate forecasting problem we encountered earlier in this chapter.

Exchange Rate Forecasts Using the General Model

Earlier in the chapter, we looked at two forecasting problems *under the assumption of flexible prices*. The first was a one-time unanticipated change in an otherwise constant U.S. money supply. Under the assumptions we made (stable real income in both countries and stable European money supply), this change caused a one-time increase in the U.S. price level but did not lead to a change in U.S. inflation (which was zero before and after the event).

The Fisher effect tells us that if inflation rates are unchanged, then, in the long run, nominal interest rates remain unchanged. Thus, the predictions of the simple model remain valid. But in the second and more complex forecasting problem, there was a one-time unanticipated change in the U.S. money growth rate that *did* lead to a change in inflation. It is here that the general model makes different predictions.

Earlier we assumed that U.S. and European real income growth rates are identical and equal to zero (0%), so real income levels are constant. We also assumed that the European money supply is constant, so that the European price level is constant, too. This allowed us to focus on changes on the U.S. side of the model, all else equal.

We now reexamine the forecasting problem for the case in which there is an increase in the U.S. rate of money growth. We learn at time T that the United States is raising the rate of money supply growth from some fixed rate μ to a slightly higher rate $\mu + \Delta\mu$.

For example, imagine an increase from 2% to 3% growth, so $\Delta\mu = 1\%$. How will the exchange rate behave in the long run? To solve the model, we make a provisional assumption that U.S. inflation rates and interest rates are constant before and after time T and focus on the differences between the two periods caused by the change in money supply growth. The story is told in Figure 11-14:

a. The money supply is growing at a constant rate. If the interest rate is constant in each period, then real money balances M/P remain constant, by assumption, because $L(i)Y$ is then a constant. If real money balances are constant, then M and P grow at the same rate. Before T that rate is $\mu = 2\%$; after T that rate is $\mu + \Delta\mu = 3\%$. That is, the U.S. inflation rate rises by an amount $\Delta\mu = 1\%$ at time T.

b. As a result of the Fisher effect, U.S. interest rates also rise by $\Delta\mu = 1\%$ at time T. Consequently, real money balances M/P must fall at time T because $L(i)Y$ will decrease as i increases.

c. In (a) we have described the path of M. In (b) we found that M/P is constant up to T, then drops suddenly, and then is constant after time T. What path must the price level P follow? Up to time T, it is a constant multiple of M; the same applies after time T, but the constant has increased. Why? The nominal money supply grows smoothly, without a jump. So if real money balances drop down discontinuously at time T, the price level must jump up discontinuously at time T. The intuition for this is that the rise in inflation and interest rates at time T prompts people to instantaneously demand less real money, but because the supply of nominal money is unchanged, the price level has to jump up. Apart from this jump, P grows at a constant rate; before T that rate is $\mu = 2\%$; after T that rate is $\mu + \Delta\mu = 3\%$.

d. PPP implies that E and P must move in the same proportion, so E is always a constant multiple of P. Thus, E jumps like P at time T. Apart from this jump, E grows at a constant rate; before T that rate is $\mu = 2\%$; after T that rate is $\mu + \Delta\mu = 3\%$.

FIGURE 11-14

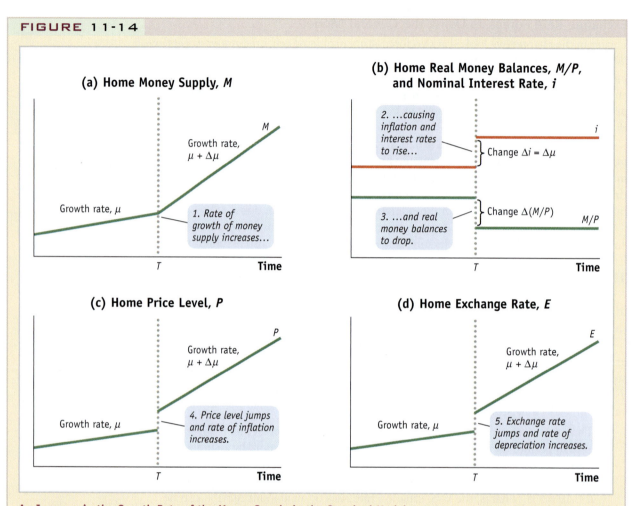

(a) Home Money Supply, M

Growth rate, $\mu + \Delta\mu$

Growth rate, μ

M

1. *Rate of growth of money supply increases...*

T — Time

(b) Home Real Money Balances, M/P, and Nominal Interest Rate, i

2. *...causing inflation and interest rates to rise...*

Change $\Delta i = \Delta\mu$

i

3. *...and real money balances to drop.*

Change $\Delta(M/P)$

M/P

T — Time

(c) Home Price Level, P

Growth rate, $\mu + \Delta\mu$

Growth rate, μ

P

4. *Price level jumps and rate of inflation increases.*

T — Time

(d) Home Exchange Rate, E

Growth rate, $\mu + \Delta\mu$

Growth rate, μ

E

5. *Exchange rate jumps and rate of depreciation increases.*

T — Time

An Increase in the Growth Rate of the Money Supply in the Standard Model Before time *T*, money, prices, and the exchange rate all grow at rate μ. Foreign prices are constant. In panel (a), we suppose at time *T* there is an increase $\Delta\mu$ in the rate of growth of home money supply *M*. This causes an increase $\Delta\mu$ in the rate of inflation; the Fisher effect means that there will be a $\Delta\mu$ increase in the nominal interest rate; as a result, as shown in panel (b), real money demand falls with a discrete jump at *T*. If real money balances are to fall when the nominal money supply expands continuously, then the domestic price level must make a discrete jump up at time *T*, as shown in panel (c). Subsequently, prices grow at the new higher rate of inflation; and given the stable foreign price level, PPP implies that the exchange rate follows a similar path to the domestic price level, as shown in panel (d).

Corresponding to these four steps, Figure 11-14 illustrates the path of the key variables in this example. (Our provisional assumption of constant inflation rates and interest rates in each period is satisfied, so the proposed solution is internally consistent.)

Comparing Figure 11-14 with Figure 11-6, we can observe the subtle qualitative differences between the predictions of the simple quantity theory and those of the more general model. Shifts in the interest rate introduce jumps in real money demand. Because money supplies evolve smoothly, these jumps end up being reflected in the price levels and hence—via PPP—in exchange rates. The Fisher effect tells us that these interest rate effects are ultimately the result of changes in expected inflation.

Looking Ahead We can learn a little more by thinking through the market mechanism that produces this result. People learn at time *T* that money growth will be more rapid in the United States. This creates expectations of higher inflation in the United States. If people believe PPP holds in the long run, they will believe higher future inflation will cause the U.S. currency to depreciate in the future. This prospect makes holding dollars less attractive, by UIP. People try to sell dollars, and invest in euros. This creates immediate downward pressure on the dollar—even though at time T itself the supply of dollars does not change at all! This lesson underlines yet again the importance of expectations in determining the exchange rate. *Even if actual economic conditions today are completely unchanged, news about the future affects today's exchange rate.* This crucial insight can help us explain many phenomena relating to the volatility and instability in spot exchange rates, an idea we develop further in the chapters that follow.

5 Monetary Regimes and Exchange Rate Regimes

The monetary approach shows that, in the long run, all nominal variables—the money supply, interest rate, price level, and exchange rate—are interlinked. Hence, monetary policy choices can radically affect some important economic outcomes, notably prices and inflation, about which policy makers, governments, and the people they represent deeply care. The approach therefore highlights issues that must be taken into account in long-run economic policy design, and we will explore these important connections between theory and policy in this final section of the chapter.

We have repeatedly stressed the importance of inflation as an economic variable. Why is it so important? High or volatile inflation rates are considered undesirable. They may destabilize an economy or retard its growth.[12] Economies with low and stable inflation generally grow faster than those with high or volatile inflation. Inflationary crises, in which inflation jumps to a high or hyperinflationary level, are very damaging indeed.[13]

Thus, an overarching aspect of a nation's economic policy is the desire to keep inflation within certain bounds. To achieve such an objective requires that policy makers be subject to some kind of constraint in the long run. Such constraints are called **nominal anchors** because they attempt to tie down a nominal variable that is potentially under the policy makers' control.

Policy makers cannot directly control prices, so the attainment of price stability in the *short run* is not feasible. The question is what can policy makers do to promote price stability in the long run and what types of flexibility, if any, they will allow themselves in the short run. Long-run nominal anchoring and short-run flexibility are the

---

[12] Macroeconomists can list numerous potential costs of inflation. Expected inflation generates a cost of holding money, a tax on transactions that adds friction to the economy; firms and workers use nominal contracts for prices and would have to change prices and recontract more often; inflation also distorts the economy when a tax system has significant nominal provisions (e.g., fixed deductions and exemptions). Unexpected inflation creates arbitrary redistributions from creditors to debtors, and this introduces risk into borrowing and lending, making interest rates and investment more costly. In short, if inflation is other than low and stable, economic life becomes at best inconvenient and at worst (as in a hyperinflation) dysfunctional. See N. Gregory Mankiw, 2007, *Macroeconomics*, 6th ed., Chap. 4 (New York: Worth).

[13] This evidence is merely suggestive: high inflation and slow growth may each be caused by other factors, such as weak institutions. Some studies have used sophisticated econometrics to address this problem. See Stanley Fischer, 1993, "The Role of Macroeconomic Factors in Growth," *Journal of Monetary Economics*, 32, 485–511; Robert J. Barro, 1997, *Determinants of Economic Growth* (Cambridge, MA: MIT Press); Michael Bruno and William Easterly, 1998, "Inflation Crises and Long-Run Growth," *Journal of Monetary Economics*, 41, 3–26.

characteristics of the policy framework that economists call the **monetary regime.** In this section, we examine different types of monetary regimes and what they mean for the exchange rate.

The Long Run: The Nominal Anchor

Which variables could policy makers use as anchors to achieve an inflation objective in the long run? To answer this key question, all we have to do is go back and rearrange the equations for relative PPP at Equation (11-2), the quantity theory in rates of change at Equation (11-6), and the Fisher effect at Equation (11-8), to obtain alternative expressions for the rate of inflation in the home country. To emphasize that these findings apply generally to all countries, we relabel the countries Home (H) and Foreign (F) instead of United States and Europe.

The three main nominal anchor choices that emerge are as follows:

■ **Exchange rate target:** Relative PPP at Equation (11-2) says that the rate of depreciation equals the inflation differential, or $\Delta E_{H/F}/E_{H/F} = \pi_H - \pi_F$. Rearranging this expression suggests one way to anchor inflation is as follows:

$$\underbrace{\pi_H}_{\text{Inflation}} = \underbrace{\frac{\Delta E_{H/F}}{E_{H/F}}}_{\substack{\text{Rate of} \\ \text{depreciation}}} + \underbrace{\pi_F}_{\substack{\text{Foreign} \\ \text{inflation}}}$$

Anchor variable

Relative PPP says that home inflation equals the rate of depreciation plus foreign inflation. A simple rule would be to set the rate of depreciation equal to a constant. Under a fixed exchange rate, that constant is set at zero (a peg). Under a crawl, it is a nonzero constant. Alternatively, there may be room for movement about a target (a band). Or there may be a vague goal to allow the exchange rate "limited flexibility." Such policies can deliver stable home inflation if PPP works well and if policy makers keep their commitment. The drawback is the final term in the equation: PPP implies that over the long run the home country "imports" inflation from the foreign country over and above the chosen rate of depreciation. For example, under a peg, if foreign inflation rises by 1% per year, then so, too, does home inflation. Thus, countries almost invariably peg to a country with a reputation for price stability (e.g., the United States). This is a common policy choice: fixed exchange rates of some form are in use in more than half of the world's countries.

■ **Money supply target:** The quantity theory suggests another way to anchor because the fundamental equation for the price level in the monetary approach says that inflation equals the excess of the rate of money supply growth over and above the rate of real income growth:

$$\underbrace{\pi_H}_{\text{Inflation}} = \underbrace{\mu_H}_{\text{Money supply growth}} - \underbrace{g_H}_{\text{Real output growth}}$$

Anchor variable

A simple rule of this sort is: set the growth rate of the money supply equal to a constant, say, 2% a year. The printing presses should be put on automatic pilot, and no human interference should be allowed. Essentially, the central bank is run by robots. This would be difficult to implement. Again the drawback is the final term in the previous equation: real income growth can be unstable. In periods of high growth, inflation will be below the desired level. In periods of low growth, inflation will be above the desired level. For this reason, money supply targets are waning in popularity or are used in conjunction with other targets. For example, the European Central Bank claims to use monetary growth rates as a partial guide to policy, but nobody is quite sure how serious it is.

■ **Inflation target plus interest rate policy:** The Fisher effect suggests yet another anchoring method:

$$\pi^e_H \quad = \quad i_H \quad - \quad r^*$$

Inflation (expected)   Nominal interest rate   World real interest rate

Anchor variable

The Fisher effect says that home inflation is the home nominal interest rate minus the foreign real interest rate. If the latter can be assumed to be constant, then as long as the average home nominal interest rate is kept stable, inflation can also be kept stable. This type of nominal anchoring framework is an increasingly common policy choice. Assuming a stable world real interest rate is not a bad assumption. (And in principle, the target level of the nominal interest rate could be adjusted if necessary.) More or less flexible versions of inflation targeting can be implemented. A central bank could in theory set the nominal interest rate at a fixed level at all times, but such rigidity is rarely seen and central banks usually adjust interest rates in the short run to meet other goals. For example, if the world real interest rate is $r^* = 2.5\%$, and the country's long-run inflation target is 2%, then its long-run nominal interest rate ought to be on average equal to 4.5% (because $2.5\% = 4.5\% - 2\%$). This would be termed the *neutral* level of the nominal interest rate. But in the short run, the central bank might desire to use some flexibility to set interest rates above or below this neutral level. How much flexibility is a matter of policy choice, as is the question of what economic objectives should drive deviations from the neutral rate (e.g., inflation performance alone, or other factors like output and employment that we shall consider in later chapters).

The Choice of a Nominal Anchor and Its Implications

Under the assumptions we have made, any of the three nominal anchor choices are valid. If a particular long-run inflation objective is to be met, then, all else equal, the first equation says it will be consistent with one particular rate of depreciation; the second equation says it will be consistent with one particular rate of money supply growth; the third equation says it will be consistent with one particular rate of interest. But if policy makers announced targets for all three variables, they would be able to match all three consistently only by chance. Two observations follow.

First, using more than one target may be problematic. Under a fixed exchange rate regime, policy makers cannot employ any target other than the exchange rate.

TABLE 11-2

Exchange Rate Regimes and Nominal Anchors This table illustrates the possible exchange rate regimes that are consistent with various types of nominal anchors. Countries that are dollarized or in a currency union have a "superfixed" exchange rate target. Pegs, bands, and crawls also target the exchange rate. Managed floats have no preset path for the exchange rate, which allows other targets to be employed. Countries that float freely or independently are judged to pay no serious attention to exchange rate targets; if they have anchors, they will involve monetary targets or inflation targets with an interest rate policy. The countries with "freely falling" exchange rates have no serious target and have high rates of inflation and depreciation. It should be noted that many countries engage in implicit targeting (e.g., inflation targeting) without announcing an explicit target and that some countries may use a mix of more than one target.

Type of Nominal Anchor	COMPATIBLE EXCHANGE RATE REGIMES				
	Countries without a Currency of Their Own	Pegs/ Bands/Crawls	Managed Floating	Freely Floating	Freely Falling (rapid depreciation)
Exchange rate target	✔	✔	✔		
Money supply target			✔	✔	
Inflation target (plus interest rate policy)			✔	✔	
None				✔	✔

However, they may be able to use a mix of different targets if they adopt an intermediate regime, such as a managed exchange rate with limited flexibility. Table 11-2 illustrates the ways in which the choice of a target as a nominal anchor affects the choice of exchange rate regime. Obviously, these are not independent choices. But a variety of choices do exist. Thus, *nominal anchoring is possible with a variety of exchange rate regimes.*

Second, whatever target choice is made, a country that commits to a target as a way of nominal anchoring is committing itself to set future money supplies and interest rates in such a way as to meet the target. Only one path for future policy will be compatible with the target in the long run. Thus, *a country with a nominal anchor sacrifices monetary policy autonomy in the long run.*

APPLICATION

Nominal Anchors in Theory and Practice

An appreciation of the importance of nominal anchors has transformed monetary policy making and inflation performance throughout the global economy in recent decades.

In the 1970s, most of the world was struggling with high inflation. An economic slowdown prompted central banks everywhere to loosen monetary policy. In advanced countries, a move to floating exchange rates allowed great freedom for them to loosen their monetary policy. Developing countries had already proven vulnerable to high inflation and now many of them were exposed to even worse inflation. Those who were pegged to major currencies imported high inflation via PPP. Those who weren't pegged struggled to find a credible nominal anchor as they faced economic downturns of their own. High oil prices everywhere contributed to inflationary pressure.

TABLE 11-3

Global Disinflation Cross-country data from 1980 to 2004 show the gradual reduction in the annual rate of inflation around the world. This disinflation process began in the advanced economies in the early 1980s. The emerging markets and developing countries suffered from even higher rates of inflation, although these finally began to fall in the 1990s.

	ANNUAL INFLATION RATE (%)				
	1980–1984	1985–1989	1990–1994	1995–1999	2000–2004
World	14.1%	15.5	30.4	8.4	3.9
Advanced economies	8.7	3.9	3.8	2.0	1.8
Emerging markets and developing countries	31.4	48.0	53.2	13.1	5.6

Source: Kenneth Rogoff, 2003, "Globalization and Global Disinflation," Economic Review, Federal Reserve Bank of Kansas City, IV, 45–78.

In the 1980s, inflationary pressure continued in many developed countries, and in many developing countries high levels of inflation, and even hyperinflations, were not uncommon. Governments were forced to respond to public demands for a more stable inflation environment. In the 1990s, policies designed to create effective nominal anchors were put in place in many countries.

One study found that the use of explicit targets grew markedly in the 1990s, replacing regimes in which there had previously been no explicit nominal anchor. The number of countries in the study with exchange rate targets increased from 30 to 47. The number with money targets increased from 18 to 39. The number with inflation targets increased most dramatically, almost sevenfold, from 8 to 54. Many countries had more than one target in use: in 1998, 55% of the sample announced an explicit target (or monitoring range) for more than one of the exchange rate, money, and inflation.[14]

Looking back from the present we can see that most, but not all, of those policies have turned out to be credible, too, thanks to political developments in many countries that have fostered **central-bank independence.** Independent central banks stand apart from the interference of politicians: they have operational freedom to try to achieve the inflation target, and they may even play a role in setting that target.

Overall, these efforts are judged to have achieved some success, although in many countries inflation had already been brought down substantially in the early to mid-1980s before inflation targets and institutional changes were implemented. Table 11-3 shows a steady decline in average levels of inflation since the early 1980s. The lowest levels of inflation are seen in the advanced economies, although developing countries have also started to make some limited progress. In the industrial countries, central-bank independence is now commonplace (it was not in the 1970s), but in developing countries it is still relatively rare.

---

[14] Gabriel Sterne, August 1999, "The Use of Explicit Targets for Monetary Policy: Practical Experiences of 91 Economies in the 1990s," *Bank of England Quarterly Bulletin*, 39(3), 272–281.

Still, one can have too much of a good thing, and the crisis of 2008–2010 prompted some second thoughts about inflation targets. Typically, such targets have been set at about 2% in developed countries, and with a world real interest rate of 2% this implies a neutral nominal interest rate of 4%. In terms of having room to maneuver, this rate permits central banks to temporarily cut their interest rates up to four percentage points below the neutral level. Prior to the crisis this range was considered ample room for central banks to take short-run actions as needed (e.g., to stimulate output or the rate of inflation if either fell too low). In the crisis, however, central banks soon hit the lower bound of zero rates and could not prevent severe output losses and declines in inflation rates to low or, at times, negative levels (*deflation*). As Irving Fisher famously noted, deflation is very damaging economically—it drives up real interest rates when nominal rates can fall no further as an offset, and falling prices make the real burden of nominal debts higher. These problems have led some economists, among them the IMF's Chief Economist, Olivier Blanchard, to question whether inflation targets should be set higher (e.g., at 4% rather than 2%).[15] The idea received a lukewarm reception, however: moving to a higher inflation target is in principle easy, but many feared its potential abuse could place at risk the hard-won credibility gains that central banks have earned for themselves in the last three decades. Indeed, even as inflation rates fell almost to zero in major economies like the United States and Eurozone, many central bankers continued to speak of their vigilance in guarding against inflation. ■

6 Conclusions

This chapter emphasized the determinants of exchange rates in the long run using the monetary approach. We employed purchasing power parity and a simple monetary model (the quantity theory) to study an equilibrium in which goods are arbitraged and prices are flexible. Under these assumptions, in the home country, changes in the money supply pass through into proportional changes in the price level and the exchange rate.

We also found that uncovered interest parity and purchasing power parity implied that real interest rates are equalized across countries. This helped us develop a monetary model that was more complex—and more realistic—because it allowed money demand to fluctuate in response to changes in the interest rate. In that setting, increases in money growth lead to higher inflation and a higher nominal interest rate and, hence, via decreases in money demand, to even higher price levels. Still, the same basic intuition holds, and one-time changes in the money supply still lead to proportionate changes in prices and exchange rates.

The monetary approach to exchange rates provides a basis for certain kinds of forecasting and policy analysis using the flexible-price model in the long run. But such forecasts matter even in the short run because today's spot exchange rate depends, like all asset prices, on the exchange rate expected to prevail in the future. To make these connections clear, in the next chapter we bring together the key ideas of arbitrage (from the previous chapter) and expectations (from this chapter) to form a complete model of the exchange rate.

---

[15] Olivier Blanchard, Giovanni Dell'Ariccia, and Paolo Mauro, "Rethinking Macroeconomic Policy," *IMF Staff Position Note*, SPN/10/03, February 12, 2010.

KEY POINTS

1. Purchasing power parity (PPP) implies that the exchange rate should equal the relative price level in the two countries, and the real exchange rate should equal 1.

2. Evidence for PPP is weak in the short run but more favorable in the long run. In the short run, deviations are common and changes in the real exchange rate do occur. The failure of PPP in the short run is primarily the result of market frictions, imperfections that limit arbitrage, and price stickiness.

3. A simple monetary model (the quantity theory) explains price levels in terms of money supply levels and real income levels. Because PPP can explain exchange rates in terms of price levels, the two together can be used to develop a monetary approach to the exchange rate.

4. If we can forecast money supply and income, we can use the monetary approach to forecast the level of the exchange rate at any time in the future. However, the monetary approach is valid only under the assumption that prices are flexible. This assumption is more likely to hold in the long run, so the monetary approach is not useful in the short run forecast. Evidence for PPP and the monetary approach is more favorable in the long run.

5. PPP theory, combined with uncovered interest parity, leads to the strong implications of the Fisher effect (interest differentials between countries should equal inflation differentials). The Fisher effect says that changes in local inflation rates pass through one for one into changes in local nominal interest rates. The result implies real interest parity (expected real interest rates should be equalized across countries). Because these results rest on PPP, they should be viewed only as long-run results, and the evidence is somewhat favorable.

6. We can augment the simple monetary model (quantity theory) to allow for the demand for real money balances to decrease as the nominal interest rate rises. This leads to the general monetary model. Its predictions are similar to those of the simple model, except that a one-time rise in money growth rates leads to a one-time rise in inflation, which leads to a one-time drop in real money demand, which in turn causes a one-time jump in the price level and the exchange rate.

7. The monetary approach to exchange rate determination in the long run has implications for economic policy. Policy makers and the public generally prefer a low-inflation environment. Various policies based on exchange rates, money growth, or interest rates have been proposed as nominal anchors. Recent decades have seen a worldwide decline in inflation thanks to the explicit recognition of the need for nominal anchors.

KEY TERMS

PROBLEMS

1. Suppose that two countries, Vietnam and Côte d'Ivoire, produce coffee. The currency unit used in Vietnam is the dong (VND). Côte d'Ivoire is a member of Communaute Financiere Africaine (CFA), a currency union of West African countries that use the CFA franc (XOF). In Vietnam, coffee sells for 5,000 dong (VND) per pound. The exchange rate is 30 VND per 1 CFA franc, $E_{VND/XOF} = 30$.

   a. If the law of one price holds, what is the price of coffee in Côte d'Ivoire, measured in CFA francs?

   b. Assume the price of coffee in Côte d'Ivoire is actually 160 CFA francs per pound of coffee. Compute the relative price of coffee in Côte d'Ivoire versus Vietnam. Where will coffee traders buy coffee? Where will they sell coffee in this case? How will these transactions affect the price of coffee in Vietnam? In Côte d'Ivoire?

2. Consider each of the following goods and services. For each, identify whether the law of one price will hold, and state whether the relative price $q^g_{US/Foreign}$ is greater than, less than, or equal to 1. Explain your answer in terms of the assumptions we make when using the law of one price.

   a. Rice traded freely in the United States and Canada

   b. Sugar traded in the United States and Mexico; the U.S. government imposes a quota on sugar imports into the United States

   c. The McDonald's Big Mac sold in the United States and Japan

   d. Haircuts in the United States and the United Kingdom

3. Use the table that follows to answer this question. Treat the country listed as the home country, and treat the United States as the foreign country. Suppose the cost of the market basket in the United States is $P_{US} = \$190$. Check to see whether purchasing power parity (PPP) holds for each of the countries listed, and determine whether we should expect a real appreciation or real depreciation for each country (relative to the United States) in the long run. For the answer, create a table similar to the one shown and fill in the blank cells. (Hint: Use a spreadsheet application such as Excel.)

Country (currency measured in FX units)	Per $, $E_{FX/\$}$	Price of Market Basket (in FX)	Price of U.S. Basket in FX (P_{us} times $E_{FX/\$}$)	Real Exchange Rate, $q_{COUNTRY/US}$	Does PPP Hold? (yes/no)	Is FX Currency Overvalued or Undervalued?	Is FX Currency Expected to Have Real Appreciation or Depreciation?
Brazil (real)	2.1893	520					
India (rupee)	46.6672	12,000					
Mexico (peso)	11.0131	1,800					
South Africa (rand)	6.9294	800					
Zimbabwe (Z$)	101,347	4,000,000					

4. Table 11-1 in the text shows the percentage undervaluation or overvaluation in the Big Mac, based on exchange rates in July 2009. Suppose purchasing power parity holds and in the long run, so that these deviations would be expected to disappear. Suppose the local currency prices of the Big Mac remained unchanged. Exchange rates in January 4, 2010, were as follows (source: IMF):

Country	Per U.S. $
Australia (A$)	0.90
Brazil (real)	1.74
Canada (C$)	1.04
Denmark (krone)	5.17
Eurozone (euro)	0.69
India (rupee)	46.51
Japan (yen)	93.05
Mexico (peso)	12.92
Sweden (krona)	7.14

Based on these data and Table 11-1, calculate the change in the exchange rate from July to January, and state whether the direction of change was consistent with the PPP-implied exchange rate using the Big Mac Index. How might you explain the failure of the Big Mac Index to correctly predict the change in the nominal exchange rate between July 2009 and January 2010?

5. You are given the following information. The current dollar-pound exchange rate is $2 per pound. A U.S. basket that costs $100 would cost $120 in the United Kingdom. For the next year, the Fed is predicted to keep U.S. inflation at 2% and the Bank of England is predicted to keep U.K. inflation at 3%. The speed of convergence to absolute PPP is 15% per year.

a. What is the expected U.S. minus U.K. inflation differential for the coming year?
b. What is the current U.S. real exchange rate $q_{US/UK}$ with the United Kingdom?
c. How much is the dollar overvalued/undervalued?
d. What do you predict the U.S. real exchange rate with the United Kingdom will be in one year's time?
e. What is the expected rate of real depreciation for the United States (versus the United Kingdom)?
f. What is the expected rate of nominal depreciation for the United States (versus the United Kingdom)?
g. What do you predict will be the dollar price of one pound a year from now?

6. Describe how each of the following factors might explain why PPP is a better guide for exchange rate movements in the long run, versus the short run: (i) transactions costs, (ii) nontraded goods, (iii) imperfect competition, (iv) price stickiness. As markets become increasingly integrated, do you suspect PPP will become a more useful guide in the future? Why or why not?

7. Consider two countries: Japan and Korea. In 1996 Japan experienced relatively slow output growth (1%), while Korea had relatively robust output growth (6%). Suppose the Bank of Japan allowed the money supply to grow by 2% each year, while the Bank of Korea chose to maintain relatively high money growth of 12% per year.

For the following questions, use the simple monetary model (where L is constant). You will find it easiest to treat Korea as the home country and Japan as the foreign country.

a. What is the inflation rate in Korea? In Japan?

b. What is the expected rate of depreciation in the Korean won relative to the Japanese yen (¥)?

c. Suppose the Bank of Korea increases the money growth rate from 12% to 15%. If nothing in Japan changes, what is the new inflation rate in Korea?

d. Using time series diagrams, illustrate how this increase in the money growth rate affects the money supply M_K, Korea's interest rate, prices P_K, real money supply, and $E_{won/¥}$ over time. (Plot each variable on the vertical axis and time on the horizontal axis.)

e. Suppose the Bank of Korea wants to maintain an exchange rate peg with the Japanese yen. What money growth rate would the Bank of Korea have to choose to keep the value of the won fixed relative to the yen?

f. Suppose the Bank of Korea sought to implement policy that would cause the Korean won to appreciate relative to the Japanese yen. What ranges of the money growth rate (assuming positive values) would allow the Bank of Korea to achieve this objective?

8. This question uses the general monetary model, where L is no longer assumed constant, and money demand is inversely related to the nominal interest rate. Consider the same scenario described at the beginning of the previous question. In addition, the bank deposits in Japan pay a 3% interest rate, $i_¥ = 3\%$.

a. Compute the interest rate paid on Korean deposits.

b. Using the definition of the real interest rate (nominal interest rate adjusted for inflation), show that the real interest rate in Korea is equal to the real interest rate in Japan. (Note that the inflation rates you computed in the previous question will be the same in this question.)

c. Suppose the Bank of Korea increases the money growth rate from 12% to 15% and the inflation rate rises proportionately (one for one) with this increase. If the nominal interest rate in Japan remains unchanged, what happens to the interest rate paid on Korean deposits?

d. Using time series diagrams, illustrate how this increase in the money growth rate affects the money supply M_K; Korea's interest rate; prices P_K; real money supply; and $E_{won/¥}$ over time. (Plot each variable on the vertical axis and time on the horizontal axis.)

9. Both advanced economics and developing countries have experienced a decrease in inflation since the 1980s (see Table 11-3 in the text). This question considers how the choice of policy regime has influenced such global disinflation. Use the monetary model to answer this question.

a. The Swiss Central Bank currently targets its money growth rate to achieve policy objectives. Suppose Switzerland has output growth of 3% and money growth of 8% each year. What is Switzerland's inflation rate in this case? Describe how the Swiss Central Bank could achieve an inflation rate of 2% in the long run through the use of a nominal anchor.

b. Like the Federal Reserve, the Reserve Bank of New Zealand uses an interest rate target.

Suppose the Reserve Bank of New Zealand maintains a 6% interest rate target and the world *real* interest rate is 1.5%. What is the New Zealand inflation rate in the long run? In 1997 New Zealand adopted a policy agreement that required the bank to maintain an inflation rate no higher than 2.5%. What interest rate targets would achieve this objective?

c. The central bank of Lithuania maintains an exchange rate band relative to the euro. This is a prerequisite for joining the Eurozone. Lithuania must keep its exchange rate within ±15% of the central parity of 3.4528 litas per euro. Compute the exchange rate values corresponding to the upper and lower edges of this band. Suppose PPP holds. Assuming Eurozone inflation is currently 2% per year and inflation in Lithuania is 5%, compute the rate of depreciation of the lita. Will Lithuania be able to maintain the band requirement? For how long? Does your answer depend on where in the band the exchange rate currently sits? A primary objective of the European Central Bank is price stability (low inflation) in the current and future Eurozone. Is an exchange rate band a necessary or sufficient condition for the attainment of this objective?

10. Several countries that have experienced hyperinflation adopt dollarization as a way to control domestic inflation. For example, Ecuador has used the U.S. dollar as its domestic currency since 2000. What does dollarization imply about the exchange rate between Ecuador and the United States? Why might countries experiencing hyperinflation adopt dollarization? Why might they do this rather than just fixing their exchange rate?

11. You are the central banker for a country that is considering the adoption of a new nominal anchor. When you take the position as chairperson, the inflation rate is 4% and your position as the central bank chairperson requires that you achieve a 2.5% inflation target within the next year. The economy's growth in real output is currently 3%. The world real interest rate is currently 1.5%. The currency used in your country is the lira. *Assume prices are flexible.*

a. Why is having a nominal anchor important for you to achieve the inflation target? What is the drawback of using a nominal anchor?

b. What is the growth rate of the money supply in this economy? If you choose to adopt a money supply target, which money supply growth rate will allow you to meet your inflation target?

c. Suppose the inflation rate in the United States is currently 2% and you adopt an exchange rate target relative to the U.S. dollar. Compute the percent appreciation/depreciation in the lira needed for you to achieve your inflation target. Will the lira appreciate or depreciate relative to the U.S. dollar?

d. Your final option is to achieve your inflation target using interest rate policy. Using the Fisher equation, compute the current nominal interest rate in your country. What nominal interest rate will allow you to achieve the inflation target?

N E T W O R K

The Big Mac Index isn't the only popular PPP gauge. In 2004 the *Economist* made a Starbuck's Tall Latte Index, which you can try to find online. (*Hint:* Google "cnn tall latte index.") In 2007 two new indices appeared: the iPod Index (based on the local prices of Apple's iPod music player) and iTunes Index (based on the local prices of a single song downloaded from Apple's iTunes store). Find those indices online and the discussions surrounding them. (*Hint:* Google "ipod itunes index big mac.") Do you think that either the iPod Index or iTunes Index is a better guide to currency overvaluation/undervaluation than the Big Mac Index? Explain your answer.

Visit the websites of some central banks around the world, for example, the U.S. Federal Reserve (http://www.federalreserve.gov/) and the European Central Bank (http://www.ecb.int/). Read their main statements of policy. Try to find out what their policy goals are *in the long run*. Who sets them? Is there more than one goal? What about a nominal anchor—is controlling inflation a long-run goal? If so, what policy is used to try to ensure that the long-run inflation goal will be met? In the short run, is the main tool they use for implementing their policy the quantity of money, the exchange rate, or the interest rate?

Exchange Rates II: The Asset Approach in the Short Run

The long run is a misleading guide to current affairs. In the long run we are all dead. Economists set themselves too easy, too useless a task if in tempestuous seasons they can only tell us that when the storm is past the ocean is flat again.

John Maynard Keynes, *A Tract on Monetary Reform*, 1923

A s we saw in the last chapter, the monetary approach to exchange rates may work in the long run, but it is a poor guide to what happens in the short run. To recap this distinction, let's return to the Canada–U.S. comparison with which we opened the last chapter—only this time we'll focus on developments in the short run.

From March 2005 to March 2006, the Canadian price level (measured by the consumer price index) rose from 126.5 to 129.3, an increase of 2.2%. The U.S. price level rose from 193.3 to 199.8, an increase of 3.4%. U.S. prices therefore increased 1.2% more than Canadian prices. But over the same period, the loonie (Canadian dollar) rose in value from $0.8267 to $0.8568, an appreciation of 3.6%.[1]

Because Canadian baskets cost 2.2% more in loonie terms, *and* each loonie cost 3.6% more in U.S. dollar terms, the change in the U.S. dollar price of the Canadian basket was approximately the sum of these two changes, or about 5.8%. But over the same period, the U.S. dollar price of U.S. baskets rose only 3.4%. Taking the difference, Canadian baskets ended up 2.4% more expensive than U.S. baskets, meaning that the U.S. *real* exchange rate with Canada rose by 2.4%, a real depreciation. This pattern was not unusual. In the previous year from March 2004 to March 2005, the real depreciation had been even larger, at 7.5%, so over two years Canadian goods rose in price by about 10% compared with U.S. goods.

---

[1] Data for this example are taken from the Bank of Canada and U.S. Bureau of Labor Statistics.

As we have already noted, evidence of this kind suggests that substantial deviations from purchasing power parity (PPP) occur in the short run: the same basket of goods generally does not cost the same everywhere at all times. These short-run failures of the monetary approach prompted economists to develop an alternative theory to explain exchange rates in the short run: the **asset approach to exchange rates,** the subject of this chapter.

The asset approach is based on the idea that currencies are assets. The price of the asset in this case is the spot exchange rate, the price of one unit of foreign exchange. Here we can draw on what we learned about how arbitrage plays a major role in the forex market by forcing the expected returns of two assets in different currencies to be equal. This insight led us to derive the uncovered interest parity (UIP) condition. Because it characterizes a forex market equilibrium, UIP is further explored and extensively applied in this chapter.

The asset approach differs from the monetary approach in its time frame and assumptions. In the monetary approach, we envisage a long run that takes several years; in the asset approach, we are typically thinking of a short run of a matter of a few months, or perhaps a year or so at most. In the monetary approach, we treat goods prices as perfectly flexible, a plausible assumption in the long run; in the asset approach, we assume that goods prices are sticky, a more appropriate assumption in the short run. Each theory is valid but only in the right context. Thus, rather than supplanting the monetary approach, the asset approach complements it, and provides us with the final building blocks necessary to construct a complete theory of exchange rates.

So far, we have assumed that exchange rates are determined by market forces in the goods, money, and foreign exchange markets—so our theory is relevant when the exchange rate floats, and the authorities leave it to find its own market-determined level. Can our theory also tell us anything about fixed exchange rates? Yes. At the end of the chapter, we see how the same theoretical framework can be applied to a fixed exchange rate regime.

1 Exchange Rates and Interest Rates in the Short Run: UIP and FX Market Equilibrium

To begin our study of exchange rates in the short run, let's recap the crucial equilibrium condition for the forex (or FX) market. In our earlier presentation, we considered a U.S. investor with two alternative investment strategies: a one-year investment in a U.S. dollar account with an interest rate $i_{\$}$, or a one-year investment in a euro account with an interest rate i_{ϵ}. Here are the essentials.

Risky Arbitrage

For the case of risky arbitrage, the foreign exchange market is in equilibrium when there is no expected difference in the rates of return on each type of currency investment. As before, we assume the Home country is the United States (US); the Foreign country is Europe (EUR, meaning the Eurozone). As we saw in the approximate uncovered interest parity condition—Equation (10-3), and repeated in this section as Equation (12-1)—this outcome requires that the dollar rate of return on the Home investment (the dollar deposit) equal the expected dollar rate of return on the Foreign investment (the euro deposit),

$$\underbrace{i_{\$}}_{\substack{\text{Interest rate} \\ \text{on dollar deposits} \\ = \\ \text{Dollar rate of return} \\ \text{on dollar deposits}}} = \underbrace{\underbrace{i_{\euro}}_{\substack{\text{Interest rate} \\ \text{on euro deposits}}} + \underbrace{\frac{(E^e_{\$/\euro} - E_{\$/\euro})}{E_{\$/\euro}}}_{\substack{\text{Expected rate of depreciation} \\ \text{of the dollar}}}}_{\substack{\text{Expected dollar rate of return} \\ \text{on euro deposits}}} \quad (12\text{-}1)$$

where each interest rate is an annual rate, $E_{\$/\euro}$ is today's exchange rate (the spot rate), and $E^e_{\$/\euro}$ is the expected future exchange rate that will prevail one year ahead.

The uncovered interest parity (UIP) equation is the **fundamental equation of the asset approach to exchange rates,** and from now on, we use it in the form of Equation (12-1). As we have seen, by rearranging this equation, we can solve it for the spot exchange rate, provided we know all of the other variables. Thus, the asset approach employs the UIP equation to determine today's spot exchange rate, as illustrated in Figure 12-1. Hence, the theory is useful only if we can assume knowledge of interest rates and the future expected exchange rate. Where does that knowledge come from?

Exchange Rate Expectations First, we need a forecast of the future level of the exchange rate $E^e_{\$/\euro}$. The asset approach itself does not provide the answer, so we must look elsewhere. Where to look? In the long-run monetary approach to the exchange rate presented in the previous chapter. We can now see how the asset approach and monetary approach fit together.

Short-Term Interest Rates The second assumption is that we know today's interest rates on deposit accounts in each country, the dollar interest rate $i_{\$}$, and the euro account interest rate $i_{\euro}$. Market participants can observe these short-term interest rates. But how are these interest rates determined, and, in particular, what is their relation to economic policy? In the next section, we explore that question to develop a fuller understanding of how exchange rates are determined.

FIGURE 12-1

Building Block: Uncovered Interest Parity—The Fundamental Equation of the Asset Approach In this model, the nominal interest rate and expected future exchange rate are treated as known exogenous variables (in green). The model uses these variables to predict the unknown endogenous variable (in red), the current spot exchange rate.

Equilibrium in the FX Market: An Example

To explore the concepts we've just studied, let's work through a numerical example to show how equilibrium in the foreign exchange market is determined.

Suppose we have made a forecast (using the long-run monetary model of exchange rates) that the expected future exchange rate $E^e_{\$/€}$ (in one year's time) is 1.224 dollars per euro. Suppose also that the current European interest rate $i_€$ is 3%, and the current U.S. interest rate $i_\$$ is 5%.

Now examine Table 12-1 to see how, for various values of the spot exchange rate $E_{\$/€}$, we can calculate the domestic rate of return and expected foreign rate of return in U.S. dollars. (Remember that 5% = 0.05, 3% = 0.03, etc.) As you work through the table, remember that the foreign returns have two components: one due to the European interest rate $i_€$ and the other due to the expected rate of depreciation of the dollar, as in Equation (12-1).

Figure 12-2 presents an **FX market diagram,** a graphical representation of these returns in the forex market. We plot the expected domestic and foreign returns (on the vertical axis) against today's spot exchange rate (on the horizontal axis). The domestic dollar return (*DR*) (which is just the Home nominal interest rate) is fixed at 5% = 0.05 and is independent of the spot exchange rate.

The foreign expected dollar return (*FR*) depends on the spot exchange rate according to Equation (12-1) and it varies as we just saw in Table 12-1. For example, we can infer from the table that a spot exchange rate of 1.224 implies a foreign return of

TABLE 12-1

Interest Rates, Exchange Rates, Expected Returns, and FX Market Equilibrium: A Numerical Example The foreign exchange (FX) market is in equilibrium when the domestic and foreign returns are equal. In this example, the dollar interest rate is 5%, the euro interest rate is 3%, and the expected future exchange rate (one year ahead) is = 1.224 $/€. The equilibrium is highlighted in bold type, where both returns are 5% in annual dollar terms. Figure 12-2 plots the domestic and foreign returns (columns 1 and 6) against the spot exchange rate (column 3). Figures are rounded in this table.

(1)	(2)	(3)	(4)	(5)	(6) = (2) + (5)
Interest Rate on Dollar Deposits (annual)	Interest Rate on Euro Deposits (annual)	Spot Exchange Rate (today)	Expected Future Exchange Rate (in 1 year)	Expected Euro Appreciation against Dollar (in 1 year)	Expected Dollar Return on Euro Deposits (annual)
Domestic Return ($)					Foreign Expected Return ($)
$i_\$$	$i_€$	$E_{\$/€}$	$E^e_{\$/€}$	$\dfrac{E^e_{\$/€} - E_{\$/€}}{E_{\$/€}}$	$i_€ + \dfrac{E^e_{\$/€} - E_{\$/€}}{E_{\$/€}}$
0.05	0.03	1.16	1.224	0.0552	0.0852
0.05	0.03	1.18	1.224	0.0373	0.0673
0.05	**0.03**	**1.20**	**1.224**	**0.02**	**0.05**
0.05	0.03	1.22	1.224	0.0033	0.0333
0.05	0.03	1.24	1.224	−0.0129	0.0171

Market equilibrium

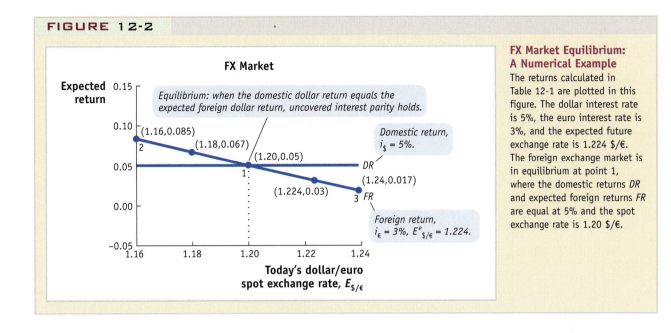

FIGURE 12-2

FX Market

Equilibrium: when the domestic dollar return equals the expected foreign dollar return, uncovered interest parity holds.

Expected return

(1.16,0.085)
(1.18,0.067)
(1.20,0.05)
(1.224,0.03)
(1.24,0.017)

Domestic return, $i_\$ = 5\%$.

Foreign return, $i_\unicode{8364} = 3\%$, $E^e_{\$/\unicode{8364}} = 1.224$.

DR
FR

Today's dollar/euro spot exchange rate, $E_{\$/\unicode{8364}}$

FX Market Equilibrium: A Numerical Example
The returns calculated in Table 12-1 are plotted in this figure. The dollar interest rate is 5%, the euro interest rate is 3%, and the expected future exchange rate is 1.224 $/€. The foreign exchange market is in equilibrium at point 1, where the domestic returns DR and expected foreign returns FR are equal at 5% and the spot exchange rate is 1.20 $/€.

3% = 0.03. Hence, the point (1.224, 0.03) is on the *FR* line, as shown. This is the special case in which there is no expected depreciation (spot and expected future exchange rates are equal to 1.224), so the foreign return equals the Foreign interest rate, 3%.

More generally, we see that the foreign return falls as the spot exchange rate $E_{\$/\unicode{8364}}$ increases, all else equal. Why? This is clear mathematically from the right side of Equation (12-1). The intuition is as follows. If the dollar depreciates today, $E_{\$/\unicode{8364}}$ rises; a euro investment is then a more expensive (and, thus, less attractive) proposition, all else equal. That is, $1 moved into a European account is worth fewer euros today; this, in turn, leaves fewer euro proceeds in a year's time after euro interest has accrued; and if expectations are fixed so that the future euro-dollar exchange rate $E^e_{\$/\unicode{8364}}$ is known and unchanged, then those fewer future euros will be worth fewer future dollars. Hence, the foreign return (in dollars) goes down as $E_{\$/\unicode{8364}}$ rises, *all else equal*. The *FR* curve is therefore downward sloping.

What is the equilibrium level of the spot exchange rate? According Table 12-1, the equilibrium exchange rate is 1.20 $/€. Only at that exchange rate are domestic returns and foreign returns equalized. To illustrate the solution graphically, domestic and foreign returns are plotted in Figure 12-2. The FX market is in equilibrium, and foreign and domestic returns are equal, at the point at which the *FR* and *DR* curves intersect. This is labeled as point 1.

Adjustment to FX Market Equilibrium

Our FX market equilibrium condition and its graphical representation should now be clear. But how is this equilibrium reached? It turns out that arbitrage automatically pushes the level of the exchange rate toward its equilibrium value.

To see this, suppose that the market is initially out of equilibrium, with the spot $E_{\$/\unicode{8364}}$ exchange rate at a level too low, so that the foreign return—the right-hand side of Equation (12-1)—exceeds the domestic return (the left-hand side).

At point 2 in Figure 12-2, foreign returns are well above domestic returns. With the spot exchange rate of 1.16 $/€ and (from Table 12-1) an expected future exchange rate as high as 1.224 $/€, the euro is expected to *appreciate* by 5.5% = 0.055 [= (1.224/1.16) − 1]. In addition, euros earn at an interest rate of 3%, for a whopping foreign expected return of 5.5% + 3% = 8.5% = 0.085, which far exceeds the domestic return of 5%. At point 2, in other words, the euro offers too high a return; equivalently, it is too cheap. Traders want to sell dollars and buy euros. These market pressures bid up the price of a euro: the dollar starts to depreciate against the euro, causing $E_{\$/€}$ to rise, which moves foreign and domestic returns into equality and forces the exchange rate back toward equilibrium at point 1.

The same idea applies to a situation in which the spot exchange rate $E_{\$/€}$ is initially too high. At point 3 in Figure 12-2, foreign and domestic returns are not equal: the exchange rate is 1.24 $/€. Given where the exchange rate is expected to be in a year's time (1.224 $/€), paying a high price of 1.24 $/€ today means the euro is expected to *depreciate* by about 1.3% = 0.013 [= 1.224/1.24 − 1]. If euro deposits pay 3%, and euros are expected to depreciate 1.3%, this makes for a net foreign return of just 1.7%, well below the domestic return of 5% = 0.05. In other words, at point 3, the euro offers too low a return; equivalently, it is too expensive today. Traders will want to sell euros.

Only at point 1 is the euro trading at a price at which the foreign return equals the domestic return. At point 1, the euro is neither too cheap nor too expensive—its price is just right for uncovered interest parity to hold, for arbitrage to cease, and for the FX market to be in equilibrium.

Changes in Domestic and Foreign Returns and FX Market Equilibrium

When economic conditions change, the two curves depicting domestic and foreign returns shift. In the case of the domestic return curve, the movements are easy to understand because the curve is a horizontal line that intersects the vertical axis at the domestic interest rate. If the domestic interest changes, the curve shifts up or down. Shifts in the foreign returns curve are a bit more complicated because there are two parts to the foreign return: the foreign interest rate plus any expected change in the exchange rate.

To gain greater familiarity with the model, let's see how the FX market example shown in Figure 12-2 responds to three separate shocks:

■ A higher domestic interest rate, $i_\$ = 7\%$

■ A lower foreign interest rate, $i_€ = 1\%$

■ A lower expected future exchange rate, $E_{\$/€}^e = 1.20$ $/€

These three cases are shown in Figure 12-3, panels (a), (b), and (c). In all three cases, the shocks make dollar deposits more attractive than euro deposits, but for different reasons. Regardless of the reason, however, the shocks we examine all lead to dollar appreciations.

A Change in the Domestic Interest Rate In Figure 12-3, panel (a), when $i_\$$ rises to 7%, the domestic return is increased by 2% so the domestic return curve *DR* shifts up by 2% = 0.02 from DR_1 to DR_2. The foreign return is unaffected. Now, at the initial equilibrium spot exchange rate of 1.20 $/€, the domestic return (point 4) is higher than the foreign return. Traders sell euros and buy dollars; the dollar appreciates to 1.177 $/€ at the new equilibrium, point 5. The foreign return and domestic return are equal once again and UIP holds once more.

FIGURE 12-3

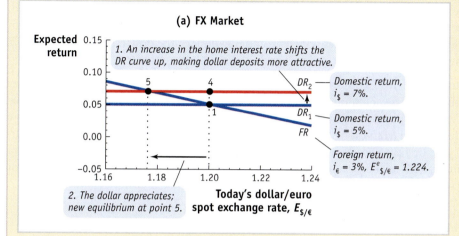

(a) FX Market

1. An increase in the home interest rate shifts the DR curve up, making dollar deposits more attractive.

Domestic return, $i_\$ = 7\%$.

Domestic return, $i_\$ = 5\%$.

Foreign return, $i_€ = 3\%$, $E^e_{\$/€} = 1.224$.

2. The dollar appreciates; new equilibrium at point 5.

Today's dollar/euro spot exchange rate, $E_{\$/€}$

(a) A Change in the Home Interest Rate A rise in the dollar interest rate from 5% to 7% increases domestic returns, shifting the DR curve up from DR_1 to DR_2. At the initial equilibrium exchange rate of 1.20 $/€ on DR_2, domestic returns are above foreign returns at point 4. Dollar deposits are more attractive and the dollar appreciates from 1.20 $/€ to 1.177 $/€. The new equilibrium is at point 5.

(b) FX Market

1. A decrease in the foreign interest rate shifts the FR curve down, making dollar deposits more attractive.

Domestic return, $i_\$ = 5\%$.

Foreign return, $i_€ = 3\%$, $E^e_{\$/€} = 1.224$.

Foreign return, $i_€ = 1\%$, $E^e_{\$/€} = 1.224$.

2. The dollar appreciates; new equilibrium at point 7.

Today's dollar/euro spot exchange rate, $E_{\$/€}$

(b) A Change in the Foreign Interest Rate A fall in the euro interest rate from 3% to 1% lowers foreign expected dollar returns, shifting the FR curve down from FR_1 to FR_2. At the initial equilibrium exchange rate of 1.20 $/€ on FR_2, foreign returns are below domestic returns at point 6. Dollar deposits are more attractive and the dollar appreciates from 1.20 $/€ to 1.177 $/€. The new equilibrium is at point 7.

(c) FX Market

1. A decrease in the expected future exchange rate shifts the FR curve down, making dollar deposits more attractive.

Domestic return, $i_\$ = 5\%$.

Foreign return, $i_€ = 3\%$, $E^e_{\$/€} = 1.224$.

Foreign return, $i_€ = 3\%$, $E^e_{\$/€} = 1.20$.

2. The dollar appreciates; new equilibrium at point 7.

Today's dollar/euro spot exchange rate, $E_{\$/€}$

(c) A Change in the Expected Future Exchange Rate A fall in the expected future exchange rate from 1.224 to 1.20 lowers foreign expected dollar returns, shifting the FR curve down from FR_1 to FR_2. At the initial equilibrium exchange rate of 1.20 $/€ on FR_2, foreign returns are below domestic returns at point 6. Dollar deposits are more attractive and the dollar appreciates from 1.20 $/€ to 1.177 $/€. The new equilibrium is at point 7.

A Change in the Foreign Interest Rate In Figure 12-3, panel (b), when $i_{\unicode{x20AC}}$ falls to 1%, euro deposits now pay a lower interest rate (1% versus 3%). The foreign return curve FR shifts down by $2\% = 0.02$ from FR_1 to FR_2. The domestic return is unaffected. Now, at the old equilibrium rate of 1.20 $/€, the foreign return (point 6) is lower than the domestic return. Traders sell euros and buy dollars; the dollar appreciates to 1.177 $/€ at the new equilibrium, point 7, and UIP holds once more.

A Change in the Expected Future Exchange Rate In Figure 12-3, panel (c), a decrease in the expected future exchange rate $E^e_{\$/\unicode{x20AC}}$ lowers the foreign return because a future euro is expected to be worth fewer dollars in the future. The foreign return curve FR shifts down from FR_1 to FR_2. The domestic return is unaffected. At the old equilibrium rate of 1.20 $/€, the foreign return (point 6) is lower than the domestic return. Again, traders sell euros and buy dollars, causing the dollar to appreciate and the spot exchange rate to fall to 1.177 $/€. The new equilibrium is point 7.

Summary

The FX market diagram, with its representation of domestic returns and foreign returns, is central to our analysis in this chapter and later in the book. Be sure that you understand that domestic returns depend only on the Home interest rate $i_\$$, but that foreign returns depend on both the Foreign interest rate $i_{\unicode{x20AC}}$ *and* the expected future exchange rate $E^e_{\$/\unicode{x20AC}}$. Remember that any change which raises (lowers) the foreign return relative to the domestic return makes euro deposits more (less) attractive to investors, so that traders will buy (sell) euro deposits. The traders' actions push the FX market toward a new equilibrium at which the dollar will have depreciated (appreciated) against the euro.

To check your understanding, you might wish to rework the three examples and the figures for the opposite cases of a *decrease* in $i_\$$, an *increase* in $i_{\unicode{x20AC}}$, and an *increase* in $E^e_{\$/\unicode{x20AC}}$; constructing the equivalent of Table 12-1 for each case may also prove helpful.

2 Interest Rates in the Short Run: Money Market Equilibrium

The previous section laid out the essentials of the asset approach to exchange rates. Figure 12-1 sums up the uncovered interest parity relationship at the heart of the asset approach. The spot exchange rate is the output (endogenous variable) of this model, and the expected future exchange rate and the home and foreign interest rates are the inputs (exogenous variables). But where do these inputs come from? In the last chapter, we developed a theory of the long-run exchange rate, the monetary approach, which can be used to forecast the future exchange rate. That leaves us with just one unanswered question: How are current interest rates determined?

Money Market Equilibrium in the Short Run: How Nominal Interest Rates Are Determined

Having seen how the supply and demand for money work in the previous chapter, we can build on that foundation here. We consider two money markets in two locations: the United States and Europe. Both markets are in equilibrium with money demand equal to money supply. In both locations, the money supply is controlled by a central bank and is taken as given; the demand for real money balances $M/P = L(i)Y$ is a function of the interest rate i and real income Y.

The Assumptions It is important to understand the key difference between the way we approach money market equilibrium in the short run (in this chapter) and the way we approached it in the long run (in the last chapter).

In the last chapter, we made the following *long-run* assumptions:

■ In the long run, the price level P is fully flexible and adjusts to bring the money market to equilibrium.

■ In the long run, the nominal interest rate i equals the world real interest rate plus domestic inflation.

In this chapter, we make *short-run* assumptions that are quite different:

■ In the short run, the price level is sticky; it is a known predetermined variable, fixed at $P = \overline{P}$ (the bar indicates a fixed value).

■ In the short run, the nominal interest rate i is fully flexible and adjusts to bring the money market to equilibrium.

Why do we make different assumptions in the short run?

First, why assume prices are now sticky? The assumption of sticky prices, also called **nominal rigidity,** is common to the study of macroeconomics in the short run. Economists have many explanations for price stickiness. Nominal wages may be sticky because of long-term labor contracts. Nominal product prices may be sticky because of *menu costs;* that is, firms may find it costly to frequently change their output prices. Thus, while it is reasonable to assume that all prices are flexible in the long run, they may not be in the short run.

Second, why assume that interest rates are now flexible? In the previous chapter, we showed that nominal interest rates are pinned down by the Fisher effect (or real interest parity) in the long run: in that case, the home nominal interest rate was equal to the world real interest rate plus the home rate of inflation. However, recall that this result does not apply in the short run because it is derived from purchasing power parity—which, as we know, only applies in the long run. Indeed, we saw evidence that in the short run real interest rates fluctuate in ways that deviate from real interest parity.

The Model With these explanations of our short-run assumptions in hand, we can now use the same general monetary model of the previous chapter and write down expressions for money market equilibrium in the two countries as follows:

$$\underbrace{\frac{M_{US}}{P_{US}}}_{\substack{\text{U.S. supply of} \\ \text{real money balances}}} = \underbrace{L(i_{\$}) \times Y_{US}}_{\substack{\text{U.S. demand for} \\ \text{real money balances}}} \tag{12-2}$$

$$\underbrace{\frac{M_{EUR}}{P_{EUR}}}_{\substack{\text{European supply of} \\ \text{real money balances}}} = \underbrace{L(i_{\unicode{x20AC}}) \times Y_{EUR}}_{\substack{\text{U.S. demand for} \\ \text{real money balances}}} \tag{12-3}$$

To recap: In the long run, prices adjust to clear the money market and bring money demand and money supply into line. In the short run, when prices are sticky, such adjustment is not possible. However, nominal interest rates *are* free to adjust. In the short run, the nominal interest rate in each country adjusts to bring money supply and money demand into equilibrium.

Money Market Equilibrium in the Short Run: Graphical Solution

Figure 12-4 represents the U.S. money market (a similar diagram applies to the European market). On the horizontal axis is the quantity of U.S. real money balances M_{US}/P_{US} and on the vertical axis is the U.S. nominal interest rate $i_\$$. The vertical line represents the supply of real money balances; this supply is fixed by the central bank at the level $M_{US}^1/\overline{P}_{US}^1$ and is independent of the level of the interest rate. The downward-sloping line represents the demand for real money balances, $L(i_\$) \times Y_{US}$. Demand decreases as the U.S. nominal interest rate increases because the opportunity cost of holding money rises and people don't want to hold high money balances. The money market is in equilibrium at point 1: the demand and supply of real money balances are equal at $M_{US}^1/\overline{P}_{US}^1$ and at a nominal interest rate $i_\$^1$.

Adjustment to Money Market Equilibrium in the Short Run

If interest rates are flexible in the short run, as we assume they are, there is nothing to prevent them from adjusting to clear the money market. But how do market forces ensure that a nominal interest rate $i_\$^1$ is attained? The adjustment process works as follows.

Suppose instead that the interest rate was $i_\$^2$, so that we were at point 2 on the real money demand curve. At this interest rate, real money demand is less than real money supply. In the aggregate, the central bank has put more money in the hands of the public than the public wishes to hold. The public will desire to reduce its cash holdings by ex-

FIGURE 12-4

Home Money Market

Equilibrium in the Home Money Market The supply and demand for real money balances determine the nominal interest rate. The money supply curve (*MS*) is vertical at $M_{US}^1/\overline{P}_{US}^1$ because the quantity of money supplied does not depend on the interest rate. The money demand curve (*MD*) is downward-sloping because an increase in the interest rate raises the cost of holding money, thus lowering the quantity demanded. The money market is in equilibrium when the nominal interest rate $i_\$^1$ is such that real money demand equals real money supply (point 1). At points 2 and 3, demand does not equal supply and the interest rate will adjust until the money market returns to equilibrium.

changing money for interest-bearing assets such as bonds, saving accounts, and so on. That is, they will save more and seek to lend their money to borrowers. But borrowers will not want to borrow more unless the cost of borrowing falls. So the interest rate will be driven down as eager lenders compete to attract scarce borrowers. As this happens, back in the money market, in Figure 12-4, we move from point 2 back toward equilibrium at point 1.

A similar story can be told if the money market is initially at point 3, where there is an excess demand for money. In this case, the public wishes to reduce their savings in the form of interest-bearing assets and turn them into cash. Now fewer loans are extended. The loan market will suffer an excess demand. But borrowers will not want to borrow less unless the cost of borrowing rises. So the interest rate will be driven up as eager borrowers compete to attract scarce lenders. These adjustments end only when point 1 is reached and there is no excess supply of real money balances.

Another Building Block: Short-Run Money Market Equilibrium

This model of the money market may be familiar from previous courses in macroeconomics. The lessons that are important for our theory of exchange rates are summed up in Figure 12-5. We treat the price level in each country as fixed and known in the short run. We also assume that the money supply and real income in each country are known. The equilibrium equations for the money market, Equations (12-2) and (12-3), then tell us the interest rates in each country. Once these are known, we can put them to use in another building block seen earlier: the interest rates can be plugged into the fundamental equation of the asset approach to exchange rate determination, Equation (12-1), along with the future expected exchange rate derived from a forecast based on the long-run monetary model of the previous chapter. In that way, the spot exchange rate can finally be determined.

Changes in Money Supply and the Nominal Interest Rate

Money market equilibrium depends on money supply and money demand. If either changes, the equilibrium will change. To help us better understand how exchange rates are determined, we need to understand how these changes occur.

FIGURE 12-5

Building Block: The Money Market Equilibrium in the Short Run In these models, the money supply and real income are known exogenous variables (in green boxes). The models use these variables to predict the unknown endogenous variables (in red boxes), the nominal interest rates in each country.

FIGURE 12-6

(a) Increase in Money Supply, MS

Nominal interest rate, $i_\$$

1. An increase in the money supply...

MS_1 → MS_2

$i_\$^1$ — 1

$i_\$^2$ — 2

2. ...lowers the nominal interest rate.

$MD_1: M_{US}/\overline{P}_{US} = L(i_\$)Y_{US}^1$

$\dfrac{M_{US}^1}{\overline{P}_{US}^1}$ $\dfrac{M_{US}^2}{\overline{P}_{US}^1}$

Real money balances, M_{US}/P_{US}

(b) Increase in Money Demand, MD

Nominal interest rate, $i_\$$

MS

1. An increase in real income causes an increase in real money demand...

$i_\$^2$ — 2

$i_\$^1$ — 1

$MD_2: M_{US}/\overline{P}_{US} = L(i_\$)Y_{US}^2$

2. ... and raises the nominal interest rate.

$MD_1: M_{US}/\overline{P}_{US} = L(i_\$)Y_{US}^1$

$\dfrac{M_{US}^1}{\overline{P}_{US}^1}$

Real money balances, M_{US}/P_{US}

Home Money Market with Changes in Money Supply and Money Demand In panel (a), with a fixed price level $\overline{P}_{US}^1$, an increase in nominal money supply from M_{US}^1 to M_{US}^2 causes an increase in real money supply from $M_{US}^1/\overline{P}_{US}^1$ to $M_{US}^2/\overline{P}_{US}^1$. The nominal interest rate falls from $i_\$^1$ to $i_\$^2$ to restore equilibrium at point 2. In panel (b), with a fixed price level $\overline{P}_{US}^1$, an increase in real income from Y_{US}^1 to Y_{US}^2 causes real money demand to increase from MD_1 to MD_2. To restore equilibrium at point 2, the interest rate rises from $i_\$^1$ to $i_\$^2$.

Figure 12-6, panel (a), shows how the money market responds to a monetary policy change consisting of an increase in the Home (U.S.) nominal money supply from M_{US}^1 to M_{US}^2. Because, by assumption, the U.S. price level is fixed in the short run at $\overline{P}_{US}^1$, the increase in nominal money supply causes an increase in real money supply from $M_{US}^1/\overline{P}_{US}^1$ to $M_{US}^2/\overline{P}_{US}^1$. In the figure, the money supply curve shifts to the right from MS_1 to MS_2. Point 1 is no longer an equilibrium; at the interest rate $i_\$^1$, there is now an excess supply of real money balances. As people move their dollars into interest-bearing assets to be loaned out, the interest rate falls from $i_\$^1$ to $i_\$^2$, at which point the money market is again in equilibrium at point 2. By the same logic, a reduction in the nominal money supply will raise the interest rate.

To sum up, *in the short run, all else equal, an increase in a country's money supply will lower the country's nominal interest rate; a decrease in a country's money supply will raise the country's nominal interest rate.*

Fortunately, our graphical analysis shows that, for a *given* money demand curve, setting a money supply level uniquely determines the interest rate and vice versa. Hence, for many purposes, *the money supply or the interest rate may be used as a policy instrument.* In practice, most central banks tend to use the interest rate as their policy instrument because the money demand curve may not be stable, and the fluctuations caused by this instability would lead to unstable interest rates if the money supply were set at a given level as the policy instrument.

Can Central Banks Always Control the Interest Rate? A Lesson from the Crisis of 2008–2009

In our analyses so far, we have assumed that central banks can control the money market interest rate, and that they can effectively do so whether they set the interest rate or the money supply. These assumptions are critical in this chapter and in the rest of this book. But are they really true? In general, perhaps, but policy operations by central banks can be undermined by financial market disruptions. Recent events in many countries illustrate the problem.

In the United States, for example, the Federal Reserve sets as its *policy rate* the interest rate that it charges banks for overnight loans. In normal times, changes in this cost of short-term funds for the banks are usually passed through into the *market rates* the banks charge to borrowers on loans such as mortgages, corporate loans, auto loans, etc., as well as on interbank loans between the banks themselves. This process is one of the most basic elements in the so-called *transmission mechanism* through which the effects of monetary policy are eventually felt in the real economy.

In the recent crisis, however, banks regarded other banks and borrowers (and even themselves) as facing potentially catastrophic risks. As a result, they lent much less freely and when they did loan, they charged much higher interest rates to compensate themselves for the risk of the loan suffering a loss or default. Thus, although the Fed brought its policy rate all the way down from 5.25% to 0% in 2007 and 2008, there was no similar decrease in market rates. In fact, market interest rates barely moved at all.

A second problem arose once policy rates hit the *zero lower bound* (ZLB). At that point, the central banks' capacity to lower interest rate further was exhausted. However, many central banks wanted to keep applying downward pressure to market rates to calm financial markets. The Fed's response was a policy of *quantitative easing*.

Usually, the Fed expands base money M0 by either lending to banks which put up safe government bonds as collateral, or by buying government bonds outright in open-market operations—although these actions are taken only in support of the Fed's interest rate target. But in the crisis, and with interest rates stuck at a floor, the Fed engaged in a number of extraordinary policy actions to push more money out more quickly:

1. It expanded the range of credit securities it would accept as collateral to include lower-grade, private-sector bonds.

2. It expanded the range of securities that it would buy outright to include private-sector credit instruments such as commercial paper and mortgage-backed securities.

3. It expanded the range of counterparties from which it would buy securities to include some nonbank institutions such as primary dealers and money market funds.

As a result of massive asset purchases along these lines, M0 in the United States more than doubled to over a trillion dollars. However, there was very little change in M1 or M2, indicating that banks had little desire to translate the cash they were receiving from the Fed into the new loans and new deposits that would expand the broad money supply.

Similar crisis actions were taken by the Bank of England and, eventually, by the European Central Bank; both expanded their collateral rules, although their outright purchase programs were more narrowly focused on aggressive use of open-market

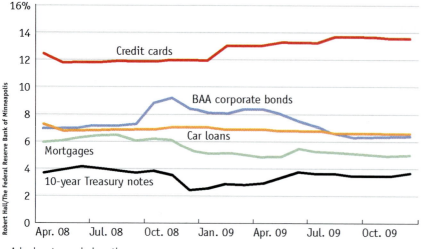

A broken transmission: the Fed's extraordinary interventions did little to change private credit market interest rates in 2008–2009.

operations to purchase large quantities of U.K. and Eurozone government bonds (though in the ECB's case this did include low-grade bonds from crisis countries such as Greece and Portgual).

To sum up, with the traditional transmission mechanism broken, central banks had to find different tools. In the Fed's case, by directly intervening in markets for different types of private credit at different maturities, policy makers hoped to circumvent the impaired transmission mechanism. Would matters have been much worse if the central banks had done nothing at all? It's hard to say (and we may not be able to attempt an answer until all the data are in once the crisis and recession are over). However, if the aim was to lower market interest rates in a meaningful way and expand broader monetary aggregates, it is as yet unclear whether these policies have had significant economic effects. ■

Changes in Real Income and the Nominal Interest Rate

Figure 12-6, panel (b), shows how the money market responds to an increase in Home (U.S.) real income from Y_{US}^1 to Y_{US}^2. The increase in real income causes real money demand to increase as reflected in the shift from MD_1 to MD_2. At the initial interest rate $i_\$^1$, there is now an excess demand for real money balances. To restore equilibrium at point 2, the interest rate rises from $i_\$^1$ to $i_\$^2$ to encourage people to hold lower dollar balances. Similarly, a reduction in real income will lower the interest rate.

To sum up, *in the short run, all else equal, an increase in a country's real income will raise the country's nominal interest rate; a decrease in a country's real income will lower the country's nominal interest rate.*

The Monetary Model: The Short Run versus the Long Run

The short-run implications of the model we have just discussed differ from the long-run implications of the monetary approach we presented in the previous chapter. It is important that we look at these differences, and understand how and why they arise.

Consider the following example: the Home central bank that previously kept the money supply constant suddenly switches to an expansionary policy. In the following year, it allows the money supply to grow at a rate of 5%.

- ■ If such expansions are expected to be a permanent policy in the long run, the predictions of the long-run monetary approach and Fisher effect are clear. All else equal, a five-percentage-point increase in the rate of Home money growth causes a five-percentage-point increase in the rate of Home inflation and a five-percentage-point increase in the Home nominal interest rate. The Home interest rate *rises* in the long run when prices are flexible.

■ If this expansion is expected to be temporary, then the short-run model we have just studied in this chapter tells a very different story. All else equal, if the Home money supply expands, the immediate effect is an excess supply of real money balances. The home interest rate will then *fall* in the short run when prices are sticky.

These different outcomes illustrate the importance of the assumptions we make about price flexibility. They also underscore the importance of the nominal anchor in monetary policy formulation and the constraints that central banks have to confront.

The different outcomes also explain some apparently puzzling linkages among money, interest rates, and exchange rates. In both of the previous cases, an expanded money supply leads to a weaker currency. However, in the short run, low interest rates and a weak currency go together, whereas in the long run, high interest rates and a weak currency go together.

What is the intuition for these findings? In the short run, when we study the impact of a lower interest rate and we say "all else equal," we have assumed that expectations have not changed concerning future exchange rates (or money supply or inflation). In other words, we envisage (implicitly) a temporary policy that does not tamper with the nominal anchor. In the long run, if the policy turns out to be permanent, this assumption is inappropriate; prices are flexible and money growth, inflation, and expected depreciation now all move in concert—in other words, the "all else" is no longer equal.

A good grasp of these key differences between the short- and long-run approaches is essential to understanding the determinants of exchange rates. To cement our understanding, in the rest of the chapter we will explore the different implications of temporary and permanent policy changes. To facilitate our applied work, we now lay out the short-run model in a succinct, graphical form.

3 The Asset Approach: Applications and Evidence

To simplify the graphical presentation of the asset approach, we focus on conditions in the Home economy; a similar approach can be used for the Foreign economy. For illustration we again assume that Home is the United States and Foreign is Europe.

The Asset Approach to Exchange Rates: Graphical Solution

Figure 12-7 shows two markets: panel (a) shows the Home money market (for the United States), and panel (b) shows the FX market diagram (for the dollar-euro market). This figure summarizes the asset approach in the short run.

The U.S. Money Market Panel (a) depicts equilibrium in the U.S. money market. The horizontal axis shows the quantity of U.S. real money balances demanded or supplied, M_{US}/P_{US}. The vertical axis shows the U.S. nominal interest rate $i_\$$. Two relationships are shown:

1. The vertical line MS represents the U.S. real money supply. The line is vertical because (i) the nominal U.S. money supply M_{US} is treated as exogenous (known), because it is set by the Home central bank, and (ii) the U.S. price level $\overline{P}_{US}$ is treated as exogenous (known) in the short run due to price stickiness.

FIGURE 12-7

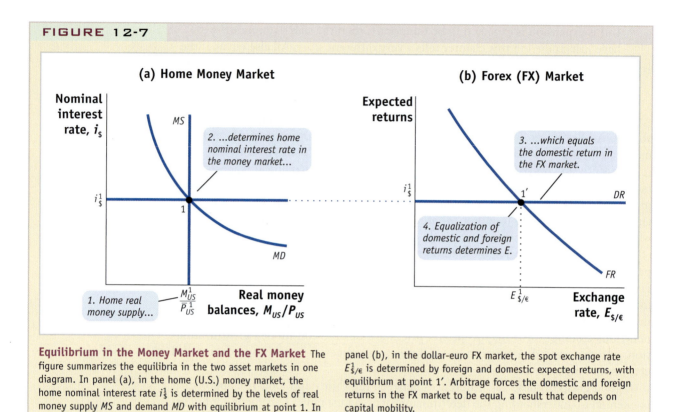

Equilibrium in the Money Market and the FX Market The figure summarizes the equilibria in the two asset markets in one diagram. In panel (a), in the home (U.S.) money market, the home nominal interest rate $i_\$^1$ is determined by the levels of real money supply MS and demand MD with equilibrium at point 1. In panel (b), in the dollar-euro FX market, the spot exchange rate $E_{\$/€}^1$ is determined by foreign and domestic expected returns, with equilibrium at point 1′. Arbitrage forces the domestic and foreign returns in the FX market to be equal, a result that depends on capital mobility.

2. The curve MD on the diagram represents the U.S. demand for real money balances, $L(i_\$)Y_{US}$. It slopes down because, when the Home nominal interest rate $i_\$$ rises, the opportunity cost of holding money increases, and demand falls. For now, we also assume that the U.S. real income level Y_{US} is exogenous (given) and fixed in the short run.

In equilibrium, money demand equals money supply, the quantity of real money demanded and supplied is $M_{US}^1/\overline{P}_{US}^1$, and the nominal interest rate is $i_\$^1$ (point 1).

The Market for Foreign Exchange Panel (b) depicts equilibrium in the FX market. The horizontal axis shows the spot exchange rate, $E_{\$/€}$. The vertical axis shows U.S. dollar returns on Home and Foreign deposits. Two relationships are shown:

1. The downward-sloping foreign return curve FR shows the relationship between the exchange rate and the expected dollar rate of return on Foreign deposits $[i_€ + (E_{\$/€}^e - E_{\$/€})/E_{\$/€}]$. The European interest rate $i_€$ is treated as exogenous (given); it is determined in the European money market, which is not shown in this figure. The expected future exchange rate $E_{\$/€}^e$ is treated as exogenous (given); it is determined by a forecast obtained from the long-run model we developed in the previous chapter.

2. The horizontal domestic return line DR shows the dollar rate of return on U.S. deposits, which is the U.S. nominal interest rate $i_\$$. It is horizontal at $i_\$^1$ because this is the U.S. interest rate determined in the Home money market in panel (a), and it is the same regardless of the spot exchange rate.

In equilibrium, foreign and domestic returns are equal (uncovered interest parity holds) and the FX market is in equilibrium at point 1'.

Capital Mobility Is Crucial We assume that the FX market is subject to the arbitrage forces we have studied and that uncovered interest parity will hold. But this is true only if there are no capital controls: as long as capital can move freely between Home and Foreign capital markets, domestic and foreign returns will be equalized. Our assumption that DR equals FR depends on capital mobility. If capital controls are imposed, there is no arbitrage and no reason why DR has to equal FR.

Putting the Model to Work With this graphical apparatus in place, it is relatively straightforward to solve for the exchange rate given knowledge of all the known (exogenous) variables we have specified previously.

To solve for the exchange rate, we start in the Home money market in panel (a) on the horizontal axis, at the level of real money supply $M_{US}^1/\overline{P}_{US}^1$; we trace upward along MS to MD at point 1, to find the current Home interest rate $i_\$^1$. We then trace right and move across from the Home money market to the FX market in panel (b), since the Home interest rate is the same as domestic return DR in the FX market. We eventually meet the FR curve at point 1'. We then trace down and read off the equilibrium exchange rate $E_{\$/€}^1$.

Our graphical treatment shows that solving the model is as simple as tracing a path around the diagrams. While we gain in simplicity, we also lose some generality because one market, the foreign money market, has been left out of the analysis. However, the same analysis also applies to the foreign country. As a quick check that you understand the logic of the asset approach to exchange rates, you might try to construct the equivalent of Figure 12-7 under the assumption that Europe is the Home economy and the United States is the Foreign economy. (Hint: In the FX market, you will need to treat the Home [European] expected future exchange rate $E_{€/\$}^e$ and the Foreign [U.S.] interest rate $i_\$$ as given. Take care with the currency units of every variable when making the switch.)

Short-Run Policy Analysis

The graphical exposition in Figure 12-7 shows how the asset approach works to determine the exchange rate. This approach can be used to analyze the impacts of economic policy or other shocks to the economy.

The most straightforward shocks we can analyze are temporary shocks because they affect only the current state of the money and foreign exchange markets and do not affect expectations about the future. In this section, we use the model to see what happens when there is a temporary, short-run increase in the money supply by the central bank.

A Temporary Shock to the Home Money Supply We take the model of Figure 12-7 and assume that, apart from the Home money supply, all exogenous variables remain unchanged and fixed at the same level. Thus, Foreign money supply, Home and Foreign real income and price levels, and the expected future exchange rate are all fixed.

The initial state of all markets is shown in Figure 12-8. The Home money market is in equilibrium at point 1 where Home money supply MS and money demand MD are equal at the Home nominal interest rate $i_\$^1$. The foreign exchange market is in

FIGURE 12-8

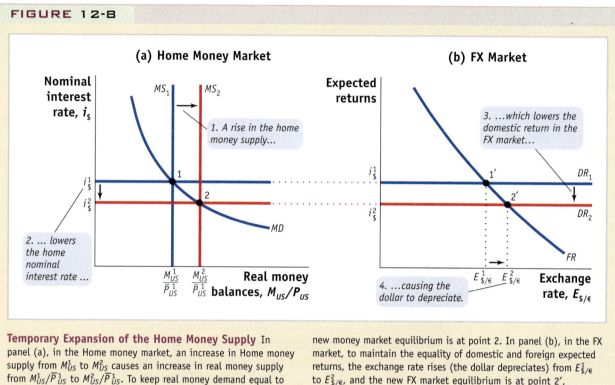

(a) Home Money Market

Nominal interest rate, $i_\$$

MS_1 MS_2

1. A rise in the home money supply...

$i_\$^1$ — 1

$i_\$^2$ — 2

2. ... lowers the home nominal interest rate ...

MD

$\dfrac{M_{US}^1}{\overline{P}_{US}^1}$ $\dfrac{M_{US}^2}{\overline{P}_{US}^1}$ **Real money balances, M_{US}/P_{US}**

(b) FX Market

Expected returns

3. ...which lowers the domestic return in the FX market...

$i_\$^1$ — 1′ DR_1

$i_\$^2$ — 2′ DR_2

FR

$E_{\$/€}^1$ $E_{\$/€}^2$ **Exchange rate, $E_{\$/€}$**

4. ...causing the dollar to depreciate.

Temporary Expansion of the Home Money Supply In panel (a), in the Home money market, an increase in Home money supply from M_{US}^1 to M_{US}^2 causes an increase in real money supply from $M_{US}^1/\overline{P}_{US}^1$ to $M_{US}^2/\overline{P}_{US}^1$. To keep real money demand equal to real money supply, the interest rate falls from to $i_\$^1$ to $i_\$^2$, and the new money market equilibrium is at point 2. In panel (b), in the FX market, to maintain the equality of domestic and foreign expected returns, the exchange rate rises (the dollar depreciates) from $E_{\$/€}^1$ to $E_{\$/€}^2$, and the new FX market equilibrium is at point 2′.

equilibrium at point 1′, where domestic return DR equals foreign return FR, where $i_\$^1 = i_€^1 + (E_{\$/€}^e - E_{\$/€}^1)/E_{\$/€}^1$, and the spot exchange rate is $E_{\$/€}^1$.

Suppose the U.S. money supply is increased temporarily from M_{US}^1 to M_{US}^2. Under the assumption of sticky prices, $\overline{P}_{US}^1$ does not change, so the U.S. real money supply will increase to $M_{US}^2/\overline{P}_{US}^1$, and the real money supply curve shifts from MS_1 to MS_2 in panel (a). U.S. real money demand is unchanged, so the money market equilibrium shifts from point 1 to point 2 and the nominal interest rate falls from $i_\$^1$ to $i_\$^2$. The expansion of the U.S. money supply causes the U.S. nominal interest rate to fall.

A *temporary* monetary policy shock leaves the long-run expected exchange rate $E_{\$/€}^e$ unchanged. Assuming all else equal, European monetary policy is also unchanged, and the euro interest rate remains fixed at $i_€$. If $E_{\$/€}^e$ and $i_€$ are unchanged, then the foreign return FR curve in panel (b) is unchanged and the new FX market equilibrium is at point 2′. The lower domestic return $i_\$^2$ is matched by a lower foreign return. The foreign return is lower because the U.S. dollar has depreciated from $E_{\$/€}^1$ to $E_{\$/€}^2$.

The result is intuitive, and we have seen each of the steps previously. We now just put them all together: a Home monetary expansion lowers the Home nominal interest rate, which is also the domestic return in the FX market. This makes Foreign deposits more attractive and makes traders wish to sell Home deposits and buy Foreign deposits. This, in turn, makes the Home exchange rate increase (depreciate). However, this depreciation makes Foreign deposits less attractive (all else equal). Eventually, the equality of foreign and domestic returns is restored, uncovered interest parity holds again, and the foreign exchange market reaches a new short-run equilibrium.

A Temporary Shock to the Foreign Money Supply We now repeat the previous analysis for a shock to the *Foreign* money supply. All other exogenous variables remain unchanged and fixed at their initial levels. Thus, Home money supply, Home and Foreign real income and price levels, and the expected future exchange rate are all fixed. The initial state of all markets is shown in Figure 12-9: the Home money market is in equilibrium at point 1 and the FX market is in equilibrium at point 2.

Let's see what happens when the Foreign money supply increases temporarily. Because changes in the Foreign money supply have no effect on the Home money market in panel (a), equilibrium remains at point 1 and the Home nominal interest rate stays at $i_\$^1$.

The shock is temporary, so long-run expectations are unchanged, and the expected exchange rate $E_{\$/\euro}^e$ stays fixed in panel (b). However, because the Foreign money supply has expanded temporarily, the euro interest rate falls from $i_\euro^1$ to $i_\euro^2$. Foreign returns are diminished, all else equal, by a fall in euro interest rates, so the foreign return curve FR shifts downward from FR_1 to FR_2. On the horizontal axis in panel (b), we can see that at the new FX market equilibrium (point 2′) the Home exchange rate has decreased (the U.S. dollar has appreciated) from $E_{\$/\euro}^1$ to $E_{\$/\euro}^2$.

FIGURE 12-9

(a) Home Money Market

(b) FX Market

1. Equilibrium in the home money market is unchanged...

2. ...but expansion of the Eurozone money supply lowers the euro interest rate, which lowers the foreign return in the FX market...

3. ...causing the dollar to appreciate.

Temporary Expansion of the Foreign Money Supply In panel (a), there is no change in the Home money market. In panel (b), an increase in the Foreign money supply causes the Foreign (euro) interest rate to fall from $i_\euro^1$ to $i_\euro^2$. For a U.S. investor, this lowers the foreign return $i_\euro + (E_{\$/\euro}^e - E_{\$/\euro})/E_{\$/\euro}$, all else equal. To maintain the equality of domestic and foreign returns in the FX market, the exchange rate falls (the dollar appreciates) from $E_{\$/\euro}^1$ to $E_{\$/\euro}^2$, and the new FX market equilibrium is at point 2′.

This result is also intuitive. A Foreign monetary expansion lowers the Foreign nominal interest rate, which lowers the foreign return in the FX market. This makes Foreign deposits less attractive and makes traders wish to buy Home deposits and sell Foreign deposits. This, in turn, makes the Home exchange rate decrease (appreciate). However, this appreciation makes Foreign deposits more attractive (all else equal). Eventually, the equality of foreign and domestic returns is restored, uncovered interest parity holds again, and the foreign exchange market reaches a new short-run equilibrium.

To ensure you have grasped the model fully, you might try two exercises. First, derive the predictions of the model for temporary *contractions* in the Home or Foreign money supplies. Second, go back to the version of Figure 12-7 that you constructed from the European perspective and generate predictions using that version of the model, first for a temporary expansion of the money supply in Europe and then for a temporary expansion in the United States. Do you get the same answers?

APPLICATION

The Rise and Fall of the Dollar, 1999–2004

In the 1990s, many developed countries adopted monetary policies that established clear, long-run nominal anchors. The European Central Bank (ECB), for example, adopted an explicit inflation target. The Federal Reserve in the United States operated with a more implicit target, but nonetheless could claim to have a credible anchor, too.

The Fisher effect tells us that nominal anchoring of this kind ought to keep nominal interest rate differentials between the United States and the Eurozone roughly constant in the long run. But in the short run, this constraint does not apply, so central banks have some freedom to temporarily change their monetary policies. In the years 2000 to 2004, such flexibility was put to use and interest rates in the United States and Europe followed very different tracks.

In later chapters, we study in more detail why central banks alter monetary policy in the short run, but for now we focus on how such changes affect exchange rates. As Figure 12-10 shows, the Fed raised interest rates from 1999 to 2001 faster than the ECB (the Fed was more worried about the U.S. economy "overheating" with higher inflation). In this period of global economic boom, the ECB's policy also tightened over time, as measured by changes in the Euro interest rate—the refinancing rate set by the ECB. But the changes were more restrained and slower in coming.

As Figure 12-10 also shows, the Fed then lowered interest rates aggressively from 2001 to 2004, with rates falling as low as 1% in 2003 to 2004 (the U.S. economy had slowed after the boom and the Fed hoped that lower interest rates would avert a recession; the terrorist attacks of September 11, 2001, led to fears of a more serious economic setback and encouraged further monetary easing). The ECB also acted similarly to lower interest rates, but again the ECB did not move rates as far or as fast as the Fed.

As a result, the ECB's interest rate, previously lower than the Fed's rate, was soon higher than the U.S. rate in 2001 and remained higher through 2004. Investors most likely viewed these policy changes as a temporary shift in monetary policy in both countries. Hence, they might be considered as an example of temporary monetary policy shocks. Do our model's predictions accord well with reality?

Up until 2001, the policy of higher rates in the United States could be seen as a temporary Home monetary contraction (relative to Foreign), and our model would predict a dollar appreciation in the short run. After 2001 the aggressive reductions in

FIGURE 12-10

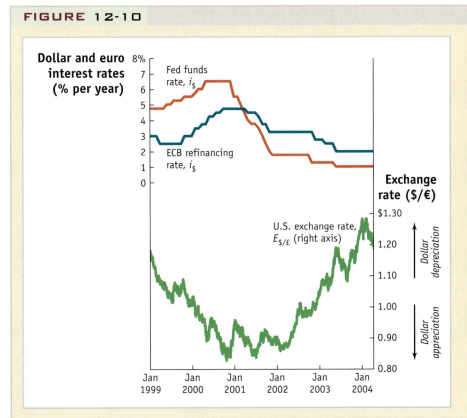

Dollar and euro interest rates (% per year)

Fed funds rate, $i_\$$

ECB refinancing rate, $i_\$$

Exchange rate ($/€)

U.S. exchange rate, $E_{\$/£}$ (right axis)

Dollar depreciation

Dollar appreciation

$1.30
1.20
1.10
1.00
0.90
0.80

Jan 1999   Jan 2000   Jan 2001   Jan 2002   Jan 2003   Jan 2004

U.S.–Eurozone Interest Rates and Exchange Rates, 1999–2004 From the euro's birth in 1999 until 2001, the dollar steadily appreciated against the euro, as interest rates in the United States were raised well above those in Europe. In early 2001, however, the Federal Reserve began a long series of interest rate reductions. By 2002 the Fed Funds rate was well below the ECB's refinancing rate. Theory predicts a dollar appreciation (1999–2001) when U.S. interest rates were relatively high, followed by a dollar depreciation (2001–2004) when U.S. interest rates were relatively low. Looking at the figure, you will see that this is what occurred.

Sources: Websites of central banks; OANDA. Exchange rate is monthly average.

U.S. interest rates could be seen as a temporary Home monetary expansion (relative to Foreign), and our model predicts a dollar depreciation in the short run. Looking at the path of the dollar-euro exchange rate in the figure, we can see that the model accords well with reality. ■

4 A Complete Theory: Unifying the Monetary and Asset Approaches

In this section, we extend our analysis from the short run to the long run, and examine permanent as well as temporary shocks. To do this, we put together a complete theory of exchange rates that couples the long-run and short-run approaches, as shown schematically in Figure 12-11:

- We need the asset approach (this chapter)—short-run money market equilibrium and uncovered interest parity:

$$\left.\begin{aligned} \overline{P}_{US} &= M_{US}/[L_{US}(i_\$)Y_{US}] \\ \overline{P}_{EUR} &= M_{EUR}/[L_{EUR}(i_€)Y_{EUR}] \\ i_\$ &= i_€ + \frac{E^e_{\$/€} - E_{\$/€}}{E_{\$/€}} \end{aligned}\right\} \quad \text{The asset approach.} \qquad (12\text{-}4)$$

There are three equations and three unknowns (two short-run nominal interest rates and the spot exchange rate). The future expected exchange rate must be known, as must the current levels of money and real income. (The price level is also treated as given.)

■ But to forecast the future expected exchange rate, we also need the long-run monetary approach from the previous chapter—a long-run monetary model and purchasing power parity:

$$\left.\begin{array}{l} P_{US}^e = M_{US}^e/[L_{US}(i_\$^e)Y_{US}^e] \\[4pt] P_{EUR}^e = M_{EUR}^e/[L_{EUR}(i_\euro^e)Y_{EUR}^e] \\[4pt] E_{\$/\euro}^e = P_{US}^e/P_{EUR}^e \end{array}\right\} \quad \text{The monetary approach.} \qquad (12\text{-}5)$$

There are three equations and three unknowns (two price levels and the exchange rate). Note that all variables here have a superscript e to denote future expected values or forecasts. We assume that forecasts of future money, real income, and nominal interest rates are known. This model can then be applied to obtain price forecasts and, hence, a forecast of the future expected exchange rate.[2]

Figure 12-11 sums up all the theory we have learned so far in the past two chapters. It shows how all the pieces fit together. In total we have six equations and six unknowns.

It is only now, with all the building blocks in place, that we can fully appreciate how the two key mechanisms of *expectations* and *arbitrage* operate in a variety of ways to determine exchange rates in both the short run and the long run. Ensure you are comfortable with all of the building blocks—how they work individually and how they connect.

After no little effort, we have arrived at a complete theory to explain exchange rates in the short run and the long run. The model incorporates all of the key economic fundamentals that affect exchange rates and, in practice, although forex markets exhibit a great deal of turbulence and uncertainty, there is evidence that these fundamentals play a major role in shaping traders' decisions (see **Side Bar: Confessions of a Forex Trader**).

Long-Run Policy Analysis

When and how can we apply the complete model? The downside of working with the complete model is that we have to keep track of multiple mechanisms and variables; the upside is that the theory is fully developed and can be applied to short-run and long-run policy shocks.

The temporary shocks we saw in the last section represent only one kind of monetary policy change, one that does not affect the long-run nominal anchor. The fact that these shocks were temporary allowed us to conduct all of the analysis under

---

[2] Recall that the previous chapter also showed us how real interest parity can be used to solve for the long-run nominal interest rate i in each country, the so-called *neutral level* of the nominal interest rate. For example, restricting our attention to the case of a stable long-run inflation rate (e.g., under nominal anchoring in which an announced inflation target is expected to be hit in each country), we have

$$\left.\begin{array}{l} i_\$ = \pi_{US,target} + r^* \\[2pt] i_\euro = \pi_{EUR,target} + r^* \end{array}\right\} \quad \text{Real interest parity.}$$

FIGURE 12-11

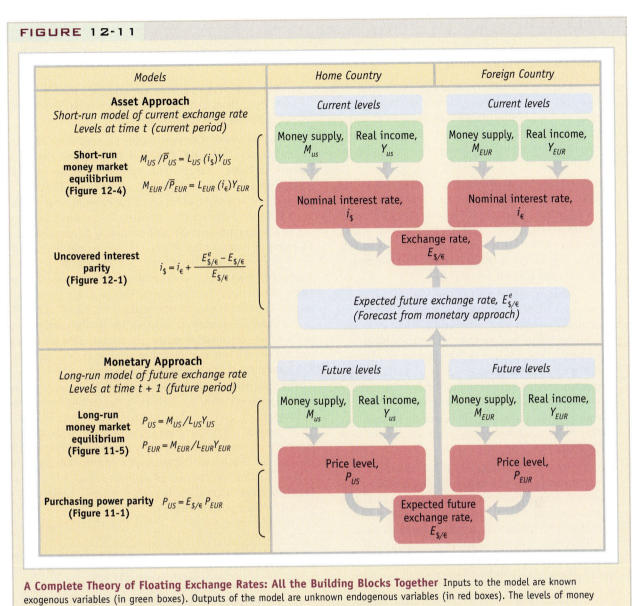

A Complete Theory of Floating Exchange Rates: All the Building Blocks Together Inputs to the model are known exogenous variables (in green boxes). Outputs of the model are unknown endogenous variables (in red boxes). The levels of money supply and real income determine exchange rates.

the assumption that the long-run expected level of the exchange rate remained unchanged.

When the monetary authorities decide to make a *permanent* change, however, this assumption of unchanged expectations is no longer appropriate. Under such a change, the authorities would cause an enduring change in all nominal variables; that is, they would be electing to change their nominal anchor policy in some way. Thus, when a monetary policy shock is permanent, the long-run expectation of the level of the exchange rate has to adjust. This change will, in turn, cause the exchange rate predictions of the short-run model to differ from those made when the policy shock was only temporary.

SIDE BAR

Confessions of a Forex Trader

Trying to forecast exchange rates is a major enterprise in financial markets and serves as the basis of any trading strategy. A tour of the industry would find many firms offering forecasting services at short, medium, and long horizons. Forecasts are generally based on three methodologies (or some mix of all three):

1. *Economic fundamentals*. Forecasts are based on ideas developed in the past two chapters. Exchange rates are determined by factors such as money, output, interest rates, and so on; hence, forecasters try to develop long- and short-range predictions of these "fundamental" variables. Example: "The exchange rate will depreciate because a looser monetary policy is expected."

2. *Politics*. Forecasts recognize that some factors that are not purely economic can affect exchange rates. One is the outbreak of war (see the application at the end of this chapter). Political crises might matter, too, if they affect perceptions of risk. Changes in risk interfere with simple interest parity and can move exchange rates. Making such forecasts is more qualitative and subjective, but is still concerned with fundamental determinants in our theory. Example: "The exchange rate will depreciate because a conflict with a neighboring state raises the probability of war and inflation."

3. *Technical methods*. Forecasts rely on extrapolations from past behavior. Trends may be assumed to continue ("momentum"), or recent maximum and minimum values may be assumed to be binding. These trading strategies assume that financial markets exhibit some persistence and, if followed, may make such an assumption self-fulfilling for a time. Nonetheless, large crashes that return asset prices back to fundamental levels can burst

such bubbles. Example: "The exchange rate has hit this level three times this year but never gone further; it will not go further this time."

A recent survey of U.K. forex traders provided some interesting insights into this world.[*] One-third described their trading as "technically based," and one-third said their trades were "fundamentals-based"; others were jobbing or trading for clients.

The survey revealed that insights from economic theory mattered little from one hour to the next. In the very short run, within the day, traders confessed that many factors unrelated to economic fundamentals affected exchange rates in the market: 29% cited "bandwagon effects," and 33% mentioned "overreaction to news." Concerning within-day changes in exchange rates, when asked, "Do you believe exchange rate movements accurately reflect changes in the fundamental value," fully 97% of the traders responded no and only 3% yes. However, in the medium run, described as within six months, 58% responded yes. And in the long run, described as more than six months, 87% thought that changes reflected fundamentals.

Which economic fundamentals mattered? News about money supplies, interest rates, and GDP levels was quickly incorporated into trading, usually in less than a minute or even in a matter of seconds. All of these are key variables in our complete model. As we would expect, PPP was deemed irrelevant within the day, but 16% thought it mattered in the medium run, and 44% in the long run. The lack of unanimity about PPP may reflect legitimate concerns about its shortcomings (which we examined in the previous chapter).

---

[*] Yin-Wong Cheung, Menzie D. Chinn, and Ian W. Marsh, 2004, "How Do UK-Based Foreign Exchange Dealers Think Their Market Operates?" *International Journal of Finance and Economics*, 9(4), 289–306.

These insights guide our analysis of permanent policy shocks. They also tell us that we cannot approach such analysis chronologically. Before we can figure out what happens in the short run, we have to know expectations; that is, what is going to happen in the long run. Thus, we have to use a technique that is common in forward-looking economic problems: we must *solve backward* from the future to the present. (This ordering mirrors the presentation of the material in this textbook—we must understand the long run before we can understand the short run.)

A Permanent Shock to the Home Money Supply We start our analysis of the Home (United States) and Foreign (Europe) economies with each economy currently at a long-run equilibrium in which all variables are steady. In this equilibrium, we assume that each country has a fixed real income, a fixed money supply, and a zero rate of inflation. Hence, there is a zero rate of depreciation because the equilibrium is characterized by purchasing power parity, and interest rates in each country are the same because the equilibrium is characterized by uncovered interest parity.

Our analysis is shown Figure 12-12. Panels (a) and (b) show the short-run impacts of a permanent increase in the money supply in the Home (U.S.) money and FX markets; panels (c) and (d) show the long-run impacts and the adjustment from the short run to the long run. We examine each of these three aspects in turn.

As shown in panels (a), (b), (c), and (d), we suppose the Home economy starts with initial equilibria in the home money and FX markets shown by points 1 and 1′, respectively. In the money market, in panels (a) and (c), at point 1, the home money market is initially in equilibrium: MS_1 corresponds to an initial real money supply of $M_{US}^1/\overline{P}_{US}^1$; given real money demand MD, the nominal interest rate is $i_\$^1$. In the FX market, in panels (b) and (d), at point 1′, the domestic return DR_1 is the nominal interest rate $i_\$^1$. Given the foreign return curve FR_1, the equilibrium exchange rate is $E_{\$/€}^1$. If both economies are at a long-run equilibrium with zero depreciation, then this is also the expected future exchange rate $E_{\$/€}^{e1} = E_{\$/€}^1$.

We now start to figure out what happens after the policy shock hits today, working backward from the future to the present.

The Long Run Refer to panels (c) and (d) of Figure 12-12. In the long run, we know from the monetary approach that an increase in the money supply will eventually lead to a proportionate increase in the price level and the exchange rate. If the money supply increases from M_{US}^1 to M_{US}^2 today, then the price level will *eventually* increase by the same proportion from P_{US}^1 to P_{US}^2, and, to maintain PPP, the exchange rate will *eventually* rise by the same proportion (and the dollar will depreciate) from $E_{\$/€}^1$ to its long-run level $E_{\$/€}^4$, in panel (d), where $E_{\$/€}^4/E_{\$/€}^1 = P_{US}^2/P_{US}^1 = M_{US}^2/M_{US}^1 > 1$. (We use "4" to denote long-run exchange rate values because there will be some short-run responses to consider in just a moment.)

Thus, in the long run, in panel (c), if money and prices both rise in the same proportion, then the real money supply will be unchanged at its original level $M_{US}^1/P_{US}^1 = M_{US}^2/P_{US}^2$, the real money supply curve will still be in its original position MS_1, and the nominal interest rate will again be $i_\$^1$. In the long run, the money market returns to where it started: long-run equilibrium is at point 4 (which is the same as point 1).

In the FX market, however, a permanent money supply shock causes some permanent changes in the long run. One thing that does not change is the domestic return, DR_1, since in the long run it returns to $i_\$^1$. But the exchange rate will rise from the initial long-run exchange rate, $E_{\$/€}^1$, to a new long-run level $E_{\$/€}^4$. Because $E_{\$/€}^4$ is a long-run stable level, it is also the new expected level of the exchange rate $E_{\$/€}^4$ that will prevail in the future. That is, the future will look like the present, under our assumptions, except that the exchange rate will be sitting at $E_{\$/€}^4$ instead of $E_{\$/€}^1$. What does this change do to the foreign return curve FR? As we know, when the expected exchange rate increases, foreign returns are higher, so the FR curve shifts up, from FR_1 to FR_2. Because in the long run $E_{\$/€}^4$ is the new stable equilibrium exchange rate, and $i_\$^1$ is the interest rate, the new FX market equilibrium is at point 4′ where FR_2 intersects DR_1.

FIGURE 12-12

(a) Short Run: Money Market

Nominal interest rate, $i_\$$

1. A permanent rise in the U.S. money supply

$MS_1 \quad \longrightarrow \quad MS_2$

$i_\$^1$

$i_\$^2$

MD

2. ...lowers the U.S. nominal interest rate in the short run.

$\dfrac{M_{US}^1}{\overline{P}_{US}^1} \quad \dfrac{M_{US}^2}{\overline{P}_{US}^1}$ **Real money balances,** M_{US}/P_{US}

(b) Short Run: FX Market

Expected returns

3. Domestic return falls (lower interest rate).

4. At the same time foreign return rises (higher expected future exchange rate).

$i_\$^1$

$i_\$^2$

DR_1

DR_2

FR_2

FR_1

$E_{\$/€}^1 \quad E_{\$/€}^3 \quad E_{\$/€}^2$ **Exchange rate,** $E_{\$/€}$

5. This causes a large short-run dollar depreciation.

Permanent Expansion of the Home Money Supply Short-Run Impact: In panel (a), the home price level is fixed, but the supply of dollar balances increases and real money supply shifts out. To restore equilibrium at point 2, the interest rate falls from $i_\$^1$ to $i_\$^2$. In panel (b), in the FX market, the home interest rate falls, so the domestic return decreases and DR shifts down. In addition, the permanent change in the home money supply implies a permanent, long-run depreciation of the dollar. Hence, there is also a permanent rise in $E_{\$/€}^e$, which causes a permanent increase in the foreign return $i_€ + (E_{\$/€}^e - E_{\$/€})/E_{\$/€}$, all else equal; FR shifts up from FR_1 to FR_2. The simultaneous fall in DR and rise in FR cause the home currency to depreciate steeply, leading to a new equilibrium at point 2′ (and not at 3′, which would be the equilibrium if the policy were temporary).

(c) Long Run: Money Market

Nominal interest rate, $i_\$$

6. Prices rise in the long run, real money supply returns to its old level...

$MS_1 \quad \longleftarrow \quad MS_2$

$i_\$^1$

$1 = 4$

$i_\$^2$

MD

7. ...and the nominal interest rate returns to its old level.

$\dfrac{M_{US}^1}{\overline{P}_{US}^1} \quad \dfrac{M_{US}^2}{\overline{P}_{US}^1}$ **Real money balances,** M_{US}/P_{US}

$= \dfrac{M_{US}^2}{\overline{P}_{US}^2}$

(d) Long Run: FX Market

Expected returns

8. Foreign return remains higher (expected future exchange rate is permanently higher).

9. But the domestic return rises to its original level.

$i_\$^1$

$i_\$^2$

DR_1

DR_2

FR_2

FR_1

$E_{\$/€}^1 \quad E_{\$/€}^4 \quad E_{\$/€}^2$ **Exchange rate,** $E_{\$/€}$

10. The dollar now appreciates to its new long-run level.

Long-Run Adjustment: In panel (c), in the long run, prices are flexible, so the home price level and the exchange rate both rise in proportion with the money supply. Prices rise to P_{US}^2, and real money supply returns to its original level M_{US}^1/P_{US}^1. The money market gradually shifts back to equilibrium at point 4 (the same as point 1). In panel (d), in the FX market, the domestic return DR, which equals the home interest rate, gradually shifts back to its original level. The foreign return curve FR does not move at all: there are no further changes in the Foreign interest rate or in the future expected exchange rate. The FX market equilibrium shifts gradually to point 4′. The exchange rate falls (and the dollar appreciates) from $E_{\$/€}^2$ to $E_{\$/€}^4$. Arrows in both graphs show the path of gradual adjustment.

The Short Run Only now that we have changes in expectations worked out can we work back through panels (a) and (b) of Figure 12-12 to see what will happen in the short run.

Look first at the FX market in panel (b). Because expectations about the future exchange rate have changed with today's policy announcement, the FX market is affected immediately. Everyone knows that the exchange rate will be $E^4_{\$/€}$ in the future. The foreign return curve shifts when the expected exchange rate changes; it rises from FR_1 to FR_2. This is the same shift we just saw in the long-run panel (d). The dollar is expected to depreciate to $E^4_{\$/€}$ (relative to $E^1_{\$/€}$) in the future, so euro deposits are more attractive today.

Now consider the impact of the change in monetary policy in the short run. Look at the money market in panel (a). In the short run, if the money supply increases from M^1_{US} to M^2_{US} but prices are sticky at P^1_{US}, then real money balances rise from M^1_{US}/P^1_{US} to M^2_{US}/P^1_{US}. The real money supply shifts from MS_1 to MS_2 and the home interest rate falls from $i^1_\$$ to $i^2_\$$, leading to a new short-run money market equilibrium at point 2.

Now look back to the FX market in panel (b). If this were a *temporary* monetary policy shock, expectations would be unchanged, and the FR_1 curve would still describe foreign returns, but domestic returns would fall from DR_1 to DR_2 as the interest rate fell and the home currency would depreciate to the level $E^3_{\$/€}$. The FX market equilibrium, after a temporary money supply shock, would be at point 3′, as we have seen before.

But this is not the case now. This time we are looking at a permanent shock to money supply. It has *two* effects on today's FX market. One impact of the money supply shock is to lower the home interest rate, decreasing domestic returns in today's FX market from DR_1 to DR_2. The other impact of the money supply shock is to increase the future expected exchange rate, increasing foreign returns in today's FX market from FR_1 to FR_2. Hence, the FX market equilibrium in the short run is where DR_2 and FR_2 intersect, now at point 2′, and the exchange rate depreciates all the way to $E^2_{\$/€}$.

Note that the short-run equilibrium level of the exchange rate ($E^2_{\$/€}$) is higher than the level that would be observed under a temporary shock ($E^3_{\$/€}$) and also higher than the level that will be observed in the long run ($E^4_{\$/€}$). To sum up, *in the short run, the permanent shock causes the exchange rate to depreciate more than it would under a temporary shock and more than it will end up depreciating in the long run.*

Adjustment from Short Run to Long Run The arrows in panels (c) and (d) of Figure 12-12 trace what happens as we move from the short run to the long run. Prices that were initially sticky in the short run become unstuck. The price level rises from P^1_{US} to P^2_{US}, and this pushes the real money supply back to its initial level, from MS_2 back to MS_1. Money demand MD is unchanged. Hence, in the home money market of panel (c), the economy moves from the short-run equilibrium at point 2 to the long-run equilibrium, which is again at point 1, following the path shown by the arrows. Hence, the interest rate gradually rises from $i^2_\$$ back to $i^1_\$$. This raises the domestic returns over in the FX market of panel (d) from DR_2 back to DR_1. So the FX market moves from the short-run equilibrium at point 2′ to the long-run equilibrium, which is again at point 4′.

An Example Let's make this very tricky experiment a bit more concrete with a numerical example. Suppose you are told that, all else equal, (i) the home money supply permanently increases by 5% today; (ii) prices are sticky in the short run, so this also causes an increase in real money supply that lowers domestic interest rates by four percentage points from 6% to 2%; (iii) prices will fully adjust in one year's time to today's monetary expansion and PPP will hold again. Based on this information, can you predict what will happen to prices and the exchange rate today and in a year's time?

Yes. Work backward from the long run to the short run, as before. In the long run, a 5% increase in M means a 5% increase in P that will be achieved in one year. By PPP, this 5% increase in P implies a 5% rise in E (a 5% depreciation in the dollar's value) over the same period. In other words, over the next year E will rise at 5% per year, which will be the rate of depreciation. Finally, in the short run, UIP tells us what happens to the exchange rate today: to compensate investors for the four-percentage-point decrease in the domestic interest rate, arbitrage in the FX market requires that the value of the home currency be expected to appreciate at 4% per year; that is, E must fall 4% in the year ahead. However, if E has to fall 4% in the next year and still end up 5% above its level at the start of today, then it must jump up 9% today: it overshoots its long-run level.

Overshooting

Compared with the temporary expansion of money supply we studied before, the permanent shock has a much greater impact on the exchange rate in the short run.

Under the temporary shock, domestic returns go down; traders want to sell the dollar for one reason only—temporarily lower dollar interest rates make dollar deposits less attractive. Under the permanent shock, domestic returns go down and foreign returns go up; traders want to sell the dollar for two reasons—temporarily lower dollar interest rates and an expected dollar depreciation make dollar deposits *much* less attractive. In the short run, the interest rate and exchange rate effects combine to create an instantaneous "double whammy" for the dollar, which gives rise to a phenomenon that economists refer to as exchange rate **overshooting.**

To better visualize the overshooting phenomenon, we show in Figure 12-13 the time path over which the key economic variables change after the permanent shock we just studied using Figure 12-12. We see the following in the four panels of Figure 12-13:

a. The nominal money supply is subject to a one-time increase at time T.

b. Real money balances rise instantaneously but revert to their initial level in the long run; the nominal interest rate falls instantaneously but reverts to its initial level in the long run.

c. The price level is sticky in the short run but rises to a new higher level in the long run, increasing in the same proportion as the nominal money supply.

d. The exchange rate rises (depreciates) to a new higher level in the long run, rising in the same proportion as the nominal money supply. In the short run, however, the exchange rate rises even more, overshooting its long-run level, then gradually decreasing to its long-run level (which is still higher than the initial level).

The overshooting result adds yet another argument for the importance of a sound long-run nominal anchor: without it, exchange rates are likely to be more volatile,

FIGURE 12-13

Responses to a Permanent Expansion of the Home Money Supply In panel (a), there is a one-time permanent increase in home (U.S.) nominal money supply at time T. In panel (b), prices are sticky in the short run, so there is a short-run increase in the real money supply and a fall in the home interest rate. In panel (c), in the long run, prices rise in the same proportion as the money supply. In panel (d), in the short run, the exchange rate overshoots its long-run value (the dollar depreciates by a large amount), but in the long run, the exchange rate will have risen only in proportion to changes in money and prices.

creating instability in the forex market and possibly in the wider economy. The wild fluctuations of exchange rates in the 1970s, at a time when exchange rate anchors were ripped loose, exposed these linkages with great clarity (see **Side Bar: Overshooting in Practice**). And new research provides evidence that the shift to a new form of anchoring, inflation targeting, might be helping to bring down exchange rate volatility in recent years.[3]

---

[3] Andrew K. Rose, 2007, "A Stable International Monetary System Emerges: Inflation Targeting Is Bretton Woods, Reversed," *Journal of International Money and Finance*, 26(5), 663–681.

SIDE BAR

Overshooting in Practice

Overshooting can happen in theory, but does it happen in the real world? The model tells us that if there is a tendency for monetary policy shocks to be more permanent than temporary, then there will be a tendency for the exchange rate to be more volatile. Thus, we might expect to see a serious increase in exchange rate volatility whenever a nominal anchoring system breaks down. Indeed, such conditions were seen in the 1970s, which is precisely when the overshooting phenomenon was discovered. How did this happen?

From the 1870s until the 1970s, except during major crises and wars, the world's major currencies were fixed against one another. Floating rates were considered anathema by policy makers and economists. Later in this book, we study the gold standard regime that began circa 1870 and fizzled out in the 1930s and the subsequent "dollar standard" of the 1950s and 1960s that was devised at a conference at Bretton Woods, New Hampshire, in 1944. As we shall see, the Bretton Woods system did not survive long for various reasons.

When floating rates reappeared in the 1970s, fears of instability returned. Concern mounted as floating exchange rates proved much more volatile than could be explained according to the prevailing flexible-price monetary approach: the models said that money supplies and real income were simply too sta-

ble to be able to generate such large fluctuations (as seen in Figure 12-14). Some feared that this was a case of *animal spirits,* John Maynard Keynes's term for irrational forces, especially in asset markets like that for foreign exchange. The challenge to economists was to derive a new model that could account for the wild swings in exchange rates.

Enter economist Rudiger Dornbusch of MIT. Building on Keynesian foundations, he published a paper in 1976 in which he showed that sticky prices and flexible exchange rates implied exchange rate overshooting.[*] Dornbusch's seminal work was a fortuitous case of a theory arriving at just the right time. In the 1970s, countries abandoned exchange rate anchors and groped for new ways to conduct monetary policy in a new economic environment. Policies varied and inflation rates grew, diverged, and persisted. Overshooting helps make sense of all this: if traders saw policies as having no well-defined anchor, monetary policy shocks might no longer be guaranteed to be temporary, so long-run expectations could swing wildly with every piece of news.

---

[*] Rudiger Dornbusch, December 1976, "Expectations and Exchange Rate Dynamics," *Journal of Political Economy*, 84, 1161–1176.

FIGURE 12-14

Exchange Rates for Major Currencies before and after 1973 Under the Bretton Woods system of fixed but adjustable dollar pegs, exchange rates were mostly stable from 1950 until 1970. The system was declared officially dead in 1973. From then on, all of these currencies have fluctuated against the dollar.

Source: International Monetary Fund (IMF), International Financial Statistics.

5 Fixed Exchange Rates and the Trilemma

We have developed a complete theory of exchange rates, based on the assumption that market forces in the money market and the foreign exchange market determine exchange rates. Our models have the most obvious application to the case of floating exchange rate regimes. But as we have seen, not every country floats. Can our theory also be applied to the equally important case of fixed exchange rate regimes and to other intermediate regimes? The answer is yes, and we conclude this chapter by adapting our existing theory for the case of fixed regimes.

What Is a Fixed Exchange Rate Regime?

To understand the crucial difference between fixing and floating, we contrast the polar cases of tight fixing (hard pegs including narrow bands) and free floating, and ignore, for now, intermediate regimes. We also set aside regimes that include controls on arbitrage (*capital controls*) because such extremes of government intervention render our theory superfluous. Instead, we focus on the case of a fixed rate regime without controls so that capital is mobile and arbitrage is free to operate in the foreign exchange market.

Here the government itself becomes an actor in the foreign exchange market and uses intervention in the market to influence the market rate. Exchange rate intervention takes the form of the central bank buying and selling foreign currency at a fixed price, thus holding the market exchange rate at a fixed level denoted $\overline{E}$.

We can explore the implications of that policy in the short run and the long run using the familiar building blocks of our theory. To give a concrete flavor to these analyses, we replace the United States and the Eurozone (whose currencies float against each other) with an example of an actual fixed exchange rate regime. The Foreign country remains the Eurozone, and the Home country is now Denmark.

We examine the implications of Denmark's decision to peg its currency, the krone, to the euro at a fixed rate $\overline{E}_{DKr/\text{€}}$.[4]

In the long run, fixing the exchange rate is one kind of nominal anchor. Yet even if it allowed the krone to float but had *some* nominal anchor, Denmark's monetary policy would still be constrained in the long run by the need to achieve its chosen nominal target. We have seen that any country with a nominal anchor faces long-run monetary policy constraints of some kind. *What we now show is that a country with a fixed exchange rate faces monetary policy constraints not just in the long run but also in the short run.*

Pegging Sacrifices Monetary Policy Autonomy in the Short Run: Example

By assumption, equilibrium in the krone-euro foreign exchange market requires that the Danish interest rate be equal to the Eurozone interest rate plus the expected rate of depreciation of the krone. But under a peg, the expected rate of depreciation is zero.

---

[4] The actual arrangement is a "narrow band" centered on 7.46038 DKr/€ and officially of width ±2.25%, according to the ERM arrangement between Denmark and the Eurozone that has been in effect since 1999. In practice, the peg is much tighter and krone usually stays within ±0.5% of the central rate.

Here uncovered interest parity reduces to the simple condition that the Danish central bank must set its interest rate equal to $i_€$, the rate set by the European Central Bank (ECB):

$$i_{DKr} = i_€ + \underbrace{\frac{E^e_{DKr/€} - E_{DKr/€}}{E_{DKr/€}}}_{\substack{\text{Equals zero for a credible} \\ \text{fixed exchange rate}}} = i_€$$

Denmark has lost control of its monetary policy: it cannot independently change its interest rate under a peg.

The same is true of money supply policy. Short-run equilibrium in Denmark's money market requires that money supply equal money demand, but once Denmark's interest rate is set equal to the Eurozone interest rate $i_€$, there is only one feasible level for money supply, as we see by imposing $i_€$ as the Danish interest rate in money market equilibrium:

$$M_{DEN} = \overline{P}_{DEN} L_{DEN}(i_{DKr}) Y_{DEN} = \overline{P}_{DEN} L_{DEN}(i_€) Y_{DEN}$$

The implications are stark. The final expression contains the euro interest rate (exogenous, as far as the Danes are concerned), the fixed price level (exogenous by assumption), and output (also exogenous by assumption). No variable in this expression is under the control of the Danish authorities in the short run, and this is the only level of the Danish money supply consistent with equilibrium in the money and forex markets at the pegged rate $\overline{\overline{E}}_{DKr/€}$. If the Danish central bank is to maintain the peg, then in the short run it must choose the level of money supply implied by the last equation.

What's going on? Arbitrage is the key force. For example, if the Danish central bank tried to supply more krone and lower interest rates, they would be foiled by arbitrage. Danes would want to sell krone deposits and buy higher-yield euro deposits, applying downward pressure on the krone. To maintain the peg, whatever krone the Danish central bank had tried to pump into circulation, it would promptly have to buy them back in the foreign exchange market.

Thus, *our short-run theory still applies, but with a different chain of causality*:

■ Under a float, the home monetary authorities pick the money supply M. In the short run, the choice of M determines the interest rate i in the money market; in turn, via UIP, the level of i determines the exchange rate E. The money supply is an input in the model (an exogenous variable), and the exchange rate is an output of the model (an endogenous variable).

■ Under a fix, this logic is reversed. Home monetary authorities pick the fixed level of the exchange rate E. In the short run, a fixed E pins down the home interest rate i via UIP (forcing i to equal the foreign interest rate i^*); in turn, the level of i determines the level of the money supply M necessary to meet money demand. The exchange rate is an input in the model (an exogenous variable), and the money supply is an output of the model (an endogenous variable).

This reversal of short-run causality is shown in a new schematic in the top part of Figure 12-15.

FIGURE 12-15

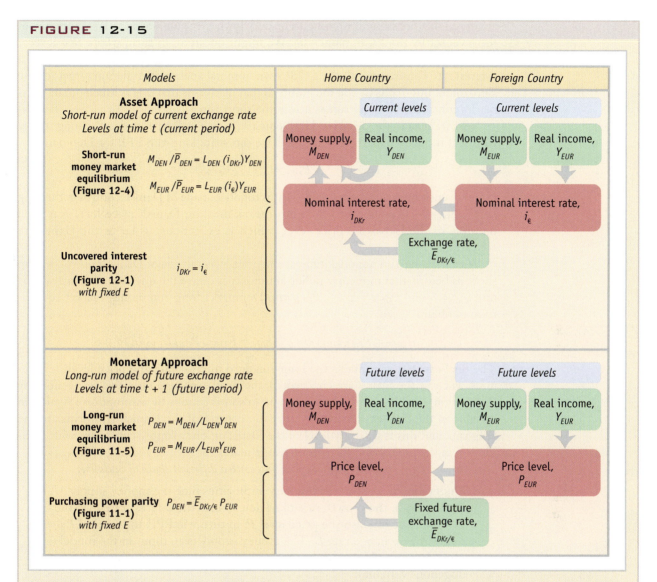

A Complete Theory of Fixed Exchange Rates: Same Building Blocks, Different Known and Unknown Variables Unlike in Figure 12-11, the Home country is now assumed to fix its exchange rate with the Foreign country. Inputs to the model are known exogenous variables (in green boxes). Outputs of the model are unknown endogenous variables (in red boxes). The levels of real income and the fixed exchange rate determine the Home money supply levels, given outcomes in the Foreign country.

Pegging Sacrifices Monetary Policy Autonomy in the Long Run: Example

As we have noted, choosing a nominal anchor implies a loss of long-run monetary policy autonomy. Let's quickly see how that works when the anchor is a fixed exchange rate.

Following our discussion of the standard monetary model, we must first ask what the nominal interest rate is going to be in Denmark in the long run. But we have already answered that question; it is going to be tied down the same way as in the short run, at the level set by the ECB, namely $i_€$. We might question, in turn, where *that* level $i_€$ comes from (the answer is that it will be related to the "neutral" level of the nominal interest rate consistent with the ECB's own nominal anchor, its inflation target for the Eurozone). But that is beside the point: all that matters is that $i_€$ is as much out of Denmark's control in the long run as it is in the short run.

Next we turn to the price level in Denmark, which is determined in the long run by PPP. But if the exchange rate is pegged, we can write long-run PPP for Denmark as

$$P_{DEN} = \overline{E}_{DKr/€}P_{EUR}$$

Here we encounter another variable that is totally outside of Danish control in the long run. Under PPP, pegging to the euro means that the Danish price level is a fixed multiple of the Eurozone price level (which is exogenous, as far as the Danes are concerned).

With the long-run nominal interest and price level outside of Danish control, we can show, as before, that monetary policy autonomy is out of the question. We just substitute $i_{DKr} = i_€$ and $P_{DEN} = \overline{E}_{DKr/€}P_{EUR}$ into Denmark's long-run money market equilibrium to obtain

$$M_{DEN} = P_{DEN}L_{DEN}(i_{DKr})Y_{DEN} = \overline{E}_{DKr/€}P_{EUR}L_{DEN}(i_€)Y_{DEN}$$

The final expression contains the long-run euro interest rate and price levels (exogenous, as far as the Danes are concerned), the fixed exchange rate level (exogenous by assumption), and long-run Danish output (also exogenous by assumption). Again, no variable in the final expression is under the control of the Danish authorities in the long run, and this is the only level of the Danish money supply consistent with equilibrium in the money and foreign exchange market at the pegged rate of $\overline{E}_{DKr/€}$.

Thus, *our long-run theory still applies, just with a different chain of causality*:

■ Under a float, the home monetary authorities pick the money supply M. In the long run, the growth rate of M determines the interest rate i via the Fisher effect and also the price level P; in turn, via PPP, the level of P determines the exchange rate E. The money supply is an input in the model (an exogenous variable), and the exchange rate is an output of the model (an endogenous variable).

■ Under a fix, this logic is reversed. Home monetary authorities pick the exchange rate E. In the long run, the choice of E determines the price level P via PPP, and also the interest rate i via UIP; these, in turn, determine the necessary level of the money supply M. The exchange rate is an input in the model (an exogenous variable), and the money supply is an output of the model (an endogenous variable).

This reversal of long-run causality is also shown in the new schematic in the bottom part of Figure 12-15.

The Trilemma

Our findings lead to the conclusion that policy makers face some tough choices. Not all desirable policy goals can be simultaneously met. These constraints are summed up in one of the most important principles in open-economy macroeconomics.

Consider the following three equations and parallel statements about desirable *policy goals*. For illustration we return to the Denmark–Eurozone example:

---

1. $\dfrac{E^e_{DKr/€} - E_{DKr/€}}{E_{DKr/€}} = 0$ *A fixed exchange rate*

      ■ May be desired as a means to promote stability in trade and investment

      ■ Represented here by zero expected depreciation

---

2. $i_{DKr} = i_€ + \dfrac{E^e_{DKr/€} - E_{DKr/€}}{E_{DKr/€}}$ *International capital mobility*

      ■ May be desired as a means to promote integration, efficiency, and risk sharing

      ■ Represented here by uncovered interest parity, which results from arbitrage

---

3. $i_{DKr} \neq i_€$ *Monetary policy autonomy*

      ■ May be desired as a means to manage the Home economy's business cycle

      ■ Represented here by the ability to set the Home interest rate independently of the Foreign interest rate

---

For a variety of reasons, as noted, governments may want to pursue all three of these policy goals. But they can't: formulae 1, 2, and 3 show that it is a *mathematical impossibility* as shown by the following statements:

- 1 and 2 imply not 3 (1 and 2 imply interest equality, contradicting 3).
- 2 and 3 imply not 1 (2 and 3 imply an expected change in *E*, contradicting 1).
- 3 and 1 imply not 2 (3 and 1 imply a difference between domestic and foreign returns, contradicting 2).

This result, known as the **trilemma,** is one of the most important ideas in international macroeconomics.[5] It tells us that the three policy goals just outlined are mutually incompatible: you cannot have all three at once. You must choose to drop one of the three (or, equivalently, you must adopt one of three pairs: 1 and 2, 2 and 3, or 3 and 1). Sadly, there is a long history of macroeconomic disasters stemming from the failure of some policy that ignored this fundamental lesson.

The trilemma can be illustrated graphically as in Figure 12-16. Each corner of the triangle represents a viable policy choice. For each corner, the label at the vertex indicates the goal that has been sacrificed, while the labels on each adjacent edge of the triangle explain the goals that can be attained (see **Side Bar: Intermediate Regimes**).

---

[5] A definition: Trilemma *noun* 1. a quandary posed by three alternative courses of action (*Collins English Dictionary* online).

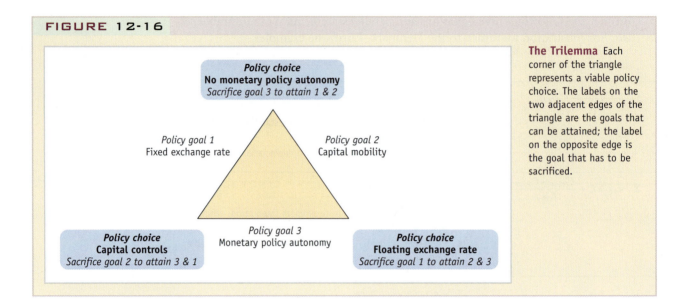

FIGURE 12-16

Policy choice
No monetary policy autonomy
Sacrifice goal 3 to attain 1 & 2

Policy goal 1
Fixed exchange rate

Policy goal 2
Capital mobility

Policy goal 3
Monetary policy autonomy

Policy choice
Capital controls
Sacrifice goal 2 to attain 3 & 1

Policy choice
Floating exchange rate
Sacrifice goal 1 to attain 2 & 3

The Trilemma Each corner of the triangle represents a viable policy choice. The labels on the two adjacent edges of the triangle are the goals that can be attained; the label on the opposite edge is the goal that has to be sacrificed.

SIDE BAR

Intermediate Regimes

The lessons of the trilemma most clearly apply when the policies are at the ends of a spectrum: a hard peg or a float, perfect capital mobility or immobility, complete autonomy or none at all. But sometimes a country may not be fully in one of the three corners: the rigidity of the peg, the degree of capital mobility, and the independence of monetary policy could be partial rather than full.

For example, in a band arrangement, the exchange rate is maintained within a range of ±X% of some central rate. The significance of the band is that some expected depreciation (i.e., a little bit of floating) is possible. As a result, a limited interest differential can open up between the two countries. For example, suppose the band is 2% wide (i.e., ±1% around a central rate). To compute home interest rates, UIP tells us that we must add the foreign interest rate (let's suppose it is 5%) to the expected rate of depreciation (which is ±2% if the exchange rate moves from one band edge to the other). Thus, Home may "fix" this way and still have the freedom to set 12-month interest rates in the range between 3% and 7%. But the home country cannot evade the trilemma forever: on average, over time, the rate of depreciation will have to be zero to keep the exchange rate within the narrow band, meaning that the Home interest rate must track the Foreign interest rate apart from small deviations.

Similar qualifications to the trilemma could result from partial capital mobility, in which barriers to arbitrage could also lead to interest differentials. And with such differentials emerging, the desire for partial monetary autonomy can be accommodated.

In practice, once these distinctions are understood, it is usually possible to make some kind of judgment about which corner best describes the country's policy choice. For example, in 2007 both Slovakia and Denmark were supposedly pegged to the euro as members of the EU's Exchange Rate Mechanism (ERM). But the similarities ended there. The Danish krone was operating in ERM bands of official width ±2.25%, but closer to ±0.5% in practice, a pretty hard peg with almost no movement. The Slovak koruna was operating with ±15% bands and at one point even shifted that band by appreciating its central rate by 8.5% in March 2007. With its perpetual narrow band, Denmark's regime was clearly fixed. With its wide and adjustable bands, Slovakia's regime was closer to managed floating.[*]

---

[*] Note that Slovakia has since joined the euro as of 2009.

The Trilemma in Europe

We motivated the trilemma with the case of Denmark, which has chosen policy goals 1 and 2. As a member of the European Union (EU), Denmark adheres to the single-market legislation that requires free movement of capital within the bloc. It also unilaterally pegs its krone to the euro under the EU's Exchange Rate Mechanism (ERM), an arrangement that ostensibly serves as a stepping-stone to Eurozone membership. Consequently, UIP predicts that the Danish central bank must set an interest rate at the same level as that set by the ECB; it has lost option 3.

The Danes could make one of two politically difficult choices if they wished to gain monetary independence from the ECB: they could abandon their commitment to the EU treaties on capital mobility (drop 2 to get 3), which is extremely unlikely, or they could abandon their ERM commitment and let the krone float against the euro (drop 1 to get 3), which is also fairly unlikely. Floating is, however, the choice of the United Kingdom, an EU country that has withdrawn from the ERM and that allows the pound to float against the euro.

Figure 12-17 shows evidence for the trilemma. Since 1999 the United Kingdom has had the ability to set interest rates independently of the ECB. But Denmark

FIGURE 12-17

The Trilemma in Europe The figure shows selected central banks' base interest rates for the period 1994 to 2010 with reference to the German mark and euro base rates. In this period, the British made a policy choice to float against the German mark and (after 1999) against the euro. This permitted monetary independence because interest rates set by the Bank of England could diverge from those set in Frankfurt. No such independence in policy making was afforded by the Danish decision to peg the krone first to the mark and then to the euro. Since 1999 the Danish interest rate has moved almost exactly in line with the ECB rate. Similar forces operated pre-1999 for other countries pegging to the mark, such as the Netherlands and Austria. Until they joined the Eurozone in 1999, their interest rates, like that of Denmark, closely tracked the German rate.

Sources: Websites of the central banks.

has not: since 1999 the Danish interest rate has tracked the ECB's rate almost exactly. (Most of the departures from equality reflect uncertainty about the euro project and Denmark's peg at two key moments: at the very start of the euro project in 1999, and during the credibility crisis of the Eurozone following the financial crash of 2008.)

These monetary policy ties to Frankfurt even predate the euro itself. Before 1999 Denmark, and some countries such as Austria and the Netherlands, pegged to the German mark with the same result: their interest rates had to track the German interest rate, but the U.K. interest rate did not. The big difference is that Austria and the Netherlands have formally abolished their national currencies, the schilling and the guilder, and have adopted the euro—an extreme and explicit renunciation of monetary independence. Meanwhile, the Danish krone lives on, showing that a national currency can suggest monetary sovereignty in theory but may deliver nothing of the sort in practice. ■

6 Conclusions

In this chapter, we drew together everything we have learned so far about exchange rates. We built on the concepts of arbitrage and equilibrium in the foreign exchange (FX) market in the short run, taking expectations as given and applying uncovered interest parity. We also relied on the purchasing power parity theory as a guide to exchange rate determination in the long run. Putting together all these building blocks provides a complete and internally consistent theory of exchange rate determination.

Exchange rates are an interesting topic in and of themselves, but at the end of the day, we also care about what they mean for the wider economy, how they relate to macroeconomic performance, and the part they play in the global monetary system. That is our goal in the next chapters in which we apply our exchange rate theories in a wider framework to help us understand how exchange rates function in the national and international economy.

The theory we've developed in the past three chapters is the first tool that economists and policy makers pick up when studying a problem involving exchange rates. This theory has served well in rich and poor countries, whether in periods of economic stability or turbulence. Remarkably, it has even been applied in wartime, and to round off our discussion of exchange rates. we digress into some colorful applications of the theory from conflicts past and present.

APPLICATION

News and the Foreign Exchange Market in Wartime

Our theory of exchange rates places expectations at center stage, but demonstrating the effect of changing expectations empirically is a challenge. However, wars dramatically expose the power of expectations to change exchange rates. War raises the risk that a currency may depreciate in value rapidly in the future, possibly all the way to zero. For one thing, the government may need to print money to finance its war effort, but how much inflation this practice will generate may be unclear. In addition, there is a risk of defeat and a decision by the victor to impose new economic arrangements such as a new currency; the existing currency may then be converted into the new currency at a rate dictated by the victors or, in a worst-case scenario, it may be declared totally worthless; that is, not legal tender. Demand for the currency will then collapse to nothing and so will its value. Investors in the foreign exchange market are continually updating their forecasts about a war's possible outcomes, and, as a result, the path of an exchange rate during wartime usually reveals a clear influence of the effects of news.

The U.S. Civil War, 1861–1865 For four years, beginning April 12, 1861, a war raged between the Union (Northern) and Confederate (Southern) forces. An important economic dimension of this conflict was the decision by the Confederate states to issue their own currency, the Confederate dollar, to help gain economic autonomy from the North and finance their war effort. The exchange rate of the Confederate dollar against the U.S. dollar is shown in Figure 12-18.

How should we interpret these data? The two currencies differed in one important respect. If the South had won, and the Confederate states had gained independence, they would have kept their Confederate dollar, and the Northern United States would have kept their U.S. dollar, too. Instead, the South was defeated, and, as expected in these circumstances, the U.S. dollar was imposed as the sole currency of the unified country; the Confederate dollar, like all liabilities of the Confederate nation, was repudiated by the victors and, hence, became worthless.

FIGURE 12-18

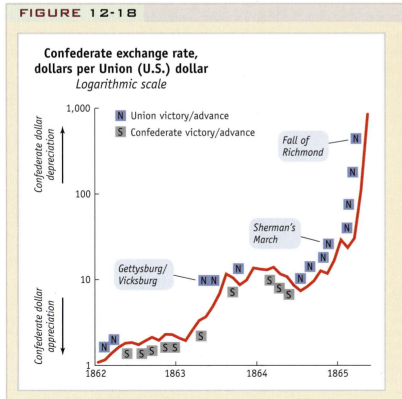

Confederate exchange rate, dollars per Union (U.S.) dollar
Logarithmic scale

N Union victory/advance
S Confederate victory/advance

Fall of Richmond

Sherman's March

Gettysburg/Vicksburg

Confederate dollar depreciation

Confederate dollar appreciation

Exchange Rates and News in the U.S. Civil War The value of the Confederate dollar fluctuated against the U.S. dollar and is shown on a logarithmic scale. Against the backdrop of a steady trend, victories and advances by the North (N) were generally associated with faster depreciation of the Confederate currency, whereas major Southern successes (S) usually led to a stronger Confederate currency.

Sources: Global Financial Data; George T. McCandless Jr., 1996, "Money, Expectations, and U.S. Civil War," American Economic Review, 86(3), 661–671.

War news regularly influenced the exchange rate.[6] As the South headed for defeat, the value of the Confederate dollar shrank. The overall trend was driven partly by inflationary war finance and partly by the probability of defeat. Major Northern victories marked "N" tended to coincide with depreciations of the Confederate dollar. Major Southern victories marked "S" were associated with appreciations or, at least, a slower depreciation. The key Union victory at Gettysburg, July 1–3, 1863, and the near simultaneous fall of Vicksburg on July 4 were followed by a dramatic depreciation of the Confederate dollar. By contrast, Southern victories (in the winter of 1862 to 1863 and the spring of 1864) were periods when the Southern currency held steady or even appreciated. But by the fall of 1864, and particularly after Sherman's March, the writing was on the wall, and the Confederate dollar began its final decline.

Currency traders in New York did good business either way. They were known to whistle "John Brown's Body" after a Union victory and "Dixie" after Confederate success, making profits all the while as they traded dollars for gold and vice versa. Abraham Lincoln was not impressed, declaring, "What do you think of those fellows in Wall Street, who are gambling in gold at such a time as this? . . . For my part, I wish every one of them had his devilish head shot off."

The Iraq War, 2002–2003 The Civil War is not the only example of such phenomena. In 2003 Iraq was invaded by a U.S.-led coalition of forces intent on overthrowing the regime of Saddam Hussein, and the effects of war on currencies were again visible.[7]

Our analysis of this case is made a little more complicated by the fact that at the time of the invasion there were *two* currencies in Iraq. Indeed, some might say there were two Iraqs. Following a 1991 war, Iraq had been divided: in the North, a de facto Kurdish government was protected by a no-fly zone enforced by the Royal Air Force and U.S. Air Force; in the South, Saddam's regime continued. The two regions developed into two distinct economies, and each had its own currency. In the North, Iraqi dinar notes called "Swiss" dinars circulated.[8] In the South, a new currency, the "Saddam" or "print" dinar, was introduced.[9]

Figure 12-19 shows the close correlation between wartime news and exchange rate movements for this modern episode. We can compare exchange rate movements with well-known events, but panel (a) allows another interesting comparison. In 2002 a company called TradeSports Exchange allowed bets on Saddam's destiny by setting up a

---

[6] This correlation was noted by Wesley Mitchell, 1903, *A History of the Greenbacks* (Chicago: University of Chicago Press). For recent econometric studies that examine this phenomenon, see George T. McCandless Jr., 1996, "Money, Expectations, and U.S. Civil War," *American Economic Review*, 86(3), 661–671; and Kristen L. Willard, Timothy W. Guinnane, and Harvey S. Rosen, 1996, "Turning Points in the Civil War: Views from the Greenback Market," *American Economic Review*, 86(4), 1001–1018.

[7] This case study draws on Mervyn King, May 2004, "The Institutions of Monetary Policy," *American Economic Review*, 94(2), 1–13.

[8] The notes were printed in Britain using plates of Swiss manufacture. The Kurds issued no new notes of their own; indeed, they had no means to do so and simply used this legacy currency after 1991. No new Swiss dinars were issued after 1989 in the South either.

[9] Once economic sanctions were imposed after the 1991 war, Baghdad had no access to the high-security technology and papers used to make modern banknotes. Instead, the Swiss dinar was retired, and the Saddam regime issued new legal tender notes in a form that it *could* print, using low-technology offset litho techniques that your local printer might use. These were the so-called Saddam or print dinars. Circulation of these notes exploded: a large volume of notes were printed by the Iraqi Central Bank and counterfeits added to this number. For these reasons, the northern currency, the Swiss dinar, was much more stable in the 1990s than the Saddam dinar.

FIGURE 12-19

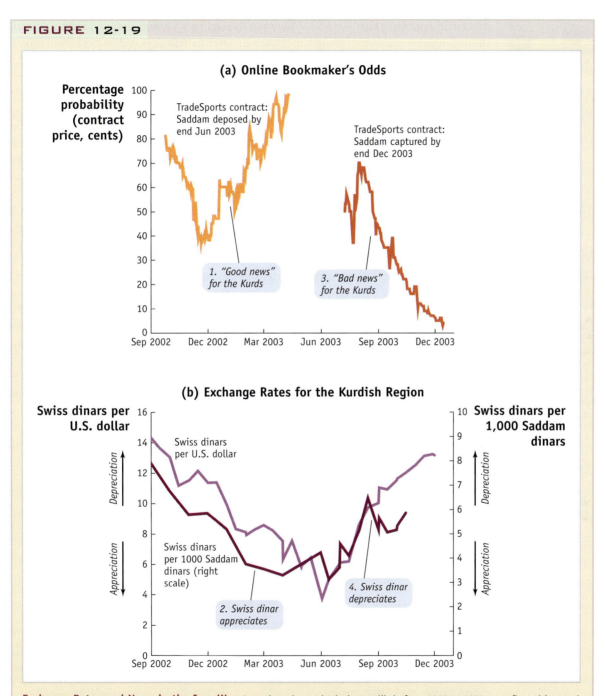

(a) Online Bookmaker's Odds

Percentage probability (contract price, cents)

TradeSports contract: Saddam deposed by end Jun 2003

TradeSports contract: Saddam captured by end Dec 2003

1. "Good news" for the Kurds

3. "Bad news" for the Kurds

(b) Exchange Rates for the Kurdish Region

Swiss dinars per U.S. dollar

Swiss dinars per 1,000 Saddam dinars

Swiss dinars per U.S. dollar

Swiss dinars per 1000 Saddam dinars (right scale)

Depreciation

Appreciation

2. Swiss dinar appreciates

4. Swiss dinar depreciates

Exchange Rates and News in the Iraq War As regime change looked more likely from 2002 to 2003, as reflected in panel (a), the Swiss dinar, the currency used by the Kurds, appreciated against the U.S. dollar and the Saddam dinar, the currency used in the south, as shown in panel (b). When the U.S. invasion ended, the difficult postwar transition began. Insurgencies and the failure to find Saddam Hussein became a cause for concern, as reflected in panel (a). The Swiss dinar depreciated against the dollar until December 2003, as shown in panel (b).

Notes: Panel (a) shows two contract prices: the value in cents of a TradeSports contract that paid 100¢ if Saddam were deposed by the end of June 2003 and 0 otherwise, and the value in cents of a contract that paid 100¢ if Saddam were captured by the end of December 2003 and 0 otherwise.

Source: Mervyn King, 2004, "The Institutions of Monetary Policy," American Economic Review, 94(2), 1–13.

Currencies in wartime:
A Confederate 2 dollar note
of 1864 issued in Richmond;
an Iraqi "Swiss" 25 dinar
from the Kurdish region;
a widely forged post-1991
Iraqi "Saddam" 25 dinar
note; a post-2003 250 new
Iraqi dinar note.

market in contracts that paid $1 if he was deposed by a certain date, and the prices of these contracts are shown using the left scale. After he was deposed, contracts that paid out upon his capture were traded, and these are also shown. If such a contract had a price of, say, 80¢, then this implied that "the market" believed the probability of overthrow or apprehension was 80%.

In panel (b), we see the exchange rates of the Swiss dinar against the U.S. dollar and the Saddam dinar from 2002 to 2003. The Kurds' Swiss dinar–U.S. dollar rate had held at 18 per U.S. dollar for several years but steadily appreciated in 2002 and 2003 as the prospect of a war to depose Saddam became more likely. By May 2003, when the invasion phase of the war ended and Saddam had been deposed, it had appreciated as far as 6 to the dollar. The war clearly drove this trend: the more likely the removal of Saddam, the more durable would be Kurdish autonomy, and the more likely it was that a postwar currency would be created that respected the value of the Kurds' Swiss dinars. Notice how the rise in the value of the Swiss dinar tracked the odds of regime change until mid-2003.

After Baghdad fell, the coalition sought to capture Saddam, who had gone into hiding. As the hunt wore on, and a militant/terrorist insurgency began, fears mounted that he would never be found and his regime might survive underground and reappear. The odds on capture fell, and, moving in parallel, so did the value of the Swiss dinar. The Kurds now faced a rising probability that the whole affair would end badly for them and their currency. (However, when Saddam Hussein was captured on December 14, 2003, the Swiss dinar appreciated again.)

We can also track related movements in the Swiss dinar against the Saddam or print dinar. Before and during the war, while the Swiss dinar was appreciating against the U.S. dollar, it was also appreciating against the Saddam dinar. It strengthened from around 10 Swiss dinars per 1,000 Saddam in early 2002 to about 3 Swiss dinars per 1,000 Saddam in mid-2003. Then, as the postwar operations dragged on, this trend was reversed. By late 2003, the market rate was about 6 Swiss dinars per 1,000 Saddam. Again, we can see how the Kurds' fortunes appeared to the market to rise and fall.

What became of all these dinars? Iraqis fared better than the holders of Confederate dollars. A new dinar was created under a currency reform announced in July 2003 and implemented from October 15, 2003, to January 15, 2004.[10] Exchange rate expectations soon moved into line with the increasingly credible official conversion rates and U.S. dollar exchange rates for the new dinar. ■

---

[10] Under this reform, all the Swiss and Saddam notes were retired and a newly designed, secure currency for Iraq was brought into circulation nationally. As long as this currency reform was seen as credible, and the market believed it would successfully take place, the market rate would have to converge to the fixed rate set in advance by the authorities for note replacement. As the reform date approached, this convergence occurred, except for what appears to be a small "forgery risk premium" on the Saddam notes—detecting a fake among these notes was by no means simple.

KEY POINTS

1. Our theory of exchange rates builds on two ideas: arbitrage and expectations. First, we developed the theory for the case of floating exchange rates.

2. In the short run, we assume prices are sticky and the asset approach to exchange rates is valid. Interest-bearing accounts in different currencies may offer different rates of nominal interest. Currencies may be expected to depreciate or appreciate against one another. There is an incentive for arbitrage: investors will shift funds from one country to another until the expected rate of return (measured in a common currency) is equalized. Arbitrage in the foreign exchange (FX) market determines today's spot exchange rate, and the FX market is in equilibrium when the uncovered interest parity condition holds. To apply the UIP condition, however, we need a forecast of the expected exchange rate in the long run.

3. In the long run, we assume prices are flexible and the monetary approach to exchange rates is valid. This approach states that in the long run, purchasing power parity (PPP) holds so that the exchange rate must equal the ratio of the price levels in the two countries. Each price level, in turn, depends on the ratio of money supply to money demand in each country. The monetary approach can be used to forecast the long-run future expected exchange rate, which, in turn, feeds

back into short-run exchange rate determination via the UIP equation.

4. Putting together all of these ingredients yields a complete theory of how exchange rates are determined in the short run and the long run.

5. This model can be used to analyze the impact of changes to monetary policy, as well as other shocks to the economy.

6. A temporary home monetary expansion causes home interest rates to fall and the home exchange rate to depreciate. This temporary policy can be consistent with a nominal anchor in the long run.

7. A permanent home monetary expansion causes home interest rates to fall and the home exchange rate to depreciate and, in the short run, overshoot what will eventually be its long-run level. This permanent policy is inconsistent with a nominal anchor in the long run.

8. The case of fixed exchange rates can also be studied using this theory. Under capital mobility, interest parity becomes very simple. In this case, the home interest rate equals the foreign interest rate. Home monetary policy loses all autonomy compared with the floating case. The only way to recover it is to impose capital controls. This is the essence of the trilemma.

KEY TERMS

asset approach to exchange rates, p. 412
fundamental equation of the asset approach to exchange rates, p. 413
FX market diagram, p. 414
nominal rigidity, p. 419
overshooting, p. 438
trilemma, p. 445

PROBLEMS

1. Use the money market and foreign exchange (FX) diagrams to answer the following questions about the relationship between the British pound (£) and the U.S. dollar ($). The exchange rate is in U.S. dollars per British pound $E_{\$/\pounds}$. We want to consider how a change in the U.S. money supply affects interest rates and exchange rates. On all graphs, label the initial equilibrium point A.

   a. Illustrate how a *temporary* decrease in the U.S. money supply affects the money and FX markets. Label your short-run equilibrium point B and your long-run equilibrium point C.

   b. Using your diagram from (a), state how each of the following variables changes in the *short run* (increase/decrease/no change): U.S. interest rate, British interest rate, $E_{\$/\pounds}$, $E^e_{\$/\pounds}$, and the U.S. price level P.

   c. Using your diagram from (a), state how each of the following variables changes in the *long run* (increase/decrease/no change relative to their initial values at point A): U.S. interest rate, British interest rate, $E_{\$/\pounds}$, $E^e_{\$/\pounds}$, and U.S. price level P.

2. Use the money market and foreign exchange (FX) diagrams to answer the following questions. This question considers the relationship between the Indian rupee (Rs) and the U.S. dollar ($). The exchange rate is in rupees per dollar, $E_{Rs/\$}$. On all graphs, label the initial equilibrium point A.

   a. Illustrate how a *permanent* increase in India's money supply affects the money and FX markets. Label your short-run equilibrium point B and your long-run equilibrium point C.

   b. By plotting them on a chart with time on the horizontal axis, illustrate how each of the following variables changes over time (for India): nominal money supply M_{IN}, price level P_{IN}, real money supply M_{IN}/P_{IN}, interest rate i_{Rs}, and the exchange rate $E_{Rs/\$}$.

   c. Using your previous analysis, state how each of the following variables changes in the *short run* (increase/decrease/no change):

India's interest rate i_{Rs}, $E_{Rs/\$}$, expected exchange rate $E^e_{Rs/\$}$, and price level P_{IN}.

   d. Using your previous analysis, state how each of the following variables changes in the *long run* (increase/decrease/no change relative to their initial values at point A): India's interest rate i_{Rs}, $E_{Rs/\$}$, $E^e_{Rs/\$}$, and India's price level P_{IN}.

   e. Explain how overshooting applies to this situation.

3. Is overshooting (in theory and in practice) consistent with purchasing power parity? Consider the reasons for the usefulness of PPP in the short run versus the long run and the assumption we've used in the asset approach (in the short run versus the long run). How does overshooting help to resolve the empirical behavior of exchange rates in the short run versus the long run?

4. Use the money market and foreign exchange (FX) diagrams to answer the following questions. This question considers the relationship between the euro (€) and the U.S. dollar ($). The exchange rate is in U.S. dollars per euro, $E_{\$/€}$. Suppose that with financial innovation in the United States, real money demand in the United States decreases. On all graphs, label the initial equilibrium point A.

   a. Assume this change in U.S. real money demand is temporary. Using the FX/money market diagrams, illustrate how this change affects the money and FX markets. Label your short-run equilibrium point B and your long-run equilibrium point C.

   b. Assume this change in U.S. real money demand is permanent. Using a new diagram, illustrate how this change affects the money and FX markets. Label your short-run equilibrium point B and your long-run equilibrium point C.

   c. Illustrate how each of the following variables changes over time in response to a permanent reduction in real money demand: nominal money supply M_{US}, price level P_{US}, real money supply M_{US}/P_{US}, U.S. interest rate $i_\$$, and the exchange rate $E_{\$/€}$.

5. This question considers how the foreign exchange (FX) market will respond to changes in monetary policy in South Korea. For these questions, define the exchange rate as South Korean won per Japanese yen, $E_{won/¥}$. Use the FX and money market diagrams to answer the following questions. On all graphs, label the initial equilibrium point A.

   a. Suppose the Bank of Korea permanently decreases its money supply. Illustrate the short-run (label equilibrium point B) and long-run effects (label equilibrium point C) of this policy.

   b. Now, suppose the Bank of Korea announces it plans to permanently decrease its money supply but doesn't actually implement this policy. How will this affect the FX market in the short run if investors believe the Bank of Korea's announcement?

   c. Finally, suppose the Bank of Korea permanently decreases its money supply, but this change is not anticipated. When the Bank of Korea implements this policy, how will this affect the FX market in the short run?

   d. Using your previous answers, evaluate the following statements:

      • If a country wants to increase the value of its currency, it can do so (temporarily) without raising domestic interest rates.

      • The central bank can reduce both the domestic price level and value of its currency in the long run.

      • The most effective way to increase the value of a currency is through surprising investors.

6. In the late 1990s, several East Asian countries used limited flexibility or currency pegs in managing their exchange rates relative to the U.S. dollar. This question considers how different countries responded to the East Asian currency crisis (1997–1998). For the following questions, treat the East Asian country as the home country and the United States as the foreign country. Also, for the diagrams, you may assume these countries maintained a currency peg (fixed rate) relative to the U.S. dollar. Also, for the following questions, you need consider only the short-run effects.

   a. In July 1997, investors expected that the Thai baht would depreciate. That is, they expected that Thailand's central bank would be unable to maintain the currency peg with the U.S. dollar. Illustrate how this change in investors' expectations affects the Thai money market and FX market, with the exchange rate defined as baht (B) per U.S. dollar, denoted $E_{B/\$}$. Assume the Thai central bank wants to maintain capital mobility and preserve the level of its interest rate, and abandons the currency peg in favor of a floating exchange rate regime.

   b. Indonesia faced the same constraints as Thailand—investors feared Indonesia would be forced to abandon its currency peg. Illustrate how this change in investors' expectations affects the Indonesian money market and FX market, with the exchange rate defined as rupiahs (Rp) per U.S. dollar, denoted $E_{Rp/\$}$. Assume that the Indonesian central bank wants to maintain capital mobility and the currency peg.

   c. Malaysia had a similar experience, except that it used capital controls to maintain its currency peg and preserve the level of its interest rate. Illustrate how this change in investors' expectations affects the Malaysian money market and FX market, with the exchange rate defined as ringgit (RM) per U.S. dollar, denoted $E_{RM/\$}$. You need show only the short-run effects of this change in investors' expectations.

   d. Compare and contrast the three approaches just outlined. As a policy maker, which would you favor? Explain.

7. Several countries have opted to join currency unions. Examples include those in the Euro area, the CFA franc union in West Africa, and the Caribbean currency union. This involves sacrificing the domestic currency in favor of using a single currency unit in multiple countries. Assuming that once a country joins a currency union, it will not leave, do these countries face the policy trilemma discussed in the text? Explain.

8. During the Great Depression, the United States remained on the international gold standard longer than other countries. This effectively

meant that the United States was committed to maintaining a fixed exchange rate at the onset of the Great Depression. The U.S. dollar was pegged to the value of gold, along with other major currencies, including the British pound, French franc, and so on. Many researchers have blamed the severity of the Great Depression on the Federal Reserve and its failure to react to economic conditions in 1929 and 1930. Discuss how the policy trilemma applies to this situation.

9. On June 20, 2007, John Authers, investment editor of the *Financial Times*, wrote the following in his column "The Short View":

> The Bank of England published minutes showing that only the narrowest possible margin, 5–4, voted down [an interest] rate hike last month. Nobody foresaw this. . . . The news took sterling back above $1.99, and to a 15-year high against the yen.

Can you explain the logic of this statement? Interest rates in the United Kingdom had remained unchanged in the weeks since the vote and were still unchanged after the minutes were released. What news was contained in the minutes that caused traders to react? Explain using the asset approach.

10. We can use the asset approach to both make predictions about how the market will react to current events and understand how important these events are to investors. Consider the behavior of the Union/Confederate exchange rate during the Civil War. How would each of the following events affect the exchange rate, defined as Confederate dollars per Union dollar, $E_{C\$/\$}$?

   a. The Confederacy increases the money supply by 2,900% between July and December 1861.
   b. The Union Army suffers a defeat in Battle of Chickamauga in September 1863.
   c. The Confederate Army suffers a major defeat with Sherman's March in the autumn of 1864.

N E T WORK

Search the Internet for websites and services offering exchange rate forecasts. (*Hint:* Google "exchange rate forecast.") How far ahead is the forecast made? What do the forecasters say about the methods that they use, if anything? Is the forecast based on fundamentals or technical methods? How much credence would you give to the forecast?

13

National and International Accounts: Income, Wealth, and the Balance of Payments

Money is sent from one country to another for various purposes: such as the payment of tributes or subsidies; remittances of revenue to or from dependencies, or of rents or other incomes to their absent owners; emigration of capital, or transmission of it for foreign investment. The most usual purpose, however, is that of payment for goods. To show in what circumstances money actually passes from country to country for this or any of the other purposes mentioned, it is necessary briefly to state the nature of the mechanism by which international trade is carried on, when it takes place not by barter but through the medium of money.

John Stuart Mill, 1848

In Chapter 10, we encountered George, the hypothetical American tourist in Paris. We learned about his use of exchange rate conversion—but how did he pay for his expenses? He traded some of his assets (such as dollar cash converted into euros, or charges on his debit card against his bank account) for goods and services (hotel, food, wine, etc.). Every day households and firms routinely trade goods, services, and assets, but when such transactions cross borders, they link the home economy with the rest of the world. In the upcoming chapters, we study economic transactions between countries, how they are undertaken, and what impact they have on the macroeconomy.

To that end, the first task of any macroeconomist is to measure economic transactions. The collection and analysis of such data can help improve research and policy formulation. In a closed economy there are important aggregate flows to consider, such as national output, consumption, investment, and so on. When an economy is open to transactions with the rest of the world, there are a host of additional economic transactions that take place across borders. In today's world economy these international flows of trade and finance have reached unprecedented levels.

Beyond barter: international transactions involve not just goods and services but also financial assets.

Cross-border flows of good, services, and capital are measured in various ways and are increasingly important subjects of discussion for economists and policy makers, for businesses, and for the well-educated citizen. There are debates about the size of the U.S. trade deficit, trade surpluses in emerging economies like China and India, the growing indebtedness of the United States to the rest of the world, and how these trends might be related to national saving and the government's budget. To understand such debates, we must first know what is being talked about. What do all these measures mean and how are they related? How does the global economy actually function?

The goals of this chapter are to explain the international system of trade and payments, to discover how international trade in *goods and services* is complemented and balanced by a parallel trade in *assets*, and to see how these transactions relate to national income and wealth. In the remainder of the book, we will use these essential tools to understand the macroeconomic linkages between nations.

1 Measuring Macroeconomic Activity: An Overview

To understand macroeconomic accounting in an open economy, we build on the principles used to track payments in a closed economy. As you may know from previous courses in economics, a closed economy is characterized by a *circular flow of payments*, in which economic resources are exchanged for payments as they move through the economy. At various points in this flow, economic activity is measured and recorded in the **national income and product accounts.** In an open economy, however, such measurements are more complicated because we have to account for cross-border flows. These additional flows are recorded in a nation's **balance of payments accounts.** In this opening section, we survey the principles behind these measurements. In later sections, we define the measurements more precisely and explore how they work in practice.

The Flow of Payments in a Closed Economy: Introducing the National Income and Product Accounts

Figure 13-1 shows how payments flow in a closed economy. At the top is **gross national expenditure (GNE),** the total expenditure on final goods and services by home entities in any given period of measurement (usually a calendar year, unless otherwise noted). It is made up of three parts: personal consumption C, investment I, and government spending G. The sum of these variables equals GNE.

Once GNE is spent, where do the payments flow next? All of this spending constitutes all payments for final goods and services within the nation's borders. Because the economy is closed, the nation's expenditure must be spent on the final goods and services it produces. More specifically, a country's **gross domestic product (GDP)** is the value of all (*intermediate* and *final*) goods and services produced as output by firms, minus the value of all goods and services purchased as inputs by firms. (GDP is also

FIGURE 13-1

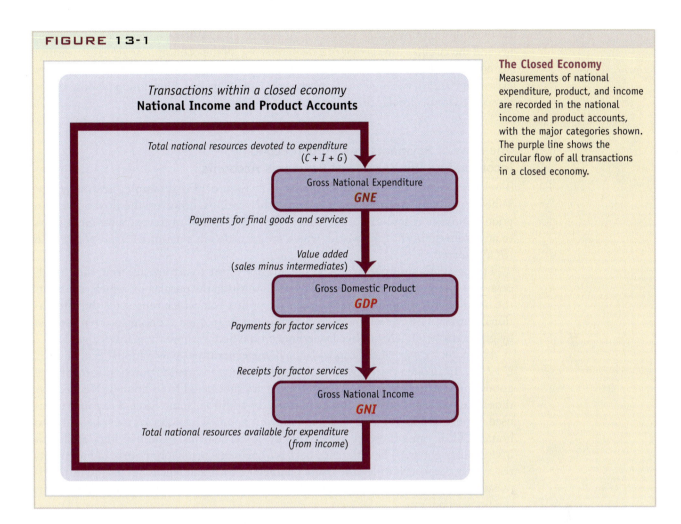

Transactions within a closed economy
National Income and Product Accounts

Total national resources devoted to expenditure
$(C + I + G)$

Gross National Expenditure
GNE

Payments for final goods and services

Value added
(sales minus intermediates)

Gross Domestic Product
GDP

Payments for factor services

Receipts for factor services

Gross National Income
GNI

Total national resources available for expenditure
(from income)

The Closed Economy
Measurements of national expenditure, product, and income are recorded in the national income and product accounts, with the major categories shown. The purple line shows the circular flow of all transactions in a closed economy.

known as *value added.*) GDP is a product measure, in contrast to GNE, which is an expenditure measure. In a closed economy, intermediate sales must equal intermediate purchases, so in GDP these two terms cancel out, leaving only the value of final goods and services produced, which equals the expenditure on final goods and services, or GNE. Thus, GDP equals GNE.

Once GDP is sold, where do the payments flow next? Because GDP measures the value of firm outputs minus the cost of firm inputs, and this remaining flow is paid by firms as income to factors such as the owners of labor, capital, and land employed by the firms. The factors may, in turn, be owned by households, government, or firms, but such distinctions are not important. The key thing in a closed economy is that all such income is paid to domestic entities. It thus equals the total income resources of the economy, also known as **gross national income (GNI).** By this point in our circular flow, we can see that in a closed economy the expenditure on total goods and services GNE equals GDP, which is then paid as income to productive factors GNI.

Once GNI is received by factors, where do the payments flow next? Clearly, there is no way for a closed economy to finance expenditure except out of its own income, so total income is, in turn, spent and must be the same as total expenditure. This is shown by the loop that flows back to the top of Figure 13-1. What we have seen in our tour around the circular flow is that *in a closed economy*, all the economic aggregate measures are equal: GNE equals GDP which equals GNI which equals GNE. *In a closed economy, expenditure is the same as product, which is the same as income.* Our understanding of the closed economy circular flow is complete.

The Flow of Payments in an Open Economy: Incorporating the Balance of Payments Accounts

The closed-economy circular flow shown in Figure 13-1 is simple, neat, and tidy. When a nation opens itself to trade with other nations, however, the flow becomes a good deal more complicated. Figure 13-2 incorporates all of the extra payment flows to and from the rest of the world, which are recorded in a nation's *balance of payments (BOP) accounts.*

The circulating purple arrows on the left side of the figure are just as in the closed-economy case in Figure 13-1. These arrows flow within the purple box, which represents the home country, and do not cross the edge of that box, which represents the international border. The cross-border flows that occur in an open economy are represented by green arrows. There are five key points on the figure where these flows appear.

As before, we start at the top with the home economy's gross national expenditure, $C + I + G$. In an open economy, some home expenditure is used to purchase foreign final goods and services. At point 1, these *imports* are subtracted from home GNE because those goods are not sold by domestic firms. In addition, some foreign expenditure is used to purchase final goods and services from home. These *exports* must be added to home GNE because those goods are sold by domestic firms. (A similar logic applies to intermediate goods.) The difference between payments made for imports and payments received for exports is called the **trade balance (TB),** and it equals net payments to domestic firms due to trade. GNE plus TB equals GDP, the total value of production in the home economy.

At point 2, some home GDP is paid to foreign entities for *factor service imports,* that is, domestic payments to capital, labor, and land owned by foreign entities. Because this income is not paid to factors at home, it is subtracted when computing home income. Similarly, some foreign GDP may be paid to domestic entities as payment for *factor service exports,* that is, foreign payments to capital, labor, and land owned by domestic entities. Because this income is paid to factors at home, it is added when computing home income. The value of factor service exports minus factor service imports is known as **net factor income from abroad (NFIA),** and thus GDP plus NFIA equals GNI, the total income earned by domestic entities from all sources, domestic and foreign.

At point 3, we see that the home country may not retain all of its earned income GNI. Why? Domestic entities might give some of it away—for example, as foreign aid or remittances by migrants to their families back home. Similarly, domestic entities might receive gifts from abroad. Such gifts may take the form of income transfers or be "in kind" transfers of goods and services. They are considered nonmarket transactions, and are referred to as *unilateral transfers.* **Net unilateral transfers (NUT)** equals the value of unilateral transfers the country receives from the rest of the world minus those it gives to the rest of the world. These net transfers have to be added to GNI to calculate **gross national disposable income (GNDI),** and thus GNI plus NUT equals GNDI, which represents the total income resources available to the home country.

FIGURE 13-2

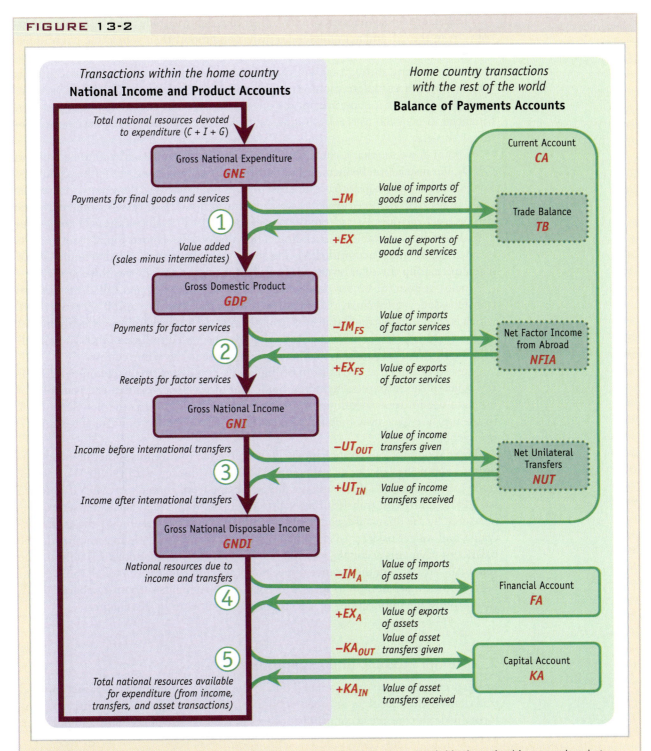

The Open Economy Measurements of national expenditure, product, and income are recorded in the national income and product accounts, with the major categories shown on the left. Measurements of international transactions are recorded in the balance of payments accounts, with the major categories shown on the right. The purple line shows the flow of transactions within the home economy; the green lines show all cross-border transactions.

The balance of payments accounts collect together the trade balance, net factor income from abroad, and net unilateral transfers and report their sum as the **current account (CA),** which is a tally of all international transactions in goods, services, and income (occurring through market transactions or transfers). The current account is not, however, a complete picture of international transactions. Resource flows of goods, services, and income are not the only items that flow between open economies. Financial assets such as stocks, bonds, or real estate are also traded across international borders.

At point 4, we see that a country's capacity to spend is not restricted to be equal to GNDI, but instead can be increased or decreased by trading assets with other countries. When foreign entities pay to acquire assets from home entities, the value of these *asset exports* increases resources available for spending at home. Conversely, when domestic entities pay to acquire assets from the rest of the world, the value of the *asset imports* decreases resources available for spending. The value of asset exports minus asset imports is called the **financial account (FA).** These net asset exports are added to home GNDI when calculating the total resources available for expenditure in the home country.

Finally, at point 5, we see that a country may not only buy and sell assets but also transfer assets as gifts. Such asset transfers are measured by the **capital account (KA),** which is the value of capital transfers from the rest of the world minus those to the rest of the world. These net asset transfers must also be added to home GNDI when calculating the total resources available for expenditure in the home country.

After some effort, at the bottom of Figure 13-2, we have finally computed the entire value of the resources, including home and foreign sources, that are available for home to use for total spending, or gross national expenditure, as the flow loops back to the top. We have now fully modified the circular flow to account for international transactions.[1]

These modifications to the circular flow in Figure 13-2 tell us something very important about the balance of payments. We start at the top with GNE. We add the trade balance to get GDP, we add net factor income from abroad to get GNI, and then we add net unilateral transfers received to get GNDI. We then add net asset exports measured by the financial account and net capital transfers measured by the capital account, and we get back to GNE. That is, we start with GNE, add in *everything* in the balance of payments accounts, and still end up with GNE. What does this tell us? The sum of all the items in the balance of payments account, the net sum of all those cross-border flows, must amount to zero! The balance of payments account *does* balance. We shall explore the implications of this important result later in this chapter.

2 Income, Product, and Expenditure

In the previous section, we sketched out all the important national and international transactions that occur in an open economy. With that overview in mind, we now formally define the key accounting concepts in the two sets of accounts and put them to use.

---

[1] In the past, both the financial and capital accounts were jointly known as "the capital account." This change should be kept in mind not only when consulting older documents but also when listening to contemporary discussion because not everyone cares for the new (and somewhat confusing) nomenclature.

Three Approaches to Measuring Economic Activity

There are three main approaches to the measurement of aggregate economic activity within a country:

- The *expenditure approach* looks at the demand for goods: it examines how much is spent on demand for final goods and services. The key measure is GNE.

- The *product approach* looks at the supply of goods: it measures the value of all goods and services produced as output minus the value of goods used as inputs in production. The key measure is GDP.

- The *income approach* focuses on payments to owners of factors: it tracks the amount of income they receive. The key measures are gross national income GNI and gross national disposable income GNDI (which includes net transfers).

It is crucial to note that in a closed economy the three approaches generate the same number: In a closed economy, GNE = GDP = GNI. In an open economy, however, this is not true.

From GNE to GDP: Accounting for Trade in Goods and Services

As before, we start with gross national expenditure, or GNE, which is *by definition* the sum of consumption *C*, investment *I*, and government consumption *G*. Formally, these three elements are defined, respectively, as follows:

- *Personal consumption expenditures* (usually called "consumption") equal total spending by private households on final goods and services, including non-durable goods such as food, durable goods such as a television, and services such as window cleaning or gardening.

- *Gross private domestic investment* (usually called "investment") equals total spending by firms or households on final goods and services to make additions to the stock of capital. Investment includes construction of a new house or a new factory, the purchase of new equipment, and net increases in inventories of goods held by firms (i.e., unsold output).

- *Government consumption expenditures and gross investment* (often called "government consumption") equal spending by the public sector on final goods and services, including spending on public works, national defense, the police, and the civil service. It does *not* include any transfer payments or income redistributions, such as Social Security or unemployment insurance payments—these are *not* purchases of goods or services, just rearrangements of private spending power.

As for GDP, it is *by definition* the value of all goods and services produced as output by firms, minus the value of all intermediate goods and services purchased as inputs by firms. It is thus a product measure, in contrast to the expenditure measure GNE. Because of trade, not all of the GNE payments go to GDP, and not all of GDP payments arise from GNE.

To adjust GNE and find the contribution going into GDP, we must *subtract* the value of final goods imported (home spending that goes to foreign firms) and we must *add* the value of final goods exported (foreign spending that goes to home firms). In addition, we can't forget about intermediate goods: we must *subtract* the value of imported intermediates (in GDP they also count as home's purchased inputs) and we must *add* the value of exported intermediates (in GDP they also count as home's produced output).[2] So, adding it all up, to get from GNE to GDP, we must add the value of *all* exports denoted *EX* and subtract the value of *all* imports *IM*. Thus,

$$\underbrace{GDP}_{\substack{\text{Gross domestic}\\\text{product}}} = \underbrace{C + I + G}_{\substack{\text{Gross national}\\\text{expenditure}\\GNE}} + \underbrace{\left(\underbrace{EX}_{\substack{\text{All exports,}\\\text{final \& intermediate}}} - \underbrace{IM}_{\substack{\text{All imports,}\\\text{final \& intermediate}}}\right)}_{\substack{\text{Trade balance}\\TB}} \quad (13\text{-}1)$$

This important formula for GDP says that *gross domestic product is equal to gross national expenditure (GNE) plus the trade balance (TB)*.

Although the adjustments for final goods trade might be more obvious or familiar in the above derivation, it is also crucial to understand and account for intermediate goods transactions properly because, due to globalization and outsourcing, trade in intermediate goods has surged in recent decades. For example, according to the 2010 *Economic Report of the President*, some estimates suggest that one-third of the growth of world trade from 1970 to 1990 was driven by intermediate trade arising from the growth of "vertically specialized" production processes (outsourcing, offshoring, etc.). More strikingly, as of 2010, it appears that—probably for the first time in world history—total world trade now consists rather more of trade in intermediate goods (60%) than in final goods (40%).

The trade balance, TB, is also often referred to as *net exports*. Because it is the net value of exports minus imports, it may be positive or negative.

If *TB* > 0, exports are greater than imports and we say a country has a *trade surplus*.

If *TB* < 0, imports are greater than exports and we say a country has a *trade deficit*.

In 2009 the United States had a trade deficit because its trade balance was −$392 billion.

From GDP to GNI: Accounting for Trade in Factor Services

Trade in factor services occurs when, say, the home country is paid income by a foreign country as compensation for the use of labor, capital, and land owned by home entities but in service in the foreign country. We say the home country is exporting factor services to the foreign country and receiving factor income in return.

An example of a labor service export is a home country professional temporarily working overseas, say, a U.S. architect freelancing in London. The wages she earns in the United Kingdom are factor income for the United States. An example of trade in capital services is *foreign direct investment*. For example, U.S.-owned factories in Ireland generate income for their U.S. owners; Japanese-owned factories in the United States generate income for their Japanese owners. Other examples of payments for

---

[2] Note that intermediate inputs sold by home firms and purchased by other home firms cancel out in GDP, in both closed and open economies. For example, suppose there are two firms A and B, and Firm A makes a $200 table (a final good) and buys $100 in wood (an intermediate input) from Firm B, and there is no trade. Total sales are $300; but GDP or value added is total sales of $300 minus the $100 of inputs purchased; so GDP is equal to $200. Now suppose Firm B makes and exports $50 of extra wood. After this change, GDP is equal to $250. You can see here that GDP *is not equal to* the value of final goods produced in an economy (although it is quite often claimed, mistakenly, that this is a definition of GDP).

capital services include income from overseas *financial* assets such as foreign securities, real estate, or loans to governments, firms, and households.

These payments are accounted for as additions to and subtractions from home GDP. Some home GDP is paid out as *income payments* to foreign entities for factor services imported by the home country IM_{FS}. In addition, domestic entities receive some income payments from foreign entities as *income receipts* for factor services exported by the home country EX_{FS}.

Accounting for these income flows, gross national income (GNI), the total income earned by domestic entities, is given by GDP plus the income from overseas EX_{FS}, minus the income going overseas IM_{FS}.[3] The last two terms, income receipts minus income payments, are the home country's *net factor income from abroad*, $NFIA = EX_{FS} - IM_{FS}$. This may be a positive or negative number, depending on whether income receipts are larger or smaller than income payments.

With the help of the GDP expression in Equation (13-1), we obtain the key formula for GNI that says the *gross national income equals gross domestic product (GDP) plus net factor income from abroad (NFIA)*.

$$ GNI = \underbrace{\underbrace{C + I + G}_{\substack{\text{Gross national expenditure} \\ GNE}} + \underbrace{(EX - IM)}_{\substack{\text{Trade balance} \\ TB}}}_{GDP} + \underbrace{(EX_{FS} - IM_{FS})}_{\substack{\text{Net factor income from abroad} \\ NFIA}} \qquad (13\text{-}2) $$

In 2009 the United States received income payments from foreigners EX_{FS} of $589 billion and made income payments to foreigners IM_{FS} of $484 billion, so the net factor income from abroad NFIA was +$105 billion. Earlier in this chapter, we computed U.S. GDP to be $14,256 billion; because of net factor income from abroad, U.S. GNI was a little higher at $14,361 billion.

APPLICATION

Celtic Tiger or Tortoise?

International trade in factor services (as measured by NFIA) can generate a difference between the product and income measures in a country's national accounts. In the United States, this difference is typically small, but at times NFIA can play a major role in the measurement of a country's economic activity.

In the 1970s, Ireland was one of the poorer countries in Europe, but over the next three decades it experienced speedy economic growth with an accompanying investment boom now known as the Irish Miracle. From 1980 to 2007, Irish real GDP per person grew at a phenomenal rate of 4.1% per year—not as rapid as in some developing countries but extremely rapid by the standards of the rich countries of the European Union (EU) or the Organization for Economic Cooperation and Development (OECD). Comparisons with fast-growing Asian economies—the "Asian Tigers"—soon had people speaking of the "Celtic Tiger" when referring to Ireland.

---

[3] GNI is the accounting concept formerly known as GNP, or *gross national product*. The term GNP is still often used, but GNI is technically more accurate because the concept is a measurement of income rather than product. Note that taxes and subsidies on production and imports are counted in GNE (both) and GDP (production taxes only). This treatment ensures that the tax income paid to the home country is properly counted as a part of home income. We simplify the presentation in this textbook by assuming there are no taxes and subsidies.

Did Irish citizens enjoy all of these gains? No. Figure 13-3 shows that in 1980 Ireland's annual net factor income from abroad was virtually nil—about €–70 per person (in 2007 real euros) or –0.5% of GDP. Yet by 2000, around 15% to 20% of Irish GDP was being used to make net factor income payments to foreigners who had invested heavily in the Irish economy by buying stocks and bonds and by purchasing land and building factories on it. (By some estimates, 75% of Ireland's industrial-sector GDP originated in foreign-owned plants in 2004.) These foreign investors expected their big Irish investments to generate income, and so they did, in the form of net factor payments abroad amounting to almost one-fifth of Irish GDP. This meant that Irish GNI (the income paid to Irish people and firms) was a lot smaller than Irish GDP.[4] Ireland's net factor income from abroad has remained large and negative ever since.

This example shows how GDP can be a misleading measure of economic performance. When ranked by GDP per person, Ireland was the 4th richest OECD economy

FIGURE 13-3

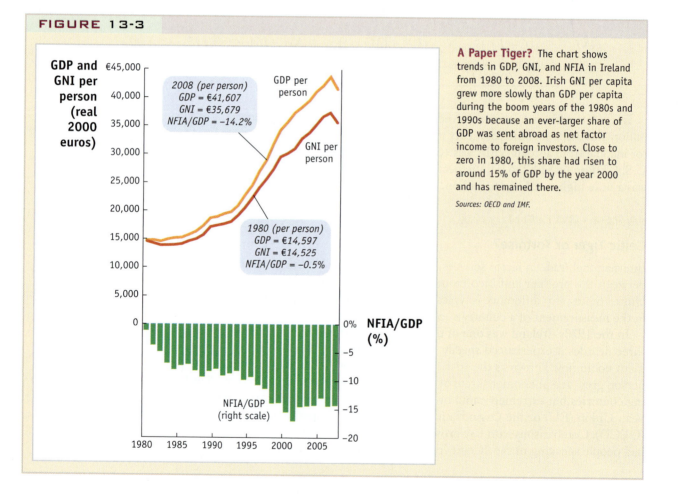

A Paper Tiger? The chart shows trends in GDP, GNI, and NFIA in Ireland from 1980 to 2008. Irish GNI per capita grew more slowly than GDP per capita during the boom years of the 1980s and 1990s because an ever-larger share of GDP was sent abroad as net factor income to foreign investors. Close to zero in 1980, this share had risen to around 15% of GDP by the year 2000 and has remained there.

Sources: OECD and IMF.

---

[4] Irish GDP might have been inflated as a result of various accounting problems. Some special factors exacerbated the difference between GDP and GNI in Ireland, such as special tax incentives that encouraged foreign firms to keep their accounts in a way which generated high profits "on paper" at their low-tax Irish subsidiaries rather than in their high-tax home country. For these reasons, many economists believe that Irish GNI, despite being more conservative, might be a truer measure of the economy's performance.

in 2004; when ranked by GNI per person, it was only 17th richest.[5] The Irish outflow of net factor payments is certainly an extreme case, but it serves to underscore an important point about income measurement in open economies. Any country that relies heavily on foreign investment to generate economic growth is not getting a free lunch. Irish GNI per person grew at "only" 3.6% from 1980 to the peak in 2007; this was 0.5% per year less than the growth rate of GDP per person over the same period. Living standards grew impressively, but the more humble GNI figures may give a more accurate measure of what the Irish Miracle actually meant for the Irish. ■

From GNI to GNDI: Accounting for Transfers of Income

So far, we have fully described market transactions in goods, services, and income. However, many international transactions take place outside of markets. International nonmarket transfers of goods, services, and income include such things as foreign aid by governments in the form of *official development assistance* (ODA) and other help, private charitable gifts to foreign recipients, and income remittances sent to relatives or friends in other countries. These transfers are "gifts" and may take the form of goods and services (food aid, volunteer medical services) or income transfers.

If a country receives transfers worth UT_{IN} and gives transfers worth UT_{OUT}, then its net unilateral transfers, NUT, are $NUT = UT_{IN} - UT_{OUT}$. Because this is a net amount, it may be positive or negative.

In general, net unilateral transfers play a small role in the income and product accounts for most high-income countries (net outgoing transfers are typically no more than 5% of GNI). But they are an important part of the gross national disposable income (GNDI) for many low-income countries that receive a great deal of foreign aid or migrant remittances, as seen in Figure 13-4.

Measuring national generosity is highly controversial and a recurring theme of current affairs (see **Headlines: Are Rich Countries "Stingy" with Foreign Aid?**). You might think that net unilateral transfers are in some ways a better measure of a country's generosity toward foreigners than official development assistance, which is but one component. For example, looking at the year 2000, a USAID report, *Foreign Aid in the National Interest*, claimed that while U.S. ODA was only $9.9 billion, other U.S. government assistance (such as contributions to global security and humanitarian assistance) amounted to $12.7 billion, and assistance from private U.S. citizens totaled $33.6 billion—for total foreign assistance equal to $56.2 billion, more than five times the level of ODA.

To include the impact of aid and all other transfers in the overall calculation of a country's income resources, we must add net unilateral transfers to gross national income. Using the definition of GNI in Equation (13-2), we obtain a full measure of national income in an open economy, known as gross national disposable income (GNDI), henceforth denoted Y:

$$\underbrace{Y}_{GNDI} = \underbrace{C + I + G}_{GNE} + \underbrace{(EX - IM)}_{\substack{\text{Trade balance} \\ TB}} + \underbrace{(EX_{FS} - IM_{FS})}_{\substack{\text{Net factor income} \\ \text{from abroad} \\ NFIA}} + \underbrace{(UT_{IN} - UT_{OUT})}_{\substack{\text{Net unilateral} \\ \text{transfers} \\ NUT}} \quad (13\text{-}3)$$

$$\underbrace{\phantom{C + I + G + (EX - IM) + (EX_{FS} - IM_{FS})}}_{GNI}$$

In general, economists and policy makers prefer to use GNDI to measure national income. Why? GDP is not a true measure of income because, unlike GNI, it does not

---

[5] Joe Cullen, "There's Lies, Damned Lies, and Wealth Statistics," *Irish Times*, May 1, 2004.

FIGURE 13-4

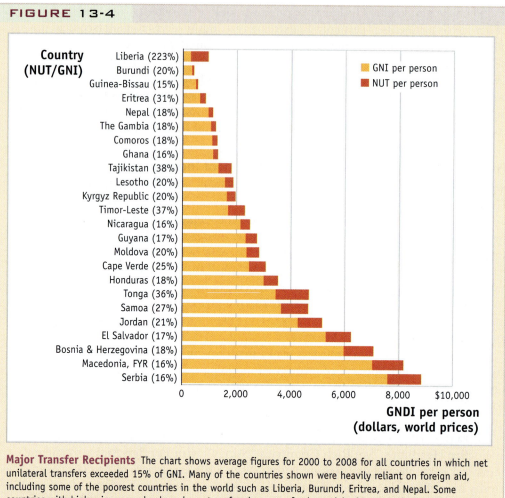

Major Transfer Recipients The chart shows average figures for 2000 to 2008 for all countries in which net unilateral transfers exceeded 15% of GNI. Many of the countries shown were heavily reliant on foreign aid, including some of the poorest countries in the world such as Liberia, Burundi, Eritrea, and Nepal. Some countries with higher incomes also have large transfers because of substantial migrant remittances from a large number of emigrant workers overseas, for example, Tonga, Jordan, El Salvador, and Cape Verde.

Source: World Bank, World Development Indicators.

include net factor income from abroad. GNI is not a perfect measure either because it leaves out international transfers. GNDI is a preferred measure because it most closely corresponds to the resources available to the nation's households, and national welfare depends most closely on this accounting measure.

What the National Economic Aggregates Tell Us

We have explained all the international flows shown in Figure 13-2 and have developed three key equations that link the important national economic aggregates in an open economy:

- To get from GNE to GDP, we add TB (Equation 13-1).
- To get from GDP to GNI, we add NFIA (Equation 13-2).
- To get from GNI to GDNI, we add NUT (Equation 13-3).

HEADLINES

Are Rich Countries "Stingy" with Foreign Aid?

The Asian tsunami on December 26, 2004, was one of the worst natural disasters of modern times. Hundreds of thousands of people were killed and billions of dollars of damage was done. Some aftershocks were felt in international politics. Jan Egeland, UN undersecretary general for humanitarian affairs and emergency relief, declared, "It is beyond me why we are so stingy." His comments rocked the boat in many rich countries, especially in the United States where official aid fell short of the UN goal of 0.7% of GNI. However, the United States gives in other ways, making judgments about stinginess far from straightforward.

Is the United States stingy when it comes to foreign aid? . . . The answer depends on how you measure. . . .

In terms of traditional foreign aid, the United States gave $16.25 billion in 2003, as measured by the Organization of Economic Cooperation and Development (OECD), the club of the world's rich industrial nations. That was almost double the aid by the next biggest net spender, Japan ($8.8 billion). Other big donors were France ($7.2 billion) and Germany ($6.8 billion).

But critics point out that the United States is much bigger than those individual nations. As a group, member nations of the European Union have a bit larger population than the United States and give a great deal more money in foreign aid—$49.2 billion altogether in 2003.

In relation to affluence, the United States lies at the bottom of the list of rich donor nations. It gave 0.15% of gross national income to official development assistance in 2003. By this measure, Norway at 0.92% was the most generous, with Denmark next at 0.84%.

Bring those numbers down to an everyday level and the average American gave 13 cents a day in government aid, according to David Roodman, a researcher at the Center for Global Development (CGD) in Washington. Throw in another nickel a day from private giving. That private giving is high by international standards, yet not enough to close the gap with Norway, whose citizens average $1.02 per day in government aid and 24 cents per day in private aid. . . .

[Also], the United States has a huge defense budget, some of which benefits

An Indonesian soldier thanks two U.S. airmen after a U.S. Navy helicopter delivered fresh water to Indonesian tsunami victims. The normal operating costs of military assets used for humanitarian purposes are not fully counted as part of official development assistance.

developing countries. Making a judgment call, the CGD includes the cost of UN peacekeeping activities and other military assistance approved by a multilateral institution, such as NATO. So the United States gets credit for its spending in Kosovo, Australia for its intervention in East Timor, and Britain for military money spent to bring more stability to Sierra Leone. . . .

"Not to belittle what we are doing, we shouldn't get too self-congratulatory," says Frederick Barton, an economist at the Center for Strategic and International Studies in Washington.

Source: "Foreign Aid: Is the U.S. Stingy?" *Christian Science Monitor/MSN Money, January 6, 2005.*

To go one step further, we can group the three cross-border terms into an umbrella term that is called the current account, CA:

$$\underbrace{Y}_{GNDI} = \underbrace{C + I + G}_{GNE} + \{\underbrace{(EX - IM)}_{\substack{\text{Trade balance}\\ TB}} + \underbrace{(EX_{FS} - IM_{FS})}_{\substack{\text{Net factor income}\\ \text{from abroad}\\ NFIA}} + \underbrace{(UT_{IN} - UT_{OUT})}_{\substack{\text{Net unilateral}\\ \text{transfers}\\ NUT}}\} \quad (13\text{-}4)$$

$$\underbrace{\phantom{(EX - IM) + (EX_{FS} - IM_{FS}) + (UT_{IN} - UT_{OUT})}}_{\substack{\text{Current account}\\ CA}}$$

It is important to understand the intuition for this expression. On the left is our full income measure, GNDI. The first term on the right is GNE, which measures payments by home entities. The other terms on the right, combined into CA, measure all net payments to home arising from the full range of international transactions in goods, services, and income.

Remember that in a closed economy, there are no international transactions so TB and NFIA and NUT (and hence CA) are all zero. Therefore, in a closed economy, the four main aggregates GNDI, GNI, GDP, and GNE are exactly equal. In an open economy, however, each of these four aggregates can differ from the others.

Understanding the Data for the National Economic Aggregates

Now that we've learned how a nation's principal economic aggregates are affected by international transactions in theory, let's see how this works in practice. In this section, we take a look at some data from the real world to see how they are recorded and presented in official statistics.

Table 13-1 shows data for the United States in 2009 reported by the Bureau of Economic Analysis in the official national income and product accounts.

Lines 1 to 3 of the table show the components of gross national expenditure, GNE. Personal consumption expenditures *C* were $10,089 billion, gross private domestic investment *I* was $1,629 billion, and government consumption *G* was $2,931 billion. Summing up, GNE was equal to $14,649 billion, which is shown on line 4.

On line 5 appears the trade balance, *TB*, which was the net export of goods and services, in the amount of −$392 billion. (That net exports are negative means that the United States imported more goods and services than it exported.) Adding this to GNE gives gross domestic product GDP on line 6, which amounted to $14,256 billion. Next we account for net factor income from abroad NFIA, equal to +$105 billion on line 7.

TABLE 13-1

U.S. Economic Aggregates in 2009 The table shows the computation of GDP, GNI, and GNDI in 2009 in billions of dollars using the components of gross national expenditure, the trade balance, international income payments, and unilateral transfers.

Line	Category	Symbol	$ billions
1	Consumption (personal consumption expenditures)	*C*	$10,089
2	+ Investment (gross private domestic investment)	*I*	1,629
3	+ Government consumption (government expenditures)	*G*	2,931
4	= Gross national expenditure	*GNE*	14,649
5	+ Trade balance	*TB*	−392
6	= Gross domestic product	*GDP*	14,256
7	+ Net factor income from abroad	*NFIA*	105
8	= Gross national income	*GNI*	14,361
9	+ Net unilateral transfers	*NUT*	−125
10	= Gross national disposable income	*GNDI*	14,236

Note: Details may not add to totals because of rounding.

Source: U.S. Bureau of Economic Analysis, NIPA Tables 1.1.5 and 4.1, using the NIPA definition of the United States.

Adding this to GDP gives gross national income GNI, equal to $14,361 billion as shown on line 8.

Finally, to get to the bottom line, we account for the fact that the United States receives net unilateral transfers from the rest of the world of −$125 billion (i.e., the United States makes net transfers to the rest of the world of $125 billion) on line 9. Adding these negative transfers to GNI results in a gross national disposable income GNDI of $14,236 billion on line 10.

Some Recent Trends Figures 13-5 and 13-6 show recent trends in various components of U.S. national income. Examining these breakdowns gives us a sense of the relative magnitude and economic significance of each component.

In Figure 13-5, GNE is shown as the sum of consumption C, investment I, and government consumption G. Consumption accounts for about 70% of GNE, while government consumption G accounts for about 15%. Both of these components are relatively stable. Investment accounts for the rest (about 15% of GNE), but investment tends to fluctuate more than C and G (e.g., it fell steeply in the great recession of 2008–2010). Over the period shown, GNE grew from $6,000 billion to about $15,000 billion in current dollars.

Figure 13-6 shows the trade balance (TB), net factor income from abroad (NFIA), and net unilateral transfers (NUT), which constitute the current account (CA). In the United States, the trade balance is the dominant component in the current account. For the entire period shown, the trade balance has been in deficit and has grown larger

---

FIGURE 13-5

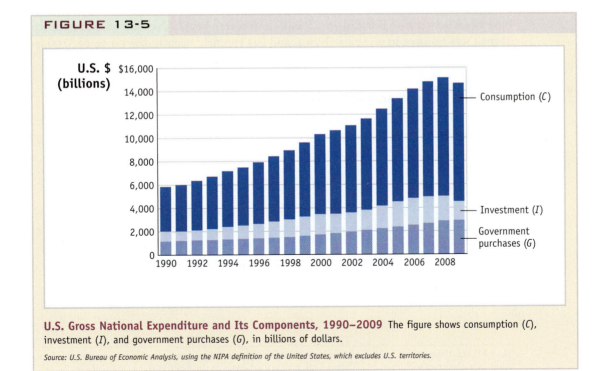

U.S. Gross National Expenditure and Its Components, 1990–2009 The figure shows consumption (C), investment (I), and government purchases (G), in billions of dollars.

Source: U.S. Bureau of Economic Analysis, using the NIPA definition of the United States, which excludes U.S. territories.

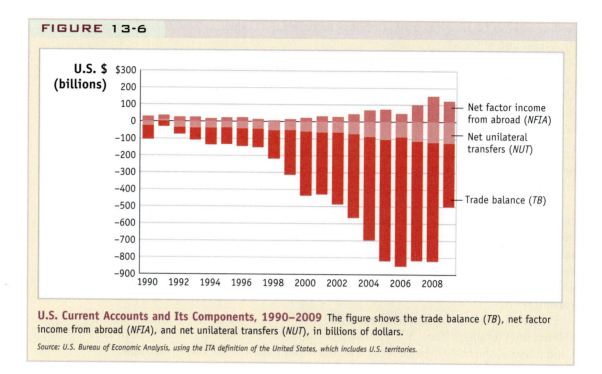

FIGURE 13-6

U.S. Current Accounts and Its Components, 1990–2009 The figure shows the trade balance (*TB*), net factor income from abroad (*NFIA*), and net unilateral transfers (*NUT*), in billions of dollars.

Source: U.S. Bureau of Economic Analysis, using the ITA definition of the United States, which includes U.S. territories.

over time. From 2004 to 2008, the trade balance was close to –$800 billion, but it fell during the recession as global trade declined. Net unilateral transfers, a smaller figure, have been between –$100 and –$125 billion in recent years.[6] Net factor income from abroad was positive in all years shown, and has recently been in the range of $100 to $150 billion.

What the Current Account Tells Us

Because it tells us, in effect, whether a nation is spending more or less than its income, the current account plays a central role in economic debates. In particular, it is important to remember that Equation (13-4) can be concisely written as

$$Y = C + I + G + CA \tag{13-5}$$

This equation is the open-economy **national income identity.** It tells us that the current account represents the difference between national income *Y* (or GNDI) and gross national expenditure GNE (or *C* + *I* + *G*). Hence,

GNDI is greater than GNE if and only if CA is positive, or in surplus.

GNDI is less than GNE if and only if CA is negative, or in deficit.

---

[6] In 1991 the United States was a net recipient of unilateral transfers, as a result of transfer payments from other rich countries willing to help defray U.S. military expenses in the Gulf War.

Subtracting $C + G$ from both sides of the last identity, we can see that the current account is also the difference between **national saving** ($S = Y - C - G$) and investment:

$$\underset{Y-C-G}{\underbrace{S}} = I + CA \qquad\qquad (13\text{-}6)$$

where national saving is defined as income minus consumption minus government consumption. This equation is called the **current account identity** even though it is just a rearrangement of the national income identity. Thus,

S is greater than I if and only if CA is positive, or in surplus.

S is less than I if and only if CA is negative, or in deficit.

These last two equations give us two ways of interpreting the current account, and tell us something important about a nation's economic condition. A current account deficit measures how much a country spends in excess of its income or—equivalently—how it saves too little relative to its investment needs. (Surpluses mean the opposite.) We can now understand the widespread use of the current account deficit in the media as a measure of how a country is "spending more than it earns" or "saving too little" or "living beyond its means."

APPLICATION

Global Imbalances

We can apply what we have learned to study some remarkable features of financial globalization in recent years, including the explosion in *global imbalances:* the widely discussed current account surpluses and deficits (seen in various countries and regions) that have been of great concern to policy makers.

Figure 13-7 shows trends since 1980 in saving, investment, and the current account for four groups of industrial countries. All flows are expressed as ratios relative to each region's GDP. Some trends stand out. First, in all regions, saving and investment have been on a marked downward trend for the past 30 years. From its peak, the ratio of saving to GDP fell by about 8 percentage points in the United States, about 15 percentage points in Japan, and about 6 percentage points in the Euro zone and other countries. Investment ratios typically followed a downward path in all regions, too. In Japan, this decline was steeper than the savings, but in the United States, there was hardly any decline in investment.

On some level, these trends reflect the recent history of the industrialized countries. The U.S. economy grew rapidly after 1990 and the Japanese economy grew very slowly, with other countries in between. The fast-growing U.S. economy generated high investment demand, while in slumping Japan investment collapsed; other regions maintained middling levels of growth and investment. Saving in all the countries reflects the demographic shift toward aging populations with fewer workers for each elderly person. This trend is commonly associated with decreased saving as the "demographic burden" of the unproductive retirees raises consumption relative to income.

The current account identity tells us that *CA* equals *S* minus *I*. Thus, investment and saving trends have a predictable impact on the current accounts of industrial countries. Because saving fell faster than investment in the United States, the current account

FIGURE 13-7

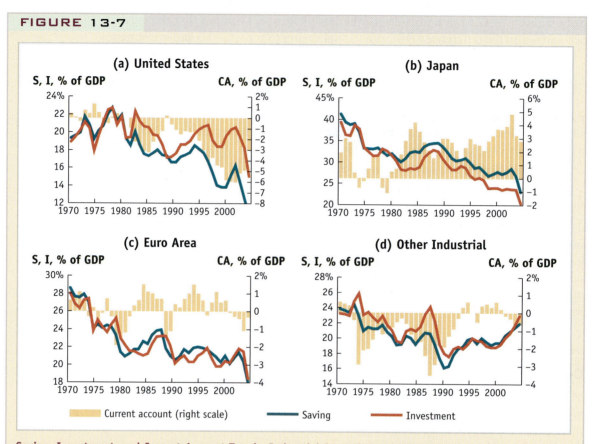

Saving, Investment, and Current Account Trends: Industrial Countries The charts show saving, investment, and the current account as a percent of each subregion's GDP for four groups of advanced countries. The United States has seen both saving and investment fall since 1980, but saving has fallen further than investment, opening up a large current account deficit approaching 6% of GDP in recent years. Japan's experience is the opposite: investment fell further than saving, opening up a large current account surplus of about 3% to 5% of GDP. The Euro area has also seen saving and investment fall but has been closer to balance overall. Other advanced countries (e.g., non-Euro area EU countries, Canada, Australia, etc.) have tended to run large current account deficits which have recently moved toward balance.

Source: IMF, World Economic Outlook, September 2005, and updates.

moved sharply into deficit, a trend that was only briefly arrested in the early 1990s. By 2003–2005 the U.S. current account was at a record deficit level close to –6% of U.S. GDP. In Japan, saving fell less than investment, so the opposite happened: a very big current account surplus opened up in the 1980s and 1990s, and it is currently near 4% of Japanese GDP. In the other industrial regions, saving and investment did not diverge so much, so the current account has recently remained closer to balance.

To uncover the sources of the trends in total saving, Figure 13-8 examines two of its components, public and private saving. We define **private saving** as that part of *after-tax* private sector disposable income that is *not* devoted to private consumption C. After-tax private sector disposable income, in turn, is defined as national income Y minus the net taxes T paid by households to the government. Hence, private saving S_p is

$$S_p = Y - T - C \tag{13-7}$$

FIGURE 13-8

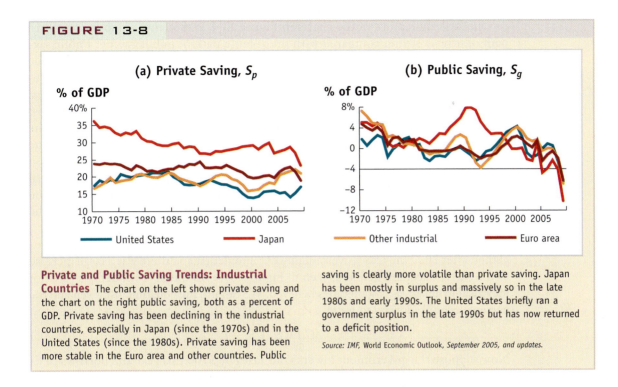

(a) Private Saving, S_p

% of GDP

(b) Public Saving, S_g

% of GDP

United States — Japan — Other industrial — Euro area

Private and Public Saving Trends: Industrial Countries The chart on the left shows private saving and the chart on the right public saving, both as a percent of GDP. Private saving has been declining in the industrial countries, especially in Japan (since the 1970s) and in the United States (since the 1980s). Private saving has been more stable in the Euro area and other countries. Public saving is clearly more volatile than private saving. Japan has been mostly in surplus and massively so in the late 1980s and early 1990s. The United States briefly ran a government surplus in the late 1990s but has now returned to a deficit position.

Source: IMF, World Economic Outlook, September 2005, and updates.

Private saving can be a positive number, but if the private sector consumption exceeds after-tax disposable income, then private saving will be negative. (Here, the private sector includes households and private firms, which are ultimately owned by households.)

Similarly, we define **government saving** or **public saving** as the difference between tax revenue T received by the government and government purchases G.[7] Hence, public saving S_g equals

$$S_g = T - G \qquad (13\text{-}8)$$

Government saving is positive when tax revenue exceeds government consumption $(T > G)$ and the government runs a *budget surplus*. If the government runs a *budget deficit*, however, government consumption exceeds tax revenue $(G > T)$, and public saving is negative.

If we add these last two equations, we see that private saving plus government saving equals total national saving, since

$$S = Y - C - G = \underbrace{(Y - T - C)}_{\text{Private saving}} + \underbrace{(T - G)}_{\text{Government saving}} = S_p + S_g \qquad (13\text{-}9)$$

In this last equation, taxes cancel out and do not affect saving in the aggregate because they are simply a transfer from the private sector to the public sector.

---

[7] Here, the government includes all levels of government: national/federal, state/regional, local/municipal, and so on.

One striking feature of the charts in Figure 13-8 is the fairly smooth downward path of private saving compared with the volatile path of public saving. Public saving is government tax revenue minus spending, and it fluctuates greatly as economic conditions change. We see that over the years private saving (by firms and households) has dropped the most in Japan, with a smaller drop seen in the United States. In other countries, the trend has been a little steadier. As for public saving, the most noticeable feature is the very large surpluses run up in Japan in the boom of the 1980s and early 1990s that subsequently disappeared during the long slump in the mid- to late 1990s and early 2000s. In other regions, surpluses in the 1970s soon gave way to deficits in the 1980s, and despite occasional improvements in the fiscal balance (as in the late 1990s), deficits have been the norm in the public sector. The United States witnessed a particularly sharp move from surplus to deficit after the year 2000.

Do government deficits cause current account deficits? Sometimes they do go together: after 2000 the U.S. government went into deficit and there was a large increase in the current account deficit as seen in Figure 13-7. But these "twin deficits" are not inextricably linked, as is sometimes believed. We can use the equation just given and the current account identity to write

$$CA = S_p + S_g - I \qquad \text{(13-10)}$$

Now suppose the government lowers your taxes by $100 this year and borrows to finance the resulting deficit but also says you will be taxed by an extra $100 plus interest next year to pay off the debt. The theory of *Ricardian equivalence* asserts that you and other households will save the tax cut to pay next year's tax increase, so a fall in public saving is fully offset by a contemporaneous rise in private saving—and in the last equation the current account is *unchanged*. However, empirical studies do not support this theory: private saving does not fully offset government saving in practice.[8]

How large is the effect of a government deficit on the current account deficit? Research suggests that a change of 1% of GDP in the government deficit (or surplus) coincides with a 0.2% to 0.4% of GDP change in the current account deficit (or surplus), a result consistent with a partial Ricardian offset.

A second reason why the current account might move independently of saving (public or private) is that there may be a contemporaneous change in the level of investment in the last equation. A comparison of Figures 13-7 and 13-8 shows this effect at work. For example, we can see from Figure 13-7 that the large U.S. current account deficits of the early to mid-1990s were driven by an investment boom, even as total saving rose slightly, driven by an increase in public saving seen in Figure 13-8. Here there was no correlation between government deficit (falling) and current account deficit (rising).

Finally, Figure 13-9 shows global trends in saving, investment, and the current account for industrial countries, developing countries that are most financially integrated into the world economy (emerging markets and oil exporters), and all countries. The large weight of the U.S. economy means that in aggregate, the industrial countries have shifted into current account deficit over this period, a trend that has been offset by a shift toward surplus in the developing countries. The industrialized

---

[8] Menzie D. Chinn and Hiro Ito, 2007, "Current Account Balances, Financial Development and Institutions: Assaying the World 'Saving Glut,'" *Journal of International Money and Finance*, 26(4): 546–569.

FIGURE 13-9

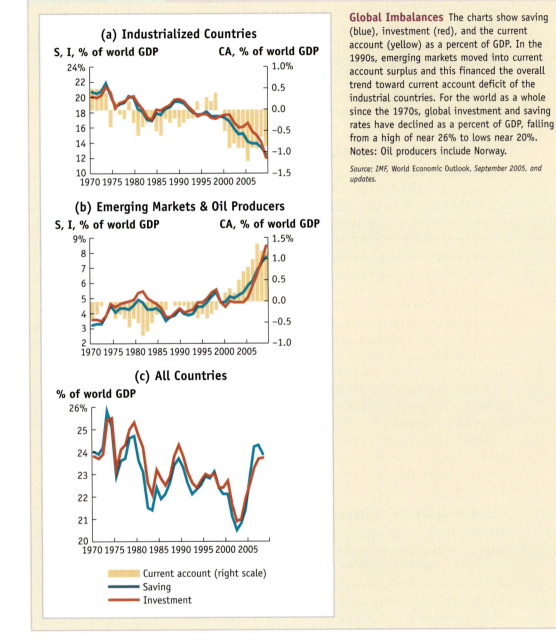

(a) Industrialized Countries

S, I, % of world GDP   CA, % of world GDP

(b) Emerging Markets & Oil Producers

S, I, % of world GDP   CA, % of world GDP

(c) All Countries

% of world GDP

Current account (right scale)
Saving
Investment

Global Imbalances The charts show saving (blue), investment (red), and the current account (yellow) as a percent of GDP. In the 1990s, emerging markets moved into current account surplus and this financed the overall trend toward current account deficit of the industrial countries. For the world as a whole since the 1970s, global investment and saving rates have declined as a percent of GDP, falling from a high of near 26% to lows near 20%. Notes: Oil producers include Norway.

Source: IMF, World Economic Outlook, September 2005, and updates.

countries all followed a trend of declining investment and saving ratios, but the developing countries saw the opposite trend: rising investment and saving ratios. For the developing countries, however, the saving increase was larger than the investment increase, allowing a current account surplus to open up. For the world as a whole, however, the industrial country trend dominates—because the GDP weight of those countries is still so large. Globally, saving and investment ratios have fallen in the past 30 years. ■

3 The Balance of Payments

In the previous section, we saw that the current account summarizes the flow of all international market transactions in goods, services, and factor services plus nonmarket transfers. In this section, we look at what's left: international transactions in assets. These transactions are of great importance because they tell us how the current account is financed and, hence, whether a country is becoming more or less indebted to the rest of the world. We begin by looking at how transactions in assets are accounted for, once again building on the intuition developed in Figure 13-2.[9]

Accounting for Asset Transactions: the Financial Account

The financial account (FA) records transactions between residents and nonresidents that involve financial assets. The total value of financial assets that are received by the rest of the world from the home country is the home country's *export of assets*, denoted EX_A (the subscript "A" stands for asset). The total value of financial assets that are received by the home country from the rest of the world in all transactions is the home country's *import of assets*, denoted IM_A.

The financial account measures all "movement" of financial assets across the international border. By this, we mean a movement from home to foreign ownership, or vice versa, even if the assets do not physically move. This definition also covers all types of assets: real assets such as land or structures, and financial assets such as debt (bonds, loans) or equity. The financial account also includes assets issued by any entity (firms, governments, households) in any country (home or overseas). Finally, the financial account includes market transactions as well as transfers, or gifts of assets.

Subtracting asset imports from asset exports yields the home country's net overall balance on asset transactions, which is known as the financial account, where $FA = EX_A - IM_A$. A negative FA means that the country has imported more assets than it has exported; a positive FA means the country has exported more assets than it has imported. The financial account therefore measures how the country accumulates or decumulates assets through international transactions.

Accounting for Asset Transactions: the Capital Account

The capital account (KA) covers two remaining areas of asset movement of minor quantitative significance. One is the acquisition and disposal of nonfinancial, nonproduced assets (e.g., patents, copyrights, trademarks, franchises, etc.). They have to be included here because such nonfinancial assets do not appear in the financial account, although like financial assets, they can be bought and sold with resulting payments flows. The other important item in the capital account is capital transfers (i.e., gifts of assets), an example of which is the forgiveness of debts.[10]

---

[9] Officially, following the 1993 revision to the System of National Accounts by the U.N. Statistical Office, the place where international transactions are recorded should be called "rest of the world account" or the "external transactions account." The United States calls it the "international transactions account." However, the older terminology was the "balance of payments account," and this usage persists, so we adopt it here.

[10] The capital account does *not* include involuntary debt cancellation, such as results from unilateral defaults. Changes in assets and liabilities due to defaults are counted as capital losses, or valuation effects, which are discussed later in this chapter.

As with unilateral income transfers, capital transfers must be accounted for properly. For example, the giver of an asset must deduct the value of the gift in the capital account to offset the export of the asset, which is recorded in the financial account, because in the case of a gift the export generates no associated payment. Similarly, recipients of capital transfers need to record them to offset the import of the asset recorded in the financial account.

Using similar notation to that employed with unilateral transfers of income, we denote capital transfers received by the home country as KA_{IN} and capital transfers given by the home country as KA_{OUT}. The capital account, $KA = KA_{IN} - KA_{OUT}$, denotes net capital transfers received. A negative KA indicates that more capital transfers were given by the home country than it received; positive KA indicates that the home country received more capital transfers than it made.

The capital account is a minor and technical accounting item for most developed countries. In some developing countries, however, the capital account can play an important role because in some years nonmarket debt forgiveness can be large, whereas market-based international financial transactions may be small.

Accounting for Home and Foreign Assets

Asset trades in the financial account can be broken down into two types: assets issued by home entities (home assets) and assets issued by foreign entities (foreign assets). This is of economic interest, and sometimes of political interest too, because the breakdown makes clear the distinction between the location of the asset issuer and the location of the asset owner, that is, who owes what to whom.

From the home perspective, a foreign asset is a claim on a foreign country. When a home entity holds such an asset, it is called an **external asset** of the home country because it represents an obligation owed to the home country by the rest of the world. Conversely, from the home country's perspective, a home asset is a claim on the home country. When a foreign entity holds such an asset, it is called an **external liability** of the home country because it represents an obligation owed by the home country to the rest of the world. For example, when a U.S. firm invests overseas and acquires a computer factory located in Ireland, the acquisition is an external asset for the United States (and an external liability for Ireland). When a Japanese firm acquires an automobile plant in the United States, the acquisition is an external liability for the United States (and an external asset for Japan). A moment's thought reveals that all other assets traded across borders have a nation in which they are located and a nation by which they are owned—this is true for bank accounts, equities, government debt, corporate bonds, and so on. (For some examples, see the **Side Bar: Double-Entry Bookkeeping in the Balance of Payments.**)

If we use superscripts "H" and "F" to denote home and foreign assets, we can break down the financial account as the sum of the net exports of each type of asset:

$$FA = \underbrace{(EX_A^H - IM_A^H)}_{\substack{\text{Net export of} \\ \text{home assets}}} + \underbrace{(EX_A^F - IM_A^F)}_{\substack{\text{Net export of} \\ \text{foreign assets}}} = \underbrace{(EX_A^H - IM_A^H)}_{\substack{\text{Net export of} \\ \text{home assets} \\ = \\ \text{Net additions to} \\ \text{external liabilities}}} - \underbrace{(IM_A^F - EX_A^F)}_{\substack{\text{Net import of} \\ \text{foreign assets} \\ = \\ \text{Net additions to} \\ \text{external assets}}} \qquad (13\text{-}11)$$

In the last part of this formula, we use the fact that net imports of foreign assets are just *minus* net exports of foreign assets, allowing us to change the sign. This reveals to us that FA equals *the additions to external liabilities* (the home-owned assets moving into foreign ownership, net) *minus the additions to external assets* (the foreign-owned assets moving into home ownership, net). This is our first indication of how flows of assets have implications for changes in a nation's wealth, a topic to which we return shortly.

How the Balance of Payments Accounts Work: A Macroeconomic View

To make further progress in our quest to understand the links between flows of goods, services, income, and assets, we have to understand how the current account, capital account, and financial account are related and why, in the end, the balance of payments accounts must, indeed, balance as suggested by the workings of the open-economy circular flow in Figure 13-2.

Recall from Equation (13-4) that gross national disposable income is

$$Y = GNDI = GNE + TB + NFIA + NUT \; = \; \underbrace{GNE + CA}_{\substack{\text{Resources available to} \\ \text{home country from income}}}$$

Does this expression represent all of the resources that are available to the home economy to finance expenditure? No. It represents only the income resources, the resources obtained from the market sale and purchase of good, services, and factor services and nonmarket transfers. In addition, the home economy can free up (or use up) resources in another way: by engaging in net sales (or purchases) of assets. We can calculate these extra resources using our previous definitions:

$$[\underbrace{EX_A}_{\substack{\text{Value of} \\ \text{all assets} \\ \text{exported}}} - \underbrace{KA_{OUT}}_{\substack{\text{Value of} \\ \text{all assets} \\ \text{exported} \\ \text{as gifts}}}] - [\underbrace{IM_A}_{\substack{\text{Value of} \\ \text{all assets} \\ \text{imported}}} - \underbrace{KA_{IN}}_{\substack{\text{Value of} \\ \text{all assets} \\ \text{imported} \\ \text{as gifts}}}] = EX_A - IM_A + KA_{IN} - KA_{OUT} = \underbrace{FA + KA}_{\substack{\text{Extra resources} \\ \text{available to the} \\ \text{home country due} \\ \text{to asset trades}}}$$

$$\underbrace{\text{Value of all assets} \atop \text{exported via sales}} \qquad \underbrace{\text{Value of all assets} \atop \text{imported via purchases}}$$

Adding the last two expressions, we arrive at the value of the total resources available to the home country for expenditure purposes. This total value must equal the total value of home expenditure on final goods and services, GNE:

$$\underbrace{GNE + CA}_{\substack{\text{Resources available} \\ \text{to home country} \\ \text{due to income}}} + \underbrace{FA + KA}_{\substack{\text{Extra resources available} \\ \text{to the home country} \\ \text{due to asset trades}}} = GNE$$

We can cancel GNE from both sides of this expression to obtain the important result known as the balance of payments identity or **BOP identity:**

$$\underbrace{CA}_{\text{Current account}} + \underbrace{KA}_{\text{Capital account}} + \underbrace{FA}_{\text{Financial account}} = 0 \qquad (13\text{-}12)$$

The balance of payments sums to zero: it does balance!

How the Balance of Payments Accounts Work: A Microeconomic View

We have just found that at the macroeconomic level, $CA + KA + FA = 0$, a very simple equation that summarizes, in three variables, every single one of the millions of international transactions a nation engages in. This is one way to look at the BOP accounts.

Another way to look at the BOP is to look behind these three variables to the specific flows we saw in Figure 13-2, and the individual transactions within each flow.

$$CA = (EX - IM) + (EX_{FS} - IM_{FS}) + (UT_{IN} - UT_{OUT})$$

$$KA = (KA_{IN} - KA_{OUT}) \qquad\qquad (13\text{-}13)$$

$$FA = (EX_A^H - IM_A^H) + (EX_A^F - IM_A^F)$$

Written this way, the components of the BOP identity allow us to see the details behind why the accounts must balance. As you can observe from these equations, there are 12 transaction types (each preceded by either a plus or minus sign) and 3 accounts (CA, KA, FA) in which they can appear.

If an item has a plus sign, it is called a balance of payments credit or **BOP credit**. Six types of transactions receive a plus (+) sign as follows:

Current account (CA):	Exports of goods and services ($+EX$);
	Exports of factor services ($+EX_{FS}$);
	Unilateral transfers received ($+UT_{IN}$).
Capital account (KA):	Capital transfers received ($+KA_{IN}$).
Financial account (FA):	Exports of home and foreign assets ($+EX_A^H$, $+EX_A^F$).

If an item has a minus sign, it is called a balance of payments debit or **BOP debit**. Six types of transactions receive a minus (−) sign as follows:

Current account (CA):	Imports of goods and services ($-IM$);
	Imports of factor services ($-IM_{FS}$);
	Unilateral transfers given ($-UT_{OUT}$).
Capital account (KA):	Capital transfers given ($-KA_{OUT}$).
Financial account (FA):	Imports of home and foreign assets ($-IM_A^H$, $-IM_A^F$).

Now, to see why the BOP accounts balance in aggregate, we have to understand one simple principle: *every market transaction (whether for goods, services, factor services, or assets) has two parts. If party A engages in a transaction with a counterparty B, then A receives from B an item of a given value, and in return B receives from A an item of equal value.*[11]

Thus, whenever a transaction generates a credit somewhere in the BOP account, it must also generate a corresponding debit somewhere else in the BOP account. Similarly, every debit generates a corresponding credit. It might not be obvious where the offsetting item is, but it must exist somewhere *if* the accounts have been measured properly. Of course, this is a big if, and we will see the consequences of mismeasurement shortly. (For more detail on this topic, see **Side Bar: Double-Entry Bookkeeping in the Balance of Payments**.)

---

[11]This principle applies not only to market transactions, but also to nonmarket transactions such as gifts and foreign aid that enter into the BOP accounts as "net unilateral transfers" or in the capital account. For example, a $100 export of food aid is not a market transaction, but appears as a credit item in total exports. This credit is offset in the BOP accounts by a −$100 debit in net unilateral transfers. In this way, nonmarket gifts, for which nothing is offered in return, are properly recorded and yet leave the BOP accounts in balance.

SIDE BAR

The Double-Entry Principle in the Balance of Payments

We can make the double-entry principle more concrete by looking at some (mostly) hypothetical international transactions and figuring out how they would be recorded in the U.S. BOP accounts.

1. Recall from Chapter 10 that our friend George was in Paris in 2003. Suppose he spent $110 (€100) on French wine one evening. This is a U.S. import of a foreign service. George pays with his American Express card. The bar is owed $110 (or €100) by American Express (and Amex is owed by George). The United States has exported an asset to France: the bar now has a claim against American Express. From the U.S. perspective, this represents an increase in U.S. assets owned by foreigners. The double entries in the U.S. BOP appear in the current account and the financial account:

CA: Drinks in Paris bar	$-IM$	$-\$110$
FA: Bar's claim on AMEX	$+EX_A^H$	$+\$110$

2. George was in the bar to meet his Danish cousin Georg. They both work as wine merchants. After a few bottles of Bordeaux, George enthuses about Arkansas chardonnay and insists Georg give it a try. Georg counters by telling George he should really try some Jutland rosé. Each cousin returns home and asks his firm to ship a case of each wine (worth $36) to the other. This barter transaction (involving no financial activity) would appear solely as two entries in the U.S. current account:

CA: Arkansas wine exported to Denmark	EX	$+\$36$
CA: Jutland wine imported to United States	$-IM$	$-\$36$

3. Later that night, George met a French entrepreneur in a smoky corner of the bar. George vaguely remembers the story: the entrepreneur's French tech company was poised for unbelievable success with an upcoming share issue. George decides to invest $10,000 to buy the French stock; he imports a French asset. The stock is sold to him through the French bank BNP, and George sends them a U.S. dollar check. BNP then has a claim against Citibank, an export of a home asset to France. Both entries fall within the financial account:

FA: George's French tech stocks	$-IM_A^F$	$-\$10,000$
FA: BNP claim against Citibank	$+EX_A^H$	$+\$10,000$

4. Rather surprisingly, George's French stocks do quite well. By December 2003 they have doubled in value. George makes a $5,000 donation to charity. His charity purchases U.S. relief supplies that will be exported to Bam, Iran, following a devastating earthquake in that city. The two entries here are entirely in the U.S. current account. The supplies are a nonmarket export of goods offset by the value of the unilateral transfer:

CA: Relief supplies exported to Bam	EX	$+\$5,000$
CA: George's charitable gift	$-UT_{OUT}$	$-\$5,000$

5. George was also pleased to see that some poor countries were benefiting from another kind of foreign assistance, debt forgiveness. In June 2003 the U.S. secretary of state announced that the United States would forgive $1 billion of debt owed by the government of Pakistan. This would decrease U.S.-owned assets overseas. The United States was exporting Pakistani assets: it hands the canceled debts back to Pakistan, a credit in the financial account. The double entries would be seen in the capital and financial accounts:

KA: U.S. grant of debt relief	$-KA_{OUT}$	$-\$1,000,000,000$
FA: Decline in U.S. external assets	$-EX_A^F$	$+\$1,000,000,000$

Understanding the Data for the Balance of Payments Account

To illustrate all the principles we've learned, let's look at the United States' balance of payments account. Table 13-2 shows an extract of the U.S. BOP accounts for 2009.[12]

---

[12] The BOP account is published each year as the "international transactions account (ITA)" by the BEA. The ITA uses a different definition of the United States territory than the national income and product accounts (NIPA), so these figures do not exactly match those in Table 13-1.

TABLE 13-2

The U.S. Balance of Payments in 2009 The table shows U.S. international transactions in 2009 in billions of dollars. Major categories are in bold type.

Major Account	Line	Category or Subcategory	Symbol	$ billions
	1	**Exports of goods and services**	$+EX$	$1,571
	1a	Of which: Goods		1,068
	1b	Services		502
	2	**Income receipts [= exports of factor services]**	$+EX_{FS}$	588
Current	3	**Imports of goods and services (−)**	$−IM$	−1,946
Account	3a	Of which: Goods (−)		−1,575
	3b	Services (−)		−370
	4	**Income payments [= imports of factor services] (−)**	$−IM_{FS}$	−467
	5	**Net unilateral transfers**	NUT	−125
	6	**Capital account net**	KA	0
	7	**U.S.-owned assets abroad net increase (−)**		−140
		[= net imports of ROW assets or financial outflow (−)]		
Capital and	7a	Of which: U.S. official reserve assets		−52
Financial	7b	Other assets		−88
Account	8	**Foreign-owned assets in U.S. net increase (+)**		306
		[= net exports of U.S. assets or financial inflow (+)]		
	8a	Of which: Foreign official assets		450
	8b	Other assets		−144
Statistical Discrepancy	9	**Statistical discrepancy (sum of 1 to 8, sign reversed)**	SD	213
		Balance on current account (lines 1, 2, 3, 4, and 5)	CA	−378
		Of which: Balance on goods and services (lines 1 and 3)	TB	−375
Summary		Balance on income (lines 2 and 4)	$NFIA$	121
Items		**Balance on financial account** (lines 7 and 8)	FA	165
		Of which: Official settlements balance (lines 7a and 8a)		398
		Nonreserve financial account (lines 7b and 8b)		−233

Notes: Details may not add to totals because of rounding. The statistical discrepancy shown here includes financial derivatives.

Source: U.S. Bureau of Economic Analysis, ITA Table 1, using the ITA definition of the United States. This includes U.S. territories, so these figures are slightly different from those in Table 13-1.

In the current account, in the top part of the table, we look first at the trade in goods and services on lines 1 and 3. Overall exports, *EX*, were +$1,571 billion (line 1, a credit), and imports, *IM*, were −$1,946 billion (line 3, a debit). In the summary items, we see the balance on goods and services, the trade balance, TB, was −$375 billion (line 1 plus line 3, or exports minus imports). Exports and imports and the trade balance are also broken down even further into goods and service components (lines 1ab and 3ab).

The next part of the current account on lines 2 and 4 deals with trade in factor services, also known as the *income account* (referring to the income paid to those factors). Income receipts for factor service exports, *EX_{FS}*, generated a credit of +$588 billion and income payments for factor service imports, *IM_{FS}*, generated a debit of −$467 billion.

Adding these two items resulted in net factor income from abroad NFIA equal to +$121 billion (line 2 plus line 4), a net credit.

Lastly, we see that net unilateral transfers, NUT, were −$125 billion, a net debit (line 5); the United States was a net donor as measured by the net transfer of goods, services, and income to the rest of the world. (Typically, in summary tables like these, unilateral transfers are shown only in net form.)

Overall, summing lines 1 through 5, the 2009 U.S. current account balance, CA, was −$378 billion, that is, a deficit of $378 billion, as shown in the summary items at the foot of the table.

A country that has a current account surplus is called a **(net) lender.** By the BOP identity, we know that it must have a deficit in its asset accounts, so like any lender, it is, on net, buying assets (acquiring IOUs from borrowers). For example, China is a large net lender. A country that has a current account deficit is called a **(net) borrower.** By the BOP identity, we know that it must have a surplus in its asset accounts, so like any borrower, it is, on net, selling assets (issuing IOUs to lenders). As we can see, the United States is a large net borrower.

Now we move to the capital and financial accounts. Typically, in summary tables like these, the capital account is shown only in net form. The United States in 2009 had a negligible capital account, KA, of less than $0.5 billion, reported as zero (line 6).

Lastly, we move to the financial account. As explained, this account can be broken down in terms of the exports and imports of two kinds of assets: U.S. assets (U.S. external liabilities) and rest of the world assets (U.S. external assets). In this summary the net trades are shown for each kind of asset.

We see that the United States was engaged in the net import of foreign assets, so that external assets (U.S.-owned assets abroad) increased by $140 billion. This net import of foreign assets is recorded as a debit of −$140 billion (line 7). Note that the minus sign maintains the convention that imports are debits.

At the same time, the United States was engaged in the net export of U.S. assets to the rest of the world so that external liabilities (foreign-owned assets in the United States) increased by $306 billion; the net export of U.S. assets is duly recorded as a credit of +$306 billion (line 8).

The sum of lines 7 and 8 gives the financial account balance, FA, of +$165 billion, recorded in the summary items.

For further information on interventions by central banks, financial account transactions are often also broken down into reserve and nonreserve components. Changes in reserves arise from official intervention in the forex market—that is, purchases and sales by home and foreign monetary authorities. The balance on all reserve transactions is called the *official settlements balance*, and the balance on all other asset trades is called the *nonreserve financial account*. We see here that U.S. authorities intervened a little: a net import of $52 billion of U.S. official reserves (line 7a) means that the Federal Reserve bought $52 billion in foreign (i.e., nondollar) exchange reserves from foreigners. In contrast, foreign central banks intervened a lot: U.S. entities sold them $450 billion in U.S. dollar reserve assets (line 8a).

Adding up the current account, the capital account, and the financial account (lines 1 through 8), we find that the total of the three accounts was −$213 billion (−$378 + $0 + $165 = −$213). The BOP accounts are supposed to balance by adding to zero— in reality, they never do. Why not? Because the statistical agencies tasked with gathering BOP data find it impossible to track every single international transaction correctly, due to measurement errors and omissions. Some problems result from the smuggling of goods or trade tax evasion. Larger errors are likely due to the mismeasured, concealed, or illicit movement of financial income flows and assets movements (e.g., money laundering and capital tax evasion).

The Statistical Discrepancy To "account" for this error, statistical agencies create an accounting item, the *statistical discrepancy* (SD) equal to minus the error $SD = -(CA + KA + FA)$. With that "correction," the amended version of the BOP identity will hold true in practice, sweeping away the real-world measurement problems. In the table, the statistical discrepancy is shown on line 9.[13] Once the statistical discrepancy is included, the balance of payments accounts always balance.

Some Recent Trends in the U.S. Balance of Payments Figure 13-10 shows recent trends in various components of the U.S. balance of payments. The sharp downward trend

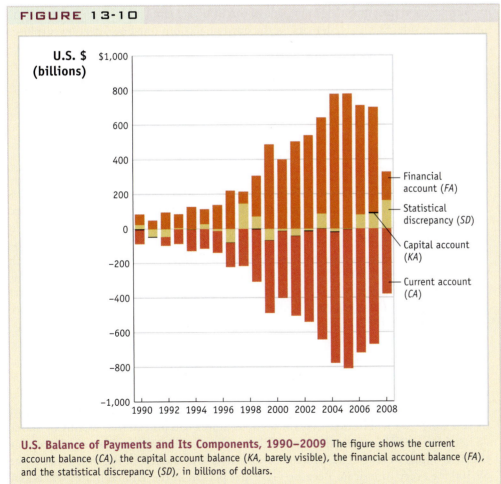

FIGURE 13-10

U.S. Balance of Payments and Its Components, 1990–2009 The figure shows the current account balance (*CA*), the capital account balance (*KA*, barely visible), the financial account balance (*FA*), and the statistical discrepancy (*SD*), in billions of dollars.

Source: U.S. Bureau of Economic Analysis, using the ITA definition of the United States, which includes U.S. territories.

---

[13] Prior to 2007, the U.S. statistical discrepancy included unmeasured financial derivatives transactions. Starting in 2007, the BEA estimates these transactions, but they are not as yet broken down in detail into home and foreign assets. For clarity, they are not reported here and are included in the statistical discrepancy in Table 13-2.

of the current account is as previously shown in Figure 13-6, so for the balance of payments identity to hold, there must be an offsetting upward trend in other parts of the BOP accounts. This is indeed the case. We can see that the United States has been financing its growing deficit on the current account primarily by running an expanding surplus on the financial account. In the mid-1990s, there was close to a $100 billion current account deficit and a comparable financial account surplus. A decade later, both figures were in the region of $800 billion, with a substantial decline only after the global financial crisis.

What the Balance of Payments Account Tells Us

The balance of payments accounts consist of the current account, which measures external imbalances in goods, services, factor services, and unilateral transfers. The financial and capital accounts measure asset trades. Using the principle that market transactions must consist of a trade of two items of equal value, we find that the balance of payments accounts really do balance.

Surpluses on the current account side of the BOP accounts must be offset by deficits on the asset side. Similarly, deficits on the current account must be offset by surpluses on the asset side. By telling us how current account imbalances are financed, the balance of payments makes the connection between a country's income and spending decisions and the evolution of that country's wealth, an important connection we develop further in the final section of this chapter.

4 External Wealth

The measurement of a nation's income flow is not the only important economic variable that must be adapted to the open-economy environment. Economists and policy makers, and the general public, also care about a nation's stock of *wealth*. And so, probably, do you.

For example, Anne has income and expenditures of $50,000 each year and savings in the bank of $10,000. But she also has a credit card debt of $20,000. Beth's life is identical to Anne's in almost every respect: she has income and expenditures of $50,000 each year and savings of $10,000, but she has no credit card debt. Who is better off? Clearly, Beth is. Her income is the same as Anne's. But Anne's wealth or "net worth" is −$10,000 (savings of $10,000 minus debt of $20,000), whereas Beth has a net worth of +$10,000. Anne's wealth is −20% of her income; Beth's wealth is +20% of her income.

Just as a household is better off with higher wealth, all else equal, so is a country. We can calculate a home country's "net worth" or **external wealth** with respect to the rest of the world (ROW) by adding up all of the home assets owned by ROW (foreigners' claims against home) and then subtracting all of the ROW assets owned by the home country (home claims against foreigners). Doing this for the United States at the end of year 2009, we would find that the United States had an external wealth of about −$2,866 billion. This made the United States the world's biggest debtor in history at the time of this writing. The United States' net debt to the rest of the world was about $9,300 for every American. Because GDP per person in the United States was about $46,400 in 2009, the external wealth of the U.S. was about −20% of GDP.

Why is U.S. external wealth at this level? How did it get there and what will happen next? To understand how the wealth levels of countries evolve, in this final section of the chapter we build on what we have learned from the national income and balance of payments accounts.

The Level of External Wealth

First, we give a definition of the level of a country's external wealth (W):

$$\underbrace{\text{External wealth}}_{W} = \underbrace{\begin{bmatrix} \text{ROW assets} \\ \text{owned by home} \end{bmatrix}}_{A} - \underbrace{\begin{bmatrix} \text{Home assets} \\ \text{owned by ROW} \end{bmatrix}}_{L} \qquad (13\text{-}14)$$

External wealth equals the value of total external assets (A) minus the value of total external liabilities (L). The former is what is owed to the home country by the rest of the world, and the latter is what is owed to the rest of the world by the home country. A country's level of external wealth is also called its *net international investment position* or *net foreign assets*. It is a stock measure, not a flow measure.

If $W > 0$, *home is a* **net creditor** *country: external assets exceed external liabilities.*

If $W < 0$, *home is a* **net debtor** *country: external liabilities exceed external assets.*

External wealth is only one part of a nation's total wealth. The other part of a nation's wealth is internal wealth, which corresponds to the total value of all nonfinancial assets in the home country. (The links between external wealth and total wealth are explored further in the appendix to this chapter.)

Because we are focusing on international economic relationships, our main emphasis is on external wealth because it measures the outstanding obligations of one country to another. Those obligations, and when and how they are paid, can be the source of great economic and political stress. Moreover, the net debts of nations, like those of individuals, ultimately carry a cost. To understand external wealth, let's look at how it is measured and how it evolves.

Changes in External Wealth

There are two reasons a country's level of external wealth changes over time.

1. *Financial flows:* As a result of asset trades, the country can increase or decrease its external assets and liabilities. How? Net exports of foreign assets cause an equal decrease in the level of external assets and hence a corresponding decrease in external wealth. Net exports of home assets cause an equal increase in the level of external liabilities and hence a corresponding decrease in external wealth. For example, if net exports of assets (whether home or foreign) are +$1 billion, then the change in external wealth is –$1 billion. The net export of assets of all kinds is measured by the financial account (FA), and this has a *negative* effect on external wealth in any period.

2. *Valuation effects:* The value of existing external assets and liabilities may change over time because of capital gains or losses. In the case of external wealth, this change in value could be due to price effects or exchange rate effects. For example, suppose, a U.S. citizen buys 100 shares of BP on the London Stock Exchange at £7 each. Suppose the exchange rate is $1.8 per pound. These U.S. external assets are worth $12.60 each (1.8 times 7), for a total of $1,260. Suppose the price of these shares then falls to £6, and the exchange rate stays the same. Each share is now worth $10.80 (1.8 times 6) and the 100 shares are valued at $1,080. Their value has fallen in dollar terms by $180 (£1 times 1.8 times 100), which is a capital loss. This is an example of a price effect. Now suppose the exchange rate rises to $2 per pound. Each share is still worth £6 in

U.K. currency but $12 in U.S. currency (2 times 6), so the total value of the shares rises to $1,200, which, relative to the $1,080 they were previously worth, implies a capital gain of $120. This is an example of an exchange rate effect. Similar effects can change the value of external liabilities.

Adding up these two contributions to the change in external wealth (ΔW), we find

$$\underbrace{\begin{bmatrix} \text{Change in} \\ \text{external wealth} \end{bmatrix}}_{\Delta W} = -\underbrace{\begin{bmatrix} \text{Financial} \\ \text{account} \end{bmatrix}}_{\substack{\text{Net export of assets} \\ = \\ FA}} + \underbrace{\begin{bmatrix} \text{Capital gains on} \\ \text{external wealth} \end{bmatrix}}_{\substack{\text{Valuation effects} \\ = \\ \text{Capital gains} \\ \text{minus capital losses}}} \qquad \text{(13-15)}$$

We gain a deeper understanding of this expression if we recall the BOP identity: the current account plus the capital account plus the financial account equals zero. Hence, minus the financial account equals the current account plus the capital account, or $-FA = CA + KA$. Substituting this identity into Equation (13-15), we obtain

$$\underbrace{\begin{bmatrix} \text{Change in} \\ \text{external wealth} \end{bmatrix}}_{\Delta W} = \underbrace{\begin{bmatrix} \text{Current} \\ \text{account} \end{bmatrix}}_{\substack{CA \\ = \\ \text{Unspent} \\ \text{income}}} + \underbrace{\begin{bmatrix} \text{Capital} \\ \text{account} \end{bmatrix}}_{\substack{KA \\ = \\ \text{Net capital} \\ \text{transfers received}}} + \underbrace{\begin{bmatrix} \text{Capital gains on} \\ \text{external wealth} \end{bmatrix}}_{\substack{\text{Valuation effects} \\ = \\ \text{Capital gains} \\ \text{minus capital losses}}} \qquad \text{(13-16)}$$

This fundamental formula tells us that a country can increase its external wealth in one of only three ways:

- Through its own thrift (a CA surplus, so expenditure is less than income)
- By the charity of others (a KA surplus, by receiving net gifts of wealth)
- With the help of windfalls (having positive capital gains)

Similarly, a country can reduce its external wealth by doing any of the opposites.

Understanding the Data on External Wealth

To track external wealth accurately, statisticians apply Equation (13-15). They face the challenge of not only keeping tabs on every trade in assets but also correctly assessing the impact of changing financial market conditions around the world on the value of the country's external assets and liabilities.

Measures of levels and changes in national external wealth are tabulated in an account known as the net international investment position. To illustrate with an example, a simplified version of this account for the United States appears in Table 13-3. The data in the table show a clear distinction between the contribution of financial flows to changes in external wealth—net trade in assets, in column (a)—and the impact of various kinds of valuation effects—columns (b), (c), and (d).

Table 13-3, line 3, column (a), shows that in 2009 the United States, on net, exported $165 billion in assets (exports of $306 billion on line 2, minus imports of $140 billion on line 1). On their own, these financial flows would have reduced U.S. external wealth by $165 billion in just one year. Yet nothing of the sort happened because more-than-offsetting valuation effects of +$953 billion—columns (b), (c), and (d)—boosted U.S. external wealth over the same period. These valuation effects were mainly driven by +$523 billion in price change effects and $277 billion in exchange rate effects.

TABLE 13-3

U.S. External Wealth in 2008–2009 The table shows changes in the U.S. net international investment position during the year 2009 in billions of dollars. The net result in row 3 equals row 1 minus row 2.

Category	Position, end 2008 ($ billions)	Financial Flows (a)	Price Changes (b)	Exchange Rate Changes (c)	Other Changes (d)	Total (a + b + c + d)	Position, end 2009 ($ billions)
			Of Which Valuation Effects				
				Changes in Position during 2009 ($ billions)			
1. External Assets	**$13,117**	**140**	**1,066**	**358**	**185**	**1,750**	**14,867**
= U.S.-owned assets abroad, of which:							
U.S. official reserve assets	294	52	57	1	0	110	404
U.S. government assets, other	624	−541	—	0	0	−541	83
U.S. private assets	12,200	630	1,009	357	185	2,181	14,380
2. External Liabilities	**16,771**	**306**	**534**	**81**	**32**	**962**	**17,733**
= Foreign-owned assets in the United States, of which:							
Foreign official assets in the United States	3,940	450	−14	0	−3	434	4,374
Other foreign assets	12,831	−144	557	81	35	528	13,359
3. External Wealth							
= Line 1 minus Line 2	−3,654	−165	523	277	153	788	−2,866
= Net international investment position of the United States							
Symbol	W (end 2008)	−FA	Capital gains				W (end 2009)

Note: Financial derivatives are excluded.

Source: U.S. Bureau of Economic Analysis.

Thus, while the United States borrowed an additional $165 billion from various nations in 2009, its external wealth actually rose by $788 billion as shown on line 3. Talk about a free lunch.

So what happened in 2009? Two main factors were at work. First, equity values rose worldwide, as the global financial crisis abated. But U.S. external assets include a larger share of equities than U.S. external liabilities, which consist of a great deal of U.S. debt. This difference in the composition of the two portfolios means that rising equity markets boosted the values of U.S. external assets much more than U.S. external liabilities. Second, about 95% of U.S. external liabilities were denominated in U.S. dollars, including vast foreign holdings of U.S. Treasury bills, held either as foreign official assets in central banks or as low-risk assets by foreign investors. These assets tended to have a stable value in dollar terms and did not experience any exchange rate valuation effects because they are denominated in dollars. In contrast, about two-thirds of U.S. external assets (foreign direct investment, bank loans, government debt) are denominated in foreign currencies, such as the euro, that were appreciating against the dollar.[14]

Some Recent Trends Over the longer run, the changes in external wealth in Equation (13-16) gradually cumulate. In the case of the United States, for the past three decades, the financial account has been almost always in surplus, reflecting a net export of assets to the rest of the world to pay for chronic current account deficits (the capital account has been negligibly small).

If there were no valuation effects, then Equation (13-15) would make a simple prediction. The change in the level of external wealth between two dates should equal the cumulative net import of assets (minus the financial account) over the intervening period. For example, if we had taken the U.S. external wealth level at the end of 1988 and added to that level all subsequent financial flows until the end of 2009, we would have estimated U.S. external wealth in 2009 at –$6,741 billion. The actual 2009 figure was a lot smaller: –$2,738 billion.

Why? Valuation effects or capital gains generated the difference of $4,003 billion in external wealth over the period, and from 1988 to 2009 these effects reduced U.S. net external indebtedness in 2009 by more than half compared with the level that financial flows alone would have predicted. The flip side of these valuation effects is that the rest of the world outside the United States suffered an equal and opposite capital loss over the same period. Why? Capital gains always have a "zero sum" property—by symmetry, an increase in the dollar value of the home country's external assets is simultaneously an increase in the dollar value of the rest of the world's external liabilities.

What External Wealth Tells Us

External wealth data tell us the net credit or debit position of a country with respect to the rest of the world. They include data on external assets (foreign assets owned by the home country) and external liabilities (home assets owned by foreigners). A creditor country has positive external wealth, a debtor country negative external wealth.

What drives external wealth? The current account told us about the imbalances in a country's external flows of goods, services, factor services, and income. The balance of payments accounts told us how these imbalances require offsetting financial flows of assets between countries. Countries with a current account surplus (deficit) must be net buyers (sellers) of assets. This buying and selling of assets has implications for external wealth. An increase in a country's external wealth results from every net import of assets; conversely, a decrease in external wealth results from every net export of assets. In addition, countries can experience capital gains or losses on their external assets and liabilities that cause changes in external wealth. All of these changes are summarized in the statement of a country's net international investment position.

---

[14] Data on the currency composition of U.S. external wealth from Cedric Tille, 2005, "Financial Integration and the Wealth Effect of Exchange Rate Fluctuations," Staff Reports 226, Federal Reserve Bank of New York.

5 Conclusions

The science of macroeconomics would be impossible without data, and the vast majority of the data we employ emerge from the efforts of official statisticians around the world. Notwithstanding the inevitable statistical discrepancies, and even the occasional errors of omission and commission (see **Side Bar: Beware of Greeks Bearing Statistics**), we would be lost without these measures of macroeconomic activity.

This chapter has illustrated some important accounting concepts and has highlighted some unusual and intriguing features of the current international economic system. We have seen how a consistent system of national income and product accounts allow for the tracking of international trade flows (including trade in intermediate goods), cross-border factor income flows, and unilateral transfers. We have also seen how these net resource flows of goods and services can be matched against a parallel set of net payment activities involving assets in the balance of payments

SIDE BAR

Beware of Greeks Bearing Statistics

It is important, but rather sad, to note that when it comes to national statistics, one cannot believe everything one reads. Over the years numerous governments have been suspected of fiddling with their official data for various purposes, as indicated by the following examples:

- *Greece.* In 2001 Greece was allowed to join the Eurozone. One of the criteria it had to meet in order to join was that its budget deficit could not be over 3% of its GDP. Greece met this requirement according to its official statistics. In November 2004, after it had been allowed to join the Eurozone, Greece admitted its 2003 budget deficit was really 3.4%, twice as large as it had previously claimed. In fact, the budget deficit had not been below 3% since 1999. The EU was not amused. Greece continued to publish incorrect or manipulated data (including a 25% upward adjustment to GDP to take into account "black economy" activity such as prostitution). By inflating its GDP, Greece made its budget deficit position look better than it was, which may have allowed Greece to borrow from other countries on favorable terms. When the euro crisis hit in 2008–2009, the full horror of Greece's weak economic and fiscal position become clear, by which point the fiasco had forced other Eurozone nations to provide emergency funding and threatened the survival of the euro project itself.

- *Italy.* In 1987 Italy was considered much poorer than northern European countries. But its statisticians also decided to increase GDP by 15% after some guesswork to account for the black economy. Instantly, Italians had a higher official GDP per person than the British, an event known as *il sorpasso*. Not that this made any Italians actually feel richer.

- *Argentina.* After its 2001 crisis, a new populist government took over but faced problems with high and persistent inflation. To "solve" this problem, the government "reorganized" its official statistical bureau, which then started publishing much lower, and highly suspicious inflation data. Lower inflation also helped the government avoid larger costs of indexed benefits and allowed the government to claim it had solved the inflation problem. Few believed these published data were true.

- *China.* In the latest International Comparison Project by the World Bank, China's own estimate of its yuan price level came in much higher than had been expected. This had various implications: dividing nominal yuan income by the price level made China look quite a bit poorer. And higher prices made China's real exchange rate less undervalued, or even overvalued. Since poorer countries usually have lower price levels, both of these impacts had the effect of making China's exchange rate look more fairly valued, given its standard of living. This came about at a time when China was under considerable political pressure to appreciate its currency. But skeptics doubted whether the data were totally plausible, because the change in the yuan price level since the previous ICP was much larger than that implied by China's own official inflation data over the same period.

accounts. Finally, we have seen how the flow of trades in assets can be combined with capital gains and losses to track the evolution of a nation's stock of external wealth, an important part of its total wealth, as recorded in the statement of the net international investment position.

We presented a fuller exposition using as an example the United States' accounts of income, balance of payments, and external wealth. In the remainder of the book, we make extensive use of the concepts introduced in this chapter to develop theories that explore the global macroeconomic linkages between nations.

KEY POINTS

1. National flows of expenditure, product, income, and wealth, and international flows of goods, services, income, and assets, together measure important aspects of a country's economic performance and describe its economy's relationship to economies in rest of the world. The records kept in the national income and product accounts, the balance of payments account, and the net international investment position track these data.

2. The key measures of economic activity are:

   • Gross national expenditure (GNE) measures an economy's total spending on final goods and services. It is the sum of consumption, investment, and government consumption: $GNE = C + I + G$.

   • Gross domestic product (GDP) measures total production (value of all output minus value of all purchased inputs).

   • Gross national income (GNI) measures the total payments to an economy's domestic factors.

   • Gross national disposable income (GNDI, also denoted Y) measures an economy's disposable income including transfers.

   In a closed economy, $GNE = GDP = GNI = GNDI$.

3. In an open economy, GDP need not equal GNE. When nations can trade, the sum of goods and services demanded by domestic residents need not be the same as the sum of goods and services supplied by domestic firms. The difference between GDP and GNE is the trade balance TB: $GDP = GNE + TB$. The trade balance is the difference between a nation's imports and exports of goods and services.

4. In an open economy, GDP need not equal GNI because imports and exports of factor services (measured by net factor income from abroad or NFIA) imply that factor income received by domestic residents need not be the same as factor payments made by domestic firms. Thus, $GNI = GDP + NFIA$.

5. In an open economy, the true level of disposable income is best measured by gross national disposable income or $Y = GNDI$. GNDI need not equal GNI because net unilateral transfers (NUT) to foreigners may be positive, due to foreign aid and other nonmarket gifts. Thus, $Y = GNDI = GNI + NUT$.

6. The sum of all the aforementioned international transactions, $TB + NFIA + NUT$, is called the current account (CA).

7. From the relationships just outlined, we find that $Y = C + I + G + CA$. This expression is known as the *national income identity*.

8. National saving S is defined as $Y - C - G$. From the national income identity, we can derive the current account identity: $S = I + CA$. The current account equals saving minus investment. Movements in investment or saving, all else equal, feed directly into the current account.

9. All international trades in goods and services and in assets are recorded in an account known as the balance of payments (BOP). As a result of double-entry bookkeeping, and allowing for gifts and transfers, the BOP must sum to zero.

10. The BOP contains the following:

   - Net exports of goods and services, TB, called the trade balance
   - Net exports of factor services, NFIA, called the net factor income from abroad
   - Net unilateral transfers received, NUT, called the net unilateral transfers

   - Net transfers of assets received, KA, called the capital account
   - Net exports of assets, FA, called the financial account

11. The first three items are the current account CA. Since the BOP accounts sum to zero, this implies the balance of payments identity: CA + FA + KA = 0.

12. External wealth is a measure of a country's credit or debt position versus the rest of the world. It equals external assets—rest of world (ROW) assets owned by home—minus external liabilities (home assets owned by ROW). The net export (import) of assets lowers (raises) a country's external wealth. External wealth is one part of a country's total wealth.

13. External wealth can change for one of two reasons: the export or import of assets (called financial flows) or changes in the value of existing assets due to capital gains or losses (called valuation effects). Both of these channels affect net external wealth.

KEY TERMS

national income and product accounts, p. 458

balance of payments accounts, p. 458

gross national expenditure (GNE), p. 458

gross domestic product (GDP), p. 458

gross national income (GNI), p. 459

trade balance (TB), p. 460

net factor income from abroad (NFIA), p. 460

net unilateral transfers (NUT), p. 460

gross national disposable income (GNDI), p. 460

current account (CA), p. 462

financial account (FA), p. 462

capital account (KA), p. 462

national income identity, p. 472

national saving, p. 473

current account identity, p. 473

private saving, p. 474

government saving, p. 475

public saving, p. 475

external asset, p. 479

external liability, p. 479

BOP identity, p. 480

BOP credit, p. 481

BOP debit, p. 481

(net) lender, p. 484

(net) borrower, p. 484

external wealth (W), p. 468

net creditor, p. 487

net debtor, p. 487

PROBLEMS

1. Below is a partial table of the OECD's 2004 ranking of member countries based on their GDP per capita. Compute the ratio of GNI to GDP in each case. What does this imply about net factor income from abroad in each country? Compute the GNI rankings of these countries. Are there any major differences between the GDP and GNI rankings? What do these differences imply? Indicate?

		GDP per Person	GNI per Person
1	Luxembourg	$64,843	$53,299
2	Norway	$41,880	$42,062
3	United States	$39,660	$39,590
4	Ireland	$36,536	$31,151
5	Switzerland	$34,740	$37,638
6	Netherlands	$33,571	$34,527
7	Iceland	$33,271	$31,897
8	Austria	$33,235	$32,843
9	Australia	$32,643	$31,462
10	Canada	$32,413	$31,751
11	Denmark	$32,335	$32,232
12	Belgium	$31,985	$31,675
13	United Kingdom	$31,780	$32,470
14	Sweden	$31,072	$31,007
15	Germany	$29,916	$28,732
16	Finland	$29,833	$30,361
17	Japan	$29,173	$29,739
18	France	$29,006	$29,287
19	Italy	$27,744	$27,586
20	Greece	$27,691	$27,412
21	Spain	$26,018	$25,672
22	New Zealand	$24,834	$23,205
23	Slovenia	$21,527	$21,268
24	Korea	$20,723	$20,771
25	Czech Republic	$19,426	$18,314
26	Portugal	$19,324	$19,029
27	Hungary	$16,519	$15,548
28	Slovak Republic	$14,651	$14,708
29	Poland	$13,089	$12,511
30	Mexico	$10,145	$9,989
31	Turkey	$7,212	$7,186

2. Note the following accounting identity for gross national income (GNI):

$$GNI = C + I + G + TB + NFIA$$

Using this expression, show that in a closed economy, gross domestic product (GDP), gross national income (GNI), and gross national expenditures (GNE) are the same. Show that domestic investment is equal to domestic savings.

3. Show how each of the following would affect the U.S. balance of payments. Include a description of the debit and credit items, and in each case identify which specific account is affected (e.g., imports of goods and services, *IM;* exports of assets, EX_A; and so on. (For this question, you may find it helpful to refer to the Appendix.)

   a. A California computer manufacturer purchases a $50 hard disk from a Malaysian company, paying the funds from a bank account in Malaysia.

   b. A U.S. tourist to Japan sells his iPod to a local resident for yen worth $100.

   c. The U.S. central bank sells $500 million of its holdings of U.S. Treasury bonds to a British financial firm and purchases pound sterling foreign reserves.

   d. A foreign owner of Apple shares receives $10,000 in dividend payments, which are paid into a New York bank.

   e. The central bank of China purchases $1 million of export earnings from a firm that has sold $1 million of toys to the United States, and the central bank holds these dollars as reserves.

   f. The U.S. government forgives a $50 million debt owed by a developing country.

4. In 2010 the country of Ikonomia has a current account deficit of $1 billion and a nonreserve financial account surplus of $750 million. Ikonomia's capital account is in a $100 million surplus. In addition, Ikonomian factories located in foreign countries earn $700 million. Ikonomia has a trade deficit of $800 million. Assume Ikonomia neither gives nor receives unilateral transfers. Ikonomia's GDP is $9 billion.

   a. What happened to Ikonomia's net foreign assets during 2010? Did it acquire or lose foreign assets during the year?

b. Compute the official settlements balance (OSB). Based on this number, what happened to the central bank's (foreign) reserves?

c. How much income did foreign factors of production earn in Ikonomia during 2010?

d. Compute net factor income from abroad (NFIA).

e. Using the identity $BOP = CA + FA + KA$, show that $BOP = 0$.

f. Compute Ikonomia's gross national expenditure (GNE), gross national income (GNI), and gross national disposable income (GNDI).

5. To answer this question, you must obtain data from the Bureau of Economic Analysis (BEA), http://www.bea.gov, on the U.S. balance of payments (BOP) tables. Go to interactive tables to obtain *annual* data for 2008 (the default setting is for quarterly data). It may take you some time to become familiar with how to navigate the website. *You need only refer to Table 1 on the BOP accounts.* Using the BOP data, compute the following for the United States:

a. Trade balance (TB), net factor income from abroad (NFIA), net unilateral transfers (NUT), and current account (CA)

b. Financial account (FA)

c. Official settlements balance (OSB), referred to as "U.S. official reserve assets" and "Foreign official assets in the U.S."

d. Nonreserve financial account (NRFA)

e. Balance of payments (BOP). Note that this may not equal zero because of statistical discrepancy. Verify that the discrepancy is the same as the one reported by the BEA.

6. Continuing from the previous question, find nominal GDP for the United States in 2008 (you can find it elsewhere on the BEA site). Use this information along with your previous calculations to compute the following:

a. Gross national expenditure (GNE), gross national income (GNI), and gross national disposable income (GNDI)

b. In macroeconomics, we often assume the U.S. economy is a closed economy when building models that describe how changes in policy and shocks affect the economy.

Based on the previous data (BOP and GDP), do you think this is a reasonable assumption to make? Do international transactions account for a large share of total transactions (involving goods and services, or income) involving the United States?

7. During the 1980s, the United States experienced "twin deficits" in the current account and government budget. Since 1998 the U.S. current account deficit has grown steadily along with rising government budget deficits. Do government budget deficits lead to current account deficits? Identify other possible sources of the current account deficits. Do current account deficits necessarily indicate problems in the economy?

8. Consider the economy of Opulenza. In Opulenza, domestic investment of $400 million earned $20 million in capital gains during 2009. Opulenzans purchased $120 million in new foreign assets during the year; foreigners purchased $160 million in Opulenzan assets. Assume the valuation effects total $1 million in capital gains.

a. Compute the change in domestic wealth in Opulenza.

b. Compute the change in external wealth for Opulenza.

c. Compute the total change in wealth for Opulenza.

d. Compute domestic savings for Opulenza.

e. Compute Opulenza's current account. Is the CA in deficit or surplus?

f. Explain the intuition for the CA deficit/surplus in terms of savings in Opulenza, financial flows, and its domestic/external wealth position.

g. How would a depreciation in Opulenza's currency affect its domestic, external, and total wealth? Assume that foreign assets owned by Opulenzans are denominated in foreign currency.

9. This question asks you to compute valuation effects for the United States in 2004, using the same methods mentioned in the chapter. Use the bea.gov website to collect the data needed for this question: look under the "International" heading.

Visit the BEA's balance of payments data page and obtain the U.S. balance of payments for 2004 in billions of dollars. Be sure to get the correct year, and annual data, not quarterly.

Visit the BEA's net international investment position data page and obtain the U.S. net international investment position for end 2003 to end 2004.

a. What was the U.S. current account for 2004?

b. What was the U.S. financial account for 2004?

c. What was the U.S. change in external wealth for 2004?

d. What was the U.S. total valuation effect for 2004?

e. Does the answer to part (d) equal the answer to part (e) minus the answer to part (c)? Why?

f. What do the BEA data indicate was the U.S. valuation effect due to exchange rate changes for 2004?

You may now assume that the U.S. dollar depreciated by 10% against major currencies in 2004, and use this average to estimate valuation effects.

g. What were end-2003 U.S. external liabilities? If 5% of these liabilities were in foreign currency and were subject to a 10% exchange rate appreciation, what decrease in U.S. external wealth resulted?

h. What were end-2003 U.S. external assets? If 65% of these assets were subject to a 10% exchange rate appreciation, what increase in U.S. external wealth resulted?

i. Using the answers to parts (g) and (h), what was the 2004 U.S. valuation effect due to exchange rate changes according to your rough calculation? Is it close to the BEA figure in part (f)?

N E T W O R K

Go to the UN website and find out what the Millennium Development Goals are (http://www.un.org/millenniumgoals). Go to the Gleneagles summit website and examine the promises made (http://www.g8.gov.uk/). Use the Web to check up on how well these G8 promises are being kept, such as the UN goal of 0.7% of GDP in official development assistance, the promise to eradicate export subsidies, and the aim to double aid by 2010. (*Hint:* Google sites such as Oxfam or the Jubilee Debt Campaign, or look for the World Bank Tools for Monitoring the Millennium Development Goals.)

Use the Web to locate the official macroeconomic statistics for your country. (In the United States, go to http://www.bea.gov.) Find the latest annual data corresponding to the measures discussed in this section. Was your country's GDP higher or lower than its GNE? Why? Was your country's GNI higher or lower than its GDP? Why? What about GNDI—was your country a net giver or receiver of transfers?

APPENDIX TO CHAPTER 13

External Wealth and Total Wealth

In this chapter, we studied external wealth. But individuals and countries care about their total wealth. How does external wealth relate to total wealth?

External wealth is only part of a country's *total wealth*, the sum of the home capital stock (all nonfinancial assets in the home economy, denoted K) plus amounts owed to home by foreigners (A) minus amounts owed foreigners by home (L):

$$\text{Total wealth} = \underbrace{K}_{\substack{\text{Home nonfinancial} \\ \text{assets}}} + \underbrace{(A - L)}_{\text{External wealth}}$$

In this definition, note that we deliberately exclude financial assets owed by one home entity to another home entity because in the aggregate these cancel out and form no part of a country's total wealth.

Changes in the value of total wealth can then be written as follows:

$$\begin{bmatrix} \text{Change in} \\ \text{total wealth} \end{bmatrix} = \underbrace{\begin{bmatrix} \text{Additions} \\ \text{to } K \end{bmatrix} + \begin{bmatrix} \text{Additions} \\ \text{to } A - L \end{bmatrix}}_{\text{Additions (acquisitions minus disposals)}} + \underbrace{\begin{bmatrix} \text{Capital gains} \\ \text{on } K \end{bmatrix} + \begin{bmatrix} \text{Capital gains} \\ \text{on } A - L \end{bmatrix}}_{\text{Valuation effects (gains minus losses)}}$$

There are two kinds of terms in this expression. The total value of wealth (of a person or a country) may change due to *additions* of assets (such as purchases, sales, or net gifts) or due to valuation effects (capital gains—or, if they are negative, capital losses—arising from changes in the prices of assets).

The previous equation can be simplified by two observations. First, additions to the domestic capital stock K have a simpler expression: they are known as investment, denoted I. (Strictly, this is the gross addition to the capital stock; the net addition would require the subtraction of depreciation, and in the previous notation that would be accounted for under valuation effects since depreciating assets fall in value.)

Second, additions to external wealth, $A - L$, also have a simpler expression: they are equal to net additions to external assets minus net additions to external liabilities, and as we saw in the main chapter, these are equal to *minus* the financial account, –FA.

Substituting, we can rewrite the last equations as

$$\begin{bmatrix} \text{Change in} \\ \text{total wealth} \end{bmatrix} = \underbrace{I}_{\substack{\text{Additions to } K \\ = \\ \text{Additions to} \\ \text{assets in the} \\ \text{home economy}}} + \underbrace{(-FA)}_{\substack{\text{Additions to} \\ A - L \\ = \\ \text{Net import of} \\ \text{assets into the} \\ \text{home economy}}} + \underbrace{\begin{bmatrix} \text{Capital gains} \\ \text{on } K \end{bmatrix} + \begin{bmatrix} \text{Capital gains} \\ \text{on } A - L \end{bmatrix}}_{\text{Valuation effects (gains minus losses)}}$$

Now, using the BOP identity, we know that $CA + KA + FA = 0$ so that minus the financial account –FA must equal $CA + KA$; hence, we can write

$$\begin{bmatrix} \text{Change in} \\ \text{total wealth} \end{bmatrix} = I + CA + KA + \underbrace{\begin{bmatrix} \text{Capital gains} \\ \text{on } K \end{bmatrix} + \begin{bmatrix} \text{Capital gains} \\ \text{on } A - L \end{bmatrix}}_{\text{Valuation effects (gains minus losses)}}$$

Notice what has happened here. The BOP identity makes the connection between external asset trade and activity in the current account. We take the connection one step further using the current account identity, $S = I + CA$, which allows us to write

$$\begin{bmatrix} \text{Change in} \\ \text{total wealth} \end{bmatrix} = S + KA + \underbrace{\begin{bmatrix} \text{Capital gains} \\ \text{on } K \end{bmatrix} + \begin{bmatrix} \text{Capital gains} \\ \text{on } A - L \end{bmatrix}}_{\text{Valuation effects (gains minus losses)}}$$

The message of this expression is clear. As we all probably know from personal experience, there are only three ways to get more (or less) wealthy: do more (or less) saving (S), receive (or give) gifts of assets (KA), or enjoy the good (bad) fortune of capital gains (losses) on your portfolio. What is true about individuals' wealth is also true for the wealth of a nation in the aggregate.

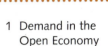

Output, Exchange Rates, and Macroeconomic Policies in the Short Run

If demand shifts from the products of country B to the products of country A, a depreciation by country B or an appreciation by country A would correct the external imbalance and also relieve unemployment in country B and restrain inflation in country A. This is the most favorable case for flexible exchange rates based on national currencies.

Robert Mundell, 1961

It is easy to understand the dislike . . . for a [fixed exchange rate] system which dictated that a slump must be aggravated by monetary reactions, although, doubtless, [people] had forgotten that the same system served to enhance booms.

Alec Ford, 1962

In November 2004, the president of the European Central Bank, Jean-Claude Trichet, declared that the large and persistent depreciation of the U.S. dollar against the euro was "not welcome from the standpoint of the ECB." He also called the exchange rate movements "brutal," the same adjective he had used a few months before. However, later the same month, Alan Greenspan, then chairman of the U.S. Federal Reserve, seemed perfectly at ease as he hinted that movements in the dollar's exchange rate were most likely to continue as an acceptable means of macroeconomic adjustment for the U.S. economy. Why was the ECB president so fretful? Why was his American counterpart so relaxed? Clearly—in the view of at least one of the central bankers—the exchange rate must matter for the economy as a whole.

Thus far our study of exchange rates has been largely disconnected from real activity and the rest of the economy. Chapters 10 through 12 developed a theory of exchange rates, in which the economy's level of output was taken as given. To gain a more complete understanding of how an open economy works, we now extend our theory and explore what happens when exchange rates and output fluctuate in the short run.

To do this, we build on the accounting framework we learned in the balance of payments chapter to understand how macroeconomic aggregates (including output, income, consumption, investment, and the trade balance) move together and in response to shocks in an open economy.

The model we study is an open-economy variant of the well-known IS-LM model that is widely used in the study of closed-economy macroeconomics. The key assumption of this type of Keynesian model is that prices are "sticky" in the short run so that output is determined by shifts in demand in the goods market. When we are finished, we will have a model that explains the relationships among all the major macroeconomic variables in an open economy in the short run.

Naturally, such a model can shed light on many policy issues. We can see how monetary and fiscal policies affect the economy, and discuss how they can be used to stabilize the economy and maintain full employment. One key lesson we learn in this chapter is that the feasibility and effectiveness of macroeconomic policies depend crucially on the type of exchange rate regime in operation.

1 Demand in the Open Economy

To understand macroeconomic fluctuations, we need to grasp how short-run disturbances affect three important markets in an economy: the goods market, the money market, and the forex market. In earlier chapters, we studied the forex market and the money market, so we will recap and apply here what we learned in those chapters. But what about the goods market? In the forex chapters, we assumed that output was fixed at a level $\overline{Y}$. We took this to be the full-employment level of output that would be expected to prevail in the long run, when all factor market prices have adjusted to ensure that all factors like labor and capital are employed. But these assumptions about output and employment are valid only in the long run. To understand short-run fluctuations in economic activity, we now develop a short-run, sticky-price Keynesian model and show how fluctuations in demand can create fluctuations in real economic activity. To start building this model, we first make our assumptions clear and then look at how demand is defined and why it fluctuates.

Preliminaries and Assumptions

Our interest in this chapter is to study short-run fluctuations in a simplified, abstract world of two countries. Our main focus is on the home economy. We use an asterisk to denote foreign variables when we need them. For our purposes, the foreign economy can be thought of as "the rest of the world" (ROW). The key assumptions we make are as follows:

- Because we are examining the short run, we assume that home and foreign price levels, $\overline{P}$ and $\overline{P}^*$, are fixed due to price stickiness. As a result of price stickiness, expected inflation is fixed at zero, $\overline{\pi}^e = 0$. If prices are fixed, all quantities can be viewed as both real and nominal quantities in the short run because there is no inflation.

- We assume that government spending $\overline{G}$ and taxes $\overline{T}$ are fixed at some constant level, which are subject to policy change.

- We assume that conditions in the foreign economy such as foreign output $\overline{Y}^*$ and the foreign interest rate $\overline{i}^*$ are fixed and taken as given. Our main interest is in the equilibrium and fluctuations in the home economy.

■ We assume that income Y is equivalent to output: that is, gross domestic product (GDP) equals gross national disposable income (GNDI). From our study of the national accounts, we know that the difference between the two equals net factor income from abroad plus net unilateral transfers. The analysis in this chapter could easily be extended to include these additional sources of income, but this added complexity would not offer any additional significant insights. We further assume that net factor income from abroad ($NFIA$) and net unilateral transfers (NUT) are zero, which implies that the current account (CA) equals the trade balance (TB); for the rest of this chapter, we shall just refer to the trade balance.

Our main objective is to understand how output (income) is determined in the home economy in the short run. As we learned from the national accounts, total expenditure or demand for home-produced goods and services is made up of four components: consumption, investment, government consumption, and the trade balance. In the following section, we see how each component is determined in the short run, and use the fact that the demand must equal supply to characterize the economy's short-run equilibrium.

Consumption

The simplest model of aggregate private consumption relates household **consumption** C to **disposable income** Y^d. As we have learned in Chapter 13, disposable income is the level of total pretax income Y received by households minus the taxes paid by households $\overline{T}$, so that $Y^d = Y - \overline{T}$. Consumers tend to consume more as their disposable income rises, a relationship that can be represented by an increasing function, called the *consumption function*:

$$\text{Consumption} = C = C(Y - \overline{T})$$

A typical consumption function of this form is graphed in Figure 14-1; it slopes upward because consumption increases when disposable income increases.

This equation is known as the *Keynesian consumption function*. In some economic theories, consumption smoothing is both desirable and feasible. That is, in any given year consumption need not depend on income in that year, but rather on total lifetime resources (wealth). In contrast, the Keynesian consumption function assumes that private consumption expenditure *is* sensitive to changes in current income. This assumption

FIGURE 14-1

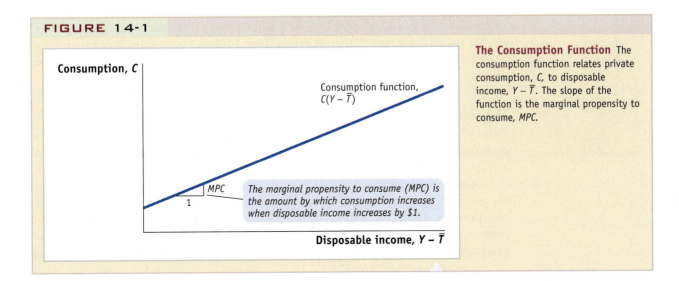

The Consumption Function The consumption function relates private consumption, C, to disposable income, $Y - \overline{T}$. The slope of the function is the marginal propensity to consume, MPC.

Consumption, C

Consumption function, $C(Y - \overline{T})$

MPC

1

The marginal propensity to consume (MPC) is the amount by which consumption increases when disposable income increases by $1.

Disposable income, $Y - \overline{T}$

seems to be a more reasonable match with reality, at least in the short run, given the empirical finding that there is very little consumption smoothing seen in practice, either at the household or national level.

Marginal Effects The consumption function relates the level of consumption to the level of disposable income, but we are more often interested in the response of such variables to small changes in equilibrium, due to policy or other shocks. For that purpose, the slope of the consumption function is called the **marginal propensity to consume (MPC),** and it tells us how much of every extra $1 of disposable income received by households is spent on consumption. We generally assume that *MPC* is between 0 and 1: when consumers receive an extra unit of disposable income (whether it's a euro, dollar, or yen), they will consume only a fraction of it and save the remainder. For example, if you elect to spend $0.75 of every extra $1 of disposable income you receive, your *MPC* is 0.75. We can also define the *marginal propensity to save (MPS)* as $1 - MPC$, so in this example $MPS = 0.25$, meaning that $0.25 of every extra $1 of disposable income is saved.

Investment

The simplest model of aggregate investment makes two key assumptions: firms face an array of possible investment projects, each of which earns a different real return; and a firm will invest capital in a project only if the real returns exceed the firm's cost of borrowing capital. The firm's borrowing cost is the **expected real interest rate** r^e, which equals the nominal interest rate i minus the expected rate of inflation π^e: $r^e = i - \pi^e$. It is important to note that, in general, the expected real interest rate depends not only on the nominal interest rate but also on expected inflation. However, under our simplifying assumption that expected inflation is zero, the expected real interest rate equals the nominal interest rate, $r^e = i$.

When the expected real interest rate in the economy falls, we expect more investment projects to be undertaken. For example, at a real interest rate of 10%, there may be only $1 billion worth of profitable investment projects that firms wish to undertake; but if the real interest rate falls to 5%, there may now be $2 billion worth of profitable projects. Hence, our model assumes that investment I is a decreasing function of the real interest rate; that is, investment falls as the real interest rate rises.

$$\text{Investment} = I = I(i)$$

Remember that this is true only because when expected inflation is zero, the real interest rate equals the nominal interest rate. Figure 14-2 shows a typical investment function of this type. It slopes downward because as the real interest rate falls, the quantity of investment rises.

The Government

To develop a basic model of economic activity in the short run, we will assume that the government's role is simple. It collects an amount T of **taxes** from private households and spends an amount G on **government consumption** of goods and services.

Note that the latter includes only actual spending on goods and services bought by the public sector at all levels. For example, G includes military equipment and personnel, transport and infrastructure, public universities and schools, and so forth. Excluded from this concept are the often huger sums involved in government **transfer programs,** such as social security, medical care, or unemployment benefit systems, that

FIGURE 14-2

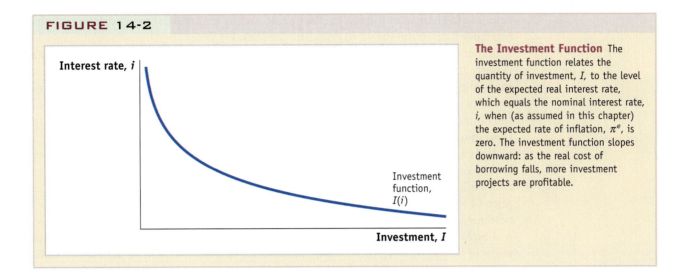

The Investment Function The investment function relates the quantity of investment, I, to the level of the expected real interest rate, which equals the nominal interest rate, i, when (as assumed in this chapter) the expected rate of inflation, π^e, is zero. The investment function slopes downward: as the real cost of borrowing falls, more investment projects are profitable.

redistribute income between households. Such transfers are excluded because we assume that *in the aggregate* they do not generate any change in the total expenditure on goods and services; they merely change who gets to engage in the act of spending.

In the unlikely event that $G = T$ exactly, government spending exactly equals taxes and we say that the government has a *balanced budget*. If $T > G$, the government is said to be running a *budget surplus* (of size $T - G$); if $G > T$, a *budget deficit* (of size $G - T$ or, equivalently, a negative surplus of $T - G$).

Fiscal policy is concerned with the levels of taxes T and spending G set by the government. In this chapter, we do not study in detail why or how governments make such policy choices; we make the simple assumption that in the short run the levels of taxes and spending are set exogenously at some fixed levels, denoted by an overbar:

$$\text{Government purchases} = G = \overline{G}$$
$$\text{Taxes} = T = \overline{T}$$

Policy makers may change these levels of taxes and spending at any time. We analyze the impact of such changes on the economy later in this chapter.

The Trade Balance

In the balance of payments chapter, we saw from an accounting standpoint that the trade balance (equal to exports minus imports) measures the impact of foreign trade on the demand for domestic output. To develop a model, however, we need to know what drives these flows, so in our simple model we now explore three key determinants of the trade balance: the real exchange rate and the level of home and foreign incomes.

The Role of the Real Exchange Rate What is the role of the real exchange rate? Recall George, the American tourist we met at the start of our study of exchange rates, who had to deal with a weaker dollar during his visits to Paris over the course of several years. If U.S. and French prices are sticky (constant in euro and U.S. dollar terms), then as the U.S. exchange rate depreciates, the prices of French goods and services became more and more expensive in dollar terms. In the end, George was ready to take a vacation in California instead. In the aggregate, when spending patterns change in response to changes in the real exchange rate, we say that there is **expenditure switching** from foreign purchases to domestic purchases.

Expenditure switching is a major factor in determining the level of a country's exports and imports. When learning about exchange rates in the long run, we saw that the real exchange rate is the price of goods and services in a foreign economy relative to the price of goods and services in the home economy. If Home's exchange rate is E, the Home price level is $\overline{P}$ (fixed in the short run), and the Foreign price level is $\overline{P}^*$ (also fixed in the short run), then the real exchange rate q of Home is defined as $q = E\overline{P}^*/\overline{P}$.

For example, suppose that the home country is the United States, and the reference basket costs \$100; suppose that in Canada the same basket costs C\$120 and the exchange rate is \$0.90 per Canadian dollar. In the expression $q = E\overline{P}^*/\overline{P}$, the numerator $E\overline{P}^*$ is the price of foreign goods converted into home currency terms, $\$108 = 120 \times 0.90$; the denominator $\overline{P}$ is the home currency price of home goods, \$100; the ratio of the two is the real exchange rate, $q = \$108/\$100 = 1.08$. This is the relative price of foreign goods in terms of home goods. In this case, Canadian goods are more expensive than U.S. goods.

A rise in the home real exchange rate (a real depreciation) signifies that foreign goods have become more expensive relative to home goods. As the real exchange rate rises, both home and foreign consumers will respond by *expenditure switching*: the home country will import less (as *home* consumers switch to buying home goods) and export more (as *foreign* consumers switch to buying home goods). These concepts are often seen in economic debates and news coverage (see **Headlines: Expenditure Switching and the Dollar Devaluation** and **The Curry Trade**) and they provide us with the following insight:

■ *We expect the trade balance of the home country to be an increasing function of the home country's real exchange rate. That is, as the home country's real exchange rate rises (depreciates), it will export more and import less, and the trade balance rises.*

The Role of Income Levels The other determinant of the trade balance we might wish to consider is the income level in each country. As we argued earlier in our discussion of the consumption function, when domestic disposable income increases, consumers tend to spend more on all forms of consumption, including consumption of foreign goods. These arguments provide a second insight:

■ *We expect an increase in home income to be associated with an increase in home imports and a fall in the home country's trade balance.*

Symmetrically, from the rest of the world's standpoint, an increase in rest of the world income ought to be associated with an increase in rest of the world spending on home goods, resulting in an increase in home exports. This is our third insight:

■ *We expect an increase in rest of the world income to be associated with an increase in home exports and a rise in the home country's trade balance.*

Combining the three insights above, we can write the trade balance as a function of three variables: the real exchange rate, home disposable income, and rest of the world disposable income:

$$TB = TB(\underbrace{E\overline{P}^*/\overline{P}}_{\substack{\text{Increasing} \\ \text{function}}}, \underbrace{Y - \overline{T}}_{\substack{\text{Decreasing} \\ \text{function}}}, \underbrace{Y^* - \overline{T}^*}_{\substack{\text{Increasing} \\ \text{function}}})$$

We show the relationship between the trade balance and the real exchange rate in Figure 14-3, for the home country, all else equal—that is, holding home and foreign disposable income fixed. The trade balance is an *increasing* function of the real

HEADLINES

Expenditure Switching and the Dollar Devaluation

From 2001 to 2004, the U.S. dollar began a sustained depreciation against many currencies. The economic impacts were reflected in the following string of pronouncements—in the space of just one week—from all corners of the globe and found in The Financial Times.

DOLLAR'S DIVE SET TO DELIGHT EXPORTERS AS WELL AS TOURISTS
January 9, 2004. Listen carefully to the crowds shuffling down New York's Fifth Avenue, and the more immediate effects of the plummeting dollar are obvious in the voices of European shoppers enjoying dramatic increases in purchasing power. One couple from London caused a stir at Saks department store by walking in and spending $25,000 on a single diamond necklace. . . . By the fourth quarter of this year, the National Association of Manufacturers expects exports to be up by 12 per cent, with its members also benefiting from falling imports as rivals abroad struggle with the other side of the exchange rate coin.

EURO'S RAPID RISE WORRIES ECB
January 9, 2004. The European Central Bank yesterday signaled its growing unease over the rapid rise of the euro against the dollar. . . . Jean Claude Trichet, bank president, said repeatedly the bank did not like "excessive volatility" in foreign exchange markets. . . . Pascal Lamy, the EU's trade commissioner, said the euro was approaching a level that could be worrying for the competitiveness of the eurozone's exporters.

EURO ERODES GERMANY'S ROLE AS AN INDUSTRIAL POWERHOUSE
January 13, 2004. The currency's seemingly unstoppable ascent against the dollar is speeding an industrial decline.

. . . Economists expect even more jobs to go as German companies struggle to cut costs and boost productivity.

STRONG CURRENCY HITS AUSTRALIANS
January 13, 2004. Almost one in five Australian manufacturers are considering moving production offshore because of the strengthening of the Australian dollar in the past two years, says a report. . . . The study, based on a survey of 800 manufacturers, found that lost sales due to import penetration were at least as significant as lower export returns. . . . "At this level exports struggle to compete on world markets," it said.

FIGURE 14-3

The Trade Balance and the Real Exchange Rate The trade balance is an increasing function of the real exchange rate, $E\bar{P}^*/\bar{P}$. When there is a real depreciation (a rise in q), foreign goods become more expensive relative to home goods, and we expect the trade balance to increase as exports rise and imports fall (a rise in TB). The trade balance may also depend on income. If home income levels rise, then some of the increase in income may be spent on the consumption of imports. For example, if home income rises from Y_1 to Y_2, then the trade balance will decrease, whatever the level of the real exchange rate, and the trade balance function will shift down.

HEADLINES

The Curry Trade

In 2009, a dramatic weakening of the pound against the euro sparked an unlikely boom in cross-Channel grocery deliveries.

If carrying coals to Newcastle is judged a pointless exercise, then importing croissants, baguettes and bottles of claret into France might seem even more absurd. But, due to the strength of the euro against the pound, hundreds of Britons living in France are now using the internet to order their food, including many French specialties, from British supermarkets.

Simon Goodenough, the director of Sterling Shopping, a delivery firm based in Brackley, Northamptonshire, says his company has 2,500 British customers in France and is running five delivery vans full of food to France each week.

"We deliver food from Waitrose, Sainsbury's and Marks and Spencer, but by far the biggest is Asda," said Goodenough ". . .We sit in our depot sometimes looking at the things people have bought and just laugh at the craziness of it all. We have

seen croissants and baguettes in people's shopping bags. And we have delivered bottles of Bergerac wine bought from Sainsbury's to a customer in Bergerac. We even have a few French customers who have now heard about what we do. They love things like curries and tacos, which they just can't get in France.". . .

Goodenough said many of his company's British customers hold pensions or savings in sterling rather than euros: "They have seen a 30% drop in their spending power over the past 18 months."

John Steventon owns La Maison Removals, a delivery company based in Rayleigh, Essex. It takes food from its warehouse to about 1,000 British customers in central France.

"We just can't cope with demand at the moment," he said. . . . "We found that friends in France were asking us to

bring over British food for them so we just thought it made sense to set up a food delivery service. . . . The savings for buying food, in particular, are amazing due to the strength of the euro. Customers tell us that for every £100 they would spend in France buying food, they save £30 buying through us, even with our 15% commission. A lot of people are using us to get things they really miss, such as bacon and sausages."

Nikki Bundy, 41, has lived near Périgueux in the Dordogne with her family for four years. . . . "It's just so much cheaper for us to buy our food this way. . . . The food in France is lovely, but you can come out of a supermarket here with just two carrier bags having spent €100. I still try and buy my fresh fruit and veg in France, but most other things I now buy from Asda."

Source: Excerpted from Leo Hickman, "Expat Orders for British Supermarket Food Surge on Strength of euro," The Guardian, June 9, 2010.

exchange rate $E\overline{P}^*/\overline{P}$. Thus, the relationship shown in Figure 14-3 is upward-sloping. The reason is that an increase in the real exchange rate (a real depreciation) increases TB by raising exports and lowering imports, implying a movement along the curve drawn.

The effect of the real exchange rate on the trade balance is now clear. What about the effects of changes in output? An illustration of the impact of an increase in home output on the trade balance is shown in Figure 14-3. At any level of the real exchange rate, an increase in home output leads to more spending on imports, lowering the trade balance. This change would be represented as a downward shift in the trade balance curve, that is, a reduction in TB for a given level of Y.

Marginal Effects Once More The impact of changes in output on the trade balance can also be thought of in terms of the marginal propensity to consume. Suppose home output (which equals home income, because of the assumptions we've made) rises by an amount $\Delta Y = \$1$ and that, all else equal, this leads to an increase in home imports of $\Delta IM = \$MPC_F$, where $MPC_F > 0$. We refer to MPC_F as the *marginal propensity to consume foreign imports*. For example, if $MPC_F = 0.1$, this means that out of every additional \$1 of income, \$0.10 are spent on imports.

How does MPC_F relate to the MPC seen earlier? After a \$1 rise in income, any additional goods consumed have to come from somewhere, home or abroad. The fraction

MPC of the $1 increment spent on all consumption must equal the sum of the incremental spending on home goods plus incremental spending on foreign goods. Let $MPC_H > 0$ be the *marginal propensity to consume home goods.* By assumption $MPC = MPC_H + MPC_F$. For example, if $MPC_F = 0.10$ and $MPC_H = 0.65$, then $MPC = 0.75$; for every extra dollar of disposable income, home consumers spend 75 cents, 10 cents on imported foreign goods and 65 cents on home goods (and they save 25 cents).[1]

APPLICATION

The Trade Balance and the Real Exchange Rate

Our theory assumes that the trade balance increases when the real exchange rate rises. Is there evidence to support this proposition? In Figure 14-4, we examine the evolution of the U.S. trade balance (as a share of GDP) in recent years as compared with the U.S. real exchange rate with the rest of the world.

FIGURE 14-4

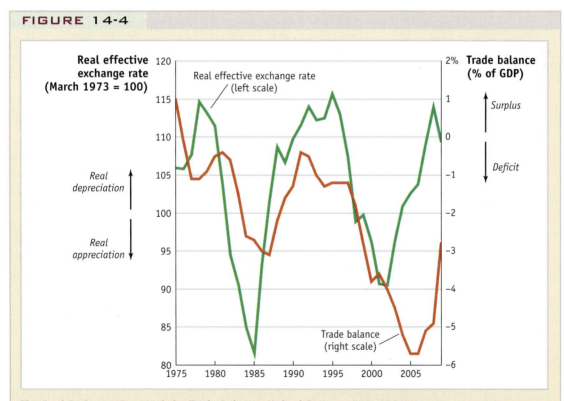

The Real Exchange Rate and the Trade Balance: United States, 1975–2006 Does the real exchange rate affect the trade balance in the way we have assumed? The data show that the U.S. trade balance is correlated with the U.S. real effective exchange rate index. Because the trade balance also depends on changes in U.S. and rest of the world disposable income (and other factors), it may respond with a lag to changes in the real exchange rate, so the correlation is not perfect (as seen in the years 2000–2006).

Sources: U.S. Federal Reserve; Bureau of Economic Analysis NIPA.

---

[1] A similar calculation can be applied to the export function, where exports will depend on the marginal propensity to consume imports in the foreign country.

By considering the home country to be the United States and the foreign "country" to be the rest of the world, we cannot use data on the *bilateral* real exchange rate q for any individual foreign country. We need a composite or weighted-average measure of the price of goods in all foreign countries relative to the price of U.S. goods. To accomplish this, economists construct *multilateral* measures of real exchange rate movement.

The most common weighting scheme uses a weight equal to that country's share in the home country's trade. If there are N foreign countries, we can write home's total trade as the sum of its trade with each foreign country: Trade = Trade$_1$ + Trade$_2$ + ⋯ + Trade$_N$. Applying a trade weight to each bilateral real exchange rate's percentage change, we obtain the percentage change in home's multilateral real exchange rate or **real effective exchange rate:**

$$\underbrace{\frac{\Delta q_{\text{effective}}}{q_{\text{effective}}}}_{\substack{\text{Real effective exchange} \\ \text{rate change (in \%)}}} = \underbrace{\left(\frac{\text{Trade}_1}{\text{Trade}}\frac{\Delta q_1}{q_1}\right) + \left(\frac{\text{Trade}_2}{\text{Trade}}\frac{\Delta q_2}{q_2}\right) + \cdots + \left(\frac{\text{Trade}_N}{\text{Trade}}\frac{\Delta q_N}{q_N}\right)}_{\text{Trade-weighted average of bilateral real exchange rate changes (in \%)}}$$

For example, if we trade 40% with country 1 and 60% with country 2, and we have a real appreciation of 10% against 1 but a real depreciation of 30% against 2, then the change in our real effective exchange rate is (40% × −10%) + (60% × 30%) = (0.4 × −0.1) + (0.6 × 0.3) = −0.04 + 0.18 = 0.14 = + 14%. That is, we have experienced an effective trade-weighted real depreciation of 14%.

Figure 14-4 shows that the U.S. multilateral real exchange rate and the U.S. trade balance have been mostly positively correlated, as predicted by our model. In periods when the United States has experienced a real depreciation, the U.S. trade balance has tended to increase. Conversely, real appreciations have usually been associated with a fall in the trade balance. However, the correlation between the real exchange rate and the trade balance is not perfect. There appears to be lag between, say, a real depreciation and a rise in the trade balance (as in the mid-1980s). Why? Import and export flows may react only slowly or weakly to changes in the real exchange rate, so the trade balance can react in unexpected ways (see **Side Bar: Barriers to Expenditure Switching: Pass-Through and J Curve**). We can also see that the trade balance and real exchange rate did not move together as much during the years 2000 to 2008 because other factors, such as tax cuts and wartime spending, may have created extra deficit pressures that spilled over into the U.S. current account during this period. ■

Exogenous Changes in Demand

We have already treated as given, or exogenous, the changes or *shocks* in demand that originate in changes to government purchases or taxes. However, other exogenous changes in demand can affect consumption, investment, or the trade balance, and it is important to know how to analyze these, too. Examples of such changes are illustrated in Figure 14-6.

■ *An exogenous change in consumption.* Suppose that at any given level of disposable income, consumers decide to spend more on consumption. After this shock, the consumption function would shift up as in Figure 14-6, panel (a). For example, an increase in household wealth following a stock market or housing market boom (as seen in expansions since 1990) could lead to a shift of this sort. This is a change in consumption demand unconnected to disposable income.

SIDE BAR

Barriers to Expenditure Switching: Pass-Through and the J Curve

The basic analysis in the text assumes that two key mechanisms are operating. First, we assume that a nominal depreciation causes a real depreciation and raises the price of foreign imports relative to home exports. Second, we assume that such a change in relative prices will lower imports, raise exports, and increase the trade balance. In reality, there are reasons why both mechanisms operate weakly or with a lag.

Trade Dollarization, Distribution, and Pass-Through

One assumption we made was that prices are sticky in local currency. But what if some *home* goods prices are set in *foreign* currency?

For example, let the foreign country be the United States and suppose a share d of the home-produced basket of goods is priced in U.S. dollars at a sticky *dollar* price $\overline{P}_1$. Suppose the remaining share, $1 - d$, is priced, as before, in local currency at a sticky *local currency* price $\overline{P}_2$. Hence,

$$\left.\begin{array}{c}\text{Price of foreign goods} \\ \text{relative to dollar-priced} \\ \text{home goods}\end{array}\right\} = \frac{E \times \overline{P}^*}{E \times \overline{P}_1} = \frac{\overline{P}^*}{\overline{P}_1} \text{ has a weight} = d$$

$$\left.\begin{array}{c}\text{Price of foreign goods} \\ \text{relative to local-currency-} \\ \text{priced home goods}\end{array}\right\} = \frac{E \times \overline{P}^*}{\overline{P}_2} \text{ has a weight} = 1 - d$$

What now is the price of all foreign-produced goods relative to all home-produced goods (the real exchange rate)? It is the weighted sum of the relative prices of the two parts of the basket. Hence, we find

$$q = \text{Home real exchange rate} = d\frac{\overline{P}^*}{\overline{P}_1} + (1 - d)\frac{E\overline{P}^*}{\overline{P}_2}$$

The first term with a weight d does not contain E because both numerator and denominator are dollar prices (already expressed in a common currency). Only the second term with a weight $(1 - d)$ contains E, since the prices are in different currencies. Thus, a 1% increase in E will lead to only a $(1 - d)$% increase in the real exchange rate.

When d is 0, all home goods are priced in local currency and we have our basic model. A 1% rise in E causes a 1% rise in q. There is full **pass-through** from changes in the nominal exchange rate to changes in the real exchange rate. But as d rises, pass-through falls. If d is 0.5, then a 1% rise in E causes just a 0.5% rise in q. The real exchange rate becomes less responsive to changes in the nominal exchange rate, and this means that expenditure switching effects will be muted.

It turns out that many countries around the world conduct a large fraction of their trade in a currency other than their own, such as U.S. dollars. The most obvious examples of goods with dollar prices are the major commodities: oil, copper, wheat, and

so on. In some Persian Gulf economies, a nominal depreciation of the exchange rate does almost nothing to change the price of exports (more than 90% of which is oil priced in dollars) relative to the price of imports (again, overwhelmingly priced in dollars).

But dollar invoicing—and in Greater Europe, euro invoicing—extends around the world, as shown in Table 14-1. Over 90% of U.S. imports are priced in dollars: all else equal, a U.S. depreciation will hardly change the prices of these imports at all. Some

TABLE 14-1

Trade Dollarization The table shows the extent to which the dollar and the euro were used in the invoicing of payments for exports and imports of different countries in the 2002–2004 period. In the United States, for example, 100% of exports are invoiced and paid in U.S. dollars but so, too, are 93% of imports. In Asia, U.S. dollar invoicing is very common, accounting for 48% of Japanese exports and more than 75% of exports and imports in Korea, Malaysia, and Thailand. In Europe the euro figures more prominently as the currency used for trade, but the U.S. dollar is still used in a sizable share of transactions.

	Exports Denominated in		Imports Denominated in	
	U.S. Dollar	Euro	U.S. Dollar	Euro
United States	100%	—	93%	—
United Kingdom	26	21%	37	27%
Australia	70	1	50	9
Asia				
Japan	48	10	9	5
Korea	83	7	80	5
Malaysia	90	—	90	—
Thailand	85	3	76	4
Eurozone				
France	34	52	47	45
Germany	24	63	34	55
Italy	18	75	25	70
Greece	46	47	55	40
Spain	30	61	36	60
EU New Accession Countries				
Czech Republic	13	70	18	66
Hungary	12	83	19	73
Latvia	27	57	—	49
Slovakia	12	74	21	60

Source: Selected data from Linda Goldberg and Cédric Tille, "The Internationalization of the Dollar and Trade Balance Adjustment," Federal Reserve Bank of New York Staff Report 255, August 2006.

Asian countries have trade flows that are 70% to 90% dollarized. Much of this is intra-Asian trade; if, say, a Korean supplier sells to a Japanese manufacturer, very often they conduct the trade not in yen or won, but entirely in U.S. dollars, which is the currency of neither the exporter nor the importer! The table also shows that many new EU member states in Eastern Europe have export shares largely denominated in euros.

Trade dollarization is not the only factor limiting pass-through in the real world. Even after an import has arrived at the port, it still has to pass through various intermediaries. The retail, wholesale, and other distribution activities all add a local currency cost or markup to the final price paid by the ultimate buyer. Suppose the markup is $100 on an import that costs $100 at the port, so the good retails for $200 in shops. Suppose a 10% depreciation of the dollar raises the port price to $110. All else equal, the retail price will rise to just $210, only a 5% increase at the point of final sale. Thus, expenditure switching by final users will be muted by the limited pass-through from port prices to final prices.

How large are these effects? A recent study of 76 developed and developing countries found that, over the period of one year, a 10% exchange rate depreciation resulted in a 6.5% rise in imported goods prices at the port of arrival but perhaps only a 4% rise in the retail prices of imported goods.[*]

The J Curve

Our model of the trade balance assumes that a real depreciation improves a country's trade balance by increasing exports and reducing imports. In reality, however, these effects may be slow to appear because orders for export and import goods are placed months in advance. Thus, at the moment of depreciation there will be no instantaneous change in export and import volumes.

What does this slow adjustment imply? Exports will continue to sell for a time in the same quantity and at the same domestic price, and so total export earnings remain fixed. What will change is the domestic price paid for the import goods. They will have become more expensive in domestic currency terms. If the same quantity of imports flows in but costs more per unit, then the home country's total import bill will rise.

As a result, if export earnings are fixed but import expenditures are rising, the trade balance will initially *fall* rather than rise, as shown in Figure 14-5. Only after time passes, and export and import orders adjust to the new relative prices, will the trade balance move in the positive direction we have assumed. Because of its distinctive shape, the curve traced out by the trade balance over time in Figure 14-5 is called the **J Curve.** Some empirical studies find that the effects of the J Curve last up to a year after the initial depreciation. Hence, the assumption that a depreciation boosts spending on the home country's goods may not hold in the very short run.

---

[*] Jeffrey A. Frankel, David C. Parsley, and Shang-Jin Wei, 2005, "Slow Passthrough around the World: A New Import for Developing Countries?" National Bureau of Economic Research (NBER) Working Paper No. 11199.

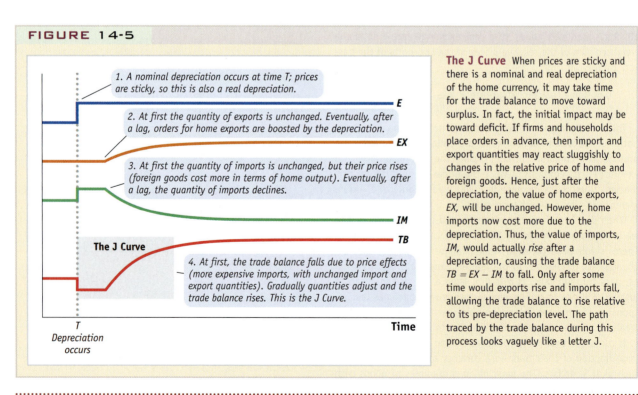

FIGURE 14-5

1. A nominal depreciation occurs at time T; prices are sticky, so this is also a real depreciation.

E

2. At first the quantity of exports is unchanged. Eventually, after a lag, orders for home exports are boosted by the depreciation.

EX

3. At first the quantity of imports is unchanged, but their price rises (foreign goods cost more in terms of home output). Eventually, after a lag, the quantity of imports declines.

IM

TB

The J Curve

4. At first, the trade balance falls due to price effects (more expensive imports, with unchanged import and export quantities). Gradually quantities adjust and the trade balance rises. This is the J Curve.

T
Depreciation occurs

Time

The J Curve When prices are sticky and there is a nominal and real depreciation of the home currency, it may take time for the trade balance to move toward surplus. In fact, the initial impact may be toward deficit. If firms and households place orders in advance, then import and export quantities may react sluggishly to changes in the relative price of home and foreign goods. Hence, just after the depreciation, the value of home exports, *EX*, will be unchanged. However, home imports now cost more due to the depreciation. Thus, the value of imports, *IM*, would actually *rise* after a depreciation, causing the trade balance $TB = EX - IM$ to fall. Only after some time would exports rise and imports fall, allowing the trade balance to rise relative to its pre-depreciation level. The path traced by the trade balance during this process looks vaguely like a letter J.

FIGURE 14-6

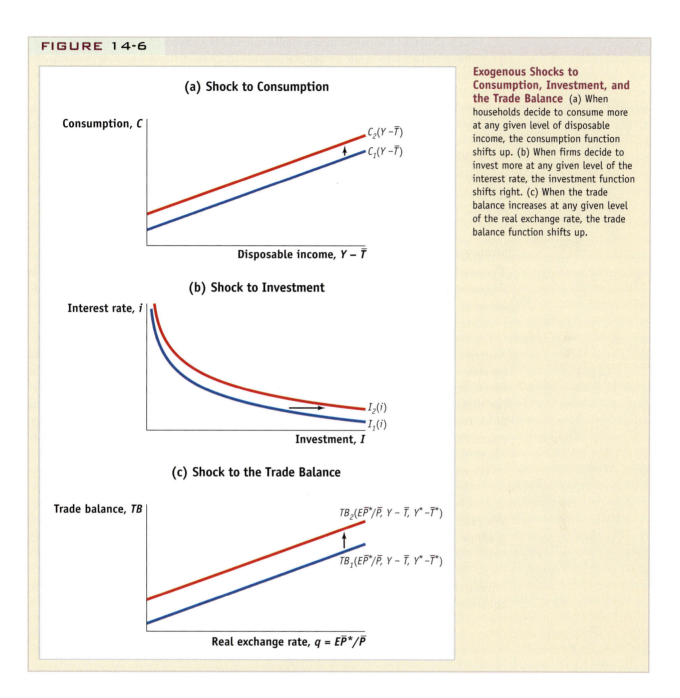

(a) Shock to Consumption

Consumption, C

$C_2(Y - \bar{T})$
$C_1(Y - \bar{T})$

Disposable income, $Y - \bar{T}$

(b) Shock to Investment

Interest rate, i

$I_2(i)$
$I_1(i)$

Investment, I

(c) Shock to the Trade Balance

Trade balance, TB

$TB_2(E\bar{P}^*/\bar{P}, Y - \bar{T}, Y^* - \bar{T}^*)$

$TB_1(E\bar{P}^*/\bar{P}, Y - \bar{T}, Y^* - \bar{T}^*)$

Real exchange rate, $q = E\bar{P}^*/\bar{P}$

Exogenous Shocks to Consumption, Investment, and the Trade Balance (a) When households decide to consume more at any given level of disposable income, the consumption function shifts up. (b) When firms decide to invest more at any given level of the interest rate, the investment function shifts right. (c) When the trade balance increases at any given level of the real exchange rate, the trade balance function shifts up.

■ *An exogenous change in investment.* Suppose that at any given level of the interest rate, firms decide to invest more. After this shock, the investment function would shift up as in Figure 14-6, panel (b). For example, a belief that high-technology companies had great prospects for success led to a large surge in investment in this sector in many countries in the 1990s. This is a change in investment demand unconnected to the interest rate.

■ *An exogenous change in the trade balance.* Suppose that at any given level of the real exchange rate, export demand rises and/or import demand falls. After one of these shocks, trade balance function would shift up as in Figure 14-6, panel (c).

Such a change happened in the 1980s when U.S. consumers' tastes shifted away from the large domestic automobiles made in Detroit toward smaller fuel-efficient imported cars manufactured in Japan. This is a switch in demand away from U.S. and toward Japanese products unconnected with the real exchange rate.

2 Goods Market Equilibrium: The Keynesian Cross

We have now studied the determinants of each component of demand. We next put all the components together and show that the goods market is in equilibrium when total demand from all these components is equal to total supply.

Supply and Demand

The total aggregate *supply* of final goods and services is equal to total national output measured by GDP. Given our assumption that the current account equals the trade balance, gross national income Y equals GDP:

$$\text{Supply} = GDP = Y$$

Aggregate demand, or just "demand," consists of all the possible sources of demand for this supply of output. In the balance of payments chapter, we studied the expenditure side of the national income accounts and saw that supply is absorbed into different uses according to the national income identity. This accounting identity *always* holds true. But an identity is not an economic model. A model must explain how, in equilibrium, the observed demands take on their desired or planned values and still satisfy the accounting identity. How can we construct such a model?

We may write total demand for GDP as

$$\text{Demand} = D = C + I + G + TB$$

We can substitute the formulae for consumption, investment, and the trade balance presented in the first section of this chapter into this total demand equation to obtain

$$D = C(Y - \overline{T}) + I(i) + \overline{G} + TB(E\overline{P}^{*}/\overline{P}, Y - \overline{T}, Y^{*} - \overline{T}^{*})$$

Finally, in an equilibrium, demand D must equal supply Y, so from the preceding two equations we can see that the **goods market equilibrium condition** is

$$Y = \underbrace{C(Y - \overline{T}) + I(i) + \overline{G} + TB(E\overline{P}^{*}/\overline{P}, Y - \overline{T}, Y^{*} - \overline{T}^{*})}_{D} \tag{14-1}$$

Determinants of Demand

The right-hand side of Equation (14-1) shows that many factors can affect demand: home and foreign output (Y and Y^{*}), home and foreign taxes (T and T^{*}), the home nominal interest rate (i), government spending ($\overline{G}$), and the real exchange rate ($E\overline{P}^{*}/\overline{P}$). Let us examine each of these in turn. We start with home output Y, and assume that all other factors remain fixed.

A rise in output Y (all else equal) will cause the right-hand side to increase. For example, suppose output increases by $\Delta Y = \$1$. This change causes consumption spending C to increase by $+\$MPC$. The change in imports will be $+MPC_F$, causing the trade balance to change by $-\$MPC_F$. So the total change in D will be $\$(MPC - MPC_F) = \$MPC_H > 0$, a positive number. This is an intuitive result: an extra \$1 of output generates some spending on home goods (an amount $\$MPC_H$), with the remainder either spent on foreign goods (an amount $\$MPC_F$) or saved (an amount $\$MPS$).

Using this result, Figure 14-7, panel (a), plots demand D, the right-hand side of Equation (14-1), as a function of income or output Y only. For the moment, we hold fixed all other determinants of D. Because D increases as Y increases, the demand function has a positive slope MPC_H, a number between 0 and 1.

Also drawn is the 45-degree line, which represents Y, the left-hand side of Equation (14-1). The 45-degree line has a slope of 1, so it is steeper than the demand function.

FIGURE 14-7

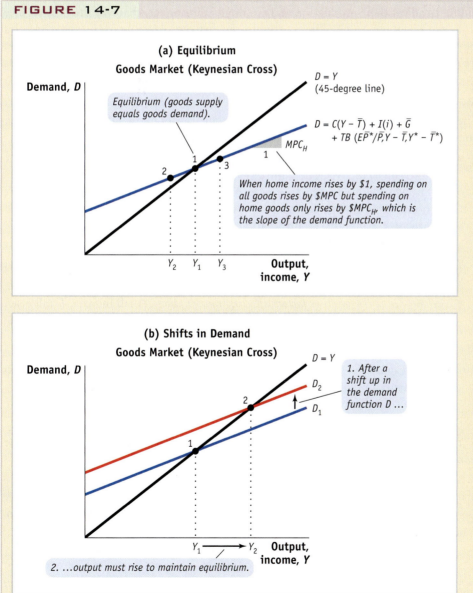

(a) Equilibrium
Goods Market (Keynesian Cross)

Demand, D

$D = Y$
(45-degree line)

Equilibrium (goods supply equals goods demand).

$D = C(Y - \bar{T}) + I(i) + \bar{G} + TB\,(E\bar{P}^*/\bar{P}, Y - \bar{T}, Y^* - \bar{T}^*)$

MPC_H

When home income rises by \$1, spending on all goods rises by $\$MPC$ but spending on home goods only rises by $\$MPC_H$, which is the slope of the demand function.

Y_2 Y_1 Y_3 Output, income, Y

(b) Shifts in Demand
Goods Market (Keynesian Cross)

Demand, D

$D = Y$

D_2

1. *After a shift up in the demand function D …*

D_1

$Y_1 \longrightarrow Y_2$ Output, income, Y

2. …*output must rise to maintain equilibrium.*

Panel (a): The Goods Market Equilibrium and the Keynesian Cross Equilibrium is where demand, D, equals real output or income, Y. In this diagram, equilibrium is a point 1, at an income or output level of Y_1. The goods market will adjust toward this equilibrium. At point 2, the output level is Y_2 and demand, D, exceeds supply, Y; as inventories fall, firms expand production and output rises toward Y_1. At point 3, the output level is Y_3 and supply Y exceeds demand; as inventories rise, firms cut production and output falls toward Y_1.

Panel (b): Shifts in Demand The goods market is initially in equilibrium at point 1, at which demand and supply both equal Y_1. An increase in demand, D, at all levels of real output, Y, shifts the demand curve up from D_1 to D_2. Equilibrium shifts to point 2, where demand and supply are higher and both equal Y_2. Such an increase in demand could result from changes in one or more of the components of demand: C, I, G, or TB.

This diagram is often called the **Keynesian cross.** It depicts the goods market equilibrium: the goods market is in equilibrium at point 1 where the two lines intersect, for that is the unique point where $D = Y$. This corresponds to an income or output level of Y_1.

Why does the goods market adjust to an equilibrium at this point? To the right of point 1, output tends to fall; to the left of point 1, output tends to rise. Why? At point 2, the output level is Y_2 and demand D exceeds supply Y; as inventories fall, firms expand production and output rises toward Y_1. At point 3, the output level is Y_3 and supply Y exceeds demand; as inventories rise, firms cut production and output falls toward Y_1. Only at point 1 are firms in an equilibrium in which production levels are stable in the short run.

Note the crucial assumptions in this model are that prices are fixed and firms are willing to adjust their production and employment to meet whatever the desired level of demand happens to be. These assumptions may be plausible in the short run, but they do not apply in the long run, when prices can adjust and output and employment are determined by the economy's ability to fully employ its technology and resources.

Factors That Shift the Demand Curve

The Keynesian cross also allows us to examine the impact of the other factors in Equation (14-1) on goods market equilibrium. Let's look at four important cases:

- *A change in government spending.* An exogenous rise in government purchases $\overline{G}$ (all else equal) increases demand at every level of output, as seen in Equation (14-1). More government purchases directly add to the total demand in the economy. This change causes an upward shift in the demand function D, as in Figure 14-7, panel (b). Goods market equilibrium shifts from point 1 to point 2, to an output level Y_2.

The lesson: any exogenous change in G (due to changes in the government budget) will cause the demand curve to shift.

- *A change in taxes (or other factors affecting consumption).* A fall in taxes $\overline{T}$ (all else equal) increases disposable income. When consumers have more disposable income, they spend more on consumption. This change raises demand at every level of output Y, because C increases as disposable income increases. This is seen in Equation (14-1) and in Figure 14-7, panel (a). Thus, a fall in taxes shifts the demand function upward from D_1 to D_2, as shown again in Figure 14-7, panel (b). The increase in D causes the goods market equilibrium to shift from point 1 to point 2, and output rises to Y_2.

The lesson: any exogenous change in C (due to changes in taxes, tastes, etc.) will cause the demand curve to shift.

- *A change in the home interest rate (or other factors affecting investment).* A fall in the interest rate i (all else equal) will lead to an increase in I, as firms find it profitable to engage in more investment projects, and spend more. This change leads to an increase in demand D at every level of output Y. The demand function D shifts upward, as seen in Figure 14-7, panel (b). The increase in demand causes the goods market equilibrium to shift from point 1 to point 2, and output rises to Y_2.

The lesson: any exogenous change in I (due to changes in interest rates, the expected profitability of investment, changes in tax policy, etc.) will cause the demand curve to shift.

■ *A change in the home exchange rate.* A rise in the nominal exchange rate E (all else equal) implies a rise in the real exchange rate EP^*/P (due to sticky prices). This is a real depreciation, and through its effects on the trade balance TB via expenditure switching, it will increase demand D at any given level of home output Y. For example, spending switches from foreign goods to American goods when the U.S. dollar depreciates. This change causes the demand function D to shift up, as seen yet again in Figure 14-7, panel (b).

The lesson: any change in the exchange rate will cause the demand curve to shift.

■ *A change in the home or foreign price level.* If prices are flexible, then a *rise* in foreign prices or a *fall* in domestic prices causes a home real depreciation, raising $q = E\overline{P}^*/\overline{P}$. This real depreciation causes TB to rise and, all else equal, it will increase demand D at any given level of home output Y. For example, spending switches from foreign goods to American goods when the U.S. prices fall. This change causes the demand function D to shift up, as seen yet again in Figure 14-7, panel (b).

The lesson: any change in P^* or P will cause the demand curve to shift.

Summary

An increase in output Y causes a move along the demand curve. But any increase in demand that is *not* due to a change in output Y will instead cause the demand curve itself to shift upward in the Keynesian cross diagram, as in Figure 14-7, panel (b). Similarly, any contraction in demand not due to output changes will cause the demand function to shift downward.

To conclude, the main factors that shift the demand curve out are as follows:

Factors That Shift the Demand Curve

Fall in taxes $\overline{T}$
Rise in government spending $\overline{G}$
Fall in the home interest rate i
Rise in the nominal exchange rate E
Rise in foreign prices P^*
Fall in home prices P
Any shift up in the consumption function C
Any shift up in the investment function I
Any shift up in the trade balance function TB

$\Rightarrow$ Demand curve D shifts up

Increase in demand D at a given level of output Y

The opposite changes lead to a decrease in demand and shift the demand curve in.

3 Goods and Forex Market Equilibria: Deriving the IS Curve

We have made an important first step in our study of the short-run behavior of exchange rates and output. Our analysis of demand shows how the level of output adjusts to ensure a goods market equilibrium, given the levels of each component of demand. Each component, in turn, has its own particular determinants, and we have examined how shifts in these determinants (or in other exogenous factors) might shift the level of demand and, hence, change the equilibrium level of output.

But there is more than one market in the economy, and a *general equilibrium* requires equilibrium in all markets—that is, equilibrium in the goods market, the money market, and the forex market. We need to bring all three markets into the analysis, and we do that next by developing a tool of macroeconomic analysis known as the IS-LM diagram. A version of this may be familiar to you from the study of closed-economy macroeconomics, but in this chapter we develop a variant of this approach for an open economy.

Analyzing equilibria in three markets simultaneously is a tall order, but it is made more manageable by proceeding one step at a time. Our first step builds on the depiction of goods market equilibrium developed in the last section using the Keynesian cross and adds on the depiction of forex market equilibrium that we developed in the earlier exchange rate chapters.

Equilibrium in Two Markets

We begin by defining the **IS curve,** which is one part of the IS-LM diagram.

The IS curve shows combinations of output Y and the interest rate i for which the goods and forex markets are in equilibrium.

In Figure 14-8, panel (b), we derive the IS curve by using the Keynesian cross to analyze goods market equilibrium. In panel (c), we impose the uncovered interest parity relationship that ensures the forex market is in equilibrium.

Before we continue, let's take a closer look at why the various graphs in this figure are oriented as they are. The Keynesian cross in panel (a) and the IS diagram in panel (b) share a common horizontal axis, the level of output or income. Hence, these figures are arranged one above the other so that these common output axes line up.

The forex market in panel (c) and the IS diagram in panel (b) share a common vertical axis, the level of the interest rate. Hence, these figures are arranged side by side so that these common interest rate axes line up.

We thus know that if output Y is at a level consistent with demand equals supply, shown in the Keynesian cross in panel (a), and if the interest rate i is at a level consistent with uncovered interest parity, shown in the forex market in panel (c), then in panel (b) we must have a combination of Y and i that is consistent with equilibrium in both goods and forex markets.

Forex Market Recap

In earlier chapters we learned that the forex market is in equilibrium when the expected returns expressed in domestic currency are the same on foreign and domestic interest-bearing (money market) bank deposits. Equation (10-3) described this condition, known as uncovered interest parity (UIP):

The expected return on the foreign deposit *measured in home currency* equals the foreign interest rate plus the expected rate of depreciation of the home currency.

Taking the foreign interest rate i^* and expectations of the future exchange rate E^e as given, we know that the right-hand side of this expression decreases as E increases: the

FIGURE 14-8

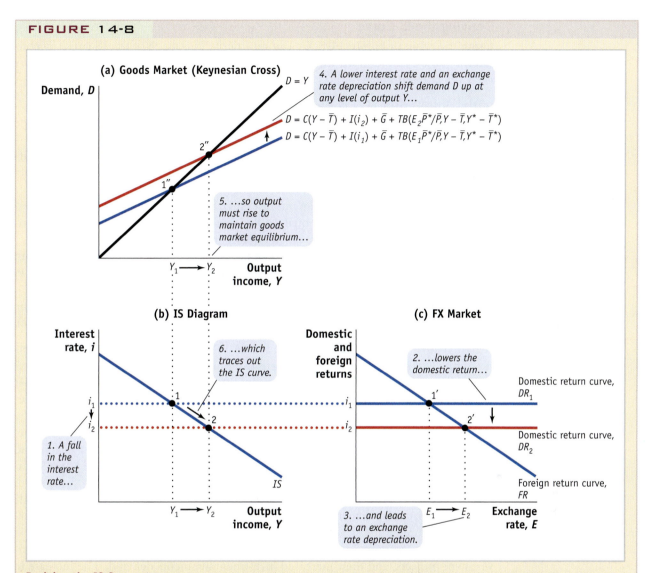

Deriving the IS Curve The Keynesian cross is in panel (a), *IS* curve in panel (b), and forex (FX) market in panel (c). The economy starts in equilibrium with output, Y_1; interest rate, i_1; and exchange rate, E_1. Consider the effect of a decrease in the interest rate from i_1 to i_2, all else equal. In panel (c), a lower interest rate causes a depreciation; equilibrium moves from 1′ to 2′. A lower interest rate boosts investment and a depreciation boosts the trade balance. In panel (a), demand shifts up from D_1 to D_2, equilibrium from 1″ to 2″, output from Y_1 to Y_2. In panel (b), we go from point 1 to point 2. The *IS* curve is thus traced out, a downward-sloping relationship between the interest rate and output. When the interest rate falls from i_1 to i_2, output rises from Y_1 to Y_2. The *IS* curve describes all combinations of *i* and *Y* consistent with goods and FX market equilibria in panels (a) and (c).

intuition for this is that the more expensive it is to purchase foreign currency today, the lower the expected return must be, all else equal.

The inverse relationship between *E* and the expected foreign return on the right-hand side of the previous equation is shown by the *FR* (foreign returns) line in panel (b) of Figure 14-8. The domestic return *DR* is the horizontal line corresponding to the level of the domestic interest rate *i*.

Deriving the IS Curve

Using the setup in Figure 14-8, we can now derive the shape of the IS curve by considering how changes in the interest rate affect output *if the goods and forex markets are to remain in equilibrium.*

Initial Equilibrium Let us suppose that the goods market and forex markets are initially in equilibrium at an interest rate i_1, an output or income level Y_1, and an exchange rate E_1.

In panel (a) by assumption, at an output level Y_1, demand equals supply, so the output level Y_1 must correspond to the point 1″, which is at the intersection of the Keynesian cross, and the figure is drawn accordingly.

In panel (c) by assumption, at an interest rate i_1 and an exchange rate E_1, the domestic and foreign returns must be equal, so this must be the point 1′, which is at the intersection of the DR_1 and FR curves, and the figure is drawn accordingly.

Finally, in panel (b) by assumption, at an interest rate i_1 and an output level Y_1, both goods and forex markets are in equilibrium. Thus, the point 1 is on the *IS* curve, *by definition.*

Lines are drawn joining the equal output levels Y_1 in panels (a) and (b). The domestic return line DR_1 traces out the home interest rate level from panel (b) across to panel (c).

A Fall in the Interest Rate Now in Figure 14-8, let us suppose that the home interest rate falls from i_1 to i_2. What happens to equilibria in the good and forex markets?

We first look at the forex market in panel (c). From our analysis of UIP in earlier chapters we know that when the home interest rate falls, domestic deposits have a lower return and look less attractive to investors. To maintain forex market equilibrium, the exchange rate must rise (the home currency must depreciate) until domestic and foreign returns are once again equal. In our example, when the home interest rate falls to i_2, the exchange rate must rise from E_1 to E_2 to equalize FR and DR_2 and restore equilibrium in the forex market at point 2′.

How do the changes in the home interest rate and the exchange rate affect demand? As shown in panel (a), demand will increase (shift up) for two reasons, as we learned earlier in this chapter.

First, when the domestic interest rate falls, firms are willing to engage in more investment projects, and their increased investment augments demand. The increase in investment, all else equal, *directly* increases demand D at any level of output Y.

Second, the exchange rate E has risen (depreciated). Because prices are sticky in the short run, this rise in the nominal exchange rate E also causes a rise in the real exchange rate $E\overline{P}^*/\overline{P}$. That is, the nominal depreciation causes a real depreciation. This increases demand D via expenditure switching. At any level of output Y consumers switch expenditure from relatively more expensive foreign goods toward relatively less expensive domestic goods. Thus, the fall in the interest rate *indirectly* boosts demand via exchange rate effects felt through the trade balance TB.

One important observation is in order: in an open economy, the phenomenon of expenditure switching operates as an additional element in demand that is not present in a closed economy. *In an open economy, lower interest rates stimulate demand through the traditional closed-economy investment channel and through the trade balance. The trade balance effect occurs because lower interest rates cause a nominal depreciation, which in the short run is also a real depreciation, which stimulates external demand via the trade balance.*

To summarize, panel (a) shows clearly that in response to a decrease in the interest rate, demand has shifted up to D_2 and the Keynesian cross goods market equilibrium is restored by a rise in output to Y_2, which corresponds to point 2″.

In panel (b), we can now derive the shape of the IS curve. At an interest rate i_1 and output level Y_1 and at an interest rate i_2 and an output level Y_2, both the goods and forex markets are in equilibrium. *We have now derived the shape of the IS curve, which describes goods and forex market equilibrium. When the interest rate falls from i_1 to i_2, output rises from Y_1 to Y_2. The IS curve is downward-sloping, which illustrates the negative relationship between the interest rate i and output Y.*

Factors That Shift the IS Curve

In deriving the IS curve, we treated various demand factors as exogenous, including fiscal policy, price levels, and the exchange rate. If any factors other than the interest rate and output change, the position of the IS curve would have to change. These effects are central in any analysis of changes in an economy's equilibrium. We now explore several changes that result in an increase in demand; that is, an upward shift in the demand curve in Figure 14-9, panel (a). (A decrease in demand would result from changes in the opposite direction.)

- *A change in government spending.* If demand shifts up because of a *rise* in $\overline{G}$, a fiscal expansion, all else equal, what happens to the IS curve? The initial equilibrium point (Y_1, i_1) would no longer be a goods market equilibrium: if the interest rate is unchanged at i_1, then I is unchanged, as are the exchange rate E and hence TB. Yet demand has risen due to the change in G. That demand has to be satisfied somehow, so more output has to be produced. Some—but not all—of that extra output will be consumed, but the rest can meet the extra demand generated by the rise in government spending. At the interest rate i_1, output must rise to Y_2 for the goods market to once again be in equilibrium. Thus, the IS curve must shift right as shown in Figure 14-9, panel (b).

The lesson: a rise in government spending shifts the IS curve out.

- *A change in taxes.* Suppose taxes were to decrease. With all other factors remaining unchanged, this tax cut makes demand shift up by boosting private consumption, all else equal. We assume that the interest rate i_1, the exchange rate E_1, and government's spending policy are all fixed. Thus, neither I nor TB nor G change. With an excess of demand, supply has to rise, so output must again increase to Y_2 and the IS curve shifts right.

The lesson: a reduction in taxes shifts the IS curve out.

- *A change in the foreign interest rate or expected future exchange rate.* A *rise* in the foreign interest rate i^* or a *rise* in the future expected exchange rate E^e causes a depreciation of the home currency, all else equal (recall that in the forex market, the FR curve shifts out because the return on foreign deposits has increased; if the home interest rate is unchanged, E must rise). A rise in E causes the real exchange rate to depreciate, because prices are sticky. As a result, TB rises via expenditure switching, and demand increases. Because C, I, and G do not change, there is an excess of demand, and supply has to rise to restore equilibrium. Output Y increases, and the IS curve shifts right.

The lesson: an increase in the foreign return (via i^* or E^e) shifts the IS curve out.

FIGURE 14-9

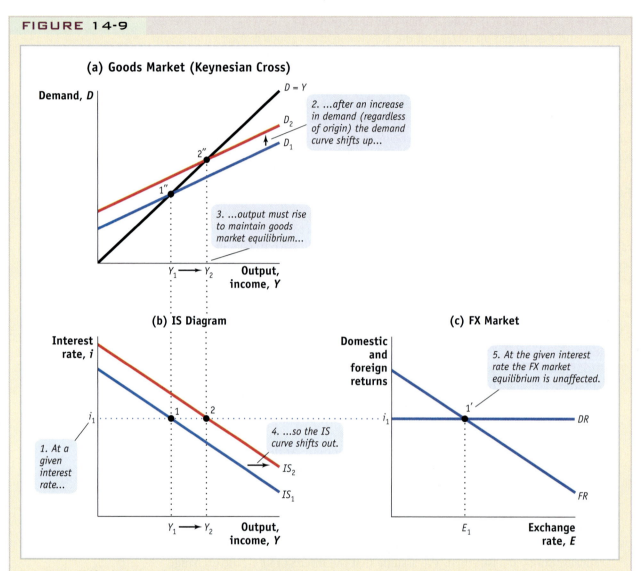

Exogenous Shifts in Demand Cause the IS Curve to Shift In the Keynesian cross in panel (a), when the interest rate is held constant at i_1, an exogenous increase in demand (due to other factors) causes the demand curve to shift up from D_1 to D_2 as shown, all else equal. This moves the equilibrium from 1″ to 2″, raising output from Y_1 to Y_2. In the IS diagram in panel (b), output has risen, with no change in the interest rate. The IS curve has therefore shifted right from IS_2 to IS_1. The nominal interest rate and hence the exchange rate are unchanged in this example, as seen in panel (c).

■ *A change in the home or foreign price level.* If prices are flexible, then a *rise* in foreign prices or a *fall* in domestic prices causes a home real depreciation, raising $q = E\overline{P}^*/\overline{P}$. This real depreciation causes *TB* to rise and, all else equal, demand will rise to a position like D_2. With an excess of demand, supply has to rise to restore equilibrium. Output *Y* must increase, and the IS curve shifts right.

The lesson: an increase P^* or a decrease in P shifts the IS curve out.

These examples show that the position of the IS curve depends on various factors that we treat as given (or exogenous). We may write this observation using the notation

$$IS = IS(G, T, i^*, E^e, P^*, P)$$

There are many other exogenous shocks to the economy that can be analyzed in a similar fashion—for example, a sudden exogenous change in consumption, investment, or the trade balance. How will the IS curve react in each case? You may have detected a pattern from the preceding discussion.

The general rule is as follows: *any type of shock that increases demand at a given level of output will shift the IS curve to the right; any shock that decreases demand will shift the IS curve down.*

Summing Up the IS Curve

When prices are sticky, the IS curve summarizes the relationship between output Y and the interest rate i necessary to keep the goods and forex markets in short-run equilibrium. The IS curve is downward-sloping. Why? Lower interest rates stimulate demand via the investment channel and, through exchange rate depreciation, via the trade balance. Higher demand can be satisfied in the short run only by higher output. Thus, when the interest rate falls, output rises, and the economy moves along the IS curve.

As for shifts in the IS curve, we have found that any factor which increases demand D at a given home interest rate i must cause the demand curve to shift up, leading to higher output Y and, as a result, an outward shift in the IS curve.

To conclude, the main factors that shift the IS curve out can be summed up as follows:

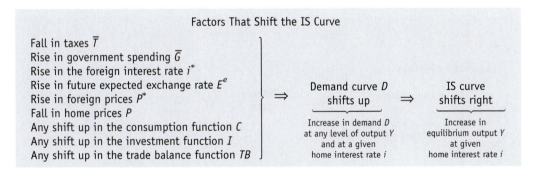

Factors That Shift the IS Curve

Fall in taxes $\overline{T}$
Rise in government spending $\overline{G}$
Rise in the foreign interest rate i^*
Rise in future expected exchange rate E^e
Rise in foreign prices P^*
Fall in home prices P
Any shift up in the consumption function C
Any shift up in the investment function I
Any shift up in the trade balance function TB

$\Rightarrow$

Demand curve D
shifts up

Increase in demand D
at any level of output Y
and at a given
home interest rate i

$\Rightarrow$

IS curve
shifts right

Increase in
equilibrium output Y
at given
home interest rate i

The opposite changes lead to a decrease in demand and shift the demand curve down and the IS curve to the left.

4 Money Market Equilibrium: Deriving the LM Curve

The IS curve links the forex market and the goods market as depicted by the Keynesian cross. It summarizes combinations of Y and i at which goods demand equals goods supply in a way that is consistent with forex market equilibrium. We have now taken care of equilibria in two out of three markets, so there is only one market left to worry about. In this section, we derive a set of combinations of Y and i that ensures equilibrium in the money market, a concept that can be represented graphically as the **LM curve**.

The LM curve is more straightforward to derive than the IS curve for a couple of reasons. First, the money market is something we have already studied in earlier chapters, so we already have all the tools we need to build the LM curve. Second, unlike the IS curve, the open-economy LM curve is no different from the closed-economy LM curve, so there will be no new material here if you have previously studied the closed-economy IS-LM model in another course.

Money Market Recap

In our earlier study of the money market, we assumed that the level of output or income Y was given. In deriving the LM curve, we now face a new question: What happens in the money market when an economy's output changes?

In the short-run, the price level is assumed to be sticky at a level $\overline{P}$, and the money market is in equilibrium when the demand for real money balances $L(i)Y$ equals the real money supply $M/\overline{P}$:

$$\underbrace{\frac{M}{\overline{P}}}_{\substack{\text{Real} \\ \text{money} \\ \text{supply}}} = \underbrace{L(i)Y}_{\substack{\text{Real} \\ \text{money} \\ \text{demand}}} \tag{14-2}$$

Figure 14-10, panel (a), shows that real money demand MD varies inversely with the nominal interest rate. As a result of this relationship, the demand curve for real money balances slopes downward. The real money supply MS is assumed to be fixed

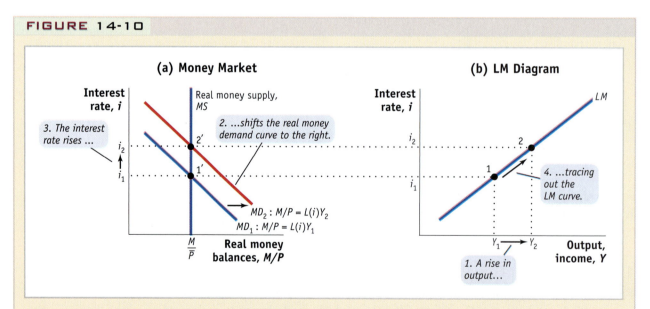

FIGURE 14-10

(a) Money Market

(b) LM Diagram

Deriving the LM Curve If there is an increase in real income or output from Y_1 to Y_2 in panel (b), the effect in the money market in panel (a) is to shift the demand for real money balances to the right, all else equal. If the real supply of money, MS, is held fixed at $M/\overline{P}$, then the interest rate rises from i_1 to i_2 and money market equilibrium moves from point 1' to point 2'. The relationship thus described between the interest rate and income, all else equal, is known as the LM curve and is depicted in panel (b) by the shift from point 1 to point 2. The LM curve is upward-sloping: when the output level rises from Y_1 to Y_2, the interest rate rises from i_1 to i_2. The LM curve in panel (b) describes all combinations of i and Y that are consistent with money market equilibrium in panel (a).

for now. Initially, the level of output is Y_1 at and the money market is in equilibrium at 1′, where real money demand is on MD_1 at $M/\overline{P} = L(i_1)Y_1$.

If output changes, the real money demand curve shifts. For example, if output rises to Y_2 and the real money supply $M/\overline{P}$ remains fixed, then real money demand increases because more output implies a larger number of transactions in the economy for which money is needed. The real money demand curve shifts right to MD_2. To keep money supply and demand equal, $M/\overline{P} = L(i_2)Y_2$, the interest rate rises from $i = i_1$ to $i = i_2$. Equilibrium moves from 1′ to 2′.

Deriving the LM Curve

This exercise can be repeated for any level of output Y. Doing so will generate a combination of interest rates i and outputs Y for which the money market is in equilibrium. This set of points, called the *LM* curve, is drawn in Figure 14-10, panel (b).

For example, if the real money supply is fixed at $M/\overline{P}$, an increase in output from Y_1 to Y_2 generates a rise in the nominal interest rate from i_1 to i_2 in panel (a), as we have just seen. This change can also be depicted as a move from point 1 to point 2 along the *LM* curve, as shown in panel (b).

We have now derived the shape of the LM curve, which describes money market equilibrium. When output rises from Y_1 to Y_2, the interest rate rises from i_1 to i_2. The LM curve is an upward-sloping relationship between the interest rate i and output Y.

The two ways of depicting the money market equilibrium are entirely equivalent. The money market diagram shows the relationship between real money balances demanded and supplied at different interest rates, holding output fixed. The *LM* curve diagram shows the relationship between output and the interest rate holding real money balances as fixed. Because the *LM* curve does *not* hold output fixed, it is important to developing our model of how output, interest rates, and exchange rates fluctuate in the short run.

Factors That Shift the LM Curve

An important reason for a shift in the LM curve is a change in the real money supply. (Changes in output result in a move *along* a given LM curve.) The LM curve tells us the interest rate i that equilibrates the money market at any given level of output Y. Given Y, we know that the equilibrium interest rate i depends on real money supply $M/\overline{P}$, and so the position of the LM curve depends on $M/\overline{P}$.

The effect of the real money supply on a nation's output or income is important because we are often interested in the impact of monetary policy changes on overall economic activity. To see how this effect operates via the LM curve, we can examine the money market diagram in Figure 14-11, panel (a). An increase in the nominal money supply M with sticky prices raises real money supply from $M_1/\overline{P}$ to $M_2/\overline{P}$ and shifts the real money supply curve MS to the right.

What happens in the LM diagram if the exogenous real money supply $M/\overline{P}$ changes in this way? For a given level of output Y, the increased supply of real money drives the interest rate down to i_2, and equilibrium in the money market shifts from point 1′ to point 2′. A decrease in the interest rate to i_2 when the level of output is unchanged at Y means that we cannot be on the same LM curve as before. There must have been a downward shift of the LM curve from LM_1 to LM_2 in Figure 14-11, panel (b).

We have shown the following: *an increase in real money supply shifts the LM curve down or to the right; a decrease in the real money supply shifts the LM curve up or to the left.*

FIGURE 14-11

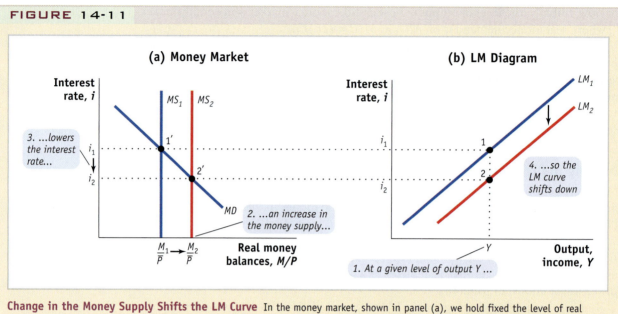

(a) Money Market

(b) LM Diagram

Change in the Money Supply Shifts the LM Curve In the money market, shown in panel (a), we hold fixed the level of real income or output, Y, and hence real money demand, MD. All else equal, we show the effect of an increase in money supply from M_1 to M_2. The real money supply curve moves out from MS_1 to MS_2. This moves the equilibrium from 1′ to 2′, lowering the interest rate from i_1 to i_2. In the LM diagram, shown in panel (b), the interest rate has fallen, with no change in the level of income or output, so the economy moves from point 1 to point 2. The LM curve has therefore shifted down from LM_1 to LM_2.

Thus, the position of the LM curve is a function of real money supply:

$$LM = LM(M/\overline{P})$$

Remember that in this short-run model of the economy, prices are sticky and treated as given, so any change in the real money supply in the short run is caused by changes in the nominal money supply M, which for now we take as given or exogenous.

Other factors can influence the position of the LM curve. In addition to changes in the money supply, exogenous changes in real money demand will also cause the LM curve to shift. For example, for a given money supply, a decrease in the demand for real money balances (an increase in the L function) at a given level of output Y will tend to lower the interest rate, all else equal, which would be depicted as a shift down or to the right in the LM curve.

Summing Up the LM Curve

When prices are sticky, the LM curve summarizes the relationship between output Y and interest rate i necessary to keep the money market in short-run equilibrium for a given level of the real money supply. The LM curve is upward-sloping. Why? In a money market equilibrium, if real money supply is constant, then real money demand must also be constant. If output rises, real money demand rises and to maintain equilibrium, real money demand must contract. This contraction in real money demand is accomplished by a rise in the interest rate. Thus, on the LM curve, when output rises, so, too, does the interest rate.

The following factors shift the LM curve:

The opposite changes lead to an increase in the home interest rate and shift the LM curve up or to the left.

5 The Short-Run IS-LM-FX Model of an Open Economy

We are now in a position to fully characterize an open economy that is in equilibrium in goods, money, and forex markets, as shown in Figure 14-12. This IS-LM-FX figure combines the goods market (the IS curve), the money market (the LM curve), and the forex (FX) market diagrams.

The *IS* and *LM* curves are both drawn in panel (a). The goods and forex markets are in equilibrium if and only if the economy is on the *IS* curve. The money market is in equilibrium if and only if the economy is on the *LM* curve. Thus, all three markets are in equilibrium if and only if the economy is at point 1, where *IS* and *LM* intersect.

FIGURE 14-12

Equilibrium in the IS-LM-FX Model In panel (a), the *IS* and *LM* curves are both drawn. The goods and forex markets are in equilibrium when the economy is on the *IS* curve. The money market is in equilibrium when the economy is on the *LM* curve. Both markets are in equilibrium if and only if the economy is at point 1, the unique point of intersection of *IS* and *LM*. In panel (b), the forex (FX) market is shown. The domestic return, *DR*, in the forex market equals the money market interest rate. Equilibrium is at point 1′ where the foreign return *FR* equals domestic return, *i*.

The forex market, or FX market, is drawn in panel (b). The domestic return DR in the forex market equals the money market interest rate. Equilibrium is at point 1′ where the foreign return FR is equal to domestic return i.

In the remainder of this chapter, and in the rest of this book, we make extensive use of this graphical depiction of the open-economy equilibrium to analyze the short-run response of an open economy to various types of shocks. In particular, we look at how government policies affect the economy and the extent to which they can be employed to enhance macroeconomic performance and stability.

Macroeconomic Policies in the Short Run

Now that we understand the open-economy IS-LM-FX model and all the factors that influence an economy's short-run equilibrium, we can use the model to look at how a nation's key macroeconomic variables (output, exchange rates, trade balance) are affected in the short run by changes in government macroeconomic policies.

We focus on the two main policy actions: changes in **monetary policy,** implemented through changes in the money supply, and changes in **fiscal policy,** involving changes in government spending or taxes. Of particular interest is the question of whether governments can use such policies to insulate the economy from fluctuations in output.

We will see that the impact of these policies is profoundly affected by a nation's choice of exchange rate regime, and we will consider the two polar cases of fixed and floating exchange rates. Many countries are on some kind of flexible exchange rate regime and many are on some kind of fixed regime, so considering policy effects under both fixed and floating systems is essential.

The key assumptions of this section are as follows. The economy begins in a state of long-run equilibrium. We then consider policy changes in the home economy, assuming that conditions in the foreign economy (i.e., the rest of the world) are unchanged. The home economy is subject to the usual short-run assumption of a sticky price level at home *and* abroad. Furthermore, we assume that the forex market operates freely and unrestricted by capital controls and that the exchange rate is determined by market forces.

Temporary Policies, Unchanged Expectations Finally, we examine only *temporary* changes in policies. We will assume that long-run expectations about the future state of the economy are unaffected by the policy changes. In particular, the future expected exchange rate E^e is held fixed. The reason for studying temporary policies is that we are primarily interested in how governments use fiscal and monetary policies to handle temporary shocks and business cycles in the short run, and our model is applicable only in the short run.[2]

The key lesson of this section is that policies matter and can have significant macroeconomic effects in the short run. Moreover, their impacts depend in a big way on the type of exchange rate regime in place. Once we understand these linkages, we will better understand the contentious and ongoing debates about exchange rates and macroeconomic policies, including the never-ending arguments over the merits of fixed and floating exchange rates (a topic covered in detail in the next chapter).

---

[2] Moreover, permanent changes may not be truly feasible given realistic constraints on governments. For example, a permanent increase in money supply, all else equal, would lead to a permanent increase in the price level, violating a money, exchange rate, or inflation target (the nominal anchor). A permanent increase in government spending, with no increase in taxes, would not be feasible given the government's long-run budget constraint.

Monetary Policy under Floating Exchange Rates

In this policy experiment, we consider a temporary monetary expansion in the home country when the exchange rate is allowed to float. Because the expansion is not permanent, we assume there is no change in long-run expectations so that the expected future exchange rate remains steady at E^e. This means that there is no change in the expected foreign return curve in the forex market.

Figure 14-13 illustrates the predictions of the model. In panel (a) in the IS-LM diagram, the goods and money markets are initially in equilibrium at point 1. The interest rate in the money market is also the domestic return DR_1 that prevails in the forex market. In panel (b), the forex market is initially in equilibrium at point 1'.

A temporary monetary expansion that increases the money supply from M_1 to M_2 would shift the LM curve to the right in panel (a) from LM_1 to LM_2, causing the interest rate to fall from i_1 to i_2. The domestic return falls from DR_1 to DR_2. In panel (b), the lower interest rate would imply that the exchange rate must depreciate, rising from E_1 to E_2. As the interest rate falls (increasing investment I) and the exchange rate depreciates (increasing the trade balance), demand increases, which corresponds to the move down the IS curve from point 1 to point 2. Output expands from Y_1 to Y_2. The new equilibrium corresponds to points 2 and 2'.

The intuition for this result is as follows: monetary expansion tends to lower the home interest rate, all else equal. A lower interest rate stimulates demand in two ways. First, directly in the goods market, it causes investment demand I to increase. Second, indirectly, it causes the exchange rate to depreciate in the forex market, which in turn

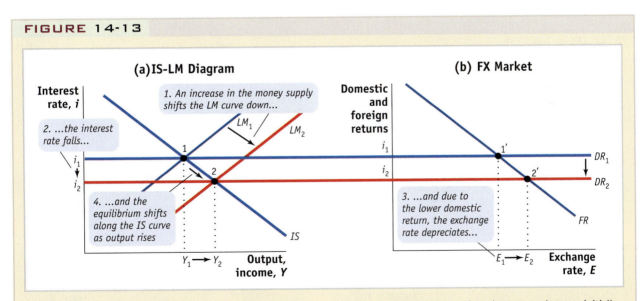

FIGURE 14-13

Monetary Policy under Floating Exchange Rates In panel (a) in the IS-LM diagram, the goods and money markets are initially in equilibrium at point 1. The interest rate in the money market is also the domestic return, DR_1, that prevails in the forex market. In panel (b), the forex market is initially in equilibrium at point 1'. A temporary monetary expansion that increases the money supply from M_1 to M_2 would shift the LM curve down in panel (a) from LM_1 to LM_2, causing the interest rate to fall from i_1 to i_2. DR falls from DR_1 to DR_2. In panel (b), the lower interest rate implies that the exchange rate must depreciate, rising from E_1 to E_2. As the interest rate falls (increasing investment, I) and the exchange rate depreciates (increasing the trade balance), demand increases, which corresponds to the move down the IS curve from point 1 to point 2. Output expands from Y_1 to Y_2. The new equilibrium corresponds to points 2 and 2'.

causes expenditure switching in the goods market, which causes the trade balance *TB* to increase. Both *I* and *TB* are sources of demand and both increase.

To sum up: a temporary monetary expansion under floating exchange rates is effective in combating economic downturns by boosting output. It raises output at home, lowers the interest rate, and causes a depreciation of the exchange rate. What happens to the trade balance cannot be predicted with certainty: increased home output will decrease the trade balance as the demand for imports will rise, but the real depreciation will increase the trade balance, because expenditure switching will tend to raise exports and diminish imports. In practice, economists tend to assume that the latter outweighs the former, so a temporary expansion of the money supply is usually predicted to increase the trade balance. (The case of a temporary contraction of monetary policy has opposite effects. As an exercise, work through this case using the same graphical apparatus.)

Monetary Policy under Fixed Exchange Rates

Now let's look at what happens when a temporary monetary expansion occurs in a home country that pegs its exchange rate with respect to the foreign country at $\overline{E}$. The key to understanding this experiment is to recall the uncovered interest parity condition: *the home interest rate must equal the foreign interest rate under a fixed exchange rate.*

Figure 14-14 puts the model to work. In panel (a) in the IS-LM diagram, the goods and money markets are initially in equilibrium at point 1. In panel (b), the forex market is initially in equilibrium at point 1'.

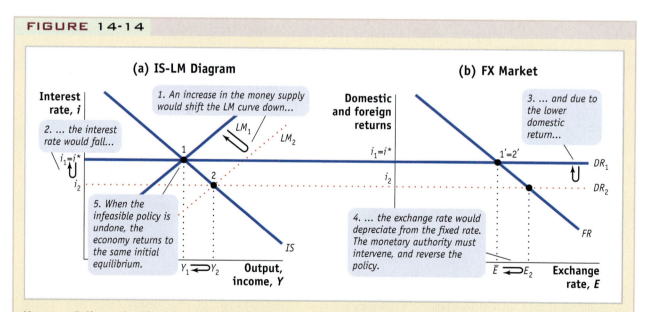

FIGURE 14-14

Monetary Policy under Fixed Exchange Rates In panel (a) in the IS-LM diagram, the goods and money markets are initially in equilibrium at point 1. In panel (b), the forex market is initially in equilibrium at point 1'. A temporary monetary expansion that increases the money supply from M_1 to M_2 would shift the *LM* curve down in panel (a). In panel (b), the lower interest rate would imply that the exchange rate must depreciate, rising from $\overline{E}$ to E_2. This depreciation is inconsistent with the pegged exchange rate, so the policy makers cannot move *LM* in this way. They must leave the money supply equal to M_1. Implication: under a fixed exchange rate, autonomous monetary policy is not an option.

A temporary monetary expansion that increases the money supply from M_1 to M_2 would shift the LM curve down and to the right in panel (a), and the interest rate would tend to fall, as we have just seen. In panel (b), the lower interest rate would imply that the exchange rate would tend to rise or depreciate toward E_2. This is inconsistent with the pegged exchange rate $\overline{E}$, so the policy makers cannot alter monetary policy and shift the LM curve in this way. They must leave the money supply equal to M_1 and the economy cannot deviate from its initial equilibrium.

This example illustrates a key lesson: under a fixed exchange rate, autonomous monetary policy is not an option. What is going on? Remember that under a fixed exchange rate, the home interest rate must exactly equal the foreign interest rate, $i = i^*$, according to the uncovered interest parity condition. Any shift in the LM curve would violate this restriction and break the fixed exchange rate.

To sum up: monetary policy under fixed exchange rates is impossible to undertake. Fixing the exchange rate means giving up monetary policy autonomy. In an earlier chapter, we learned about the trilemma: countries cannot simultaneously allow capital mobility, maintain fixed exchange rates, and pursue an autonomous monetary policy. We have now just seen the trilemma at work in the IS-LM-FX framework. By illustrating a potential benefit of autonomous monetary policy (the ability to use monetary policy to increase output), the model clearly exposes one of the major costs of fixed exchange rates. Monetary policy, which in principle could be used to influence the economy in the short run, is ruled out by a fixed exchange rate.

Fiscal Policy under Floating Exchange Rates

We now turn to fiscal policy under a floating exchange rate. In this example, we consider a temporary increase in government spending from $\overline{G}_1$ to $\overline{G}_2$ in the home economy. Again, the effect is not permanent, so there are no changes in long-run expectations, and in particular the expected future exchange rate remains steady at E^e. Figure 14-15 shows what happens in our model. In panel (a) in the IS-LM diagram, the goods and money markets are initially in equilibrium at point 1. The interest rate in the money market is also the domestic return DR_1 that prevails in the forex market. In panel (b), the forex market is initially in equilibrium at point 1'.

A temporary fiscal expansion that increases government spending from $\overline{G}_1$ to $\overline{G}_2$ would shift the IS curve to the right in panel (a) from IS_1 to IS_2, causing the interest rate to rise from i_1 to i_2. The domestic return rises from DR_1 to DR_2. In panel (b), the higher interest rate would imply that the exchange rate must appreciate, falling from to E_1 to E_2. As the interest rate rises (decreasing investment I) and the exchange rate appreciates (decreasing the trade balance TB), demand falls, which corresponds to the move up the LM curve from point 1 to point 2. Output expands from Y_1 to Y_2. The new equilibrium is at points 2 and 2'.

What is happening here? The fiscal expansion raises output as the IS curve shifts right. But the increases in output will raise interest rates, all else equal, given a fixed money supply. The resulting higher interest rates will reduce the investment component of demand, and this limits the rise in demand to less than the increase in government spending. This impact of fiscal expansion on investment is often referred to as *crowding out* by economists.

The higher interest rate also causes the home currency to appreciate. As home consumers switch their consumption to now less expensive foreign goods, the trade balance will fall. Thus, the higher interest rate also (indirectly) leads to a *crowding out* of net

FIGURE 14-15

Fiscal Policy under Floating Exchange Rates In panel (a) in the IS-LM diagram, the goods and money markets are initially in equilibrium at point 1. The interest rate in the money market is also the domestic return, DR_1, that prevails in the forex market. In panel (b), the forex market is initially in equilibrium at point 1'. A temporary fiscal expansion that increases government spending from $\bar{G}_1$ to $\bar{G}_2$ would shift the IS curve to the right in panel (a) from IS_1 to IS_2, causing the interest rate to rise from i_1 to i_2. The domestic return shifts up from DR_1 to DR_2. In panel (b), the higher interest rate would imply that the exchange rate must appreciate, falling from E_1 to E_2. As the interest rate rises (decreasing investment, I) and the exchange rate appreciates (decreasing the trade balance), demand falls, which corresponds to the move along the LM curve from point 1 to point 2. Output expands from Y_1 to Y_2. The new equilibrium corresponds to points 2 and 2'.

exports, and this too limits the rise in output to less than the increase in government spending. Thus, in an open economy, fiscal expansion not only crowds out investment (by raising the interest rate) but also crowds out net exports (by causing the exchange rate to appreciate).

To sum up: a temporary expansion of fiscal policy under floating exchange rates is effective. It raises output at home, raises the interest rate, causes an appreciation of the exchange rate, and decreases the trade balance. (A temporary contraction of fiscal policy has opposite effects. As an exercise, work through the contraction case using the same graphical apparatus.)

Fiscal Policy under Fixed Exchange Rates

Now let's see how the outcomes differ when the home country pegs its exchange rate with respect to the foreign country at $\bar{E}$. The key is to recall the parity condition: the home interest rate must remain exactly equal to the foreign interest rate for the peg to hold.

Figure 14-16 shows what happens in this case. In panel (a) in the IS-LM diagram, the goods and money markets are initially in equilibrium at point 1. The interest rate in the money market is also the domestic return DR_1 that prevails in the forex market. In panel (b), the forex market is initially in equilibrium at point 1'.

FIGURE 14-16

Fiscal Policy under Fixed Exchange Rates In panel (a) in the IS-LM diagram, the goods and money markets are initially in equilibrium at point 1. The interest rate in the money market is also the domestic return, DR_1, that prevails in the forex market. In panel (b), the forex market is initially in equilibrium at point 1'. A temporary fiscal expansion on its own increases government spending from $\overline{G}_1$ to $\overline{G}_2$ and would shift the IS curve to the right in panel (a) from IS_1 to IS_2, causing the interest rate to rise from i_1 to i_2. The domestic return would then rise from DR_1 to DR_2. In panel (b), the higher interest rate would imply that the exchange rate must appreciate, falling from $\overline{E}$ to E_2. To maintain the peg, the monetary authority must now intervene, shifting the LM curve down, from LM_1 to LM_2. The fiscal expansion thus prompts a monetary expansion. In the end, the interest rate and exchange rate are left unchanged, and output expands *dramatically* from Y_1 to Y_2. The new equilibrium corresponds to points 2 and 2'.

A temporary fiscal expansion that increases government spending from $\overline{G}_1$ to $\overline{G}_2$ would shift the IS curve to the right in panel (a) from IS_1 to IS_2, causing the interest rate to rise from i_1 to i_2. The domestic return would rise from DR_1 to DR_2. In panel (b), the higher interest rate would imply that the exchange rate must appreciate, falling from $\overline{E}$ to E_2. To maintain the peg, the monetary authority must intervene, shifting the LM curve to the right also, from LM_1 to LM_2. The fiscal expansion thus prompts a monetary expansion. In the end, the interest rate and exchange rate are left unchanged, and output expands *dramatically* from Y_1 to Y_2. The new equilibrium corresponds to points 2 and 2'.

What is happening here? From the last example, we know that there is appreciation pressure associated with a fiscal expansion if the currency is allowed to float. To maintain the peg, the monetary authority must immediately alter its monetary policy at the very moment the fiscal expansion occurs so that the LM curve shifts from LM_1 to LM_2. The way to do this is to expand the money supply, and this generates pressure for depreciation, offsetting the appreciation pressure. If the monetary authority pulls this off, the market exchange rate will stay at the initial pegged level $\overline{E}$.

Thus, when a country is operating under a fixed exchange, fiscal policy is super-effective because any fiscal expansion by the government forces an immediate monetary expansion by the central bank to keep the exchange rate steady. The double, and simultaneous, expansion of demand by the fiscal and monetary authorities imposes a huge stimulus on the economy, and output rises from Y_1 to Y_2 (beyond the level achieved by the same fiscal expansion under a floating exchange rate).

To sum up: a temporary expansion of fiscal policy under fixed exchange rates raises output at home by a considerable amount. (The case of a temporary contraction of fiscal policy would have similar but opposite effects. As an exercise, work through this case using the same graphical apparatus.)

Summary

We have now examined the operation of fiscal and monetary policies under both fixed and flexible exchange rates and have seen how the impacts of these policies differ dramatically depending on the exchange rate regime. The outcomes can be summarized as follows:

Responses to Policy Shocks in the IS-LM-FX Model						
Exchange Rate Regime	Policy	i	E	I	TB	Y
Floating	Monetary expansion	↓	↑	↑	↑?	↑
	Fiscal expansion	↑	↓	↓	↓	↑
Fixed	Monetary expansion	0	0	0	0	0
	Fiscal expansion	0	0	0	↓	↑

In this table, an up arrow ↑ indicates that the variable rises; a down arrow ↓, indicates that the variables falls; and a zero indicates no effect. The effects would be reversed for contractionary policies. The row of zeros for monetary expansion under fixed rates reflects the fact that this infeasible policy cannot be undertaken.

In a floating exchange rate regime, autonomous monetary and fiscal policy is feasible. The power of monetary policy to expand demand comes from two forces in the short run: lower interest rates boost investment and a depreciated exchange rate boosts the trade balance, all else equal. In the end, though, the trade balance will experience downward pressure from an import rise due to the increase in home output and income. The net effect on output and investment is positive, and the net effect on the trade balance is unclear—but in practice it, too, is likely to be positive.

Expansionary fiscal policy is also effective under a floating regime, even though the impact of extra spending is offset by crowding out in two areas: investment is crowded out by higher interest rates, and the trade balance is crowded out by an appreciated exchange rate. Thus, on net, investment falls and the trade balance also falls, and the latter effect is unambiguously amplified by additional import demand arising from increased home output.

In a fixed exchange rate regime, monetary policy loses its power for two reasons. First, interest parity implies that the domestic interest rate cannot move independently of the foreign rate, so investment demand cannot be manipulated. Second, the peg means that there can be no movement in the exchange rate, so the trade balance cannot be manipulated by expenditure switching.

Only fiscal policy is feasible under a fixed regime. Tax cuts or spending increases by the government can generate additional demand. But fiscal expansion then requires a monetary expansion to keep interest rates steady and maintain the peg. Fiscal policy becomes ultra-powerful in a fixed exchange rate setting—the reason for this is that if interest rates and exchange rates are held steady by the central bank, investment and the trade balance are never crowded out by fiscal policy. Monetary policy follows fiscal policy and amplifies it.

6 Stabilization Policy

We now have seen that macroeconomic policies can effect economic activity in the short run. These effects open up the possibility that the authorities can use changes in policies to try to keep the economy at or near its full-employment level of output. This is the essence of **stabilization policy.** If the economy is hit by a temporary adverse shock, policy makers could use expansionary monetary and fiscal policies to prevent a deep recession. Conversely, if the economy is pushed by a shock above its full employment level of output, contractionary policies could tame the boom.

For example, suppose a temporary adverse shock such as a sudden decline in investment, consumption, or export demand shifts the IS curve to the left. Or suppose an adverse shock such as a sudden increase in money demand suddenly moves the LM curve up. Either shock would cause home output to fall. In principle, the home policy makers could offset these shocks by using fiscal policy to shift either the IS curve or LM curve (or both) to cause an offsetting increase in output. When used judiciously, monetary and fiscal policies can thus be used to stabilize the economy and absorb shocks.

The policies must be used with care, however. If the economy is stable and growing, an additional temporary monetary or fiscal stimulus may cause an unsustainable boom that will, when the stimulus is withdrawn, turn into an undesirable bust. In their efforts to do good, policy makers must be careful not to destabilize the economy through the ill-timed, inappropriate, or excessive use of monetary and fiscal policies.

APPLICATION

Australia, New Zealand, and the Asian Crisis of 1997

At the end of 1997, many observers would have predicted economic difficulties for Australia and New Zealand in the short run. Both countries were very open to trade, and a large part of the demand for their exports was generated by a group of industrializing East Asian economies, including Korea, Thailand, and Indonesia. The problem was that all of these major trading partners suffered serious economic crises in 1997, which caused a large economic contraction in each country characterized by significant declines in output and the demand for foreign goods. To some extent, the East Asian and Pacific region as a whole was likely to be dragged into recession by these events.

In our framework, the demand for Australia's and New Zealand's exports declined as a result of a contraction in foreign output Y^*. All else equal, they would have suffered an exogenous decline in their trade balance: at every real exchange rate, the demand for exports declined, and demand fell. These events would be represented by a leftward shift of Australia's and New Zealand's IS curves, which we show in Figure 14-17.

Our model tells us that if the governments of Australia and New Zealand had chosen to ignore the Asian crisis, their economies would have contracted, home interest rates would have fallen, and the value of their currencies would have fallen. In

FIGURE 14-17

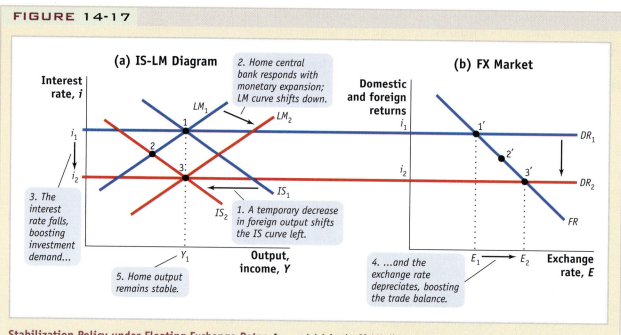

Stabilization Policy under Floating Exchange Rates In panel (a) in the IS-LM diagram, the goods and money markets are initially in equilibrium at point 1. The interest rate in the money market is also the domestic return, DR_1, that prevails in the forex market. In panel (b), the forex market is initially in equilibrium at point 1′. An exogenous negative shock to the trade balance (e.g., due to a collapse in foreign income) causes the IS curve to shift in from IS_1 to IS_2. Without further action, output and interest rates would fall and the exchange rate would tend to depreciate. The central bank can stabilize output at its former level by responding with a monetary policy expansion, increasing the money supply from M_1 to M_2. This causes the LM curve to shift down from LM_1 to LM_2. The new equilibrium corresponds to points 3 and 3′. Output is now stabilized at the original level Y_1. The interest rate falls further. The domestic return falls from DR_1 to DR_2, and the exchange rate depreciates all the way from E_1 to E_2.

Figure 14-17, panel (a), the IS-LM equilibrium shifts from point 1 to point 2, and the initial deterioration in trade balance would be only partially offset by the induced depreciation and increased investment. The forex market equilibrium would be at 2′. In the end, demand would still be below its initial level and a recession would result.

However, this did not happen. The central banks of both Australia and New Zealand responded to the Asian crisis with expansionary monetary policy. This would be depicted in our model by a down or right shift in the LM curve. The IS-LM equilibrium in the economy shifts from point 2 to point 3 in Figure 14-17, panel (a). At point 3, the further reduction in the home interest rate exacerbates the depreciation of the currency and stimulates demand through both the investment and expenditure-switching channels. Recession is avoided and output is sustained at its original level. The forex market in panel (b) ends up at 3′ with a large depreciation.

Figure 14-18 shows data for the Australian and New Zealand economies in this period. The home exchange rates were allowed to depreciate substantially, and as a result, the trade balances in both countries held up, partly due to export growth to non-Asian markets that was made possible by the temporary weakening of the real exchange rate. This episode provides a good example of how policy makers can use a floating exchange rate to cushion the blows of external macroeconomic shocks. Policy makers in Australia and New Zealand knew that after the Asian crisis had passed—in a few years'

FIGURE 14-18

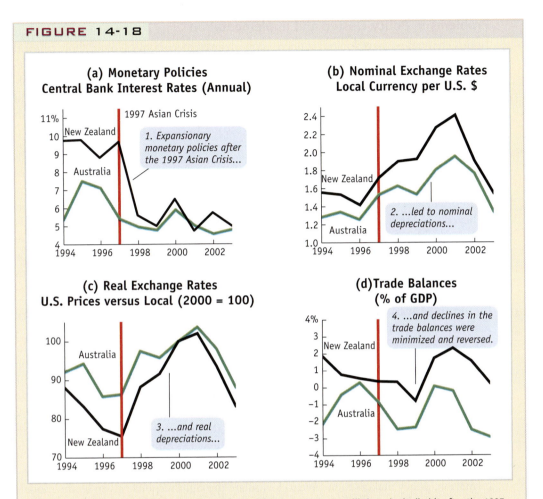

Demand Shocks Down Under Australian and New Zealand exports were likely to be badly hit after the 1997 Asian crisis as the incomes of their key trading partners contracted. Both countries were operating on a floating exchange rate, however. To bolster demand, the central banks in both countries pursued an expansionary monetary policy, lowering interest rates, as shown in panel (a), and allowing the domestic currency to depreciate about 30% in nominal terms, as shown in panel (b). This contributed to a real depreciation of about 20% to 30% in the short run, panel (c). As a result, the trade balance of both countries moved strongly toward surplus, illustrated in panel (d), and thus demand was higher than it would otherwise have been. In each country, a recession was avoided.

Sources: IMF, International Financial Statistics; World Bank, World Development Indicators.

time—there would be renewed demand for their goods. In the short run, the problem was to manage a temporary drop in aggregate demand.

This response was widely praised in economic policy-making circles, as in the following quotation from the OECD's 1999 *Economic Survey of Australia*:

Australia has continued to grow above its trend rate over the past two years with the economy proving to be remarkably resilient in the face of significant weakness in many of its trading partners, especially in Asia. At the same time, inflation remained low and the rate of unemployment was reduced further. This performance was helped by dynamic growth of domestic demand at the time when the crisis broke out, and a credible mix of macro-policies which allowed the exchange rate to move freely, kept monetary conditions expansionary and maintained fiscal retrenchment. ■

A case study: exports of wine and other Australian goods boomed after the real depreciation.

Problems in Policy Design and Implementation

In this chapter, we have looked at open-economy macroeconomics in the short run and at the role that monetary and fiscal policies can play in determining economic outcomes. The simple models we used have clear consequences. On the face of it, if policy makers were really operating in such an uncomplicated environment, they would have the ability to exert substantial control and could always keep output steady with no unemployed resources and no inflation pressure. In reality, life is more complicated for policy makers for a variety of reasons.

Policy Constraints Policy makers may not always be free to apply the policies they desire. A fixed exchange rate rules out any use of monetary policy. Other firm monetary or fiscal policy rules, such as interest rate rules or balanced-budget rules, place limits on policy. Even if policy makers decide to act, other constraints may bind them. While it is always feasible to print money, it may not be possible (technically or politically) to raise the real resources necessary for a fiscal expansion. Countries with weak tax systems or poor creditworthiness—problems that afflict developing countries—may find themselves unable to tax or borrow to finance an expansion of spending even if they wished to do so.

Incomplete Information and the Inside Lag Our models assume that the policy makers have full knowledge of the state of the economy before they take corrective action: they observe the economy's IS and LM curves and know what shocks have hit. In reality, macroeconomic data are compiled slowly and it may take weeks or months for policy makers to fully understand the state of the economy today. Even then, it will take time to formulate a policy response (the lag between shock and policy actions is called the *inside lag*). On the monetary side, there may be a delay between policy meetings. On the fiscal side, it may take time to pass a bill through the legislature and then enable a real change in spending or taxing activity by the public sector.

Policy Response and the Outside Lag Even if they finally receive the correct information, policy makers then have to formulate the right response given by the model. In particular, they must not be distracted by other policies or agendas, nor subject to influence by interest groups that might wish to see different policies enacted. Finally, it takes time for whatever policies are enacted to have any effect on the economy, through the spending decisions of the public and private sectors (the lag between policy actions and effects is called the *outside lag*).

Long-Horizon Plans Other factors may make investment and the trade balance less sensitive to policy. If the private sector understands that a policy change is temporary, then there may be reasons not to change consumption or investment expenditure. Suppose a firm can either build and operate a plant for several years or else not build at all (e.g., the investment might be of an irreversible form). For example, a firm may not care about a higher real interest rate this year and may base its decision on the expected real interest rate that will affect its financing over many years ahead. Similarly, a temporary real appreciation may have little effect on whether a firm can profit in the long run from sales in the foreign market. In such circumstances, firms' investment and export activities may not be very sensitive to short-run policy changes.

Weak Links from the Nominal Exchange Rate to the Real Exchange Rate Our discussion assumed that changes in the nominal exchange rate lead to real exchange rate changes, but the reality can be somewhat different for some goods and services. For example, the dollar depreciated 42% against the euro from 2002 to 2004, but the U.S.

prices of German cars, like BMWs, barely changed. Why? There are a number of reasons for this weak *pass-through* phenomenon, including the dollarization of trade and the distribution margins that separate retail prices from port prices (as we saw in **Side Bar: Barriers to Expenditure Switching: Pass-Through and the J Curve**). The forces of arbitrage may also be weak as a result of noncompetitive market structures: for example, BMW sells through exclusive dealers and government regulation requires that cars meet different standards in Europe versus the United States. These obstacles allow a firm like BMW to *price to market:* to charge a steady U.S. price even as the exchange rate moves temporarily. If a firm can bear (or hedge) the exchange rate risk, it might do this to avoid the volatile sales and alienated customers that might result from repeatedly changing its U.S. retail price list.

Pegged Currency Blocs Our model's predictions are also affected by the fact that for some major countries in the real world, their exchange rate arrangements are characterized—often not as a result of their own choice—by a mix of floating and fixed exchange rate systems with different trading partners. From 2002 to 2004, the dollar depreciated markedly against the euro, pound, and several other floating currencies, but in the "Dollar Bloc" (Japan, China, India, and others), the monetary authorities have ensured that the variation in the value of their currencies against the dollar is small or zero. When a large bloc of other countries pegs to the U.S. dollar, this limits the ability of the United States to engineer a real effective depreciation.

Weak Links from the Real Exchange Rate to the Trade Balance Our discussion also assumed that real exchange rate changes lead to changes in the trade balance. There may be several reasons why these linkages are weak in reality. One major reason is transaction costs in trade. Suppose the exchange rate is $1 per euro and an American is consuming a domestic good that costs $100 as opposed to a European good costing €100 = $100. If the dollar appreciates to $0.95 per euro, then the European good looks cheaper on paper, only $95. Should the American switch to the import? Yes, if the good can be moved without cost—but there are few such goods! If shipping costs $10, it still makes sense to consume the domestic good until the exchange rate falls below $0.90 per euro. Practically, this means that expenditure switching may be a nonlinear phenomenon: it will be weak at first and then much stronger as the real exchange rate change grows larger. This phenomenon, coupled with the J Curve effects discussed earlier, may cause the response of the trade balance in the short run to be small or even in the wrong direction.

APPLICATION

Macroeconomic Policies in the Liquidity Trap

Undoubtedly, one of the most controversial experiments in macroeconomic policy-making began in 2008–2010 as monetary and fiscal authorities around the world tried to respond to the major recession that followed the global financial crisis. In this application, even as the story continues to unfold, we look at the initial U.S. policy response and interpret events using the IS-LM-FX model of this chapter.

The unusual aspect of this crisis was the very rapid realization that monetary policy alone could not fully offset the magnitude of the shock to demand. In the context of our IS-LM-FX model, as consumption and investment fell for exogenous reasons, the shock moved the IS curve very far leftward. One major source of the demand shock was that, as we saw in an earlier chapter, banks were very afraid of taking on risk and sharply reduced their lending to firms and households—and even when they did lend, they were still charging very high interest rates. Thus, even with very expansionary monetary policy, that is, large rightward shifts of the LM curve, low policy rates did not translate into cheap borrowing for the private sector. Once the U.S. Federal Reserve had brought its policy rate to zero in December 2008, there was little more it could do to stimulate demand using conventional monetary policies.

This peculiar situation is depicted by the blue lines in Figure 14-19 and differs from the normal IS-LM-FX setup we have seen so far. After the demand shock and the Fed's response to it, the IS curve has moved so far in (to IS_1) and the LM curve has moved so far out (to LM_1), that the IS and LM curves now intersect at a very low interest rate: so low that it is equal to zero. In the money market, nominal interest rates can't fall below zero, so another way of describing this situation is to say that the economy was at an IS-LM equilibrium at which the LM curve was absolutely flat and resting on the horizontal axis (at a 0% interest rate) in the diagram.

[Note that in the FX diagram this would place the domestic return DR at zero. Also, note that interest rates were by this time at zero in all developed countries, for similar

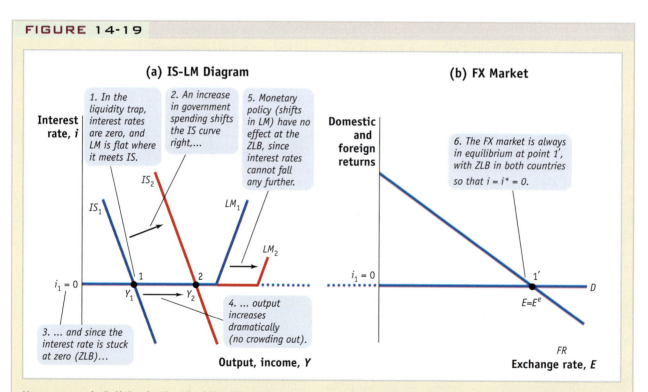

FIGURE 14-19

(a) IS-LM Diagram

1. In the liquidity trap, interest rates are zero, and LM is flat where it meets IS.

2. An increase in government spending shifts the IS curve right,...

5. Monetary policy (shifts in LM) have no effect at the ZLB, since interest rates cannot fall any further.

3. ... and since the interest rate is stuck at zero (ZLB)...

4. ... output increases dramatically (no crowding out).

(b) FX Market

6. The FX market is always in equilibrium at point 1', with ZLB in both countries so that $i = i^* = 0$.

Macroeconomic Policies in the Liquidity Trap After a severe negative shock to demand, the IS curve may move very far to the left (IS_1). The nominal interest rate may then fall all the way to the zero lower bound (ZLB), with IS_1 intersecting the flat portion of the LM_1 curve at point 1, on the horizontal axis, in panel (a). Output is depressed at a level Y_1. In this scenario, monetary policy is impotent because expansionary monetary policy (e.g., a rightward shift from LM_1 to LM_2) cannot lower the interest rate any further. However, fiscal policy may be very effective, and a shift right from IS_1 to IS_2 leaves the economy still at the ZLB, but with a higher level of output Y_2. (The figure is drawn assuming the ZLB holds in both home and foreign economies, so the FX market is in equilibrium at point 1' with $E = E^e$ at all times.)

reasons. Thus, it is also appropriate to think of the foreign (e.g., euro) interest rate as also stuck at zero, which in the FX diagram would lower the foreign return *FR*.]

The situation just described is unusual in several ways. First, monetary policy is powerless in this situation: it cannot be used to lower interest rates because interest rates can't go any lower. In the diagram, moving the LM curve out to LM_2 does not dislodge the economy from the horizontal portion of the LM curve. We are still stuck on the IS_1 curve at a point 1 and a 0% percent interest rate. This unfortunate state of affairs is known as the *zero lower bound* (ZLB). It is also known as a *liquidity trap* because liquid money and interest-bearing assets have the same interest rate of zero, so there is no opportunity cost to holding money, and thus changes in the supply of central bank money have no effect on the incentive to switch between money and interest-bearing assets.

Can anything be done? Yes. The bad news is that fiscal policy is the only tool now available to increase demand. The good news is that fiscal policy has the potential to be super powerful in this situation. The reason is that as long as interest rates are stuck at zero, and the monetary authorities keep them there, government spending will not crowd out investment or net exports, in contrast to the typical situation we studied earlier in this chapter.[3] In 2009 because the Fed and the private sector anticipated more than a year or two of very high unemployment and falling inflation, everyone had expectations of zero interest rates for a long period.

Did the United States use fiscal policy to try to counteract the recession? Yes. Did it work? Not as well as one might have hoped.

The government's fiscal response took two forms. First was the *automatic stabilizer* built into existing fiscal policies. In the models that we have studied so far in this chapter, we have assumed that taxes and spending are fixed. In reality, however, they are not fixed, but vary systematically with income. Most importantly, when income *Y* falls in a recession, receipts from income taxes, sales taxes, and so on, all tend to fall as well. In addition, transfer expenditures (like unemployment benefits) tend to go up: a rise in negative taxes, as it were. This decline does not depend on any policy response, and in the 2008–2010 period the fall in tax revenues (plus the rise in transfers) was enormous.

The second fiscal response was a discretionary policy, the American Recovery and Reinvestment Act (ARRA), better known as the "stimulus" bill. This policy was one of the first actions undertaken by the Obama administration and it was signed into law on February 17, 2009. Some of the president's advisors had originally hoped for a $1.4 trillion package, mostly for extra government consumption and investment spending, and also for aid to states. This was to be spread over 2 to 3 years from 2009–2011. However, the final compromise deal with Congress was only half as big, $787 billion over three years, and was tilted more toward temporary tax cuts. Most of the stimulus was scheduled to take effect in 2010, not 2009, reflecting the policy lags we noted above. On average, the package amounted to about 1.5% of GDP in spending and tax cuts.

Construction work on an interstate highway in Cleveland, Ohio, funded by government stimulus money.

Some key outcomes are shown in Figure 14-20. As panel (a) shows, the size of the gap between actual and potential output left a huge hole to be filled by fiscal policy. By mid-2009 this hole was about 6% of potential GDP or over $1 trillion at an annual rate. *Even if the entire stimulus was spent*, the fiscal package could at best have filled only

---

[3]Note that, at the ZLB, the model resembles the fixed exchange rate model, not the floating exchange rate model, because being stuck at the ZLB pegs the interest rate (in this case at zero, rather than at i^*).

FIGURE 14-20

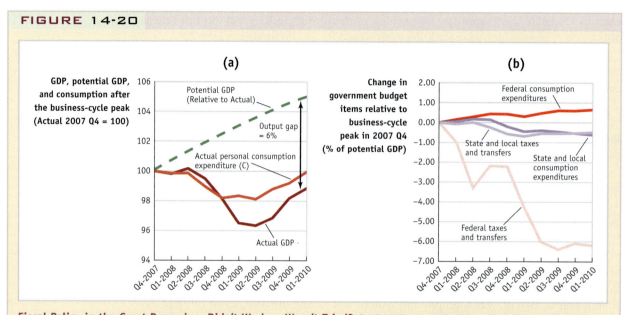

Fiscal Policy in the Great Recession: Didn't Work or Wasn't Tried? In the U.S. economic slump of 2008–2010, output had fallen 6% below the estimate of potential (full-employment) level of GDP by the first quarter of 2009, as seen in panel (a). This was the worst U.S. recession since the 1930s. Policy responses included automatic fiscal expansion (increases in spending and reductions in taxes), plus an additional discretionary stimulus (the 2009 American Recovery and Reinvestment Act or ARRA). The tax part of the stimulus appeared to do very little: significant reductions in taxes seen in panel (b) were insufficient to prop up consumption expenditure, as seen in panel (a), as consumers saved the extra disposable income. And on the government spending side there was no stimulus at all in the aggregate: increases in federal government expenditure were fully offset by cuts in state and local government expenditure, as seen in panel (b).

Sources: Federal Reserve Economic Indicators (FRED). Potential output from Congressional Budget Office; all other data from the Bureau of Economic Analysis.

about one-quarter of the collapse in demand or 1.5% of GDP. Policy makers in the government, and many observers, knew the package was too small, but politics stood in the way of a larger package.

The data in panel (a) also show that private consumption fell precipitously. One intention of ARRA was to support private spending through tax cuts. Tax revenues T did fall considerably [largely at the federal level as shown in panel (b), because states were getting some offsetting transfers via ARRA]. But tax cuts did not appear to generate much extra private spending, certainly not enough to offset the initial collapse in consumption expenditure. Many consumers were unsure about the economic recovery, worried about the risks of unemployment, and trying to use whatever "extra" money they got from tax cuts to pay down their debts or save. In addition, because people were trying to hold onto their money (precautionary motives were high), the marginal propensity to consume was probably low. Furthermore, for non-Keynesian consumers, the temporary nature of many of the tax cuts meant that anyone following the principles of *Ricardian equivalence* would be likely to save the tax cut to pay off an expected future tax liability.

This left government spending G to do a great deal of the stimulation, but problems arose because of the contrary effects of state and local government policies. As the figure shows, federal expenditures went up, rising by 0.5% of GDP in 2010. Leaving aside the miniscule size of this change, a big source of trouble was that state and local government expenditures went down by just as much. States and localities imposed austerity spending cuts, which were made necessary by calamitous declines in their tax revenues, by their limited ability to borrow, and by the feeble amount of aid to states authorized in the final ARRA package. The net change in overall government expenditures was thus, in the end, zero.

To sum up, the aggregate U.S. fiscal stimulus had four major weaknesses: it was rolled out too slowly, due to policy lags; the overall package was too small, given the magnitude of the decline in aggregate demand; the government spending portion of the stimulus, for which positive expenditure effects were certain, ended up being close to zero, due to state and local cuts; and this left almost all the work to tax cuts (automatic and discretionary) that recipients, for good reasons, were more likely to save rather than spend. With monetary policy impotent and fiscal policy weak and ill designed, the economy remained mired in its worst slump since the 1930s Great Depression.[4] ■

7 Conclusions

The analysis of macroeconomic policy is different in an open economy than in a closed economy. The trade balance generates an additional source of demand, and its fluctuations are driven by changes in output and the real exchange rate. Expenditure switching is a key mechanism at work here: as international relative prices change, demand shifts from foreign to home goods and vice versa.

The open economy IS-LM-FX framework is a workhorse model for analyzing the macroeconomic responses to shocks and to changes in monetary and fiscal policies. Exploring these responses, in turn, draws out some clear contrasts between the operation of fixed and flexible exchange rate regimes.

Under flexible exchange rates, monetary and fiscal policies can be used. Monetary expansions raise output and also lower the interest rate, which stimulates investment and causes a depreciation, which in turn stimulates the trade balance. Fiscal expansions raise output; raise the interest rate, which depresses investment; and cause an appreciation, which in turn lowers the trade balance.

With two policy tools available, the authorities have considerable flexibility. In particular, their ability to let the exchange rate adjust to absorb shocks makes a strong case for a floating exchange rate. Now we can understand the logic behind Robert Mundell's quote at the start of the chapter.

Under fixed exchange rates, monetary policy cannot be used because the home interest rate has to remain equal to the foreign interest rate in order for the exchange rate to remain fixed. But fiscal policy has great power under a fixed exchange rate. Fiscal expansions raise output and force the monetary authority to expand the money supply to prevent any rise in the interest rate and any appreciation of the exchange rate. In contrast to the floating case, in which interest rate increases and exchange rate appreciation put downward pressure on investment and the trade balance, the demand stimulus is even greater.

---

[4] The size of the output gap was understood early on, even before President Obama took office. At the start of January 2009 the Congressional Budget Office forecast that, without a stimulus, unemployment would rise above 9% by early 2010, and remain there for several years, with an output gap projected to be 6.8% of GDP in 2010 and 2011 (numbers very close to what has transpired). In that context, some economists pointed out the problems with the size and design of the ARRA package, especially the use of temporary tax cuts. See, for example, Martin Feldstein, Statement for the House Democratic Steering and Policy Committee, January 7, 2009; and Paul Krugman, "The Obama Gap," *The New York Times*, January 8, 2009.

With only one policy tool available, the authorities in fixed rate regimes have much less flexibility. They also expose the economy to more volatility because any demand shock will entail an immediate and reinforcing monetary shock. The tendency of fixed exchange rate systems to amplify demand shocks helps us understand the logic behind Alec Ford's quote at the start of the chapter.

Whatever the regime, fixed or floating, our findings suggest that macroeconomic policy can *in principle* be used to stabilize an open economy when it suffers from external shocks. Under floating exchange rates, however, more policy options are available (monetary and fiscal policy responses are feasible) than under fixed exchange rates (only a fiscal policy response is feasible).

Despite these relatively simple lessons, real-world policy design is not straightforward. Policy makers have difficulty identifying shocks, devising the right response, and acting quickly enough to ensure that policy actions have a timely effect. Even then, under some conditions, the economy may respond in unusual ways.

KEY POINTS

1. In the short run, we assume prices are sticky at some preset level P. There is thus no inflation, and nominal and real quantities can be considered equivalent. We assume output GDP equals income Y or GDNI and that the trade balance equals the current account (there are no transfers or factor income from abroad).

2. The Keynesian consumption function says that private consumption spending C is an increasing function of household disposable income $Y - T$.

3. The investment function says that total investment I is a decreasing function of the real or nominal interest rate i.

4. Government spending is assumed to be exogenously given at a level G.

5. The trade balance is assumed to be an increasing function of the real exchange rate EP^*/P, where P^* denotes the foreign price level.

6. The national income identity says that national income or output equals private consumption C, plus investment I, plus government spending G, plus the trade balance TB: $Y = C + I + G + TB$. The right-hand side of this expression is called

demand, and its components depend on income, interest rates, and the real exchange rate. In equilibrium, demand must equal the left-hand side, supply, or total output Y.

7. If the interest rate falls in an open economy, demand is stimulated for two reasons. A lower interest rate directly stimulates investment. A lower interest rate also leads to an exchange rate depreciation, all else equal, which increases the trade balance. This demand must be satisfied for the goods market to remain in equilibrium, so output rises. This is the basis of the IS curve: declines in interest rates must call forth extra output to keep the goods market in equilibrium. Each point on the IS curve represents a combination of output Y and interest rate i at which the goods and FX markets are in equilibrium. Because Y increases as i decreases, the IS curve is downward-sloping.

8. Real money demand arises primarily from transactions requirements. It increases when the volume of transactions (represented by national income Y) increases, and decreases when the opportunity cost of holding money, the nominal interest rate i, increases.

9. The money market equilibrium says that the demand for real money balances L must equal the real money supply: $M/P = L(i)Y$. This equation is the basis for the LM curve: any increases in output Y must cause the interest rate to rise, all else equal (e.g., holding fixed real money M/P). Each point on the LM curve represents a combination of output Y and interest rate i at which the money market is in equilibrium. Because i increases as Y increases, the LM curve is upward-sloping.

10. The IS-LM diagram combines the IS and LM curves on one figure and shows the unique short-run equilibrium for output Y and the interest rate i that describes simultaneous equilibrium in the goods and money markets. The IS-LM diagram can be coupled with the forex market diagram to summarize conditions in all three markets: goods, money, and forex. This combined IS-LM-FX diagram can then be used to assess the impact of various macroeconomic policies in the short run.

11. Under a floating exchange rate, the interest rate and exchange rate are free to adjust to maintain equilibrium. Thus, government policy is free to move either the IS or LM curves. The impacts are as follows:

- Monetary expansion: LM shifts to the right, output rises, interest rate falls, exchange rate rises/depreciates.

- Fiscal expansion: IS shifts to the right, output rises, interest rate rises, exchange rate falls/appreciates.

12. Under a fixed exchange rate, the interest rate always equals the foreign interest rate and the exchange rate is pegged. Thus, the government is not free to move the LM curve: monetary policy must be adjusted to ensure that LM is in such a position that these exchange rate and interest rate conditions hold. The impacts are as follows:

- Monetary expansion: not feasible.
- Fiscal expansion: IS shifts to the right, LM follows it and also shifts to the right, output rises strongly, interest rate and exchange rate are unchanged.

13. The ability to manipulate the IS and LM curves gives the government the capacity to engage in stabilization policies to offset shocks to the economy and to try to maintain a full-employment level of output. This is easier said than done, however, because it is difficult to diagnose the correct policy response, and policies often take some time to have an impact, so that by the time the policy effects are felt, they may be ineffective or even counterproductive.

KEY TERMS

PROBLEMS

1. In 2001 President George W. Bush and Federal Reserve Chairman Alan Greenspan were both concerned about a sluggish U.S. economy. They also were concerned about the large U.S. current account deficit. To help stimulate the economy, President Bush proposed a tax cut, while the Fed had been increasing U.S. money supply. Compare the effects of these two policies in terms of their implications for the current account. If policy makers are concerned about the current account deficit, discuss whether stimulatory fiscal policy or monetary policy makes more sense in this case. Then, reconsider similar issues for 2009–2010, when the economy was in a deep slump, the Fed had taken interest rates to zero, and the Obama administration was arguing for larger fiscal stimulus.

2. Suppose that American firms become more optimistic and decide to increase investment expenditure today in new factories and office space.

   a. How will this increase in investment affect output, interest rates, and the current account?

   b. Now repeat part (a), assuming that domestic investment is very responsive to the interest rate so that U.S. firms will cancel most of their new investment plans if the interest rate rises. How will this affect the answer you gave previously?

3. For each of the following situations, use the IS-LM-FX model to illustrate the effects of the shock. For each case, state the effect of the shock on the following variables (increase, decrease, no change, or ambiguous): Y, i, E, C, I, and TB. Assume the government allows the exchange rate to float and makes no policy response.

   a. Foreign output decreases.
   b. Investors expect a depreciation of the home currency.
   c. The money supply increases.
   d. Government spending increases.

4. How would a decrease in the money supply of Paraguay (currency unit is the "guaraní") affect its own output and its exchange rate with Brazil (currency unit is the "real"). Do you think this policy in Paraguay might also affect output across the border in Brazil? Explain.

5. For each of the following situations, use the IS-LM-FX model to illustrate the effects of the shock and the policy response. *Note:* Assume the government responds by using monetary policy to stabilize output, unlike question 3, and assume the exchange rate is floating. For each case, state the effect of the shock on the following variables (increase, decrease, no change, or ambiguous): Y, i, E, C, I, and TB.

   a. Foreign output decreases.
   b. Investors expect a depreciation of the home currency.
   c. The money supply increases.
   d. Government spending increases.

6. Repeat the previous question, assuming the central bank responds in order to maintain a fixed exchange rate. In which case or cases will the government response be the same as in the previous question?

7. This question explores IS and FX equilibria in a numerical example.

   a. The consumption function is $C = 1.5 + 0.75(Y - T)$. What is the marginal propensity to consume MPC? What is the marginal propensity to save MPS?

   b. The trade balance is $TB = 5(1-[1/E]) - 0.25(Y - 8)$. What is the marginal propensity to consume foreign goods $MPCF$? What is the marginal propensity to consume home goods $MPCH$?

   c. The investment function is $I = 2 - 10i$. What is investment when the interest rate i is equal to $0.10 = 10\%$?

   d. Assume government spending is G. Add up the four components of demand and write down the expression for D.

e. Assume forex market equilibrium is given by $i = ([1/E] - 1) + 0.10$, where the two foreign return terms on the right are expected depreciation and the foreign interest rate. What is the foreign interest rate? What is the expected future exchange rate?

8. [More difficult] Continuing the last question, solve for the IS curve: obtain an expression for Y in terms of i, G, and T (eliminate E).

9. Assume that initially the *IS* curve is given by

$$IS_1: Y = 12 - 1.5T - 30i + 2G$$

and that the price level P is 1, and the *LM* curve is given by

$$LM_1: M = Y(1 - i)$$

The home central bank uses the interest rate as its policy instrument. Initially, the home interest rate equals the foreign interest rate of 10% or 0.1. Taxes and government spending both equal 2. Call this case 1.

a. According to the IS_1 curve, what is the level of output Y? Assume this is the desired full-employment level of output.

b. According to the LM_1 curve, at this level of output, what is the level of the home money supply?

c. Plot the IS_1 and LM_1 curves for case 1 on a chart. Label the axes, and the equilibrium values.

d. Assume that forex market equilibrium is given by $i = ([1/E] - 1) + 0.10$, where the two foreign return terms on the right are expected depreciation and the foreign interest rate. The expected future exchange rate is 1. What is today's spot exchange rate?

e. There is now a foreign demand shock, such that the IS curve shifts left by 1.5 units at all levels of the interest rate, and the new IS curve is given by

$$IS_2: Y = 10.5 - 1.5T - 30i + 2G$$

The government asks the central bank to stabilize the economy at full employment. To stabilize and return output back to the desired level, according to this new IS curve, by how much must the interest rate be lowered from its initial level of 0.1? (Assume taxes and government spending remain at 2.) Call this case 2.

f. At the new lower interest rate and at full employment, on the new *LM* curve (LM_2), what is the new level of the money supply?

g. According to the forex market equilibrium, what is the new level of the spot exchange rate? How large is the depreciation of the home currency?

h. Plot the new IS_2 and LM_2 curves for case 2 on a chart. Label the axes, and the equilibrium values.

i. Return to part (e). Now assume that the central bank refuses to change the interest rate from 10%. In this case, what is the new level of output? What is the money supply? And if the government decides to use fiscal policy instead to stabilize output, then, according to the new *IS* curve, by how much must government spending be increased to achieve this goal? Call this case 3.

j. Plot the new IS_3 and LM_3 curves for case 3 on a chart. Label the axes, and the equilibrium values.

10. In this chapter, we've studied how policy responses affect economic variables in an open economy. Consider each of the problems in policy design and implementation discussed in this chapter. Compare and contrast each problem as it applies to monetary policy stabilization versus fiscal policy stabilization.

APPENDIX 1 TO CHAPTER 14

The Marshall-Lerner Condition

The model developed in this chapter assumes that a depreciation of a country's currency (a rise in q) will cause the trade balance to move toward surplus (a rise in TB). Is this assumption justified?

Let's look at a simple example. Consider a hypothetical two-country world in which trade is initially balanced, so $TB = 0$ or $EX = IM$. The question of how the trade balance changes then simplifies to a question of whether the change in exports is greater or less than the change in imports. Let us consider a small percentage change in the real exchange rate, say, $\Delta q/q = +1\%$, that is, a home real depreciation of 1%. Note that this is, approximately, a foreign real appreciation of 1%, since the foreign real exchange rate $q^* = 1/q$ is simply the inverse of the home real exchange rate, implying that $\Delta q^*/q^* = -1\%$.

As we have argued, when home exports look cheaper to foreigners, the real value of home exports expressed in home units of output will *unambiguously* rise. This effect is described by the elasticity of home exports with respect to the home real exchange rate, denoted η, where

$$\frac{\Delta EX}{EX} = \eta \times \frac{\Delta q}{q} = \eta\%$$

That is, if the home country experiences a 1% real depreciation, its real exports (measured in home units) rise by $\eta\%$.

The same logic applies to the foreign country, with exports EX^*, real exchange rate $q^* = 1/q$, and elasticity η^*, so that

$$\frac{\Delta EX^*}{EX^*} = \eta^* \times \frac{\Delta q^*}{q^*} = \eta^*\%$$

Now consider the trade link between the two countries. Foreign exports must equal home imports, measured in any consistent units. In home real output units

$$\underbrace{\begin{array}{c}\text{Home imports}\\\text{in units of home output}\end{array} = \underbrace{IM(q)}_{\substack{\text{Home imports}\\\text{(real)}}}}$$

$$\begin{array}{c}\text{Foreign exports}\\\text{in units of home output}\end{array} = \underbrace{\underbrace{(1/P)}_{\substack{\text{Divide by home}\\\text{price level to}\\\text{convert to home}\\\text{output units}}} \times \underbrace{E}_{\substack{\text{Exchange rate}\\\text{converts}\\\text{foreign to}\\\text{domestic}\\\text{currency}}} \times \underbrace{\underbrace{P^*}_{\substack{\text{Price of}\\\text{foreign basket}\\\text{in foreign}\\\text{currency}}} \times \underbrace{EX^*(q^*)}_{\substack{\text{Foreign exports}\\\text{(real)}}}}_{\substack{\text{Value of foreign exports in}\\\text{foreign currency}}}}_{\text{Value of foreign exports in home currency}}$$

Equating these two terms, we find that $IM(q) = (EP^*/P) \times EX^*(q^*)$. Thus,

$$IM(q) = q \times EX^*(q^*)$$

This expression makes intuitive sense for the stylized two-country world that we are studying. It states that IM, the quantity of home imports (measured in *home* output units), must equal the quantity of foreign exports EX^* (measured in *foreign* output units) multiplied by a factor q that converts units of foreign goods to units of home goods (since q is the relative price of foreign goods, that is home goods per unit of foreign goods).

For a small change, we may write the percentage change in the previous equation as follows. On the left is the percentage change in imports; on the right is the percentage change in q *times* EX^*, which equals the percentage change in q *plus* the percentage change in EX^*:

$$\frac{\Delta IM}{IM} = \frac{\Delta q}{q} + \frac{\Delta EX^*}{EX^*} = \frac{\Delta q}{q} + \left[\eta^* \times \frac{\Delta q^*}{q^*}\right] = 1\% + \left[\eta^* \times (-1\%)\right] = (1 - \eta^*)\%$$

What is going on here? On the home import side, two effects come into play. Foreigners export a lower volume of their more expensive goods measured in foreign output units (a volume effect of $-\eta^*\%$), but those goods will cost more for home importers in terms of home output (a price effect of 1%). The price effect follows because the real exchange rate (the relative price of the foreign goods in terms of domestic goods) has increased (by 1%), and this makes every unit of imports cost more in real terms.

Starting from balanced trade with $EX = IM$, a 1% home real depreciation will cause EX to change by $\eta\%$ and IM to change by $1 - \eta^*\%$. The trade balance (initially zero) will increase (to become positive) if and only if the former impact on EX exceeds the latter impact on IM. This occurs if and only if $\eta > 1 - \eta^*$, or, equivalently,

$$\eta + \eta^* > 1$$

The last expression is known as the *Marshall-Lerner condition:* it says that the trade balance will increase only after a real depreciation if the responsiveness of trade volumes to real exchange rate changes is sufficiently large (or sufficiently elastic) to ensure that the volume effects exceed the price effects.

APPENDIX 2 TO CHAPTER 14

Multilateral Real Exchange Rates

How do the predictions of our model change when a country trades with multiple countries or regions? Can our theory be extended to this more realistic case? Can we make a sensible aggregation of trade flows, trade balances, and real exchange rates across, say, N different countries?

Suppose that for trade with any foreign country (say, country 1), the fractional change in home exports EX_1 and imports IM_1 given a small change in the real exchange rate q_1 is

$$\frac{\Delta EX_1}{EX_1} = \varepsilon \times \frac{\Delta q_1}{q_1}; \qquad \frac{\Delta IM_1}{IM_1} = -\varepsilon \times \frac{\Delta q_1}{q_1}$$

The parameter $\varepsilon > 0$ is an *elasticity*. In this case, it is the elasticity of exports and imports with respect to the real exchange rate. When q rises by 1% (a real depreciation), exports rise by ε% and imports fall by ε%. (A more complicated analysis is needed when the import and export elasticities differ; see the first appendix.)

From these relationships, we find the following by rearranging:

$$\Delta TB_1 = \Delta EX_1 - \Delta IM_1 = \varepsilon \frac{\Delta q_1}{q_1} EX_1 + \varepsilon \frac{\Delta q_1}{q_1} IM_1$$

$$= \varepsilon \times (EX_1 + IM_1) \times \frac{\Delta q_1}{q_1}$$

$$= \varepsilon \times \text{Trade}_1 \times \frac{\Delta q_1}{q_1}$$

where $\text{Trade}_i = [EX_i + IM_i]$ is the total trade of the home country with country i.

Adding up this last equation across all countries, the change in the home trade balance is given by $\Delta TB = \Delta TB_1 + \Delta TB_2 + \cdots + \Delta TB_N$, which we can write as

$$\Delta TB = \varepsilon \times \left[\text{Trade}_1 \frac{\Delta q_1}{q_1} + \text{Trade}_2 \frac{\Delta q_2}{q_2} + \cdots + \text{Trade}_N \frac{\Delta q_N}{q_N} \right]$$

We normalize by total trade, where $\text{Trade} = \text{Trade}_1 + \text{Trade}_2 + \cdots + \text{Trade}_N$, to obtain

$$\Delta TB = \varepsilon \times \text{Trade} \times \left[\frac{\text{Trade}_1}{\text{Trade}} \frac{\Delta q_1}{q_1} + \frac{\text{Trade}_1}{\text{Trade}} \frac{\Delta q_2}{q_2} + \cdots + \frac{\text{Trade}_1}{\text{Trade}} \frac{\Delta q_N}{q_N} \right]$$

The expression in brackets might look familiar. In Chapter 10, we introduced the concept of a *trade-weighted change in the nominal exchange rate*—the change in the value of a currency against a basket of currencies, where the change in each country-pair's nominal exchange rate was weighted by that particular country-pair's share of trade volume. The preceding expression is similar, only with nominal exchange rates replaced by real exchange rates. The expression shows that (with some assumptions) our model can be extended to more realistic scenarios with many countries by using the change in a trade-weighted real exchange rate covering all trading partners.

15

Fixed versus Floating: International Monetary Experience

In truth, the gold standard is already a barbarous relic. All of us, from the Governor of the Bank of England downwards, are now primarily interested in preserving the stability of business, prices, and employment, and are not likely, when the choice is forced on us, deliberately to sacrifice these to the outworn dogma. . . . Advocates of the ancient standard do not observe how remote it now is from the spirit and the requirements of the age.

John Maynard Keynes, 1923

How many more fiascoes will it take before responsible people are finally convinced that a system of pegged exchange rates is not a satisfactory financial arrangement for a group of large countries with independent political systems and independent national policies?

Milton Friedman, 1992

The gold standard in particular—and even pegged exchange rates in general—have a bad name. But the gold standard's having lost her name in the 1920s and 1930s should not lead one to forget her 19th century virtues. . . . Can these lost long-term virtues be retrieved without the world again being in thrall to the barbarous relic? . . . In an integrated world economy, the choice of an exchange rate regime—and thus the common price level—should not be left to an individual country. The spillover effects are so high that it should be a matter of collective choice.

Ronald McKinnon, 2002

A century ago, economists and policy makers may have had their differences of opinion, but—unlike today—they were virtually unanimous in their agreement about the ideal choice of exchange rate regime. Fixed exchange rates were viewed as the best choice. Even if some countries occasionally adopted a floating rate, it was usually with the expectation that they would soon return to a fixed or pegged rate.

The preferred method for fixing the exchange rate was also more or less agreed upon. It was the **gold standard,** a system in which the value of a country's currency was fixed relative to an ounce of gold and, hence, relative to all other currencies that were also pegged to gold. The requirements of the gold standard were strict: although monetary authorities could issue paper money, they were obliged to freely exchange paper currency for gold at the official fixed rate.

Figure 15-1 documents more than 100 years of exchange rate arrangements around the world. From 1870 to 1913, most of the world converged on the gold standard. At the peak in 1913, approximately 70% of countries were part of the gold standard system; very few floated (about 20%) or used other metallic standards (about 10%). Since 1913 much has changed. Adherence to the gold standard weakened during World War I, waxed and waned in the 1920s and 1930s, then was never seen again. John Maynard Keynes and other policy makers designed a new system, but one in which exchange rates were still fixed.

In the period after World War II, the figure shows that many currencies were pegged to the U.S. dollar. The British pound, the French franc, and the German mark were also somewhat popular peg choices. Yet because the pound, franc, and mark were all pegged to the dollar at this time, the vast majority of the world's currencies ended up, directly or indirectly, on what amounted to a "dollar standard" system.

Like the gold standard, the dollar-based system didn't endure either. Beginning in the early 1970s, floating exchange rates became more common, and they now account

FIGURE 15-1

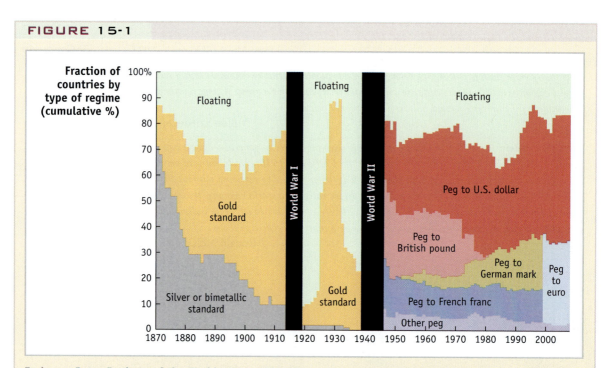

Exchange Rates Regimes of the World, 1870–2007 The shaded regions show the fraction of countries on each type of regime by year, and they add up to 100%. From 1870 to 1913, the gold standard became the dominant regime. During World War I (1914–1918), most countries suspended the gold standard, and resumptions in the late 1920s were brief. After further suspensions in World War II (1939–1945), most countries were fixed against the U.S. dollar (the pound, franc, and mark blocs were indirectly pegged to the dollar). Starting in the 1970s, more countries opted to float. In 1999 the euro replaced the franc and the mark as the base currency for many pegs.

Sources: Christopher M. Meissner, 2005, "A New World Order: Explaining the International Diffusion of the Gold Standard, 1870–1913," Journal of International Economics, 66(2), 385–406; Christopher M. Meissner and Nienke Oomes, 2006, "Why Do Countries Peg the Way They Peg? The Determinants of Anchor Currency Choice," Cambridge Working Papers in Economics 0643, Faculty of Economics, University of Cambridge, and later updates.

for about 30% of all currency regimes. Remember that these data count all countries' currencies equally, without any weighting for economic size (measured by GDP). In the larger economies of the world, and especially among the major currencies, floating regimes are even more prevalent.

Why do some countries choose to fix and others to float? Why do they change their minds at different times? These are the main questions we confront in this chapter, and they are among the most enduring and controversial questions in international macroeconomics. They have been the cause of conflicts among economists, policy makers, and commentators for many years.

On one side of the debate are those like Milton Friedman (quoted at the start of this chapter) who in the 1950s, against the prevailing gold standard orthodoxy, argued that floating rates are obviously to be preferred, have clear economic advantages, and are the only politically feasible solution. On the opposing side of the debate are figures such as Ronald McKinnon (also quoted above) who think that only a system of fixed rates can prevent noncooperative policy making, keep prices and output stable, and encourage international flows of trade and finance.

What are the pros and cons of different exchange rate regimes? Are the answers black and white? And why should we care?

1 Exchange Rate Regime Choice: Key Issues

In previous chapters, we have examined the workings of the economy under fixed and floating exchange rates. One advantage of understanding the workings of these regimes in such detail is that we are now in a position to address a perennially important macroeconomic policy question: What is the best exchange rate regime choice for a given country at a given time? In this section, we explore the pros and cons of fixed and floating exchange rates by combining the models we have developed with additional theory and evidence. We begin with an application about Germany and Britain in the early 1990s. This story highlights the choices policy makers face as they choose between fixed exchange rates (pegs) and floating exchange rates (floats).

APPLICATION

Britain and Europe: The Big Issues

One way to begin to understand the choice between fixed and floating regimes is to look at countries that have sometimes floated and sometimes fixed and to examine their reasons for switching. In this case study, we look behind the British decision to switch from an exchange rate peg to floating in September 1992.

We start by asking, why did Britain first adopt a peg? The answer derives from Britain's membership in the European Union (EU) since the 1970s and the steps being taken in the 1980s and 1990s by EU member states to move toward a common currency, the euro, which arrived in 1999. For now, we note that the push for a common currency was part of a larger program to create a single market across Europe. Fixed exchange rates, and ultimately a common currency, were seen as a means to promote trade and other forms of cross-border exchange by lowering transaction costs. In addition, it was also felt that an exchange rate anchor might help lower British inflation.

An important stepping-stone along the way to the euro was a fixed exchange rate system created in 1979 called the Exchange Rate Mechanism (ERM), which tied together all member currencies at fixed rates. The most important currency in the ERM was the German mark or deutsche mark (DM). Effectively, in the 1980s and 1990s, the German central bank, the Bundesbank, retained monetary autonomy and had the freedom to set its own money supply levels and nominal interest rates. For other countries, joining the ERM meant that, in effect, they had to *unilaterally* peg to the DM.[1] Thus, we would say that the DM was the **base currency** or **center currency** (or Germany was the *base country* or *center country*) in the fixed exchange rate system.

Britain joined the ERM in 1990. Based on our analysis of fixed exchange rates in the previous chapter, we can understand the implications of that choice using Figure 15-2. This figure shows the familiar one-country IS-LM-FX diagram for Britain and another IS-LM diagram for the center country, Germany. We treat Britain as the home country and Germany as the foreign country, and denote foreign variables with an asterisk.

Panel (a) shows an IS-LM diagram for Germany, with German output on the horizontal axis and the German DM interest rate on the vertical axis. Panel (b) shows the British IS-LM diagram, with British output on the horizontal axis. Panel (c) shows the British forex market, with the exchange rate in pounds per mark. The vertical axes of panels (b) and (c) show returns in pounds, the home currency.

Initially, we suppose the three diagrams are in equilibrium as follows. In panel (b), at point 1, British output is Y_1 and the pound interest rate is i_1. In panel (a), at point 1″, German output is Y_1^* and the DM interest rate i_1^*. In panel (c), at point 1′, the pound is pegged to the DM at the fixed rate $\overline{E}$ and expected depreciation is zero. The trilemma tells us that monetary policy autonomy is lost in Britain: the British interest rate must equal the German interest rate, so there is uncovered interest parity with $i_1 = i_1^*$.

A Shock in Germany With the scene set, our story begins with a threat to the ERM from an unexpected source. The countries of Eastern Europe began their transition away from Communism, a process that famously began with the fall of the Berlin Wall in 1989. After the wall fell, the reunification of East and West Germany was soon under way. Because the economically backward East Germany required significant funds to support social services, pay unemployment benefits, modernize infrastructure, and so on, the reunification imposed large fiscal costs on Germany, but West Germans were willing to pay these costs to see their country united. As we know from the previous chapter, an increase in German government consumption G^* can be represented as a shift to the right in the German IS curve, from IS_1^* to IS_2^* in panel (a). This shift would have moved the German economy's equilibrium from point 1″ to point 3″. All else equal, the model predicts an increase in German interest rates from i_1^* to i_3^* and a boom in German output from Y_1^* to Y_3^*.[2] This was indeed what started to happen.

The next chapter in the story involves the Bundesbank's response to the German government's expansionary fiscal policy. The Bundesbank was deeply afraid that the boom in output might cause an increase in German rates of inflation, and it wished to

---

[1] Officially, all currencies in the ERM pegged to a virtual basket of currencies called the ecu (European currency unit), the precursor of the euro. In practice, though, the DM was the predominant reserve currency and, in effect, the base currency.

[2] All else would not have been equal under this shift, given the ERM; Germany's interest rate increase would have been matched by other ERM members to preserve their pegs. For Germany, those shifts would be increases in the foreign interest rate (from Germany's perspective), and those responses would, in turn, have shifted Germany's IS curve a tiny bit farther. These extra effects make no substantive difference to the analysis, so the extra shift is not shown here, for clarity.

FIGURE 15-2

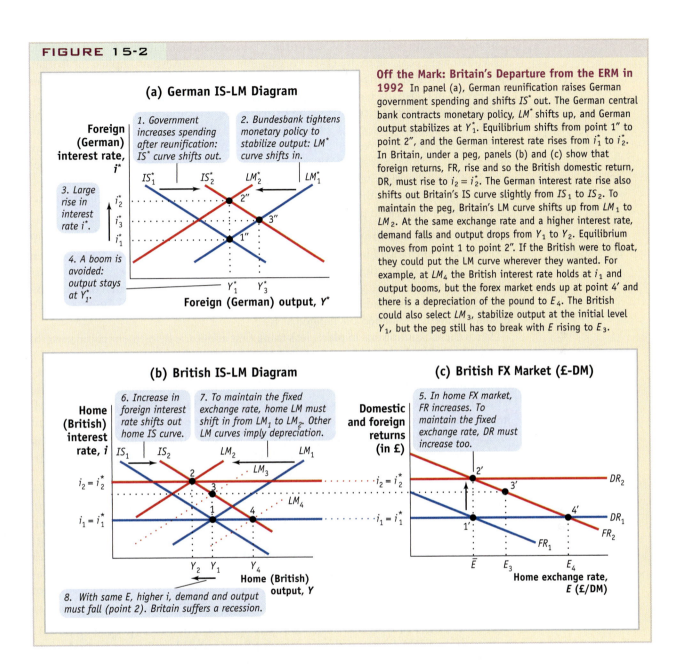

(a) German IS-LM Diagram

Foreign (German) interest rate, i^*

1. Government increases spending after reunification: IS^* curve shifts out.

2. Bundesbank tightens monetary policy to stabilize output: LM^* curve shifts in.

3. Large rise in interest rate i^*.

4. A boom is avoided: output stays at Y_1^*.

IS_1^* IS_2^* LM_2^* LM_1^*

i_2^* i_3^* i_1^*

Foreign (German) output, Y^*

Y_1^* Y_3^*

Off the Mark: Britain's Departure from the ERM in 1992 In panel (a), German reunification raises German government spending and shifts IS^* out. The German central bank contracts monetary policy, LM^* shifts up, and German output stabilizes at Y_1^*. Equilibrium shifts from point 1″ to point 2″, and the German interest rate rises from i_1^* to i_2^*. In Britain, under a peg, panels (b) and (c) show that foreign returns, FR, rise and so the British domestic return, DR, must rise to $i_2 = i_2^*$. The German interest rate rise also shifts out Britain's IS curve slightly from IS_1 to IS_2. To maintain the peg, Britain's LM curve shifts up from LM_1 to LM_2. At the same exchange rate and a higher interest rate, demand falls and output drops from Y_1 to Y_2. Equilibrium moves from point 1 to point 2″. If the British were to float, they could put the LM curve wherever they wanted. For example, at LM_4 the British interest rate holds at i_1 and output booms, but the forex market ends up at point 4′ and there is a depreciation of the pound to E_4. The British could also select LM_3, stabilize output at the initial level Y_1, but the peg still has to break with E rising to E_3.

(b) British IS-LM Diagram

Home (British) interest rate, i

6. Increase in foreign interest rate shifts out home IS curve.

7. To maintain the fixed exchange rate, home LM must shift in from LM_1 to LM_2. Other LM curves imply depreciation.

IS_1 IS_2 LM_2 LM_1 LM_3

LM_4

$i_2 = i_2^*$

$i_1 = i_1^*$

Y_2 Y_1 Y_4

Home (British) output, Y

8. With same E, higher i, demand and output must fall (point 2). Britain suffers a recession.

(c) British FX Market (£-DM)

Domestic and foreign returns (in £)

5. In home FX market, FR increases. To maintain the fixed exchange rate, DR must increase too.

$i_2 = i_2^*$

$i_1 = i_1^*$

DR_2
DR_1
FR_2
FR_1

$\bar{E}$ E_3 E_4

Home exchange rate, E (£/DM)

take steps to head off that risk. Using its policy autonomy, the Bundesbank elected to tighten monetary policy: it contracted the money supply and raised interest rates. This policy change is seen in the upward shift of the German LM curve, from LM_1^* to LM_2^* in panel (a). We suppose that the Bundesbank stabilizes German output at its initial level Y_1^* by raising German interest rates to the even higher level of i_2^*, as shown in the diagram.[3]

---

[3] Interest rate responses in the ERM (described in footnote 2) would, in turn, have moved Germany's IS curve out yet farther, requiring a bit more tightening from the Bundesbank. Again, these indirect effects do not affect the analysis and are not shown, for clarity.

Choices for the Other ERM Countries What happened in the countries of the ERM that were pegging to the DM? We examine what these events implied for Britain, but the other ERM members faced the same problems. The IS-LM-FX model tells us that events in Germany have two implications for the British IS-LM-FX model. First, as the German interest rate i^* rises, the British foreign return curve FR shifts up in the British forex market (to recap: German deposits pay higher interest, all else equal). Second, as the German interest rate i^* rises, the British IS curve also moves out (to recap: at any given British interest rate, the pound has to depreciate more, boosting British demand via expenditure switching). Now we only have to figure out how much the British IS curve shifts, what the British LM curve is up to, and hence how the equilibrium outcome depends on British policy choices.

Choice 1: Float and Prosper? First, let us suppose that the Bank of England had left interest rates unchanged in Britain at i_1 and suppose British fiscal policy had also been left unchanged. In addition, we assume that Britain would allow the pound-DM exchange rate to float in the short run, but for simplicity we also assume that the same expected exchange rate would prevail in the long run, so that the long-run future expected exchange rate E^e remained unchanged at $\overline{E}$.

With these assumptions in place, let's think first about the investment component of demand: I in Britain would be unchanged at $I(i_1)$. But in the forex market in panel (c), with the domestic return DR_1 held at i_1 by the Bank of England and with the foreign return rising from FR_1 to FR_2, the new equilibrium would be at 4′ and the exchange rate would rise temporarily to E_4: the pound would have to depreciate to E_4 against the DM, implying an exit from the ERM system. Now think about the trade balance component of demand: the British trade balance would rise because a nominal depreciation is also a real depreciation in the short run, given sticky prices.[4] As we saw in the previous chapter, British demand would therefore increase, as would British equilibrium output.

To sum up the result after all these adjustments occur, an increase in the foreign interest rate always shifts out the home IS curve, all else equal. We see this in panel (b): British interest rates would still be at i_1, and British output would have risen to Y_4, on the new IS curve IS_2. To keep the interest rate at i_1, as output rises, the Bank of England would have had to expand the money supply and the British LM curve would shift out from LM_1 to LM_4, and the pound would depreciate to E_4. If Britain were to float and depreciate, Britain would experience a boom. But this course of action would not have been compatible with Britain's continued ERM membership.

Choice 2: Peg and Suffer? If Britain's exchange rate were to stay pegged to the DM because of the ERM, however, the outcome for Britain would not be so rosy. In this scenario, the trilemma means that in order to maintain the peg, Britain would have to increase its interest rate and follow the lead of the center country, Germany. In panel (b), the pound interest rate would have to rise to the level $i_2 = i_2^*$ to maintain the peg. In panel (c), the domestic return would rise from DR_1 to DR_2 in step with the foreign return's rise from FR_1 to FR_2, and the new FX market equilibrium would be at 2′. The Bank of England would accomplish this rise in DR by tightening its monetary policy and lowering the British money supply. In panel (b), under a peg, the new position of the IS

---

[4] This is true in a pure two-country model, and, from the British perspective, Germany is the "rest of the world." With many countries, however, the direction of change is still the same. All else equal, a British real depreciation against Germany will still imply a depreciation of the British real effective exchange rate against the rest of the world.

curve at IS_2 would imply an upward shift in the British LM curve, as shown by the move from LM_1 to LM_2. So the British IS-LM equilibrium would now be at point 2, with output at Y_2. The adverse consequences for the British economy now become apparent. At point 2, as compared with the initial point 1, British demand has fallen. Why? British interest rates have risen (depressing investment demand I), but the exchange rate has remained at its pegged level $\bar{E}$ (so there is no change in the trade balance). To sum up, what we have shown in this scenario is that the IS curve may have moved right a bit, but the opposing shift in the LM curve would have been even larger. If Britain were to stay pegged and keep its membership in the ERM, Britain would experience a recession.

In 1992 Britain found itself facing these exact choices. As we have noted, if the British pound had been floating against the DM, then leaving interest rates unchanged would have been an option, and Britain could have achieved equilibrium at point 4 with a higher output, Y_4. Indeed, as we know, the whole range of monetary policy options would have been opened up by floating, including, for example, the choice of a mild monetary contraction, shifting the British LM curve from LM_1 to LM_3, moving equilibrium in panel (b) to point 3, stabilizing U.K. output at its initial level Y_1, with the FX market in panel (c) settling at point 3' with a mild depreciation of the exchange rate to E_3.

What Happened Next? Following an economic slowdown, and after considerable last-minute dithering and chaos, in September 1992 the British Conservative government finally came to the conclusion that the benefits of being in ERM and the euro project were smaller than costs suffered due to a German interest rate hike that was a reaction to Germany-specific events. Two years after joining the ERM, Britain opted out.

Did Britain make the right choice? In Figure 15-3, we compare the economic performance of Britain with that of France, a large EU economy that maintained its ERM peg. After leaving the ERM in September 1992, Britain lowered interest rates [panel (a)]

FIGURE 15-3

(a) Interest Rates

(b) Exchange Rate Movements

(c) Real GDP Growth

Floating Away: Britain versus France after 1992 Britain's decision to exit the ERM allowed for more expansionary British monetary policy after September 1992. In other ERM countries that remained pegged to the mark, such as France, monetary policy had to be kept tighter to maintain the peg. Consistent with the model, the data show lower interest rates, a more depreciated currency, and faster output growth in Britain compared with France after 1992.

Note: Interest rates are three-month LIBOR, annualized rates.

Sources: Data from Global Financial Data; econstats.com; IMF, International Financial Statistics.

Stefan Rousseau/PA Archive/PA Photos

Most Britons are opposed to the euro, some vehemently so.

in the short run and depreciated its exchange rate against the DM [panel (b)]. In comparison, France never depreciated and had to maintain higher interest rates to keep the franc pegged to the DM until German monetary policy eased a year or two later. As our model would predict, the British economy boomed in subsequent years (panel c). The French suffered slower growth, a fate shared by most of the other countries that stayed in the ERM.

The British choice stands to this day. Although the option to rejoin the ERM has remained open since 1992, the British have not shown much interest. The idea of pegging to, much less joining, the euro, is deeply unpopular. All subsequent British governments have decided that the benefits of increased trade and economic integration with Europe were smaller than the associated costs of sacrificing British monetary autonomy.[5] ■

Key Factors in Exchange Rate Regime Choice: Integration and Similarity

We started this chapter with an application about the policy choice and tradeoffs Britain faced in 1992 when it needed to decide between a fixed exchange rate (peg) and a floating exchange rate (float).

At different times and with differing degrees of enthusiasm, British authorities could see the potential benefits of participating fully in an economically integrated single European market, including the gains that would flow from being in the ERM fixed exchange rate system. The fixed exchange rate promised to lower the costs of economic transactions among the members of the ERM zone. But the British could also see—as the events of 1992 made clear—that there would be times when the monetary policy being pursued by authorities in Germany would be out of line with policy that was best for Britain. The fundamental source of this divergence between what Britain wanted and what Germany wanted was that each country faced different shocks. The fiscal shock that Germany experienced after reunification was not felt in Britain or any other ERM country.

To better understand these trade-offs, and hence the decision to fix or float, we now examine the issues that are at the heart of this decision: economic *integration* as measured by trade and other transactions, and economic *similarity*, as measured by the similarity of shocks.

Economic Integration and the Gains in Efficiency

The term "economic integration" refers to the growth of market linkages in goods, capital, and labor markets among regions and countries. We have argued that by lowering transaction costs, a fixed exchange rate might promote integration and hence increase economic efficiency. Why?

---

[5] Even the Liberal Democrats, for a long time pro-euro while just a small party perpetually in opposition, effectively dropped their stance once they had the opportunity to join a coalition government with the Conservatives in 2010.

Trade is the most obvious example of an activity that volatile exchange rates might discourage. Stable exchange rates and prices encourage arbitrage and lower the costs of trade. But trade is not the only type of international economic activity likely to be discouraged by exchange rate fluctuations. Currency-related transaction costs and uncertainty also act as barriers to cross-border capital and labor flows.

■ The lesson: *the greater the degree of economic integration between markets in the home country and the base country, the greater will be the volume of transactions between the two, and the greater will be the benefits the home country gains from fixing its exchange rate with the base country. As integration rises, the efficiency benefits of a common currency increase.*

Economic Similarity and the Costs of Asymmetric Shocks

We have also argued that a fixed exchange rate can lead to costs. Our argument depended on the assumption that one country experienced a country-specific shock or **asymmetric shock** that was not shared by the other country: the shocks were dissimilar.

The application on Britain and Germany showed why an *asymmetric* shock causes problems: it leads to a conflict between the policy goals of the two countries. In our example, German policy makers wanted to tighten monetary policy to offset a boom caused by a positive demand shock due to their expansionary fiscal policy. British policy makers did not want to implement the same policy because they had not experienced the same shock.

Now we can begin to see why similar or *symmetric* shocks cause no problems. Imagine a different scenario in which both countries experience an identical demand shock. Both monetary authorities would like to respond identically, raising interest rates in each country by the same amount to stabilize output. Fortunately, this desired symmetric increase in interest rates does not conflict with Britain's fixed exchange rate commitment. If interest rates were initially set at a low common level, $i_1 = i_1^*$, they would just be raised to a new higher level, $i_2 = i_2^*$. Here, Britain can stabilize output *and* stay pegged because uncovered interest parity is still satisfied! The exchange rate $\overline{E}$ does not change, and even though Britain is pegging unilaterally to Germany, Britain has the interest rate it would choose even if it floated and were free to make an independent monetary policy choice.

The simple, general lesson we can draw is that for a home country that unilaterally pegs to a foreign country, asymmetric shocks impose costs in terms of lost output. Desired foreign and home monetary policies will sometimes differ, but the peg means that foreign's policy choice will be imposed on home. In contrast, symmetric shocks do not impose any costs because desired foreign and home monetary policies will be the same, and foreign's imposed choice will suit home perfectly.

In reality, the application of this idea is more complex. The countries may not be identical and the shocks may be a mix of symmetric and asymmetric shocks of different magnitudes. It is possible, although algebraically tedious, to account for these complexities in the same framework. At the end of the day, however, the main point holds true.

■ The lesson: *if there is a greater degree of economic similarity between the home country and the base country, meaning that the countries face more symmetric shocks and fewer asymmetric shocks, then the economic stabilization costs to home of fixing its exchange rate to the base become smaller. As economic similarity rises, the stability costs of common currency decrease.*

Simple Criteria for a Fixed Exchange Rate

We can now set out a simple theory of exchange rate regime choice by considering the *net benefits* (benefits minus the costs) of pegging versus floating. Our discussions about integration and similarity have shown the following:

- *As integration rises, the efficiency benefits of a common currency increase.*
- *As symmetry rises, the stability costs of a common currency decrease.*

Our theory says that if market integration or symmetry increases, the net benefits of a fixed exchange rate also increase. If the net benefits are negative, the home country ought to float if the decision is based solely on its economic interests. If the net benefits turn positive, the home country ought to fix.

Figure 15-4 illustrates the theory graphically in an **symmetry-integration diagram** in which the horizontal axis measures the degree of economic integration between a pair of locations, say, A and B, and the vertical axis measures the symmetry of the shocks experienced by the pair A and B.

We use the figure to consider the question of whether A should peg unilaterally to B (or vice versa). Suppose conditions change and the pair moves up and to the right, for example, from point 1 toward point 6. Along this path, integration and symmetry are both increasing, so the net benefits of fixing are increasing. At some critical point (point 2 in the graph), the net benefits turn positive. Before that point, floating is best. After that point, fixing is best.

Our argument is more general: whatever the direction of the path, as long as it moves up and to the right, it must cross some threshold like point 2 beyond which ben-

---

FIGURE 15-4

A Theory of Fixed Exchange Rates Points 1 to 6 in the figure represent a pair of locations. Suppose one location is considering pegging its exchange rate to its partner. If their markets become more integrated (a move to the right along the horizontal axis) or if the economic shocks they experience become more symmetric (a move up on the vertical axis), the net economic benefits of fixing increase. If the pair moves far enough up or to the right, then the benefits of fixing exceed costs (net benefits are positive), and the pair will cross the fixing threshold shown by the *FIX* line. Above the line, it is optimal for the region to fix. Below the line, it is optimal for the region to float.

efits outweigh costs. Thus, there will exist a set of points—a downward-sloping line passing through point 2—that delineates this threshold. We refer to this threshold as the *FIX* line. Points above the *FIX* line satisfy the economic criteria for a fixed exchange rate.

What might different points on this chart mean? To give an example, if we are at point 6, we might think of A and B as neighborhoods in a city—they are very well integrated and an economic shock is usually felt by all neighborhoods in the city. If A and B were at point 5, they might be two cities. If A and B were at point 4, they might be the regions of a country, still above the *FIX* line. If A and B were at point 3, they might be neighboring, well-integrated countries with few asymmetric shocks. Point 2 is right on the borderline. If A and B were at point 1, they might be less well-integrated countries with more asymmetric shocks and our theory says they ought to float.

The key prediction of our theory is this: *pairs of countries above the FIX line (more integrated, more similar shocks) will gain economically from adopting a fixed exchange rate. Those below the FIX line (less integrated, less similar shocks) will not.*

In a moment, we develop and apply this theory further. But first, let's see if there is evidence to support the theory's two main assumptions: Do fixed exchange rates deliver gains through integration? Do they also impose costs by obstructing stabilization policy?

APPLICATION

Do Fixed Exchange Rates Promote Trade?

Probably the single most powerful argument *for* a fixed exchange rate is that it might boost trade by eliminating trade-hindering frictions. The idea is an old one. In 1878 the United States had yet to rejoin the gold standard following the Civil War. Policy makers were debating whether going back on gold made sense, and J. S. Moore, a U.S. Treasury official testifying before Congress, was questioned on the subject:

Question: Do you not think that the use of a common standard of value has a tendency to promote a free commercial interchange between the various countries using it?

Answer: If two countries, be they ever so distant from each other should have the same standard of money . . . there would be no greater harmonizer than such an exchange.

Benefits Measured by Trade Levels As we have noted, this was the conventional wisdom among policy makers in the late nineteenth and early twentieth centuries, and research by economic historians has found strong support for their views: all else equal, a pair of countries adopting the gold standard had bilateral trade levels 30% to 100% higher than comparable pairs of countries that were off the gold standard.[6] Thus, it appears that the gold standard *did* promote trade.

What about fixed exchange rates today? Do they promote trade? Economists have exhaustively tested this hypothesis using increasingly sophisticated statistical methods.

---

[6] J. Ernesto López Córdova and Christopher M. Meissner, March 2003, "Exchange Rate Regimes and International Trade: Evidence from the Classical Gold Standard Era, 1870–1913," *American Economic Review*, 93(1), 344–353; Antoni Estevadeordal, Brian Frantz, and Alan M. Taylor, May 2003, "The Rise and Fall of World Trade, 1870–1939," *Quarterly Journal of Economics*, 118(2), 359–407; Marc Flandreau and Mathilde Maurel, January 2005, "Monetary Union, Trade Integration, and Business Cycles in 19th Century Europe," *Open Economies Review*, 16(2), 135–152. The quotation is cited in an earlier draft of the paper by López Córdova and Meissner.

We can look at some evidence from a recent study in which country pairs A–B were classified in four different ways:

a. The two countries are using a *common currency* (i.e., A and B are in a currency union or A has unilaterally adopted B's currency).

b. The two countries are linked by a *direct* exchange rate peg (i.e., A's currency is pegged to B's).

c. The two countries are linked by an *indirect* exchange rate peg, via a third currency (i.e., A and B have currencies pegged to C but not directly to each other).

d. The two countries are not linked by any type of peg (i.e., their currencies *float* against one another, even if one or both might be pegged to some other third currency).

Using this classification and trade data from 1973 to 1999, economists Jay Shambaugh and Michael Klein compared bilateral trade volumes for all pairs under the three pegged regimes (a) through (c) with the benchmark level of trade under a floating regime (d) to see if there were any systematic differences. They also used careful statistical techniques to control for other factors and to address possible reverse causality (i.e., to eliminate the possibility that higher trade might have caused countries to fix their exchange rates). Figure 15-5 shows their key estimates, according to which currency unions increased bilateral trade by 38% relative to floating regimes. They also found that the adoption of a fixed exchange rate would promote trade, but only for the case of *direct* pegs. Adopting a direct peg increased bilateral trade by 21% compared with a floating exchange rate. Indirect pegs had a negligible and statistically insignificant effect.[7]

FIGURE 15-5

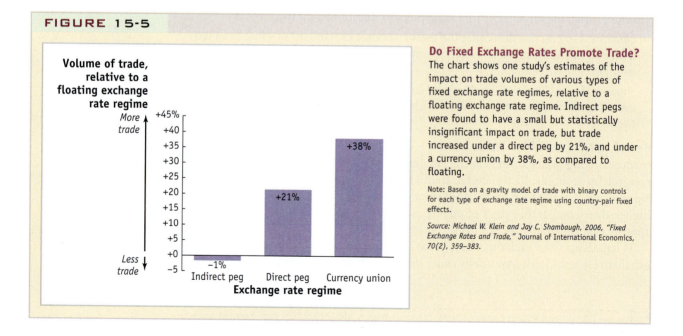

Do Fixed Exchange Rates Promote Trade? The chart shows one study's estimates of the impact on trade volumes of various types of fixed exchange rate regimes, relative to a floating exchange rate regime. Indirect pegs were found to have a small but statistically insignificant impact on trade, but trade increased under a direct peg by 21%, and under a currency union by 38%, as compared to floating.

Note: Based on a gravity model of trade with binary controls for each type of exchange rate regime using country-pair fixed effects.

Source: Michael W. Klein and Jay C. Shambaugh, 2006, "Fixed Exchange Rates and Trade," Journal of International Economics, 70(2), 359–383.

[7]Michael W. Klein and Jay C. Shambaugh, 2006, "Fixed Exchange Rates and Trade," *Journal of International Economics*, 70(2), 359–383.

Benefits Measured by Price Convergence Examining the effect of exchange rate regimes on trade levels is just one way to evaluate the impact of currency arrangements on international market integration, and it has been extensively researched. An alternative and growing empirical literature examines the relationship between exchange rate regimes and price convergence. These studies use the law of one price (LOOP) and purchasing power parity (PPP), which we saw first in our exchange rate chapters, as their benchmark criteria for an integrated market. If fixed exchange rates promote trade by lowering transaction costs, then we would expect to find that differences between prices (measured in a common currency) ought to be smaller among countries with pegged rates than among countries with floating rates. In other words, under a fixed exchange rate, we should find that LOOP and PPP are more likely to hold than under a floating regime. (Recall that it is convergence in prices that underlies the gains-from-trade argument.)

Statistical methods can be used to detect how large price differences have to be between two locations before arbitrage begins. Research on prices of baskets of goods shows that as exchange rate volatility increases, the price differences widen and the speed at which prices in the two markets converge decreases. These findings offer support for the hypothesis that fixed exchange rates promote arbitrage and price convergence.[8]

At a more microeconomic level, economists have also studied convergence in the prices of individual goods. For example, several studies focused on Europe have looked at the prices of various goods in different countries (e.g., retail prices of cars and TV sets, and the prices of Marlboro cigarettes in duty-free shops) and have concluded that higher exchange rate volatility is associated with larger price differentials between locations. In particular, while price gaps still remain for many goods, the "in" countries that maintained membership in the ERM (and now the Eurozone) saw prices converge much more than the "out" countries.[9] ■

Do Fixed Exchange Rates Diminish Monetary Autonomy and Stability?

Probably the single most powerful argument *against* a fixed exchange rate is provided by the trilemma. An economy that unilaterally pegs to a foreign currency sacrifices its monetary policy autonomy.

We have seen the result many times now. If capital markets are open, arbitrage in the forex market implies uncovered interest parity. If the exchange rate is fixed, expected depreciation is zero, and the home interest rate must equal the foreign interest rate. The stark implication is that when a country pegs, it relinquishes its independent monetary policy: it has to adjust the money supply M at all times to ensure that the home interest rate i equals the foreign interest rate i^* (plus any risk premium).

---

[8] Maurice Obstfeld and Alan M. Taylor, 1997, "Nonlinear Aspects of Goods-Market Arbitrage and Adjustment: Heckscher's Commodity Points Revisited," *Journal of the Japanese and International Economies*, 11(4), 441–479.

[9] Marcus Asplund and Richard Friberg, 2001, "The Law of One Price in Scandinavian Duty-Free Stores," *American Economic Review*, 91(4), 1072–1083; Pinelopi Koujianou Goldberg and Frank Verboven, 2004, "Cross-Country Price Dispersion in the Euro Era: A Case Study of the European Car Market," *Economic Policy*, 19(40), 483–521; Jean Imbs, Haroon Mumtaz, Morten O. Ravn, and Hélène Rey, 2009, "One TV, One Price?" NBER Working Papers 15418.

The preceding case study of Britain and the ERM is one more example: Britain wanted to decouple the British interest rate from the German interest rate. To do so, it had to stop pegging the pound to the deutsche mark. Once it had done that, instead of having to contract the British economy as a result of unrelated events in Germany, it could maintain whatever interest rate it thought was best suited to British economic interests.

The Trilemma, Policy Constraints, and Interest Rate Correlations

Is the trilemma truly a binding constraint? Economist Jay Shambaugh tested this proposition, and Figure 15-6 shows some evidence using his data. As we have seen, there are three main solutions to the trilemma. A country can do the following:

1. Opt for open capital markets, with fixed exchange rates (an "open peg").
2. Opt to open its capital market but allow the currency to float (an "open nonpeg").
3. Opt to close its capital markets ("closed").

In case 1, changes in the country's interest rate should match changes in the interest rate of the base country to which it is pegging. In cases 2 and 3, there is no need for the country's interest rate to move in step with the base.

Figure 15-6 displays evidence for the trilemma. On the vertical axis is the annual change in the domestic interest rate; on the horizontal axis is the annual change in the base country interest rate. The trilemma says that in an open peg the two changes should be same and the points should lie on the 45-degree line. Indeed, for open pegs, shown in panel (a), the correlation of domestic and base interest rates is high and the line of best fit has a slope very close to 1. There are some deviations (possibly due to some pegs being more like bands), but these findings show that open pegs have very little monetary policy autonomy. In contrast, for the open nonpegs, shown in panel (b), and closed economies, shown in panel (c), domestic interest rates do not move as much in line with the base interest rate, the correlation is weak, and the slopes are much smaller than 1. These two regimes allow for some monetary policy autonomy.[10]

Costs of Fixing Measured by Output Volatility

The preceding evidence suggests that nations with open pegs have less monetary independence. But it does not tell us directly whether they suffer from greater output instability because their monetary authorities cannot use monetary policy to stabilize output when shocks hit. Some studies have found that, on average, the volatility of output growth *is* much higher under fixed regimes.[11] However, a problem in such studies is that countries

---

[10] The correlation isn't perfect for open pegs, nor is it zero for the other cases. This may not be surprising. Pegs are defined as de facto fixed within a ±2% band. The band allows central banks a little bit of flexibility with their exchange rates and interest rates that would be lacking in a strict peg (a band of zero width). As for nonpegs and closed countries, there may be reasons why their correlation with the base isn't zero. For example, they may have inflation targets or other guides to monetary policy that cause their interest rates to follow paths similar to those of the base country. In other words, these countries have some room for maneuver that open pegs don't have, but how much they choose to use it is another matter.

[11] Atish R. Ghosh, Anne-Marie Gulde, Jonathan D. Ostry, and Holger C. Wolf, 1997, "Does the Nominal Exchange Rate Regime Matter?" NBER Working Paper No. 5874.

FIGURE 15-6

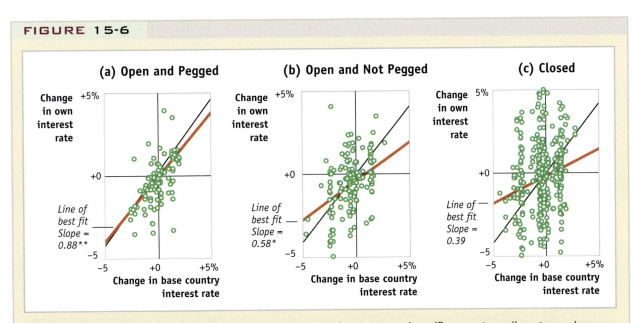

(a) Open and Pegged

(b) Open and Not Pegged

(c) Closed

The Trilemma in Action The trilemma says that if the home country is an open peg, it sacrifices monetary policy autonomy because changes in its own interest rate must match changes in the interest rate of the base country. Panel (a) shows that this is the case. The trilemma also says that there are two ways to get that autonomy back: switch to a floating exchange rate or impose capital controls. Panels (b) and (c) show that either of these two policies permits home interest rates to move more independently of the base country.

Notes: ** Statistically significant at 1% level. * Statistically significant at 5% level. Hyperinflations excluded.

Source: Data from Jay C. Shambaugh, 2004, "The Effect of Fixed Exchange Rates on Monetary Policy," Quarterly Journal of Economics, *119(1), 300–351.*

often differ in all kinds of characteristics that may affect output volatility, not just the exchange rate regime—and the results can be sensitive to how one controls for all these other factors.[12]

In the search for cleaner evidence, some recent research has focused on a key prediction of the IS-LM-FX model: all else equal, an increase in the base-country interest rate should lead output to fall in a country that fixes its exchange rate to the base country. This decline in output occurs because countries that fix have to tighten their monetary policy and raise their interest rates to match that of the base country. In contrast, countries that float do not have to follow the base country's rate increase and can use their monetary policy autonomy to stabilize, by lowering their interest rate and/or allowing their currency to depreciate. Economists Julian di Giovanni and Jay Shambaugh looked at changes in base-country interest rates (say, the U.S. dollar or euro rates) and examined the correlation of these base interest rate changes with changes in GDP in a large sample of fixed and floating nonbase countries. The results, shown in Figure 15-7,

---

[12] See, for example, Eduardo Levy-Yeyati and Federico Sturzenegger, September 2003, "To Float or to Fix: Evidence on the Impact of Exchange Rate Regimes on Growth," *American Economic Review*, 93(4), 1173–1193; Kenneth Rogoff, Ashoka Mody, Nienke Oomes, Robin Brooks, and Aasim M. Husain, 2004, "Evolution and Performance of Exchange Rate Regimes," IMF Occasional Paper No. 229, International Monetary Fund.

FIGURE 15-7

Output Costs of Fixed Exchange Rates Recent empirical work finds that shocks which raise base country interest rates are associated with large output losses in countries that fix their currencies to the base, but not in countries that float. For example, as seen here, when a base country raises its interest rate by one percentage point, a country that floats experiences an average increase in its real GDP growth rate of 0.05% (not statistically significantly different from zero), whereas a country that fixes sees its real GDP growth rate slow on average by a significant 0.12%.

Source: Julian di Giovanni and Jay C. Shambaugh, 2008, "The Impact of Foreign Interest Rates on the Economy: The Role of the Exchange Rate Regime," Journal of International Economics, *74(2), 341–361. See Table 3.*

clearly confirm the theory's predictions: when a base country hikes its interest rate, it spreads economic pain to those countries pegging to it, but not to the countries that are floating. These findings confirm that one cost of a fixed exchange rate regime is a more volatile level of output, a cost that is consistent with the theory we have developed. ■

2 Other Benefits of Fixing

We began the chapter by emphasizing two key factors that influence the choice of fixed versus floating rate regimes: economic integration (market linkages) and economic similarity (symmetry of shocks). But other factors can play a role and in this section, we explore some other benefits of a fixed exchange rate regime, benefits that can be particularly important in emerging markets and developing countries.

Fiscal Discipline, Seigniorage, and Inflation

One common argument in favor of fixed exchange rate regimes in developing countries is that an exchange rate peg prevents the government from printing money to finance government expenditure. Under such a financing scheme, the central bank is called upon to *monetize* the government's deficit (i.e., give money to the government in exchange for debt). This process increases the money supply and leads to high inflation. The source of the government's revenue is, in effect, an inflation tax (called *seigniorage*) levied on the members of the public who hold money (see **Side Bar: The Inflation Tax**).

SIDE BAR

The Inflation Tax

How does the inflation tax work? Consider a situation in which a country with a floating exchange rate faces a constant budget deficit and is unable to finance this deficit through domestic or foreign borrowing. To cover the deficit, the treasury department calls on the central bank to "monetize" the deficit by purchasing an amount of government bonds equal to the deficit.

For simplicity, suppose output is fixed at Y, prices are completely flexible, and inflation and the nominal interest rate are constant. At any instant, money grows at a rate $\Delta M/M = \Delta P/P = \pi$, so the price level rises at a rate of inflation π equal to the rate of money growth. The Fisher effect tells us that the nominal interest rate is $i = r^* + \pi$, where r^* is the real world interest rate.

This ongoing inflation erodes the real value of money held by households. If a household holds M/P in real money balances, then a moment later when prices have increased by an amount $\Delta M/M = \Delta P/P = \pi$, a fraction π of the real value of the original M/P is lost to inflation. The cost of the inflation tax to the household is $\pi \times M/P$. For example, if I hold \$100, the price level is currently 1, and inflation is 1%, then after one period the initial \$100 is worth only \$99 in real (inflation-adjusted) terms, and prices are 1.01.

What is the inflation tax worth to the government? It can spend the extra money printed ΔM to buy real goods and services worth $\Delta M/P = (\Delta M/M) \times (M/P) = \pi \times (M/P)$. For the preceding example, the money supply expands from \$100 to \$101, and this would provide financing worth \$1 to the government. The real gain for the government equals the real loss to the households.

The amount that the inflation tax transfers from household to the government is called seigniorage, which can be written as

$$\underbrace{\text{Seigniorage}}_{\text{Inflation tax}} = \underbrace{\pi}_{\text{Tax rate}} \times \underbrace{\frac{M}{P}}_{\text{Tax base}} = \pi \times L(r^* + \pi)Y$$

The two terms are often viewed as the tax rate (here, inflation) and the tax base (the thing being taxed; here, money). The first term rises as inflation π rises, but the second term goes to zero as π gets large because if inflation becomes very high, people try to hold almost no money, and real money demand $L(r^* + \pi)Y$ falls to zero.

Because of these two offsetting effects, the inflation tax tends to hit diminishing returns as a source of real revenue: as inflation increases, the tax generates increasing real revenues at first, but eventually the rise in the first term is overwhelmed by the fall in the second term. Once a country is in a hyperinflation, the economy is usually well beyond the point at which real inflation tax revenues are maximized.

High inflation and hyperinflation (inflation in excess of 50% *per month*) are undesirable. If nothing else (such as fiscal discipline) can prevent them, a fixed exchange rate may start to look more attractive. Does a fixed exchange rate rule out inflationary finance and the abuse of seigniorage by the government? In principle, yes, but this anti-inflationary effect is not unique to a fixed exchange rate. As we saw in an earlier chapter on the monetary approach to exchange rates, any nominal anchor will have the same effect.

If a country's currency floats, its central bank can print a lot or a little money, with very different inflation outcomes. If a country's currency is pegged, the central bank might run the peg well, with fairly stable prices, or run the peg so badly that a crisis occurs, the exchange rate ends up in free fall, and inflation erupts.

Nominal anchors—whether money targets, exchange rate targets, or inflation targets—imply a "promise" by the government to ensure certain monetary policy outcomes in the long run. However, these promises do not guarantee that the country will achieve these outcomes. All policy announcements including a fixed exchange rate are to some extent "cheap talk." If pressure from the treasury to monetize deficits gets too strong, the commitment to any kind of anchor could fail.

The debate over whether fixed exchange rates improve inflation performance cannot be settled by theory alone—it is an empirical question. What has happened in reality? Table 15-1 lays out the evidence on the world inflation performance from 1970 to 1999. Average inflation rates are computed for all countries and for subgroups of countries:

TABLE 15-1

Inflation Performance and the Exchange Rate Regime Cross-country annual data from the period 1970 to 1999 can be used to explore the relationship, if any, between the exchange rate regime and the inflation performance of an economy. Floating is associated with slightly lower inflation in the world as a whole (9.9%) and in the advanced countries (3.5%) (columns 1 and 2). In emerging markets and developing countries, a fixed regime eventually delivers lower inflation outcomes, but not right away (columns 3 and 4).

Regime Type	Annual Inflation Rate (%)			
	World	Advanced Countries	Emerging Markets and Developing Countries	Emerging Markets and Developing Countries (Excluding the Year after a Regime Change)
Fixed	17.4%	4.8%	19.6%	8.8%
Limited flexibility	11.1	8.3	12.4	10.8
Managed floating	14.0	7.8	15.1	14.7
Freely floating	9.9	3.5	21.2	15.8
Freely falling	387.8	47.9	396.1	482.9

Source: Author's calculations based on the dataset from Kenneth Rogoff, Ashoka Mody, Nienke Oomes, Robin Brooks, and Aasim M. Husain, 2004, "Evolution and Performance of Exchange Rate Regimes," IMF Occasional Paper No. 229, International Monetary Fund.

advanced economies (rich countries), emerging markets (middle-income countries integrated in world capital markets), and developing countries (other countries).

For all countries (column 1), we can see that average inflation performance appears largely unrelated to the exchange rate regime, whether the choice is a peg (17.4%), limited flexibility (11.1%), managed floating (14.0%), or freely floating (9.9%). Only the "freely falling" has astronomical rates of inflation (387.8%). Similar results hold for the advanced countries (column 2) and for the emerging markets and developing countries (column 3). Although average inflation rates are higher in the latter sample, the first four regimes have fairly similar inflation rates, with fixed and freely floating almost indistinguishable.

We may conclude that as long as monetary policy is guided by *some* kind of nominal anchor, the particular choice of fixed and floating may not matter that much.[13] Possibly the only place where the old conventional wisdom remains intact is in the developing countries, where fixed exchange rates can help to deliver lower inflation rates after high inflations or hyperinflations. Why? In those situations, people may need to see the government tie its own hands in a very open and verifiable way for expectations of perpetually high inflation to be lowered, and a peg is one way to do that. This can be seen in Table 15-1, column 4. If we exclude the first year after a change in the exchange rate regime, we exclude chaotic periods after high inflations and hyperinflations when inflation (and inflationary expectations) may still persist even after the monetary and exchange rate policies have changed. We can then see that once things settle down in

---

[13] Kenneth Rogoff, Ashoka Mody, Nienke Oomes, Robin Brooks, and Aasim M. Husain, 2004, "Evolution and Performance of Exchange Rate Regimes," IMF Occasional Paper No. 229, International Monetary Fund.

years two and later, fixed exchange rates generally do deliver lower (single-digit) inflation rates than other regimes.

■ The lesson: *it appears that fixed exchange rates are neither necessary nor sufficient to ensure good inflation performance in many countries. The main exception appears to be in developing countries beset by high inflation, where an exchange rate peg may be the only credible anchor.*

Liability Dollarization, National Wealth, and Contractionary Depreciations

As we learned in the balance of payments chapter, exchange rate changes can have a big effect on a nation's wealth. External assets and liabilities are never entirely denominated in local currency, so movements in the exchange rate can affect their value. For developing countries and emerging markets afflicted by the problem of *liability dollarization*, the wealth effects can be large and destabilizing, providing another argument for fixing the exchange rate, as we now show.

Suppose there are just two countries and two currencies, Home and Foreign. Home has external assets A_H denominated in Home currency (say, pesos) and A_F denominated in Foreign currency (say, U.S. dollars). Similarly, it has external liabilities L_H denominated in Home currency and L_F denominated in Foreign currency. The nominal exchange rate is E (with the units being Home currency per unit of Foreign currency—here, pesos per dollar).

The value of Home's dollar external assets and liabilities can be expressed in pesos as EA_F and EL_F, respectively, using an exchange rate conversion. Hence, the Home country's total external wealth is the sum total of assets minus liabilities expressed in local currency:

$$W = \underbrace{(A_H + EA_F)}_{\text{Assets}} - \underbrace{(L_H + EL_F)}_{\text{Liabilities}}$$

Now suppose there is a small change ΔE in the exchange rate, all else equal. This does not affect the values of A_H and L_H, but it *does* change the values of EA_F and EL_F expressed in pesos. We can express the resulting change in national wealth as

$$\Delta W \quad = \quad \underbrace{\Delta E}_{\substack{\text{Change in} \\ \text{exchange rate}}} \quad \times \quad \underbrace{[A_F - L_F]}_{\substack{\text{Net international} \\ \text{credit(+) or debit(−)} \\ \text{position in dollar assets}}} \qquad (15\text{-}1)$$

The expression is intuitive and revealing. After a depreciation ($\Delta E > 0$), the wealth effect is positive if Foreign currency assets exceed Foreign currency liabilities (the net dollar position in brackets is positive) and negative if Foreign currency liabilities exceed Foreign currency assets (the net dollar position in brackets is negative).

For example, consider first the case in which Home experiences a 10% depreciation, with assets of $100 billion and liabilities of $100 billion. What happens to Home wealth if it has half or $50 billion of assets in dollars and no liabilities in dollars? It has a net credit position in dollars, so it ought to gain. Half of assets and all liabilities are expressed in pesos, so their value does not change. But the value of the half of assets denominated in dollars will rise in peso terms by 10% times $50 billion. In this case, a 10% depreciation increases national wealth by 5% or $5 billion because it increases the value of a net foreign currency credit position.

Now look at the case in which Home experiences a 10% depreciation, as in the preceding example, but now Home has zero assets in dollars and half or $50 billion of liabilities in dollars. All assets and half of liabilities are expressed in pesos, so their value does not change. But the value of the half of liabilities denominated in dollars will rise in peso terms by 10% times $50 billion. In this case, a depreciation decreases national wealth by 5% or $5 billion because it increases the value of a net foreign currency debit position.

Destabilizing Wealth Shocks Why do these wealth effects have implications for stabilization policy? In the previous chapter, we saw that nominal exchange rate depreciation can be used as a short-run stabilization tool in the IS-LM-FX model. In the face of an adverse demand shock in the Home country, for example, a depreciation will boost Home aggregate demand by switching expenditure toward Home goods. Now we can see that exchange rate movements might also affect aggregate demand by affecting wealth.

These impacts matter because it is easy to imagine more complex short-run models of the economy in which wealth affects the demand for goods. For example,

- Consumers might spend more when they have more wealth. In this case, the consumption function would become $C(Y - T,$ Total wealth), and consumption would depend not just on after-tax income but also on wealth.

- Firms might find it easier to borrow if their wealth increases (e.g., wealth increases the net worth of firms, increasing the collateral available for loans). The investment function would then become $I(i,$ Total wealth), and investment would depend on both the interest rate and wealth.

We can now begin to understand the importance of the exchange rate valuation effects summarized in Equation (15-1). This equation says that countries have to satisfy a very special condition to avoid changes in external wealth whenever the exchange rate moves: the value of their foreign currency external assets must exactly equal foreign currency liabilities. If foreign currency external assets do not equal foreign currency external liabilities, the country is said to have a *currency mismatch* on its external balance sheet, and exchange rate changes will affect national wealth.

If foreign currency assets exceed foreign currency liabilities, then the country experiences an increase in wealth when the exchange rate depreciates. From the point of view of stabilization, this is likely to be beneficial: additional wealth will complement the direct stimulus to aggregate demand caused by a depreciation, making the effect of the depreciation *even more* expansionary. This benign scenario applies to only a few countries, most notably the United States.

However, if foreign currency liabilities exceed foreign currency assets, then the country experiences a *decrease* in wealth when the exchange rate depreciates. From the point of view of stabilization policy, this wealth effect is unhelpful because the fall in wealth will tend to offset the conventional stimulus to aggregate demand caused by a depreciation. In principle, if the valuation effects are large enough, the overall effect of a depreciation can be contractionary! For example, while an interest rate cut might boost investment, and the ensuing depreciation might also boost the trade balance, such upward pressure on aggregate demand may well be offset partially or fully (or even outweighed) by adverse wealth changes that put downward pressure on demand.

We now see that if a country has an adverse (i.e., negative) net position in foreign currency assets, then the conventional arguments for stabilization policy (and the need for floating) are at best weak and at worst invalid. For many emerging market and developing economies, this is a serious problem. Most of these poorer countries are net debtors, so their external wealth shows a net debit position overall. But their net position in foreign currency is often just as much in debit, or even more so, because their liabilities are often close to 100% dollarized.

Evidence Based on Changes in Wealth When emerging markets experience large depreciations, they often suffer serious collapses in external wealth. To illustrate the severity of this problem, Figure 15-8 shows the impact of exchange rate valuation effects on wealth in eight countries. All the countries witnessed exchange rate crises during the period in which the domestic currency lost much of its value relative to the U.S. dollar. Following the 1997 Asian crisis, Korea, the Philippines, and Thailand saw their currencies depreciate by about 50%; Indonesia's currency depreciated by 75%. In 1999 the Brazilian real depreciated by almost 50%. In 2001 Turkey's lira depreciated suddenly by about 50%, after a long slide. And in Argentina, the peso depreciated by about 75% in 2002.

All of these countries also had a problem of liability dollarization, with large levels of currency mismatch. In the case of the Asian countries, they had borrowed a great deal in yen and U.S. dollars. In the cases of Turkey, Brazil, and Argentina, they had borrowed extensively in U.S. dollars. We would predict, therefore, that all the countries ought to have seen large declines in external wealth as a result of the valuation effects, and indeed this was the case. Countries such as Brazil and Korea escaped lightly, with wealth falling cumulatively by only 5% to 10% of GDP. Countries with larger exposure to foreign currency debt, or with larger depreciations, suffered much more: in Argentina, the Philippines, and Thailand, the losses were 20% to 30% of one year's GDP and in Indonesia almost 40% of one year's GDP.

Evidence Based on Output Contractions Figure 15-8 tells us that countries with large liability dollarization suffered large wealth effects. But do these wealth effects cause serious economic damage—serious enough to warrant consideration as a factor in exchange rate regime choice?

FIGURE 15-8

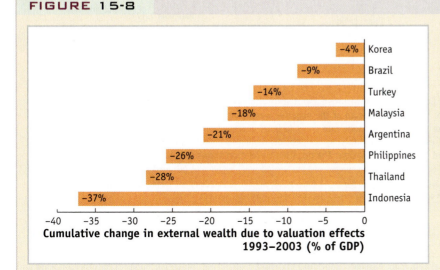

Cumulative change in external wealth due to valuation effects 1993–2003 (% of GDP)

Korea −4%
Brazil −9%
Turkey −14%
Malaysia −18%
Argentina −21%
Philippines −26%
Thailand −28%
Indonesia −37%

Exchange Rate Depreciations and Changes in Wealth These countries experienced crises and large depreciations of between 50% and 75% against the U.S. dollar and other major currencies from 1993 to 2003. Because large fractions of their external debt were denominated in foreign currencies, all suffered negative valuation effects causing their external wealth to fall, in some cases (such as Indonesia) quite dramatically.

Source: IMF, World Economic Outlook, April 2005, Figure 3.6.

Figure 15-9 suggests that wealth effects are associated with contractions and that the damage is fairly serious. Economists Michele Cavallo, Kate Kisselev, Fabrizio Perri, and Nouriel Roubini looked at the correlation between wealth losses on net foreign currency liabilities suffered during the large depreciations seen after an exchange rate crisis, and a measure of the subsequent fall in real output.[14] There is clearly a strong correlation. For example, after 1992 Britain barely suffered any negative wealth effect and, as we noted earlier, did rather well in its subsequent economic performance: Britain in 1992 sits in the upper left part of this scatterplot (very small wealth loss, no negative impact on GDP). At the other extreme sit cases like Indonesia, where liability dollarization led to massive wealth losses after the 1997 crisis: Indonesia in 1997 sits in the lower right part of this scatterplot (large wealth loss, large negative impact on GDP).

Original Sin Such findings have had a profound influence among professional international macroeconomists in recent years. Previously, external wealth effects were largely ignored and poorly understood. But now, especially after the adverse consequences of recent large depreciations, it is universally recognized that the problem of

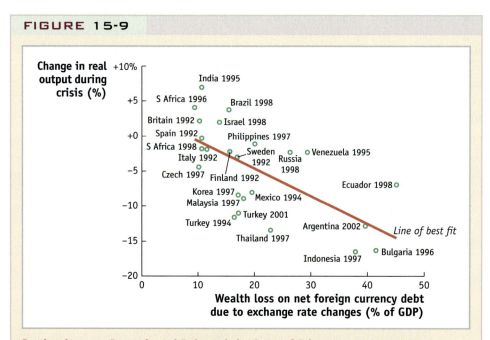

FIGURE 15-9

Foreign Currency Denominated Debt and the Costs of Crises This chart shows the correlation between a measure of the negative wealth impact of a real depreciation and the real output costs after an exchange rate crisis (a large depreciation). On the horizontal axis, the wealth impact is estimated by multiplying net debt denominated in foreign currency (as a fraction of GDP) by the size of the real depreciation. The negative correlation shows that larger losses on foreign currency debt due to exchange rate changes are associated with larger real output losses.

Source: Michele Cavallo, Kate Kisselev, Fabrizio Perri, and Nouriel Roubini, "Exchange Rate Overshooting and the Costs of Floating," Federal Reserve Bank of San Francisco Working Paper Series, Working Paper 2005-07, May 2005.

---

[14] Michele Cavallo, Kate Kisselev, Fabrizio Perri, and Nouriel Roubini, "Exchange Rate Overshooting and the Costs of Floating," Federal Reserve Bank of San Francisco Working Paper Series, Working Paper 2005-07, May 2005.

currency mismatch, driven by liability dollarization, plays a profound role in many developing countries and is a legitimate factor to be considered during any debate over the choice of exchange rate regime.

It is an old problem. In the long history of international investment, one remarkably constant feature has been the inability of most countries—especially poor countries on the periphery of global capital markets—to borrow from abroad in their own currencies. In the late nineteenth century, such countries had to borrow in gold, or in a "hard currency" such as British pounds or U.S. dollars. The same is true today, as is apparent from Table 15-2. In the world's financial centers and the Eurozone, only a small fraction of external liabilities are denominated in foreign currency. In other countries, the fraction is much higher; in developing countries, it is close to 100% on average.

Economists Barry Eichengreen, Ricardo Hausmann, and Ugo Panizza used the term "original sin" to refer to a country's inability to borrow in its own currency.[15] As the provocative name suggests, an historical perspective reveals that the "sin" is highly persistent and originates deep in a country's historical past. Countries that have a weak record of macroeconomic management—often due to institutional or political weakness—have in the past been unable to follow prudent monetary and fiscal policies. Domestic currency debts were frequently diluted in real value by periods of high inflation. Creditors were then unwilling to hold such debt, obstructing the development of a domestic currency bond market. Creditors were then willing to lend only in foreign currency, that is, to hold debt that promised a more stable long-term value.

Still, sinners can find redemption. Another view argues that the problem is one of global capital market failure: for many small countries, the pool of their domestic

TABLE 15-2

Measures of "Original Sin" Only a few developed countries can issue external liabilities denominated in their own currency. In the financial centers and the Eurozone, the fraction of external liabilities denominated in foreign currency is less than 10%. In the remaining developed countries, it averages about 70%. In developing countries, external liabilities denominated in foreign currency are close to 100% on average.

	External Liabilities Denominated in Foreign Currency (average, %)
Financial centers (United States, United Kingdom, Switzerland, Japan)	8%
Eurozone countries	9
Other developed countries	72
Eastern European countries	84
Middle East and African countries	90
Developing countries	93
Asia/Pacific countries	94
Latin American and Caribbean countries	100

Source: Barry Eichengreen, Ricardo Hausmann, and Ugo Panizza, "The Pain of Original Sin." In Barry Eichengreen and Ricardo Hausmann, eds., 2005, Other People's Money: Debt Denomination and Financial Instability in Emerging-Market Economies (Chicago: University of Chicago Press).

---

[15] Barry Eichengreen, Ricardo Hausmann, and Ugo Panizza, 2005, "The Pain of Original Sin." In Barry Eichengreen and Ricardo Hausmann, eds., *Other People's Money: Debt Denomination and Financial Instability in Emerging-Market Economies* (Chicago: University of Chicago Press).

Two Russian bonds: a 100 ruble bond of 1915 and a 1,000 U.S. dollar bond of 1916. Creditors knew the dollar value of the ruble bond could be eroded by ruble depreciation. Only default could erode the value of the dollar bond.

currency liabilities may be too small to offer any significant risk diversification benefits to foreign investors. In this case, multinational institutions might step in to create markets for securities in the currencies of small countries, or in baskets of such currencies. An alternative view argues that as such countries reform—improve their institutional quality, design better policies, secure a low-inflation environment, and develop a better reputation—they will eventually free themselves from original sin and be able to issue external debt in their own currency. Many observers think this is already happening. Habitual "sinners" such as Mexico, Brazil, Colombia, and Uruguay have recently been able to issue some debt in their own currency. In addition, many countries are also reducing currency mismatch by piling up large stocks of foreign currency assets in central bank reserves and sovereign wealth funds. The recent trends indicate substantial progress in reducing this problem as compared with the 1990s.[16]

Yet any optimism must be tempered with caution. Only time will tell whether countries have really turned the corner and put their "sinful" ways behind them. Progress on domestic-currency borrowing is still very slow in many countries, and this still leaves the problem of mismatches in the private sector. While private sector exposure could be insured by the government, that insurance could, in turn, introduce the risk of abuse in the form of *moral hazard*, the risk that an insured entity (here, private borrowers) will engage in excessive risk taking, knowing that it will be bailed out if they incur losses. This could then create massive political problems, because it may not be clear who, in a crisis, would receive a public-sector rescue, and who would not. Why can't the private sector simply hedge all its exchange rate risk? This solution would be ideal, but in many emerging markets and developing countries, currency derivative markets are underdeveloped because many currencies cannot be hedged at all, and for others the markets are poorly developed, and the costs high.

If developing countries are unable to avoid currency mismatches, they must try to cope with them. One option is to reduce or stop external borrowing, but countries are not eager to forsake all borrowing in world capital markets. A more feasible—and perhaps only—alternative is for developing countries to minimize or eliminate valuation effects by limiting the movement of the exchange rate. This is indeed what we observe, and evidence shows that the larger a country's stock of foreign currency liabilities relative to GDP, the more likely that country is to peg its currency to the currency in which the external debt is issued.[17]

■ The lesson: *in countries that cannot borrow in their own currency, floating exchange rates are less useful as a stabilization tool and may be destabilizing. This outcome applies particularly to developing countries, and these countries will prefer fixed exchange rates to floating exchange rates, all else equal.*

[16] Barry Eichengreen and Ricardo Hausmann, 2005, "Original Sin: The Road to Redemption." In Barry Eichengreen and Ricardo Hausmann, eds., *Other People's Money: Debt Denomination and Financial Instability in Emerging-Market Economies* (Chicago: University of Chicago Press); John D. Burger and Francis E. Warnock, 2003, "Diversification, Original Sin, and International Bond Portfolios," International Finance Discussion Papers 755, Board of Governors of the Federal Reserve System (U.S.); Camilo E. Tovar, 2005, "International Government Debt Denominated in Local Currency: Recent Developments in Latin America," *BIS Quarterly Review*, 109–118; Philip E. Lane and Jay C. Shambaugh, 2007, "Financial Exchange Rates and International Currency Exposures," NBER Working Paper No. 13433.
[17] Ricardo Hausmann, Ugo Panizza, and Ernesto Stein, 2001, "Why Do Countries Float the Way They Float?" *Journal of Development Economics*, 66(2), 387–414; Christopher M. Meissner and Nienke Oomes, 2006, "Why Do Countries Peg the Way They Peg? The Determinants of Anchor Currency Choice," Cambridge Working Papers in Economics 0643, Faculty of Economics, University of Cambridge.

Summary

We began the chapter by emphasizing the two key factors that influence the choice of fixed versus floating rate regimes: economic integration (market linkages) and economic similarity (symmetry of shocks). But we now see that many other factors can affect the benefits of fixing relative to floating.

A fixed exchange rate may have some additional benefits in some situations. It may be the only transparent and credible way to attain and maintain a nominal anchor—which may be particularly important in emerging markets and developing countries with weak institutions, a lack of central bank independence, strong temptations to use the inflation tax, and poor reputations for monetary stability. A fixed exchange rate may also be the only way to avoid large fluctuations in external wealth, which can be a problem in emerging markets and developing countries with high levels of liability dollarization. These may be powerful additional reasons to fix, and they seem to apply with extra force in developing countries. Therefore, such countries may be less willing to allow their exchange rates to float—a situation that some economists describe as a **fear of floating.**

To illustrate the influence of additional costs and benefits in our graphical representation, consider a Home country thinking of pegging to the U.S. dollar as a base currency. Such a Home country with a fear of floating would perceive additional benefits to a fixed exchange rate. So it would be willing to peg its exchange at lower levels of integration and similarity. We would represent this as in Figure 15-10 by an inward shift of the FIX line from FIX_1 to FIX_2. Without fear of floating, based on FIX_1, the Home country would float with symmetry-integration measures given by points 1 and 2, and fix at point 3. But if it had fear of floating, based on FIX_2, it would elect to fix at point 2 because the extra benefits of a fixed rate lower the threshold.

FIGURE 15-10

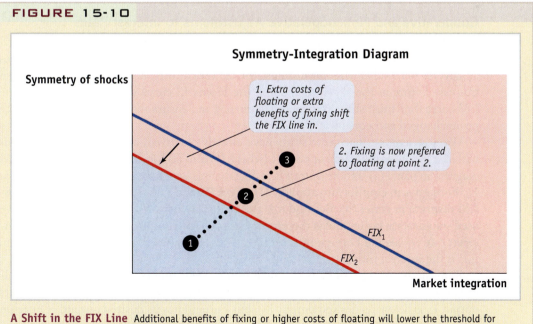

Symmetry-Integration Diagram

Symmetry of shocks

1. Extra costs of floating or extra benefits of fixing shift the FIX line in.

2. Fixing is now preferred to floating at point 2.

FIX_1

FIX_2

Market integration

A Shift in the FIX Line Additional benefits of fixing or higher costs of floating will lower the threshold for choosing a fixed exchange rate. The FIX line moves down. Choosing a fixed rate now makes sense, even at lower levels of symmetry or integration (e.g., at point 2).

3 Fixed Exchange Rate Systems

To provide a foundation, our discussion so far has considered only the simplest type of fixed exchange rate: a single home country that unilaterally pegs to a foreign base country. In reality there are more complex arrangements, called **fixed exchange rate systems,** which involve multiple countries. Examples include the global *Bretton Woods system* in the 1950s and 1960s and the European *Exchange Rate Mechanism* (ERM) through which all potential euro members must pass.

These systems were based on a **reserve currency system** in which there are N countries $(1, 2, \ldots, N)$ participating. One of the countries, the center country (the Nth country), provides the reserve currency, which is the base or center currency to which all the other countries peg. In the Bretton Woods system, for example, N was the U.S. dollar; in the ERM, N was the German mark until 1999, and is now the euro.

Throughout this chapter, we have assumed that a country pegs unilaterally to a center country, and we know that this leads to a fundamental asymmetry. The center country has monetary policy autonomy and can set its own interest rate i^* as it pleases. The other noncenter country, which is pegging, then has to adjust its own interest rate so that i equals i^* in order to maintain the peg. The noncenter country loses its ability to conduct stabilization policy, but the center country keeps that power. The asymmetry can be a recipe for political conflict and is known as the *Nth currency problem.*

Are these problems serious? And is there a better arrangement that can be devised? In this section, we show that **cooperative arrangements** may be the answer. We study two kinds of cooperation. One form of cooperation is based on mutual agreement and compromise between center and noncenter countries on the setting of interest rates. The other form of cooperation is based on mutual agreements about adjustments to the levels of the fixed exchange rates themselves.

Cooperative and Noncooperative Adjustments to Interest Rates

Figure 15-11, panel (a), illustrates the possibility of policy conflict between center and noncenter countries. Suppose that Home, which is the noncenter country, experiences an adverse demand shock, but Foreign, the center country, does not. We have studied this case before in the previous chapter: the Home IS curve shifts left and the Home LM curve then must shift up to maintain the peg and ensure that the Home interest rate i is unchanged and equal to i^*.

We now assume that these shifts have already occurred, and we start the analysis with the Home equilibrium at point 1 (where IS_1 and LM_1 intersect) in Home's IS-LM diagram in panel (a). Home output is at Y_1, which is lower than Home's desired output Y_0. Foreign is in equilibrium at point 1' (where IS_1^* and LM_1^* intersect) in Foreign's IS-LM diagram in panel (b). Because it is the center country, Foreign is assumed to have used stabilization policy and is therefore at its preferred output level Y_0^*. The Home interest rate equals the Foreign interest rate, $i_1 = i_1^*$, because Home is pegged to Foreign; this is the interest rate shown on both vertical axes.

Because this is a unilateral peg, only Foreign, the center country, has monetary policy autonomy and the freedom to set nominal interest rates. Home is in recession (its output Y_1 is below its desired output Y_0), but Foreign has its desired output. If Foreign makes no policy concession to help Home out of its recession, this would be the noncooperative outcome. There would be no burden sharing between the two countries: Home is the only country to suffer.

FIGURE 15-11

(a) Home IS-LM Diagram (noncenter)

(b) Foreign IS-LM Diagram (center)

Cooperative and Noncooperative Interest Rate Policies by the Center Country In panel (a), the noncenter home country is initially in equilibrium at point 1 with output at Y_1, which is lower than desired output Y_0. In panel (b), the center foreign country is in equilibrium at its desired output level Y_0^* at point 1'. Home and foreign interest rates are equal, $i_1 = i_1^*$, and home is unilaterally pegged to foreign. Foreign has monetary policy autonomy. If the center country makes no policy concession, this is the noncooperative outcome.

With cooperation, the foreign country can make a policy concession and lower its interest rate and home can do the same and maintain the peg. Lower interest rates in the other country shift each country's IS curve in, but the easing of monetary policy in both countries shifts each country's LM curve down. The net effect is to boost output in both countries. The new equilibria at points 2 and 2' lie to the right of points 1 and 1'. Under this cooperative outcome, the foreign center country accepts a rise in output away from its desired level, from Y_0^* to Y_2^*. Meanwhile, home output gets closer to its desired level, rising from Y_1 to Y_2.

Now suppose we shift to a cooperative outcome in which the center country makes a policy concession. How? Suppose Foreign lowers its interest rate from to $i_1^* = i_2^*$. Home can now do the same, and indeed must do so to maintain the peg. How do the IS curves shift? A lower Foreign interest rate implies that, *all else equal*, Home demand is lower, so the Home IS curve shifts in to IS_2; similarly, in panel (b), a lower Home interest rate implies that, *all else equal*, Foreign demand is lower, so the Foreign IS* curve shifts in to IS_2^* in panel (b). However, the easing of monetary policy in both countries means that the LM curves shift down in both countries to LM_2 and LM_2^*.

What is the net result of all these shifts? To figure out the extent of the shift in the IS curve, we can think back to the Keynesian cross and the elements of demand that underlie points on the IS curve. The peg is being maintained. Because the nominal exchange rate is unchanged, the real exchange rate is unchanged, so neither country sees a shift in its Keynesian cross demand curve due to a change in the trade balance. But both countries do see a rise in the Keynesian cross demand curve, as investment demand rises thanks to lower interest rates. The rise in demand tells us that new equilibrium points 2 and 2' lie to the right of points 1 and 1': even though the IS curves have shifted in, the downward shifts in the LM curves dominate, and so output in each country will rise in equilibrium.

Compared with the noncooperative equilibrium outcome at points 1 and 1', Foreign now accepts a rise in output away from its preferred stable level, as output booms from Y_0^* to Y_2^*. Meanwhile, Home is still in recession, but the recession is not as deep, and output is at a level Y_2 that is higher than Y_1. In the noncooperative case, Foreign achieves its ideal output level and Home suffers a deep recession. In the cooperative case, Foreign suffers a slightly higher output level than it would like and Home suffers a slightly lower output level than it would like. The burden of the adverse shock to Home has been shared with Foreign.

Caveats Why would Home and Foreign agree to a cooperative arrangement in the first place? Cooperation might be possible in principle if neither country wants to suffer too much exchange rate volatility against the other—that is, if they are *close* to wanting to be in a fixed arrangement but neither wants to unilaterally peg to the other. A unilateral peg by either country gives all the benefits of fixing to both countries but imposes a stability cost on the noncenter country alone. If neither country is willing to pay that price, there can be no unilateral peg by either country. They could simply float, but they would then lose the efficiency gains from fixing. But if they can somehow set up a peg with a system of policy cooperation, then they could achieve a lower instability burden than under a unilateral peg and this benefit could tip the scales enough to allow the gains from fixing to materialize for both countries.

Cooperation sounds great on paper. But the historical record casts doubt on the ability of countries to even get as far as announcing cooperation on fixed rates, let alone actually backing that up with true cooperative behavior. Indeed, it is rare to see credible cooperative announcements under *floating* rates, where much less is at stake. Why?

A major problem is that, at any given time, the shocks that hit a group of economies are typically asymmetric. A country at its ideal output level not suffering a shock may be unwilling to change its monetary policies just to help out a neighbor suffering a shock and keep a peg going. In theory, cooperation rests on the idea that my shock today could be your shock tomorrow, and we can all do better if we even out the burdens with the understanding that they will "average out" in the long run. But policy makers have to be able to make credible long-run commitments to make this work and suffer short-run pain for long-run gain. History shows that these abilities are often sadly lacking: short-sighted political goals commonly trump longer-term economic considerations.

For example, consider the European Exchange Rate Mechanism (ERM), which was effectively a set of unilateral pegs to the German mark. The ERM was very clearly built around the idea of safeguarding gains from trade in Europe through fixed rates, but the designers knew that it had to incorporate some burden-sharing measures to ensure that the burden of absorbing shocks didn't fall on every country but Germany. The measures proved inadequate, however, and in the crisis of 1992 the German Bundesbank ignored pleas from Italy, Britain, and other countries for an easing of German monetary policy as recessions took hold in the bloc of countries pegging to the German mark. When the test of cooperation came along, Germany wanted to stabilize Germany's output, not anybody else's. Thus, even in a group of countries as geographically and politically united as the European Union, it was tremendously difficult to make this kind of cooperation work. (This problem was alleviated by true monetary union, with the arrival of the euro and the creation of the European Central Bank.)

The main conclusion is that, in practice, the center country in a reserve currency system has tremendous autonomy, which it may be unwilling to give up lightly, thus making cooperative outcomes hard to achieve consistently.

Cooperative and Noncooperative Adjustments to Exchange Rates

We have studied interest rate cooperation. Is there scope for cooperation in other ways? Yes. Countries may decide to adjust the level of the fixed exchange rate. Such an adjustment is (supposedly) a "one-shot" jump or change in the exchange rate at a particular time, which for now we assume to be unanticipated by investors. Apart from that single jump, at all times before and after the change, the exchange rate is left fixed and Home and Foreign interest rates remain equal.

Suppose a country that was previously pegging at a rate $\bar{E}_1$ announces that it will henceforth peg at a different rate, $\bar{E}_2 \neq \bar{E}_1$. By definition, if $\bar{E}_2 > \bar{E}_1$, there is a **devaluation** of the home currency; if $\bar{E}_2 < \bar{E}_1$, there is a **revaluation** of the home currency.

These terms are similar to the terms "depreciation" and "appreciation," which also describe exchange rate changes. Strictly speaking, the terms "devaluation" and "revaluation" should be used only when pegs are being adjusted; "depreciation" and "appreciation" should be used to describe exchange rates that float up or down. Note, however, that these terms are often used loosely and interchangeably.

A framework for understanding peg adjustment is shown in Figure 15-12. We assume now that both Home and Foreign are noncenter countries in a pegged exchange rate system and that each is pegged to a third center currency, say, the U.S. dollar.

(Why this change in the setup compared with the last section? Interest rate adjustment required us to study moves by the center country to help noncenter countries; with exchange rate adjustment, it is only noncenter countries who change their exchange rates vis-à-vis the center, so in this problem our focus shifts mostly away from the center country.)

We assume that the center (the United States) is a large country with monetary policy autonomy that has set its interest rate at $i_\$$. Home is pegged to the U.S. dollar at $\bar{E}_{\text{home}/\$}$ and Foreign is pegged at $\bar{E}^*_{\text{foreign}/\$}$. In Home's IS-LM diagram in panel (a), equilibrium is initially at point 1 (where IS_1 and LM_1 intersect). Again, due to a prior adverse demand shock, Home output is at Y_1 and is lower than Home's desired output Y_0. In Foreign's IS-LM diagram in panel (b), equilibrium is at Foreign's desired output level Y_0^* at point 1' (where IS_1^* and LM_1^* intersect). Because Home and Foreign peg to the center currency (here, the U.S. dollar), Home and Foreign interest rates equal the dollar interest rate, $i_1 = i_1^* = i_\$$.

Now suppose that in a cooperative arrangement, Home devalues against the dollar (and against Foreign) and maintains a peg at a new, higher exchange rate. That is, there is an unanticipated rise $\bar{E}_{\text{home}/\$}$. The Home and Foreign interest rates remain equal to the dollar interest rate, $i_1 = i_1^* = i_\$$, because both countries still peg. We can think back to the IS-LM model, or back to the Keynesian cross that we used to construct the IS curve, if necessary, to figure out the impact of the change. Because the nominal depreciation by Home is also a real depreciation, Home sees demand increase: the Home IS curve shifts out to IS_2. Furthermore, the real depreciation for Home is also a real appreciation for Foreign, so Foreign demand *decreases*: the IS* curve shifts in to IS_2^*. The outcome is cooperative because the burden of the adverse demand shock is being shared: Home output at Y_2 is lower than the ideal Y_0 but not as low as at Y_1; and Foreign has accepted output lower at Y_2^* than its ideal Y_0^*.

Why might this kind of cooperation work? Home and Foreign could agree that Home would devalue a little (but not too much) so that both countries would jointly feel the pain. Some other time, when Foreign has a nasty shock, Home would "repay" by feeling some of Foreign's pain.

FIGURE 15-12

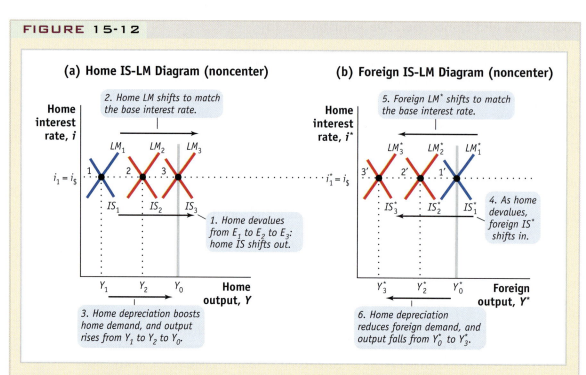

(a) Home IS-LM Diagram (noncenter)

2. Home LM shifts to match the base interest rate.

Home interest rate, i

LM_1 LM_2 LM_3

$i_1 = i_\$$

IS_1 IS_2 IS_3

1. Home devalues from E_1 to E_2 to E_3: home IS shifts out.

Y_1 Y_2 Y_0

Home output, Y

3. Home depreciation boosts home demand, and output rises from Y_1 to Y_2 to Y_0.

(b) Foreign IS-LM Diagram (noncenter)

5. Foreign LM^* shifts to match the base interest rate.

Home interest rate, i^*

LM_3^* LM_2^* LM_1^*

$i_1^* = i_\$$

IS_3^* IS_2^* IS_1^*

4. As home devalues, foreign IS^* shifts in.

Y_3^* Y_2^* Y_0^*

Foreign output, Y^*

6. Home depreciation reduces foreign demand, and output falls from Y_0^* to Y_3^*.

Cooperative and Noncooperative Exchange Rate Adjustments by Noncenter Countries In panel (a), the noncenter home country is initially in equilibrium at point 1 with output at Y_1, which is lower than desired output Y_0. In panel (b), the noncenter foreign country is in equilibrium at its desired output level Y_0^* at point 1'. Home and foreign interest rates are equal to the base (dollar) interest rate and to each other, $i_1 = i_1^* = i_\$$, and home and foreign are unilaterally pegged to the base.

With cooperation, home devalues slightly against the dollar (and against foreign) and maintains a peg at a higher exchange rate. The home interest and foreign interest rates remain the same. But the home real depreciation causes home demand to increase: IS shifts out to IS_2. This is also a foreign real appreciation, so foreign demand decreases: IS^* shifts in to IS_2^*. Under this cooperative outcome at points 2 and 2', foreign accepts a fall in output away from its desired level, from Y_0^* to Y_2^*. Meanwhile, home output gets closer to its desired level, rising from Y_1 to Y_2.

With noncooperation, home devalues more aggressively against the dollar. After a large home real depreciation, IS shifts out to IS_3 and IS^* shifts in to IS_3^*. Under this noncooperative outcome at points 3 and 3', home gets its desired output Y_0 by "exporting" the recession to foreign, where output falls all the way to Y_3^*.

Now suppose we shift to a noncooperative outcome in which Home devalues more aggressively against the dollar. After a large real depreciation by Home, Home demand is greatly boosted, and the Home IS curve shifts out a long way to IS_3. Home's real depreciation is also a large real appreciation for Foreign, where demand is greatly reduced, so the Foreign IS^* curve shifts in a long way to IS_3^*. The outcome is noncooperative: Home now gets its preferred outcome with output at its ideal level Y_0; it achieves this by "exporting" the recession to Foreign, where output falls all the way to Y_3^*.

There are two qualifications to this analysis. First, we have only considered a situation in which Home wishes to devalue to offset a negative demand shock. But the same logic applies when Home's economy is "overheating" and policy makers fear that output is above the ideal level, perhaps creating a risk of inflationary pressures. In that case, Home may wish to revalue its currency and export the overheating to Foreign.

Second, we have not considered the center country, here the United States. In reality, the center country also suffers some decrease in demand if Home devalues because the center will experience a real appreciation against Home. However, there is less to worry about in this instance: because the United States is the center country, it has policy autonomy, and can always use stabilization policy to boost demand. Thus, there may be a monetary easing in the center country, a secondary effect that we do not consider here.

Caveats We can now see that adjusting the peg is a policy that may be cooperative or noncooperative in nature. If noncooperative, it is usually referred to as a **beggar-thy-neighbor policy**: Home can improve its position at the expense of Foreign and without Foreign's agreement. When Home is in recession, and its policy makers choose a devaluation and real depreciation, they are engineering a diversion of some of world demand toward Home goods and away from the rest of the world's goods.

This finding brings us to the main drawback of admitting noncooperative adjustments into a fixed exchange rate system. Two can play this game! If Home engages in such a policy, it is possible for Foreign to respond with a devaluation of its own in a tit-for-tat way. Down that road lies exchange rate mayhem, and the pretense of a fixed exchange rate system is over. The countries will no longer be pegging and will be playing a new noncooperative game against each other with floating exchange rates.

Cooperation may be most needed to sustain a fixed exchange rate system with adjustable pegs, so as to restrain beggar-thy-neighbor devaluations. But can it work? Consider continental Europe since World War II, under both the Bretton Woods system and the later European systems such as ERM (which predated the euro). A persistent concern of European policy makers in this period was the threat of beggar-thy-neighbor devaluations. For example, the British pound and the Italian lira devalued against the dollar and later the German mark on numerous occasions from the 1960s to the 1990s. Although some of these peg adjustments had the veneer of official multilateral decisions, some (like the 1992 ERM crisis) occurred when cooperation broke down.

The Gold Standard

Our analysis in this section has focused on the problems of policy conflict in a reserve currency system in which there is one center country issuing a currency (e.g., the dollar or euro) to which all other noncenter countries peg. As we know from Figure 15-1, this is an apt description of most fixed exchange rate arrangements at the present time and going back as far as World War II. A key issue in such systems is the asymmetry between the center country, which retains monetary autonomy, and the noncenter countries, which forsake it.

Are there symmetric fixed exchange rate systems, in which there is no center country and the asymmetry created by the Nth currency problem can be avoided? In theory the ERM system worked this way before the advent of the euro in 1999, but, as the 1992 crisis showed, there was, in practice, a marked asymmetry between Germany and the other ERM countries. Historically, the only true symmetric systems have been those in which countries fixed the value of their currency relative to some commodity. The most famous and important of these systems was the gold standard, and this system had no center country because countries did not peg the exchange rate at $\overline{E}$, the local currency price of some base currency, but instead they pegged at $\overline{P_g}$, the local currency price of gold.

How did this system work? Under the gold standard, gold and money were seamlessly interchangeable, and the combined value of gold and money in the hands of the public was the relevant measure of money supply (M). For example, consider two countries,

The U.S. gold parity was $20.67 per troy ounce from 1834 to 1933, so a $20 gold coin like this 1907 Saint Gaudens Double Eagle contained 20/20.67 = 0.9675 ounces of gold.

Britain pegging to gold at $\overline{P}_g$ (pounds per ounce of gold) and France pegging to gold at $\overline{P}_g^*$ (francs per ounce of gold). Under this system, one pound cost $1/\overline{P}_g$ ounces of gold, and each ounce of gold cost $\overline{P}_g$ francs, according to the fixed gold prices set by the central banks in each country. Thus, one pound cost $E_{\text{par}} = \overline{P}_g^*/\overline{P}_g$ francs, and this ratio defined the *par* exchange rate implied by the gold prices in each country.

The gold standard rested on the principle of free convertibility. This meant that central banks in both countries stood ready to buy and sell gold in exchange for paper money at these mint prices, and the export and import of gold were unrestricted. This allowed arbitrage forces to stabilize the system. How?

Suppose the market exchange rate in Paris (the price of one pound in francs) was E francs per pound and deviated from the par level, with $E < E_{\text{par}}$ francs per pound. This would create an arbitrage opportunity. The franc has appreciated relative to pounds, and arbitrageurs could change 1 ounce of gold into $\overline{P}_g^*$ francs at the central bank, and then into $\overline{P}_g^*/E$ pounds in the market, which could be shipped to London and converted into $\overline{P}_g^*/(E\overline{P}_g)$ ounces of gold, which could then be brought back to Paris. Because we assumed that $E < E_{\text{par}}$, $\overline{P}_g^*/(E\overline{P}_g) = E_{\text{par}}/E > 1$, and the trader ends up with more than an ounce of gold and makes a profit.

As a result of this trade, gold would leave Britain and the British money supply would fall (pounds would be redeemed at the Bank of England by the French traders, who would export the gold back to France). As gold entered France, the French money supply would expand (because the traders could leave it in gold form, or freely change it into franc notes at the Banque de France).

We can note how the result tends to stabilize the foreign exchange market (just as interest arbitrage did in the chapters on exchange rates). Here, the pound was depreciated relative to par and the arbitrage mechanism caused the British money supply to contract and the French money supply to expand. The arbitrage mechanism depended on French investors buying "cheap" pounds. This would bid up the price of pounds in Paris, so E would rise toward E_{par}, stabilizing the exchange rate at its par level.

Four observations are worth noting. First, the process of arbitrage was not really costless, so if the exchange rate deviated only slightly from parity, the profit from arbitrage might be zero or negative (i.e., a loss). Thus, there was a small band around the par rate in which the exchange rate might fluctuate without any arbitrage occurring. However, this band, delineated by limits known as the upper and lower "gold points," was typically small, permitting perhaps at most ±1% fluctuations in E on either side of E_{par}. The exchange rate was, therefore, very stable. For example, from 1879 to 1914, when Britain and the United States were pegged to gold at a par rate of $4.86 per pound, the daily dollar-pound market exchange rate in New York was within 1% of its par value 99.97% of the time (and within half a percent 77% of the time).[18]

Second, in our example we examined arbitrage in only one direction, but, naturally, there would have been a similar profitable arbitrage opportunity—subject to transaction costs—in the opposite direction if E had been above E_{par} and the franc had been depreciated relative to parity. (Working out how one makes a profit in that case, and what the net effect would be on each country's money supply, is left as an exercise.)

Third, gold arbitrage would enforce a fixed exchange rate at E_{par} (plus or minus small deviations within the gold points), thus setting expected depreciation to zero.

[18] Eugene Canjels, Gauri Prakash-Canjels, and Alan M. Taylor, 2004, "Measuring Market Integration: Foreign Exchange Arbitrage and the Gold Standard, 1879–1913," *Review of Economics and Statistics*, 86(4), 868–882.

Interest arbitrage between the two countries' money markets would equalize the interest rates in each country (subject to risk premiums). So our earlier approach to the study of fixed exchange rates remains valid, including a central principle, the trilemma.

Fourth, and most important, we see the inherent symmetry of the gold standard system when operated according to these principles. Both countries share in the adjustment mechanism, with the money supply contracting in the gold outflow country (here, Britain) and the money supply expanding in the gold inflow country (here, France). In theory, if these principles were adhered to, neither country has the privileged position of being able to not change its monetary policy, in marked contrast to a center country in a reserve currency system. But in reality, the gold standard did not always operate quite so smoothly, as we see in the next section. ■

4 International Monetary Experience

A vast diversity of exchange rate arrangements have been used throughout history. In the chapter that introduced exchange rates, we saw how different countries fix or float at present; at the start of this chapter, we saw how exchange rate arrangements have fluctuated over more than a century. These observations motivated us to study how countries choose to fix or float.

To try to better understand the international monetary experience and how we got to where we are today, we now apply what we have learned in the book so far.[19] In particular, we rely on the trilemma, which tells us that countries cannot simultaneously meet the three policy goals of a fixed exchange rate, capital mobility, and monetary policy autonomy. With the feasible policy choices thus set out, we draw on the ideas of this chapter about the costs and benefits of fixed and floating regimes to try to understand why various countries have made the choices they have at different times.

The Rise and Fall of the Gold Standard

As we saw in Figure 15-1, the history of international monetary arrangements from 1870 to 1939 was dominated by one story: the rise and fall of the gold standard regime. In 1870 about 15% of countries were on gold, rising to about 70% in 1913 and almost 90% during a brief period of resumption in the 1920s. But by 1939, only about 25% of the world was pegged to gold. What happened? The analysis in this chapter provides insights into one of the grand narratives of economic history.[20]

The period from 1870 to 1914 was the first era of globalization, with increasingly large flows of trade, capital, and people between countries. Depending on the countries in question, some of these developments were attributable to technological developments in transport and communications (such as steamships, the telegraph, etc.); some were a result of policy change (such as tariff reductions). Our model suggests that as the volume of trade and other economic transactions between nations increase, there will be more to gain from adopting a fixed exchange rate (as in Figure 15-4).

---

[19] Barry Eichengreen, 1996, *Globalizing Capital: A History of the International Monetary System* (Princeton, NJ: Princeton University Press); Maurice Obstfeld and Alan M. Taylor, 2004, *Global Capital Markets: Integration, Crisis, and Growth* (Cambridge: Cambridge University Press).
[20] Lawrence Officer, October 1, 2001, "Gold Standard," *EH.Net Encyclopedia*, edited by Robert Whaples, http://eh.net/encyclopedia/article/officer.gold.standard.

Thus, as nineteenth-century globalization proceeded, it is likely that more countries crossed the FIX line and met the economic criteria for fixing.

There were also other forces at work encouraging a switch to the gold peg before 1914. The stabilization costs of pegging were either seen as insignificant—because the pace of economic growth was not that unstable—or else politically irrelevant—because the majority of those adversely affected by business cycles and unemployment were from the mostly disenfranchised working classes. With the exception of some emerging markets, price stability was the major goal and the inflation tax was not seen as useful except in emergencies.

As for the question, why peg to gold? (as opposed to silver, or something else), note that once a gold peg became established in a few countries, the benefits of adoption in other countries would increase further. If you are the second country to go on the gold standard, it lowers your trade costs with one other country; if you are the 10th or 20th country to go on, it lowers your trade costs with 10 or 20 other countries; and so on. This can be thought of as a "snowball effect" (a *network externality*, as economists say), where only one standard can dominate in the end.[21]

This is not to say that all was plain sailing before 1914. Many countries joined gold, only to leave temporarily due to a crisis. Even in countries that stayed on gold, not everyone loved the gold standard. The benefits were often less palpable than the costs, particularly in times of deflation or in recessions. For example, in the United States, prices and output stagnated in the 1890s, drawing support to populists who wanted to leave the gold standard and escape its monetary strictures. The tensions reached a head in 1896 at the Democratic Convention in Chicago, when presidential candidate William Jennings Bryan ended his speech saying: "Having behind us the producing masses of this nation and the world, supported by the commercial interests, the laboring interests and the toilers everywhere, we will answer their demand for a gold standard by saying to them: You shall not press down upon the brow of labor this crown of thorns, you shall not crucify mankind upon a cross of gold." (Bryan lost, the pro-gold McKinley became president, the Gold Standard Act of 1900 was passed to bury any doubts, and tensions defused as economic growth and gold discoveries raised output and prices.)

The Granger Collection

Bryan's "cross of gold."

These trends were upset by World War I. For belligerent countries, the war required financing. The inflation tax was heavily used, and this implied exit from the gold standard. In addition, once a war began in Europe (and later drew in the United States), the majority of global trade was affected by conflict: trade was almost 100% wiped out between belligerents, and fell by 50% between belligerents and neutrals. This effect persisted long after the war ended, and it was exacerbated by protectionism (higher tariffs and quotas) in the 1920s. By the 1930s, world trade had fallen to close to half of its 1914 level. All of these developments meant that the rationale for fixing based on gains from trade was being weakened.[22]

[21] Christopher M. Meissner, 2005, "A New World Order: Explaining the International Diffusion of the Gold Standard, 1870–1913," *Journal of International Economics*, 66(2), 385–406.

[22] Reuven Glick and Alan M. Taylor, 2010, "Collateral Damage: Trade Disruption and the Economic Impact of War," *Review of Economics and Statistics*, 92(1), 102–127; Antoni Estevadeordal, Brian Frantz, and Alan M. Taylor, 2003, "The Rise and Fall of World Trade, 1870–1939," *Quarterly Journal of Economics*, 118(2), 359–407.

Then, from 1929 on, the Great Depression undermined the stability argument for pegging to gold. The 1920s and 1930s featured much more violent economic fluctuations than had been seen prior to 1914, raising the costs of pegging. Moreover, politically speaking, these costs could no longer be ignored. The rise of labor movements and political parties of the left started to give voice and electoral weight to constituencies that cared much more about the instability costs of a fixed exchange rate.[23]

Other factors also played a role. The Great Depression was accompanied by severe deflation, so to stay on gold might have risked further deflation given the slow growth of gold supplies to which all money supplies were linked. Deflation linked to inadequate gold supplies therefore undermined the usefulness of gold as a nominal anchor.[24] Many countries had followed beggar-thy-neighbor policies in the 1920s, choosing to re-peg their currencies to gold at devalued rates, making further devaluations tempting. Among developing countries, many economies were in recession before 1929 because of poor conditions in commodity markets, so they had another reason to devalue (as some did as early as 1929). The war had also left gold reserves distributed in a highly asymmetric fashion, leaving some countries with few reserves for intervention to support their pegs; as backup, many countries now used major currencies as reserves, too, but the value of these reserves depended on everyone else's commitment to the gold peg, a commitment that was increasingly questionable.

All of these weaknesses undermined the confidence and credibility of the commitment to gold pegs in many countries, making the collapse of the pegs more likely. Currency traders would then speculate against various currencies, raising the risk of a crisis. In the face of such speculation, in 1931 both Germany and Austria imposed capital controls, and Britain floated the pound against gold. The gold standard system then unraveled in a largely uncoordinated, uncooperative, and destructive fashion.

In the language of the trilemma, with its three solutions or "corners," the 1930s saw a movement by policy makers away from the "open capital market/fixed exchange rate" corner, and the other two corners came to dominate. Countries unwilling to close their capital markets by imposing controls opted to abandon the gold peg and moved to the open capital market/floating exchange rate solution, allowing them to regain monetary policy autonomy: Britain and the United States among others made this choice. Countries willing to adopt capital controls but unwilling to suffer the volatility of a floating rate moved to the "closed capital market/fixed exchange rate" solution, allowing them to regain monetary policy autonomy in a different way: Germany and many countries in South America made this choice. Gaining monetary autonomy gave all of these countries the freedom to pursue more expansionary monetary policies to try to revive their economies, and most of them did just that. Finally, a few countries remained on the gold standard and did not devalue or impose controls, in part because they were not forced off gold (they had large reserves) and in part because they were worried about the inflationary consequences of floating. France was such a country. Countries that stuck with the gold standard paid a heavy price: compared with 1929, countries that floated had 26% higher output in 1935, and countries that

---

[23] Barry Eichengreen, 1992, *Golden Fetters: The Gold Standard and the Great Depression* (New York: Oxford University Press).

[24] World gold production more or less kept pace with output growth in the nineteenth century, but output grew much faster than gold stocks in the twentieth century. If gold gets scarcer, its relative price must rise. But if the money price of gold is pegged, the only way for the relative price of gold to rise is for all other prices to fall—that is, by economy-wide price deflation.

adopted capital controls had 21% higher output, as compared with the countries that stayed on gold.[25]

Figure 15-13 shows these outcomes diagrammatically. To sum up: although many other factors were important, trade gains and an absence of (or political indifference to) stability costs helped bring the gold standard into being before 1914; reduced trade gains and stability costs that were higher (or more politically relevant) help explain the ultimate demise of the gold standard in the interwar period.

Bretton Woods to the Present

The international monetary system of the 1930s was utterly chaotic. Near the end of World War II, allied economic policy makers gathered in the United States, at Bretton Woods, New Hampshire, to try to ensure that the postwar economy fared better. The architects of the postwar order, notably Harry Dexter White and John Maynard Keynes, constructed a system that preserved one key tenet of the gold standard regime—by keeping fixed rates—but discarded the other by imposing capital controls.

FIGURE 15-13

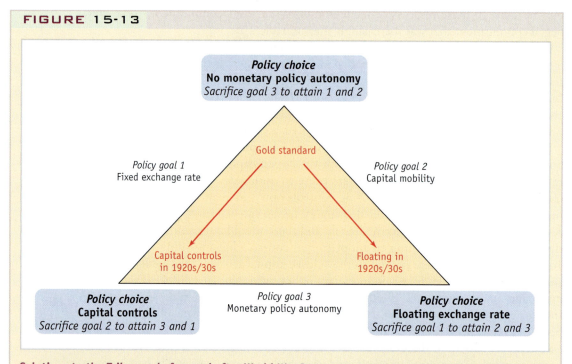

Solutions to the Trilemma before and after World War I Each corner of the triangle represents a viable policy choice. The labels on the two adjacent edges of the triangle are the goals that can be attained; the label on the opposite edge is the goal that has to be sacrificed. Trade gains and an absence of (or political indifference to) stability costs help explain how the gold standard came into being before 1914 (top corner). Subsequently, reduced trade gains and higher actual (or politically relevant) stability costs help explain the ultimate demise of the gold standard in the 1920s and 1930s. Countries sought new solutions to the trilemma to achieve policy autonomy, either by floating (bottom right corner) or by adopting capital controls (bottom left corner).

---

[25] Maurice Obstfeld and Alan M. Taylor, 2004, *Global Capital Markets: Integration, Crisis, and Growth* (Cambridge: Cambridge University Press). The output cost estimates are from page 143.

The trilemma was resolved in favor of exchange rate stability to encourage the rebuilding of trade in the postwar period. Countries would peg to the U.S. dollar; this made the U.S. dollar the center currency and the United States the center country. The U.S. dollar was, in turn, pegged to gold at a fixed price, a last vestige of the gold standard.

In Figure 15-14, the postwar period starts with the world firmly in the "closed capital market/fixed exchange rate" corner on the left. At Bretton Woods, the interests of international finance were seemingly dismissed, amid disdain for the speculators who had destabilized the gold standard in the 1920s and 1930s: U.S. Treasury Secretary Henry Morgenthau pronounced that the new institutions would "drive . . . the usurious money lenders from the temple of international finance." At the time, only the United States allowed full freedom of international capital movement, but this was soon to change.

It was obvious that to have trade one needed to have payments, so some kind of system for credit was needed, at least on a short-term basis. By the late 1950s, after getting by with half measures, many countries in Europe and elsewhere were ready to liberalize financial transactions related to current account transactions to free up the trade and payments system. At the same time, they sought to limit speculative financial transactions that were purely asset trades within the financial account (e.g., interest arbitrage by forex traders).

FIGURE 15-14

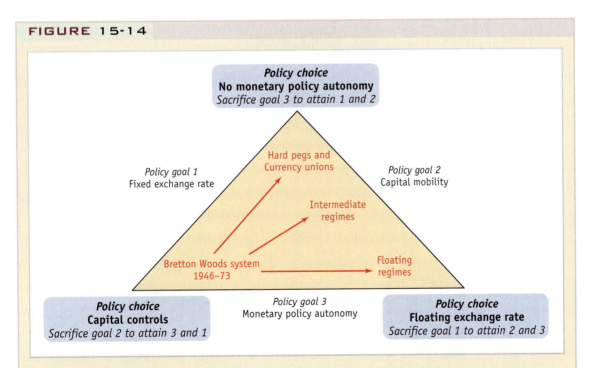

Solutions to the Trilemma since World War II In the 1960s, the Bretton Woods system became unsustainable because capital mobility could not be contained. Thus, countries could no longer have fixed rates and monetary autonomy (bottom left corner). In the advanced countries, the trilemma was resolved by a shift to floating rates, which preserved autonomy and allowed for the present era of capital mobility (bottom right corner). The main exception was the currency union of the Eurozone. In developing countries and emerging markets, the "fear of floating" was stronger; when capital markets were opened, monetary policy autonomy was more often sacrificed and fixed exchange rates were maintained (top corner).

Unfortunately, in practice it proved difficult then (and has proved so ever since) to put watertight controls on financial transactions. Controls in the 1960s were very leaky and investors found ways to circumvent them and move money offshore from local currency deposits into foreign currency deposits. Some used accounting tricks such as over- or underinvoicing trade transactions to move money from one currency to another. Others took advantage of the largely unregulated offshore currency markets that had emerged in London and elsewhere in the late 1950s.

As capital mobility grew and controls failed to hold, the trilemma tells us that countries pegged to the dollar stood to lose their monetary policy autonomy. This was already a reason for them to think about exiting the dollar peg. With autonomy evaporating, the devaluation option came to be seen as the most important way of achieving policy compromise in a "fixed but adjustable" system. But increasingly frequent devaluations (and some revaluations) undermined the notion of a truly fixed rate system, made it more unstable, generated beggar-thy-neighbor policies, and—if anticipated—encouraged speculators.

The downsides became more and more apparent as the 1960s went on. Other factors included a growing unwillingness in many countries to peg to the U.S. dollar, after inflation in the Vietnam War era undermined the dollar's previously strong claim to be the best nominal anchor currency. It was also believed that this inflation would eventually conflict with the goal of fixing the dollar price of gold and that the United States would eventually abandon its commitment to convert dollars into gold, which happened in August 1971. By then it had become clear that U.S. policy was geared to U.S. interests, and if the rest of the world needed a reminder about asymmetry, they got it from U.S. Treasury Secretary John Connally, who in 1971 uttered the memorable words, "The dollar is our currency, but it's your problem."

Figure 15-14 tells us what must happen in an international monetary system once capital mobility reasserts itself, as happened to the Bretton Woods system in the 1960s. The "closed capital market/fixed exchange rate" corner on the left is no longer an option. Countries must make a choice: they can stay fixed and have no monetary autonomy (move to the top corner), or they can float and recover monetary autonomy (move to the right corner).

These choices came to the fore after the Bretton Woods system collapsed from 1971 to 1973. How did the world react? There have been a variety of outcomes, and the tools developed in this chapter help us to understand them:

■ Most advanced countries have opted to float and preserve monetary policy autonomy. This group includes the United States, Japan, United Kingdom, Australia, and Canada. They account for the growing share of floating regimes in Figure 15-1. For these countries, stability costs outweigh integration benefits. They are at the bottom right corner of the trilemma diagram.

■ A group of European countries instead decided to try to preserve a fixed exchange rate system among themselves, first via the ERM and now "irrevocably" through the adoption of a common currency, the euro. Integration gains in the closely integrated European market might, in part, explain this choice. This group of countries is at the top corner of the trilemma diagram.

■ Some developing countries have maintained capital controls, but many of them (especially the emerging markets) have opened their capital markets. Given the "fear of floating" phenomenon, their desire to choose fixed rates (and sacrifice monetary autonomy) is much stronger than in the advanced countries, all else equal. These countries are also at the top corner of the trilemma diagram.

■ Some countries, both developed and developing, have camped in the middle ground: they have attempted to maintain intermediate regimes, such as "dirty floats" or pegs with "limited flexibility." India is often considered to be a case of an intermediate regime somewhere between floating or fixed. Such countries are somewhere in the middle on the right side of the trilemma diagram.

■ Finally, some countries still impose some capital controls rather than embrace globalization. China has been in this position, although change is afoot. These countries, mostly developing countries, are clinging to the bottom left corner of the trilemma diagram.

5 Conclusions

Exchange rate regimes have varied greatly across countries and across time and continue to do so. Explaining why this is the case, and figuring out the optimal choice of exchange rate regime, are major tasks in international macroeconomics.

We began this chapter by studying the main costs and benefits of fixed versus floating regimes. Fixing enhances the economic efficiency of international transactions. Floating allows authorities to stabilize an economy with monetary policy. The clash between these two goals creates a trade-off. Only with enough economic integration (more gains on transactions) and sufficiently symmetric shocks (less need for policy autonomy) do fixed exchange rates make sense, as shown in the symmetry-integration diagram.

However, other factors also affect the trade-off, especially in emerging markets and developing countries: fixed exchange rates may provide the only credible nominal anchor after a high inflation, and they insulate countries with net foreign currency debt from the adverse wealth effects of depreciations.

Finally, we examined exchange rate systems in theory and in practice. Over the years, fixed rate systems such as the gold standard and the Bretton Woods system have come and gone, with collapses driven, at least in part, by failures of cooperation. That leaves us today with no real international monetary "system" at all, but rather many countries, and occasionally groups of countries, pursuing their own interests and trying to make the best choice of regime given their particular circumstances. As this chapter has shown, there may be good reasons why "one size fits all" will never apply to exchange rate regimes.

KEY POINTS

1. A wide variety of exchange rate regimes have been in operation throughout history to the present.

2. The benefits for the home country from a fixed exchange rate include lower transaction costs and increased trade, investment, and migration with the base or center country.

3. The costs to the home country from a fixed exchange rate arise primarily when the two countries experience different economic shocks and home would want to pursue monetary policies different from those of the base or center country.

4. The costs and benefits of fixing can be summed up on a symmetry-integration diagram. At high levels of symmetry and/or integration, above the FIX line, it makes sense to fix. At low levels of symmetry and/or integration, below the FIX line, it makes sense to float.

5. A fixed rate may confer extra benefits if it is the only viable nominal anchor in a high-inflation country and if it prevents adverse wealth shocks caused by depreciation in countries suffering from a currency mismatch.

6. Using these tools and the trilemma, we can better understand exchange rate regime choices in the past and in the present. Before 1914 it appears the gold standard did promote integration, and political concern for the loss of stabilization policies was limited. In the 1920s and 1930s, increased isolationism, economic instability, and political realignments undermined the gold standard. After 1945 and up to the late 1960s, the Bretton Woods system of fixed dollar exchange rates was feasible, with strict controls on capital mobility, and was attractive as long as U.S. policies were not at odds with the rest of the world. Since 1973 different countries and groups of countries have gone their own way, and exchange rate regimes reflect the sovereign choice of each country.

KEY TERMS

gold standard, p. 549
base currency, p. 552
center currency, p. 552
asymmetric shock, p. 557
symmetry-integration diagram, p. 558
fear of floating, p. 573
fixed exchange rate systems, p. 574
reserve currency system, p. 574
cooperative arrangements, p. 574
devaluation, p. 577
revaluation, p. 577
beggar-thy-neighbor policy, p. 579

PROBLEMS

1. Using the IS-LM-FX model, illustrate how each of the following scenarios affects the home country. Compare the outcomes when the home country has a fixed exchange rate with the outcomes when the home currency floats.

   a. The foreign country increases the money supply.

   b. The home country cuts taxes.

   c. Investors expect a future appreciation in the home currency.

2. The Lithuanian lita is currently pegged to the euro. Using the IS-LM-FX model for Home (Lithuania) and Foreign (Eurozone), illustrate how each of the following scenarios affect Lithuania:

   a. The Eurozone reduces its money supply.

   b. Lithuania cuts government spending to reduce its budget deficit.

   c. The Eurozone countries increase their taxes.

3. Consider two countries that are currently pegged to the euro: Latvia and Comoros. Latvia is a member of the European Union, allowing it to trade freely with other EU countries. Exports to the Eurozone account for the majority of Latvia's outbound trade, which mainly consists of manufacturing goods, services, and wood. In contrast, Comoros is an archipelago of islands off the eastern coast of southern Africa that exports food commodities primarily to the United States and France. Comoros historically maintained a peg with the French franc, switching to the euro when France joined the Eurozone. Compare and contrast Latvia and Comoros in terms of their likely degree of integration symmetry with the Eurozone. Plot Comoros and Latvia on a symmetry-integration diagram as in Figure 15-4.

4. Use the symmetry-integration diagram as in Figure 15-4 to explore the evolution of international monetary regimes from 1870 to 1939—that is, during the rise and fall of the gold standard.

   a. From 1870 to 1913, world trade flows doubled in size relative to GDP, from about 10% to 20%. Many economic historians believe this was driven by exogenous declines in transaction costs, some of which were caused by changes in transport technology. How would you depict this shift for a pair of countries in the symmetry-integration diagram that started off just below the FIX line in 1870? Use the letter A to label your starting point in 1870 and use B to label the end point in 1913.

b. From 1913 to 1939, world trade flows collapsed, falling in half relative to GDP, from about 20% back to 10%. Many economic historians think this was driven by exogenous increases in transaction costs from rising transport costs and increases in tariffs and quotas. How would you depict this shift for a pair of countries in the symmetry-integration diagram that started off just above the FIX line in 1913? Use the letter B to label your starting point in 1913 and use C to label the end point in 1939.

c. Other economic historians contend that these changes in transaction costs arose endogenously. When countries went on the gold standard, they lowered their transaction costs and boosted trade. When they left gold, costs increased. If this is true, then do points A, B, and C represent unique solutions to the problem of choosing an exchange rate regime?

d. Changes in other factors in the 1920s and 1930s had an impact on the sustainability of the gold standard. These included the following:

   i. An increase in country-specific shocks

   ii. An increase in democracy

   iii. Growth of world output relative to the supply of gold

In each case, explain why these changes might have undermined commitment to the gold standard.

5. Many countries experiencing high and rising inflation, or even hyperinflation, will adopt a fixed exchange rate regime. Discuss the potential costs and benefits of a fixed exchange rate regime in this case. Comment on fiscal discipline, seigniorage, and expected future inflation.

6. In the late 1970s, several countries in Latin America, notably Mexico, Brazil, and Argentina, had accumulated large external debt burdens. A significant share of this debt was denominated in U.S. dollars. The United States pursued contractionary monetary policy from 1979 to 1982, raising dollar interest rates. How would this affect the value of the Latin American currencies relative to the U.S. dollar? How would this affect their external debt in local currency terms? If these countries had wanted to prevent a change in their external debt, what would have been the appropriate policy response, and what would be the drawbacks?

7. Home's currency is the peso and trades at 1 peso per dollar. Home has external assets of $200 billion, all of which are denominated in dollars. It has external liabilities of $400 billion, 75% of which are denominated in dollars.

a. Is Home a net creditor or debtor? What is Home's external wealth?

b. What is Home's net position in dollar-denominated assets?

c. If the peso depreciates to 1.2 pesos per dollar, what is the change in Home's external wealth in pesos?

8. Evaluate the empirical evidence on how currency depreciation affects wealth and output across countries. How does the decision of maintaining a fixed versus floating exchange rate regime depend on a country's external wealth position?

9. Home signs a free-trade agreement with Foreign, which lowers tariffs and other barriers to trade. Both countries are very similar in terms of economic shocks, as they each produce very similar goods. Use a symmetry-integration diagram as in Figure 15-4 as part of your answer to the following questions:

a. Initially, trade rises. Does the rise in trade make Home more or less likely to peg its currency to the Foreign currency? Why?

b. In the longer run, freer trade causes the countries to follow their comparative advantage and specialize in producing very different types of goods. Does the rise in specialization make Home more or less likely to peg its currency to the Foreign currency? Why?

NETWORK

Visit the International Monetary Fund's website (http://www.imf.org) and locate the latest classification of exchange rate regimes in all countries around the world. How many countries are fixing and how many are floating?

Find the photo of the $20 gold coin on page 580 and the specifications in its caption. Calculate the U.S. dollar price of 1 ounce of gold under the pre-1913 gold standard. Now use the Internet to find details, including gold content, of a British gold sovereign coin worth £1 in the same era. Calculate the British pound price of 1 ounce of gold under the pre-1913 gold standard. Now compute the implied pound-dollar exchange rate. Check your answer against the value given in the text.

Index

Note: Page numbers followed by f indicate figures; page numbers followed by n indicate notes; page numbers followed by t indicate tables; key terms are in **boldface** type.